YEARBOOK OF INTERNATIONAL HUMANITARIAN LAW

Yearbook of International Humanitarian Law

Volume 1
1998

T.M.C. Asser Press

Cover photograph courtesy of the ICRC, Geneva.

ISBN 90-6704-107-6
ISSN 1389-1359

T.M.C. Asser Instituut - Institute for Private and Public International Law, International Commercial Arbitration and European Law
Institute Address: R.J. Schimmelpennincklaan 20-22, The Hague, The Netherlands; Mailing Address: P.O. Box 30461, 2500 GL The Hague, The Netherlands; Tel.: (31-70)3420300; Fax: (31-70)3420359; Internet: www.asser.nl.
Over thirty years, the T.M.C. Asser Institute has developed into a leading scientific research institute in the field of international law. It covers private international law, public international law, including international humanitarian law, the law of the European Union, the law of international commercial arbitration and increasingly, also, international economic law and the law of international commerce. Conducting scientific research, either fundamental or applied, in the aforementioned domains, is the main activity of the Institute. In addition, the Institute organizes congresses and postgraduate courses, undertakes contract-research and operates its own publishing house.
Because of its inter-university background, the Institute often cooperates with Dutch law faculties as well as with various national and foreign institutions. The Institute organizes *Asser College Europe*, a project in cooperation with East and Central European countries whereby research and educational projects are organized and implemented.

Editorial Office:
Yearbook of International Humanitarian Law
T.M.C. Asser Instituut
P.O. Box 30461
2500 GL The Hague, The Netherlands
Tel. +31(70)3420300; Fax +31(70)3420359; E-mail: A.J.M.McDonald@asser.nl

CORRESPONDENTS

The *Yearbook of International Humanitarian Law* extends it sincere thanks and appreciation to its correspondents, without whose assistance the compilation of this volume would not have been possible:

AFRICA

Professor Larbi Chaht Abdelkader, *Algeria*
Professor Ahmed Abou El Wafa, *Egypt*
Mr. Michael Ibanga, *Nigeria*
Dr. B. O. Okere, *Nigeria*
Professor Amechi Uchegbu, *Nigeria*
Professor Michael G. Cowling, *South Africa*

ASIA-PACIFIC

Professor Tim McCormack, *Australia*
Dr. Borhan Uddin Khan, *Bangladesh*
Professor Zhang Yong, *China*
Mr. Fadillah Agus, *Indonesia*
Professor Hideyuki Kasutani, *Japan*
Mr. Jayantha W. Atukorala, *Sri Lanka*

EUROPE

Dr. Thomas Desch, *Austria*
Mag. Peter Kustor, *Austria*
Professor Marc Cogen, *Belgium*
Professor Eric David, *Belgium*
Professor Ivo Josipović, *Croatia*
Professor Maja Seršić, *Croatia*
Mr. Tanel Kerikmäe, *Estonia*
Professor Konstantin Obradović, *Federal Republic of Yugoslavia*
Professor Lauri Hannikainen, *Finland*
Mr. Juhani Parkkari, *Finland*
Professor Paul Tavernier, *France*
Assistant Professor Beate Rudolf, *Germany*
Dr. Maria Gavouneli, *Greece*
Professor Péter Kovács, *Hungary*
Professor Colm Campbell, *Ireland*
Mr. Ray Murphy, *Ireland*
Professor Paolo Benvenuti, *Italy*
Professor Sergio Marchisio, *Italy*
Drs. Astrid Delissen, *Netherlands*
Professor Nico Keijzer, *The Netherlands*
Professor Dr. Jerzy Menkes, *Poland*
Ms. Joanna Nowakowska, *Poland*
Professor Igor Blischchenko, *Russian Federation*
Dr. Rosario Huesa, *Spain*
Professor Antoni Pigrau i Solé, *Spain*
Mr. Frederik Danelius, *Sweden*
Dr. Alain Dennis Henchoz, *Switzerland*
Ms. Anne-Marie La Rosa, *Switzerland*
Mr. Paul Berman, *United Kingdom*
Professor Françoise Hampson, *United Kingdom*
Dr. K. H. Kaikobad, *United Kingdom*
Dr. Danesh Sarooshi, *United Kingdom*

MIDDLE EAST

Professor Djamchid Momtaz, *Iran*
Professor Eyal Benvenisti, *Israel*
Professor Ruth Lapidoth, *Israel*

NORTH AMERICA

Professor Katia Boustany, *Canada*
Professor René Provost, *Canada*
Professor William A. Schabas, *Canada*
Lt. Col. (ret.) Burrus M. Carnahan, *USA*
Professor em. Howard S. Levie, *USA*
Commander Ronald Neubauer, *USA*

SOUTH AMERICA

Professor José Alejandro Consigli, *Argentina*
Mr. Gabriel Valladares, *Argentina*
Mr. Francisco Orrego Bauzá, *Chile*
Professor Hernán Salinas Burgos, *Chile*
Mr. Juan Pablo Olmedo, *Chile*
Professor Alfonso Velázquez, *Paraguay*

PREFACE

To publish and produce the first comprehensive and really international Yearbook on international humanitarian law! That idea and challenge emerged during the aftermath of the Geneva War Victims Conference in 1993 at the Legal Department of the Netherlands Ministry for Foreign Affairs. It would take another five years, numerous discussions with experts in the Netherlands and abroad, and the expertise and knowledge of the staff of the T.M.C. Asser Instituut, before the first volume could be presented. A major inducement for the publication and the preparatory work was also the research which was undertaken at our Institute by young, dedicated scholars in the field of humanitarian law, including state practice, the frequent contacts with Professor Dr. Horst Fischer and his 'Institute for International Humanitarian Law' at the University of Bochum and the cooperation in the publication of the Bofax Newsletter. It was Alan Stephens of Kluwer Law International who came up with most useful comments and suggestions concerning the focus and structure of the new *Yearbook*.

Gradually, the 'idea' turned into a reality and all ingredients for the official project launch were present when the search for a competent and enthusiastic managing editor was successful: Avril McDonald, with research experience and having been employed at the Yugoslav Tribunal, turned out to be the right person at the right place at the right time. The only missing, but crucial, element was the formation of an Editorial Board and Board of Recommendation which could provide the necessary input for the Yearbook in order for it to be able to reach its aims and goals. These aims were set out during the first meeting of the Board of Editors:

> It is the Board of Editors' intention to make this Yearbook a truly international endeavour and to guarantee its high academic quality. The most important task nowadays concerning international humanitarian law is to promote compliance, in particular through implementation and education. The Yearbook's aim is to serve worldwide practice, which is understood to include the implementation, research and development and the teaching of the law.
>
> All aspects of international law applicable in times of armed conflict should be covered by the Yearbook, including interesting developments taking place outside the traditional body of international humanitarian law. This is understood to include relevant aspects of human rights law, refugee law, disarmament law, humanitarian assistance, conflict resolution policy, etc.

The ambition to make the Yearbook a truly international endeavour has been realised not only by the appointment of a multinational Board of Editors but also through the creation of a worldwide network of correspondents, representing almost every continent and region. The T.M.C. Asser Instituut feels privileged to cooperate with such esteemed experts and organisations in international humanitarian law. With the guidance and experience of the Board of Editors and Board of Recommendation, the organisational structure seems a guarantee for a high-quality, readable and informative Yearbook.

I feel that the commencement of this project and the publication of a Yearbook on international humanitarian law comes at a very appropriate moment. It is a paradoxical situation that history repeats itself; despite the fact that, with hindsight, almost every war seems futile and pointless, we are still faced with war-like situations in almost every continent and with a growing intensity. There is a widespread conviction that the international community is impotent to abide by the basic rules of humanity, yet an awareness that respect for these basic rules is essential for humanity's survival.

The establishment and work of the International Tribunals for the Former Yugoslavia and Rwanda and the recent adoption of a Statute to create a permanent International Criminal Court emphasise the growing interest of the international community in international humanitarian law. At the same time, governments, politicians and academics increasingly refer to current relevant legal developments.

The *Yearbook of International Humanitarian Law*, as the world's first-ever annual academic publication devoted to this field, wishes to provide a 'truly international forum' for articles, commentaries and documentation that have international humanitarian law as their focal point.

I wish to congratulate the Board of Editors on this first volume and to express my sincere wish that we will witness many more examples of such academic craftsmanship.

Gerard J. Tanja
General Director, T.M.C. Asser Instituut, The Hague
Advisor to the Editorial Board

The Hague, November 1998

TABLE OF CONTENTS

ABBREVIATIONS

ABl	Amtsblatt
AD	Annual Digest of Public International Law Cases
AFDI	Annuaire français de droit international
AJIL	American Journal of International Law
AP	Associated Press
APL(s)	Anti-personnel landmine(s)
ASEAN	Association of South East Asian Nations
ATCA	Alien Tort Crimes Act (USA)
BGBl	Bundesgesetzblatt (Austria)
BLDP	(Cambodian) Buddhist Liberal Democratic Party
BlgNR	Beilagen zu den Stenographischen Protokollen des Nationalrates (Austria)
B.O.	Boletín Oficial de la República Argentina
BRA	Bougainville Revolutionary Army
BTG	Bougainville Transitional Government
BYIL	British Yearbook of International Law
CAR	Canadian Airborne Regiment
CCW	Certain Conventional Weapons (Convention)
CF	Canadian Forces
CGDK	Coalition Government of Democratic Kampuchea
CHR	(United Nations) Centre for Human Rights
CICR	Comité International de la Croix Rouge
CIS	Commonwealth of Independent States
CJCS	Chairman of the Joint Chiefs of Staff (USA)
CMAC	Court Martial Appeal Court
c.p.m.g	(Italian) Codice Penale Militare de Guerra (Military Penal Code of War)
c.p.m.p.	(Italian) Codice Penale Militare de Pace (Military Penal Code of Peace)
CPP	Cambodian People's Party
CRA	Conzinc Riotinto Australia
CRC	Convention on the Rights of the Child
CTS	Commonwealth Treaty Series
CWC	Chemical Weapons Convention
CTBT	Comprehensive Test Ban Treaty
DK	Democratic Kampuchea
DOD	Department of Defense
EJIL	European Journal of International Law
ECHR	European Convention on Human Rights
EHRR	European Human Rights Reports
Eur. Comm. H.R.	European Commission of Human Rights

Eur. Ct. H.R.	European Court of Human Rights
F.C.J.	Federal Court of Justice (Canada)
FRY	Federal Republic of Yugoslavia
FSIA	Foreign Sovereign Immunities Act (USA)
FUNCINPEC	National United Front for a Neutral, Peaceful and Cooperative Cambodia
GA	General Assembly
GAOR	UN General Assembly Official Records
GC	Geneva Conventions
GrCC	Greek Criminal Code
G.U.	Gazzetta Ufficiale (Italian Official Gazette)
HCJ	High Court of Justice
HRLJ	Human Rights Law Journal
Hum.Rts. Q	Human Rights Quarterly
I/A Comm. H.R.	Inter-American Commission of Human Rights
I/A Court H.R	Inter-American Court of Human Rights
ICA	International Council on Archives
ICBS	International Committee of the Blue Shield
ICC	International Criminal Court
ICCPR	International Protocol on Civil and Political Rights
ICJ	International Court of Justice
ICJ Reps	International Court of Justice Reports
ICLQ	International and Comparative Law Quarterly
ICBL	International Campaign to Ban Landmines
ICOM	International Council of Museums
ICOMOS	International Council on Monuments and Sites
ICRC	International Committee of the Red Cross
ICTR	International Criminal Tribunal for [...] Rwanda
ICTY	International Criminal Tribunal for [...] the Former Yugoslavia
IHL	International Humanitarian Law
ILM	International Legal Materials
ILR	International Law Reports
IMT	International Military Tribunal
IRA	Irish Republican Army
IRRC	International Review of the Red Cross
Israel Y.B. Human Rights	Israel Yearbook on Human Rights
JNA	Yugoslav People's Army
JPI	Judicial Police Inspectors
KR	Khmer Rouge
LAS	League of Arab States
LNTS	League of Nations Treaty Series
LOAC	Law of Armed Conflict
Loy. L.A. Int'l & Comp. L.J.	Loyola Los Angeles International and Comparative Law Journal
MCC	Military Criminal Code
MLR	Modern Law Review

M.R.N.D.	Mouvement Révolutionaire National pour la Démocratie
NATO	North Atlantic Treaty Organisation
NCOs	Non-Commissioned Officers
NGO(s)	Non-Governmental Organisation(s)
nm	Nanometres
NSD	Non-Self-Destructing
NPC	New Penal Code
ÖAD	Österreichische Außenpolitische Dokumentation (Austria)
OAS	Organisation of American States
OIOS	(UN) Office of Internal Oversight Services
ONU	Organisation Nations Unies
ONUC	United Nations Force in the Congo
OPCW	Organisation for the Prohibition of Chemical Weapons
OTP	Office of the Prosecutor (of the ICTR and/or ICTY)
PC	Privy Council
PLA	People's Liberation Army (China)
PMG	Peace Monitoring Group
PNG	Papua New Guinea
PNGDF	Papua New Guinea Defence Forces
POW	Prisoner of War
PRC	People's Republic of China
RICR	Revue International de la Croix Rouge
ROE	Rules of Engagement
RPF	Rwandan Patriotic Front
SC	Security Council
SD	Self-Destruction
SDA	Self-Deactivating
SFRY	Socialist Federal Republic of Yugoslavia
SG	(United Nations) Secretary-General
SIPRI	Stockholm International Peace Research Institute
SRSGHRC	Special Representative of the UN Secretary-General in Cambodia
SS	SchutzStaffel
Texas L Rev	Texas Law Review
TMG	Truce Monitoring Group
TVPA	Torture Victims Protection Act (USA)
UK	United Kingdom
UN	United Nations
UNAMIR	United Nations Assistance Mission for Rwanda
UNCHR	United Nations Commission on Human Rights
UN Doc.	United Nations Documents Series
UNDP	United Nations Development Program
UNEF	United Nations Emergency Force (in the Sinai)
UNESCO	United Nations Educational, Scientific and Cultural Organisation
UNFICYP	United Nations Force in Cyprus
UNHCR	United Nations High Commission for Refugees
UNHFOR	United Nations Human Rights Field Office in Rwanda
UNICEF	United Nations (International) Children's (Emergency) Fund

UNIDIR	United Nations Institute for Disarmament Research
UNIFIL	United Nations Interim Force in Lebanon
UNIIMOG	United Nations Iran/Iraq Military Observer Group
UNIKOM	United Nations Iraq/Kuwait Observer Mission
UNITAF	United Nations Task Force (in Somalia)
UNOMSIL	United Nations Observer Mission in Sierra Leone
UNOSOM	United Nations Operation in Somalia
UNPF	United Nations Peacekeeping Force
UNPROFOR	United Nations Protection Force (in Bosnia and Herzegovina)
UNSC	United Nations Security Council
UNTAC	United Nations Transitional Authority in Cambodia
UNTS	United Nations Treaty Series
UNWCC	United Nations War Crimes Commission
US	United States (of America)
USA	United States of America
UXO	Unexploded Ordinance
Virginia JIL	Virgina Journal of International Law
VRS	Bosnian Serb Army
WCR	War Crimes Reports
WHO	World Health Organisation
WWII	World War Two
YIHL	Yearbook of International Humanitarian Law

ARTICLES

INTERNATIONAL HUMANITARIAN LAW AND UNITED NATIONS MILITARY OPERATIONS*

Christopher Greenwood**

1. INTRODUCTION

The application of international humanitarian law to United Nations military operations is a subject that has attracted considerable interest almost from the inception of the United Nations.[1] While the basic premise that United Nations

** Professor of International Law, London School of Economics; member of the Board of Editors, *Yearbook of International Humanitarian Law*. The author gratefully acknowledges the assistance of Mr. Christoph Safferling, LL.M., who helped to compile materials for this article, and Ms. Avril McDonald, Managing Editor of the *Yearbook of International Humanitarian Law*, who made a number of helpful suggestions regarding recent developments at the United Nations, as well as providing valuable encouragement. The responsibility for any errors remains that of the author alone.

1. See in particular, D.W. Bowett, *United Nations Forces* (London, Sweet and Maxwell 1964) pp. 484-516; F. Seyersted, *United Nations Forces in the Law of Peace and War* (Leiden, Sijthoff 1966); ICRC, *Symposium on Humanitarian Action and Peace-Keeping Operations* (Geneva, ICRC 1994); L. Condorelli et al, eds., *The United Nations and International Humanitarian Law* (Paris, Editions Pedone 1996); D. Schindler, 'United Nations Forces and International Humanitarian Law' in C. Swinarski, ed., *Studies and Essays on International Humanitarian Law* (The Hague, Martinus Nijhoff 1984) p. 521; P. Benvenuti, 'The Implementation of International Humanitarian Law in the Framework of United Nations Peace-keeping Operations' in European Commission, *Law in Humanitarian Crises* (Luxembourg, Office for Official Publications of the European Communities 1995) vol. I, p. 83; G.-J. van Hegelsom, 'The Law of Armed Conflict and United Nations Peace-Keeping and Peace-Enforcing Operations' 6 *Hague Yearbook of International Law* (1993) p. 45; and U. Palwankar, 'Applicability of international humanitarian law to United Nations peace-keeping forces', 33 *International Review of the Red Cross* (1993) p. 227 See also the two resolutions adopted by the Institut de droit international: Resolution on the Conditions of Application of Humanitarian Rules of Armed Conflict to Hostilities in which United Nations Forces may be Engaged, adopted at Zagreb in 1971 ('the Zagreb Resolution'), 54 (II) *Annuaire de l'institut de droit international* (1971) p. 465, and the Resolution on the Conditions of Application of Rules other than Humanitarian Rules of Armed Conflict to Hostilities in which United Nations Forces may be

forces should, at the very least, respect the 'principles and spirit' of international humanitarian law conventions has long commanded general acceptance, there has been considerable controversy both about the legal basis for this proposition – in particular, whether this duty of respect is something derived from general international law or the result of a specific and voluntary undertaking by the United Nations – and about the exact meaning of 'principles and spirit' in this context. Developments during the last decade, in particular, the greatly increased level of United Nations military activity in the period 1990-95; the adoption of the Convention on the Safety of United Nations and Associated Personnel, 1994[2]; the prosecution of members of United Nations forces for acts committed during some of these recent operations[3]; and the attempts to elaborate a set of principles applicable to all United Nations military operations suggest that the time is ripe to reexamine the relationship between international humanitarian law and United Nations military operations.

As the terms 'international humanitarian law' and 'United Nations operations' are used in a variety of ways, it is important at the outset to make clear how they are used here. 'International humanitarian law' (IHL) denotes the whole body of law applicable during hostilities (the *jus in bello* or law of armed conflict), rather than being confined to those parts of the *jus in bello* which are regarded as humanitarian in character.[4] By 'United Nations operations' is meant primarily military operations established by the competent organ of the United Nations and conducted under United Nations command and control (e.g., UNPROFOR (United Nations Protection Force) in Yugoslavia or UNOSOM (United Nations Operation in Somalia) in Somalia). However, military operations authorized by the Security Council but conducted entirely by national contingents operating

---

Engaged, adopted in Wiesbaden in 1975 ('the Wiesbaden Resolution'), 56 *Annuaire de l'institut de droit international* (1975) p. 540.

2. United Nations General Assembly Resolution 49/59, 34 *ILM* (1995) p. 482. For an example of implementing legislation, see the United Nations Personnel Act (United Kingdom) 1997. Although reference will be made to this Convention in so far as it is relevant to the application of international humanitarian law to United Nations operations, it is not intended to analyse it in detail. For discussion of the Convention, see E. Bloom, 'Protecting Peacekeepers: The Convention on the Safety of United Nations and Associated Personnel' 89 *AJIL* (1995) p. 621, C. Bourloyannis-Vrailas, 'The Convention on the Safety of United Nations and Associated Personnel', 44 *ICLQ* (1995) p. 560, C. Greenwood, 'Protection of Peacekeepers: The Legal Regime', 7 *Duke Journal of Comparative and International Law* (1996) p. 185; and W.G. Sharp, 'Protecting the Avatars of International Peace and Security', loc. cit., *Duke Journal of Comparative and International Law* p. 93.

3. See the articles by Boustany, Young and Siekmann, *infra* pp. 371, 362, and 301 respectively.

4. Although the two resolutions of the Institut de droit international (loc. cit. n. 1) distinguish between rules of a humanitarian character and other rules of the law of armed conflict, so much disagreement exists as to the classification of individual rules that the distinction tends to confuse rather than clarify.

under national command and control (e.g., the coalition forces in the Gulf during 1990-91) will also be considered.

In discussing the relationship between IHL and United Nations operations, it is not enough simply to ask whether IHL is applicable to United Nations military operations. Such an approach overlooks important differences between the several types of United Nations operations, as well as variations which may be material between different rules of IHL. Moreover, even when allowance is made for those differences, at least three separate questions have to be considered:

(1) to what extent do the rules of IHL operate as a constraint on the freedom of action of United Nations operations?

(2) in what ways do the rules of IHL offer a degree of protection to those serving in United Nations operations? and

(3) quite apart from their duty to respect IHL, do persons serving in a United Nations operation have a duty to take action to ensure that others respect IHL?

This article will address these questions in the following way. In order to deal with certain preliminary issues, section 2 will examine the scope of application of IHL and section 3 will briefly survey the different types of United Nations operations and the legal framework within which they take place. Section 4 will then consider the principle of the applicability of IHL to United Nations operations. In doing so, it will examine both the theoretical basis for holding that the United Nations might be subject to international humanitarian law and the practice of the United Nations itself in this respect. The question when a United Nations force should be regarded as a party to an armed conflict is considered in section 5. Section 6 then examines the extent to which international humanitarian law operates as a constraint upon the conduct of United Nations military operations. The protection afforded to United Nations and associated personnel by IHL is the subject of section 7, while the question whether such personnel have a duty to ensure that others comply with IHL will be considered in section 8. The conclusions of this study are set out in section 9.

2. THE SCOPE OF APPLICATION OF INTERNATIONAL HUMANITARIAN LAW

Before examining the applicability of international humanitarian law to United Nations operations, it is necessary to say a little about the normal conditions for the application of that law. As is well known, there are two separate bodies of international humanitarian law. The first is applicable to armed conflicts of an international character. Its principal sources today are the four Geneva Conventions of 12 August 1949[5] the first Additional Protocol to those Conventions,[6] the Hague Convention for the Protection of Cultural Property in the Event of Armed Conflict, 1954, and the Protocol of the same date[7] and a number of conventions relating to weaponry,[8] together with the rules of customary law, many of which are codified in the Hague Conventions of 1907, in particular Hague Convention No. IV and the annexed Regulations on the Laws and Customs of War on Land.[9]

Whatever the position may once have been, this body of international humanitarian law is today applicable to any armed conflict between two or more states, irrespective of whether there is a formal state of war; it is the fact of hostilities, not the existence of a formal legal condition which brings the law into operation.[10] While the term 'armed conflict' is not defined in any of the conventions, it has generally been given a very broad definition. Thus, the authoritative

5. Geneva Convention No. I for the Amelioration of the Condition of the Wounded and Sick in Armed Forces in the Field, 1949, 75 *UNTS* (1950) 31 (A. Roberts and R. Guelff, *Documents on the Laws of War* (Oxford, Clarendon Press, 2nd edn., 1989) p. 169); Geneva Convention No II for the Amelioration of the Condition of Wounded, Sick and Shipwrecked Members of the Armed Forces at Sea, 1949, 75 *UNTS* (1950) 85 (Roberts and Guelff, p. 193); Geneva Convention No. III Relative to the Treatment of Prisoners of War, 1949, 75 UNTS (1950) 135 (Roberts and Guelff, p. 215); and Geneva Convention No. IV Relative to the Protection of Civilian Persons in Time of War, 1949, 75 UNTS (1950) 287 (Roberts and Guelff, p. 271).

6. Additional Protocol I, relating to the Protection of Victims of International Armed Conflicts, 1125 UNTS (1979) 3 (Roberts and Guelff, op. cit. n. 5, p. 385).

7. 249 UNTS (1954) p. 240 (Roberts and Guelff, op. cit. n. 5, p. 339). The Convention and Protocol were adopted under the auspices of UNESCO. Revision of the Convention and the Protocol was under discussion at the time of writing. For a discussion of the review process, see Hladik, *infra*, p. 313; Year in Review at p. 135.

8. In particular, the Geneva Protocol for the Prohibition of the Use in War of Asphyxiating, Poisonous or Other Gases, and of Bacteriological Methods of Warfare, 1925, XCIV LNTS (1929) 65 (Roberts and Guelff, op. cit. n. 5, p. 137); the United Nations Convention on Prohibitions or Restrictions on the Use of Certain Conventional Weapons which may be Deemed to be Excessively Injurious or to have Indiscriminate Effects ('The Weapons Convention') and the Protocols thereto, 1981, 19 *ILM* (1980) p. 1523 (Roberts and Guelff, ibid., p. 471); and the Chemical Weapons Convention, 1993, 32 *ILM* (1993) p. 800.

9. 205 CTS (1907) p. 227 (Roberts and Guelff, op. cit n. 5, p. 43).

10. Art. 2 common to the four Geneva Conventions provides that the Conventions shall apply 'to all cases of declared war or of any other armed conflict which may arise between two or more of the High Contracting Parties, even if the state of war is not recognized by one of them'. In practice, the Conventions have been applied to armed conflicts even if none of the parties have recognized the existence of a state of war. Additional Protocol I applies in the same circumstances, as well as to what are known as 'wars of national liberation' (Art. 1 (4)). It is now generally accepted that the rules of customary international humanitarian law apply to any international armed conflict, irrespective of the existence of a formal state of war; see C. Greenwood, 'The Concept of War in Modern International Law,' 36 *ICLQ* (1987) p. 283.

commentary on the 1949 Geneva Conventions, published by the ICRC, states that:

> Any difference between two States and leading to the intervention of members of the armed forces is an armed conflict within the meaning of Article 2 [common to the four Geneva Conventions], even if one of the parties denies the existence of a state of war. It makes no difference how long the conflict lasts, how much slaughter takes place, or how numerous are the participating forces . . .'[11]

A similar view has been expressed by the Appeals Chamber of the International Criminal Tribunal for the Former Yugoslavia (ICTY) in its decision in *Prosecutor* v. *Tadić (Jurisdiction)*, in which it stated that 'an armed conflict exists whenever there is a resort to armed force between States.'[12] There is also some support for this approach in state practice. The United States, for example, considered that an armed conflict triggering the application of IHL had come into being between itself and Syria when Syrian anti-aircraft batteries in Lebanon shot down a United States naval aircraft in 1983 and captured the pilot.[13]

While the various treaties on international humanitarian law are stated to apply to conflicts only between states (or powers) which are parties to those treaties, it is at least arguable that, under customary law, it is not a precondition of the existence of an international armed conflict that all the parties must be states, although it is necessary that they possess some kind of international status, at least *de facto*.[14]

Once an international armed conflict exists, the rules of international humanitarian law apply equally to all the parties to that conflict, irrespective of which party acted illegally in resorting to force – no distinction in this regard is drawn between aggressor and victim. Prosecution attempts to argue that Germany did not benefit from provisions of IHL in the Second World War, because it had been the aggressor, were rejected in a number of war crimes trials and other cases.[15]

11. J.S. Pictet, ed., *Commentary on Geneva Convention III* (Geneva, ICRC 1960) p. 23.

12. *The Prosecutor* v. *Duško Tadić*, Decision on the Defence Motion for Interlocutory Appeal on Jurisdiction, Case No. IT-94-1-AR72, 2 October 1995, 105 *ILR* 419 at 453, para. 70. For comment, see C. Greenwood, 'International Humanitarian Law and the *Tadić* case,' 7 *EJIL* (1996) p. 265.

13. *Digest of United States Practice in International Law* (1981-88) Vol. III, p. 3456.

14. H. Lauterpacht, *Oppenheim's International Law*, Vol. II (London, Longmans 7th edn., 1952) pp. 203-204; L. Kotszch, *The Concept of War* (1956) p. 56.

15. See in particular, *United States* v. *List* 15 *AD* (1948) p. 632, *United States* v. *Krupp* 15 *AD* (1948) p. 620 and the decision of the Court of Appeal of Singapore applying the same principle to Japan in *NV de Bataafsche Petroleum Maatschappij* v. *War Damages Commission (the 'Singapore Oil Stocks Case')*, 23 *ILR* (1956) p. 810.

This conclusion was reaffirmed in the era of the Charter by Sir Hersch Lauterpacht[16] and other writers and was expressly incorporated in the preamble to Additional Protocol I to the Geneva Conventions, which reaffirms that:

> 'the provisions of the Geneva Conventions of 12 August 1949 and of this Protocol must be applied in all circumstances to all persons who are protected by those instruments, without any adverse distinction based on the nature or origin of the armed conflict or on the causes espoused by or attributed to the parties to the conflict.'

The principle has not been seriously questioned in recent years. An important consequence is that a combatant, even if serving in the armed forces of an aggressor, is not liable to punishment for acts of violence which do not themselves contravene IHL. Such a combatant is not, therefore, liable to punishment for killing an adversary in open combat and with weapons which are not prohibited.

The law applicable to non-international armed conflicts is a separate body of IHL, more limited in scope than that applicable to international conflicts. The principal treaty provision is common Article 3 of the four Geneva Conventions, which applies 'in the case of armed conflict not of an international character occurring in the territory of one of the High Contracting Parties'. In its decision on jurisdiction in the *Tadić* case, the Appeals Chamber of ICTY, considered that such a conflict exists whenever there occurs 'protracted armed violence between governmental authorities and organized armed groups or between such groups within a State'.[17] Additional Protocol II of 1977 contains more detailed treaty provisions for the regulation of non-international conflicts.[18] However, its provisions do not apply in all situations covered by common Article 3 but only in conflicts between government and dissident forces and even then only if the dissident forces exercise control over a part of the territory of the state concerned.[19] In *Tadić*, the Appeals Chamber of the ICTY considered that there is also a substantial body of customary international law applicable to non-international armed conflicts which applies to any conflict to which common Article 3 is applicable.[20] When foreign armed forces intervene in an internal conflict on the side of the government forces and become involved in fighting with dissident

16. H. Lauterpacht, 'The Limits of the Operation of the Law of War,' 30 *BYIL* (1953) p. 206.

17. 105 *ILR* 419 at 453, para. 70.

18. Additional Protocol II to the Geneva Conventions of 1949, relating to the Protection of Victims of Non-International Armed Conflicts, 1125 UNTS (1979) p. 609 (Roberts and Guelff, op. cit. n. 5, p. 447).

19. Art. 1(1). Art. 1(2) also raises the threshold for the application of the Protocol.

20. See *supra* n. 12.

forces, it is unclear whether that fighting is to be considered as an international armed conflict or not.

The rules of IHL applicable during an internal armed conflict are skeletal compared with those which apply to international conflicts. Moreover, although they apply equally to government and non-government factions, the laws of internal armed conflict do not preclude treating the mere act of bearing arms as criminal under the domestic law of the state concerned. Unlike soldiers in an international armed conflict, combatants in internal conflicts may be punished for the mere act of combatancy and very often are.

In addition to the rules of IHL applicable during the two types of armed conflict, numerous provisions of the Geneva Conventions and Additional Protocols require action to be taken in time of peace, for example, the enactment of legislation to make possible the punishment of grave breaches of the Conventions.[21]

Finally, it is important to note that the obligations of states under the Geneva Conventions and Additional Protocol I may extend beyond a duty to ensure that their own forces comply with those agreements and require them to take action to prevent violations by others. Common Article 1 of the Conventions provides that 'the High Contracting Parties undertake to respect *and to ensure respect* for the present Convention in all circumstances' [emphasis added]. It has been argued that this provision requires all parties to the Conventions 'to do everything in their power to ensure that the humanitarian principles underlying the Conventions are applied universally' and thus to take action in the face of violations by others.[22] This extensive interpretation of common Article 1 has, however, been criticised by other writers as having no basis in the *travaux préparatoires* of the article.[23] Certainly, there is little evidence in the practice of states since 1949

21. Geneva Convention No. I, Art. 49; No. II, Art. 50; No. III, Art. 129; No. IV, Art. 146; and Additional Protocol No. I, Art. 85.

22. J.S. Pictet, *Commentary on Geneva Convention IV* (Geneva, ICRC 1958) p. 16. See also L. Condorelli and L. Boisson de Chazournes, 'Quelques remarques à propos de l'obligation des Etats de 'respecter et faire respecter' le droit international humanitaire 'en toute circonstances' in Swinarski, op. cit. n. 1, p. 17.

23. Thus, Professor Roberts comments: 'This interpretation of article 1 does not appear to have a basis in the negotiating history of the 1949 Geneva Conventions. In the various meetings at Stockholm and Geneva, the words 'to ensure respect' had another meaning: to ensure that the whole population of a country which was party to the Conventions would respect the law in all circumstances, even perhaps in the case of civil war. There appears to be little or nothing in the records of the Diplomatic Conference to suggest an awareness on the part of government delegates, or indeed ICRC participants, that the phrase 'to ensure respect' implied anything beyond this. (A. Roberts, 'The Laws of War: Problems of Implementation' in European Commission, op. cit. n. 1, p. 13 at pp. 31-2).

that supports the conclusion that states have regarded themselves as obliged to intervene to prevent violations of IHL by others.

3. THE NATURE AND LEGAL FRAMEWORK OF UNITED NATIONS OPERATIONS

The Charter of the United Nations envisages that the Security Council should determine the existence of threats to the peace, breaches of the peace or acts of aggression and should then take action to restore the peace (including, where it deems it appropriate, military action against those responsible).[24] In order to undertake enforcement action of this kind, it was envisaged that it would have the right to call upon national contingents made available to it on a standing basis under agreements between the United Nations and the major military Powers.[25] No such agreements have ever been concluded, however, and before 1990, the military powers of the Council under Chapter VII of the Charter were invoked only in the case of Korea in 1950, where the Council, after condemning the North Korean invasion of the South, established a Unified Command under the leadership of the United States and called upon Members to contribute forces to that command.[26] Instead, the United Nations improvised a concept of peacekeeping by consent, the legal basis of which was rooted in the consent of the states on whose territory each force operated and not in the provisions of Chapter VII of the Charter. It was only after Iraq's invasion of Kuwait in August 1990 that the Security Council began once again to use its Chapter VII powers to authorize enforcement action.

Analyses of United Nations military operations in recent years have tended to divide such operations into a variety of categories, such as 'peacekeeping' and 'peace-enforcement'[27] and to focus upon the Charter provisions which supplied the mandate for a particular operation. While this approach is obviously valuable in helping to analyse the objectives of each operation and its place within the United Nations system, it is of limited assistance in determining the applicability

24. Arts. 39-42 of the Charter.

25. Art. 43. For a description of this system and the ambitious plans discussed in the first years of the United Nations, see Bowett, op. cit. n. 1, pp. 12-28.

26. See Bowett, op. cit. n. 1, pp. 29-60 and R. Higgins, *United Nations Peacekeeping 1946-1967*, Vol. II (Oxford, Oxford University Press 1970) pp. 153-314. The United Nations force in the Congo, ONUC, is also considered by some commentators to have been a Chapter VII operation, Higgins, ibid., Vol. III (1980) p. 54.

27. The best known is probably that in the Secretary-General's *Agenda for Peace*, UN Doc. S/24111 (17 June 1992).

of IHL. As was seen in Part II of this article, IHL applies in the event of an armed conflict, a factual concept which exists when certain hostilities take place. If, therefore, IHL can apply to United Nations operations at all (a matter which is considered below), whether or not it is applicable to a particular operation will be dependent upon the existence of an armed conflict to which the relevant United Nations force is a party, not on how the United Nations operation is classified for other United Nations purposes. It is the *fact* of participation in hostilities, not the existence of *authority* to do so which is significant.

It is necessary, therefore, to adopt a different approach for the purposes of this article. At first sight, the critical distinction for present purposes would appear to be that between Chapter VII operations and others, since only the former envisage the initiation of hostilities by the United Nations force.[28] The distinction between Chapter VII and other operations is, of course, important but it is not sufficient. It has long been the practice of the United Nations that even a United Nations force which is not established under Chapter VII is entitled to use force in self-defence. At least in theory, the United Nations interprets self-defence in a very broad manner. Thus, in a report on the operations of UNPROFOR in the former Yugoslavia, the Secretary-General stated:

> 'It is to be noted that, in this context, self-defence is deemed to include situations in which armed persons attempt by force to prevent United Nations troops from carrying out their mandate.'[29]

This means that even a force established and operating without any Chapter VII mandate can be drawn into hostilities on a large scale if, for example, its mandate is to ensure the delivery of relief supplies and it elects to use force in order to overcome armed resistance to the passage of a relief convoy. Moreover, in a number of recent operations, the Security Council has used its powers under Chapter VII to provide a mandate for the use of force in support of certain objectives within the context of an operation which was not primarily an enforcement operation.[30] The result is that a category of operations which contains elements of both peacekeeping and enforcement actions has emerged. Conversely,

28. Bowett, op. cit. n. 1, p. 485.

29. UN Doc. S/24540 (10 September 1992) para. 9. A similar approach had earlier been adopted in the case of UNIFIL in Lebanon, UN Doc. S/1 2611 (19 March 1978), para. 4 (d).

30. That was the case with the United Nations operations in the former Yugoslavia, where UNPROFOR was not established as an enforcement operation but was subsequently given a Chapter VII mandate to use 'all necessary means' to achieve certain of its objectives, such as the protection of safe areas. In addition, the Council authorized NATO to use force in order to enforce a ban on flights over Bosnia-Herzegovina and later in more general support of UNPROFOR.

the Security Council may have recourse to Chapter VII not because it envisages the use of force but because there is no government in the host state from which consent to the operation can be obtained.[31]

For the purposes of this article, therefore, United Nations operations will be divided into three categories:

(1) Operations established as enforcement actions, where the United Nations force is authorized to take the initiative in combat and where it does, in fact, become involved in hostilities.

(2) Operations established for peacekeeping or similar purposes, where a right to use force in self-defence may exist but it is not envisaged that force will be used and where the United Nations force does not, in fact, become involved in hostilities with other organized armed forces.

(3) Operations established for peacekeeping or similar purposes but in which the United Nations force becomes involved in hostilities with other organized armed forces, either because it employs force in self-defence (within the extended sense in which that term has come to be used in the United Nations) or because a specific authority to use force is added to its mandate and that authority is employed.

These are not hard and fast categories and it will frequently be difficult to determine whether an operation which initially fell into the second category has crossed the line into the third.

Another feature of many recent United Nations operations must also be borne in mind. Whereas the Charter envisaged United Nations operations being conducted under the command and control of the United Nations itself, that has not always been the case in practice. Until 1990, most operations came under United Nations command and control, although in the Korean conflict, the Security Council effectively nominated the United States as commander of all forces fighting with United Nations authority and the United States exercised effective command and control with minimal involvement by United Nations organs.[32] Since 1990, however, the practice of the Council authorizing action to be taken by national contingents under national command and control has become far more widespread. Three different models can be identified:

(1) Operations under United Nations command and control, in which a force is composed of national contingents placed under United Nations command and control pursuant to agreements between the Participating States and the United

31. That was the reason for the initial decision to adopt a Chapter VII resolution (Res. No. 794(1992)) in Somalia. Fighting involving the United Nations and associated forces broke out only some time after the deployment pursuant to that resolution.

32. Higgins, op. cit. n. 26, Vol. II, p. 195.

Nations.[33] This has been the model employed for such forces as UNIFIL (United Nations Interim Force in Lebanon); UNFICYP (United Nations Force in Cyprus); UNIKOM (United Nations Iraq/Kuwait Observer Mission); and UNIIMOG (United Nations Iran/Iraq Military Observer Group).

(2) Operations conducted under national command and control but authorized by the Security Council. This was the model adopted in the Gulf conflict, where Security Council Resolution No. 678 (1990) authorized 'States co-operating with the Government of Kuwait' to 'use all necessary means' to achieve the objectives set out in the resolution.[34] Given the resources presently available to the United Nations and the views of the states most likely to provide the forces for any major enforcement operation, it seems likely that, for the foreseeable future, this is the model which will apply to any operation falling within the first category set out above.

(3) Operations in which a force under United Nations command has operated alongside other forces under national command and control. Thus, in Somalia, UNOSOM I and UNOSOM II operated under United Nations command but alongside separate forces which remained under national command. Similarly, in Bosnia-Herzegovina, UNPROFOR was a United Nations force but the NATO air force units which conducted air strikes in support of UNPROFOR did not come under United Nations command and control, even though they operated under authorization from the Security Council and in response to requests from the United Nations for assistance.

The differences between these three models may be of considerable significance for the application of IHL both in theory and in practice.

33. See the model agreement between the United Nations and Participating States, UN Doc. A/46/185 (23 May 1991).

34. See C. Greenwood 'New World Order or Old? The Invasion of Kuwait and the Rule of Law', 55 *MLR* (1992) p. 153. Although it has been argued by some commentators (e.g., O. Schachter, 'United Nations Law in the Gulf Conflict' 85 *AJIL* (1991) p. 452 and N. Rostow, 'Until What? Enforcement Action or Collective Self-Defence?', 85 *AJIL* (1991) p. 506) that the Security Council approved an action by way of collective self-defence, rather than authorizing enforcement action, the United Kingdom considered that the legal basis for the military action which followed was derived from the resolution, not from the right of collective self-defence; 62 *BYIL* (1991) p. 704 et seq., a view supported by Professor Bowett, 'Collective Security and Collective Self-Defence: the Errors and Risks in Identification' in M. Rama-Montaldo, ed., *International Law in an Evolving World: Liber Amicorum Eduardo Jimenez de Arechaga* (Montevideo, Fundaçion de Cultura Universitaria 1994), Vol. 1, p. 425.

4. THE APPLICABILITY OF INTERNATIONAL HUMANITARIAN LAW TO UNITED NATIONS OPERATIONS

The early debates regarding the applicability of IHL to United Nations operations were dominated by concern over whether a body of law devised for conflicts between states could be applicable to what were perceived as qualitatively different military operations. Thus, it was suggested that even if the United Nations launched a major military offensive against an aggressor, in the exercise of Chapter VII powers, its action was that of a law-enforcer, not a belligerent, and the ensuing hostilities did not, therefore, possess the character of war. Whether United Nations operations could possess the character of 'war' in the formal sense of that term is an interesting question but not one which can be regarded as decisive today. As was demonstrated in Part II of this article, the application of IHL is nowadays dependent upon the fact of hostilities occurring, not on the characterization of those hostilities as amounting to a formal state of war. There is no material difference between hostilities conducted by (or on behalf of) the United Nations and any other hostilities.

A discrete, though related, objection to the applicability of IHL to United Nations operations was that it presupposes a degree of equality between the warring parties, whereas no such equality could exist between the forces of the global organization charged with the maintenance of international peace and security and those of an aggressor whose resort to force was in violation of the most fundamental rules of the international legal order. This argument is important but it is not a reason for rejecting the applicability of IHL to United Nations operations. It has already been seen that the justice of a party's cause has not been accepted as a reason for modifying the application to it of the rules of IHL.[35] There are sound reasons why that should be so. It is likely that the principal effect of holding that one side in a conflict was not subject to the same obligations as the other would be that both sides would come to disregard the law. As Sir Hersch Lauterpacht explained,

> '... it is impossible to visualize the conduct of hostilities in which one side would be bound by rules of warfare without benefiting from them and the other side would benefit from them without being bound by them.'[36]

Moreover, the majority of provisions of IHL are intended to protect the individual, not to benefit the state, and while individual soldiers or even civilians may

35. For a more detailed analysis of this question, see C. Greenwood, 'The Relationship between *Ius ad Bellum* and *Ius in Bello*', 9 *Review of International Studies* (1983) p. 221.

36. Lauterpacht, loc. cit. n. 16, p. 212.

support the aims of an aggressor, it should not be presumed that all persons dependent upon the aggressor also partake of his guilt. These arguments also apply to hostilities involving the United Nations.[37]

That is not to say that no consequences flow from the imbalance between the legal position of the United Nations and an aggressor. Since the aggressor's resort to force is unlawful, it incurs international responsibility for all the consequences of its use of force. It therefore has a duty to compensate not only those who have suffered loss as a result of the violations of IHL committed by its forces but also those injured by acts of the same forces which were not contrary to IHL. In the latter case, the illegality which gives rise to the responsibility lies in the original wrongful resort to force. Moreover, since opposition to an illegal resort to force is an entirely foreseeable consequence of that unlawful act, the aggressor is also responsible for damage caused by lawful acts of war on the part of its opponents. This was the approach adopted in the aftermath of the Gulf conflict, when the Security Council reaffirmed, in Resolution No. 687 (1991), that Iraq was 'liable under international law for any direct loss, damage ... or injury to foreign Governments, nationals or corporations as a result of its unlawful invasion and occupation of Kuwait.'[38] That has been interpreted by the United Nations Compensation Commission as including losses caused by military action or the threat of military action by the coalition forces.[39] In addition, the special status of the United Nations may have a bearing upon the application of the law relating to belligerent occupation. This question is considered in Part VI, below. The legal imbalance between the United Nations and an aggressor does not, however, mean that the United Nations is not to be regarded as subject to rules of international humanitarian law which are undoubtedly applicable to the aggressor.

A somewhat different argument is that the United Nations is incapable of complying with some of the obligations imposed by international humanitarian law, since these presuppose the existence of a state structure. In particular, the United Nations has no courts or system of criminal law by which it could try and punish persons responsible for war crimes. It could not, therefore, undertake certain essential steps by way of ensuring compliance by its own forces with IHL or discharging a responsibility to bring to justice others responsible for violations. This is clearly a relevant factor in determining how IHL is to be applied by United Nations forces but it is not a reason for holding that the law cannot be applicable to such forces. Since the United Nations does not recruit service

37. Bowett, op. cit. n. 1, pp. 493-495.

38. Para. 16.

39. Governing Council Decision No. 7, para. 21(a), UN Doc. S/AC.26/1991/7/Rev. 1, 109 *ILR*, and the Report and Recommendations of the Panel of Commissioners in the *Well Blowout Control Claim* (18 December 1996) UN Doc. S/AC.26/1996/5, 109 *ILR* 479.

personnel directly but relies instead upon national contingents made available to it,[40] the obligation to ensure that discipline is maintained and that violations of IHL are punished can be and is discharged by the various contributing states.[41]

There is, therefore, no reason why the United Nations cannot be subject to IHL if its forces become engaged in an armed conflict. It is, however, necessary to consider the juridical basis upon which that law may become applicable. The United Nations is not, of course, party to the Geneva Conventions or any of the other treaties concerning IHL. It is probably the case that the United Nations could not become party to such treaties, which are open only to 'Powers', although this has been questioned.[42] The United Nations is not, therefore, bound by any of these treaties as such.

Nevertheless, the International Court of Justice has held that the United Nations is 'a subject of international law and capable of possessing international rights and duties'.[43] It is therefore subject to IHL insofar as it engages in activities of the kind regulated by IHL. Accordingly, the United Nations is subject to customary international humanitarian law, even if it not bound by the IHL treaties, to the extent that it engages in armed conflict.[44] Most of the provisions of the 1907 Conventions were regarded as declaratory of custom at the time of the Second World War, while the majority of the substantive provisions of the

40. Although there have been proposals for the direct recruitment of a United Nations force, these have never come to anything. The United Nations does, of course, have its own force of security guards at Headquarters and members of this force have been used in certain operations abroad. It is not, however, a military force.

41. See below, p. 18. See also M. Bothe in B. Simma, ed., *The Charter of the United Nations: A Commentary* (Oxford, University Press 1994) pp. 598-600.

42. The Holy See is a party to the Geneva Conventions and Additional Protocols, as well as to the Hague Convention on Cultural property and its Protocol. The Byelorussian and Ukrainian Soviet Socialist Republics were also parties before they became independent from the USSR in 1992. These were, however, special cases, since the Holy See had all the attributes of statehood prior to 1870 (J. Crawford, *Creation of States in International Law* (Oxford, Clarendon Press 1979) pp. 152-160), while Byelorussia and the Ukraine were founding members of the United Nations. By contrast, in 1989 when the Swiss Government received a document by which Palestine purported to become party to the Geneva Conventions and the Additional Protocols, it responded by informing all parties that 'due to the uncertainty within the international community as to the existence or non-existence of a State of Palestine' it was not in a position to decide whether this communication constituted an instrument of accession. (ICRC, 'Geneva Conventions of 12 August 1949 and Additional Protocols of 8 June 1977: Ratifications, Accessions and Successions', p. 3). It is implicit in this statement that only states were considered as capable of becoming parties to the Conventions and Protocols.

43. *Advisory Opinions on Reparations*, *ICJ Rep.* (1949) p. 174 at p. 179.

44. Schindler, loc. cit. n. 1, at p. 526.

Geneva Conventions and some, though not all, of those in the two Additional Protocols have now achieved that status.[45]

Moreover, the question whether the United Nations is bound by particular provisions of IHL is not the same as whether the members of a United Nations force are obliged to comply with those provisions. Although the United Nations is not a party to the Geneva Conventions or Additional Protocols, a United Nations force is composed of national contingents contributed by states which are invariably parties to the Conventions and most of whom are also parties to the Protocols.[46] Those states are required by Article 1 of the Conventions and Article 1 of Additional Protocol I to ensure that the members of their armed forces respect the provisions of the Conventions and the Protocol 'in all circumstances'. This requirement certainly applies to cases in which a state becomes involved in hostilities as a result of using its armed forces under national command and control but with the authorization of the Security Council. In those circumstances, the state itself will be a party to the armed conflict and will be subject to IHL in exactly the same way as if it had acted without any United Nations authority. Thus, the coalition states which engaged in hostilities with Iraq under the mandate conferred by Resolution 678 regarded themselves as parties to an armed conflict and subject to the Geneva Conventions and the customary rules of IHL.[47]

45. T. Meron, *Human Rights and Humanitarian Norms as Customary Law* (Oxford, Clarendon Press 1989) pp. 3-78, R. Baxter, 'Treaties and Custom', 129 *Hague Receuil* (1970-I) p. 27, C. Greenwood, 'Customary Law Status of the 1977 Additional Protocols' in A. Delissen and G. Tanja, eds., *Humanitarian Law of Armed Conflict: Challenges Ahead* (Dordrecht, Martinus Nijhoff 1991) p. 93.

46. Of the 185 Members of the United Nations, only Eritrea, the Marshall Islands and Nauru were not parties to the Geneva Conventions at 1 January 1998 (ICRC, loc. cit. n. 42). 148 States were parties to Additional Protocol I and 140 to Additional Protocol II. A number of important military Powers, including the United States, France, India and Pakistan, were not parties to the Protocols.

47. The Parliamentary Under-Secretary of State at the United Kingdom Ministry of Defence stated in a written Parliamentary answer that:

'It was the common understanding, reflected at all times in the practice of coalition forces, that member States acting under [the authorization given by Resolution 678] remained bound by the principles and rules of international law regulating the conduct of armed conflict.' HC Debs, Vol. 531, WA 43-4, 22 July 1991; 62 *BYIL* (1991) p. 676.

The same approach was taken by the other coalition states; see e.g., United States Department of Defense, *Conduct of the Persian Gulf War: Final report to Congress* (Washington, USGPO 1992), Appendix 0. In addition, the ICRC stated:

'The Middle East conflict is beyond any doubt an international armed conflict as defined in Article 2 common to the Geneva Conventions of 12 August 1949. The fact that military action has been authorized by Security Council resolution 678 does not affect this definition or the application of the laws of armed conflict.' (ICRC, 'Outline of the Legal Aspects of the Conflict in the Middle East',

The implications of common Article 1, however, go further than that. Even if a state's armed forces serve in a force under United Nations command and control, it is arguable that the state is still under an obligation to ensure that they respect the provisions of the relevant conventions in any armed conflict in which they become engaged.[48] This argument is open to the objection that the United Nations cannot be held internationally responsible for a violation of obligations to which the United Nations itself is not subject, while the state cannot be held responsible for the acts of members of its armed forces serving in a force under United Nations command and control, because it has relinquished control over them to such an extent that they are no longer its organs but have become agents of the United Nations. However, that argument is not convincing. First, the attribution of responsibility should not be confused with the existence of the obligation. State (or United Nations) responsibility is not the only, or even the most important, means for ensuring compliance with the rules of IHL, which can be enforced directly against individuals. Secondly, as will be seen, the United Nations has included in its agreements with contributing states a requirement that each state ensures that its contingents comply with the principles and spirit of the relevant IHL conventions. It is therefore implicit in those agreements that the United Nations will not require a national contingent to act in a way which is contrary to the obligations of the state under those conventions.

The result is that, in principle, once armed forces under the command of the United Nations or acting under United Nations authorization become involved in an armed conflict, they are obliged to observe the customary IHL (because that is binding upon both the states from which they come and the United Nations) and the relevant IHL conventions (because these are binding upon the states concerned). This appears to be the conclusion reached by the Institut de droit international which has adopted resolutions concluding that:

> 'The humanitarian rules of the law of armed conflict apply to the United Nations as of right and they must be complied with in every circumstance by United Nations forces which are engaged in hostilities.'[49]

---

21 January 1991, reproduced in M. Weller, ed., *Iraq and Kuwait: Hostilities and their Aftermath* (Cambridge, Grotius Publications 1993) p. 332).
Additional Protocol I did not apply, because neither Iraq, nor some of the most prominent members of the coalition were parties to it; ibid.

48. Bowett, op. cit. n. 1, p. 504, concludes that 'national contingents in the service of the United Nations are bound to the same extent and degree, to all those rules of warfare which would obtain if the same forces were engaged in international armed conflict for the State alone.' See also Schindler, loc. cit. n. 1, p. 528 and Higgins, op. cit. n. 26, Vol. II, p. 194.

49. Zagreb Resolution, loc. cit. n. 1, Art. 2.

and

> 'Subject to the exceptions provided for in the following Articles, the rules of armed conflict shall apply to hostilities in which United Nations forces are engaged, even if those rules are not specifically humanitarian in character.'[50]

One problem, of course, is that although customary IHL and the Geneva Conventions bind all states likely to contribute to a United Nations operation, the same is not true of Additional Protocol I and some of the other IHL treaties. It is possible, therefore, that different contingents in the same force could be subject to different legal obligations, thus creating serious problems of interoperability.[51]

In the light of this discussion about the principle of applicability, it becomes necessary to consider the extent to which the practice of the United Nations has been consistent with that principle. In the Korean conflict, the Security Council established an armed force under United States command with a mandate to engage in armed conflict on a substantial scale. It was an enforcement action which was one of the clearest possible examples of the first category of United Nations operation, set out at page 12 above. The United States announced that it would be guided by the humanitarian principles of the Geneva Conventions and, in particular, the principles in common Article 3.[52] The Unified Command at various times stated that it would comply with the provisions of the Third Geneva Convention (on POWs) and gave instructions to that effect, and in 1951 the United States stated that United Nations forces in Korea had been instructed to comply with the provisions of all four Geneva Conventions.[53] There has remained an element of doubt as to whether the United Nations regarded the four Conventions as binding on the United Nations forces or considered that it was required only to apply certain principles contained therein.[54] Nevertheless, it should be remembered that at the time of the Korean War, the 1949 Conventions had only just been adopted and none of the major participants except for South Korea had become party to them. Moreover, as Professor Bowett has pointed out, 'there is, in fact, no known case in which the United Nations Command ever claimed exemption from any of the accepted rules of the laws of war, customary or conventional'.[55]

50. Weisbaden Resolution, loc. cit. n. 1, Art. 2.
51. In practice, it is Additional Protocol I which is most likely to give rise to such problems.
52. Higgins, op. cit. n. 26, p. 191.
53. Ibid. and documents quoted there, especially UN Doc S/2232 (6 July 1951).
54. S. Bailey, *How Wars End* (Oxford, Clarendon Press 1982) Vol. II, p 444.
55. Bowett, op. cit. n. 1, p. 56.

Since the time of Korea, it seems to have been generally accepted that if the United Nations established or authorized an enforcement operation which was designed to, and did, in fact, engage in hostilities on a large scale, the whole of the relevant IHL would apply to that operation.[56] The acceptance of this position is recognized in the Convention on the Safety of United Nations and Associated Personnel, 1994, Article 2(2) of which provides that:

> 'This Convention shall not apply to a United Nations operation authorised by the Security Council as an enforcement action under Chapter VII of the Charter of the United Nations in which any of the personnel are engaged as combatants against organized armed forces and *to which the law of international armed conflict applies*' [emphasis added].

It seems, therefore, to be admitted that IHL is applicable to the first category of operations outlined on page 12.[57] There may, however, be less to this admission than meets the eye, since, for the reasons given in section 3 above, major operations of this kind are likely to be conducted by forces authorized by the Security Council but operating under national command and control and, as the Gulf case demonstrated, there has never been any doubt about the applicability of IHL to operations conducted in this way.

Nor has there been any difficulty about operations falling within the second category outlined on page 12. If a United Nations operation, whatever its command and control structure, does not become a party to an armed conflict, national or international, then it is not required to comply with IHL, since the conditions for the application of that law are not present. That does not mean, however, that IHL has no relevance to such an operation. The members of this type of operation may derive a degree of protection from IHL. In addition, it is arguable that they have a duty to take steps to ensure that others respect the principles of the law. These issues are considered in sections 7 and 8 of this article.

The problems have tended to arise in the third category of operations, i.e., those in which the basic mandate of the force is not to engage in combat but it becomes involved in hostilities either because it acts in self-defence or because it is authorized to use force for certain specific objectives (perhaps, as in the former Yugoslavia, by way of additions grafted onto its original mandate).

56. See e.g., D. Shraga, in Condorelli, loc. cit. n. 1, at p. 323.

57. Whether the degree of United Nations involvement makes any difference to the application of specific provisions of international humanitarian law is another matter, which is considered in section 6, below.

With regard to this category of operations, the position taken by the United Nations has been that a force under United Nations command and control should observe the 'principles and spirit' of IHL. It has not conceded that the force is under a legal obligation to comply with the entire body of IHL. This approach is now embodied in the model agreement drawn up for use between the United Nations and the states contributing contingents to the force. Article 28 of the model agreement provides that the operation:

> '. . . shall observe and respect the principles and spirit of the general international conventions applicable to the conduct of military personnel. The international conventions referred to above include the four Geneva Conventions of 12 August 1949 and their Additional Protocols of 8 June 1977 and the UNESCO Convention of 14 May 1954 on the Protection of Cultural Property in the event of Armed Conflict. [The contributor State] shall therefore ensure that the members of its national contingent serving with the [operation] be fully acquainted with the principles and spirit of these Conventions.'[58]

The same agreement requires the contributing state to 'exercise jurisdiction with respect to crimes or offences which may be committed by its military personnel' serving with the operation.[59] This requirement would include violations of the principles and spirit of the Conventions listed in Article 28.

More recently, the United Nations has included in the Status of Forces Agreements which it has concluded with host states in respect of certain operations a clause by which both the United Nations and the host state agree to act in accordance with the principles and spirit of these Conventions. Thus, Article 17 of the Agreement between the United Nations and the Government of the Republic of Rwanda on the Status of the United Nations Assistance Mission for Rwanda (UNAMIR) of 5 November 1993, provided that:

> 'Without prejudice to the mandate of UNAMIR and its international status:
> (a) The United Nations shall ensure that UNAMIR shall conduct its operations in Rwanda with full respect for the principles and spirit of the general conventions applicable to the conduct of military personnel. These international conventions include the four Geneva Conventions of 12 August 1949 and their Additional Protocols of 8 June 1977 and the UNESCO Convention of 14 May 1954 on the Protection of Cultural Property in the event of Armed Conflict;

58. UN Doc. A/46/185 (23 May 1991). Similar provisions had been included in earlier agreements; see e.g., the Exchange of Notes between the United Nations and Canada regarding the participation of Canadian units in UNFICYP (1966) 555 *UNTS* 120.

59. Art. 25.

(b) The Government undertakes to treat at all times the military personnel of UNAMIR with full respect for the principles and spirit of the general conventions applicable to the conduct of military personnel. These international conventions include the four Geneva Conventions of 12 August 1949 and their Additional Protocols of 8 June 1977; UNAMIR and the Government shall therefore ensure that members of their respective military personnel are fully acquainted with the principles and spirit of the above-mentioned international instruments.'[60]

The presence of this clause in the Rwanda Agreement is all the more remarkable since no comparable provision appeared in the model status of forces agreement drafted in 1990. Moreover, UNAMIR was not established under Chapter VII of the Charter but was a classical peacekeeping force which was not intended to be involved in hostilities of any kind.[61] Similar provisions have subsequently been included in agreements with Haiti, Angola and Croatia.

While provisions of this kind in the status of forces and contributors' agreements are laudable, they are not without difficulty. First, the commitment to observe the 'principles and spirit' of the various conventions, rather than the entirety of those treaties, is difficult to understand or to justify. It has already been seen that if a United Nations force is established to conduct an enforcement operation engages in hostilities, it is obliged to comply with *all* the relevant provisions of IHL, not just with the principles and spirit thereof. As was demonstrated in sections 2 and 3 of this article, that is because the force in question has become a party to an armed conflict, so that the criteria for the application of IHL are satisfied. It is the fact of that participation in armed conflict, not the legal character of the force's mandate which leads to that conclusion. If, therefore, a United Nations force established for peacekeeping or other purposes becomes a party to an armed conflict, it should also be regarded as bound to comply with the whole of the applicable IHL. The only conventions in respect of which an element of discretion would exist would be those which are not automatically applicable, either because some of the contributor states are not parties thereto or the forces ranged against them are not bound by those treaties. If, on the other hand, the force does not participate in an armed conflict, then the criteria for application of IHL to its operations are not met. In the former

60. Quoted in Shraga, in Condorelli, loc. cit. n. 1, at p. 325 note 16. The Agreement was also communicated to the Rwandan Patriotic Front (at that time the forces fighting the Government of Rwanda, the RPF, overthrew the then-Government in 1994) 'which confirmed its readiness to co-operate in the implementation of its provisions', Report of the Secretary-General of the United Nations, UN Doc. S/26927, 30 December 1993, para. 7.

61. See SC Res. No. 872 (1993). The tragic events of 1994 showed that this assumption was false and also demonstrated the worthlessness of the undertakings given by the-then Government of Rwanda in the provision quoted above.

case, a commitment to observe the 'principles and spirit' of the conventions is insufficient; in the latter it is unnecessary.

Secondly, it is unclear what a commitment to observe the principles and spirit of the Conventions means in practice. In particular, how does it differ from the normal obligation to respect the Conventions in all circumstances? A particular problem is whether an individual acting in a manner contrary to the principles and spirit of, for example, the Geneva Conventions could be prosecuted under national legislation regarding grave breaches.[62]

Finally, the reference to the principles and spirit of the treaties listed in the status of forces and contributors' agreements leaves open the question whether customary IHL is also regarded as applicable.

In an attempt to address these questions, section 5 of this article will examine the circumstances in which a United Nations force should be regarded as participating in an armed conflict and whether such a conflict is always to be characterized as international or may sometimes constitute an 'armed conflict not of an international character' for the purposes of common Article 3 of the Geneva Conventions. Section 6 will then consider the rules of IHL actually to be applied.

5. UNITED NATIONS FORCES AS PARTIES TO ARMED CONFLICT

It has already been seen that the term 'armed conflict' is nowhere defined in the various treaties on IHL but that it is a factual term, referring to the fact of hostilities taking place, rather than to the intention with which they are conducted. In addition, there is considerable support for the view that 'armed conflict' should be given a broad interpretation and that the existence of an international armed conflict should not be regarded as contingent upon hostilities reaching a particular level of intensity.[63] If that test were to be applied to the activities of United Nations forces, then the threshold of armed conflict would be passed as soon as any fighting which went beyond purely sporadic acts of violence occurred between the members of the United Nations force and organized armed forces.

If one applies that test to the fighting in Bosnia-Herzegovina, then there is no doubt that the threshold was crossed, at the latest, by the summer of 1994. Soon after UNPROFOR forces first deployed in Bosnia-Herzegovina at the beginning of 1992, a series of conflicts broke out between the Government of Bosnia-Herzegovina and the Bosnian Serb forces (assisted to a degree which is still in issue

62. See the discussion of a related question by Professor Boustany in connection with United Nations operations in Somalia, *infra* p. 371.

63. See page 6 et seq. above.

in cases before the ICTY by the Federal Republic of Yugoslavia); Bosnia-Herzegovina and Croatia and the Bosnian Croat forces; and Croatia and the Bosnian Croat forces against the Bosnian Serb forces.[64] Unlike the coalition forces in the Gulf conflict, UNPROFOR did not enter any of these conflicts as an ally of one of the existing parties. It did, however, become involved in increasingly severe bouts of fighting with Bosnian Serb units, and in 1994 and 1995, NATO air force units operating under a mandate from the Security Council and in support of UNPROFOR bombed numerous targets in Serb-held areas of Bosnia.[65] The level of fighting was well in excess of that regarded in other cases as sufficient to amount to an armed conflict and it undoubtedly meets the criteria suggested by Pictet's *Commentaries* and the Appeals Chamber of the ICTY in *Tadić*.[66]

It is difficult, therefore, to resist the conclusion that if one applied the normal criteria for determining whether or not an armed conflict existed, it would be found that both UNPROFOR and the NATO states concerned were parties to an armed conflict with the Bosnian Serb forces (albeit a conflict separate from those already in existence). The suggestion - which has sometimes been made - that a distinction can be drawn in this case between the NATO States and UNPROFOR is based on a pretence since the two forces, although constitutionally separate, operated together and at the request of the same organ of the United Nations. It is clear, however, that neither the United Nations nor the states involved in the NATO operations regarded themselves as parties to an armed conflict.[67] There was also great reluctance to regard UNOSOM or the United States forces in Somalia as parties to an armed conflict. It seems, therefore, that there is a tendency to treat the threshold for determining whether a force has become party to an armed conflict as being somewhat higher in the case of United Nations and associated forces engaged in a mission which has a primarily peace-keeping or humanitarian character than in the normal case of conflicts between states.

This tendency is likely to be reinforced by the recent adoption of the Convention on the Safety of United Nations and Associated Personnel, 1994. That

64. *Prosecutor* v. *Tadić (Jurisdiction)* 105 *ILR* 419 and *Prosecutor* v. *Tadić (Merits)*, Case IT-94-1-T, decision of 7 May 1997. This decision will be reported in volume 112 of *International Law Reports*.

65. See Report of the Secretary-General pursuant to Res. 982 (1995) and 987 (1995), UN Doc. S/1995/444 (30 May 1995).

66. See *supra* note 12.

67. Nor, it would appear, did the Trial Chamber of the International Criminal Tribunal for the Former Yugoslavia in the Rule 61 proceedings regarding *Karadžić and Mladić*, 108 *ILR* 85; see C. Greenwood, 'The Development of International Humanitarian Law by the International Criminal Tribunal for the Former Yugoslavia' 2 *Year Book of United Nations Law* (1998), p. 97.

Convention makes attacks upon United Nations and associated personnel criminal offences which all states have a duty to punish. It has already been seen that Article 2(2) of that Convention[68] provides that the Convention shall cease to apply when the personnel of a United Nations force are 'engaged as combatants against organized armed forces and to which the law of international armed conflict applies.' The Convention and the law of international armed conflict are treated as mutually exclusive regimes.[69] The threshold for the application of the law of international armed conflict thus becomes the ceiling for the application of the Convention.[70] Since the Convention has been regarded as an important and necessary step in increasing the protection afforded to peacekeepers, it is to be expected that the United Nations and those states which contribute large numbers of personnel to United Nations operations will be extremely reluctant to accept that it has ceased to apply in any operation, no matter how intense the fighting has become.[71]

It appears, therefore, that a United Nations force and national units operating in association with it but under national command will be regarded as parties to an armed conflict only when they have engaged in hostilities on a scale comparable to those of a force established for the purpose of enforcement action. That scale will be considerably higher than that which is used to define an armed conflict for other purposes.

A closely related question is whether a particular armed conflict should be characterized as international or internal. Obviously, this question does not arise if United Nations forces or national forces operating with United Nations authority are engaged in hostilities against a state (as in the Gulf conflict) or an entity possessing a degree of international status and *de facto* statehood (as in the Korean conflict). In such a case, the conflict will undoubtedly possess an international character. The difficult case arises when a United Nations force

68. Quoted at page 20, *supra*.

69. Bloom, loc. cit. n. 2, at p. 625.

70. At least, it seems that that was the intention. The drafting is, however, less than satisfactory since the application of the laws of international armed conflict brings the Convention's application to an end only in respect of 'a United Nations operation authorized by the Security Council as an enforcement action under Chapter VII of the Charter.' Yet it has been seen that a United Nations operation which was not established under Chapter VII may have certain Chapter VII powers or may engage in heavy fighting merely in the exercise of its right of self-defence. See Greenwood, loc. cit. n. 2, at p. 198.

71. The United States stated in the debate on the draft Convention that the draft would cover the personnel in Rwanda, Somalia and Bosnia and even went so far as say that NATO personnel operating in support of UNPROFOR would have been covered by the Convention, UN Doc. A/49/PV 84, p. 15.

present in a particular state becomes involved in fighting with a rebel group or dissident faction, as happened in Somalia.

The practice of the United Nations here has varied over time. In the Congo in 1960-1963, ONUC became involved in fighting with the secessionist Katanga forces which were already engaged in an internal armed conflict with the Government of Congo. The United Nations considered itself to be bound by (and to benefit from) the entire body of the Geneva Conventions and not just common Article 3 (the only provision in the Conventions which applies to non-international conflicts).[72] This interpretation is strengthened by the fact that there is a strong element of fiction in claiming that a conflict in which forces from several different states are involved is a conflict of a non-international character.

On the other hand, in Somalia, the United Nations and the United States did not regard themselves as parties to an international armed conflict. The fighting in which they became involved was against an entity, the Aideed faction, which was not the government of a state and did not claim to be such. Moreover, unlike, for example, the North Korean forces in the Korean conflict or even the Bosnian Serb forces in Bosnia-Herzegovina, the Aideed faction did not possess the military, political or judicial organization of a state. In these circumstances, to have maintained that both sides were obliged to apply the Prisoners of War Convention would have had an air of unreality. It would also have been difficult to reconcile with the determination of the United Nations to put on trial those Aideed supporters who had attacked United Nations and United States personnel, without, it appears, any regard for whether these attacks would constitute war crimes.[73] In so far as the United Nations or the United States regarded themselves as parties to an armed conflict at all, it seems, therefore, that they characterized that conflict as internal, in contrast to the approach taken in the Congo a generation earlier.

The ambiguity about when a United Nations force is to be considered as a party to an armed conflict and how that conflict should be characterized is regrettable, to say the least, and cannot be reconciled with principle.[74] It is, however, an inevitable product of the tension between the approach on the one hand of IHL in treating all parties to a conflict equally and, at least in the case of an international conflict, excluding the punishment of combatants for the mere act of combatancy and the understandable desire of the United Nations and contributor states both to maintain at least a facade of neutrality and to insist upon punishment of those who attack their personnel.

72. Bowett, op. cit. n. 1, at pp. 509-10.

73. See SC Res. Nos. 837 and 885 (1993).

74. It is e.g., contrary to the approach adopted by the Institut in its Zagreb and Weisbaden Resolutions, n. 1, *supra*.

6. THE RULES OF INTERNATIONAL HUMANITARIAN LAW APPLICABLE TO UNITED NATIONS OPERATIONS

It is necessary, therefore, to examine the rules of IHL which are actually applied in United Nations operations under two different heads – those which apply when the United Nations force or those associated with it are parties to an armed conflict and those which apply when those forces become involved in fighting but are not treated as parties to a conflict.

The first head is largely straightforward. In cases where the United Nations force is a party to an international armed conflict, IHL applicable to international conflicts applies in its entirety. The only question is whether the involvement of the United Nations leads to any difference in the application of those rules. One such difference has already been the subject of comment. The lack of a criminal law or court system in the United Nations means that even where an operation is conducted entirely under United Nations command and control, certain obligations derived from IHL must be the responsibility of the contributing states and not of the United Nations.

A second difference is that the law of neutrality and, therefore, certain rules of IHL referring to neutral states cannot be applied in the same way in a conflict in which the United Nations is directly involved, since a member state of the United Nations cannot be regarded as wholly neutral in such a conflict. A member state which declines to become directly involved in such a conflict may nevertheless render assistance to the United Nations, and in certain circumstances may be obliged to do so, without violating the law of neutrality. Moreover, if the Security Council has used its powers under Chapter VII of the Charter to impose economic sanctions upon a state and, as in the Gulf conflict and the former Yugoslavia, to authorize naval forces to take action to prevent sanctions-breaking, those sanctions are binding upon all member states by virtue of Articles 2(5) and 25 of the Charter (and arguably bind non-member states as well). It follows that, as the Institut has said,

> '... Member States of the Organization may not take advantage of the general rules of the law of neutrality in order to evade obligations laid upon them in pursuance of a decision of the Security Council acting in accordance with the Charter, nor may they depart from the rules of neutrality for the benefit of a party opposing the United Nations forces.'[75]

75. Weisbaden Resolution, loc. cit. n. 1, Art. 4.

These considerations are likely to be particularly important in the law of naval warfare.[76] It is also relevant that the United Nations may adopt means for the enforcement of sanctions which do not entirely correspond with the traditional concepts of the law of naval warfare. The embargo imposed upon Iraq during the Gulf War had many of the features of a blockade but differed from the classic concept of blockade in that it was applied to 'neutral' as well as 'enemy' ports and ships which were intercepted trying to violate the embargo were not taken in prize but merely turned back (some of them on more than one occasion).

The other area of IHL which requires comment is the law of belligerent occupation. It is perfectly possible that the United Nations itself or a state or states acting under its authority could occupy part or all of the territory of an adversary in the course of an international armed conflict.[77] In such a case, the law of belligerent occupation would apply but only unless and until the Security Council used its Chapter VII powers to impose a different regime as part of the measures which it considered necessary for the restoration of peace and security.[78] Such a regime could set aside those parts of the law of belligerent occupation designed to protect the interests of the displaced sovereign (rather than the population). While a resolution of the kind here envisaged has some of the features of an armistice or even a peace treaty, it differs from them in that it derives its legal force from the decision-making powers conferred by the Charter upon the Security Council and not from the agreement of the other party.

In the event that a United Nations force becomes a party to an internal armed conflict, the rules of IHL applicable to such a conflict would apply in the same way as if the United Nations had not been involved.

The more difficult task is to determine how the rules of IHL might be applicable to a United Nations operation which has involved the United Nations in fighting but where the United Nations has not been regarded as a party to an armed conflict. Although, for the reasons given earlier, this situation should not exist at all – either the United Nations force is a party to the conflict and should apply IHL in its entirety (subject only to the observations in the preceding four paragraphs), or it is not, in which case it is not bound by IHL at all – the existence of such a situation is now so commonly accepted that it must be treated as a fact. The task of determining how IHL applies to such a case becomes, in effect, one of ascertaining the content of the 'principles and spirit' which the United Nations has accepted are applicable.

Several attempts have been made to give greater content to the undertaking to respect the 'principles and spirit' of the IHL conventions. In 1995 the Special Committee on Peace-keeping Operations requested the Secretary-General to draw up

76. See L. Doswald-Beck, ed., *San Remo Manual on International Law Applicable to Armed Conflicts at Sea* (Cambridge, Grotius Publications 1995) paras. 7-9.

77. The coalition states occupied about 15 percent of Iraq at the end of the Gulf Conflict.

78. As was done in the Gulf conflict in Res. Nos. 686 and 687 (1991).

a code of conduct for peacekeeping personnel consistent with applicable IHL, so as to ensure the highest standards of conduct.[79] That same year, a meeting of Experts convened by the ICRC produced a preliminary report on the subject.[80] In 1996 the ICRC submitted to the Secretary-General a 32-paragraph set of draft guidelines based on the proposals of the Meeting of Experts. Those guidelines, in turn, formed the basis for a draft directive on IHL prepared by the Secretariat of the United Nations in 1997.[81] At the time of going to press, the draft directive had not been adopted in final form and it was likely that changes would be made to it before it was adopted. Detailed comment upon the draft would therefore be inappropriate.[82]

It is, however, worth noting that there appears to be agreement that certain principles of IHL are applicable to United Nations operations which fall below the level of participation in an armed conflict. That is particularly the case with the principles concerning methods and means of warfare, in particular, the principles of distinction and proportionality. The application of the relevant parts of IHL on this subject should not be controversial, since it is difficult to see how it could be argued that a United Nations force not participating in an armed conflict should be entitled to employ weapons or to attack targets which would be forbidden to that same force if it were to become a party to an armed conflict. The only danger of the approach adopted in the draft directive is that the attempt to reduce a series of quite elaborate rules to more straightforward principles may end up by stating in an unqualified form principles which in Additional Protocol I and other texts are subject to certain exceptions and qualifications.

A second body of principles which is generally accepted as applicable is that relating to the treatment of the wounded, sick and shipwrecked. The rules on this subject in the First and Second Geneva Conventions are almost entirely uncontroversial and serve a purely humanitarian goal. It should, therefore, be possible to go beyond the very brief statement in the draft directive and include most of the provisions of the two conventions.

Finally, there are a number of rules relating to the treatment of detainees. This is a far more difficult subject, since the classification of a detainee as a prisoner of war would lead to the application of the Third Convention and involve a degree of recognition of the status of the party which he served and his right to participate in combat. It has long been one of the most contentious questions regarding the applicability of IHL to United Nations operations. The application of the Fourth Convention would also raise difficult questions regarding belligerent occupation. The

79. UN Doc. A/50/230, 22 June 1995.

80. ICRC, *Report of a Meeting of Experts on the Applicability of International Humanitarian Law to United Nations Forces* (Geneva, ICRC 1995).

81. Directives for UN Forces Regarding Respect for International Humanitarian Law.

82. It is hoped to comment in a later volume on any final directive or guidelines issued by the United Nations.

approach adopted in the draft directive is therefore based upon that employed in Article 75 of Additional Protocol I, which lays down certain fundamental guarantees for any person detained in time of conflict who does not benefit from better protection under another regime.

The law of belligerent occupation is rightly considered not to apply when a United Nations force is involved in administering territory but has not been a party to an international armed conflict. That was the case, for example, in Somalia.[83]

7. INTERNATIONAL HUMANITARIAN LAW AND THE PROTECTION OF UNITED NATIONS AND ASSOCIATED PERSONNEL

So far, this article has concentrated upon the application of IHL as a constraint upon the operations of United Nations forces. The relationship between United Nations forces and IHL also, however, involves consideration of the extent to which the law may provide protection for the members of such forces and personnel associated with them. This is a large subject in its own right and space permits only a brief examination.

Where a United Nations force is a party to an international armed conflict, its members benefit from the same protection under the Geneva Conventions and the rest of IHL which applies to members of a belligerent state's forces. Thus, if captured, they are entitled to the protection of the Third Convention regarding the treatment of prisoners of war. Their murder or ill-treatment after capture would thus be a grave breach of the Convention. They are, however, liable to be attacked by legitimate combatants and may be killed or wounded without any violation of IHL so long as no prohibited weapons or methods of warfare are employed. Civilian personnel with such a force would benefit from the provisions of the Fourth Convention.

A more difficult case arises where a United Nations force is not a party to an armed conflict but is nevertheless subjected to attacks by one or more of the belligerent forces. International Humanitarian Law make virtually no express provision for such a case. A rare exception is Article 37(1)(d) of Additional Protocol I, which prohibits 'the feigning of protected status by the use of signs, emblems or uniforms of the United Nations'. This provision assumes that members of a United Nations force have some degree of 'protected status'[84] but it seems that that is not a special

83. For an interesting discussion of the administration of Somalia and the law of belligerent occupation, see M.J. Kelly, *Peace Operations* (Canberra, Australian Government Printing Service 1997), Chapter 4. Major Kelly, a legal officer with the Australian Defence Force, served in the United Nations operation in Somalia.

84. The *travaux préparatoires* of the provision make clear that it was not intended to apply to situations in which United Nations forces were engaged as combatants.

status but merely the right to enjoy the same protection afforded to civilians and others not involved in the conflict as combatants.

Nevertheless, it is possible to infer certain other protections. The parties to an international conflict have a duty under Articles 69-71 of Additional Protocol I to respect and protect United Nations personnel engaged in relief operations. More generally, since United Nations personnel not directly engaged in the conflict and their buildings, equipment etc., would not constitute a military objective within the definition in Additional Protocol I, Articles 48 and 50-52, attacks upon them would be unlawful. If taken prisoner, such personnel would, at the very least, be entitled to the fundamental guarantees in Additional Protocol I, Article 75 Since all of these provisions of Additional Protocol I are regarded as largely declaratory of customary law, it would matter little whether or not the belligerents are party to the Protocol. In addition, the protocol on landmines attached to the United Nations Convention on Prohibitions and Restrictions on the Use of Certain Conventional Weapons, 1981, entitles United Nations personnel to a degree of protection from the use of land-mines.[85]

Where a United Nations force becomes subject to attack in an internal armed conflict to which it is not a party, a limited degree of protection is also implicit in the relevant rules of IHL. Thus, members of such a United Nations force would be 'persons taking no active part in hostilities' for the purposes of common Article 3 of the Geneva Conventions. Acts of violence against them and hostage-taking would therefore be unlawful. The massacre of members of the Belgian contingent in UNAMIR in April 1994 during the Rwandan civil war was thus a clear violation of Article 3. The Security Council's condemnation of that attack as a violation of IHL should be interpreted as a reference to that provision, as well as to the status of forces agreement concluded only a few months earlier.[86] Members of a United Nations force which is not a party to the conflict may also benefit from more detailed protection under Articles 4 and 5 of Additional Protocol II.

The problem is that these provisions presuppose that the United Nations force is taking no active part in hostilities. Clearly this will often be the case, as it was in Rwanda. Equally, if the United Nations force has become a party to the conflict, quite different rules will apply. As we have seen, there is, however, a grey area in the middle. The United Nations may have considered that it was not a party to the conflict in Somalia but it is difficult to see that UNOSOM and associated forces were 'taking no active part in the hostilities', at least after their intervention to arrest General

85. Protocol II, Article 8. An amended version of this Protocol was adopted in 1996, 35 *ILM* (1996) p. 1209. A treaty banning the use of anti-personnel land mines was adopted in 1997. The former entered into force on 3 December 1998, the latter will enter into force on 1 March 1999.

86. Res. 912 (1994) para. 5. On the status of forces agreement, see above, pp. 21-22.

Aideed.[87] It was because the provisions of IHL were considered to offer inadequate protection to members of United Nations operations that the 1994 Convention was adopted.

8. DO UNITED NATIONS FORCES HAVE A DUTY TO TAKE ACTION AGAINST VIOLATIONS OF INTERNATIONAL HUMANITARIAN LAW BY OTHERS?

It has frequently been suggested that, quite apart from the question whether IHL operates as a constraint upon what acts a United Nations operation may itself perform, a United Nations force has a duty to take action against violations of IHL by others, irrespective of whether it is itself a party to an armed conflict. This duty is said to be derived from common Article 1 to the Geneva Conventions and the corresponding provision in Additional Protocol I.[88]

In some cases, the right and the duty to ensure respect is an express part of the mandate of the force concerned. It is now generally accepted that large scale violations of human rights taking place within a state are capable in principle of constituting a threat to international peace and security which the Security Council is entitled to take measures to address. It would thus be lawful – and is, today, a practical possibility – for the Security Council to establish an operation with a specific humanitarian mandate or a mandate which included a duty to ensure that warring parties complied with the principles of IHL or human rights law.

A much more difficult question arises, however, where a United Nations operation is not set up with the specific purpose of enforcing humanitarian law or human rights but rather to conduct traditional peacekeeping activities or the delivery of humanitarian supplies. The forces involved in such an operation may well, in the course of their functions, come across serious violations of IHL. In those circumstances, do they have a right or a duty to take action, including military action, to put an end to such violations? It should be clear that a *right* to take such action is implicit, not only in the mandate of the United Nations force itself, but also in the Geneva Conventions. Whether there is a legal *duty* to take such action is a different matter. There is no obvious legal basis for the existence of such a duty. For the reasons given in Part 2, above, it is suggested that the argument that such a duty can be derived from the duty to 'ensure respect' in common Article I is unsound. The very general terms of

87. See *Report of the Commission of Inquiry established pursuant to Security Council Resolutions 885* (1993). UN Doc. S/1994/653.

88. For a moving argument to this effect, see J. A. MacInnis, 'Peacekeeping and International Humanitarian Law', 3 *International Peacekeeping* (1996) p. 92. Major-General MacInnis was deputy Force Commander of UNPROFOR. See, however, the different perspective offered by Siekmann, p. 301.

that provision are being asked to bear a weight which they were never intended to carry and which has never been acknowledged in state practice.

Moreover, while it is attractive from a humanitarian standpoint to argue that a legal duty to take action of this kind exists, considerable practical difficulties arise. The prevention of violations of IHL involves far more than simply the act of interceding in a particular case. Where there are systematic abuses taking place, their prevention may require the initiation of combat operations on a large scale. Many United Nations forces are simply not equipped for an operation of that kind. In addition, intervention by military means to prevent violations of IHL, even if it was, in principle, impartial, would almost certainly be seen by those on the receiving end of such intervention as compromising that impartiality. It would therefore make the discharge of the force's mandate even more difficult. To give a practical example, a lightly armed United Nations force charged with the responsibility for delivering relief supplies will almost certainly be forced to negotiate safe passage with a variety of local forces. If the United Nations force then intervenes to prevent one of those local forces from violating IHL, it is highly likely that that action will prejudice the ability of the force to continue delivering relief supplies and thus fulfilling the mandate which the Security Council gave it.

Consequently, if it is to be said that there is a duty for a United Nations force to intervene, at whatever cost, to prevent violations of IHL, then that duty has to be recognised not by the force commander but by the Security Council and the principal states in setting up the operation in the first place and determining the force levels and the nature of the equipment with which that force is to be provided.

9. CONCLUSIONS

Perhaps inevitably, this study has shown that the relationship between IHL and United Nations military operations remains the subject of considerable uncertainty. Nevertheless, a few conclusions can be suggested.

(1) In principle, a United Nations force, or a force authorized by the United Nations, is required, if it becomes party to an armed conflict, to apply as a matter of law the relevant body of IHL, customary and conventional, subject only to the fact that the application of certain rules of the law of naval warfare and belligerent occupation may be modified as a result of the United Nations involvement.

(2) The character of the conflict will determine whether the relevant body of law is that applicable to international or non-international conflicts.

(3) The mandate of the United Nations force and whether it is classified as an enforcement, peace-enforcement or peacekeeping operation is not decisive of whether IHL is applicable, since any class of United Nations operation is capable of becoming involved in hostilities. Nevertheless, an enforcement action is, as a practical matter, more likely to lead to involvement in a conflict than a peacekeeping operation.

(4) In practice, however, there is a great reluctance to acknowledge that a United Nations force which was not established in order to carry out enforcement action has become a party to an armed conflict even if it has become involved in quite heavy fighting. The consequence is that a higher threshold for determining the existence of armed conflict is applied in such cases than in relation to fighting between states.

(5) It is therefore possible for a United Nations force to engage in combat operations without being treated as a party to an armed conflict. In such a case, it is accepted that the force has a duty to comply with the principles and spirit of the principal conventions on IHL. Attempts are being made to give greater substance to this reference to principles and spirit.

(6) International humanitarian law offers some protection to the members of a United Nations force which is not a party to a conflict but that protection is insufficient and is to be supplemented by the 1994 Convention.

(7) In the absence of a specific provision in the mandate, a United Nations force has no legal duty to take action against violations of IHL by other persons or groups, although it has a right to do so.

IMPLEMENTING LEGISLATION FOR THE APPLICATION OF THE LAW ON THE INTERNATIONAL CRIMINAL TRIBUNAL FOR THE FORMER YUGOSLAVIA AND CRITERIA FOR ITS EVALUATION*

Ivo Josipović**

1. LEGAL NATURE OF THE INTERNATIONAL CRIMINAL TRIBUNAL AS THE BASIS OF THE EXISTENCE OF IMPLEMENTATION LEGISLATION

The establishment of the International Tribunal for the Prosecution of Persons Responsible for Serious Violations of International Humanitarian Law Committed in the Territory of the Former Yugoslavia Since 1991 (ICTY) and the adoption of its Statute heralded a new page in the history of international, particularly international criminal, law.[1] For the first time since World War II, an international criminal court was established. The Tribunal was created in order to achieve important legal and political goals: to punish perpetrators of serious violations of international humanitarian law committed in the former Yugoslavia

** Ivo Josipović is Assistant Professor of Criminal Procedure, Faculty of Law, University of Zagreb.

1. The International Criminal Tribunal for the Prosecution of Persons Responsible for Serious Violations of International Humanitarian Law Committed in the Territory of Former Yugoslavia Since 1991 (hereinafter, the ICTY or the Tribunal) was founded and its Statute was enacted by Security Council Resolution 827/1993 of 25 May 1993. For the development of an international criminal court, see M.C. Bassiouni, 'Introduction to the History of Establishing an International Criminal Court', in *International Criminal Law,* part 3 (1986) p. 181 et seq.; H Grebing, 'Zur Frage der Schaffung eines Internationalen Gerichthofs' [Problems Relating to Establishment of International Criminal Tribunal] in Goldtdammer's *Archiv für Strafrecht* (1976) p. 97; and M C. Bassiouni, 'From Versailles to Rwanda in Seventy-Five Years: The Need to Establish a Permanent International Criminal Court', 10 *Harvard Human Rights Journal* (1997) pp. 11-62.

Yearbook of International Humanitarian Law
Volume 1 - 1998 - pp. 35-68

since 1991[2]; to prevent further crimes; to facilitate the peace process; and to serve as a test for a future permanent international criminal court.

The establishment of the ICTY redefines some of the fundamental principles of international law, including the principle of state sovereignty.[3] A condition for coexistence of a reasonably efficient international court with sovereign states is that states adopt and perform certain obligations originating from the new international criminal law. International obligations of a state may be created either voluntarily, by acceptance of an international treaty or another legal instrument, or by imposition of certain obligations by another state, a group of states or international organisations.[4]

Earlier international criminal adjudication was based on the dictates of the victorious forces in the First and the Second World Wars. After World War I, Articles 227 and 228 of the Treaty of Versailles, signed on 28 June 1919, provided for the trial on war crimes charges of the German Emperor Wilhelm II Hohenzollern and the highest officers of his army.[5] Despite the fact that the formal legal framework for the obligation was a treaty, it is clear that the obligation of Germany was created by the dictate of the victorious forces. The same can be said of the peace treaty between Finland and the Soviet Union signed after World War II, where an obligation was imposed on Finland to prosecute its politicians and military officers responsible for the Finnish-Soviet war.[6] Trials

2. See M.C. Bassiouni, 'The Commission of Experts Established Pursuant to Security Council Resolution 780: Investigating Violations of International Humanitarian Law in the Former Yugoslavia', 5 *Criminal Law Forum* (1994) pp. 279-340.

3. See J.B. Attanasio, 'Reporter's Overview and Conclusions: Of Soveignty, Globalisation and Court', 28 *Journal of International Law and Politics* (1996).

4. On the notion of *jus cogens* in international law, see extensively in L. Hannikaninen, *Peremptory Norms (IUS COGENS)* in *International Law* (Finnish Lawyers' Publishing Company, Helsinki 1988).

5. The Emperor was granted asylum in the Netherlands and legal proceedings against him were never instituted. As no international criminal court existed, the procedure was entrusted to the Supreme Court in Leipzig. Due to various legal and actual obstacles and the disinterestedness of the victorious forces, this court punished only a small number of perpetrators of war crimes. See D. Krapac, *Međunarodni sud za ratne zločine na području bivše Jugoslavije* [International War Crimes Tribunal for the Former Yugoslavia] (Hrvatski helsinški odbor i Hrvatski pravni centar, Zagreb 1995) p. 9.

6. Conflict between Finland and Russia in respect of the border in Eastern Karjala dates back to 1918 when Finnish troops failed to realise the idea of their political leaders concerning new borders with Russia. During World War II, conflict between Finland and Russia (then the USSR) developed in two phases. The first was the so-called 'Winter War' (1939-1940), when the USSR attacked Finland and, following three and a half months of war, managed to sign the Moscow Peace Accord and to make significant territorial gains. In 1941, Finland became a German ally and entered into war against the USSR in the hope of a quick success and recapture of the lost territory. The initial success of the Finnish army, which at first managed to regain the lost territory and to capture

in Nürnberg and Tokyo were conducted on the basis of decisions of victorious forces, particularly on the basis of the London Agreement of 1945; the Statute of the International Military Tribunal; Law No. 10, enacted by the Supervising Council for Germany; and the Decision of General McArthur on the establishment of the International Military Tribunal for the Far East[7]. It should be noted that the above-mentioned decisions were applied as autonomously accepted rules of international law in some states, whereas other states had to apply the same rules as imposed by virtue of authority of the victorious states.

The project of an international criminal court involved establishment of the court by an international convention to which states shall accede voluntarily.[8] Conversely, the ICTY was established on the basis of Chapter VII of the United Nations Charter as a compulsory, generally binding measure, undertaken under the authority of the Security Council to prevent a breach of the peace. The Security Council used the authority specified in Article 41 of the UN Charter to take necessary measures in order to maintain peace and prevent armed conflict. By invoking Article 29 of the UN Charter, enabling it to establish bodies for assistance, the Security Council established the ICTY as its subsidiary organ. The fact that the ICTY was established pursuant to Chapter VII of the UN Charter and the fact that Security Council Resolution 827 invokes Chapter VII means that all decisions of the Security Council related to the operation of the ICTY are mandatory for all states (Arts. 2(2) and 25 of the UN Charter).

Before proceeding to an analysis of national legislation enabling performance of the obligations of the respective states arising from Resolution 827, from the Statute of the ICTY and from the Tribunal's Rules of Procedure and Evidence,[9] it is necessary to reiterate that these obligations were not created, as it is dominant in international law, by voluntary acceptance by these states, but by

---

Eastern Karjala, finally turned to failure. In 1944, Finland admitted defeat in the Moscow Peace Treaty and undertook to try politicians responsible for the war. See L. Hannikainen and A. Raija-Rosas, *Implementing Humanitarian Law Applicable in Armed Conflicts: The Case of Finland* (Martinus Nijhoff Publishers, Dordrecht 1992) pp. 41-48. See also I. Josipović, 'The International Criminal Tribunal and the Croatian Legal System', II *Croatian International Relations Review* (1996) pp. 2-3.

7. See B.V.A. Röling and A. Cassese, *The Tokyo Trial and Beyond* (Polity Press, Cambridge 1993) pp. 1-6. There were several national criminal courts acting in the Far East. They are outside the scope of this article, which considers only international tribunals. E.g., see R.J. Pritchard, 'The Gift of Clemency following British War Crimes Trials in the Far East, 1946-1948', 7 *Criminal Law Forum*, No. 1 (1996) pp. 15-49.

8. For details see: M.C. Bassiouni, *A Draft International Criminal Code and Draft Statute for an International Criminal Tribunal* (Martinus Nijhoff Publishers, Dordrecht 1987). M.C. Bassiouni, *Draft statute international criminal tribunal* (Nouvelles études pénales, Toulouse, Eres 1992).

9. Hereinafter, Rules.

a generally binding decision of the Security Council. Furthermore, it is often forgotten that the mandatory character of Resolution 827 and provisions of the Statute and the Rules means that they are binding not only on the states that were involved in the armed conflict on the territory of the former Yugoslavia since 1991 but on all states. To what extent such a concept of a criminal court changes the traditional understanding of sovereignty can best be seen from the ICTY decisions in respect of the two principal issues: the issue of jurisdiction of the Court[10] and the issue of *subpoenae* to states and their officials[11].

Unlike the ICTY, it was always envisaged that the legal basis of any permanent court would be a multilateral convention. This method has both advantages and disadvantages when compared to the way the ICTY was created. The futue will show which of the two shall prevail.[12]

2. GENERAL REVIEW OF IMPLEMENTING LAWS OF INDIVIDUAL STATES

The fact that the ICTY has its seat in the Netherlands, whereas the crimes over which it has jurisdiction were committed on the territory of the former Yugoslavia, as well as the fact that perpetrators are located in different states where the ICTY has neither its own police force nor the possibility of direct action, clearly indicates that the efficiency of the Court depends on cooperation of states with the Court and on national implementation of its decisions and orders.[13] Most states take the position that rules of international law are not self-executing but have to be incorporated into national legislation. Considering that international law creates obligations for states, the objection that internal law, including national constitutional law, prevents performance of their obligations in respect of the ICTY is unacceptable. In case of conflict of national legal systems and rules of international law, a state, depending on its understanding

10. *Prosecutor* v. *Duško Tadić*, Decision on Defence Motion for Interlocutory Appeal on Jurisdiction, Case No. IT-94-1-T, 2 October 1995.

11. See Judgment on the Request of the Republic of Croatia for Review of the Decision of Trial Chamber II of 18 July 1997, Case No. IT-14-AR108 *bis*. See Malanczuk, *infra* at. p. 229.

12. Such an analysis is beyond the scope of this paper.

13. Art. 29 of the ICTY Statute provides '1. States shall cooperate with the International Tribunal in the investigation and prosecution of persons accused of committing serious violations of international humanitarian law.
2. States shall comply without undue delay with any request for assistance or an order issued by a Trial Chamber, including but not limited to: (a) the identification and location of persons; (b) the taking of testimony and the production of evidence; (c) the service of documents; (d) the arrest or detention of persons; (e) the surrender or the transfer of the accused to the International Tribunal.'

of the relationship between national and international law, either directly applies the rules of international law, or has an obligation to amend its legislation, including its Constitution, if necessary, in order to ensure compliance.

The number of states that have enacted implementing legislation seems to be rather small. However, when one considers the number of states which could come into a position to perform the orders of the ICTY in practice, one can be relatively satisfied with the number of states that have adopted the necessary legislation. Certainly, the enactment and enforcement of appropriate implementing laws by the states which were directly involved in the conflicts and by the states where indicted persons and witnesses are likely to be found is of paramount importance.

In order to meet their obligations in respect of the ICTY, the following states have enacted specific laws:[14] Australia[15]; Austria[16]; Belgium[17]; Bosnia and Herzegovina[18]; Croatia[19]; Hungary[20]; Denmark[21]; Finland[22]; France[23];

14. Information concerning laws of particular states and their English translations were obtained courtesy of the Registrar of the ICTY and reflects the situation as of 1 November 1997. A further source of information concerning the laws of some states was 'State Cooperation Implementing Legislation,' Update 1 November 1996, produced by the ICTY. For the sake of brevity, all laws shall be quoted in abbreviated form according to the state of origin. E.g., Italian Law, German Law, Austrian Law, etc. The Federal Republic of Yugoslavia has entered into a special agreement with the ICTY on operation of the Office of the Prosecutor of the ICTY on its territory. However this agreement cannot be considered implementing legislation.

15. International War Crimes Tribunals Act of 24 August 1995. Australian law is interesting as it applies not only to the ICTY but to all international war crimes tribunals. In addition, unlike the laws of other states, which regulate the matter rather superficially, mainly referring to analogous application of appropriate domestic legislation (procedures, extradition), Australian law is quite extensive and regulates the subject matter in detail in 85 elaborate articles.

16. Austrian Federal Law on Cooperation with the International Tribunals, effective as of 1 June 1996.

17. *Projet de loi relatif à la coopération judicarie avec le tribunal international pour l'ex-Yougoslavie et le tribunal international pour le Ruanda* [Law on Recognition of the International Criminal Tribunal for the former Yugoslavia and the International Criminal Tribunal for Rwanda and Cooperation with these Tribunals] of 1 February 1996, effective as of 22 March 1996.

18. The Government of the Republic of Bosnia and Herzegovina (the Assembly elected during pre-war elections was not active at that time) has enacted the *Uredba sa zakonskom snagom o izručenju po molbi Međunarodnog suda* [Decree with Force of Law on Deferral Upon Request by the International Tribunal], Službeni list BiH No. 12/1995 of 10 April 1995), and the *Odluka o izražavanju spremnosti Republike Bosne i Hercegovine Savjetu sigurnosti UN-a o prihvatanju osoba osuđenih presudama međunarodnog suda za ratne zločine na izdržavanje izrečenih kazni* [Decision expressing readiness of the Republic of Bosnia and Herzegovina to accept persons sentenced by the International War Crimes Tribunal], Službeni list BiH No. 2/1995 of 15 January 1995. In addition, Bosnia and Herzegovina has entered into a special agreement of cooperation with the ICTY which merely enumerates obligations in accordance with the Statute and confirms the adherence of Bosnia and Herzegovina thereto.

19. *Ustavni zakon o suradnji Republike Hrvatske s Međunarodnim kaznenim sudom* [Constitutional Act on the Cooperation with the International Criminal Tribunal], *Narodne novine* No. 32/1996, hereinafter, the Constitutional Act. On the basis of the Constitutional Act, the Government

Germany[24]; Iceland[25]; Italy[26]; the Netherlands[27]; New Zealand[28]; Norway[29];

of the Republic of Croatia has enacted the *Uredba o uredu za suradnju s Međunarodnim kaznenim sudom* [Decree About an Office for Cooperation with the International Criminal Tribunal], *Narodne novine* No. 61/1996.

20. Act XXXIX of 1996 on the fulfillment of obligations deriving from the Statute of the International Tribunal Established for Punishing the Serious Violations of International Humanitarian Law Committed in the Territory of the Former Yugoslavia. Available only in English.

21. *Lov om straforolgning ved det internationale tribunal til padommelse af krigsforbrydelser i det tidligere Jugoslavien* [Act on Criminal Proceedings before the International Tribunal for the Prosecution of Persons Responsible for War Crimes Committed in the Territory of Former Yugoslavia] Act No. 1099 of 21 December 1994.

22. *Laki entisen Jugoslavian alucella tehtyjä rikoksia käsittelevän sotarikostuomioistuimen toimivallasta ja tuomioistuimelle annettaviasta oikeusavusta* [Act on Jurisdiction of the International Tribunal for the Prosecution of Persons Responsible for Crimes Committed in the Territory of the Former Yugoslavia and on Legal Assistance to the International Tribunal] 5 January 1994/12.

23. *Loi no. 95-1 du 2 janvier 1995 portant adaption de la législation française aux dispositions de la résolution 827 du Conseil de sécurité des Nations Unies instituant un tribunal international en vue de juter les personnes présumées responsable de violations graves du droit international humanitaire commises sur le territoire de l'ex-Yougoslavie depuis 1991* [Law no. 95-1 of 2 January 1995 on adapting French law to the provisions of United Nations Security Council Resolution 827 establishing an International Tribunal for the Prosecution of Persons Responsible for Crimes Committed in the Territory of the Former Yugoslavia since 1991].

24. *Gesetz über die Zusammenarbeit mit dem Internationalen Strafgericht für das ehemalige Jugoslawien, Bundesgesetzblatt Nr. 18/1995, 31.3.1995* [Law on regulating the co-operation with the International Tribunal for the Former Yugoslavia of 31 March 1995].

25. Law enacted on 9 May 1994, English version not available.

26. *Disposizioni in materia di cooperazione con il Tribunale internazionale competente per gravi violazioni del diritto umanitario commesse nei territori della ex Jugoslavia* [Provisions on Cooperation with the International Tribunal for the Prosecution of Serious Violations of International Humanitarian Law Committed in the Territory of the Former Yugoslavia] Decree-Law no. 544 of 28 December 1993 and no. 120 of 14 February 1994. Italy was the first state to enact an implementing law.

27. *Wet van 21 april 1994, houdende bepalingen verband houdende met de instelling van het International Tribunaal voor de vervolging van personen aansprakelijk voor ernstige schendingen van het internatiionale humanitaire recht, begaan op het grondgebied van het voormalige Joegoslaviën sedert 1991* [Provisions relating to the Establishment of the International Tribunal for the Prosecution of Persons Responsible for Serious Violations of International Humanitarian Law Committed in the Territory of the Former Yugoslavia Since 1991, of 21 April 1994].

28. The 1995 International War Crimes Tribunals Act.

29. Act relating to the incorporation into Norwegian law of UN SC Resolution on the establishment of an International Tribunal for Crimes committed in the former Yugoslavia of 1 June 1994. Available only in English.

Spain[30]; Sweden[31]; Switzerland[32]; the United Kingdom[33]; and the United States of America[34].

Some states have informed the Court that they are preparing appropriate laws (e.g., Turkey and Sri Lanka). Russia, Korea, Singapore and Venezuela informed the ICTY that their performance of obligations in respect of the ICTY does not require enactment of any special legal rules. Other states, when asked by the ICTY, had not issued any statement at the time of writing. It should also be mentioned that the Council of Europe has prepared a Model Law for Implementation of Provisions of Resolution 827 (including the Statute of the ICTY, which is an integral part thereof) to National Legislation.[35] In addition to the above-mentioned, agreements with the Court on execution of prison sentences in respect of convicted persons, which can be understood as implementation legislation in the broader sense, were signed by some states. Such an obligation was already introduced to implementation legislation by thirteen

30. *12552 Ley Orgánica 15/94, de l junio para la cooperación con el Tribunal Internacional para el enjuiciamento de los presuntos responsables de violaciones graves del derecho internacional humanitario cometidas en el territoriao de la ex Yugoslavia, 2 junio 1994* [Act 15/1994 on co-operation with the International Tribunal for the Prosecution of Persons Responsible for Serious Violations of International Humanitarian Law Committed in the Territory of the Former Yugoslavia, Law of 2 June 1994].

31. Act relating to establishment of an International Tribunal for Trial of Crimes Committed in former Yugoslavia, of 1 June 1994. Available only in English.

32. *Arréte fédéral relatif a la coopération avec les tribunaux internationaux chartésde poursuivre les violations graves du droit international humanitaire, 21 decembre 1995* [Federal Law on co-operation with International Tribunal for the Prosecution of Persons Responsible for Serious Violations of International Humanitarian Law Committed in the Territory of the Former Yugoslavia since 1991, of 21 December 1995].

33. United Nations (International Tribunal) (Former Yugoslavia) Order 1996, entered into force on 15 March 1996.

34. On 5 October 1994, the USA signed with the ICTY 'Agreement on the Surrender of Persons', on the basis of which the US President signed the National Defense Authorization Act for Fiscal Year 1996 on 22 January 1996. Section 1342 of this Act is titled 'Judicial Assistance to the International Tribunal for Yugoslavia and the International Tribunal for Rwanda'. The Agreement and the Act itself regulate only one of the required aspects of cooperation with the Tribunal. A decision of the United States District Court for the Southern District of Texas, Laredo Division (1997 US Dist. LEXIS 20714) of 17 December 1997 which shall be discussed below, completely overruled American implementation legislation.

35. The Model itself actually transcribes provisions of the Statute and the Rules and determines methods of communication with the ICTY through the Ministry of Foreign Affairs or the Ministry of Justice. Therefore, the Model does not require any specific elaboration short of remarking that, in respect of performance of obligation to surrender, it envisages control of the highest court in the state, but only in respect of formal requirements for surrender, without a right to decide on the merits (Art. 5, point 6 of the Model).

states.[36] Some of these states have specifically informed the Court of their readiness to accept convicts.[37] The Netherlands has not only enacted a law on performance of obligations arising out of the Statute of the ICTY, but, as the host state of the ICTY, on 27 May 1994, entered into a separate agreement with the United Nations regulating the status of the ICTY in respect of Dutch state authorities.[38]

3. CRITERIA FOR EVALUATION OF IMPLEMENTATION LEGISLATION

3.1 General remarks

The main criterion for the evaluation of the implementation legislation of each particular state is whether this legislation entirely enables the cooperation of the respective state with the ICTY and the fulfilment of states' obligations on the

36. Austria; Belgium; Bosnia and Herzegovina; Croatia; Denmark; Finland; Germany; Italy; the Netherlands; Norway; Spain; Sweden; and Switzerland.

37. Bosnia and Herzegovina; Croatia; Denmark; Finland; Germany; Italy; The Netherlands; Norway; and Sweden. Two other states (Iran and Pakistan) which did not enact special implementing legislation did likewise. The ICTY enters into agreements on execution of prison sentences with individual states. Such agreements contain the same conditions as specified by the Rules. Some states have agreed to accept prisoners but with reservations. For example, Spain expressed her readiness to accept convicts as a matter of principle, but not at the present time (Letter dated 28 March 1995). Germany, Sweden and Switzerland are willing to accept their citizens only. Denmark shall decide on its readiness to accept a convict in each particular case, whereas Finland will accept a maximum of five convicts. Norway shall accept a limited number of convicts depending on 'individual assessment in each particular case'. See State Cooperation Implementing Legislation, Update, 1 November 1996, edited by the ICTY, pp. 3-4. On the other hand, The Bahamas; Belarus; Belize; Burkina Faso; Ecuador; Liechtenstein; Malaysia; Poland; and Slovenia have explicitly indicated that they are not in a position to accept convicts in execution of prison sentences. Information according to Internet www page of the ICTY, Fact Sheet of 22 December 1997, http://www. un.org/icty/subla-e.htm.

38. Agreement between the United Nations and the Kingdom of the Netherlands concerning the headquarters of the International Tribunal for the Prosecution of Persons Responsible for Serious Violations of International Humanitarian Law Committed in the Territory of the Former Yugoslavia since 1991. Since the Agreement does not relate to the subject matter of criminal law and to implementation of rules enabling performance of obligations in respect of the ICTY, but to mutual rights and obligations originating from the fact that the Netherlands is the host state to the seat of the Tribunal, it shall not be discussed any further.

basis of Resolution 827, the Statute and the Rules.[39] States' most important obligations *vis-à-vis* the ICTY are the following[40]:

a) General duty of full cooperation with the ICTY and its bodies, and, in accordance with this, the obligation to harmonise national legal systems with obligations in respect of the ICTY;[41]

b) Acceptance of jurisdiction of the ICTY and its primacy in respect of the trial of crime perpetrators, including deferral of cases which are *sub judice* before national courts to the ICTY.[42]

c) Provision of legal assistance by enforcing requests and orders issued by the ICTY.[43] Possible forms of legal assistance are enumerated in an non-exhaustive list either in the quoted provision of the Statute or in the Rules:

c.i) Obligations related to production and conservation of evidence; identification of locations and persons; taking witness testimonies; and production of other evidence and service of documents. Rule 8 of the Rules envisages an obligation of states to supply the Prosecutor with information within the framework of the obligation specified by Article 29 of the Statute,[44] as well as the right of the Prosecutor (which means, as a corollary, a duty of states) to require states and international organisations to cooperate in investigations[45] and to require states to perform urgent actions in respect of conservation of evidence and arrest and protection of witnesses and victims of crimes.

c.ii) Arrest, detention and surrender of indicted persons to the ICTY. The obligation to arrest and surrender accused persons is regulated by Rules 55 to 59 of the Rules and by rules regulating provisional measures requested by the

39. Certainly, other criteria for evaluation applicable to any legal system could also be applied (e.g., nomotechnical quality). However, they are not the subject of this paper. Bearing in mind the aim of this study, I shall limit myself to the above-mentioned basic criteria of evaluation. It should be remembered that Resolution 780 (1992) of 6. Oct. 1992, establishing the Commission of Experts, introduced certain obligations for states. As it does not relate directly to the work of the ICTY, and because Resolution 827, the Statute and the Rules include obligations specified in it, it shall not be further discussed.

40. For details see I. Josipović, 'The International Criminal Tribunal and the Croatian Legal System', op. cit. n. 6, at pp. 5-6.

41. Para. 4 of Resolution 827 and Art. 29(1) of the Statute.

42. Arts. 9 and 10 of the Statute; Arts. 9-13 of the Rules.

43. Art. 29(2) of the Statute.

44. It should be noted that the Prosecutor is an integral part of the Tribunal, an approach which can be faulted. Regardless of the fact that arrest, detention and surrender of accused persons to the ICTY are listed within the framework of provision of legal assistance, in this paper I shall deal with them separately from other forms of legal assistance, due to their specificities.

45. Rule 39(iii).

prosecutor.[46] In relation to the obligation to arrest, detain and surrender accused persons, Rule 60 regulates the obligation to advertise the indictment when an accused is at large.

c.iii) A specific form of assistance to the ICTY is the possibility for states to appear before the Court as *Amici Curiae*[47] through their representatives;

d) Recognition of status, privileges and immunities to officials of the Court, including the Prosecutor, the Registrar and their staff, to the same extent as is accorded to officials of the United Nations (Art. 30 of the Statute);[48]

e) Obligation to protect witnesses and victims pursuant to Article 22 of the Statute and Rules 75 and 39(iii) of the Rules of Procedure and Evidence;

f) Obligations in respect of restitution of property and compensation of damages (Rules 105 and 106);

g) Two facilitative contributions to the operation of the ICTY which cannot be defined as obligations, but as voluntary contributions to the mission of the ICTY:

g.i) Contributions of states in money, equipment, services and staff (point 5 of Resolution 827), and

g.ii) Enforcement of sentences of imprisonment (Art. 27 of the Statute and Rules 103 and 123).

Although, when evaluating implementation legislation, one has to take into account all of the above-mentioned obligations, bearing in mind the limitations of this paper, national legal systems shall be evaluated on the basis of the following three criteria, which we deem the most fundamental:

a) acceptance of jurisdiction of the ICTY in all its aspects;

b) arrest and surrender of accused persons; and

c) cooperation of states in taking evidence.

46. Rule 40: Provisional Measures and Rule 40 *bis*: Transfer and Provisional Detention of Suspects.

47. Pursuant to Rule 74, individuals and organizations can act as *amici curiae*. The first such appearance was during the *Tadić* case, when a representative of the German Government appeared before the ICTY to speak to the extradition of Tadić from Germany to the Tribunal. This representative explained the legal (im)possibility of extraditing Mr. Tadić from Germany prior to amendment of German legislation. As the *Amicus Curiae* explained, the decision of Trial Chamber I of the ICTY contained not only an order to Germany to surrender Mr. Tadić but also to undertake legislative, administrative and judicial measures in order to enable the surrender. See Decision of the Trial Chamber on the application by the prosecutor for a formal request for deferral to the competence of the International Criminal Tribunal for the Former Yugoslavia, Case No. IT-94-1-D of 8 November 1994.

48. Considering that this obligation does not refer directly to obligations of states to the ICTY as far as aspects of criminal procedure are concerned, I shall not deal with it in more detail in this paper.

It is important to correctly determine what precisely are the the obligations of states and whether their implementation legislation enables their performance. The fact that states can find themselves in a situation where their legislation is not completely harmonised with the Rules, due to their frequent amendments by the ICTY, has to be taken into account. It is not realistic to expect states to change their legislation every time the Rules are amended.[49]

When discussing each of the aforementioned criteria for evaluation of implementation legislation, I shall not consider in detail the laws of all states, especially where certain laws follows the requirements of the Statute and the Rules entirely. I shall primarily pinpoint the instances where implementation legislation does not meet the specified criteria. However, some implementation laws cannot be assessed as to whether legislation of the respective state is in accordance with the Statute and the Rules or not. It shall be so in cases where implementation legislation refers to application of domestic legislation *mutatis mutandis*. Certainly, it would be possible to analyse the laws which the implementation legislation refers to in each particular case. However, such a great effort would not lead to adequate results as their application *mutatis mutandis* depends on judicial practice. Without the analysis of case-law, any assessment would necessarily remain incomplete.[50]

3.2 Recognition of the jurisdiction of the ICTY – the fundamental obligation of the implementation legislation

Existence of national implementation legislation in a particular state implies, by itself, that the respective state recognises the jurisdiction of the ICTY.[51] However, general recognition of jurisdiction is not enough Acceptance of jurisdiction in the full sense, pursuant to the Statute and to the Rules, includes very specific obligations:

49. Frequent amendment of the Rules – 12 by 12 November 1997 – clearly indicates initial incompleteness of the legal framework for adjudication before the ICTY. One of the major legal problems of the ICTY is the significant lack of regulation which not only necessitates frequent supplementation of the Rules, but jeopardizes legal certainty in respect of accused and other persons who appear before the ICTY in different roles.

50. So long as case-law in states which invoke application of their general rules *mutatis mutandis* does not exist or at least is not accessible to experts.

51. In the *Tadić* case, the Defense lodged an appeal challenging the jurisdiction of the ICTY based on, a) the illegal foundation of the ICTY, b) wrongful primacy of the ICTY over national courts, and c) lack of jurisdiction *ratione materiae*. The Appeal was rejected. See *supra* n. 10. See also 'Decision on the Defence Motion for Interlocutory Appeal on Jurisdiction', 7 *Criminal Law Forum* (1996) pp. 51-138.

a) there is an obligation on states to defer competence in pending proceedings to the ICTY at its request;[52]

b) proceedings against persons for crimes for which they have already been *tried* by the ICTY must not be instituted before national courts.[53] If the ICTY receives reliable information that a state has acted to the contrary, it shall issue an order asking a national court to terminate the proceedings, and, if it does not comply, shall inform the UN Security Council;[54]

c) states have an obligation to recognise the jurisdiction of the ICTY even where a final judgment of a national court already exists. In accordance with the modified *non-bis-in-idem* rule,[55] the ICTY may proceed even following the finality of the judgment of a national court and it is possible that the proceedings may be renewed, to the detriment of the accused.[56] Proceedings can be renewed before the ICTY in the following instances: when a crime was tried before a national court as an ordinary crime[57], or where the national court did not proceed impartially and independently or where the case was not handled conscientiously or the proceedings were conducted for the purpose of enabling the accused to avoid international criminal responsibility[58];

d) states have an obligation to recognise the legal effects of a sentence. Although this is not set forth explicitly, it follows from the obligation of states to surrender accused persons for the purpose of execution of sentence[59], to implement restitution of property and to exempt the judgment in respect of guilt from claims in civil proceedings where civil courts are authorised to solve prejudicial issues autonomously (including the issue of guilt for a crime)[60].

The above-mentioned superficiality of regulation of the operation of the ICTY has led to the situation where neither the Statute nor the Rules explicitly regulate

52. Art. 9(2) of the Statute.
53. Art. 10(1) of the Statute.
54. Rule 13 of the Rules.
55. Art. 10 of the Statute.
56. Art. 10 of the Statute should, according to its substance, rather be titled '*bis-in-idem*'. There are no legal arguments in favor of setting aside the elementary and internationally recognized right of the accused not to be tried (to his or her detriment) for the same crime once again. This right is guaranteed by important international instruments such as the International Covenant on Civil and Political Rights, Article 14(7). However, the motivation for such a solution is clear and lies in the described distrust of the international community of the states involved in the armed conflict in the former Yugoslavia. The authors of the Statute estimated that the importance of punishing the perpetrators of war crimes outweighed, in a moral, political and strategic sense, the protection of the rights of accused persons.
57. Art. 10(a) of the Statute.
58. Art. 10(b) of the Statute.
59. Art. 29 of the Statute in relation to Rule 102 B.
60. Art. 24(3) of the Statute and Rules 105 and 106.

the possibility of concurrent proceedings before the ICTY and before a national court. One could envisage a situation where the ICTY institutes proceedings and a national court follows. Furthermore, it is not explicitly set forth that, in cases where the ICTY enacts a decision pursuant to Article 10(2) of the Statute after the sentence was delivered before a national court, the first-in-time (national) judgment should lose its legal effects. This is particularly important in cases where a national court delivers a convicting sentence and the ICTY an acquitting one. By the nature of things, it has to be construed that states have an obligation to terminate all proceedings not only in instances where a judgment of the ICTY already exists but also where proceedings before the ICTY are underway. By the same token, the later-in-time judgment of the ICTY renders an earlier sentence delivered by a national court without legal effect. The mistake made by the authors of the Statute who failed to provide for these instances in the Statute can be best seen by looking at the Italian implementing law, which sets forth in Article 7(2)(c) that Italy shall not recognise a judgment of the ICTY 'if for the same fact and in respect of the same person a final judgment has been rendered in the state'.[61]

The way in which the Rules regulate the situation in which the ICTY takes over the proceedings instituted before national courts gives rise to special doubts. Namely, Article 9(2) of the Statute envisages that the ICTY may assume jurisdiction from national courts at any time, and does not envisage any specific requirements short of a formal request. However, Rule 9 makes such deference subject to three conditions: a) that, in the proceedings before a national court, the crime is characterised as an ordinary crime; b) that there is a lack of impartiality or independence, or national investigation or proceedings are designed to shield the accused from international criminal responsibility; or, c) that the issue is closely related to or otherwise involves significant factual or legal questions which are already being considered by the ICTY. Conditions specified *ad* a) and b) entirely correspond to those envisaged by Article 10 of the Statute in respect of renewal of proceedings which were *completed* by a national court. Considering that regulation of deferral of proceedings which were not completed before a national court, as regulated by Rule 9, is contrary to the basic idea of primary jurisdiction of the ICTY, as specified by Article 9(2) of the Statute, Rule 9 can be considered to be contrary to Article 9(2). It seems that the authors of the Rules have either confused a situation in which *pendent* proceedings are to be assumed by the ICTY with renewal of the *completed* proceedings which are

61. In the same article, the Italian legislators determined the procedure for recognition of judgements of the ICTY in accordance with Italian regulations, which is contrary to the Statute and to the spirit of Resolution 827. Namely, acceptance of judgments of the ICTY should be unconditional in all states.

fundamentally different, or wanted to narrow the possibility of the ICTY to assume pendent proceedings. The latter option seems highly improbable and it appears that Rule 9 resulted from insufficiently prudent normative activities of the ICTY.[62] The other possible assumption concerning reasons for such regulation is that the authors of the Rules considered that assumption of pendent proceedings by the ICTY degrades a respective state to the same extent as a renewed trial following delivery of a judgment by a national court, and that, for this reason, the authors of the Rules wanted to remedy the omission made by the authors of the Statute: they have envisaged, in principle, the same conditions which are otherwise applicable to renewal of the proceedings. One can notice in literature that regulation of priority of jurisdiction of the ICTY before national courts is not consistent with the principle *aut dedere aut judicare*[63], and has imposed on states the obligation to enforce decisions of the ICTY and to defer their jurisdiction instead[64].

By participating in the preparatory work on drafting of the Statute of the ICTY; in procedures for appointment of the Prosecutor and Judges; in preparations for commencement of its operations and selection of its staff; and by enactment of specific laws regulating the performance of obligations in respect of the ICTY, almost all states have recognised the jurisdiction of the ICTY, either explicitly or implicitly. The only state which has explicitly refused to recognise a part of the ICTY's jurisdiction is the Federal Republic of Yugoslavia.[65] The same position is taken by the Bosnian-Serb entity (Republika Srpska) of the

62. The first request for deferral of jurisdiction was directed to Bosnia and Herzegovina in the procedure against Ratko Mladić, Radovan Karadžić and Mića Stanišić (Order of the Prosecutor of the ICTY No. IT-95-5-d of 24 April 1995). Surrender of Dusan Tadić from the Federal Republic of Germany was requested before commencement of the procedure in Germany. See *supra* n. 47.

63. See D. Krapac, 'Elemanti prava mednarodne kaznenskopravne pomoèi' [Basis of Judicial Assistence] in Lj. Bavcon, *Mednarodno kaznensko pravo* [International Criminal Law] (ÈZ Uradni list R Slovenije, Ljubljana 1997) p. 152.

64. Cf., K.S. Gallant, 'Securing the Presence of Defendants before the International Tribunal for the Former Yugoslavia: Breaking with Extradition', 5 *Criminal Law Forum* (1994) pp. 557-588.

65. Allegations which can be periodically heard that the FRY does not recognize the jurisdiction of the ICTY at all are not accurate. She does not recognize it only in cases of concurrent jurisdiction of her bodies. This follows from the letter of Mr. Uroš Klikovac, the vice-president of the Government of the FRY to the Security Council of the United Nations of 29 December 1994 (1994/1450). His two basic propositions are the following: a) the so-called FRY shall process its citizens who have committed crimes herself, and b) the so-called FRY shall, within limits of the proposition, a) provide legal assistance to the ICTY in accordance with rules of her national law. Had the FRY not recognized the jurisdiction of the ICTY at all, she would not have established bodies for cooperation with the ICTY, or envisaged the possibility of rendering legal assistance. Regardless of later concessions to the international community, the attitude of the FRY towards the jurisdiction of the ICTY had not fundamentally changed at the time of writing.

Republic of Bosnia and Herzegovina.[66] An assessment as to what extent other states reduce the jurisdiction of the ICTY when compared to their respective courts will be possible when judicial practice shows how particular states, when exercising obligations in respect of the ICTY, apply national legislation *mutatis mutandis*.[67]

3.3 Arrest and surrender of suspects/accused to the ICTY: extradition *sui generis*

Amongst other obligations that states have in respect of the ICTY, Article 29 of the Statute requires states to perform the following, subject to a request of the ICTY, without delay: a) to identify and locate persons, b) to arrest or detain such persons, and c) to surrender suspects/accused and transfer them to the ICTY.[68] Arrest, detention and surrender of suspects/accused to the Tribunal is performed on the basis of a written order issued by the ICTY. Following arrest, states have an obligation to inform the Registrar of the ICTY, while the method of surrender of the accused to the ICTY has to be solved by a special agreement between a state and the ICTY.[69] Rule 58 has correctly envisaged possible legal and political problems which may arise in the course of surrender of the accused to the Tribunal. This Rule declares that the performance of the obligation of surrender of an accused person to the ICTY pursuant to Article 29 of the Statute prevails over any legal impediment in national law which could obstruct the performance of the said obligation. Problems were expected to emerge, especially in respect of states involved in the conflict. Such states could have political and legal (constitutional) grounds not to surrender their citizens to the ICTY.[70] Due to this situation, a theory was developed in expert circles

66. This was the case at the time of writing.

67. Laws of several states that have enacted a law on performance of obligations to the ICTY invoke application of general rules of criminal procedure and of extradition *mutatis mutandis*.

68. Art.29(2) mentions arrest or detention of *persons* and surrender or transfer of the *accused*. Did the authors of the Statute want to imply that persons who are not accused could be arrested or detained? It could not be justified, unless in respect of the arrest and compulsory bringing before the ICTY of witnesses who are trying to avoid testifying. On the other hand, Rule 55 implies that an arrest and surrender warrant can be issued exclusively in respect of an accused. But, Rule 40 *bis* changed this position.

69. Rules 55-57.

70. According to Art. 9(2) of the Croatian Constitution, 'A citizen of the Republic of Croatia may not be expelled from the Republic, cannot be divested of his or her citizenship, and cannot be extradited to another state.' The Constitution of the former SFRY contained a similar provision: 'A citizen of the Socialist Federal Republic of Yugoslavia cannot be deprived of citizenship, expelled from the country or extradited.' (Art. 200(2) of the Constitution of former SFRY of 1974, Službeni

that the surrender of suspects/accused does not amount to extradition[71] in the classical sense. Extradition means handing over of a person to another state for trial or execution of sentence, whereas surrender within the meaning of the Statute of the ICTY does not involve a state to state but a state to ICTY relationship, where the ICTY represents a supranational body. Therefore, in accordance with this theory, constitutional prohibition of extradition of citizens does not prevent surrender to the ICTY.

The obligation to arrest and to surrender persons who are not indicted but are suspected of committing a crime falling within the jurisdiction of the ICTY is the best example of how frequent amendment of the Rules leads to the situation where the implementation legislation of certain states, which entirely complied with the requirements of the Statute and the Rules, 'overnight' becomes incompatible. As one of the provisional measures, Rule 40(i) provides for the right of the Prosecutor to ask states to arrest a suspect provisionally. The surrender of such person would follow on the basis of a judicial warrant following endorsement of the indictment. However, the 8th Revision of the Rules of 25 April 1996 introduced the new Rule 40 *bis,* authorising the Prosecutor to ask a judge, determined pursuant to Rule 28, to issue a warrant for surrender of the suspect to the Court. Such suspect can be subject to detention which can last, with extensions, for up to 90 days.[72]

3.4 Legal assistance to the ICTY

The Rules of evidence of the ICTY are framed according to accusatory proceedings of the Anglo-American type. Procedural acts for collection of particular evidence (investigation, taking statements of witnesses, suspects and

list, Beograd 1988, p. 92). The same wording is contained in the Constitution of the Republic of Serbia of 1990. The Constitution of the Republic of Slovenia of 1991, in Art. 47(2), like the Croatian Constitution, prohibits extradition to *another state*. German Grundgesetz of 1949 in Art. 16(2) prohibits extradition 'to abroad'. Cf., D. Krapac, ICTY, *supra* n. 5 at p. 49.

71. For the notion, legal nature and history of extradition see D. Krapac, and V. Birin, *Međunarodna krivičnopravna pomoć* [International Judicial Assistance] (Informator, Zagreb 1987) p. 23 et seq., D. Krapac, ICTY, *supra* n. 5 at p. 50, points to an historical precedent for the argument that surrender to an international tribunal does not amount to extradition (Case of Wilhelm II and his extradition following World War I). See also A. Jones, *Jones on Extradition* (Sweet and Maxwell, London 1995) for historical development and the present situation of extradition in England; M.C. Bassiouni, *Extradition: US law and practice,* (Oceana, New York 1993); J. Schutte, 'Transfer of criminal proceedings, the European system', in *International criminal law* Vol. II, M.C. Bassiouni, ed., (Transnational Publishers, Dobbs Ferry, New York 1986) pp. 317-348.

72. Rule 40 *bis* (D). On arrest and detention before the ICTY, see I. Josipović, *Uhićenje i pritvor* [Arrest and Pre-trial Detention] (Targa, Zagreb 1998) pp. 101-125.

expert witnesses, production of documents, technical recordings) shall, in most instances, be performed in the same states where the crimes were committed (the Republic of Croatia and the Republic of Bosnia and Herzegovina) or in the states in which particular witnesses have found refuge. Legal assistance that states are obliged to render to the ICTY and to its Prosecutor has to be understood extensively. In addition to customary legal assistance among states, states have an obligation to enable the prosecution to perform on-site investigations. This has to be understood as a right of the Prosecutor to perform necessary acts in the territory of the respective state on his or her own. As will be seen, many states either failed to envisage such a possibility at all or restricted it by their respective implementation laws. In addition to these legal limitations, it is clear that the Prosecutor cannot perform all procedural acts which could be successfully performed by a state on its territory. The wording of Article 29 of the Statute, which sets forth the basis of the obligation of states to *render* all forms of legal assistance and to *perform* orders issued by the Court, implies that states are expected to have the necessary acts performed by their respective bodies. The Statute does not explicitly mention autonomous taking of evidence by the Prosecutor. On the other hand, Rule 39 speaks not only of the right of the Prosecutor to ask for assistance of states and international organisations[73] but also sets forth his or her right to question persons and to record their statements; to take evidence; to perform on-site investigation; and to take other necessary measures in order to complete investigation and prepare and lead prosecution at the hearing[74]. Namely, having regard to what was said in respect of the legal force and compulsory nature of the Statute and the Rules with respect to particular states, the Prosecutor's authority to conduct procedures and collect evidence autonomously would follow from the Rules. The logic and principles of nomotechnics show that the Rules regulate beyond the Statute. Being the higher legal rule, the Statute sets forth an obligation of states to provide legal assistance to the ICTY and to enforce its orders. At the same time, the Rules implicitly (by regulating the authority of the Prosecutor) specify a more demanding obligation: to enable the Prosecutor to perform procedural acts independently on states' territory. However, in this instance, the conflict of the Statute and the Rules is of a somewhat milder nature since logic leads to the conclusion that the prosecutor should be able to perform procedural acts autonomously. This logic is based on the fact that the Prosecutor is a part of the ICTY, which is a supranational body, which, however, necessarily acts in the territory of individual states. There is no territory in which the prosecutor could act (except in the most

73. Rule 39(iii).
74. Rule 39(i) and (ii).

radical theoretical discussions) that would not be a part of territory of some state. If one rejects the position that the Prosecutor is authorised to perform an action in particular states autonomously, it would mean that he or she cannot perform any individual acts alone, but only by using the assistance offered by authorised bodies of the respective state. Such a conclusion would be contrary to the spirit of organisation of the ICTY and to the position of the Prosecutor in relation to his tasks envisaged by the Statute and by the Rules.

4. SHORT ANALYSIS OF IMPLEMENTING LEGISLATION OF DIFFERENT STATES

4.1 Model legislation of the Council of Europe

In order to facilitate enactment of adequate implementing legislation within its Member States, the Council of Europe drafted Guidelines for National Implementing Legislation of the United Nations Security Council Resolution 827 of May 1993 (hereinafter, the Guidelines). The Guidelines are a part of Annex 3 to Recommendation 1218 (1993) of 27 September 1993 and serve as a kind of model for implementing legislation.

Firstly, the Guidelines specify the obligation of full cooperation with the ICTY[75] and regulate the parallel and primary jurisdiction of the ICTY. However, provisions on the consequences of deferral of proceedings for continued procedure before national courts are absent.

The provisions on *arrest, detention and surrender* of the accused provide for an obligation of states to comply with an order of the ICTY. Competent judicial authorities may review formal requirements, short of review of whether indictments or requests for arrest and surrender are founded or not.[76] Understandably, the Guidelines do not consider details such as possible length of detention, possible appeal, etc., since such details depend on different national legal systems. The Guidelines envisage provisional arrest (Art. 6), but not surrender of suspects who have not been indicted. This means that, like most national laws, the Guidelines do not comply with Rule 40 *bis* of the Rules of Procedure and Evidence, which was adopted later.

Legal assistance to the ICTY is regulated in a summary way and includes: identification and location of persons, taking testimonies and production of evidence and service of documents (Art. 7); assistance in examination of

75. Art. 2.
76. Art. 5.

witnesses and experts and in bringing them before the ICTY (Art. 8); collecting police information (Art. 9); and seizure (Art. 11). The Guidelines do not regulate on-site investigations and the right of the ICTY to act in the territory of individual states. This represents a major defect. Being relatively general and brief, the Guidelines have to be understood as a mere framework model which indicates the necessary substance of implementing legislation and, as we have just seen, has its defects.

4.2 States involved in the armed conflicts in the Former Yugoslavia (Bosnia and Herzegovina, Croatia, Federal Republic of Yugoslavia)

It is clear that the implementing laws of these three states created by collapse of the Socialist Federal Republic of Yugoslavia (SFRY) are the most interesting, considering that Croatia, Bosnia and Herzegovina and the Federal Republic of Yugoslavia (FRY) participated in the armed conflicts on the territory of the Former Yugoslavia since 1991 and that the ICTY tries war crimes committed in the territory of Former SFRY.[77] The success of the ICTY's mission directly depends on cooperation of these states[78]. The Dayton Agreement is considered as a very important mechanism imposing obligations on the Parties to the Agreement to cooperate with the ICTY[79], but, in fact, it contains very few and general norms concerning cooperation. In respect of the obligation to cooperate, Resolution 827 (1993) and the Statute of ICTY are much stronger and more precise.

Bosnia and Herzegovina enacted a Decree with Force of Law on Deferral upon Request by the International Tribunal in 1995. The very title of the said regulation implies that it does not deal with all aspects of cooperation with the ICTY but only with arrest and surrender of the accused to the ICTY. However, Article 29 speaks about 'transfer of items used for commission of a crime and items which can be used as evidence'. The transfer procedure is fast, provides for short deadlines and comes under the jurisdiction of the Supreme Court. There are no explicit provisions regulating the parallel and primary jurisdiction of the ICTY. However, recognition of jurisdiction in accordance with the Statute can

77. The war took place on the territory of Croatia and Bosnia and Herzegovina. However, it is likely that certain acts, such as preparing and inciting, were committed in the territory of the FRY, military units of which participated in fighting in the territory of Croatia and Bosnia and Herzegovina.

78. This study shall deal with the normative aspect of cooperation. Actual cooperation of particular states was, at different time periods, assessed differently by the ICTY. See *ICTY Yearbook* (1995) pp. 317-322.

79. See *ICTY Yearbook* (1995) p. 321.

be inferred from rules regulating surrender of the accused. Legal assistance to the ICTY, including the right of the ICTY to perform procedural acts in the territory of Bosnia and Herzegovina, is not regulated. Thus it can be said that the implementing legislation of Bosnia and Herzegovina is not satisfactory. However, on 3 December 1994, Bosnia and Herzegovina and Mr. Richard Goldstone, the then-Prosecutor of the ICTY, signed a Memorandum of Consent in Respect of Cooperation of the Government of Bosnia and Herzegovina with the Tribunal in Respect of Prosecution of Persons Responsible for Serious Breaches of International Humanitarian Law.[80] By this Memorandum, Bosnia and Herzegovina has undertaken to cooperate with the Prosecutor of the ICTY in accordance with the Statute and the Rules. The Memorandum includes the Request for Assistance addressed by the Prosecutor to Bosnia and Herzegovina which contains: provisions on parallel jurisdiction, including primary jurisdiction of the ICTY; provisions on legal assistance; the right of the Prosecutor to perform investigations in the territory of Bosnia and Herzegovina (including taking testimonies of witnesses; the handing over of documents; exhumations; etc.); the obligation of Bosnia and Herzegovina to arrest and surrender accused persons subject to an order of the Tribunal; the right of the ICTY to have its observers present during trials before Bosnian courts; and other provisions which are not of particular interest for this study. Regardless of the doubtful legal effect of the Memorandum, it has to be said that it represents a solid basis for the cooperation of Bosnia and Herzegovina with the ICTY. In addition, international military forces are present in Bosnia and Herzegovina and can implement orders of the ICTY independently from the authorities of Bosnia and Herzegovina. However, it must be remembered that the Republic of Srpska, which is a constituent part of Bosnia and Herzegovina but which, in fact, acts independently from central authorities, does not recognise the jurisdiction of the ICTY and does not enforce its orders. After the election of the government of Prime Minister Milorad Dodik, there were significant signs of change. Some voluntary surrenders were performed. But, at the legal level, there had been no change at the time of writing. International forces have occasionally enforced some of the ICTY orders. However, the arrest of the two most-wanted accused (Karadžić and Mladić) is still awaited. Herzeg-Bosnia, a part of the Federation of Bosnia and Herzegovina with a majority Croat population, has also shown great independence from central authorities. This part of Bosnia and Herzegovina recognises the jurisdiction of

80. A new Memorandum of Consent was prepared in 1997. It was supposed to be signed by the two entities (the Federation of Bosnia and Herzegovina and the Republic of Srpska) and by the Republic of Bosnia and Herzegovina. However, the text of the Memorandum was never agreed upon and was never signed. The reason for proposing the new Memorandum was to make it obligatory for the Republic of Srpska, which did not accept the ICTY, to cooperate.

the ICTY in principle, but for a long time significant problems in the enforcement of ICTY orders existed. Voluntary surrender of the majority of the accused of Croatian or Bosnian-Croat nationality has been performed by mediation of the Republic of Croatia, while some arrests have been made by international forces.

In 1996, the *Republic of Croatia* enacted the Constitutional Act on Cooperation of the Republic of Croatia with the International Criminal Tribunal. Since its enactment, the cooperation of Croatia with the ICTY has significantly improved. Cooperation with the ICTY is performed by the Government of the Republic of Croatia.[81] The Constitutional Act entirely adopted the concept of parallel jurisdiction, including primary jurisdiction of the ICTY. Articles 9 to 12 regulate the procedure of deferral to the ICTY in detail. The Constitutional Act consequently implemented the concept of primary jurisdiction of the ICTY even in respect of the impossibility of renewed trial before national courts following the procedure before the ICTY. The provisions relating to the arrest and surrender of the accused (Arts. 13 to 24) envisage the possibility of surrender of accused persons regardless of their citizenship. Surrender of the accused is subject to jurisdiction of County Courts and to an appeal before the Supreme Court of the Republic of Croatia. When deciding the issue, Croatian courts shall review only the existence of formal requirements and not whether the request of the ICTY was founded or not. As the Constitutional Act was enacted after introduction of Rule 40 *bis*, it speaks about surrender of accused persons, and not of suspects. Once the appeals process has been exhausted, an accused person may file a constitutional complaint with the Constitutional Court.[82] Legal assistance to the ICTY is to be provided by the competent authorities (courts, police, the State Attorney, etc.). At their request, representatives of the ICTY can be present during the proceedings, so that they can ask questions, make suggestions, and make video and audio recordings.[83] In the territory of the Republic of Croatia, the ICTY may act directly, and may, subject to the consent of the Government of the Republic of Croatia, open its special office. The government has established the Office for Cooperation with the International Criminal Tribunal which cooperates directly, subject to supervision of the government. This office was opened in Zagreb even before enactment of the Constitutional Act.[84] The ICTY may perform on-site investigations. In practice, the ICTY mainly takes testimonies of witnesses; collects documents; performs exhumations; and other necessary investigational acts. The Constitutional Act

81. Art. 2.

82. Art. 23.

83. Art. 25.

84. Another Office of the ICTY operates in Sarajevo (Bosnia and Herzegovina) and another in Belgrade (FR Yugoslavia). However, these two have different authority.

is fully compatible with the Statute and with the Rules of Procedure and Evidence, and enables the widest cooperation of the Republic of Croatia and the ICTY. Dissatisfaction with cooperation of the Republic of Croatia with the ICTY, which was occasionally expressed by the officials of the ICTY, has extra-legal origins.

The *Federal Republic of Yugoslavia* recognises the jurisdiction of the ICTY to a limited extent only. Restrictive recognition of jurisdiction of the ICTY is reflected in the fact that the FRY considers that its citizens should be tried by national courts and, consequently, arrest and surrender of the accused citizens of the FRY is not accepted.[85] Moreover, the Yugoslav Constitution prohibits extradition of Yugoslav citizens. Since the FRY considers surrender to the ICTY as tantamount to extradition, it has refused to surrender its citizens to the ICTY. It follows that the FRY recognises the jurisdiction of the ICTY only where Yugoslav courts do not have competing jurisdiction. As a result, the FRY does not have implementing legislation. However, in respect of legal assistance, Yugoslavia has entered into a special agreement with the United Nations in the form of an exchange of letters. This agreement enables partial cooperation of the FRY with the ICTY and its limited activities in the territory of Yugoslavia. Pursuant to this agreement, the ICTY may have a Liaison Officer in the FRY, but only in the capacity of a staff member of the United Nations, and not of that of a representative of the Tribunal. The Liaison Officer and other staff members of the ICTY are vested with immunity equivalent to that belonging to other staff members of the United Nations, and are permitted to collect information and take evidence, including interviews with victims and witnesses. They have access to documents of a public nature and are authorised to contact local and central authorities through the Federal Ministry of Justice. As to why the ICTY and the United Nations may have entered into agreements with the FRY providing for such limited possibilities of action in the FRY, the reasons are probably of a political nature. Such an attitude, however, raises the question of equal treatment of all states by the ICTY.

4.3 Common Law States (Australia, New Zealand, United Kingdom, United States of America)

The *Australian Law* is the most extensive of all implementing laws and regulates in detail the cooperation of Australia not only with the ICTY but also with all other existing or future international war crimes courts. Unlike many other laws, which invoke application of general procedural rules *mutatis mutandis*, the

85. Compare the above-mentioned letter of Mr. Uroš Klikovac, *supra* n. 65.

Australian law has the character of a genuine codification, which regulates the subject matter entirely and in detail, starting with definition of terms, the rights and obligations of the subjects to the proceedings and forms of particular procedural acts. For these reasons, the Australian Law deserves more attention. However, due to the limited scope of this paper, it shall be analysed from the viewpoint of the three aforementioned criteria.

The conclusion that the Australian Law recognises the jurisdiction of the ICTY follows from the entire text of the Law and from the fact that Resolution 827/93 and the Statutes of the ICTY and ICTR represent its constituent parts. However, the Law has several shortcomings. Namely, despite the fact that the said Law deals with certain issues in almost too much detail, it does not explicitly regulate instances where the ICTY wants Australian courts to defer proceedings already pending before them, or the consequences of such deferral. Considering that the Statute of the ICTY is a constituent part of the Law, one must assume that Australian judicial practice would follow its spirit. Legal assistance to the ICTY is regulated in detail, including procedural acts which can hardly ever be applied in practice (e.g., stop and frisk). On the other hand, provision of legal assistance and execution of orders of the ICTY are subject to important restrictions which are contrary to the spirit of the Statute and of the Rules, as well as to the decision of the Appeals Chamber on applicability of *subpoenae* in respect of states in the *Blaškić* case[86]. For example, the Attorney-General can deny a request of the ICTY to hand over documents or to produce other evidence[87]; refuse to arrange for service in Australia of a process relating to proceedings before the ICTY[88]; and refuse to make arrangements for the enforcement of forfeiture orders[89] if, in the opinion of the Attorney-General: (a) complying with the request would prejudice Australia's sovereignty, or (b) there are special circumstances justifying

86. At the hearing held on 22 September 1997, when discussing whether a state can withhold documents which it deems important for national security, the then-President of the Tribunal, Judge Antonio Cassese, mentioned that the Australian law envisaged a possibility of non-delivery of documents related to military secrets. The Prosecutor replied that 'if the decision of this court was that the national security interest cannot be asserted as an absolute bar to the duty to produce evidence, any domestic law to the contrary would have to yield.' (Draft transcript of the hearing on 22 September 1997. Not official, not corrected), pp. 126-127. In Judgment on the request of the Republic of Croatia for review of the decision of Trial Chamber II of 18 July 1997, Blaškić case (IT-95-14), 29 October 1997, the Appeals Chamber unanimously found that 'states are not allowed, on claim of national security interests, to withhold documents and other evidentiary material requested by the ICTY; however, practical arrangements may be adopted by a Trial Chamber to make allowance for legitimate and *bona fide* concerns of states' (Disposition, sub (4)).

87. Art. 26.

88. Art. 40.

89. Art. 44.

non-compliance. The Australian Law explicitly envisages sessions of the Tribunal in Australia for the purpose of taking evidence, conducting or continuing of proceedings before the Tribunal or giving judgment in proceedings before the Tribunal.[90] The Australian Law contains nothing specific regarding the arrest and surrender of accused persons to the ICTY, except the aforementioned wide-ranging and detailed regulation.

Like Australia, *New Zealand* has enacted a very detailed law regulating cooperation with all war crimes tribunals, present and future. The concept of the New Zealand Law is similar to the Australian one. It does not contain provisions concerning deferral of pendent proceedings to the ICTY (parallel jurisdiction, including primary jurisdiction of the ICTY). However, it does include detailed provisions regulating legal assistance to the ICTY, without the restrictions contained in the Australian Law. Legal assistance related to the service of process by the ICTY, including production of necessary documents, has to be approved by the Attorney-General if a crime falling within the jurisdiction of the ICTY is concerned, and if 'there are reasonable grounds for believing that the person to be served is located in New Zealand.'[91] Interestingly, acts shall be performed pursuant to procedures proposed by the ICTY, and, if the process would be illegal or inappropriate from the viewpoint of national law or without a regulated procedure, New Zealand law applies. The possibility for the ICTY to have a session in New Zealand, and to take evidence, conduct proceedings and deliver a decision, is explicitly envisaged.[92] The Law specifically mentions that orders made by the Tribunal are not subject to review by domestic authorities.[93] *Surrender of accused persons* to the ICTY is regulated in a standard and satisfactory way.

The implementing legislation of the *United Kingdom* is consequent in following the requirements of the Statute and of the Rules of Procedure and Evidence. It applies in the entire territory of the United Kingdom, and respects certain organisational and procedural specific characteristics of Scotland and Northern Ireland. The only objection concerns recognition of jurisdiction of the ICTY[94], which enables subsequent continuation of the procedure before national courts regardless of the fact that the procedure was terminated because of deferral of jurisdiction to the ICTY. The Law envisages provision of legal assistance to the ICTY in detail and without reservation, including handing-over of documents and arrest and surrender of witnesses who do not fulfil their obligations to give

90. Art. 41(4).
91. Art. 55(1).
92. Art. 36.
93. Art. 39.
94. Pursuant to Art. 14(6).

testimony. Surrender of accused persons can be denied in case of mistaken identity, if a crime is not within the jurisdiction of the ICTY or if the person would – if he were charged with it in the United Kingdom – be entitled to be discharged under any rule of law relating to previous acquittal or conviction.[95] This provision could possibly be abused by national courts.

In addition to solving many other issues falling within the subject matter of national security, the *United States of America's Law* regulates, in a form of law, the Agreement on Surrender of Persons Between the US Government and the ICTY of 5 October 1994. There is a similar agreement between the US and the ICTR.[96] As far as its substance is concerned, the Agreement (and the Law) refers only to one obligation in respect of the ICTY: surrender of accused persons, including American citizens. The Agreement envisages surrender of two categories of persons: accused persons[97] and convicts[98]. The Agreement does not envisage surrender of suspects pursuant to Rule 40 *bis* of the Rules of Procedure and Evidence. The Agreement remains silent about other forms of cooperation (performance of other obligations in respect of the ICTY). Therefore, American implementing regulations (the Agreement and the Law) deserve to be criticised due to their insufficiency. Due to the extent of the presence of American military forces in Bosnia and Herzegovina, it is probable that a need for taking evidence from the US will emerge (*inter alia*, interviewing witnesses and collecting documents).

The reputation of the United States as a state which has otherwise significantly contributed to the work of the ICTY by its political engagement was not enhanced by the fact that one American court neglected the Agreement and, as a practical matter, included the United States among those States which do not meet their obligations to international tribunals. The US District Court for the Southern District of Texas, Laredo Division, denied the request of the ICTR to surrender an accused person on the grounds that the American Government was not authorised to enter into any agreement with the ICTR, and that the Agreement was unconstitutional and, therefore, inapplicable. Moreover, the Court deemed that evidence enclosed with the request for surrender by the ICTR was not of such a nature to show a probable cause. By this decision, the American court set a dangerous precedent, according to which a national court is entitled to question whether a request of an international court is founded or not as to the

95. Art. 6(5).

96. Agreement on Surrender of Persons between the Government of the United States and the International Tribunal for the Prosecution of Persons Responsible for Serious Violations of International Humanitarian Law in the Territory of Rwanda, 24 January 1995.

97. Art. 2(2) and (3).

98. Art. 2(4).

fact whether evidence that an accused has actually committed a crime or not was sufficient.[99] At the time of writing, a Decision on Appeal was pending.

4.4 Scandinavian states

Scandinavian countries' legislation[100] mainly follow the Guidelines for National Implementing Legislation prepared by the Council of Europe. The *Swedish Law* is a model of good regulation of cooperation with the ICTY. The parallel jurisdiction of the ICTY is adequately regulated and the primary jurisdiction of the ICTY is recognised. Unlike many other laws which prohibit a retrial before national courts only where the ICTY has delivered judgment, the Swedish Law correctly sets forth that if the question of liability for a certain criminal act *has been tried* at the Tribunal, prosecution for the same act may not be instituted in Sweden.[101] Arrest and surrender of suspects/accused is regulated in a way which satisfies the requirements of Rule 40 *bis* of the Rules. The sole reason envisaged by the Swedish Law for non-execution of a detention order or judgment, duly pronounced by the ICTY, is when it is clear that the detention order or judgment was manifestly incorrect.[102] It is anticipated that judicial practice in Sweden shall not abuse the said possibility. Legal assistance to the ICTY includes all necessary procedural acts, including the possibility that, at the request of the Tribunal, a hearing may be held in accordance with the provisions of Chapter 23 of the Code of Judicial Procedure.[103]

The *Finnish Law* also correctly follows the requirements of the Statute and the Rules. Jurisdiction of the Tribunal is recognised according to the criterion of parallel jurisdiction, as specified by the Statute. However, trial by Finnish courts after the Tribunal has already decided upon a matter is prohibited.[104] Pursuant to the Finnish Law, arrest and surrender are regulated in respect of a person who is suspected of a crime, i.e., in compliance with Rule 40 *bis*. Application of the Extradition Act[105] *mutatis mutandis* in respect of Section 4(2) makes possible inconsistencies with the Statute and the Rules non-transparent for the time being. Sections 6, 7 and 8 of the Finnish law entirely enable the

99. 1997 US Dist. LEXIS 20714, Decision in the Matter of Surrender of Elizaphant Ntakirutimana, MISC, MO.L-96-5. For an analysis of this case, see Paust, *infra* at page 205.

100. An English translation of the Icelandic law was not accessible to the author, so that law shall not be discussed.

101. Section 13(2).

102. Section 3(2).

103. Section 11(1).

104. Section 3(2).

105. 456/70.

rendering of legal assistance to the ICTY and enable the ICTY to perform all necessary procedural acts in Finnish territory autonomously.

The *Norwegian Law*, consisting of nine short articles, falls within a group of the shortest implementing laws. It regulates parallel jurisdiction of domestic courts and the ICTY in a somewhat obscure way. Article 5 of the Law excludes the conduct of a procedure in Norway for crimes which are to be tried before the ICTY or in respect of which the ICTY has delivered a final judgment. Such regulation is deficient in that it does not extend to cases where the ICTY leads investigations but the trial has not commenced, or to cases where the procedure before the ICTY was completed without a judgment (e.g., where the Prosecutor dropped charges). Arrest and surrender of suspects/accused and provision of legal assistance, including the right of the ICTY to perform certain acts on Norwegian territory, are regulated in a generally appropriate way. *Mutatis mutandis* application of domestic legislation on extradition, on international legal assistance and on courts and criminal procedure in general, is envisaged.

The *Danish Law* is even shorter and more scarce. It generally invokes provisions of the Statute and Rules and provides for *mutatis mutandis* application of national law in respect of all important issues, such as deferral, arrest and surrender of suspects and legal assistance. This makes it entirely non-transparent for evaluation. Its specificity is that all decisions related to cooperation with the ICTY and possible application of the law for purposes of other international war crime tribunals come under the jurisdiction of the Minister of Justice. However, certain procedural decisions of the Minister of Justice shall be submitted to the court for approval by its judgment.[106]

4.5 European (civil law) states

Austrian law applicable to both the ICTY and the ICTR generally recognises the jurisdiction of the Courts and specifies that Austrian authorities are obliged to cooperate extensively with the ICTY (and ICTR). The Law envisages subsidiary application of the Law on Extradition and Judicial Assistance and of the Code of Criminal Procedure.[107] Paragraph 4 sets forth the parallel jurisdiction of Austrian courts and of the ICTY, which nevertheless has primacy. Austrian courts shall not have jurisdiction if the ICTY has either convicted or acquitted the accused. If the ICTY requires deferral of the proceedings, Austrian courts shall suspend the procedure, collect all necessary evidence and hand it over to the

106. Art. 4(4).

107. *Auslieferungs und Rechtshilfegesetz and Strafprozessordnung*. General provisions on jurisdiction are contained in paras. 1 to 3.

ICTY. If the ICTY decides not to bring an indictment or withdraws one, or, after review, dismisses the indictment or, if the ICTY finds that it has no jurisdiction, an Austrian court shall continue the procedure. Austrian Law specifies that Austrian citizenship is not an obstacle for surrender of an accused person to the ICTY.[108] By the same token, Paragraph 6 of the Law regulates methods and channels of legal assistance by Austrian authorities (courts, prosecution, police) to the ICTY. Legal assistance itself is regulated in detail in Section Two of the Law, and includes performance of all procedural acts necessary for the ICTY in the form envisaged by Austrian Law.[109] It is especially interesting that Paragraph 11(1) of the Law enables the Tribunal to send summons and other documents to individuals in Austria directly by mail. Paragraph 12, which also has a constitutional character, envisages delivery of documents to the ICTY: where documents contain confidential information which amounts to a state secret, particularly related to national security and the military, the ICTY shall be asked to guarantee their confidentiality. The Minister of Foreign Affairs may refuse to hand over the documents if the guarantees for maintenance of their confidentiality are not satisfactory. The Law also specifies that the ICTY shall have authority to hear witnesses and accused persons in Austria independently, and to inspect locations and take other evidence. The Ministry of Foreign Affairs has to be informed in advance about the intention of the ICTY to undertake certain investigational acts, and Austrian authorities shall provide assistance to the ICTY if necessary. The ICTY shall have authority to hold proceedings in Austria unless the Federal Minister for Foreign Affairs objects, because of serious misgivings related to the security of the Republic of Austria. The arrest and surrender of accused persons is resolved in accordance with the Statute and the Rules. The rights of arrested persons are protected by the mechanism of constitutional review.[110] Interestingly, the Austrian Law specifies that the investigating judge shall lift the detention and revoke the transfer order without delay for acceptable reasons, such as cancellation of the request for surrender by the ICTY; obviously mistaken identity of a person; and failure to perform surrender within 14 days following the arrest[111]. Such restriction is not in accordance with the spirit of the Statute and the Rules. The Austrian Law speaks

108. Para. 5 of the Law. This provision is of a constitutional character and is enacted pursuant to the constitution-making procedure.

109. Para. 10.

110. Arrest and surrender of accused persons subject to a request of the ICTY is regulated by Arts. 16 and 17 of the Austrian Law. 'A right of appeal against rulings on detention and transfer exist only under Art. 1. para. 1 of the Law on the Constitutional Right of Appeal' (Art. 16 para. 3).

111. Art. 16(5).

of arrest and surrender 'of the accused person' and not of 'the suspect'. This means that, subject to Austrian Law, Rule 40 *bis* on arrest and surrender of suspects could not be applied. This situation resulted from subsequent amendments of the Rules, as was mentioned earlier.

The *Dutch Law* does not explicitly regulate jurisdiction of the Tribunal. Indeed, in its 18 articles, the Dutch Law fails to regulate many important aspects of cooperation with the ICTY. Deferral of cases to the Tribunal and the relationship of national jurisdiction with the jurisdiction of the ICTY are not even mentioned. However, Dutch recognition of jurisdiction of the ICTY can be inferred from the entire context of the Law, which follows the Model, though not very precisely. It is difficult to conclude how possible conflicts of jurisdiction would be resolved in the Netherlands. The Law regulates arrest and surrender of suspects in detail[112], and the only two mentioned reasons for denial of surrender of suspects to the ICTY are mistaken identity and fact that the request refers to a crime which is not within the jurisdiction of the ICTY[113]. Requests for *legal assistance to the ICTY* 'shall be met whenever possible', and the provisions of the Criminal Procedure Act and the Extradition Act shall be applied *mutatis mutandis*. Representatives of the ICTY shall be enabled to attend performance of procedural acts[114], but the Law does not envisage a possibility for representatives of the ICTY to perform certain procedural acts on their own. In addition, the Law regulates treatment of witnesses before the ICTY, transfer of persons and execution of sentences of the ICTY.

As France plays an important role in international relations and politics (including a decisive role in decision-making in respect of conflict in the territory of the former SFRY) the *French Law* is of particular interest. France also played an extremely important role in international military forces in Bosnia and Herzegovina. French members of military forces may possibly appear as witnesses before the ICTY. Unfortunately, in many respects, the French Law does not meet the criteria used for evaluation of implementation legislation in this paper. Parallel jurisdiction of the ICTY and French courts and deferral of cases to the ICTY are regulated by Articles 3 to 6 of the French Law in an untypical way. Subject to a request of the ICTY, a French court shall declare its lack of jurisdiction and forward the file to the Prosecutor. The French Law does not say anything about the possibility of continuing the procedure before French courts. Provisions related to legal assistance to the ICTY are also insufficient. Article 6(1) regulates provision of legal assistance in a similar way

112. Arts. 3 to 5.
113. Art. 3(3).
114. Art. 9.

as is applicable to legal assistance among states, i.e., on the basis of requests of the ICTY, which has to forward evidence showing that the request is justified. *A contrario,* it follows that the French Public Prosecutor and the court having jurisdiction in the matter are authorised to examine whether the request was justified, which is not in the spirit of the Statute and Rules. Another deficiency of the law is that it does not permit the ICTY to perform on-site investigations. Indeed, certain problems emerged between France and the ICTY following the statement of the French Minister of Defence, who announced that members of French military forces would not be permitted to appear as witnesses before the ICTY.[115] However, after meeting with the ICTY's Chief Prosecutor Louise Arbour, French Foreign Minister Hubert Vedrine announced a policy reversal and stated that French military officers could testify before the ICTY under normal court procedures.[116]

Under the French Law, arrest and surrender of accused persons is subject to guarantees for protection of the rights of accused persons, which especially refers to short deadlines for performance of certain acts in the surrender procedure and duration of detention.[117] A request for surrender of accused persons has to be substantiated by evidence supporting its justifiability.[118] This can be evaluated in the same way as the identical request for legal assistance.

The *German Law* regulates parallel *jurisdiction* and provides, without exception, for primary jurisdiction of the ICTY in accordance with the Statute and the Rules of Procedure and Evidence.[119] *Arrest and surrender* of accused persons for purpose of criminal procedure or execution of sentences is to be conducted pursuant to provisions of the International Legal Assistance in Criminal Cases Act. Legal Assistance to the ICTY is also regulated in full compliance with the Statute and Rules. The ICTY staff can perform acts in order to take evidence on their own, subject to special permission and the consent of the relevant

115. This statement gave rise to great concern in the ICTY and the Prosecutor Ms. Louise Arbour held a special talk with the French Minister of Foreign Affairs, advocating for a change of the French position. See Statement by the Prosecutor Louise Arbour following her meeting with the French Minister of foreign affairs, Mr. Hubert Vedrine, ICTY Press Release, CC/PIO/275-E, of 15 December 1997.

116. See 'France to allow officers to testify before UN war crimes court' (Agence France Presse, 16 March 1998). During a visit to Bosnia and Herzegovina in April 1998, French President Jacques Chirac stated that, 'Naturally, France is cooperating and will cooperate fully with the ICTY. It goes without saying that we consider that war criminals must be tried and punished.' 'France's Chirac urges Bosnians to "build model country"', (Agence France Presse, 7 April 1998).

117. Compare Arts. 10(1), 11(1), 12(1), 13(2), 15(2).

118. Art. 9(1).

119. Art. 2.

German authorities. The ICTY does not have authority to take compulsory measures, which have to be taken by German authorities exclusively.[120]

The *Hungarian Law*, which is, with its five articles, one of the shorter implementation laws, recognises the jurisdiction of the ICTY mostly to the extent required by the Statute and by the Rules. Article 1(1) sets forth, as a matter of principle, that criminal action shall be deferred to the ICTY subject to its request to such effect. Proceedings before Hungarian courts can be instituted or continued in the three following cases: a) if the ICTY finds that it has no jurisdiction in a case, b) if the Prosecutor does not indict, c) if the indictment of the Prosecutor has been dismissed by the Trial Chamber.[121] In Hungary, once the ICTY passes a final judgment, the same person cannot be tried again for the same crime. Article 2 of the Law, regulating legal assistance to the ICTY, provides for *mutatis mutandis* application of the Act of International Criminal Legal Assistance. The Law is not explicit about the details of certain procedural actions or about the possibility for the Prosecutor to perform certain actions autonomously on Hungarian territory.

Italy was the first state to enact an implementing law, back in 1993. Jurisdiction of the ICTY is accepted in a satisfactory way. Subject to the request of the ICTY, Italian courts shall enact a decision on deferral of the case to the ICTY due to the primacy of its jurisdiction.[122] A new trial before Italian courts is not possible if the ICTY has delivered a final decision in a particular case.[123] A new trial is possible if the Prosecutor of the ICTY did not indict, if the ICTY rejected the indictment or if the ICTY declares its lack of jurisdiction.[124] The most significant deficiency of the Italian Law obstructing the primary jurisdiction of the ICTY is contained in Article 7(2)(b) and (c). Pursuant to these provisions, a judgement of the ICTY shall not be recognised in Italy if the crime was not envisaged by Italian law or if a final decision has already been delivered in Italy, which is contrary to the primary jurisdiction of the ICTY. Legal assistance to the ICTY shall be provided by Italian courts, subject to rules of national law.[125] The possibility for the ICTY to perform certain procedural actions in Italy (on-site investigation) is not envisaged. Rules regulating arrest and surrender refer to accused persons and not to suspects, meaning that they do not comply with Rule 40 *bis*. This is hardly surprising as the Italian Law was enacted prior to adoption of Rule 40 *bis*. Arrest and detention of indicted persons is subject to

120. Art. 4(4).
121. Art. 1(2).
122. Art. 3.
123. Art. 5.
124. Art. 4(1).
125. Art. 10.

relatively short detention periods and includes remedies from the detention decision.[126] However, the fact that the Italian law, among other things,[127] specifies that execution of arrest warrants issued by the ICTY can be denied if a crime is not within the jurisdiction of the ICTY *ratione temporis* or *ratione loci*, or if an act is not considered a crime subject to Italian Law, or if a final judgment for the same crime has already been delivered in Italy[128], makes it incompatible with the Rules of the ICTY. The said legal rules envisage the possibility for Italian courts to review decisions of the ICTY on its jurisdiction and to establish primacy of national law in respect of the law of the ICTY. Therefore, it can be said that the Italian Law is highly incompatible with the norms of the Statute and the Rules.

The *Spanish Law* solved the issue of parallel *jurisdiction* and the primary jurisdiction of the ICTY precisely.[129] A request for deferral of jurisdiction can be denied only if the case does not fall within the jurisdiction of the ICTY *ratione territoriae or ratione temporis*.[130] The Spanish law, which was enacted prior to the adoption of Rule 40 *bis*, restricts *arrest and surrender* to persons who have been indicted. *Legal assistance* is not regulated in detail. It explicitly mentions only assistance in respect of appearance of witnesses before the ICTY.[131] Other kinds of cooperation can be said to be covered by general provisions of Articles 1 and 2, where it is specified that Spain shall cooperate with the ICTY *entirely*, in accordance with Resolution 827 and the Statute, subject to subsidiary application of national substantive and procedural criminal law. It would have been even better had it mentioned the Rules as a subsidiary source of law.

5. CONCLUDING REMARKS CONCERNING IMPLEMENTING LEGISLATION

Implementing legislation enacted by particular states for purpose of performance of their obligations in respect of the ICTY indicates a degree of acceptance of the system of international criminal litigation. It represents a connection of states with this system. The Statute, the Rules and other legal rules and authority which should follow from fair and impartial adjudication of the ICTY have to affect

126. Arts. 11 to 13.

127. Art. 11(3) specifies the following reasons for denial of an arrest warrant: inexistence of a decision of the ICTY and mistaken identity of the accused.

128. Art. 11(3c, c-bis, c-ter).

129. Arts. 4 and 5.

130. Art. 4(3).

131. Art. 7.

acceptance of certain values and standards and influence the process of globalisation of criminal law. In addition to its legal implications, this process has enormous political ones, primarily due to the fundamental redefinition of the classical understanding of sovereignty. Therefore, assessment of implementing legislation of a particular state may serve as a significant indicator of her readiness to accept the new concept of globalisation of criminal justice and of the 'new world order' based on global human values and a different understanding of state sovereignty.

Generally speaking, implementing legislation can be organised into three classes[132]: a) one comprising legislation complying with the Statute and the Rules in their entirety[133], b) another comprising legislation which suffers certain defects but can be considered satisfactory[134], and c) the third class comprising legislation which is contrary to the requirements set forth by the Statute and the Rules to such an extent that they lead to the conclusion that they do not correspond to the idea of supranational international adjudication[135]. All assessments have to be made cautiously, considering several important facts. First, it is not enough for a state to have implementing legislation which complies with the Statute and the Rules. Practice also has to comply, and the respective state has to apply the implementing legislation habitually.[136] Second, certain minor inconsistencies of legislation with the Statute and the Rules must not be understood as unwillingness of states to accept the system of international criminal justice, but may result from the fact that the ICTY amends its legal framework frequently (frequent amendments of the Rules), and that states cannot

132. In our analysis of each particular legal system, we have pointed out their possible defects. We shall not repeat these assessments here but just mention legal systems which can be classified in each particular group as a matter of example.

133. For example, such is the situation in Germany, New Zealand, Austria, Sweden, Finland and Croatia.

134. Examples of such legislation can be found in the United Kingdom, France, Spain, the Netherlands and Australia.

135. For example, the United States and Italy. Certainly, states which have not enacted implementing legislation (e.g., FRY) should be put in this group in case their respective internal legislation does not enable performance of obligations in respect of the ICTY without special implementing legislation. It also has to be borne in mind that some states did not enact implementing legislation due to their geographic remoteness or for other reasons which make actual cooperation with the ICTY improbable.

136. For example, despite its good legislation, Croatia was occasionally singled out as a state which did not cooperate with the ICTY to a satisfactory extent. It is encouraging to notice that such assessments have recently changed. Application of national legislation *mutatis mutandis* envisaged by many implementing laws in states which were not in a position to do so, makes assessment of legislation and practice of the respective state impossible.

always follow such amendments without delay.[137] Third, the quality of implementing laws related to the operation of the ICTY and the readiness of states to apply them amount to a significant indicator for anticipating the relationship of a particular state with the future, general and permanent international criminal court.[138] The efficiency of the ICTY depends directly on cooperation of states, i.e., on the quality of implementing legislation and the will of states to cooperate with the Court. Implementing legislation and cooperation of states with the ICTY depends not only on legal rules, but on the political will of a particular state and the international community in general. Strengthening the legal and weakening the political components in the international criminal justice system, the greatest professionalism possible, and the equal treatment of all states are the best ways to make a success of the ICTY and the idea of international criminal adjudication in general.

137. The best example is subsequent introduction of Rule 40 *bis* to the Rules of Procedure and Evidence. By the same token, enactment and application of implementing rules can either have strong political implications in some states, or procedure for their enactment can be complicated. Therefore, states cannot be expected to follow a fast pace of change of the Rules of Procedure and Evidence.

138. The behavior of states which are very active in persuading other states to perform their obligations in respect of the ICTY while they do not perform such obligations themselves is not encouraging. We have already mentioned cases where French military officers refused to testify as well as the denial of an American court of the surrender request of the US Government in relation to a person accused by the ICTR.

INTERFACE, CORRESPONDENCE AND CONVERGENCE OF HUMAN RIGHTS AND INTERNATIONAL HUMANITARIAN LAW*

Raúl Emilio Vinuesa**

1. INTRODUCTION

From a doctrinal point of view, the relationship between human rights and international humanitarian law (IHL) seems like a settled issue in terms of the correspondence of basic objectives and common aims.[1]

Different theories have tried to explain that relationship, taking into consideration either that human rights and IHL are separate systems or that they are

** Professor of International Law and Human Rights, Faculty of Law, University of Buenos Aires.

1. See J. Pictet, *Développement et Principes du Droit International Humanitaire* (Genève, Institut Henry Dunant 1983); M. El Kouhene, *Les garanties fondamentales de la personne en droit humanitaire et droit de l'homme* (Dordrecht, Nijhoff 1986); D. Schindler, 'El Comité Internacional de la Cruz Roja y los Derechos Humanos' [International Committee of the Red Cross and Human Rights], 116 *International Review of the Red Cross* (1979) p. 99 at p. 126; D. Weissbrodt and P. Hicks, 'Aplicación de los derechos humanos y del derecho humanitario en caso de conflicto armado' [Human Rights and International Humanitarian Law Application during Armed Conflicts] 116 *International Review of the Red Cross* (1979) p. 127 at p. 147; T. Meron, *Human Rights and Humanitarian Norms as Customary Law* (Oxford, Clarendon Press 1989); 'The Protection of the Human Person under Human Rights Law and Humanitarian Law', 91/1 *Bulletin of Human Rights* (New York, United Nations 1992); C. Cerna, 'Human Rights in Armed Conflict: Implementation of International Humanitarian Law Norms by Regional Intergovernmental Human Rights Bodies' in F. Kalshoven and Y. Sandoz, eds., *Implementation of International Humanitarian Law/Mise en oeuvre du Droit International Humanitaire* (Dordrecht, Nijhoff 1989); H. Gros Espiell, 'Derechos Humanos, Derecho Internacional Humanitario y Derecho Internacional de los Refugiados' [Human Rights, International Humanitarian Law and International Refugee Law], in C. Swinarski, ed., *Etudes et essais sur le droit international humanitaire et sur les principes de la Croix Rouge en l'honneur de Jean Pictet* (Genève, The Hague, ICRC, Nijhoff) p. 706 et seq.

Yearbook of International Humanitarian Law
Volume 1 - 1998 - pp. 69-110

completely integrated within international law. Most recent positions emphasize their convergence into a scheme of mutual coordination and complementarity.[2]

In our view, none of these positions clearly characterize the day-to-day interface between human rights and IHL. Taking that premise as a point of departure, our purpose is to demonstrate that there is no rational or organized convergence between the two systems of law, that similitude and correspondence are sometimes overwhelmed by diversity, and that gaps and overlaps between their rules are a common feature of their interrelations.

The main objective of this paper is to consider the differences and similarities between human rights and IHL, paying special attention to the effects of derogations from human rights. We will take account of normative reiterations or duplicity of rules and will explore areas that are not necessarily covered either by human rights or IHL. Finally, we will attempt to make some general observations on the basis of each system's particularities.

2. DIFFERENCES AND SIMILARITIES

Although human rights and IHL share as a common objective the protection of the human person, they differ in terms of structure, means of implementation and the situations to which they apply.

Human rights and IHL are both part of international law. They recognize the same international law sources for the generation of their rules, and general principles of international responsibility are applicable when due observance of any of their rules is challenged or violated. Within this common legal framework, however, human rights and IHL have a separate origin and a distinct outcome as a result of the different situations or circumstances to which they apply. In that sense, the protection of the human person through separate legal schemes, each one with its own principles and particularities, has generated constant practical and theoretical contacts, resulting in some cases in a normative overlap. At the same time, interactions between human rights and IHL could evidence the existence of gaps or *lacunae* in the implementation of a proper and comprehensive system of protection of individuals in all circumstances.

2. See A. Cançado Trindade, 'Aproximaciones o convergencias entre el derecho internacional humanitario y la protección internacional de los derechos humanos' [Approximations or Convergences between International Humanitarian Law and International Protection of Human Rights], in *Seminario Interamericano sobre la Protección de la Persona en Situaciones de Emergencia* (San José de Costa Rica, Instituto Interamericano de Derechos Humanos 1996) p. 33 at p. 88.

2.1 The origins and scope of human rights law

Human rights law, which basically concerns the relationship of states with their own nationals or with individuals who are under their territorial jurisdiction, was only introduced as part of international law in recent times.[3] Protection of human rights has its origins in domestic law. Practically all human rights recognized at the international level are prescribed within the domestic law of most countries of the international community, and the day-to-day implementation of human rights still continues primarily within the internal sphere of state functions and competences. Since World War II, however, international concerns about human rights have developed as a response to states' non-compliance with their own domestic laws. Moreover, systematic violations of basic human rights within a state began to be considered as affecting international peace and security.

International human rights law has thus generated different levels of regional and universal schemes for the supervision and control of states, enabling monitoring of internal enforcement of human rights recognized under international customary or treaty law.

International human rights accomplishments have traditionally been influenced by political discourse. Drawing on diverse presumptions and with various aims, different theories have tried to monopolise human rights fundamentals. Human rights law thus developed under the umbrella of contradictory ideologies that privileged the observance of certain rights to the detriment of others. Considering that there are several categories or generations of human rights, and considering states' varying approaches to and acknowledgment of the concept of universal human rights, not all states have an identical level of generalised acceptance.

Regional as opposed to international implementation of human rights has tolerated different standards in the observance of the same rights as applied in different countries. Although basic human rights have generally been considered as having a common universal and indivisible nature, cultural relativism in the interpretation and direct operational application of those rights cannot be ignored.

3. See P. Alston, ed., *The United Nations and Human Rights: A Critical Appraisal* (Oxford, Clarendon Press 1992); T. Buergenthal, *International Human Rights in a Nutshell* (St. Paul, West Publishing Co. 1995); A. Cassese, *Human Rights in a Changing World* (Philadelphia, Temple University Press 1990); Centre for Human Rights, *United Nations Action in the Field of Human Rights* (New York, United Nations 1995); J. Donnelly, *International Human Rights* (Boulder, Westview Press 1993); H. Hannum, ed., *Guide to International Human Rights Practice* (Philadelphia, University of Pennsylvania Press 1992); L. Henkin, ed., *The International Bill of Rights: The Covenant on Civil and Political Rights* (New York, Columbia University Press 1981); A. Robertson and J. Merrills, *Human Rights in the World* (New York, Manchester University Press 1989); P. Sieghart, *The International Law of Human Rights* (Oxford, Clarendon Press 1983); K. Vassak and P. Alston, eds., *The International Dimensions of Human Rights*, (Westport, Greenwood Press 1982).

Conversely, issues of political divergencies or cultural particularities in the implementation of specific rules are unknown within IHL implementation.

2.2 Origins of IHL and convergence with and divergence from human rights

International humanitarian law, has a longer history, having originated in the middle of the nineteen century as a substantial part of international law.[4] It was conceived to be applied during armed conflicts in order to protect the victims of hostilities. That set of rules regulating specific protections for individuals affected by war was identified as humanitarian law *strictu sensu*. Those rules were also known as the 'Law of Geneva'.

Customary and then treaty rules prescribing methods and mean of combat and also regulating the conduct of hostilities developed as part of traditional international law at the beginning of the twentieth century. This later series of rules was originally known as the law of war or as 'Hague Law'. Later, both groups of norms converged as an integral part of customary rules and treaty law, nowadays universally identified as IHL.

At first sight it seems that there is no possible compatibility between human rights and that part of IHL prescribing means and methods of combat. Considering that the killing of combatants is permitted under IHL, and even more so that civilian casualties or damage to property or to the environment are allowed as collateral effects of military necessity, it seems that there is not too much room to work out a reasonable scheme of convergence between IHL and human rights law. Rules expressing the content of military necessity or the legality of certain collateral effects of military attacks would be incompatible within human rights law. It could thus reasonably be argued that IHL and human rights are separate systems within international law. Even if both systems interact, they maintain their independence and autonomy.

International humanitarian law basically concerns the adequate treatment of civilians and combatants of the other belligerent state(s). But considering that

4. See A. Delissen, et al, eds., *Humanitarian Law of Armed Conflict: Challenges Ahead. Essays in Honor of Frits Kalshoven* (Dordrecht, Nijhoff 1991); *International Dimensions of Humanitarian Law* (Geneva, Henry Dunant Institute (Dordrecht, Nijhoff 1988); T. Meron, *Human Rights in Internal Strife: Their International Protection* (Cambridge, Grotius 1987); Y. Sandoz, et al, eds., *Commentary on the Additional Protocols of 1977 to the Geneva Conventions of 1949* (Geneva, The Hague, ICRC, Nijhoff 1987); Swinarski, ed., op. cit. n. 1.

it has been created and is constantly evolving with the aim of safeguarding and protecting victims or non-combatant persons during extraordinary situations such as armed conflicts, either of an internal or international character, the possibility of ensuring at least minimum standards of humane treatment during these extreme situations becomes a paramount objective, common and fundamental to both systems. Mitigation of unnecessary suffering and the promotion of humanitarian treatment of civilians or combatants *hors de combat* during armed conflicts are essential for the consolidation of basic human rights recognized and applied under all circumstances. At present, humanitarian law regulates, on a residual basis, the rights of all persons without special protection, who do not participate in the hostilities or who are *hors de combat.*

Human rights generate direct obligations for states to protect and to guarantee the enjoyment of the civil, political, economic, social and cultural rights of individuals, to whom they directly apply. Treaties recognizing human rights are special agreements in which rights of individuals are secured by states parties, creating a direct relationship between them and individuals as subjects with specific rights under international law.[5] The idea is that individuals are thereby protected from abuses perpetrated by their own state authorities. Human rights law also creates duties binding on individuals, who must, in particular, ensure that their enjoyment of their human rights does not impinge on or infringe the rights of others. Human rights, which apply to all persons without distinction, tend to consolidate the role of individuals within an organized community of interest within a democratic society. Full compliance with human rights and freedoms depends upon a stabilized institutional environment where the rule of law applies. Further, peace, as opposed to war, is a fundamental prerequisite for the full protection of human rights.

Humanitarian law in general terms generates rights and obligations binding on states, and also creates rights and duties binding on individual combatants, who are obliged to observe the rules of IHL. In addition, it confers rights upon special categories of protected persons and on a residual basis to all persons not involved in hostilities. In the sense of granting rights to or imposing duties on individuals under international law, there is no particular differentiation with human rights law.

Humanitarian law rules have been and continue to be created and developed as a response to traumatic experiences in time of war. Unnecessary suffering and the special protection of individuals directly affected by armed conflicts have

5. I/A Court H.R., *The Effect of Reservations on the Entry into Force of the American Convention on Human Rights (Arts. 74 and 75)*, Advisory Opinion OC-2/82 of 24 September 1982, Series A No. 2.

determined the existence of clearly identifiable groups of people to whom a particular set of safeguards is applicable during armed conflicts. As international humanitarian law applies to all persons included within a special category of protected persons, in principle it discriminates in favour of groups of vulnerable persons or victims within an armed conflict. The history of humanitarian law has witnessed the gradual incorporation of new categories of protected individuals. At present, humanitarian law regulates, on a residual basis, the rights of all persons without special protection who do not participate in the hostilities or who are *hors de combat*. Although the principle of distinction is vital for a differentiated treatment of protected persons during armed conflicts, the incorporation of residual protection for those who do not have other more favourable treatment has considerably extended the personal scope of humanitarian law.

The application of humanitarian law rules to internal armed conflicts or to conflicts without an international character has also reached and embraced individuals affected by these conflicts, without distinguishing between particular categories of protected persons.

2.3 Harmonization and implementation of IHL and human rights

In consideration of the independence of IHL and human rights, during the discussions at the Diplomatic Conference that finally approved Protocols I and II to the Geneva Conventions of 1949, it was decided to incorporate fundamental human rights into the Protocols, in the form of fundamental minimum guarantees.[6] Negotiations concerned the harmonization of the Protocols with the United Nations Covenants.[7] The latter being applicable in all circumstances, except, in the case of some rights guaranteed, during states of siege or emergency, it was important to use the same language in the Protocols. This equation tends to eradicate the factual possibility of situations not contemplated by one legal scheme or the other. Their reciprocal complement is not related to equalization or fusion of norms but to the superimposition of the same normative content as expressed by different systems of law. In that sense, it has already been stated that fundamental rights of individuals, as accepted and prescribed by international law through international instruments, are applicable during armed conflicts.[8]

6. See Art. 75 of Protocol I and Arts. 4 to 6 of Protocol II to the Geneva Conventions of 1977 (hereinafter, Protocols I and II).

7. S. Junod, 'Los derechos humanos y el derecho internacional humanitario' [Human Rights and International Humanitarian Law], in *Primer Seminario sobre Derecho Internacional Humanitario* (Buenos Aires, Instituto de Derecho Internacional Público, U.B.A. 1981) p. 17 at p. 23.

8. UNGA Res. 2675 (XXV).

In the same way, the preamble to Protocol II recognized the continuity of human rights application during internal armed conflicts.[9]

The interface of human rights and IHL is expressed in the duplicity of regulations dealing with the protection of individuals during armed conflicts. The characterization of humanitarian law as human rights applicable during armed conflicts[10], however, could distort the real scope and independence of humanitarian law.

The independence of both systems is reflected in the mechanisms designed to implement them. Humanitarian law is meant to be applied by states. States involved in hostilities may be assisted by Protecting Powers or by the ICRC. Humanitarian law has a predominant preventative function and has been designed to allow its prompt and almost automatic implementation during international armed conflicts through the actions of states or the ICRC. Even where, during an internal armed conflict, there is no possible control by Protecting Powers, there is always a possibility for the ICRC to intervene.

On the other hand, mechanisms for the international implementation of human rights include promotion and monitoring functions, as well as negotiation, conciliation and judicial functions to be performed by regional or international organs. States and individuals have access to these mechanisms that, in most cases, are activated *ex post facto* and eventually oriented towards restoration of the *status quo ante* or due compensation.

International humanitarian law basically prescribes states' obligations 'to respect and ensure respect' for rights and obligations recognised *vis-à-vis* other states.[11] Responsibilities 'to respect and ensure respect' have customary roots in state decentralised practices. International human rights law prescribes states' obligations 'to respect and to guarantee' rights of individuals *vis-à-vis* each state.[12] Human rights obligations should be internally implemented by the same state that, in practice, is potentially in a position to violate them.

State violations of human rights primarily concern individuals directly affected by such violations. International and regional monitoring and control of human

9. The Preamble of Protocol II prescribes that, 'Recalling furthermore that international instruments relating to human rights offer a basic protection to the human person.'

10. See Proclamation of Teheran, proclaimed by the International Conference on Human Rights at Teheran, 13 May 1968; see also Y. Dinstein, 'Human Rights in Armed Conflicts: International Humanitarian Law', in T. Meron, ed., *Human Rights in International Law* (Oxford, Clarendon Press 1984) p. 345 et seq.

11. L. Condorelli and L. Boisson de Chazournes, 'Quelques remarques a propos de l'obligation des Etats de "respecter et faire respecter" le Droit International Humanitaire "en toutes circonstances"', in Swinarski, ed., op. cit. n. 1.

12. T. Buergenthal, 'To Respect and to Ensure State Obligations and Permissible Derogations', in Henkin, ed., op. cit. n. 3.

rights violations, as performed by treaty organs, would principally aim towards effective internal compliance and eventual reparation. International humanitarian law violations, on the other hand, primarily concern affected states. State obligations and responsibilities for such violations are related to other belligerent or neutral states. State responsibility for violations of international humanitarian law does not, however, preclude responsibility of individuals.

As we have said, humanitarian law has developed as a legal system worked out of limits and restrictions to prevent unnecessary suffering during armed conflicts. The safeguarding of elemental principles of humanity relates humanitarian law with human rights. Both systems recognise a minimum level of protection that all human beings should have, irrespective of circumstances of peace or war. In any particular situation, duplicity of rules would generate overlaps among human rights and humanitarian law rules.

But, in between peace and war, there are other situations in which internal violence or disturbances do not qualify as internal armed conflicts in order to trigger the application of humanitarian law. Taking into consideration that human rights are subject to restrictions and temporary derogations or suspensions, there is a chance that *lacunae* in the applicable law could cause lack of protection either from human rights (suspended or restricted) or from humanitarian law (in respect to situations not covered by it). We thus consider it most relevant to refer to permissible derogations of rights in order to detect complementarity effects between human rights and humanitarian law and to identify where these *lacunae* may arise.

3. DEROGATION FROM RIGHTS UNDER HUMAN RIGHTS INSTRUMENTS

Most relevant international and regional instruments for the protection of human rights entitle states to suspend temporarily and under special circumstances the rights and guarantees recognized by them.

The International Covenant on Civil and Political Rights (ICCPR), the European Convention for the Protection of Human Rights and Fundamental Freedoms (ECHR), the European Social Charter and the American Convention on Human Rights (American Convention) all contain clauses that specifically provide for derogations from the rights guaranteed. The African Charter on Human and Peoples' Rights and the International Covenant on Economic, Social and Cultural Rights, conversely, have no provision related to derogation.

The philosophy underpinning the right of states to derogate from or to temporarily suspend human rights is founded on the very essence of the principle of state sovereignty. That is why states have basically agreed on the possibility of derogating from the application of human rights when there is a threat to the life of the nation. The territorial integrity or political independence of a state, its institutional stability and its internal public order prevail over human rights during emergency situations.

Human rights treaty law has predetermined state compliance with basic requirements for the acceptance of derogations as a licit state prerogative. These requirements refer to reasons for derogations, formal notification and extension of tolerated derogations. There is also a well-defined group of basic human rights that have been conventionally recognised as not subject to derogation.

Conversely, as IHL has been created and developed to be applied during certain well-defined circumstances, there is no room to consider the possibility of endowing states with the power to derogate from the rights recognized as applicable in those specific situations. The acceptance of the principle of non-reciprocity as the basis of the legal system for the observance and compliance of humanitarian law, as well as the normative limitations on reprisals, have evidenced the non-derogable character of rights and guarantees afforded to individuals under IHL.

That basic difference within the legal structure of human rights and humanitarian law is most relevant in the context of the reasons and arguments advanced by states when proclaiming their need to derogate from the application of human rights, considering that the same reasons that justify derogation from human rights could determine the immediate application of humanitarian law rules, which, by definition, are non-derogable.

3.1 Announcing and justifying emergencies

The ICCPR entitles states parties to take measures derogating from their obligations under the Covenant during public emergencies which threaten the life of the nation.[13] The European Convention allows derogations 'in time of war or other public emergency threatening the life of the nation.'[14] The American Convention is even more specific when authorising derogations 'in time of war, public danger, or other emergency that threatens the independence or security of a State Party'.[15] Although the language of these instruments differs, the criteria used are common. A threat of war also qualifies as a threat to the life of the nation. Both the ICCPR and the American Convention prohibit derogation

13. Art. 4(1) ICCPR.

14. Art. 15(1) Council of Europe Convention for the Protection of Human Rights and Fundamental Freedoms 1950 (hereafter, European Convention).

15. Art. 27(1) American Convention on Human Rights 1969 (hereafter, American Convention).

measures that involve discrimination on the ground of race, colour, sex, language, religion or social origin.

Suspension of human rights could be defined as a discretional power of states that implies the possibility of taking measures derogating from their obligations under international human rights law. States have a broad margin of appreciation when implementing derogations as long as they officially announce the causes of a public emergency. States wishing to derogate must notify the relevant States Parties, through the appropriate intermediary.[16] Compliance or non-compliance with the obligation to notify is related to the possibility of establishing an international control for eventual abuses and is not necessary for a probable validation of the measures taken under cover of an authorised derogation.[17] In all circumstances, minimum standards must be respected, whether or not a state of emergency has been proclaimed.[18]

In most cases under domestic law, the declaration of a state of emergency is a discretional power of the executive branch, not subject to judicial control. The requirement of an official proclamation of a public emergency prescribed by Article 4(1) of the ICCPR is an attempt to ensure that human right suspensions are only implemented to the extent strictly required by the exigencies of the situation. In practice, that requires objective criteria to restrict measures derogating from human rights commitments.

16. Art. 4(3) of the ICCPR contemplates that '... Any State Party to the present Covenant availing itself of the right to derogation shall immediately inform the other State Parties to the present Covenant, through the intermediary of the Secretary-General of the United Nations, of the provisions from which it has derogated and of the reasons by which it was actuated. A further communication shall be made, through the same intermediary, on the date on which it terminates such derogation'.
Art. 15(3) of the European Convention prescribes that '... Any High Contracting Party availing itself of this right of derogation shall keep the Secretary-General of the Council of Europe fully informed of the measures that it has taken and the reasons therefor. It shall also inform the Secretary-General of the Council of Europe when such measures have ceased to operate and the provisions of the Convention are again being fully executed.'
Art. 27(3) American Convention expresses that '...Any State Party availing itself of the right of suspension shall immediately inform the other States Parties, through the Secretary General of the Organisation of American States, of the provisions the application of which it has suspended, the reasons that gave rise to the suspension, and the date set for the termination of such suspension.'

17. The European Court of Human Rights in the *Brannigan and McBride* case has declared that 'The power of extended detention with such judicial control and the derogation of 23 December 1988 being clearly linked to the persistence of the emergency situation, there is no indication that the derogation was other than a genuine response', *Branningan and McBride* v. *United Kingdom*, Judgment of 26 May 1993, Series A, No 258=B (1994) 17 *EHRR* 539.

18. Declaration of Minimum Humanitarian Standards adopted by a Group of Experts at Turku, Finland, 1990. Text reproduced at 89 *AJIL* (1995) p. 218 et seq.

The UN Human Rights Committee has stated that domestic measures taken under Article 4 of the ICCPR are of a temporal and exceptional character.[19] While every state has the sovereign right to declare a state of emergency, it is the function of the United Nations Human Rights Committee to control state parties' compliance with the ICCPR and its Optional Protocol. If full and comprehensive information required in conformity with Article 4(3) has not been provided, the Committee cannot conclude that a valid reason exists to legitimise derogation.[20]

At a regional level, the European Court of Human Rights has established that the customary meaning of the term 'public emergency threatening the life of the nation' is clear, referring to exceptional situations of crisis or emergency, that are actual or imminent, affect the whole population and constitute a threat to the organised life of the state as a community.[21] Thus, measures and restrictions permitted under the European Convention for the maintenance of public safety and order are plainly inadequate if those requirements are not objectively met.[22]

The European Commission has concluded that each government has its own responsibility to secure the life of the nation and to determine whether that life is threatened by a public emergency.[23] Even though the government has a discretional power and some margin of appreciation in determining the existence of a public emergency threatening the life of the nation, the Commission has determined that it has the competence and the duty to examine and pronounce upon a government determination of the existence of such an exceptional situation.[24]

In that context, the European Court concluded that it is its function to determine whether the conditions lay down in Article 15 of the European Convention for the existence of the exceptional right of derogation have been fulfilled.[25] The domestic margin of appreciation is thus accompanied by a European supervision.[26]

Turning to specific cases, the European Commission resolved in *Denmark, Norway, Sweden and the Netherlands* v. *Greece* that, on 21 April 1967, there was not in Greece a public emergency threatening the life of the nation, despite

19. GC 5/13, United Nations Human Rights Committee 36, 110.

20. *Silva, et al* v. *Uruguay* (E.8/34) *HRC* 36, 130.

21. Eur. Ct. HR, *Lawless* v. *Ireland* (322/57), Judgment: 1 *EHRR* 15.

22. Eur. Comm. HR, in *Denmark, Norway, Sweden and the Netherlands* v. *Greece*, (3321-3/67; 3344/67) Report: 5 November 1969.

23. Eur. Comm. HR, *Ireland* v. *United Kingdom* (5310/71) 2 *EHRR* 25.

24. Eur. Comm. HR, *Greece* v. *United Kingdom* (176/56) Unpublished Report.

25. *Lawless* v. *Ireland*, see *supra* n. 21.

26. *Ireland* v. *United Kingdom*, see *supra* n. 23.

three factors that were argued by the government which had seized power by military force and overthrown the legitimate government: the threat of a Communist takeover of the government by force; the state of public order; and the constitutional crisis immediately preceding the general election scheduled for May 1967.[27]

In another case, the European Court observed that a law which provided for detention without trial, subject to certain safeguards announced by the respondent government, appeared to be a measure strictly required by the exigencies of the situation under Article 15 of the European Convention. The application of ordinary law had proven unable to check the growing danger which threatened the state; and the assembling of the necessary evidence to convict persons involved in activities of the Irish Republican Army (IRA) and its splinter groups was meeting with great difficulties caused by the military, secret, and terrorist character of those groups and the fear they sowed in the population.[28]

Within European experience, justification under Article 15 does not follow automatically from a high level of violence. There must be a link between the facts of the emergency on the one hand and the measures applied to deal with it on the other.[29] The state facing the emergency must choose its means and prescribe its safeguards against executive branch abuse, subject to Article 15 requirements and to the control machinery under the Convention.[30]

At the same time, the European Court has observed that 'when a State is struggling against a public emergency threatening the life of the nation, it would be rendered defenceless if it were required to accomplish everything at once ... The interpretation [of Article 15 of the European Convention] must leave a place for progressive adaptations.'[31]

The European Court has maintained that it is not its function to substitute for the government's assessment any other assessment of what might be the most prudent or most expedient policy to combat terrorism. However, the Court has the power to review the lawfulness of the measures adopted in conformity with the Convention, taking into accounts the conditions and circumstances existing when the measures were taken and during the time they continued to apply.

From all previous European experience restricting derogations of human rights, there is no direct confrontation with probable IHL applications.

27. *Denmark, Norway, Sweden and the Netherlands* v. *Greece*, see *supra* n. 22.
28. *Lawless* v. *Ireland*, see *supra* n. 21.
29. *Ireland* v. *United Kingdom*, see *supra* n. 23.
30. Ibid.
31. Ibid.

Treaty law[32] also requires that state measures derogating from obligations under international human rights law cannot be inconsistent with other state obligations under international law. This is a strong limitation on effects of derogation in as much as the norms authorising derogation from human rights cannot be opposed to other international obligations assumed customarily or conventionally by the state involved.

International humanitarian law will be applicable during armed conflicts of an international or an internal character, irrespective of the existence of the above-mentioned requirement. What have been authorised are derogations from human rights treaty law, not derogation from rights recognised by other international norms. Even if that requirement was not prescribed, IHL would be applicable during certain states of emergencies amounting to internal or international armed conflicts. This illustrates the independence of IHL and human rights law. International humanitarian law will apply not because there is a limitation on the right to derogate within human rights law but because an autonomous source of law prescribes its direct application.

3.2 Extension of non-derogable rights: judicial guarantees

Judicial guarantees are not included as non-derogable rights within human rights treaty law, except in the American Convention on Human Rights. But non-derogability of judicial remedies within the American system is a consequence of exceptional previous situations, not necessarily linked to armed conflicts *per se.*

Concerning derogation from judicial guarantees during states of emergency, in 1987 the Inter-American Commission on Human Rights asked the Court if the writ of *habeas corpus* is one of the judicial guarantees that may not be suspended by a state party to the American Convention.[33] As the basis for its request to the Court, the Commission took into consideration the fact that some states parties to the American Convention on Human Rights have assumed that one of the rights that may be suspended in emergency situations is the right to judicial protection afforded by the writ of *habeas corpus*. The Commission pointed out that some states have promulgated laws or have developed practices enabling them to hold a detainee incommunicado for a prolonged period of time.

32. Art. 4(1) UN Covenant on Civil and Political rights; Art. 15(1) European Convention; Art. 27(1) American Convention.

33. I/A Court HR, *Habeas Corpus in Emergency Situations* (Arts. 27(2), 25(1) and 7(6) American Convention on Human Rights), Advisory Opinion OC-8/87 of 29 January 1987.

During that time, the detainee may even be refused permission to contact anyone, in order to prevent resort to the writ of *habeas corpus*.[34]

The Commission was aware that within the American Convention the right of personal liberty may be temporarily suspended in time of war, public danger or during any other emergency that threatens the independence or security of a state party.[35] The Commission also recognised that the executive branch of a state has the authority to temporarily detain a person on the mere presumption that she or he endangers the independence or security of the state.[36]

The Commission stressed the idea that the essence of *habeas corpus* as a legal remedy is to bring the detainee before a judge in order to verify whether he or she is still alive and whether he or she has been subjected to torture. That remedy is directly related to the right to humane treatment, which is one of the rights recognised by the American Convention that cannot be suspended under any circumstances.[37]

The Commission also argued that, even during states of emergency, there is an obligation to give reasons for a detention ordered by the executive branch. The intervention of the judiciary would prevent the '... violation of the principle of separation of powers, a basic characteristic of the rule of law and of democratic systems.'[38]

The Court, when interpreting the American Convention[39], constantly referred to the Vienna Convention on the Law of Treaties to stress that its text must be interpreted in good faith, keeping in mind the object and the purpose of the Convention and the need to prevent a conclusion that could give rise to the suppression of the enjoyment or exercise of the rights and freedoms recognised in the Convention or restrict them to a greater extent than is provided for therein.[40]

When interpreting Article 27 of the American Convention, the Court found that the term 'suspension of Guarantees' ('suspension of articles' in the English version) does not have an absolute meaning because the rights protected by this

34. Ibid., para. 12, p. 31.
35. Cf., Art. 27 American Convention.
36. See *supra* n. 33, para. 12, p. 32.
37. See *supra* n. 33, para. 12, p. 32. Cf., Arts. 27 and 5 American Convention.
38. See *supra* n. 33, para. 12, p. 33.
39. Cf., I/A Court HR, *Restrictions to the death penalty (Arts. 4(2) and 4(4) American Convention on Human Rights)*, Advisory Opinion OC-3/83 of 8 September 1983, Series A No. 3, para. 48.
40. Art. 29 American Convention; OC-3/83, see *supra* n. 33, para. 16, p. 36.

provision are inherent to man. What could be suspended or limited, said the Court, is their full and effective exercise.[41]

When dealing with suspension of guarantees, Article 27 of the Convention recognises that it only applies during exceptional situations, such as in time of war, public danger, or other emergency that threatens the independence or security of a state party. The suspension of certain rights is only permitted to the extent and for the period of time strictly required by the exigencies of the situation, provided that such measures are not inconsistent with states' other obligations under international law and do not involve discrimination on the ground of race, colour, sex, language, religion, or social origin.

The Court stated that previous experience in the Americas has shown that abuses may result from the application of emergency measures not objectively justified under the requirements of Article 27 or under the principles prescribed by other relevant instruments. The Court seemed to justify suspension of guarantees in order to preserve the values of a democratic society. It emphasised that the suspension of guarantees cannot be disassociated from the effective exercise of representative democracy referred to in Article 3 of the OAS Charter.[42] The suspension of guarantees lacks all legitimacy, however, whenever it is resorted to for the purpose of undermining the democratic system. That system establishes limits that may not be transgressed, thus ensuring that certain fundamental human rights remain permanently protected.

The Court concluded that all rights recognised by the American Convention must be guaranteed and enforced unless special circumstances justify the suspension of some. Certain rights may never be suspended, irrespective of the emergency.

The Court accepted that what might be permissible in one type of emergency would not be tolerable in another. The lawfulness of the measures taken to deal with each of the special situations referred to in Article 27(1) will depend upon the nature and particularities of the emergency and upon the proportionality and reasonableness of the measures.[43] In that sense, the Court, although having in mind the previous experience of American states in relation to democracy, allows for the possibility of legally imposing more severe suspensions during certain

41. See *supra* n. 33, para. 17, p. 37.

42. See *supra* n. 33, para. 20, p. 38: the Court states that '... the soundness of this conclusion gains special validity given the context of the Convention, whose Preamble reaffirms the intention (of the American States) ... to consolidate in this hemisphere, within the framework of democratic institutions, a system of personal liberty and social justice based on respect for the essential rights of man.'

43. See *supra* n. 33, para. 22, p. 39.

emergency situations, for instance, during a foreign military occupation or an internal or international armed conflict.

The Convention also prescribes limitations on the right of states parties to suspend rights and freedoms. No derogation is permitted under any circumstances for certain rights and freedoms, including the judicial guarantees essential for the protection of such rights.[44]

The suspension of guarantees does not imply a temporary suspension of the rule of law, nor does it authorise those in power to act in disregard of the principle of legality, by which they are bound at all times.[45] When enforcing human rights derogations, governments do not perform an absolute and unrestricted function that goes beyond the circumstances justifying the possibility to apply such exceptional legal measures. The Court has already noted, in this connection, that an inseparable bond exists between the principles of legality, democratic institutions and the rule of law.[46]

The Court concluded that, in serious emergency situations, it is lawful to temporarily suspend certain rights and freedoms whose free exercise must, under normal circumstances, be respected and guaranteed by the state. However, since not all of these rights and freedoms may be suspended even temporarily, it is imperative that the judicial guarantees essential for their protection remain in force. Article 17(2) does not link these judicial guarantees to any specific provision of the Convention, which indicates that what is important is that these judicial remedies have the character of being essential to ensure the protection of those rights.[47]

The Court then found that judicial remedies recognised by Article 7(6) (*habeas corpus*) and Article 25(1) *(amparo)*, although not specifically mentioned in Article

44. Art. 27(2) American Convention: '... The foregoing provision does not authorize any suspension of the following articles: Art. 3 (Right to Judicial Personality), Art. 4 (Right to Life), Art. 5 (Right to Humane Treatment), Art. 6 (Freedom from Slavery), Art. 9 (Freedom from Ex Post Facto Laws), Art. 12 (Freedom of Conscience and Religion), Art. 17 (Rights of the Family), Art. 18 (Right to a Name), Art. 19 (Rights of the Child), Art. 20 (Right to Nationality) and Art. 23 (Right to participate in Government), or of the judicial guarantees essential for the protection of such rights ...'

45. See *supra* n. 33, para. 24, p. 40.

46. See *supra* n. 33, para. 2 and para. 24, p. 40; Cf., I/A Court HR, *The Word 'Laws' in Article 30 of the American Convention on Human Rights,* Advisory Opinion OC-6/86 of 9 May 1986, Series A. No. 6, para. 32; '... in a democratic society, the rights and freedoms inherent in the human person, the guarantees applicable to them and the rule of law form a triad. Each component thereof defines itself, complements and depends on the other for its meaning, idem, p. 41.

47. See *supra* n. 33, para. 27, p. 41.

27(2), are non-derogable judicial guarantees, essential for the protection of non-derogable rights.[48]

The Commission request referred to judicial remedies recognised by Articles 25(1) (*amparo*) and Article 7(6) (*habeas corpus*) in relation to non-derogable guarantees recognised by Article 27(2). The concept of 'guarantee' as used in Article 27(2) is designed to protect, to ensure or to assert the entitlement to a right or the exercise thereof.[49]

The Court recognised that its conclusion is buttressed by the realities that have been the experience of some of the peoples of this hemisphere in recent decades, particularly disappearances, torture and murder committed or tolerated by some governments. This experience has demonstrated over and over again that the right to life and to humane treatment are threatened whenever the right to *habeas corpus* is partially or wholly suspended.[50]

The Court also declared that, '... It follows that in a system governed by the rule of law it is entirely in order for an autonomous and independent judicial order to exercise control over the lawfulness of such measures by verifying, for example, whether a detention based on the suspension of personal freedom complies with the legislation authorised by the state of emergency. In this context, *habeas corpus* acquires a new dimension of fundamental importance.'[51] But if all that the judiciary could review is the compatibility of the detention with the domestic legislation authorised by the state of emergency, the role of the judge would not necessarily imply a control of arbitrary detention, if arbitrary detention is legally foreseen within the legal limits required to deal with the emergency. Then it could be argued that the declaration of a state of emergency is not necessary under a strict judicial control. The executive branch could define a broad margin of discretion as part of its internal declaration of emergency. The judge seems only entitled to control actions or omissions of government authorities in relation to emergency legislation. In that context, the Court concluded that '... the suspension of guarantees may not exceed the limits of that strictly required to deal with the emergency, any action on the part of the public authorities that goes beyond those limits, which must be specified with precision

48. See *supra* n. 33, para. 29, p. 42: '... the judicial remedies that must be considered to be essential within the meaning of article 27(2) are those that ordinarily will effectively guarantee the full exercise of the rights and freedoms protected by that provision and whose denial or restriction would endanger their full enjoyment.'

49. See *supra* n. 33, para. 25, p. 40.

50. See *supra* n. 33, para. 36, p. 44; 'Those who drafted the Convention were aware of these realities, which may well explain why the Pact of San José is the first international human rights instrument to include among the rights that may not be suspended essential judicial guarantees for the protection of non-derogable rights', idem, para. 36, p. 45.

51. See *supra* n. 33, para. 40, p. 46.

in the decree promulgating the state of emergency, would also be unlawful notwithstanding the existence of the emergency situation.'[52]

Herewith the Court recognised the possibility of a broad margin of discretion being granted to governments when declaring a state of emergency. In that case, the judge would only be entitled to control emergency legislation in the context of its practical application, without having the possibility to declare that legislation is in itself in excess of what the circumstances requires. The Court would have no possibility to recognise that the declaration of emergency is in itself under judicial revision. But it is important to note that non-derogable rights could not be affected within that internal legislation granting special powers to the government. A second important judicial test would relate to the violation of other international instruments which ban or limit the discretion of states during emergencies.

The Court finally concluded that 'from what has been said before, it follows that writs of *habeas corpus* and of "amparo" are among those judicial remedies that are essential for the protection of various rights whose derogation is prohibited by Article 27(2) and that serve, moreover, to preserve legality in a democratic society.'[53] The Court also observed that 'the Constitutions and legal systems of the States Parties that authorise, expressly or by implication, the suspension of the legal remedies of *habeas corpus* or of "amparo" in emergency situations cannot be deemed to be compatible with the international obligations imposed on these States by the Convention.'[54]

A difficult test for the doctrine behind this Advisory Opinion will be to foresee its potential effects during exceptional states of emergencies derived from internal or international armed conflicts. We might presume that judicial remedies would be enforced during those situations under terms and conditions prescribed by IHL and not necessarily within the scope proposed by the Advisory Opinion interpretation, based on specific political and historical contexts not necessarily linked to armed conflicts.

That assumption takes into consideration the fact that those legal extensions of derogations depend directly upon what is strictly required by the exigencies of the situation. The Court's conclusions have been strongly motivated, in accordance with the text of the American Convention, by recent experiences of systematic violations of human rights during Latin-American military governments.

52. See *supra* n. 33, para. 38, p. 46.
53. See *supra* n. 33, para. 42, p. 48 (formalities versus respect and guarantees of rights).
54. See *supra* n. 33, para. 43, p. 48.

In the same vein, the Court, in a later Advisory Opinion concerning Judicial Guarantees in States of Emergency, declared that the question raised by the Government of Uruguay is related to a specific juridical, historical and political context, in that states of exception or emergency, and of human rights and the essential guarantees in those situations, were a critical problem in the Americas. The Court understood that its opinion could be useful within a reality in which basic principles of the system have often been questioned.[55]

In neither Advisory Opinion does the Court make reference to judicial guarantees prescribed by IHL which, by definition, are non-derogable rights applicable during armed conflicts.

4. HARD CORE GROUP OF HUMAN RIGHTS AND FUNDAMENTAL GUARANTEES: EXCEPTIONS TO DEROGATION

It has already been stated that human rights and IHL have a common objective in the protection of human beings. We will now try to identify international rules that have a common content.

Besides the European Social Charter, all other international treaties dealing with derogations precisely enumerate the rights not subject to derogation.

The European Convention has a limited number of rights exempted from derogation.[56] It is the only international human rights treaty reflecting a direct determination to deal with war situations.

The American Convention prescribes a much broader list of rights not subject to derogation.[57] This extensive list of non-derogable rights is a consequence of

55. Advisory Opinion OC-9/87 of October 6, 1987 on Judicial Guarantees in States of Emergency, (Arts. 27(2), 25 and 8) at para. 17 p. 29. The government of Uruguay asked the Court 'to interpret the scope of the convention's prohibition of the suspension of the judicial guarantees essential for the protection of such rights. Because even in time of war, public danger, or other emergency that threatens the independence or security of a State Party (Art. 27(1)) it is not possible to suspend the judicial guarantees essential for the protection of such rights, the Government of Uruguay requests the Court's opinion, in particular regarding: (a) which of these judicial guarantees are "essential" and (b) the relationship between Art. 27(2), in that regard, and Arts. 25 and 8 of the American Convention'.

56. Derogation from Art. 2 (Right to Life), except in respect of death resulting from lawful acts of war; from Art. 3 (Torture or other Ill Treatment); Art. 4(1) (Slavery or Servitude); and Art. 7 (Retroactive Penal Law) are not permitted under Art. 15(2).

57. Art. 27(2) prescribes that '...The foregoing provision does not authorise any suspension of the following articles: Art. 3 (Right to Judicial Personality); Art. 4 (Right to Life); Art. 5 (Right to Humane Treatment); Art. 6 (Freedom from Slavery); Art. 9 (Freedom from Ex Post Facto Laws); Art. 12 (Freedom of Conscience and Religion); Art. 17 (Rights of the Family); Art. 18 (Right to a Name); Art. 19 (Rights of the Child); Art. 20 (Right to Nationality); and Art. 23 (Right to

Latin America's recent negative experiences during state of emergencies imposed by *de facto* governments. Special protection of the right to nationality or of the right to participate in government seem to be rather difficult to be secured or implemented by states during an armed conflict, especially considering that these rights have been recognised as part of international human rights and not necessarily as part of IHL.

The ICCPR's Article 4(2) enumerates a short list of core rights from which derogations may not be made.[58]

From a comparison of rights not subject to derogation under the above-mentioned treaties, it is possible to conclude that there is a limited number of rights that could easily be identified as the hard core of human rights. These rights are universally recognised under customary international human right law as well as under treaty law.

The right to life, protection from torture and other ill treatment, freedom from slavery and servitude and freedom from retroactive penal laws have been considered as part of the essence of human rights, with a universal and indivisible character.[59] But at the same time, this hard core group of human rights has been recognised as applicable during armed conflicts because they are also prescribed by IHL. That implies that the same rights have a dual enforcement scheme. This is a positive reassurance that the content of the norms would be observed or at least would have a better chance of being implemented during states of emergency, including armed conflicts.

If applicability of these rights during an armed conflict depended exclusively on human rights law, its enforceability would be limited to the schemes developed to enforce that law. On the contrary, because they have also been recognised by IHL, they benefit from the aforesaid dual schemes in order to be observed. Overlaps of norms of a humanitarian and human rights nature are welcome, as long as they provide extra mechanisms to assure compliance.

The presumption that a basic hard core group of human rights could only be deduced by strict recognition and correspondences among major international human rights treaty instruments when defining non-derogable rights undermines accomplishments produced by IHL developments in the field of human rights

---

Participate in Government), or of the judicial guarantees essential for the protection of such rights'.

58. It prescribes that no derogation from Art. 6 (Right to Life); Art. 7 (Freedom from Torture, Cruel or Inhuman Treatment); Art. 8(1) (Freedom from Slavery); Art. 8(2) (Freedom from Servitude); Art. 11 (Freedom from Imprisonment for Debts); Art. 15 (Freedom from Ex Post Facto Penal Laws); Art. 16 (Recognition of Personality); and Art. 18 (Freedom of Thought, Conscience and Religion); may be made.

59. See United Nations World Conference on Human Rights: Vienna Declaration and Programme of Action, 25 June 1993, 32 *ILM* (1993), p. 1661 et seq.

protection during armed conflicts. Even if these normative developments have been inspired by human rights law, their independence and autonomy precludes the exclusion of humanitarian law mechanisms to implement them during armed conflicts.[60]

Examination of humanitarian treaty law reveals several rights that correspond directly with human rights recognised as part of the so-called hard core group of fundamental rights.[61]

A comparison of the hard core of rights guaranteed under human rights and IHL reveals that fundamental humanitarian law guarantees coincide with non-derogable human rights, with the exception of several rights that, in spite of being considered derogable under certain regional and international human rights instruments, will be treated as non-derogable during armed conflicts as a result of humanitarian law enforcement.

Within that latter category, judicial guarantees, specially penal due process, are only secured to be always applicable during time of armed conflicts. As an exception among treaty law, judicial guarantees are considered as non-derogable under the American Convention of Human Rights, but within a particular context.

60. Cf., International Criminal Tribunal for the Former Yugoslavia, *Prosecutor* v. *Tadić* a/k/a/"Dule", Decision on the Defence Motion for Interlocutory Appeal on Jurisdiction, Case IT-94-I-AR 72; reproduced at 91 *ILM* (1996) pp. 32 et seq.

61. For example, Art. 3 common to the four Geneva Conventions of 1949 and applicable during internal armed conflicts prescribes the right to life, to freedom from torture and cruel treatment, *inter alia*. Principles of legality, due process and of non-retroactivity are also recognised by common Art. 3. The same article prescribes that persons protected under it shall in all circumstances be treated humanely, without any adverse distinction founded on race, colour, religion or faith, sex, birth or wealth, or any other similar criteria. Common Art. 3 implies that states have accepted their obligation to protect their own nationals during internal armed conflicts.

Art. 75 of Protocol I lays down minimum guarantees applicable to persons in the power of a party to an international conflict, including that they shall be treated humanely in all circumstances and shall enjoy these rights without discrimination and with due respect for the person, honour, convictions and religious practices of all protected persons. The rights guaranteed include violence to life, health, or physical or mental well-being of persons, in particular, murder; torture; corporal punishment; mutilation; outrages upon personal dignity; humiliating and degrading treatment; enforced prostitution and any form of indecent assault; the taking of hostages; collective punishments; and threats to commit any of the foregoing acts, shall remain prohibited whether committed by civilian or by military agents. Due process and other relevant judicial guarantees, such as non-retroactivity of penal laws, as well as special protection of women and children are considered as fundamental guarantees applicable under the general terms and conditions of Protocol I. Fundamental rights are also prescribed in Art. 4 of Protocol II, which reiterates the fundamental guarantees recognised under Art. 75 of Protocol I, adding acts of terrorism, slavery and the slave trade and pillage as acts that shall remain prohibited at any time and in any place whatsoever.

Protocol II also recognises the principle of legality, the principle of non-retroactivity and the right to due process for penal prosecution and punishment of criminal offences related to armed conflicts.

Other rights secured exclusively by humanitarian law as non-derogable guarantees in time of war include special protection of children and women; prohibition of the taking of hostages; prohibition of medical experiments; acts of terrorism; and prohibition of collective punishments.

Considering that the duplication of rights enables different and independent enforcement mechanisms to be activated, we find that this reiteration of norms protecting fundamental rights is a reasonable and convenient means of producing effective compliance and eventually determining legal consequences for violations, as a reassurance of their effectiveness.

Although it has been universally recognised that human rights will continue to apply during armed conflicts, states' prerogatives to derogate from certain categories of rights have been, in practice, commonly used and even extended beyond tolerable limits. It should also be remembered that the special protection granted under IHL is of a humanitarian character, depending upon the particular situation and qualification of persons as subjects to be protected.

5. GAPS AND OVERLAPS

5.1 A Minimum Humanitarian Standard

As the law stands today, there are different situations of violence or use of force within a state that are not necessarily covered by international humanitarian treaty law. These situations could include, amongst others: internal violence, domestic states of emergency, localised commotion, or internal strife without the required intensity to properly apply Protocol II or common Article 3. In those cases, it appears that, besides domestic law, only international law relating to human rights will be applicable. Recent developments, however, seem to signify the need to deal with IHL even in situations of internal violence that were not traditionally covered by it.

In that context, beginning as an academic exercise, in 1990, a group of experts adopted a Declaration of Minimum Humanitarian Standards[62] in which all situations, including internal violence; ethic, religious and national conflicts; disturbances; tensions; and public emergencies were contemplated. The Declaration is an acknowledgement of the lack of adequate protection of human beings in extreme internal situations not covered by either IHL or human rights law. It attempts to solve legal problems derived from complicated technical and juridical definitions of armed conflicts. The Declaration is directed to all persons,

62. *Supra* n. 18.

groups and authorities, irrespective of their legal status and without any adverse discrimination. It deduces an irreducible core group of humanitarian and human rights rules that must be respected in all circumstances, irrespective of defining the particularities of situations to which they should apply. The Declaration is intended to give a legal framework to situations not necessarily contemplated by IHL. Even if international human rights instruments provide a regulatory scheme to deal with those particular situations, it is well known that their observance and compliance during situations of internal violence would be difficult, considering especially that human rights treaty law is primarily directed to governments, and that certain governments have already demonstrated their reluctance to observe and respect minimum standards during those extreme situations. The Declaration has been considered as a reaffirmation of already existing rules of human rights and IHL and as declaratory of customary law.[63]

The need for such minimum humanitarian standards becomes clear when one turns to state practice, in particular the experience of some Latin American countries. Regarding the so-called 'dirty wars' waged in some of these states during the 1970s and 1980s, it is relevant to note the recognition by some successor governments that previous fighting against subversive movements or guerrilla warfare even not amounting to traditional internal armed conflicts should also be considered under the scope of the basic rules of IHL. Conversely, military governments in Latin America tried to avoid their responsibility to comply with IHL by not recognising the existence of formal internal armed conflicts at all.

There are reasons why a state might derogate from the application of certain human rights during extraordinary situations that could not be identified as an internal armed conflict. At the same time, the lack of required intensity of hostilities, or the lack of effective control over territory necessary to maintain such hostilities, or even the lack of capacity to apply international humanitarian rules as defined by Protocol II are some of the causes that evidence the existence of undefined zones in which treaty law is insufficient. Even more, the strict application of Article 3 common to the four Geneva Conventions of 1949 requires the existence of an internal armed conflict.

Beyond limitations in treaty law, state practice has developed an increasing concern with the application of basic IHL to situations of internal violence not covered by formal states' agreements.

In that context, we will now consider Argentina's recent practice related to repeated, even systematic, acts of violence performed by state authorities during

63. Cf., A. Eide, et al., 'Combating lawlessness in gray zone conflicts through minimum humanitarian standards', 89 *AJIL* (1995) p. 216.

military governments as a consequence of subversive activities, and subsequent repression involving the use of force.

5.2 The experience of Argentina

During successive military governments in Argentina, it was systematically denied by state authorities that IHL or human rights were violated. Government authorities referred to a dirty war (*'guerra sucia'*) in order to justify excesses in the repression of subversive activities.

The Military Junta, before handing over power to the democratic government, enforced an amnesty law in order to protect all members of the military from future prosecution for crimes allegedly committed during the repression of 'subversion'.[64]

The democratic government thus had to consider how to prosecute military leaders for violations of human rights without violating basic human rights principles protected by the amnesty law. The National Constitution prohibits retroactive abrogations of penal laws (Art. 18), and the Penal Code (Art. 2) prescribes that any changes in the law after a criminal act has been committed oblige the judge to apply the law most beneficial to the defendant.

In December 1983, the recently-elected democratic government ordered, through a presidential Decree, the investigation and prosecution of former military commanders for human rights violations on the grounds of violations of the Penal Code and the Code of Military Justice. Under the terms of the Decree, military leaders were not charged with war crimes, genocide or crimes against humanity.

The government argued that the amnesty law violated the National Constitution that prohibits the concentration of all powers in one of the branches of the government (Art. 29) and was also contrary to the constitutional principle that ensures equal protection before the law (Art. 16). Finally, the Congress passed a law nullifying the Amnesty Law.[65]

Judicial proceedings were then commenced pursuant to Decree No. 158 issued by the National Executive Power on 13 December 1983, ordering previous military leaders to be brought to justice before the Supreme Council of the Armed Forces on charges of homicide, unlawful deprivation of freedom and torture. The Decree also prescribed that trials on those charges shall in no way prejudice later

64. Ley [Law] No. 22.924 (*B.O.* 27/09/83).

65. Ley [Law] No. 23.040 (*B.O.* 29/12/83): A National Appeals Court declared the constitutionality of Law No 23.040 and the illegality of the so-called self-amnesty law; Cámara Nacional de Apelaciones en lo Criminal y Correccional Federal, judgment of 4 October 1984 in re Fernández Marino, Amador.

trials for other crimes which the above-mentioned superior officers may have perpetrated as primary or secondary parties, instigators or accomplices.[66]

In October 1984, the Supreme Council declared its inability to continue the proceedings and concluded that orders and directives given to pursue military operations against subversion were correct in form and content.

As all decisions of the Military Tribunals were under revision by civilian courts, the Federal Appeals Court took over the proceedings.[67] Before the Appeals Court, the prosecutor argued that the Military Junta was responsible for all the planning, direction and supervision of the campaign against subversion.[68] The Appeals Court concluded that, although the Military Junta assumed the command of the Armed Forces, and in spite of the fact that the eradication of subversion was one of the basic objectives of the Military Government, the Military Junta did not seem to have taken part in the decision-making process concerning the war against subversion. The evidence showed that, with respect of the chain of command in each of the armed forces, the former commanders were not subordinated to anyone.[69]

The Appeals Court observed that the orders and directives addressed to each force were not issued by the Military Junta, but rather by the commanders-in-chief of each branch of the services. According to the testimony of all the superior officers, the information regarding the conduct of the operations was received through the natural chain of command.[70]

Human rights violations were part of a system of operations ordered by the commanders-in-chief of the armed forces. Even if the commanders did not individually abduct, torture or murder, they had to face criminal charges based on their responsibilities for acts committed by others.

The Appeals Court observed that the operating structure of the armed forces continued to function in the same manner as before, but those subordinated to the accused detained a large number of people, lodged them clandestinely in military units or in places controlled by the armed forces, subjected them to

66. Decreto [Decree] No. 158/83 (B.O. 15/11/83). The Decree was passed in accordance with powers granted to the President by the National Constitution (Art. 86.15).

67. See amendments to the Code of Military Justice approved by Law No 23.049 (*B.O.* 15/02/84); the law amending the Code of Military Justice conferred jurisdiction on the federal courts of appeal to intervene in military proceedings by appeal or by removing the case from military courts and assuming jurisdiction in the case, regardless of the stage of proceedings (Art. 10).

68. *Causa originalmente instruida por el Consejo Supremo de las Fuerzas Armadas en cumplimiento del Decreto 158/83 del Poder Ejecutivo Nacional,* Cámara Nacional de Apelaciones en lo Criminal y Correccional, sentencia del 9 de Diciembre de 1985, *Fallos* CSJN, v. 309-I, p. 33 et seq. At p. 288.

69. Ibid., at pp. 289-290.

70. Ibid., at pp. 294-295.

interrogation under torture, kept them in captivity under inhumane conditions, and, finally, either submitted those persons to the courts or to the National Executive Power, released them, or killed them. These proceedings, which assume secret derogation from the laws in force, were carried out in accordance with plans approved and implemented by the military commanders.[71]

The Appeals Court proved that the system chosen to fight subversion departed from the rule of law, even from those laws of exception which were designed for times of emergency. On the basis of the evidence discussed in the proceedings, the Appeals Court concluded that the defendants deliberately concealed the facts from the courts, from the families of the victims, from national and foreign institutions and organizations, from the church, from governments of foreign countries, and from society at large.[72]

On the reasoning of the Appeals Court, the commanders secretly established a criminal method for fighting terrorism. Low-ranking officers of the armed forces were granted broad discretion to deprive of freedom whoever appeared to be, according to intelligence information, an agent of subversion. The system implemented to fight subversion also granted immunity to those primarily involved in it.[73]

Referring to the terrorist phenomenon in Argentina before 1976, the Appeals Court observed that it has been sufficiently proven that terrorism went back as far as 1960. It further stated that this situation engendered a general sense of fear on the part of the population and serious concern on part of the authorities. It was also beyond discussion that by the beginning of the 1970s terrorist activities increased significantly. This growth became evident in the methods resorted to by the insurgents, the number of terrorist acts, the military structure of the operations, the offensive capabilities of terrorist groups; the financial resources acquired through theft, kidnaping and other crimes; the operational infrastructure and means of communication used by the commandos; the organization which provided those groups with immunity from prosecution; the indiscriminate and irrational terrorist attacks perpetrated by surprise; the insurgents' capacity to intercept the mass media; and their ability to take over police stations and military units.[74]

71. Ibid., at p. 295.

72. Ibid., at p. 297: 'The unlawfulness of the actions taken is reflected not only in the violence characterizing the operations but also in the measures which were taken for the purpose of concealing the arrests and the fate of the detainees, submitting them to unacceptable conditions of captivity.'

73. Ibid., at pp. 297-298: 'There was not enough evidence as to determine the existence of a similar systematic plan as to ascertain criminal responsibility to the defendants in reference to abduction of minors, bribery, kidnapping for ransom, extortion and crimes against property.'

74. Ibid., at p. 1538.

During the period that the military *de facto* government fought against subversion (1976-1979), the Junta granted broad powers to itself and to others in order to legalize their actions. Once the commanders of the armed forces took over the government of Argentina in 1976, the National Congress was dissolved, members of the Supreme Court were replaced and the authority of the president was vested in a Military Junta. Provincial governors as well as all other administrative authorities were also replaced.

The Court confirmed that the Code of Military Justice was in force during that time. It recognized military jurisdiction in time of war over civilians who commit severe crimes within the area of operations or zones of war. Military jurisdiction is also recognized in respect of other acts that are punished by orders issued by the commanders of the different zones. The Code also prescribed that the commanders-in-chief of the military forces during time of war were vested with the disciplinary powers recognized by the President of the Nation. During time of war, those regulations may be enacted in order to provide for the security of troops and materials, for the success of the operations, and in order to police those areas.[75]

Besides the Code of Military Justice, the Law on National Defense[76] and the Criminal Code were also in force. In its preamble, that law announced the need to have an adequate response to face the possibility of external attack or internal commotion providing for the creation of special zones under military control.

Evaluating the content of those regulations, the Court of Appeals concluded that, before as well as after 1976, the state has adequate legal means to protect itself, and military commanders had legal means available for the struggle against subversion. During that entire period, constitutional guarantees remained in force. Suspension of certain constitutional rights was only affected by a declaration of a state of siege.

In that context, the Court of Appeals observed that other individual rights which continued to be protected under the Constitution included: the right of equality before the law and the right of due process; the right not to be convicted without previous trial founded on a law predating the act for which the trial is

75. Art. 131 of the Code of Military Justice. Its regulations were binding on all persons who were found within the military zones. The Code also prescribed that when those regulations are used to punish criminal behaviour, they shall be published in newspapers and printed on signs and posted in public places. The regulations prescribe the death penalty for the crimes of vandalism, rape, arson and other crimes of a similar nature. The procedure to be followed once the accused has been apprehended should be oral and speedy safeguarding of the rights of the defense, which may be reasonably exercised by the defendant. The Code also provided that sentences imposing grave penalties may be appealed before the higher military authorities of the area (Art. 139).

76. Ley [Law] No. 16.970 (*B.O.* 10/10/66); see *supra* n. 68 at p. 1537.

held; not to be tried by special commissions; not to be arrested except upon an order in writing from a competent authority; and the right to inviolability of property and of domicile.[77]

Next, the Appeals Court had to determine whether the means used by former commanders to fight subversion were in accordance with legal means available at that time, and if not, whether there were causes or justification to excuse illegal behavior.

The defense advanced several causes of justification, including state of necessity; obedience to the law; self-defense; and state of war.

The defense of state of necessity is recognized by the Criminal Code as a justification for committing a crime under certain circumstances. Criminal charges in the extant case included illegal detentions, torture, disappearances and homicides. All of them produced great harm. That harm was inflicted by those who were in command of the armed forces of the state in order to avoid another harm provoked by subversive activities.

On that point, the Court of Appeals stated that if the idea was to kill and kidnap in order to prevent the subversive groups from continuing to kill and kidnap, then this would not be a situation where a 'lesser' evil is being resorted to in order to avoid a 'greater' evil. Both evils would have produced, at best, equal damage. Therefore the defense of necessity does not apply.[78]

The Court assumed that the 'subversives' had not occupied or overtaken any portion of the national territory. Their acts had not been acknowledged in this country or abroad as producing a state of war. Their acts were not manifestly supported by a foreign power. Subversives lacked the support of the population: 'in brief, the terrorists were far from been able to take over the government of the country, an evil that could have eventually justified the reaction of the Junta. Moreover, the defense based on an existing state of necessity must be rejected for the reason that the defendants failed to exhaust less damaging means to control subversive activities.'[79] On that point it could be considered that there was no chance, whatever the circumstances, to legally justify the sort of actions taken or authorized by the military commanders when fighting subversion.

The struggle against subversion as planned and executed by the armed forces was considered by the Appeals Court as a question of self defense, pride and revenge rather than a question of protecting Argentine society and institutions.[80]

Considering the broad legislative and executive powers concentrated in the Junta, military leaders could have implemented methods and means to accomplish

77. See *supra* n. 68 at p. 1544.
78. Ibid., at p. 1542.
79. Ibid., at p. 1543.
80. Ibid., at p. 1545.

their objectives which were less harmful than the ones used. On that point, we disagree with the Appeals Court, reasoning that individual responsibilities should be related to the illegality of actions or omissions and irrespective of the intensity of harm produced.

The Appeals Court also rejected the defense of compliance with a legal duty as a justification for crimes committed pursuant to the legitimate exercise of a right or a duty. Defendants argued that if a rule of law tolerates the production of harm, the conduct that, in accordance with that law, produces harm could not be incriminated.

Defendants referred to Decree No. 2770, enacted under a constitutional government. The Decree prescribed that the armed forces under the command of the President and the Council of Defense shall proceed to execute the military and security operations which are necessary in order 'to exterminate' the capacity of the subversive elements to act throughout the national territory.

The Appeals Court expressed the view that if authorization 'to exterminate' was meant to legalize physical eliminations, disappearances or killings of subversives, the Decree would have been considered unconstitutional and unenforceable because such a provision would have been beyond the competence of any authority and in contradiction with the rest of the legal order.[81]

In reference to allegations of self defense, the Court of Appeals rejected the argument based on the necessity to resort to unprecedented methods that were justified as effective enough to face an aggression which was equally unprecedented and illegal. For the Court, those methods could not pass the test of reasonability of means employed from a moral as well as from a legal point of view.[82]

81. Ibid., at pp. 1547-1548: 'In order to understand the legal context within which the presidential order 'to exterminate' subversives was issued, it must be recalled that article 31 of the national constitution was still in force. According to this article, the National Constitution, the laws enacted as a consequence of constitutional prescriptions and treaties concluded with foreign nations, are the supreme law of the land. Consequently, even if the President would have desired to issue an administrative act derogating the supreme law of the land, he was not in a position to do so because it was beyond the powers granted to him by the Constitution.'

82. See *supra* n. 68 at p. 1555: 'The discrepancy between the acts that were carried out and what is admissible to a civilized society appears to have been recognized by the commanders themselves. For this reason, they choose to keep covert the procedures they had employed, even after the fight was over.' The Court added at p. 1557 that, 'The means with which the defendants conducted the fight against subversion do not correspond to the notion of excessive use of defensive force. Excess, as said above, stems from fear, surprise and an agitated state of mind. The terrorist aggression was grave, serious and it had to be stopped; however, it cannot be accepted that a government which held all the power of law and of force, behaved as it did out of a change in the state of mind of its members. The acts in question were planned, directed and ordered ... In no way can it be accepted that the defendants subjectively acted using excessive defensive force.'

In connection with the 'state of war' defense, the Court of Appeal distinguished international war from internal armed conflicts. Such distinction ranges from internal disorder to international war. Acts committed by rebels whose state of belligerence has not been recognized constitute a case of insurrection. If the corresponding government has recognized the state of belligerence, it is a case of domestic civil war. Finally, if a foreign state recognizes the belligerence of the party or armed group, it is assumed that the situation would be assimilated to an international civil war. The Court justified its distinctions on old-fashioned and inaccurate legal literature dating back to 1926.[83]

The Court also recognized that, after World War II, new types of internal armed conflicts developed. One of these new forms of conflicts is referred to as 'revolutionary war'. For the Court, a revolutionary war is a form of war allowing a small and ruthless minority to gain control over a country through force, taking power through violent and unconstitutional means.[84]

The Court expressed the view that experts on the subject are largely in agreement in distinguishing five stages within revolutionary war: Stage one includes alignment and infiltration in the targeted country, clandestine organization of the revolutionary apparatus and social agitation. Stage two includes intimidation of the population through various acts of terrorism, as a means of placing the government in disrepute and depriving it of its leadership. Stage three calls for control of the population by instilling it with Marxism or by securing its passivity. Stage four includes taking control of a populated region in order to set up a revolutionary government and to promote that government's international recognition. Stage five includes mobilizing a general offensive, civil war and the takeover of the country.[85]

The court concluded that, in view of the evidence gathered in the proceedings regarding the intensity of terrorism in Argentina, the armed conflict that took place in the country might be characterized as a state of revolutionary war. But there is no evidence that the subversive forces exercised effective control over territorial areas as a necessary condition to proclaim a revolutionary government. There was no recognition of belligerence and rebels did not receive international recognition as such.[86]

The above reasoning of the Court of Appeals assumed that because the struggle was purely domestic any notion of war should be excluded.[87] When the Court

83. See *supra* n. 68, at p. 1560.

84. Ibid., at pp. 1560-1561; the Court of Appeals quoted R. Thompson, *Guerra Revolucionaria y Estrategia Mundial* (Buenos Aires, Paidós 1969) p. 20.

85. See *supra* n. 68, at p. 1561.

86. Ibid., at p. 1562.

87. Ibid., at pp. 1562-1563.

referred to the notion of war, it meant that a state of war only refers to armed conflicts among sovereign states. It also concluded that it was not a case of international civil war, due to the lack of external recognition of belligerent groups.

There is some terminological confusion in the Court's reasoning. It did not formally accept the existence of a state of war, but it already presumed a war situation as to justify the necessary applicability of the Code of Military Justice.

Even if historically, military Juntas denied the existence of an armed conflict, they constantly referred to a dirty war. In that sense, defendants claimed the existence of a state of war in order to argue that there is no domestic, international or natural law applicable during war. They further observed that terrorist aggression provoked a war in which the armed forces had the duty to intervene. Such a war had to be won and it left no room for law, moderation, ethics, religion or humanitarian principles.[88]

Regarding the rules of law applicable to the case, the Court of Appeals stated that notions such as state of necessity, emergency situations, internal commotion, sedition and war have been incorporated within the legal system: 'thus all those concepts must be examined in light of the rule of law. The rule of law cannot be ignored for the sake of destroying an evil enemy, nor it can be set aside by winners or losers in a war. No one who wants to keep alive the permanent values of society ... may ignore the rule of law ... Perhaps methods chosen by the defendants to fight subversion accelerated the victory.' However, on the Court's reasoning, it was not the victory of law or civilization. Only force won.[89]

The Court of Appeals stressed that the commanders were not being tried because they won the war against subversion, but rather because of the methods they used in accomplishing their goals. They were tried because they have downgraded values that are deeply ingrained in Argentine culture, traditions and way of being.[90]

The Court acknowledged that, according to prevailing legal doctrine, the applicability of international (humanitarian) law requires the existence of a condition that is lacking in the present case, which is the acknowledgment of a state of belligerence. The Court seemed to be afraid to recognize in the rebels a special status that would result in granting them certain rights. In that context should be read Podestá Costa's passage quoted by the Court to the effect that 'an armed uprising ceases to be a crime in order to become a right *vis-à-vis* the

88. Ibid., at p. 1563: 'A war cannot be tried in court. And if it were, only the defeated side could be brought to justice. In no way can this court accept such a theory, which obviously disregards a legal and cultural tradition that also pertains to the armed forces.'

89. See *supra* n. 68 at pp. 1563-1564.

90. Ibid.

established government, and that right must be exercised pursuant to certain predetermined rules.'[91]

In reference to the application of international law to internal armed conflicts, the Court of Appeals relied on part of the doctrine that considered the necessary application of international rules only when belligerent status has been recognized or when the intensity of the conflict is equivalent to a civil war.[92] The Court also referred to the laws and customs of war recognized in the Hague Conventions of 1907[93] as well as the application of the four Geneva Conventions of 1949.[94]

The Criminal Appeals Court concluded that it is understood that there is no war situation, no relevant internal strife or commotion, or grave insurrection, in spite of its intensity or gravity, that could be dealt with outside the rule of law.[95]

Grave breaches of the four Geneva Conventions were compared by the Criminal Appeals Court with internal penal legislation in order to conclude that domestic law as well as international law had an adequate answer in order to determine individual responsibilities. After recognising the existence of a duplication of norms, internal and international, dealing with same issues, the Court manifested its decision to apply internal law, stating that it was unnecessary to have recourse to international law.[96]

The Court declared that one thing must remain absolutely clear: 'the Court's decision rests on the Argentine legal system that is currently in force. Under this legal system this Court is compelled to conclude, beyond the shadow of a doubt, that the conduct of the defendants which is subject to examination in this case is contrary to law.'[97]

What the Court completely omitted was a consideration of the scope and limitations for the applicability of Article 3 common to the four 1949 Geneva Conventions. Common Article 3 prescribes that in the case of an armed conflict

91. Ibid., at p. 1566.

92. Ibid., at p. 1572: 'When the government has recognized the opposing forces as belligerent, or treats the rebel party as a *de facto* government; or when without reaching any of such instances the government must resort to measures of war in view of the magnitude of the armed rebellion, it can be said that the situation is one of civil war. Then, there are no political criminals, but only enemies. Both belligerent parties stand on equal footing and must be ruled by the laws and usages of war as if the conflict is international ... G. Bidart Campos, *Derecho Constitucional*, Vol. 1, p. 582'.

93. Ibid., at pp. 1528 and 1577.

94. Ibid., at pp. 1574-1576 and 1578.

95. Ibid., at p. 1568.

96. Ibid., at pp. 1583 and 1584.

97. Ibid., at p. 1584.

not of an international character, a state party is obligated to apply at least minimum standards. Such application would not affect the legal status of the parties to the conflict. Recourse to common Article 3 would not suffice in itself to grant belligerent status to subversive groups.

Instead, the Court, after determining not to apply international law, defined which domestic law rules would specifically apply to insurrection, internal civil fighting or to a revolutionary war. The Court did not elaborate on the possibility of applying international law standards as part of Argentine domestic law.

The Court observed that national constitutional rules dealing with exceptional situations or internal uprising should apply. In that context it stated that within the Constitution all the appropriate means and tools in order to consolidate domestic peace were granted. Therefore, the government cannot resort to means that are not authorized by the Constitution. In case of internal unrest, the Constitution provides for a state of siege rather than the imposition of martial law.[98]

Besides the National Constitution, the Court noted that there were domestic laws such as the Code of Military Justice, the Law of National Defense and the Criminal Code that offered a legal framework apt to deal with states of internal emergency.[99]

The Court also referred to regulations issued by the armed forces determining specific means and ways to fight against subversion. Among those regulations,

98. See *supra* n. 68 at p. 1566; Quoting González Calderón, *Curso de Derecho Internacional*, (Buenos Aires, Depalma 1974), at p. 280. A state of siege was declared on November 1974 by Presidential Decree No. 1368. (*Gaceta Oficial*, 7 November 1974). That state of siege was also in force during the *de facto* military government. The National Constitution prescribes the legal framework within which a state of siege should be applied. Art. 23 of the National Constitution provides that 'in the event of internal disorder or foreign attack endangering the functioning of this Constitution and the authorities created thereby, the province or territory in which the disturbance of order exists shall be declared to be in a state of siege and the constitutional guarantees shall be suspended therein. But during such suspension the President of the Republic shall not convict or punish upon his own authority. His power shall be limited, in such a case, with respect to persons, to arresting or transferring them from one point of the nation to another, if they do not prefer to leave Argentine territory.' The judiciary has defined the declaration of a state of siege as a political act. Such act is not subject to any approval nor is it subject to judicial review.(See *supra* n. 68 at p. 1568: *Fallos* Vol. 233, p. 206). A state of siege did not allow the armed forces to arrest without trial, to torture or to provoke a massive disappearance of persons. The Court added that it cannot be accepted that a *de facto* government, that concentrated all power in its hands and even bestowed on itself the ability to alter the Constitution, had no other way to curb terrorism than to act beyond the legal framework and to resort to clandestine operations and to a regime of terror equal to the one which it was supposed to curb. (See *supra* n. 68 at pp. 1569/1577).

99. See *supra* n. 68 at pp. 1575-1576.

Annex 1 on Legal Classification of Subversive Elements[100], prescribed that individuals who participate in subversion are never governed by public international law. Accordingly, those individuals do not enjoy the right to be treated as prisoners of war. They shall be considered as ordinary criminals, to be tried and convicted as such, in accordance with domestic law.

The Court speculated with the idea developed by certain publicists that in cases of domestic armed conflicts of an insurrectional nature, as well as in the case of international war, the actions of the parties are governed either by the municipal or international legal order, and that there are no justification for acting outside the boundaries of the legal order.[101] However, the Court did not go as far as accepting the application of international law to the present case although it had already defined the existence of a revolutionary war.

It stressed that it had examined the applicability of the positive rules of domestic law and the written rules of the *jus gentium*. It had analyzed the opinions of legal scholars on constitutional law and public international law, as well as different theories concerning conventional warfare and revolutionary war. It had also taken into account the usages of civilized nations concerning war and had concluded 'that not even one rule has been found that could justify, or pardon at least, those authorizing the acts reviewed during the present proceedings'.[102] It also stressed that homicide, torture, robbery, indiscriminate injury and illegal deprivation of freedom find in written or customary laws or in the opinion of legal scholars not a single note of justification or exculpation. The acts in question are illegal under Argentine domestic law and they violate international law: they find no justification in our cultural patterns; they contradict ethical and religious principles.[103]

What the Criminal Appeal Court finally seems to accept is that there is a coincidence in the content of internal rules dealing with individual responsibilities for violations of human rights law as well as for violations of basic rules of IHL, both applicable to the very same situation, irrespective of its classification as internal violence or as armed conflict. In that sense, the uncertainty generated by domestic situations of violence that are difficult to categorise in order to apply IHL rules will disappear.

This assertion was confirmed and reiterated by the General Commander of the Argentine armed forces during a public speech given in February 1998, in the context of a extremely sensitive political issue, that is, the possible future

100. Regulations RC-9-1 of the Argentine Army, at p. 173, See *supra* n. 68 at p. 1571.
101. Ibid., n. 68 at p. 1578.
102. Ibid., at p. 1583.
103. Ibid., at pp. 1583-1584.

derogation from 'due obedience'[104] and 'final point'[105] laws. Regarding actions undertaken by armed forces during repression of subversive activities in the seventies, he stressed the obligation of the regular armed forces to comply with and observe under all circumstances the basic rules of IHL.[106]

In our view, the democratic government that prosecuted members of military juntas for gross violations of human rights dealt with the problem from a domestic law perspective, in spite of having recognised that international human rights and IHL had also been violated. On the reasoning of the Criminal Appeals Court, there was no need to refer to international norms. These norms are reiterated and embraced within internal human rights regulations. The Appeals Court implicitly accepted the existence of a sort of equal and duplicated set of rules as part of human rights law and IHL. It was obviously acting *ex post facto* in order to determine individual responsibility. What it could not ignore is the fact that IHL as well as human rights law have different mechanisms than domestic law, in order to ensure proper and adequate protection of potential victims.

A positive consequence of the above case is the recognition, even if not directly applied by the courts, that state authorities should comply with IHL rules in spite of whatever official qualifications of internal emergency situations involving the use of force might be predetermined.

This development is most relevant because IHL enforcement mechanisms could be, in certain cases, more effective than human rights mechanisms in terms of preventive actions towards the protection of potential victims and vulnerable persons. Rule overlaps will provide better prospects of effective compliance with state obligations and responsibilities in relation to adequate protection of persons under all circumstances.

Progressive advancement towards generalised protection is one of the constant objectives of human rights law. New challenges in the protection of human rights have provoked almost immediate answers, in order to accomplish a sound response, as required by new situations. Humanitarian law, however, has always developed as an *ex post facto* reaction to ameliorate unnecessary sufferings.

104. Ley de Obediencia Debida [Due Obedience Act] No. 23.521 (*B.O.* 09/06/87).

105. Ley [Act] No. 23.492 (*B.O.* 29/12/86]

106. '...At that time - in reference to internal violence during the seventies - war was not mentioned but fighting against delinquent subversive bands, which was a fact. But as soldiers we know that hostilities should be conducted with due respect to the Geneva Conventions. Many of you present here ... know to what I particularly referred to, because you have been prisoners of war in the Malvinas and the rest of the army knows because of the knowledge of international humanitarian law ...' Discourse pronounced by General M. Balza on 12 February 1998, text reproduced in *El Soldado Journal* (Buenos Aires, 13 February 1998).

Accomplishments in human rights law have not necessarily been followed up by international humanitarian law developments.

5.3 Relevant jurisprudence of the ICTY

Other examples of grey zones in which there is no straightforward possibility to apply either international humanitarian or human rights law have been provided by a non-coherent jurisprudence of the International Criminal Tribunal for the former Yugoslavia (ICTY).

From the judgement of the ICTY in the case of *Prosecutor* v. *Tadić*[107] (Merits), it could be presumed that there has been a step backwards in terms of an extended application of rules created to protect individuals during an international armed conflict and not necessarily applicable during internal conflicts.[108]

The *Tadić* judgement also reveals the lack of direct interdependence of human rights and IHL in relation to the legal consequences of disappearances. On the reasoning of the Trial Chamber, it could be inferred that disappearance is a human rights violation, not necessarily a humanitarian law violation. The court conclusion demonstrates the lack of reciprocal intercourse in catching up with new developments towards the complete protection of individuals.

In reference to the content of norms, there is no direct interconnection between human rights law and humanitarian law. That is why it is always necessary for a rule to be applied as part of either system and for this rule to have been previously incorporated or prescribed as part of both systems.

Application of norms by analogy is always possible but would depend on the will of the parties involved and not be a direct consequence of what it is considered to be the law.

In the *Tadić* case[109], the accused, a Bosnian Serb, was charged on 31 counts of grave breaches of the Geneva Conventions, violations of the laws or customs of war and crimes against humanity. In relation to the charge of torture and murder of four Muslims at the Omarska Hangar building in June 1992, the Trial Chamber finally concluded that, in spite of being convinced that Tadić took part in the incidents, '... the Prosecution failed to elicit clear and definitive evidence from witnesses about the condition of the four prisoners after they have been

107. International Criminal Tribunal for the Former Yugoslavia, *Prosecutor* v. *Tadić* Opinion and Judgment, Case No. IT-94-1-T, Judgment 7 May 1997, at 36 *ILM* (1997) p. 908 et seq.

108. On the contrary, the Swiss Military Tribunal gave an broad interpretation of the applicability of IHL to internal armed conflicts, *In re. G.*, Military Tribunal, Division 1, Lausanne, Switzerland, 18 April 1997. See commentary at 92 *AJIL* (1998) p. 78 et seq.

109. *Supra* n. 68.

assaulted, let alone that they died or that death resulted from the assault upon them.'[110]

The Trial Chamber's application of the *corpus delicti* rule did not take into account that the four prisoners did not return to their cells or that no witnesses had seen them again. The Trial Chamber ignored the legal consequences of forced disappearances as developed under human rights law.[111] If the Chamber had the authority to apply human rights law, it could not avoid dealing with the effects of disappearances or at least it would be forced to investigate if there was a systematic policy followed by the authorities with control of the territory where disappearances occurred. However, the ICTY was empowered to deal only with IHL violations.[112]

It could also be argued that the Trial Chamber was obliged to recognise the legal effects of disappearances as part of customary humanitarian law. In that case, the Trial Chamber would have had at its disposal relevant precedents of state practice concerning situations of internal violence, state of emergencies and armed conflicts of both an internal and international character.

In other situations dealt with by the ICTY, issues of 'protected persons' have evidenced the difference between IHL, which is applicable only to certain categories of individuals, even if in the same situation as others, and human rights applicable to all persons under the same circumstances and without discrimination.

In *Tadić*, the majority of the Trial Chamber found that, after 19 May 1992, when the Yugoslav National Army (JNA) withdrew from Bosnia, the victims of the conflict in Bosnia were not protected persons within the meaning of the Fourth Geneva Convention Relative to the Protection of Civilian Persons since they were not in the hands of an occupying power of which they were not nationals. The majority of the Chamber concluded that Tadić could not be found guilty of committing grave breaches of the Geneva Convention because the prosecution had not proved that the conflict continued to be international and that Serbia had exercised effective control over Bosnian Serb forces after this date.[113] The Majority cited the ICJ's Judgement in *Nicaragua* v. *United States* asserting that the acts of the *contras* could not be imputed to the United States

110. Ibid., at para. 238.

111. Declaration on the Protection of all Persons from enforced Disappearances, 18 December 1992, A/RES/47/133; see also Art. 3.2.(d) Declaration of Minimum Humanitarian Standards, *supra* n. 32.

112. Statute of the International Criminal Tribunal for the Former Yugoslavia, S/RES/808 (1993).

113. See *supra* n. 107 at para. 595.

because they were not under the control of the United States.[114] The dissenting Judge, however, argued that the conflict in Bosnia was international and that the creation of the Bosnian Serb forces was a legal fiction.[115]

On the other hand, in an earlier Rule 61 Decision in the case of *Prosecutor* v. *Rajić*[116], Trial Chamber II concluded that the test to prove agency applied by the ICJ in *Nicaragua* v. *United States* was not applicable to the question whether Croatia was in effective control of Bosnian Croat forces in the area they occupied at the relevant time. The Chamber declared that, '[t]he ICJ was considering State responsibility for violations of international humanitarian law and therefore focused on US operational control over the *contras*, whereas the Chamber was not considering Croatia's liability for acts committed by Bosnian Croats but merely whether the Bosnian Croats could be considered agents of Croatia for the purpose of establishing subject matter jurisdiction regarding acts alleged to violate the grave breaches provisions of the Geneva Conventions, for which specific operational control was not of paramount importance.'[117] The Trial Chamber concluded that it had subject matter jurisdiction regarding grave breaches charges in conformity with Article 2 of the ICTY Statute because there was *prima facie* evidence both that the crimes had occurred within the context of an international armed conflict, by virtue of Croatia's direct military involvement in the conflict and its control over the Bosnian Croats forces, and that the civilian and property were protected in conformity with the Geneva Conventions.[118]

The Tribunal has not dealt with violations committed by Bosnian government forces against Bosnian Croats civilians that could be characterised as grave breaches. Taking into account that Bosnian Croats are nationals of Bosnia and Herzegovina, they would be considered as non-protected persons under the Fourth Geneva Convention.[119] If the Tribunal had also been authorised to prosecute on the grounds of grave human rights violations, the result would be substantially different regarding protected persons.

114. *Military and Paramilitary Activities in and against Nicaragua, Nicaragua* v. *United States*, Merits, 1986, *ICJ Rep.* 14.

115. See *supra* n. 107, Dissenting opinion of Judge McDonald, para. 7.

116. International Criminal Tribunal for the Former Yugoslavia, *Prosecutor* v. *Rajić*, Review of Indictment Pursuant to Rule 61 of the Rules of Procedure and Evidence, case No. IT-95-12-R61, 13 September 1996, para. 22.

117. Ibid. para. 14.

118. Ibid., at para. 21.

119. See *contra*, G. Aldrich, 'Jurisdiction of the International Criminal Tribunal for the Former Yugoslavia', 90 *AJIL* (1996) p. 64 et seq.; see also *Prosecutor* v. *Tadić*, Decision on the Defence Motion for Interlocutory Appeal on Jurisdiction, Case No. IT-94-1-AR72, 2 October 1995, para. 76, at 35 *ILM* (1996) p. 57.

In determining subject matter jurisdiction, the Trial Chamber in *Prosecutor* v. *Rajić* seems to have asserted that once the conflict has been characterised as international it follows that almost all civilian persons and property will be immediately protected from the beginning of hostilities. This conclusion constitutes a new trend towards an extended protection of civilians and property during armed conflicts. It could be argued that control needed for defining the international character of an armed conflict is different from control defined for purposes of identifying protected persons as well as for defining protected property.[120]

The Appeals Chamber in *Prosecutor* v. *Tadić* (judgement on jurisdiction) took a most progressive position when it provided an extended interpretation of protected persons during internal armed conflicts when determining the application of customary international humanitarian law to such conflicts.[121]

The situation concerning the dual application of IHL and human rights to internal situations, far from having been settled, however, seems to have become subject to increased doubts and uncertainties.

6. FINAL REMARKS

There is a common pattern of daily interface among traditional international actors other than states when dealing either with human rights or with IHL issues. For instance, ICRC activities in the field of human rights (for example, visits to political detainees) do not transform such activities into a humanitarian law concern. On the other hand, United Nations Security Council functions related to the implementation of humanitarian law do not convert that political organ into a humanitarian agent. In much the same way, human rights activism in the field of internal or international armed conflicts remains basically a human rights subject matter.

The consolidation of independent legal structures for human rights, as for international humanitarian law, as well as the recognition of their own principles and the existence of different mechanisms for the observance and compliance of their own rules, are obviously based on the common objective of protecting

120. O. Swaak-Goldman, '*Prosecutor* v. *Rajić*, Review of the Indictment Pursuant to Rule 61 of the Rules of Procedure and Evidence', 91 *AJIL* (1997) p. 523 et seq., see at p. 531: 'Another aspect of this decision that deserves comment is the Trial Chamber's conclusion, in its discussion of protected property, that control equals occupation and that this occurs almost immediately. This finding seems to make the phrasing in the Four Geneva Conventions related to protected persons - "in the hands of a party to the conflict or Occupying Power"- redundant.'

121. See *supra* n. 119, paras. 127 and 128.

human beings in all circumstances. The existence of common principles for both systems, such as inviolability, non-discrimination and personal security, as identified by Jean Pictet[122], does not lessen their differences created by the recognition of military necessity as an excuse for the non-observance of these basic principles in relation to certain persons (combatants, civilians affected by collateral effects of military necessity) during armed conflicts.[123]

The UN World Conference on Human Rights evidenced the need to coordinate efforts geared to the due protection of basic human rights under all circumstances, including armed conflicts. It recommended that '... the United Nations assume a more active role in the promotion and protection of human rights in ensuring full respect for international humanitarian law in all situations of armed conflict, in accordance with the purposes and principles of the Charter of the United Nations.'[124]

Coordination of efforts does not mean fusion of human rights and IHL's own standards and principles into a single set of rules. The World Conference acknowledged their separate structure when expressing its '... grave concern about continuing human rights violations in all parts of the world in disregard of standards as contained in international human rights instruments and international humanitarian law ...'[125]

Common concerns and interests of human rights and IHL should not affect their legal independence. In that sense, the maintenance of their own identity will assure the possibility of duplication of rules, furthering the protection of human beings by different means. That assumption is not oriented to intensify duplication of efforts but to generate different ways to accomplish the same objectives.

The mirror effect on rule developments within each system will most certainly help to avoid undesired *lacunae*. Normative repetitions and overlaps will motivate future coordination efforts that must not minimise perceptions of due protection of individuals from a non-uniform approach.[126]

After World War II, one of the most important changes in international law was the influence of human rights doctrines in approaching problems traditionally dealt with through the principle of equality of states, state sovereignty and the principle of non-intervention in the domestic jurisdiction of states. That tendency

122. See Pictet, op. cit. n. 1, at p. 75.

123. L. Doswald-Beck and S. Vité, 'Derecho internacional humanitario y derecho de los derechos humanos' [International Humanitarian Law and Human Rights Law], 116 *International Review of the Red Cross* (1993) p. 99 at p. 124.

124. See *supra* n. 59, Part II, para. 96, at p. 1687.

125. See *supra* n. 59, para. 29, at p. 1671.

126. Cf., Address by the President of the ICRC, Cornelio Somaruga, UN World Conference on Human Rights, Vienna, 14-25 June 1993, Internal Document of the Conference, pp. 2 and 3.

is clearly evidenced in recent customary law rules which emerged to govern internal armed conflicts and internal strife. Reflecting this, the Appeals Chamber of the ICTY declared in the *Tadić* case (Jurisdiction) that, 'A State-sovereignty-oriented approach has been gradually supplanted by a human-being-oriented approach ... it follows that in the area of armed conflict the distinction between inter-state wars and civil wars is losing its value as far as human beings are concerned ... If international law, while of course duly safeguarding the legitimate interests of States, must gradually turn to the protection of human beings, it is only natural that the aforementioned dichotomy should gradually lose its weight.'[127]

After all, state practices leading towards the formation of customary rules in areas of human rights and international humanitarian law convergence, such as internal violence or internal strife, would not necessary predetermine the identification of that practice as part of one or the other system.

Customary rule accomplishments in areas not covered by treaty law and aiming for the protection of human beings in general, if developed during armed conflicts or internal violence situations, have the chance to qualify as rules pertaining to both systems. Rational exercises in order to identify during those situations new customary law rules as part of human rights or IHL will essentially remain an academic activity.

International humanitarian law's main current and short-term interest will continue to be framed within the context of armed conflicts. It will concentrate on the development of new restrictions on the use of force by states through adequate expansion of limitations on conventional weapons; restrictions on means and methods of warfare; regulation of economic warfare and neutrality; effects on the environment; and extension of humanitarian principles to internal violence situations not traditionally covered by treaty law.

Human rights' main interest has expanded and will continue to expand towards acceptance of new generations of rights. Human rights activism is committed towards due recognition of the universal and indivisible character of basic and fundamental rights (hard-core group of rights).

In that sense, human rights and IHL have taken different directions: one creating and extending rights of individuals, the other restricting the discretion of states in the use of force. As both systems continue to concentrate on limiting state sovereignty, new areas of convergence might appear, although at present it seems reduced to situations of internal violence.

From a strictly doctrinal point of view, a possible integration of human rights and IHL's common principles and values could stimulate a positive nexus that

127. See *supra* n. 119, at p. 32 et seq. and para. 97, at p. 63.

would facilitate an increased influence of rule accomplishments from one system to the other. That would not necessarily imply reference to legal analogy but to the development of a philosophy of common and shared values, so as to promote reciprocal interdependence.

CURRENT DEVELOPMENTS

THE YEAR IN REVIEW*

Avril McDonald**

**. Avril McDonald, LL.B. (Trinity College Dublin), LL.M. (Queen's University of Belfast), Dip. Journ. (Dublin City University) is Managing Editor of the *Yearbook of International Humanitarian Law*, T.M.C. Asser Instituut, The Hague, and a Ph.D. candidate in the field of IHL at the Queen's University of Belfast, Northern Ireland.

The review is based on the classification scheme used in the Documentation section, although the numbering scheme used differs.

Yearbook of International Humanitarian Law
Volume 1 - 1998 - pp. 113-160

1. INTRODUCTION

Since the breakthrough adoption in 1977 of Protocols I and II Additional to the Geneva Conventions of 1949[1], the major issue and biggest challenge facing international humanitarian law (IHL) has been its implementation. The two Additional Protocols addressed many, though not all, of the *lacunae* left in IHL after the adoption of the Geneva Conventions in 1949. As one commentator has noted: 'There is, however, a particularly acute contrast between humanitarian law's highly developed rules, many of which enjoy nearly universal acceptance, and the repeated violations of those rules in conflicts around the world.'[2]

The past several years have seen fairly vigorous activity, both internationally and nationally, to implement IHL. These initiatives have proceeded at a number of levels and on a number of fronts; some high profile, others less conspicuous.

The most prominent and perhaps unexpected development of the past few years has been the adoption of a Statute for a permanent International Criminal Court (ICC) on 17 July 1998[3] in Rome, where all roads supposedly lead, although this

1. The 20th anniversary of the adoption of the Additional Protocols of 1977 was marked by the *International Review of the Red Cross* with a special issue, in which several veterans of the 1974-1977 Diplomatic Conference gave their views on the Protocols, 20 years on. See *IRRC* No. 320, (September-October 1997).

2. See Paul Berman, 'The ICRC's Advisory Service on International Humanitarian Law: the challenge of national implementation', *IRRC* No. 312, (May-June 1996) p. 338; see also Adam Roberts, 'The Law of War: Problems in Implementation in Contemporary Conflicts', in *Law in Humanitarian Crises: How can international humanitarian law be made effective in armed conflicts?* Vol. 1 (European Commission Brussels 1995) p. 13; see also Dutli *infra* at p. 245.

3. A/CONF.183.9. 17 July 1998. Available online at http://www.un.org/icc. The Statute was adopted by the United Nations Diplomatic Conference of Plenipotentiaries on the Establishment of

has been a particularly long and winding one[4]. In the short-term at least, this development may be of more symbolic than practical value. The Statute needs the ratifications of 60 states before it enters into force[5]; a process that could take many years, and the Court, when functional, will be subject to limitations contained within its Statute that will severely restrict its scope and effectiveness. Moreover, the Court will most likely start life with the USA not only not behind it but strongly opposed.[6] Only time will tell whether the ICC will become known as the little (or big) court that could or that couldn't. One should not, however, let the scale and seriousness of the problems and the challenges ahead blind one to the scale of the achievement. As UN Secretary-General Kofi Annan remarked during his speech at the official signing ceremony of the ICC Statute on 18 July 1998: 'No doubt, many of us would have liked a Court vested with even more far-reaching powers, but that should not lead us to minimize the breakthrough you have achieved. The establishment of the Court is still a gift of hope for future generations, and a giant step forward in the march towards universal human rights and the rule of law. It is an achievement which, only a few years ago, nobody would have thought possible.'[7]

The ICC will build on the work of the *ad hoc* International Criminal Tribunals for the Former Yugoslavia (ICTY) and Rwanda (ICTR), which are in the process of developing the jurisprudence of IHL and have already rendered several important decisions, including the first conviction by an international criminal court for the crime of genocide[8] and the first sentences for genocide[9].

---

an International Criminal Court on 17 July 1998, following an unrecorded vote requested by the USA. The results of the vote were 120 states in favour, 7 against and 21 abstentions. Following its adoption, 10 states immediately signed the Statute and 127 delegations signed the Final Act. The Statute is reprinted in 37 *ILM* 999 (1998).

4. With the first proposal to establish an international criminal court apparently made by Gustave Moynier in Geneva in 1872. See Christopher Keith Hall, 'The first proposal for a permanent international criminal court', *IRRC* No. 322 (March 1998) p. 57. The Statute is the fruit of almost four years of negotiations by the Preparatory Committee at UN Headquarters in New York, and five weeks of intense debate at the Rome Treaty Conference, held from 15 June to 17 July 1998; 156 States and over 100 NGOs participated in the Conference.

5. Under Art. 126 of the ICC Statute, the Statute will enter into force 60 days after the 60th instrument of ratification has been deposited with the Secretary-General of the United Nations.

6. The USA voted against the ICC Statute and has indicated that it will actively lobby against the court.

7. Statement by the United Nations Secretary-General Kofi Annan at the ceremony held at the Campidoglio celebrating the adoption of the Statute of the International Criminal Court, 18 July 1998. Available online at http://www.un.org/icc/speeches/718sg.htm.

8. *Prosecutor* v. *Jean-Paul Akayesu*, Judgement, Case No. ICTR-96-4-T, 2 September 1998.

9. *Prosecutor* v. *Jean Kambanda*, Sentencing Judgement, Case No. ICTR-97-23-S, 4 September 1998; *Prosecutor* v. *Jean-Paul Akayesu*, Sentencing Judgement, Case No. ICTR-96-4-T, 2 October 1998.

Important developments have also occurred regarding the application of IHL to several categories of weapons. New prohibitions extend not only to weapons in widespread use (landmines) but also weapons that have not yet been deployed (blinding laser weapons)[10] or widely used (chemical weapons).

Both the Chemical Weapons Convention of 1993[11] and the Landmines Convention of 1997[12] completely ban ('never under any circumstances'[13]) the development, production, acquisition, stockpiling, retaining or transfer of their respective weapons categories. Both treaties acknowledge that the right of the parties to an armed conflict to choose their methods and means of warfare is not unlimited; that it is prohibited to use weapons that can cause superfluous injury or unnecessary suffering; and that the principle of distinction between civilians and combatants must be respected.[14]

During the Review Conference on the 1980 Certain Conventional Weapons Convention (CCW Convention)[15], an entirely new Protocol IV on Blinding Laser Weapons was adopted and Protocol II on Landmines was amended to include new restrictions on the use of antipersonnel landmines.

10. 'It is the first time since 1868 that a weapon has been prohibited before it has been used on the battlefield. It has also stigmatized deliberate blinding.' Louise Doswald-Beck, 'New Protocol on Blinding Laser Weapons,' *IRRC* No. 312 (May-June 1996) p. 272 at p. 296. See also 'The Vienna Review Conference: success on blinding laser weapons but deadlock on landmines', *IRRC* No. 309, p. 672.

11. Convention on the Prohibition of the Development, Production, Stockpiling and Use of Chemical Weapons and on their Destruction (hereinafter, Chemical Weapons Convention), opened for signature in Paris on 13 January 1993. Entered into force on 29 April 1997. UN Doc. CD/CW/WP.400/Rev.

12. Convention on the Prohibition of the Use, Stockpiling, Production and Transfer of Anti-Personnel Mines and on Their Destruction (hereinafter, Landmines Convention), 18 September 1997, Oslo, Norway. Reprinted at p. 539 of this volume.

13. Arts. 1(1) of, respectively, the Chemical Weapons Convention and the Landmines Convention.

14. These principles are directly alluded to in the Preamble of the Landmines Convention. For a discussion of methods of warfare that cause unnecessary suffering, see Roger S. Clarke, 'Methods of Warfare that Cause Unnecessary Suffering or Are Inherently Indiscriminate: A Memorial Tribute to Howard Berman', 28 *California Western International Law Journal* (1998) p. 379.

15. The Review Conference was requested by France, pursuant to Art. 8(3)(a) of the CCW Convention. See Louise Doswald-Beck, *supra* n. 10 at p. 227, fn. 28.

At the level of states, which have the primary responsibility for implementing IHL, relevant developments have occurred in a number of areas. During the reporting period[16], a number of states, including two Security Council members, adopted legislation to implement IHL: Britain ratified and adopted legislation to implement Protocols I and II[17], while the USA adopted legislation to implement the Grave Breaches provisions of the Geneva Conventions[18], common Article 3 of the Geneva Conventions and certain provisions of the 1907 Hague Regulations on Land Warfare.[19] The USA still has not signed the Additional Protocols of 1977, however. In March 1998, France indicated its intention to sign Protocol I, although, as of early October 1998, it had not done so.[20] Its signing of this Protocol would leave the USA as the only member of the SC not to have signed, and the USA and Turkey as the only NATO members to remain outside the Protocol.

Some states have recently amended their criminal and penal codes to include jurisdiction over certain violations of IHL; a number of prosecutions have been undertaken and others are proceeding or pending for violations of IHL, including against non-nationals for violations of IHL committed against non-nationals. Quite a number of states have recently established commissions to study IHL and to draft implementation measures, which, in several cases, have resulted in the adoption of implementing legislation, concerning, *inter alia*, legislation to implement treaty law; legislation to cooperate with the International Criminal Tribunals; and legislation to protect the emblem. Several states made a declaration under Article 90(2)(a) of Protocol I recognising the competence of the Fact-Finding Commission.[21] Meanwhile, education and training in IHL for the armed forces is being conducted within many states, with the International Institute of International Humanitarian Law at San Remo in Italy and the ICRC continuing to play an important educative role *vis-à-vis* the armed forces of many states. Some defence forces are taking concrete

16. This review, exceptionally, takes note of developments of the past few years; future reviews will cover a single year only.

17. Geneva Conventions (Amendment) Act, 1995 [amending Geneva Conventions Act of 1957 to enable effect to be given to the Additional Protocols of 1977], Chapter 27, 19 July 1995.

18. United States War Crimes Act of 1996 (Public Law 104-192, 110 Stat 2104, 18 U.S.C. 2401/35 *ILM*, p. 1540). Reprinted at p. 643 of this volume. See Carnahan at p. 518; Dutli at p. 258.

19. Expanded War Crimes Act of 1997. Section 583 of Foreign Operations, Export Financing, and Related Programs Appropriations Act, 1998 (Public Law: 105-118 (11/26/97) (H.R.2159)). Reprinted at p. 643 of this volume. For commentary, see Carnahan in Correspondents' Reports at p. 519 of this volume.

20. France signed Protocol II in 1984. See Correspondents' Reports at p. 443.

21. Information about various recent implementation measures within states is provided in *National Implementation of International Humanitarian Law*, Advisory Service on International Humanitarian Law, Annual Report 1996, ICRC, 1997, and in Correspondents' Reports at p. 393 et seq.

steps to incorporate awareness of and respect for IHL into their national codes of conduct for the Armed Forces.

To 'strengthen its support for states engaged in implementation of the law at national level'[22], in early 1996 the ICRC established an Advisory Service on International Humanitarian Law, further to a recommendation of the 26th Conference of the Red Cross and Red Crescent held in Geneva in December 1995. The need to promote full respect for and compliance with IHL and to strengthen advisory services to states was earlier acknowledged in the Final Declaration of the International Conference for the Protection of War Victims, held from 30 August to 1 September 1993, at the Preparatory Meeting of Experts from 26 to 28 September 1994, and at the Meeting of the Intergovernmental Group of Experts held in Geneva from 23 to 27 January 1995.[23]

Below, some recent implementation measures and other developments in IHL are outlined. Because of limitations of space and to avoid repetition, the review will be selective, with the emphasis on developments not otherwise treated of in this volume. Because of its historic and symbolic importance, and the fact that it is not discussed elsewhere in this volume, special attention is paid to the Statute of the International Criminal Court.

2. SOURCES AND GENERAL PRINCIPLES - POST-1977 DEVELOPMENTS

2.1 Minimum Humanitarian Standards

It is widely recognised that 'international law relating to human rights and humanitarian norms applicable in armed conflicts do not adequately protect human beings in situations of internal violence, disturbances, tensions and public emergency'.[24] Following on the adoption of the Turku Declaration on Minimum Humanitarian Standards by a group of experts in 1990[25], which was designed to cover situations of internal violence and emergency which fall outside Protocol II and common

22. Advisory Service Annual Report, ibid., at p. 11. See Dutli *infra* at pp. 252-253.

23. See 'Follow-Up to the International Conference for the Protection of War Victims, *IRRC*, No. 304 (January-February 1995), pp. 4-38.

24. *Preamble, Declaration of Minimum Humanitarian Standards*, 2nd, rev. edn., (Institute for Human Rights, Åbo Akademi University, Turku/Åbo 1996) p. 7.

25. Ibid. See also Vinuesa at pp. 90-92 of this volume.

Article 3, in January 1998 the UN Secretary-General presented a report on the subject of minimum humanitarian standards[26], building on related initiatives since the early 1990s[27]. The purpose of the report was 'not to reach firm conclusions but rather to set the framework for future discussions on the issue of fundamental standards of humanity'.[28] Some states and NGOs have submitted responses to the SG; most support, in general terms, the development of minimum humanitarian standards.[29]

According to the Secretary-General, 'the main issue concerns the difficulties in determining in which situations the rules regulating non-international armed conflict become operable, and the fact that some situations of internal violence fall outside existing treaty law. In addition, there is the question of the adequacy of the existing rules even in cases where the situation meets the thresholds set out in international humanitarian law.'[30]

As the report notes: 'The need for identifying fundamental standards of humanity arises from the observation that, at the present time, it is often situations of internal violence that pose the greatest threat to human dignity and freedom'.[31] The massive scale of the violence and devastation wrought by situations of internal violence and disturbances[32] evidences the need for taking steps to extend the reach of IHL applicable in these situations.[33]

The problem with the development of minimum humanitarian standards, such as the Turku Declaration, or fundamental standards of humanity is, as Rosemary Abi-Saab points out, 'that by going, perhaps into too much detail and mentioning specific rights to be protected in the context of internal disturbances, it has produced a declaration that is much more elaborate than common article 3, applicable in the case of internal *armed* conflicts, and even in some respects than

26. Sub-Commission on Prevention of Discrimination and Protection of Minorities, Minimum Humanitarian Standards, Analytical report of the Secretary-General submitted pursuant to Commission on Human Rights resolution 1997/21, E/CN.4/1998/87, 5 January 1998. This follows an earlier report submitted by the SG on this subject, see UN Doc. E/CN.4/1996/80

27. See *supra* n. 24 at pp. 4-6.

28. *Supra* n. 26 at para. 2.

29. The views and information received from states and United Nations bodies in response to the SG's report of 1998 are contained in E/CN.4/1998/87/Add.1, 12 January 1998.

30. *Supra* n. 26 at para. 41.

31. Ibid., at para. 8.

32. According to the SG, 'in 1996 there were 19 situations of internal violence in which at least 1,000 people were killed (. . .) and which, cumulatively (. . .) had led to between 6.5 and 8.4 million deaths. If one includes situations of internal violence which, in 1996 had de-escalated or ended, another 2 million deaths could be added. In addition, in 1996 there were approximately 40 other internal situations causing between 100 and 1,000 deaths (. . .) which cumulatively have also led to thousands of deaths.' Ibid., at para. 18.

33. Ibid., at para. 13.

Protocol II, which met with very serious resistance on the part of governments at the 1974-1977 Diplomatic Conference; resistance that would be much greater in cases of internal disturbances and tensions. However, such initiatives remain very useful for bringing the international community to agree on what is meant by "humane treatment" and the nature and content of prohibited acts from both a humanitarian and human rights point of view.'[34]

2.2 Customary International Humanitarian Law

In order to elucidate the content of customary IHL applicable in both international and non-international armed conflicts, in December 1995 the 26th International Conference of the Red Cross and Red Crescent endorsed the recommendations of the Intergovernmental group of experts for the Protection of War Victims, among which were that the ICRC undertake a study on customary IHL.[35] It is considered that 'the establishment of customary law will be particularly useful for (i) conflicts where the parties are not bound by the Additional Protocols of 1977 and (ii) cases before courts and tribunals where only customary law can be used.'[36]

While the establishment of a list of customary law rules, derived from the *opinio juris* and practice of states, will be helpful in establishing a basic legal foundation in the absence of any applicable treaty law, there is a danger that excess reliance on customary law could undermine the Additional Protocols. The ICRC report will be presented to the 27th International Conference of the Red Cross and Red Crescent in Geneva in November 1999, and it is expected to be officially published in early 2000.

3. CONFLICTS, ARMED FORCES AND NON-STATE ACTORS

'The nature of conflicts has changed from set-piece international confrontations to a bewildering array of separatist and counter-insurgency wars, border disputes,

34. Rosemary Abi-Saab, 'Human Rights and Humanitarian Law in Internal Conflicts,' in Daniel Warner, ed., *Human Rights and Humanitarian Law: The Quest for Universality*(Martinus Nijhoff, The Hague 1997) at p. 119.

35. Recommendation II of the Group proposed that, 'the ICRC be invited to prepare, with the assistance of experts on IHL representing various geographical regions and different legal systems, and in consultation with experts from governments and international organisations, a report on customary rules of IHL, applicable in international and non-international armed conflicts and to circulate the report to States and competent international bodies.'

36. In 'Study on customary rules of international humanitarian law, Plan of action'. Copy on file with the author.

ethnic and religious violence, *coups de'ètat*, national and counter-revolutionary operations,' stated Oxfam in a report issued in April 1998, listing as some examples the conflicts in Afghanistan, Kashmir, Mexico, East Timor, Sri Lanka, Rwanda and the Balkans.[37] A disproportionate number of conflicts were waged in Africa, 14 of whose 53 states were engaged in armed conflict in 1996.[38]

The Stockholm International Peace Research Institute (SIPRI) reported in its 1998 *Yearbook* that 25 major armed conflicts were waged in 1997[39], compared with 27 in 1996[40]; all but one - that between India and Kashmir - were internal. However, many were internationalised in some way.

The predominance of internal armed conflicts means that many persons fighting in today's armed conflicts are not members of regular armed forces but are 'attached' to rebel or paramilitary groups, *inter alia.* In many cases there is no proper chain of command through which to monitor and enforce respect for IHL. Paramilitaries are not always fighting against states, however; often states employ irregulars over whom they deliberately exercise little control to carry out acts that constitute violations of IHL. It becomes harder to distinguish between regular armed forces and non-state actors. Where paramilitary groups are retained by a state but are not necessarily subject to a central command, their obligations under IHL and the responsibility of the state concerned are not always clear.

With the increase in the number of internal and internationalised armed conflicts is coming greater recognition that a strict division of conflicts into internal and international is scarcely possible, if it ever was, and that the distinction between grave breaches and other war crimes is becoming increasingly blurred and irrelevant from a practical point of view - although it is still exists juridically especially given the trend towards recognising that war crimes committed in internal armed conflicts

37. E. Cairns, *Conflict and Emergencies 1998* (Oxfam, London 1998); see also E. Cairns, *A Safer Future: Reducing the Human Cost of War* (Oxfam, London 1998).

38. 'The Causes of Conflict and the Promotion of Durable Peace and Sustainable Development in Africa', Secretary-General's Report to the United Nations Security Council, 16 April 1998, part I, Introduction. Available online at http://www.un.org/ecosocdev/geninfo/afrec/sgreport/report.htm.

39. *SIPRI Yearbook 1998: Armaments, Disarmament and International Security*, (Oxford University Press, Oxford 1998).

40. *SIPRI Yearbook 1997: Armaments, Disarmament and International Security*, (Oxford University Press, Oxford 1997).

can give rise to individual criminal responsibility[41], and that grave breaches might also be committed in internal armed conflicts[42].

As noted in the Decision on Jurisdiction in the *Tadić* case before the ICTY, the practice of some states indicates a move towards recognising that violations of common Article 3 during internal conflicts give rise to individual criminal responsibility and that universal jurisdiction may extend to violations of IHL committed in both internal as well as international armed conflicts. In 1993, Belgium became the first state to pass a law classifying as war crimes certain violations of IHL committed in the course of a non-international armed conflict (Protocol II situations).[43] The Spanish Penal Code of 1995 considers as protected persons those who are protected by virtue of Protocol II.[44] In an *amicus* brief submitted to Trial Chamber II of the ICTY in the *Tadić* case, the US government stated that the provisions concerning grave breaches of the Geneva Conventions (referred to in Article 2 of the Statute of the ICTY) also cover non-international armed conflicts.[45] The US Expanded War Crimes Act of 1997[46] amends the War Crimes Act of 1996[47] to include jurisdiction over violations of common Article 3, and defines as war crimes acts constituting a grave breach of the Geneva Conventions or a violation of common Article 3. And in a Danish case in 1994, the court refused to distinguish

41. This was affirmed by the establishment of the ICTR and by the jurisprudence of both *ad hoc* Tribunals. See Cissé *infra* at p. 167; Rowe at pp. 222-225.

42. In the Appeals Decision in *Tadić*, while the majority found that grave breaches are only applicable during international armed conflicts (at paras. 81-83), it noted that this area of the law

43. Loi du 16 juin 1993 relative à la repression des infractions graves aux Conventions internationales de Genève du 12 août 1949 et aux Protocols I et II du 8 juin 1977, additionnels a ces Convention. Published in *Moniteur belge*, 5 août 1993. This law and other legislation recognising individual criminal responsibility for violations of IHL committed in internal armed conflicts is analysed by Thomas Graditzky in 'Individual criminal responsibility for violations of international humanitarian law committed in non-international armed conflicts', *IRRC* No. 322 (March 1998) p. 29.

44. Código Penal, Law 10/1995, 23 November 1995. Title XXIV, Crimes Against the International Community, Chapter III, Crimes against Protected People and Property in the Event of Armed Conflict, Article 608. Title XXIV is in the Documentation section at p. 633. For commentary, see Antonio Pigrau i Solé in Correspondents' Reports at p. 502.

45. Submission by the Government of the United States of America concerning Certain Arguments made by Counsel for the Accused in the Case of *The Prosecutor of the Tribunal* v. *Dusan Tadić* (Case No. IT-94-I-T), 17 July 1995, pp. 35-36.

46. *Supra* n. 19.

47. *Supra* n. 18.

between grave breaches and other violations but considered 'all counts related to the Convention as a whole', and found that 'the requirements set out in the Convention as to "grave breaches" have been met in the case of all counts of the indictment.'[48]

4. PROTECTED PERSONS

4.1 Civilians Generally

Civilians are increasingly becoming targets of attack during armed conflicts. Ninety percent of today's casualties are civilians, compared with five percent in World War I and about 48 percent in World War II. As noted by Ambassador Otunnu, the UN Special Representation for Children in Armed Conflict, '[i]n so many conflicts today: children, women, the elderly, crops, granary stocks, live stock; they are all fair game in the single minded struggle for power.'[49]

This trend was also remarked upon by the UN Secretary-General in his report entitled 'The Causes of Conflict and the Promotion of Durable Peace and Sustainable Development in Africa': 'In the past, civilian populations were chiefly indirect victims of fighting between hostile armies. Today, they are often the main targets, with women suffering in disproportionate numbers while often also being subjected to atrocities that include organized rape and sexual exploitation. Increasingly, relief workers, including United Nations staff, have also been directly targeted. Such attacks are unconscionable and undermine the basic conditions of humanitarian assistance.'[50]

4.2 Women

The widespread and routine nature of rape and other forms of sexual abuse, including enforced prostitution, during armed conflicts has been documented in several recent UN reports.

48. *The Director of Public Prosecutions* v. *T.* Sentence passed by the Eastern High Court (3rd Division) on 22 November 1994 (unpublished). English translation on file with the *YIHL*.

49. Speech by Olara A. Otunnu, Special Representative of the Secretary-General of the United Nations for Children in Armed Conflict, in Child Soldiers, proceedings of the Conference on Child Soldiers, The Hague, 20 November 1997, published by Watoto wa Amani, January 1998, p. 7 at p. 8.

50. *Supra* n. 38 at para. 49.

In the preliminary report of the Special Rapporteur on the situation of systematic rape, sexual slavery and slavery-like practices during periods of armed conflicts, presented to the 48th session of the Sub-Commission on Prevention of Discrimination and Protection of Minorities[51], Ms. Linda Chavez noted the systematic manner in which sexual abuses were perpetrated in several recent conflicts, including the Iraqi invasion and occupation of Kuwait, in Peru, in Haiti, in the former Yugoslavia and in Rwanda, and stated that the rape and sexual abuse of women and girls in both international and internal armed conflicts constitutes a grave breach of IHL.[52] '[T]here is growing recognition that acts of rape committed in wartime constitute war crimes and crimes against humanity.'[53] The report concludes that, although 'there exists a very substantial body of international law relating to systematic rape, sexual slavery and slavery-like practices during warfare, including internal armed conflict', nonetheless, 'there is a need for further inquiry as to how those international legal standards can be disseminated broadly, used to prevent further violations, applied to past misconduct, and invoked to provide remedies for victims.'[54]

Ms. Chavez's research was continued by Special Rapporteur Ms. Gay J. McDougall, who submitted the Final Report on systematic rape, sexual slavery and slavery-like practices during armed conflict on 22 June 1998.[55]

Ms. McDougall asserted that an appropriate response to violations of the human rights of women in situations of armed conflict 'requires that acts of sexual violence and slavery must be properly documented, the perpetrators brought to justice, and the victims provided with full and effective redress. The appropriate characterizations of these acts as international crimes of slavery, crimes against humanity, genocide, grave breaches of the Geneva Conventions, war crimes or torture is also essential.' The Special Rapporteur asserted that these crimes 'have particular legal consequences as *jus cogens* crimes (...).'[56]

The Special Rapporteur's definition of rape is broader than in some national jurisdictions; it includes any forced penetration, by any object, including a penis, into

51. See Preliminary Report of the Special Rapporteur on the situation of systematic rape, sexual slavery and slavery-like practices during periods of armed conflict, Ms. Linda Chavez, UN Doc. E/CN.4/Sub.2/1996/26, 16 July 1996. By a letter dated 13 May 1997, the Special Rapporteur informed the High Commissioner for Human Rights that she was not in a position to submit her final report, resigned as Special Rapporteur and requested that another member of the Sub-Commission continue the study. UN Doc. E/CN.4/Sub.2/1997/12, 17 June 1997.

52. Ibid., at para. 14.

53. Ibid., at para. 25.

54. Ibid., at para. 86.

55. UN Doc. E/CN.4/Sub.2/1998/13.

56. Ibid., at para. 8.

a victim's vagina, anus or mouth, and is gender-neutral.[57] She stated that 'the manifestly coercive circumstances that exist in all armed conflict situations establish a presumption of non-consent and negates the need for the prosecution to establish a lack of consent as an element of the crime.'[58] The report goes on to document the legal framework for prosecuting rape and sexual violence and offers a series of recommendations for ending the cycle of impunity concerning sexual crimes. An appendix to the report analyses the legal liability of the Japanese Government in respect of the so-called 'Comfort Women'; that is, Korean women, *inter alia*, who were forced into sexual slavery for the Japanese army during WWII.

Further research into the situation surrounding women in armed conflicts, *inter alia*, was conducted by the Special Rapporteur on violence against women, its causes and consequences, Ms. Radhika Coomaraswamy, who presented her report to the 54th session of the Commission on Human Rights in January of this year.[59] Noting that today's conflicts are overwhelmingly non-international, it observed that '[t]he State is under a due diligence standard to prevent, prosecute and punish offenders who violate the rights of others, whether they are acting as official agents of the State or as paramilitaries. (. . .) Since women are often the victims of violence perpetrated by non-State actors during armed conflicts (. . .) [i]t is imperative that the international community evolve unequivocal standards which ensure human rights protection to victims who live in areas not under the control of formal State authorities.'[60] The report also observed that, for the first time in history, women are perpetrating and being charged with crimes of sexual violence.[61]

The Statutes of the *ad hoc* Tribunals for the former Yugoslavia and Rwanda for the first time criminalised rape as a crime against humanity under international treaty

57. Ibid., at para. 24.

58. Ibid., at para. 25.

59. Report of the Special Rapporteur on violence against women, its causes and consequences, Ms. Radhika Coomaraswamy, submitted in accordance with Commission resolution 1997/44. UN Doc. E/CN.4/1998/54, 26 January 1998, Part I. See also the Report of the Special Rapporteur on violence against women, its causes and consequences, on the mission to Rwanda on the issues of violence against women in situations of armed conflict. UN Doc. E/CN.4/1998/54/Add.1.

60. Ibid., at paras. 9 and 10.

61. Ibid., at para. 11. The ICTR became the first international criminal tribunal ever to charge a women with sex crimes when it charged Pauline Nyiramasuhuko, Rwanda's former Minister of Family Welfare and the Advancement of Women with crimes against humanity and violations of common Article 3 and Protocol II in respect of sex crimes. Nyiramasuhuko's son, Arsène Shalom Ntahobali, is also charged with sex crimes.

law[62], and rape has been charged as a crime against humanity by both Tribunals.[63] The absence of explicit reference to rape or sexual assault in Articles 2 (grave breaches) and 3 (violations of the laws or customs of war) of the ICTY Statute has not prevented the Prosecutor of the ICTY from charging these crimes under these provisions.[64] The Statute of the ICTR includes rape as a war crime in Article 4(e), which incorporates serious violations of common Article 3 and Protocol II.

Several cases of which the ICTY is currently seized involve charges of rape and sexual assault, including *Čelebići*, where Delić is charged with both command and personal responsibility for rape; *Furundžija*[65], where the accused is charged with failure to prevent a rape; and *Kunarać*[66], where the accused is charged with both personal and command responsibility for rape and sexual assaults. At the time of writing, the ICTY had yet to issue a judgement on charges of rape and sexual assault, although a decision in the *Čelebići* case was expected on 16 November 1998. However, the ICTR, in September 1998, became the first international criminal court since the International Tribunal for the Far East (Tokyo Tribunal) to pronounce on rape and sexual violence in its landmark judgement in the *Akayesu* case.[67]

This judgement defines rape, 'as there is no commonly accepted definition of this term in international law'.[68] According to the Trial Chamber, it is a 'physical invasion of a sexual nature, committed on a person under circumstances which

62. In Arts. 5(g) and 3(g) respectively. Rape was, however, previously enumerated as a crime against humanity in Article II of Control Council Law No. 10 although it was not prosecuted in any of the 12 subsequent trials.

63. For example, by the ICTY in the indictment *Gagović and Others* ("Foča"), Case No. IT-96-23-I, 26 June 1996 and by the ICTR in the case of *The Prosecutor* v. *Jean-Paul Akayesu*. Case No. ICTR-96-4-T.

64. For example, in the *Čelebići* Indictment, Delić is charged with two grave breaches (torture) arising out of an act of rape. Both counts 18 and 21 use the word rape. Case No. IT-96-21-I. In the indictment *Gagović and Others* ("Foča"), rape and other forms of sexual assault are charged, *inter alia*, as the grave breaches of torture and wilfully causing great suffering. Ibid.

65. Case No. IT-95-17.

66. Kunarać is charged in the *Gagović* indictment, *supra* n. 63.

67. *Supra* n. 8. Only those parts of the *Akayesu* judgement specifically pertaining to women are considered here; other aspects of the judgement are considered in Section 6.1.2 below, dealing with the ICTR generally.

68. Ibid., at para. 596.

are coercive.'[69] 'While rape has been defined in certain national jurisdictions as non-consensual intercourse, variations on the act of rape may include acts which involve the insertion of objects and/or the use of bodily orifices not considered to be intrinsically sexual.'[70] 'Sexual violence, which includes rape, is considered to be any act of a sexual nature which is committed on a person under circumstances which are coercive.'[71] '[It] is not limited to physical invasion of the human body and may include acts which do not involve penetration or even physical contact.'[72] The Chamber explained that coercive circumstances did not need to be evidenced by a show of physical force. 'Threats, intimidation, extortion and other forms of duress which prey on fear or desperation may constitute coercion, and coercion may be inherent in certain circumstances, such as an armed conflict or the military presence of *Interahamwe*[73] among refugee Tuti women (. . .).'[74]

The Trial Chamber also pronounced on the controversial question of whether rape and sexual violence can constitute genocide, as argued by the Prosecutor during the trial. It found that rape and sexual violence 'constitute genocide in the same way as any other act as long as they were committed with intent to destroy a particular group targeted as such. Indeed, rape and sexual violence certainly constitute infliction of serious bodily and mental harm on the victims and are even, according to the Chamber, one of the worst ways of inflict [sic] harm on the victim as he or she suffers both bodily and mental harm.'[75] The court held that sexual violence was 'an integral part of the part of the process of the destruction (. . .) specifically contributing to the destruction of the Tutsi group as a whole.'[76]

The Trial Chamber also held that, within a patriarchal society, rape could constitute genocide, as a measure to prevent births within the group, where 'a woman of the said group is deliberately impregnated by a man of another group, with the intent to have her give birth to a child who will consequently not belong to the mother's group'.[77] Furthermore, the Chamber noted that measures intended to prevent births within the group could be mental as well as physical. 'For example, rape can be a measure intended to prevent births when the person raped refuses subsequently to procreate (. . .).'[78] The crime of transferring children to another group could also be committed by the sanctioning of 'acts of threats or trauma which would lead to the forcible transfer of children from one group to

69. Ibid., at para. 597 and at para. 688.
70. Ibid., at para. 596.
71. Ibid., at para. 598.
72. Ibid., at para. 688.
73. 'Those who work together'. The *Interahamwe* was a militia active in the genocide in Rwanda.
74. *Supra* n. 8 at para. 688.
75. Ibid., at para. 731.
76. Ibid., at para. 731.
77. Ibid., at para. 507.
78. Ibid., at para. 508.

another'.[79] Measures to prevent births within the group could also include 'sexual mutilation, the practice of sterilization, forced birth control, separation of the sexes and prohibition of marriages.'[80]

The position of the Statute of the ICC *vis-à-vis* women is discussed below in section 6.1.3.

4.3 Children

The affects of conflict on children are equally if not more devastating. According to Ambassador Otunnu: 'In the decade from 1987 till 1997 more than 2 million children have been killed in wars. Between 4 and 5 million have been disabled, 12 million have been left homeless. More than a million children have been left orphans or separated in some permanent way from their parents. More than 10 million are psychologically traumatized in a serious way. Of the 53 million people uprooted by conflicts, half are children. There are 23 million refugees and internally displaced persons. (. . .) 50 percent of those (. . .) are children.'[81]

Children are also at risk of being forcibly abducted, press-ganged or conscripted and made to serve in rebel armies[82] and sometimes in government forces.[83] One NGO has estimated that 'as many as 250,000 children under the age of 18 serve in government forces or armed rebel groups. The participation of child soldiers has been reported in 33 current or recent armed conflicts in almost every region of the world. In 26 of these cases, children under 15 and as young as ten have been used as soldiers'.[84]

A major difficulty in trying to address the problem of child soldiers is in winning recognition of its existence. According to UN expert, Graça Machel, who was tasked by the UN Secretary-General to study the situation of children in armed conflicts: 'No peace treaty to date has formally recognized the existence of child combatants. As a result, their special needs are unlikely to be taken into account

79. Ibid., at para. 509.

80. Ibid., at para. 507.

81. *Supra* n. 49. See also the Promotion and Protection of the Rights of Children, Impact of armed conflict on children, Report of the Expert of the Secretary-General, Ms. Graça Machel, submitted pursuant to General Assembly resolution 48/157, A/51/306, 26 August 1996, at para. 2. Available online at gopher://gopher.un.org:70/00/ga/docs/51/plenary/A51-306.EN.

82. For a report on the abduction of children to serve in a rebel army see *The Scars of Death: Children Abducted by the Lord's Resistance Army in Uganda*, Human Rights Watch/Africa, (September 1997).

83. For example, children have been recruited in Algeria, Angola, Burundi, Djibouti, Liberia, Rwanda, Sierra Leone, South Africa, Sudan and Uganda. Report of Conference on Child Soldiers, *supra* n. 49 at pp. 26-37.

84. Human Rights Watch, Stop the Use of Child Soldiers! Campaign Page http://hrw.org/hrw/campaigns/crp/facts.htm. See also the report of the Committee on the Rights of the Child, UN Doc. E/CN.4/1997/96, para. 45.

in demobilization programmes. (. . .) Official acknowledgement of children's part in a war is a vital step.'[85]

Recruiting children younger than 15 or involving them in hostilities is illegal under IHL and under the Convention on the Rights of the Child (CRC).[86] The CRC, while defining a child as anyone under the age of 18, introduces the lower age limit in the context of armed conflicts, a situation in which children could be considered to be most at risk. Article 38 of the CRC prohibits the direct participation of children under the age of 15 in hostilities, giving rise to questions as to the meaning of direct participation[87], and leaving unprotected children not directly participating.

Since 1992, a worldwide campaign has been underway to draw attention to the problem of child combatants and to lobby for the adoption of an Optional Protocol to the CRC which would raise the minimum age at which children can be recruited into armies from 15 to 18[88], and which would prohibit the participation of children under the age of 18 years in hostilities.[89]

There have been four sessions of the working group established by the UN to develop new international standards which would help protect children from war, but so far the group has been unable to achieve a document that is satisfactory to all participating states. The last meeting, which was held in Geneva from 2-10 February 1998, ended in 'disagreement and stalemate (. . .). While those supporting the initiative included a broad coalition of NGOs, a group of European Governments and some from Africa and Latin America, many other important states remained opposed, including Cuba, Bangladesh, Israel, Republic of Korea, Pakistan, the United Kingdom and the United States. Of these, most would not block an international consensus for a higher age. However, the US in particular will not accept a minimum age higher than 17, as it claims that the Pentagon can more easily reach

85. Machel report, *supra* n. 81 at para. 49. See also Rachel Brett and Margaret McCallin, *Children: The invisible soldiers*, Rädda Barnen (Swedish Save the Children) (Stockholm 1996).

86. See Stéphane Jeannet and Joël Mermet, 'The Involvement of Children in Armed Conflict', *IRRC*, No. 322 (March 1998) p. 105 at 106.

87. 'Optional Protocol to the Convention on the Rights of the Child concerning involvement of children in armed conflict, Position of the International Committee of the Red Cross,' Geneva 27 October 1997, *IRRC* No. 322 (March 1998) p. 107 at pp. 114-117.

88. In 1992, the Committee on the Rights of the Child recommended that an Optional Protocol to the Convention on the Rights of the Child be adopted which would raise the minimum age of recruitment and participation in hostilities from 15 (Art. 38 of the CRC) to 18, and also that a study on the impact of armed conflict on children be undertaken. This became the Machel report.

89. In fact, the Draft Optional Protocol itself contains the possibility of a limit of 17 years for direct participation in hostilities and a limit of either 16 or 17 for recruiting children into the armed forces. See Arts. 1 and 2 of the Draft Optional Protocol to the CRC, reprinted in proceedings of the Conference on Child Soldiers (Watoto wa Amani, The Hague 20 November 1997) , Annex 2. However, most campaigners prefer 18 as the legal minimum age for both recruitment and participation, either direct or indirect, in hostilities.

its recruiting goals without it.'[90] However the US, while blocking a consensus, would not be able to sign the Optional Protocol as it has not signed the CRC.

Many children's rights advocates and the ICRC lobbied for and hoped that the ICC Statute would include a provision raising the minimum age of recruitment and participation in hostilities to 18. Instead, the Statute retains the 15 year limit for both recruiting and participation in hostilities.[91]

5. METHODS, MEANS AND TYPES OF WARFARE

5.1 Use of Weapons

5.1.1 *Blinding Laser Weapons*[92]

The Blinding Laser Weapons Protocol (Protocol IV) to the CCW Convention prohibits weapons that are 'specifically designed, as their sole combat function or as one of their combat functions' to cause blinding. The focus on the weapon itself, rather than on the act of blinding, and particularly the use of the wording 'specifically designed', seems to exclude the use of laser weapons that can be used for blinding but that are not specifically designed for this purpose.[93]

The Protocol does not prohibit the production of blinding laser weapons. At the Review Conference, it was considered that the inclusion of such a provision would require intrusive verification measures which there was no time to debate. It was decided to leave this issue for a future Review Conference. Fortunately, the ban

90. Kenneth Roth, 'New Minefields for NGOs: After a big win, global citizen power gears up for the next fight', *The Nation* (13 April 1998).

91. Art. 8(2)(b)(xxvi) proscribes as a war crime when committed in an international armed conflict, 'Conscripting or enlisting children under the age of fifteen years into the national armed forces or using them to participate in hostilities.' Art. 8(2)(e)(vii) prohibits when committed during an internal armed conflict 'within the established framework of international law', 'Conscripting or enlisting children under the age of fifteen years into armed forces or groups or using them to participate actively in hostilities.'

92. For an analysis of Protocol IV to the CCW Convention concerning Blinding Laser Weapons, see Zöcker at p. 333 of this volume.

93. This is recognised in the USA Department of Defence's policy statement on Blinding Lasers, which states that 'accidental or incidental eye injuries may occur on the battlefield as a result of the use of lasers not specifically designed to cause permanent blindness'. DOD Policy Statement on Blinding Lasers, 17 January 1997, reprinted at p. 595 of this volume.

on transfer of such weapons to any state or non-state entity includes non-state parties.[94]

Article 2 caused the greatest difficulty at the Review Conference. Its wording underwent several transmutations before the current version emerged, on 5 October 1995, as a proposal of the Netherlands.[95] As desired by many delegates, including the USA and UK, 'the duty has been placed on the level of the State, (...) and takes the form of appropriate training and "other practical measures". This clearly means that orders cannot be given to use lasers to blind combatants and that efforts must be made to train soldiers to use laser equipment so as to avoid such a result as far as possible. It also means that, if lasers were to be used to counter optical equipment, particular efforts would have to be made to avoid blinding individuals, as in practice, such lasers would be the most serious hazard to eyesight.'[96]

Article 3 permits blinding as a collateral or incidental effect of the legitimate military employment of laser systems, including those used against optical equipment. This gives rise to some problems of interpretation, such as concerning whether blinding as a result of lasers used against direct optics is covered.[97]

The Convention entered into force on 30 July 1998 when 20 states ratified it. As of 14 September 1998, 29 states had ratified Protocol IV.[98]

5.1.2 *Landmines*

The Review Conference of the CCW Convention was convened primarily to look into the question of amending Protocol II concerning landmines. However, despite widespread support for stronger prohibitions, 'only minimal restrictions on the use of anti-personnel landmines were finally adopted'.[99]

Amended Protocol II expands Protocol II in several ways: it introduces a specific definition of anti-personnel mines; it extends its reach to non-international armed conflicts[100]; it assigns clearance responsibility to those who plant mines, and provides that the location of all mines must be mapped and recorded in all circum-

94. 'Austria strongly argued in favour of this proposal, pointing out the particular danger of a state party to the Protocol transferring the weapon to a non-party State which might well then use it.' Doswald-Beck, *supra* n. 10 at p. 289.

95. Doswald-Beck, ibid., p. 292.

96. Doswald-Beck, ibid., p. 292.

97. Louise Doswald-Beck argues that 'according to a normal interpretation of Article 3 the phrase "including laser systems used against optical equipment" could not be used to legitimize the deliberate blinding of persons using binoculars or other direct optics'. *Supra* n. 10 at p. 294

98. Source: ICRC IHL Treaty database: http://www.icrc.org.

99. Peter Herby, 'Third Session of the Review Conference of States Parties to the 1980 United Nations Convention on Certain Conventional Weapons,' Geneva, 22 April-3 May 1996, *IRRC* No. 312, (May-June 1996) p. 361.

100. Art. 1(2) states that the Protocol shall apply to situations covered by common Art. 3.

stances. New protection is given to humanitarian workers. Long and short-lived anti-personnel mines are still permitted under the amended Protocol, provided they are detectable, are placed in clearly identified areas, and, in the case of short-lived mines, self-destruct within 30 days. The situation regarding anti-tank mines remains the same.[101]

Although there is a new provision prohibiting the transfer of non-detectable anti-personnel landmines, and of any mine, to entities other than states, transfers of non-detectable anti-personnel mines to entities other than states is permitted if they 'agree to apply' the provisions of the Protocol. State parties are to enact penal legislation to suppress serious violations of the Protocol. 'The amended Protocol does not, however, contain any provisions for the verification of either the reliability of its technical requirements (. . .) or of possible violations of its provisions on the use of landmines.'[102]

The ICRC has been very critical of amended Protocol II, stating that 'not only does [it] *not* prohibit the use of a weapon with indiscriminate effects but even indirectly promotes the development and use of new weapons which will have precisely the same effects, at least in the short term. This is the first time that a humanitarian law instrument may have the effect of promoting the use of a new weapon'[103] [referring to the fact that amended Protocol II places fewer restrictions on smart mines than on ordinary, 'dumb' mines, thus perhaps encouraging their use]. Protocol II, which was adopted on 3 May 1996, entered into force on 3 December 1998, six months following the deposit of the 20th instrument of ratification. As of 14 September 1998, 25 states had ratified Protocol II.[104]

While amended Protocol II is an improvement on its predecessor, it did not offer what was increasingly being demanded: a complete ban on landmines.[105] This was achieved through the Ottawa Process which led to the adoption of the Convention on the Prohibition of the Use, Stockpiling, Production and Transfer of Anti-Personnel Mines and on their Destruction in October 1997.[106] On 16 September 1998, Burkina Faso became the 40th state to deposit its instrument of ratification with the UN SG, thus triggering the entry into force of the Convention. On 1 March

101. Herby, *supra* n. 99 at p. 363.

102. Herby, ibid., at p. 364.

103. Herby, ibid., at p. 366.

104. Source: ICRC IHL Treaty database: http://www.icrc.org.

105. In December 1996, 157 states supported a UN General Assembly resolution calling for the urgent negotiation of a legally binding ban on anti-personnel landmines.

106. For a discussion of the Ottawa Process and the Landmines Treaty, see Goose at p. 269.

1999, the Landmines Convention will become binding on a third of the 130 states that have signed it.

There are now, therefore, three separate international legal regimes governing the use of anti-personnel landmines: Protocol II to the CCW Convention of 1980, amended Protocol II of 3 May 1996 and the 1997 Landmines Treaty.

5.1.3 *Nuclear Weapons*

On 8 July 1996, the International Court of Justice issued two advisory opinions entitled, 'Legality of the threat or use of nuclear weapons' in response to questions submitted to it by the General Assembly and the WHO.[107] It was the first time since the *Nicaragua* case of 1986 that the ICJ dwelt so extensively on questions relevant to IHL. Those looking to the Court for a judicial pronouncement on the illegality of nuclear weapons were disappointed. The Court's *non liquet*, that is, its inability to state whether the use of nuclear weapons was illegal or not, has been described by one commentator as merely apparent.[108] While the Court stated that it could not say whether 'the threat of nuclear weapons would be lawful or unlawful in an extreme circumstance of self-defence, in which the very survival of a State would be at stake'[109], 'at least one thing is certain, namely, that by a tiny majority the Court did indeed refuse to reject the nuclear powers' argument that in such circumstances the use of nuclear weapons would not be prohibited by law'[110]. The majority Opinion was only formed with the President's casting vote, and with every Judge issuing either Separate or Dissenting Opinions, the range of views represented

107. *Legality of the Use of Nuclear Weapons*. International Court of Justice, Advisory Opinion of 8 July 1996 in response to resolution 49/75K adopted by the General Assembly on 15 December 1994; *Legality of the Use of Nuclear Weapons*. Advisory Opinion of 8 July 1996 in response to resolution WHA46.40 adopted by the World Health Assembly on 14 May 1993

108. See Luigi Condorelli, 'Nuclear weapons: a weighty matter for the International Court of Justice, JURA NON NOVIT CURIA?' *IRRC* No. 316 (January-February 1997) p. 9 at 11. This is recognised by Judge Guillaume in his Separate Opinion in which he chastises the Court for failing to say explicitly what it meant implicitly. The *IRRC* devotes almost all of issue 316 to the Nuclear Weapons Advisory Opinions, with an introduction by Judge Geza Herczegh.

109. Advisory Opinion, para. 2E, clause 2.

110. *Supra* n. 108, at p. 10. Condorelli goes on to state: 'the mere fact that, for whatever reason, the Court did not decide that nuclear weapons are always forbidden implies that those who held them to be illegal have been totally defeated. They did not get what they wanted, that is, a ruling by the Court that the nuclear powers are not in any circumstances entitled to use the weapon they possess. And vice-versa: the very fact that the Court did not rule that the threat or use of nuclear weapons is prohibited in all circumstances means that those who hold it to be legal mainly the nuclear powers - in effect triumphed. Their dearest wish (that their policy of nuclear deterrence should not be labelled *hic et nunc* illegal) was granted to the full.' At p. 12.

is broad. Despite not declaring nuclear weapons to be illegal, the Advisory Opinions clarify that the use of nuclear weapons has to respect the rules of IHL.

5.1.4 *Chemical Weapons*

On 29 April 1997 the Chemical Weapons Convention entered into force when the 65th signatory nation deposited its instrument of ratification.[111] As of 31 August 1998, 169 states had signed and 114 states had ratified or acceded to the Convention.[112]

The organisation charged with monitoring the Convention, the Organisation for the Prohibition of Chemical Weapons (OPCW), was established and began its work of conducting inspections of declared facilities in states parties. Within 30 days after the coming into force of the Convention, states parties were required to submit to the OPCW initial declarations regarding their stockpiles of chemical weapons and other information. Within the first four months of its existence, the OPCW had conducted 70 inspections.[113]

The Chemical Weapons Convention 'complements and reinforces' the 1925 Geneva Protocol prohibiting the use of chemical and biological weapons by also banning the development, production, stockpiling and use of chemical weapons, and also requires the destruction of existing stockpiles.[114]

5.1.5 *Bacteriological/Biological Weapons*

In 1997, the 1972 Convention on the Prohibition of the Development, Production and Stockpiling of Bacteriological (Biological) and Toxin Weapons and on their Destruction celebrated its 25th Anniversary.[115] By September 1998, 151 states were party to the Biological Weapons Convention. While the 1972 Convention went beyond the 1925 Geneva Protocol in not only prohibiting the use but also the development, production, acquisition and stockpiling of biological weapons, its major deficiency is its lack of provision for verification of compliance.

111. The 65th state, Hungary, deposited its notice of ratification on 31 October 1996. See Peter Herby, 'Chemical Weapons Convention enters into force', *IRRC* No. 317 (March-April 1997) p. 208.

112. Current figures on ratifications can be obtained at http://www.opcw.nl.

113. Source: ibid.

114. Herby, loc. cit. n. 111. For a discussion of the long-standing taboo against the use of chemical weapons, see Richard M. Price, *The Chemical Weapons Taboo* (Cornell University Press, 1997).

115. The *International Review of the Red Cross* marked this anniversary with a special issue on the subject of the Convention. See *IRRC* No. 318 (May-June 1997).

After admissions by first the Russian Federation (in 1992) and subsequently Iraq (in 1995) that they had breached the 1972 Convention, the international community was stirred to begin a review of the Convention and steps that could be taken to monitor compliance. In June 1997, the *Ad Hoc* Group charged with this task issued a rolling text that is to form the basis of a future verification protocol.[116]

5.2 Protected Objects

5.2.1 *Protection of Cultural Property*

Since the beginning of the decade, efforts have been underway to revise the 1954 Hague Convention for the Protection of Cultural Property in the Event of Armed Conflict.[117] The latest meeting of the governmental experts on the revision of the Convention was held in Vienna from 11 to 13 May 1998, with a view to the convening of a Diplomatic Conference of the High Contracting Parties in the first half of 1999.[118] The purpose of this meeting was to consider five main issues, which had already been discussed at the earlier meetings: the form of the new instrument; special protection; military necessity; jurisdiction and responsibility; and institutional matters.

Most experts agreed that the 1954 Convention should be retained as the basis of the protection for cultural property in armed conflict and that revisions should be contained within a new optional protocol. It was proposed to establish an enhanced regime of special protection providing more flexibility regarding the eligibility of cultural property to becoming specially protected, although it was acknowledged that any new initiatives in this regard at an international level should be matched by national legislation.

A majority of the experts were in favour of retaining the concept of military necessity within any new optional protocol, 'but this concept should appear in the text rather as a barrier against destruction than the opposite'.[119] The working group examined a number of elements which could limit the application of the concept, and it was agreed that such elements should appear in the optional protocol and should refer both to general principles and procedural limitations.

116. *Human Rights Watch World Report 1998*, p. 368. See also Michael Weston, 'Giving Teeth to the Biological Weapons Convention', 45 *NATO Review* (1997) p. 33.

117. The review process is considered by Hladik at p. 313 of this volume.

118. See Report by the Director-General on the Results of the Meeting of Governmental Experts on the Revision of the Hague Convention for the Protection of Cultural Property in the Event of Armed Conflict 1954, Vienna, 11-13 May 1998, UNESCO, 155th session, 155EX/51, Paris, 17 August 1998.

119. Ibid., Annex p. 3.

On the question of jurisdiction and responsibility, a majority of experts stated that while a duplication of international efforts should be avoided, provisions on individual criminal responsibility should be included and the provision of the 1954 Convention concerning the principle *aut dedere aut judicare* should be retained.

At the close of the meeting, the government of the Netherlands indicated that it would convene a Diplomatic Conference at The Hague from 14 to 26 March 1999.

6. ENFORCEMENT OF IHL

6.1 International Criminal Prosecution

6.1.1 *The International Tribunal for the Former Yugoslavia*

The ICTY, which got off to a slow start, appears to have turned the corner, although it would be exaggerating to say that it is now coasting along. As of October 1998, one judicial process had been completed – concerning *Dražen Ěrdemović*, who confessed.[120] That concluded after going to the Appeals Chamber, there to be sent back to the Trial Chamber so that Ěrdemović, who had initially pleaded guilty to a crime against humanity, but which plea was found not to be informed, could reenter a plea. Ěrdemović, who the second time around confessed to a war crime, was sentenced to five years for his part in the execution of about 1,000 unarmed Bosnian Muslim civilians. Ěrdemović himself killed up to seventy people.[121] The judgement is primarily concerned with questions of duress and superior orders and ponders whether these can be raised as defences or considered only in mitigation of sentence.[122]

The Tribunal has also secured its first conviction at trial, in the case of *Duško Tadić*, who was found guilty of crimes against humanity and violations and the laws or customs of war[123] and sentenced to 20 years imprisonment[124].

No verdict had been rendered, at the time of writing, in the second trial to have concluded before the ICTY, that concerning the four defendants accused in the

120. As Ěrdemović confessed, under Rule 62(iv) there could be no trial and his case proceeded directly to sentencing.

121. *Prosecutor* v. *Dražen Erdemović*, Judgement of the Appeals Chamber, 7 October 1997, Case No. IT-96-22-A at para. 8.

122. The Appeals Judgement is analysed by Rowe at p. 210 of this volume.

123. *Prosecutor* v. *Duško Tadić*, Opinion and Judgment, Case No. IT-94-1-T, 7 May 1997.

124. *Prosecutor* v. *Duško Tadić*, Sentencing Judgement, Case No. IT-94-1-T, 14 July 1997.

Čelebići Indictment.[125] *Čelebići* will be the first judgement in which the Tribunal will consider in depth the question of command responsibility, with which three of the four accused are charged. It will also be the first case in which the ICTY will pronounce on charges of rape.

Several trials are ongoing. The trial of General *Tihomir Blaškić*, who is charged with command responsibility for grave breaches of the Geneva Conventions, violations of the laws or customs of war and crimes against humanity, opened on 24 June 1997. The Defence case opened on 7 September 1998. The *Aleksovski* trial began on 6 January 1998 and was expected to conclude at the end of November 1998. The joint trial of the six persons accused in the indictment *Kupreškić* and others began on 17 August 1998. The trial of *Anto Furundžija* concluded on 22 June 1998 after seven days of hearings but reopened in November at the Prosecutor's request.[126] Furundžija is charged with failure to prevent a rape. A couple of other trials were prematurely terminated by the deaths of the accused. One, *Slavko Dokmanović*, hanged himself in his cell, prompting an investigation into the conditions of detention[127], while the other, *Milan Kovacević*, whose trial was the first before the ICTY on charges of genocide, died of a heart attack[128].

With Kovacević dead, only one other accused in Tribunal custody is facing genocide charges, *Goran Jelisić*.[129] The trial of the most high-ranking defendant in Tribunal custody, *Dario Kordić*, is also pending. Kordić, who was Vice-President of the Croatian Community of Herceg-Bosna, is charged with command responsibility for grave breaches, crimes against humanity and violations of the laws or customs of war.[130]

As of the end of October 1998, 26 persons were in custody, and one was on provisional release[131], out of 56 individuals accused in 19 public indictments.[132] The

125. The Judgement in this case was expected on 16 November 1998.

126. ICTY CC/PIO/332-E, The Hague, 14 July 1998.

127. An inquiry into the death of Mr. Dokmanović, led by Judge Almiro Rodrigues, found no negligent behaviour on the part of detention unit staff. Judge Rodriguez has set up a working group which will study the issue of suicides in prison and review the preventative measures applied in various detention systems. See http://www.un.org/icty/bulletin21-e/dokman.htm.

128. An investigation into the circumstances of Dr. Kovacević's death was undertaken by the Tribunal and a report was prepared by Judge Almiro Rodriques and published on 27 August 1998. It cleared the ICTY and the persons involved, including the duty doctor, of any negligence. Available online at http://www.un.org/icty/pressreal/inquiry/htm.

129. Case No. IT-95-10-PT. On 29 Oct. 1998, Jelisić pleaded quilty to 31 out of 33 counts with which he is charged in a second amended indictment. See ICTY press release JL/PIU/357-E.

130. Case No. IT-95-14/2-PT.

131. *Milan Simić*, Case No. IT-95-9-PT.

132. Indictments were withdrawn against four accused: Marinko Katava (named in the indictment, *Kupreskić & others*); Pero Skopljak (*Kordić & others*); Ivan Santić (*Kordić &* others) and Stipo Alilović *(Kupresić & others)*. In the case of the first three, the Prosecutor stated that 'there is insufficient basis to justify proceeding to trial against [them] and in the interests of justice the

Prosecutor has adopted a strategy of issuing sealed indictments, in order to retain the element of surprise in apprehending suspects.

To address the problem of what to do in case of failure to execute an indictment, the Tribunal has held five public hearings under Rule 61 of its Rules of Procedure and Evidence, which allows it to convene a public hearing to consider the evidence and to issue international arrest warrants. Eight such warrants have been issued as a result of these hearings[133], including against the two most wanted, *Radovan Karadžić* and *Ratko Mladić*.

Recognising the need to hasten proceedings before the ICTY, the SC voted to create a third Trial Chamber[134], and the Judges of the ICTY, at their 18th Plenary Session held on 9 and 10 July 1998, made a series of amendments to the Rules 'with the aim of streamlining and expediting proceedings'. These changes include assigning a single judge of a Trial Chamber to act as the pre-trial judge, with responsibility for ruling on all pre-trial motions; issuing a single judgement determining both culpability, and, in the case of guilt, the sentence; amendment of the indictment by the confirming jud
ge; and other changes that will assist in streamlining the pre-trial and trial proceedings.[135] However, the Tribunal is also considering adding to its workload, by issuing indictments concerning the war in Kosovo.[136]

The most important decisions rendered to date are the Decision on the Defence Motion for Appeal in the *Tadić* Case[137]; the Decision on *Subpoena* in the *Blaškić*

indictment should now be withdrawn.' In the case of the fourth, Alilović, '[t]he Prosecutor has received confirmation that the accused is dead. He died on 25 October 1995 in Amsterdam.' See ICTY Press Release CC/PIO/278-E, 19 December 1997. Alilović was indicted on 10 November 1995. The figure of 19 public indictments does not include *Erdemović* – whose case has now concluded – *Dokmanović*, *Kovacević*, *Djukić* or *Miljković* (the latter four died and although their indictments have not yet officially been withdrawn, they are not included in the list of public indictments).

133. The Rule 61 hearings were held in the cases of *Dragan Nikolić*, *Milan Martić*, *Vukovar Hospital* (Mile Mrksić, Miroslav Radić and Veselin Šljivanćanin), *Ivica Rajić*, and *Radovan Karadžić* and *Ratko Mladić* (jointly accused).

134. UN SC Resolution 1166 (1998), 13 May 1998.

135. See ICTY Press Release CC/PIO/333-E, 16 July 1998.

136. See ICTY Press Release CC/PIO/301-E, 10 March 1998 in which the Prosecutor asserted the Tribunal's jurisdiction over the violence in Kosovo.

137. *Supra* n. 42.

case[138]; the Appeals Decision in the *Erdemović* case[139]; and the Opinion and Judgment in the *Tadić* case[140]. The first has been considered at length elsewhere.[141] The second and third are discussed elsewhere in this volume.[142] We will thus confine ourselves to a brief consideration of the judgement in the *Tadić* case.[143]

In his original indictment, Tadić was accused of 34 counts of grave breaches, crimes against humanity and violations of the laws or customs of war. Three counts were dropped before the opening of the trial when the victim of a rape refused to testify. Tadić was convicted on 11 of the remaining 31 charges. He was acquitted of 9 counts of murder because of insufficient evidence, and 11 charges of grave breaches were dropped when the majority found that an international armed conflict did not exist in Bosnia and Herzegovina at the time the crimes were committed.

The majority opinion on the question of the applicability of Article 2 of the ICTY Statute, incorporating the grave breaches provisions of the Geneva Conventions, found that the conflict could not be considered as international and the grave breaches provisions did not apply in this case as the victims of the crimes could not be considered as protected persons, as defined in Article 4 of the Fourth Geneva Convention of 1949. That is, they were not persons in the hands of a party to the conflict or an Occupying Power of which they were non-nationals. It came to this conclusion because it considered that the relevant party to the conflict, that is, the Bosnian Serb Army (VRS) could not be considered to be an agent of the Federal Republic of Yugoslavia (FRY). Despite admitting that there was evidence that the FRY had created the VRS as a force of non-nationals to take over from the JNA (Yugoslav Army) after its withdrawal from Bosnia on 19 May 1992, and that it had provided it with essential men and *materiel;* that coordination between the VRS and Belgrade existed at the highest levels; and that Belgrade paid the salaries of all senior VRS Commanders, the majority concluded that this did not amount to a relationship of agency.

138. Judgement on the Request of the Republic of Croatia for Review of the Decision of Trial Chamber II of 18 July 1997, *Prosecutor* v. *Tihomir Blaškić*, Case No. IT-95-14-AR108 *bis*, 29 October 1997.

139. *Supra* n. 121.

140. *Supra* n. 123.

141. See *inter alia* George H. Aldrich, 'Jurisdiction of the International Tribunal for the Former Yugoslavia', 90 *AJIL* (1996) p. 64; Geoffrey R. Watson, 'The Humanitarian Law of the Yugoslav War Crimes Tribunal: jurisdiction in *Prosecutor* v. *Tadić*', 36 *Virginia JIL* (1996) p. 687.

142. On *Erdemović*, see Rowe *supra* at p. 210 and on the *Subpoena* Decision see Malanczuk at p. 229 of this volume.

143. The decision is currently under appeal by both the Prosecutor and the Defence. The *YIHL* will offer an in-depth analysis of the case once the Appeals decision has been rendered.

The majority applied an onerous test of agency, based on that applied by the ICJ in the *Nicaragua* case.[144] Applied to the *Tadić* case it became, whether the relationship was so much one of dependence on the one side and control on the other that it would be right to equate the VRS, for legal purposes, with an organ of the government of the FRY, or as acting on behalf of that government. The majority concluded that it would not be right to consider the VRS as agents of the JNA or the government of FRY as, despite the fact that there was a relationship of dependency on the one side, there was no evidence that the FRY, through the JNA, 'made use of the potential for control inherent in that dependence, or was otherwise given effective control over those forces . . .'[145]

The majority was not blind to the possibility that the acts of the JNA and the FRY after 19 May 1992 were 'nothing more than a cynical and intentional creation of the objective factors necessary to distance themselves from direct legal responsibility for the acts of the armed forces of *Republika Srpska*, while doing everything to ensure that the material factors necessary to ensure the successful continuation of the armed conflict to achieve the same military and political goals were kept in place', although it doubted whether 'fraudulent intent' could vitiate the legal effect of creating such objective factors and found in any event that 'this is not the only nor the most reasonable conclusion open on the evidence presented.' There was, in short, no evidence on which the Trial Chamber could confidently conclude that the VRS and the JNA were anything more than mere allies, albeit highly dependent ones, of the government of the FRY in its plan to achieve a greater Serbia, according to the majority.[146]

The possibility of a legal fiction was not so easily dismissed by Judge McDonald in her Dissenting Opinion. Judge McDonald found that the conflict was international in character after 19 May 1992 and that the victims continued to be protected persons after that date as the VRS was an agent of the JNA and by extension, the FRY government, and that the grave breaches provisions were therefore applicable. Judge McDonald reasoned that the majority had incorrectly applied the test of agency articulated in the *Nicaragua* case by requiring a showing of 'effective control', a higher standard than that required in *Nicaragua*.[147] While arguing that the evidence in fact supported a finding of effective control, Judge McDonald said

144. *ICJ Rep.* 1986.
145. *Supra* n. 123 at para. 605.
146. Ibid., at para. 606.
147. At para. 3 of her Dissenting Opinion.

that 'the appropriate test of agency from *Nicaragua* is one of 'dependency and control' and a showing of effective control is not required'.[148]

Professor Meron has argued that the chamber erred in its resort to the *Nicaragua* case for the applicable legal standard of agency: '... the *Nicaragua* case dealt with quite a different legal question - whether, for legal purposes, the contras either constituted an organ of the United States Government or were acting on its behalf. If so, their acts could be attributed to the United States for the purposes of state responsibility.'[149] While *Nicaragua* was concerned with the question of state responsibility, the *Tadić* case was concerned with individual criminal responsibility, and the identification of the foreign intervenor 'was only relevant to characterising the conflict. Thus, the problem in the trial chamber's approach lay not in its interpretation of *Nicaragua*, but in applying *Nicaragua* to *Tadić* at all.'[150]

The Judgment is also controversial in its finding that discriminatory intent is an element of all crimes against humanity and not just persecution. Despite acknowledging that neither the Nuremberg or Tokyo Charters nor Control Council Law No. 10, nor the International Law Commission's Draft Code of Crimes against the Peace and Security of Mankind require such an element, the Chamber stated that, '[n]evertheless, because the requirement of discriminatory intent on national, political, ethnic, racial or religious grounds for all crimes against humanity was included in the Report of the Secretary-General, and since several Security Council members stated that they interpreted Article 5 as referring to acts taken on a discriminatory basis, the Trial Chamber adopts the requirement of discriminatory intent for all crimes against humanity under Article 5.'[151]

While crimes against humanity must be committed pursuant to a policy, 'such a policy need not be formalized and can be deduced from the way in which the acts occur. Notably, if the acts occur on a widespread or systematic basis that demonstrates a policy to commit those acts, whether formalized or not.'[152] The Chamber also stated that crimes against humanity can be committed by non-governmental forces which have *de facto* control over, or are able to move freely within, defined territory[153]; in other words, although there must be a policy to commit such crimes, it need not be the policy of a government. Furthermore, while crimes against

148. At para. 4 of her Dissenting Opinion.

149. T. Meron, 'Classification of Armed Conflict in the Former Yugoslavia: Nicaragua's Fallout', 92 *AJIL* (1998) p. 236.

150. Ibid., at p. 237. See also Vinuesa at p. 106.

151. *Supra* n. 123 at para. 652.

152. Ibid., at para. 653.

153. Ibid., at para. 654.

humanity must be committed against a civilian population, the Chamber adopted a broad definition of civilian population: 'Thus the presence of those actively involved in the conflict should not prevent the characterization of a population as civilian and those actively involved in a resistance movement can qualify as victims of crimes against humanity.'[154] 'The presence of certain non-civilians in their midst does not change the character of the population.'[155] Finally, the Chamber endorsed the finding of the Trial Chamber in the Rule 61 hearing in the *Vukovar Hospital* case[156] that even a single act by a perpetrator could constitute a crime against humanity if it was committed with the requisite intent.[157]

6.1.2 *The International Criminal Tribunal for Rwanda*[158]

Due to the good cooperation it has enjoyed with those African states to which accused persons fled after the genocide in Rwanda, the ICTR has had relatively more success than the ICTY at taking custody of its accused, with 26 of 35 accused persons on remand at the ICTR's detention centre in Arusha, and another one awaiting surrender by the USA to the Tribunal.[159] In contrast with the ICTY, most of its accused in custody are leaders, the majority of which are accused of genocide and/or complicity in genocide. On 30 April 1998, the UN SC voted to create a third Trial Chamber for the ICTR, further to a request of the President of the Tribunal.[160]

As of the beginning of October 1998, the ICTR had concluded one trial – that of Jean-Paul Akayesu – and the joint trial of Clement Kayishema and Obed Ruzinda was expected to conclude in November 1998; rendered one conviction; and two sentences in the cases of *Jean-Paul Akayesu* and *Jean Kambanda.*

The Trial Chamber in its judgement in the *Akayesu* case, rendered on 2 September 1998, reaffirmed that the Genocide Convention is 'undoubtedly part of interna -

154. Ibid., at p. 643.

155. Ibid., at p. 638.

156. *The Prosecutor* v. *Mile Msksić, Miroslav Radić and Veselin Šljivančanin*, Review of the Indictment Pursuant to Rule 61 of the Rules of Procedure and Evidence, Case No. IT-95-13-R61. The hearing was held on 20, 26, 27 and 28 March 1996 and the Decision was rendered on 3 April 1996. See Review of Indictment Pursuant to Rule 61 of the Rules of Procedure and Evidence.

157. *Supra* n. 123 at para. 649.

158. For a more detailed consideration of the work of the ICTR, and its relationship with the judicial processes in Rwanda, see Cissé at p. 161 of this volume.

159. On 5 August 1998, a US District Court Judge ordered the surrender to the ICTR of Elizaphan Ntakirutimana. For background to this case, see Paust at p. 205 of this volume.

160. See UN Doc. S/RES/1165 (1998), 30 April 1998.

tional law'[161], and that 'contrary to popular belief, the crime of genocide does not imply the actual extermination of [the] group in its entirety, but is understood as such once any one of the acts mentioned in Article 2(2)(a) through 2(2)(e) is committed with the specific intent to destroy "in whole or in part" a national, ethnical, racial or religious group'[162].

'Causing serious bodily or mental harm to members of the group does not necessarily mean that the harm is permanent or irremediable.'[163] 'For purposes of interpreting Article 2(2)(b) of the Statute, the Chamber takes serious bodily or mental harm, without limiting itself thereto, to mean acts of torture, be they bodily or mental, inhumane or degrading treatment, persecution.'[164]

The expression 'deliberately inflicting on the group conditions of life calculated to bring about the group's physical destruction in whole or in part, should be construed as the methods of destruction by which the perpetrator does not immediately kill the members of the group, but which, ultimately, seek their physical destruction.'[165] The means of inflicting such conditions of life on the protected groups include subjecting the group to a subsistence diet; systematic expulsion from homes and the reduction of essential medical services below minimum requirements.[166]

The Chamber emphasised that the victim of the act of genocide is 'a member of a group, chosen as such, which, hence, means that the victim of the crime of genocide is the group itself and not only the individual. The perpetration of the act charged therefore extends beyond its actual commission, for example, the murder of a particular individual, for the realisation of an ulterior motive, which is to destroy, in whole or in part, the group of which the individual is just one element.'[167]

Finally, the Chamber noted that intent to commit genocide could be inferred 'from a certain number of presumptions of fact. The Chamber considers that it is possible to deduce the genocidal intent inherent in a particular act charged from the general context of the perpetration of other culpable acts systematically directed against that same group, whether those acts were committed by the same offender

161. *Supra* n. 8. at para. 495. In the *Case concerning application of the Convention on the Prevention and Punishment of the Crime of Genocide* (*Bosnia and Herzegovina* v. *Yugoslavia*), Preliminary Objections, Judgment of 11 July 1996, para. 31, the ICJ stated that the duty incumbent on states to prevent and punish genocide does not depend on the nature of the conflict and is the same whether the conflict is international or internal.

162. Ibid., at para. 497.

163. Ibid., at para. 502.

164. Ibid., at para. 504.

165. Ibid., at para. 505.

166. Ibid., at para. 506.

167. Ibid., at paras. 521 and 522.

or by others. Other factors include the scale of the atrocities committed, their general nature, in a region or country, or furthermore, the fact of deliberately and systematically targeting victims on account of their membership of a particular group, while excluding the members of other groups, can enable the Chamber to infer the genocidal intent of a particular act.'[168] The Court also pronounced on the question of complicity in genocide, finding that 'an accomplice to genocide need not necessarily possess the *dolus specialis* of genocide, namely the specific intent to destroy, in whole or in part, a national, ethnic, racial or religious group, as such'.[169]

The Trial Chamber acquitted Akayesu of violations of common Article 3 and Additional Protocol II on the basis that the Prosecutor failed to establish beyond a reasonable doubt that Akayesu was 'either a member of the armed forces under the military command of either of the belligerent parties, or that he was legitimately mandated and expected, as a public official or agent or person otherwise holding public authority or *de facto* representing the Government, to support or fulfill the war efforts.'[170] Both Akayesu and the Prosecutor have appealed the judgement.[171]

On 2 October 1998, the ICTR sentenced Akayesu to three life sentences for genocide, calling it 'the crime of crimes', and an additional 80 years for other war crimes. These sentences are to be served concurrently. Akayesu has indicated that he will appeal this sentence.

Jean Kambanda probably thought that by pleading guilty and cooperating fully with the Prosecutor he could expect some indulgence from the Trial Chamber. Indeed, he requested just two years during the pre-sentencing hearing. Instead, despite recognising Kambanda's cooperation with the Prosecutor, that his guilty plea 'is likely to encourage other individuals to recognize their responsibilities during the tragic events which occurred in Rwanda in 1994', and that in Rwanda, as in most national jurisdictions, a guilty plea is regarded as a mitigating circumstance, the Trial Chamber sentenced him to the maximum sentence of life imprisonment. In so doing, it stated that, despite mitigating circumstances, these were outweighed by several aggravating factors, in particular, that Kambanda occupied a high position as Prime Minister of the Interim Government, that the crimes which he committed are of intrinsic gravity and shock the human conscience, and that he committed them knowingly and with premeditation.[172] Moreover, it noted that Kambanda never

168. Ibid., at para. 523.
169. Ibid., at paras. 540 and 541.
170. Ibid., at para. 640.
171. ICTR/INFO-9-2-144, Arusha 7 October 1998.
172. *Supra* n. 9 at para. 61.

showed any remorse or apologised to his victims, despite having the opportunity to do so. Kambanda has appealed the sentence.

Kambanda's sentence will not encourage others in high positions to come forward and to confess and to cooperate with the Prosecutor of the ICTR. On the other hand, Erdemović's sentence by the ICTY is not going to give any lowly potential mass murders much cause for pause before pulling the trigger, although it will certainly encourage them to come forward, confess and cooperate fully with the Prosecutor.

6.1.3 *Permanent International Criminal Court*

The adoption of a Statute for a permanent International Criminal Court opens a new chapter in the enforcement of IHL.

The Statute confers jurisdiction over four categories of crimes: (a) the crime of genocide; (b) crimes against humanity; (c) war crimes; and (d) the crime of aggression.[173]

There was widespread support for the inclusion of the crime of *aggression* as long as there was agreement on an acceptable definition of the term and on the role of the SC as provided for in the UN Charter.[174] The main stumbling block to the inclusion of aggression was the inability to agree on a definition of the crime. The Statute sidesteps this problem by providing in Article 5(2) that the Court shall exercise jurisdiction over aggression only once the crime and the conditions of the Court's jurisdiction over it are defined, as provided for in the Statute. Such provision should be consistent with the relevant provisions of the UN Charter.

The crime of *genocide* is defined in Article 6. The definition is a verbatim of Article II of the Genocide Convention. The provision omits, however, Article III of the Genocide Convention, expressly giving the Court jurisdiction over the named acts, although Article III is incorporated in the equivalent provisions of the Statutes of the *ad hoc* Tribunals.[175]

Article 7 confers jurisdiction over *crimes against humanity*. The *chapeau* states that they are the named acts 'when committed as part of a widespread or systematic attack directed against any civilian population, with knowledge of the attack'.

173. Art. 5(1)(a) - (d).

174. During the discussions in the Committee of the Whole on the Bureau Discussion Paper (A/CONF.183/C.1/L.53, 6 July 1998) on 8 July 1998.

175. In the ICTY's and ICTR's Arts. 4 and 2 respectively.

The Statute follows the ICTR Statute in not requiring a nexus to an armed conflict.[176] The ICTY, conversely, retained the nexus to armed conflict[177], although the ICTY has found that customary international law no longer requires any nexus between crimes against humanity and armed conflict'[178] and that 'the Security Council may have defined the crime in Article 5 of the ICTY Statute more narrowly than necessary under customary international law'.[179]

The ICC Statute follows the ICTY Statute in not requiring that crimes against humanity be directed against a civilian population with a particular intent, such as 'on national, political, ethnic, racial or religious grounds', whereas the ICTR Statute does contain such a requirement. As noted above, however, the Trial Chamber in its Opinion and Judgment in the *Tadić* case in fact required such discriminatory intent for all crimes against humanity, and not just persecution.

Crimes against humanity must be carried out in a systematic and widespread manner. This is intended to exclude isolated and random acts, not linked to a policy of commission of crimes against humanity although in the *Vukovar Hospital* and *Tadić* cases before the ICTY the Trial Chamber stated that even a single act could constitute a crime against humanity if the requisite intention was present (see above).

The use of the phrase 'civilian population' makes it unclear whether persons *hors de combat* are covered by this provision, although the Decision in the *Vukovar Hospital* Rule 61 hearing indicated that soldiers who have laid down their arms are protected under IHL.[180]

The *chapeau* of Article 7 introduces an element not present in the Statutes of the ICTY or ICTR, that the individual crime against humanity be committed, 'with knowledge of the widespread and systematic attack'. During the Diplomatic Conference, this provision proved very controversial, with many delegates and

176. The *chapeau* of Art. 3 of the ICTR Statute (crimes against humanity) states that they are the following crimes, 'when committed as part of a widespread or systematic attack against any civilian population, on national, ethnic, racial or religious grounds'.

177. Art. 5 (Crimes against humanity) of the ICTY Statute provides that they are the following crimes, 'when committed in armed conflict, whether international or internal in character, and directed against the civilian population'.

178. *Supra* n. 42 at para. 78. Later in the same Decision, the Trial Chamber states that 'customary international law may not require a connection between crimes against humanity and any conflict at all'. At para. 141.

179. Ibid., at para. 141.

180. The Chamber noted that: 'Although according to the terms of Article 5 of the Statute of this Tribunal, the combatants in the traditional sense of the term cannot be victims of a crime against humanity, this does not apply to individuals who, at one particular point in time, carried out acts of resistance.' It added that this conclusion was supported by the Commission of Experts established pursuant to Security Council Resolution 780 and with certain case law, particularly the *Barbie* case. *Supra* n. 156 at para. 29.

NGOs fearing that it would 'seriously weaken the court's ability to deter and punish atrocities'.[181] The Canadian delegation, which drafted the compromise proposal on crimes against humanity, responded by saying that 'this concern had been recognised and addressed by the text. The current reference to knowledge (. . .) simply means that the *mens rea* (intention) corresponds to the *actus reus* (action) - which is the essence of a criminal act.'[182] According to the ICTY, an element of a crime against humanity is that 'the perpetrator must have knowledge of the wider context in which his act occurs'.[183]

The list of acts constituting crimes against humanity when the elements are the *chapeau* are met is more extensive in the ICC Statute than in the equivalent provisions of the ICTY and ICTR Statutes. While subparagraphs (a), (b), (c) and (f)[184] are identical to the equivalent provisions of the ICTY and ICTR Statutes, all the remaining subparagraphs introduce expanded definitions or new subcategories of crimes against humanity.[185] Article 7 also goes beyond the Statutes of the *ad hoc* Tribunals in featuring a series of explanatory paragraphs, including Article 7(1)(b) 'Extermination', which the explanatory subparagraph (2)(b) states 'includes the intentional infliction of conditions of life, *inter alia*, the deprivation of access to food and medicine, calculated to bring about the destruction of part of a population,' and a definition of 'enslavement' which states that it means the exercise of any or all of the powers attaching to the right of ownership over a person and includes the exercise of such power in the course of trafficking in persons, in particular women and children.' Definitions are also provided of 'deportation or forcible transfer of the population'; 'torture'; 'forced pregnancy'; 'persecution'; 'apartheid'; 'attack'; 'enforced disappearance of persons'; 'gender' and 'forced pregnancy'.[186]

181. In 'Canadian Compromise Proposal Seriously Criticized,' In *On the Record*, p. 1, published in *Terra Viva* during the Rome Conference, Rome, No. 15, 3 July 1998.

182. 'Crimes against Humanity Compromise,' In *On the Record*, p. 1, published in *Terra Viva* during the Rome Conference, Rome, No. 22, 14 July 1998.

183. *Tadić* Opinion and Judgment, *supra* n. 123 at para. 626.

184. (a) Murder; (b) Extermination; (c) Enslavement; and (f) Torture.

185. (d) *Deportation* or forcible transfer of population; (e) *Imprisonment* or other severe deprivation of physical liberty in violation of fundamental rules of international law; (g) rape, sexual slavery, enforced prostitution, forced pregnancy, enforced sterilization, or any other form of sexual violence of comparable gravity, (h) *Persecution* against any identifiable group or collectivity *on political, racial*, national, ethnic, cultural, *religious*, gender as defined in paragraph 3, or other groups that are universally recognized as impermissible under international law in connection with any act referred to in this paragraph or any crime within the jurisdiction of the Court; (i) Enforced disappearance of persons; (j) The crime of apartheid; (k) *Other inhumane acts* of a similar character intentionally causing great suffering, or serious injury to body or to physical or to mental or physical health. [Provisions in roman type are new; provisions in italics correspond with Articles 5 and 3 of the Statutes of the ICTY and ICTR.]

186. Art. 7(2)(d) - (i) respectively.

It is noteworthy that Article 7 considerably expands the range of acts committed against women that are now to be considered as crimes against humanity under treaty law. Whereas, the *ad hoc* Tribunals' Statutes specify only 'rape' as a crime against humanity, Article 7(1)(g) proscribes as crimes against humanity, '[r]ape, sexual slavery, enforced prostitution, forced pregnancy, enforced sterilization, or other forms of sexual violence of comparable gravity. While the codification of rape as a crime against humanity flows naturally from its inclusion in the Statutes of the *ad hoc* Tribunals, and many would argue that rape has long constituted a crime against humanity under customary international law, it is the first time that most of these other acts have been explicitly criminalised under international treaty law.

Article 8 of the Statute confers jurisdiction over *war crimes*. Unlike the Statute of the ICTY, which separates grave breaches and violations of the laws or customs of war in two separate articles, emphasising their continuing juridical distinction, the ICC Statute groups all war crimes under the general heading, 'war crimes'.

Paragraph 1 contains a troubling restriction, that is, the requirement that the Court 'shall have jurisdiction in respect of war crimes *in particular* when committed as a part of a plan or policy or as part of a large-scale commission of such crimes' [italics added]. During the Diplomatic Conference, several options were tabled regarding this provision, including that the Court should have jurisdiction *only* when war crimes were committed as part of a plan or policy or as part of a large-scale commission of such crimes, as well as a proposal that would have had this provision deleted. During a debate in the Committee of the Whole on 8 July 1998, a great majority of the delegations supported the 'in particular' option over the 'only option' or the third option to delete the provision.[187]

This jurisdictional requirement has no basis in customary or statutory international humanitarian law. Neither the Nuremberg or Tokyo Tribunal Statutes nor the *ad hoc* Tribunals required such an element. Before the adoption of the ICC Statute, the then-head of the ICRC's legal division, Toni Pfanner, stated that 'to add any further requirement to the list of war crimes would (...) not only be superfluous, but it would also risk blurring the very notion of such crimes.'[188] It is submitted that this is precisely what has happened. The inclusion of this element confuses war crimes with crimes against humanity, which are quantitatively and

187. See Daily Summary of the ICC Conference, 8 July 1998. http://www.un.org/icc/pressrel/087dsum.htm.

188. 'Establishment of a Permanent International Criminal Court,' in *IRRC* No. 322 (March 1998) p. 23.

qualitatively different, and will discourage the prosecution of isolated war crimes of whatever gravity.

Article 8 of the ICC Statute seems to be an all-inclusive provision. It prohibits, 'namely, any of the following acts'; there follow 26 subparagraphs listing the prohibited acts. It is the first time that many of these acts have been explicitly criminalised under international law, although they are prohibited under IHL. We will note just a couple here.

Article 8 explicitly criminalises not only rape but a whole range of other forms of sexual abuse[189]; the first time that many of these acts have been specifically codified as war crimes in the Statute of an International Criminal Court when committed in international armed conflicts.[190] The allusion in Article 8(2)(b)(xxii) to 'any other form of sexual violence also constituting a grave breach of the Geneva Conventions', suggests that while the ICC Statute does not itself explicitly include rape as a grave breach, it recognises that rape and other forms of sexual assault do constitute grave breaches.

Subparagraph (iii) prohibits '[i]ntentionally directing attacks against personnel, installations, material, units or vehicles involved in a humanitarian assistance or peacekeeping mission in accordance with the Charter of the United Nations, as long as they are entitled to the protection given to civilians or civilian objects under the laws of armed conflict.' The last part of the subparagraph is particularly interesting considering the current debate regarding the status of UN peacekeepers.[191] It means that if UN peacekeepers were to lose their current civilian status and become parties to the conflict, they would not only become responsible under IHL for their crimes but they would also lose the protection they enjoy as civilians and become in effect legitimate targets for the armed parties.

Paragraphs (c) and (e) give the Court jurisdiction over war crimes committed in internal armed conflicts. The inclusion of jurisdiction over such conflicts in the ICC Statute was widely supported.[192] Under paragraph (c), the Court has jurisdiction over serious violations of common Article 3. Subparagraph (d) states that Article 8(2)(c) does not apply to situations of internal disturbances or tensions, such as riots, isolated and sporadic acts of violence or other acts of a similar nature, a restriction not contained in common Article 3. Paragraph (e) gives the Court

189. Art. 8(2)(b)(xxii) prohibits, 'Committing rape, sexual slavery, enforced prostitution, forced pregnancy, as defined in Art. 8, Para. 2(f), enforced sterilization, or any other form of sexual violence also constituting a grave breach of the Geneva Conventions.

190. Although they have been prosecuted as war crimes when committed in either international or internal armed conflicts before the ICTY.

191. See *infra*, Section 8.2; see also Greenwood at p. 3 of this volume.

192. During the Committee of the Whole meeting on the Bureau Discussion Paper, 8 July 1998.

jurisdiction over 'Other serious violations of the laws and customs applicable in armed conflicts not of an international character, within the established framework of international law (. . .)'. Its 12 subparagraphs give the Court jurisdiction over a range of acts when committed in internal conflicts, most likely within a Protocol II situation. As there is no direct reference to Protocol II in the paragraph, it is not clear if the Court will apply the high threshold requirements of Protocol II, which would exclude many kinds of conflicts. This would be unfortunate considering that subparagraph (e) contains a far more elaborate list of prohibitions than subparagraph (c). Like subparagraph (b) applicable to international armed conflicts, subparagraph (e)(vii) makes the 'Conscripting or enlisting of children under the age of fifteen years into armed forces or groups or using them to participate actively in hostilities' a crime, although, as with the relevant subparagraph of Paragraph (b)(xxvi) dealing with international conflicts, it is unfortunate that the drafters could not go further and raise the age limit to 18, as well as to broaden the applicability of the provision by making clear that it also applies to non-state parties. Paragraph 8(2)(e)(iii) also criminalises attacks on peacekeepers in internal armed conflicts.[193] The implications of a change in UN peacekeepers' status under IHL, mentioned above, are also apposite here.

Subparagraph (e)(vi) prohibits 'rape, sexual slavery, enforced prostitution, forced pregnancy, as defined in article 7, paragraph 2 (f), enforced sterilization, and any other form of sexual violence also constituting a serious violation of article 3 common to the four Geneva Conventions.'

There are many serious omissions in the range of crimes prohibited in internal armed conflicts under Article 8(2)(e)(i)-(xii), but which are prohibited when committed in international armed conflicts under the Statute. There is also no reference to the use of weapons during internal armed conflicts, unlike regarding international armed conflicts.[194] While it was always unlikely that the Statute would considerably expand the scope of Protocol II, the omissions are serious considering that these are precisely the types of tactics used and crimes committed during many internal armed conflicts.

As for the elements of each of these crimes, Article 9 provides that they shall be adopted at a later date by a two-thirds majority of the Assembly of States Parties.

Under Article 11, the Court's jurisdiction is non-retroactive, so the creation of the Court will not provide a solution to the problem of massive violations of IHL committed before the entry into force of the Statute.

The question of how the Court should exercise its jurisdiction, and in particular, whether the Court should exercise automatic jurisdiction in respect of the core crimes of genocide, crimes against humanity and war crimes or whether its

193. Art. 8(2)(e)(iii).
194. In Art. 8(2)(b)(xvii)-(xx).

jurisdiction should be automatic only in the case of genocide and subject to state consent in respect of the other categories of crimes, was one of the most difficult to resolve at the ICC Conference. While the like-minded states supported the Court having automatic jurisdiction over genocide, crimes against humanity and war crimes, the US in particular was strongly opposed to the ICC having automatic jurisdiction over war crimes.

During the Conference debates on the Bureau's Discussion paper, on 8 and 9 July 1998, there was broad support for a Court with automatic jurisdiction over the core crimes of genocide, crimes against humanity and war crimes, and for some form of state consent over treaty crimes, if those crimes were to be included in the Statute (they were not). In fact, the ICC Statute gives the Court automatic jurisdiction over the core crimes, without distinguishing between genocide and the other crimes.[195]

While there was widespread support for states parties being immediately subject to the Court's jurisdiction, it was proposed that the consent of at least one of the following states be required for the court to exercise jurisdiction: the state where the crime was committed; the state with custody of the accused; the state of the suspect's citizenship; and the state of the victim's nationality - this was the so-called Korean proposal. In the end, in an attempt to persuade certain states to support the Statute, this proposal was whittled down and the Statute permits the Court to exercise its jurisdiction over all of the core crimes referred to in Article 5 (when referred either by a state or initiated by the Prosecutor) only if either the state where the act occurred or the state of nationality of the accused is a state party[196], or, in the case of a relevant third non-state party (such as one with custody of the accused), which has notified its acceptance of the exercise of jurisdiction by the Court.

The question of how the Court's jurisdiction should be triggered was contentious from beginning to end of the Conference. The American delegation was determined that cases should be referrable to the court only by states parties or the Security Council, claiming that a Prosecutor with *ex officio* powers might initiative politically-motivated or frivolous proceedings. However, there was widespread support for an independent, *ex officio* prosecutor[197], and the Statute provides for

195. Under Art. 15.

196. Under Art. 12.

197. During the meeting of the Committee of the Whole of 9 July 1998.

the initiation of an investigation by the Prosecutor *proprio motu* on the basis of information of crimes within the jurisdiction of the Court.[198] Situations can also be referred by the SC, acting under Chapter VII[199], or by a state party[200]. In order to placate states wishing to give the Security Council the power to block action by the Court, the Statute adopted the so-called 'Singapore' proposal under which the SC can block an investigation or prosecution for a renewable period of 12 months.[201] Although the Statute does not state how many times the 12-month period can be renewed, as this provision is termed 'deferral of investigation or prosecution', it is presumably not *ad infinitum*.

The Court is not intended to usurp national jurisdiction; it is intended to be complementary to it[202] and indeed to function as a spur to national prosecutions[203]. Cases are inadmissible before the ICC where they are already being investigated by a state with jurisdiction, unless the state is unable or unwilling to carry out the investigation or prosecution.[204] Where a national jurisdiction has investigated and dismissed the case, the ICC cannot assume jurisdiction, unless 'the decision resulted from the unwillingness or inability or the State genuinely to prosecute'.[205] Defendants should not be subject to double jeopardy[206], unless the national trial was designed to shield the accused from justice or was otherwise not in conformity with the norms of due process recognized by international law.[207] Article 17 also states that the Court should declare a case inadmissible where it 'is not of sufficient gravity to justify further action by the Court'.[208] This suggests that the Court will focus on particularly serious cases and may pursue a strategy of only prosecuting leaders.

198. Under Art. 15(1), further to Art. 13(c).

199. Art. 13(b). During the ICC Conference debates, some states expressed the wish that the SC should also be able to refer situations under Chapter VI, while some suggested that the SC should only be able to refer matters related to the crime of aggression. Some states were in favour of other bodies, including the UN Commission on Human Rights and the ICRC, being able to refer situations to the Court.

200. Art. 14.

201. Art. 16.

202. Art. 1 states that the court 'shall be complementary to national criminal jurisdictions'.

203. This can be seen in the Preamble of the Statute, which states, *inter alia*, 'Affirming that the most serious crimes of concern to the international community as a whole must not go unpunished and that their effective prosecution must be ensured by taking measures at the national level and by enhancing international cooperation', and 'Recalling that it is the duty of every State to exercise its criminal jurisdiction over those responsible for international crimes'.

204. Art. 17(1)(a).

205. Art. 17(1)(b).

206. Under Arts. 17(1)(c) and 20 (ne bis in idem).

207. Art. 20(3)(b).

208. Art. 17(1)(i).

Another aspect of the Statute that deserves mention are the provisions relating to compensation to victims and the efforts to incorporate consideration for victims into the Statute generally. Unlike the ICTY and the ICTR, where compensation to victims was not provided for in the Statute directly but instead was relegated to the Rules[209], the ICC Statute provides for reparations to victims and goes some considerable way beyond the Tribunals' provisions. While the ICTY is competent only to transmit a guilty verdict to the competent authorities of the state concerned, with a view to the victim then pursuing an action in his or her national courts or before other competent bodies, Article 75 enables the Court 'to establish principles relating to reparations to, or in respect of, victims, including restitution, compensation and rehabilitation'. On this basis, in its decision the Court may, either upon request or on its own motion in exceptional circumstances, determine the scope and extent of any damage, loss and injury to, or in respect or, victims and will state the principles upon which it is acting.'[210] The Court may itself make an order against a convicted person, specifying appropriate reparations to, or in respect of, victims, including restitution, compensation and rehabilitation. The Court may also order awards to be made through the Trust Fund for victims provided for in Article 79.[211] Before making awards, the Court may hear directly from victims, other interested persons or states and from the convicted person or his representatives.[212] These complement other victim-centred provisions in the Statute, such as the provision to establish a victim and witnesses unit[213], the possibility of special measures to protect victims and witnesses[214] and provisions for victims to be involved at all stages of the judicial process.

There is much in the Statute to criticise, including the transitional opt-out clause concerning war crimes, in Article 124 and some of the permitted defences, in particular, the possibility of superior orders providing a complete defence. We can only note them here, confident that these and all aspects of the Statute will generate extensive scholarship, as merits an international legal development of this importance.

209. Rule 106 ICTY Rules of Procedure and Evidence.

210. Art. 75(1) ICC Statute.

211. Ibid., Art. 75(2).

212. Ibid., Art. 75(3).

213. Provision for whose establishment is made in Art. 43(6).

214. Such as under Art. 68 (Protection of the victims and witnesses and their participation in the proceedings).

6.2 National Courts

Several states have undertaken prosecutions of both nationals and non-nationals for violations of IHL under their national legislation, in particular relating to the conflicts in the former Yugoslavia and Rwanda, but also concerning some alleged Nazi war criminals. Regarding the latter, trials were held of Karl Hass and Erich Priebke in Italy[215]; Maurice Papon in France[216]; and Aleksandras Likeikis in Lithuania. Trials in Croatia of the Croatian suspected war criminals Dinko and Esperanza Sakić, and of retired British Rail worker Andrzej Sawoniuk in England are expected over the coming months.[217] There were two extradition cases in Argentina involving Erich Priebke[218] and Dinko Sakić[219], with another one expected in the case of Mrs. Sakić. The Priebke extradition case is significant for upholding the principle that crimes against humanity are not subject to statutory limitations. This principle was also confirmed by the Military Tribunal in Rome that tried Priebke.[220]

Regarding persons accused of war crimes in the Former Yugoslavia, the Danish case has been already mentioned. A trial in Switzerland of a man accused of crimes committed in Bosnia and Herzegovina, found, contrary to the opinion of the majority in the *Tadić* case, that 'the conflict in the former Yugoslavia shall be considered and qualified globally as an international conflict'.[221] This was also the view of the courts in the *Jorgić* and *Djajić* cases in Germany.[222]

In France, in cases concerning both Rwandan and Bosnian Serb defendants, the Cour de Cassation, Criminal, found that while a French judge is competent to examine an offence committed in a foreign country, by a foreigner, if it covers facts which, under a different qualification, would come under his competence[223], a court could not exercise jurisdiction where, although the victims were present in France, the accused was not.[224] This is tantamount to saying that the court cannot justify an *in absentia* proceeding. In the USA, several relevant cases were brought by

215. Judgement of the Corte Militare di Appello of 7 March 1998, published 15 April 1998.

216. Sentence of 2 April 1998. Cour d'Assises de la Gironede, sitting at Bordeaux.

217. Information about trials in specific countries is available in Correspondents' Reports.

218. Decision of the Argentine Supreme Court on Priebke, Erich's extradition request. Case 16.063/94, 2 November 1995. Published as Priebke Erich's Extradicción. Fallos de la Corte Supreme de Justicia. Tomo 318/3, pp. 2149-2228. For commentary on this case, see Consigli at p. 341 of this volume.

219. Decision of the Federal Judge on the extradition request of Croatia in respect of Dinko *Sakić*. See Correspondents' Reports at p. 404

220. See Marchisio at p. 344 of this volume.

221. *In re G.* First Division Military Tribunal, Lausanne. Hearings held from 14 to 18 April 1997. Decision, 18 April 1997. See La Rosa and Henchoz at p. 513 of Correspondents' Report.

222. See Fischer at p. 380 of this volume.

223. *Munyeshyaka.* Cour de Cassation, crim., 6 January 1998. Reprinted at p. 598.

224. *Javor* e.a. Cour de Cassation, crim. 26 Mars 1996.

victims under the Alien Tort Crimes Act and Torture Victims Protection Act, as noted in Correspondents' Reports.

There was other interesting case law, not involving prosecutions. In Hungary, a Decision of the Constitutional Court on the direct applicability of the Geneva Conventions found that the Geneva Conventions were self-executing in Hungary, and that persons accused of war crimes and crimes against humanity during the totalitarian regimes could be prosecuted and punished by the state based on international law as contained in the Geneva Conventions.[225]

In Slovenia, a decision of the Slovene Supreme Court in the case of 'the Stolen Children' was pending at the time of writing. The Stolen Children is the name given to the group of 250 plaintiffs from eastern Slovenia who were taken away from their parents during the Second World War while they were still children because they were recognised as Ayran. Their parents were later executed. The plaintiffs brought an action against Germany in Celje, the city where the crime was committed. However, Germany contests the competence of the Slovene courts, *acta iure imperii.* [226]

In Colombia, the Constitutional Court issued an important judgement which examined the scope and application of Protocol II[227], following its earlier scrutiny of Additional Protocol I[228]. This judgment confirms, *inter alia*, that minimum standards of humanity apply to all persons fighting in conflicts, including irregulars, and that the legal obligation to respect IHL does not depend on reciprocal treatment.

In several states, prosecutions were undertaken of persons who had served in UN peacekeeping missions in Somalia and Rwanda. These are noted below in section 8.2.

225. Alkotmánybíróság 36/1996 (IX.4.) AB határozata (Magyar Közlöny:1996/75 pp. 4673-4675). Decision n°36/1996 (IX.4) AB of the Constitutional Court (*Official Journal*:1996/75 pp. 4673-4675). For commentary see Kovács in Correspondents' Reports at p. 451

226. From a letter dated 15/4/98 to the author from Aleš Rojs, attorney at law, in the law firm of Odvetniška Pisarna of Ljubljana, which is representing the 'Stolen Children'. In the files of the author.

227. Judgement of Constitutional Court of 18 May 1995. Sentencia No. C-225, Revisión constitucional del 'Protocolo adicional a los conflictos armados sin carácter internacional (Protocolo II)'. Unpublished. For commentary on this case see Kalshoven at p. 262 of this volume.

228. Judgement of Constitutional Court of 29 October 1992. Sentencia No. C-574/92, Revisión oficiosa del Protocolo Adicional a los Convenios de Ginebra del 12 de agosto de 1949, relativo a la protección de las víctimas de los conflictos armados internacionales (Protocol I)

7. IMPLEMENTATION

7.1 Implementation by States

Over the past few years, several states have taken measures to implement IHL at various levels. In terms of implementing treaty law, in 1995 Britain introduced the Geneva Conventions (Amendment) Act, amending the Geneva Conventions Act of 1957 to enable effect to be given to the Additional Protocols of 1977. Several reservations and declarations were made by the UK in respect of the Protocol[229], including that it was the UK's understanding that the rules contained in Protocol I apply only to conventional weapons and do not regulate or prohibit nuclear weapons, and that the UK reserves for itself the right of reprisals if attacks were to be made against the civilian population or civilian objects.[230]

The USA's War Crimes and Expanded War Crimes Acts have been noted, as has the Belgian law of 1993. In 1996, Zimbabwe introduced the Geneva Conventions Amendment Act 1996, incorporating the Additional Protocols into Zimbabwean law.[231]

On 1 November 1995, Argentina approved the Convention on the Imprescriptibility of War Crimes and Crimes against Humanity, and on 23 November, the President promulgated the law.[232]

During the reporting period, several states adopted legislation to implement the Chemical Weapons Convention; the Landmines Convention; amended Protocol II of the CCW Convention on Landmines; Protocol IV on Blinding Laser Weapons; and the Safety Convention including *inter alia*: Chemical Weapons Convention - Argentina, Austria, Ireland, Italy, and Switzerland; Landmines - Argentina, Austria, Germany, Italy, Switzerland and the UK; Blinding Laser Weapons - Argentina, Austria, Germany and Switzerland; and the Safety Convention - the UK and Germany.

Several states adopted legislation to cooperate with the International Criminal Tribunals, including Australia, Austria, Belgium, Croatia, Denmark, Finland, Hungary, Iceland, Italy, the Netherlands, New Zealand, Norway, Sweden, Switzerland, the United Kingdom and the United States.[233]

229. Which are set out in the Geneva Conventions Act (First Protocol) Order 1998, 1998 *Statutory Instruments* No. 1754. Reprinted at p. 640 of this volume.

230. See also Written Answers, 28 January 1998, Hansard, p. 270.

231. Details about these laws can be found in the section Correspondents' Reports. For comment on the Zimbabwean law, see Dutli at pp. 254-257 of this volume.

232. Law concerning the imprescriptibility of war crimes and crimes against humanity, adopted 1 November 1995, promulgated 23 November 1995. Published in the *Boletín Oficial de la República Argentina*, 29 November 1995.

233. For an analysis for implementing legislation to cooperate with the ICTY, see Josipović at p. 35 of this volume.

Several states have revised their penal codes to include war crimes and crimes against humanity, including Finland, Nicaragua, Paraguay, Peru, Rwanda, Slovenia, and Spain. The Military Criminal Code that was introduced to Greece in 1995 implements Greece's obligations *vis-à-vis* the Third Geneva Convention concerning prisoners of war.[234]

Some states adopted legislation to protect the emblem and to promote cooperation with the ICRC, including Armenia, Cameroon and Georgia.

In addition, several states established national commissions or committees to explore the implementation and application of IHL, including Albania, Argentina, Belarus, Cambodia, Colombia, Côte d'Ivoire, Dominican Republic, El Salvador, Ethiopia, France, Latvia, Lithuania, Moldova, Namibia, Panama, Paraguay, Portugal, Senegal, South Africa, Sweden, Togo, Uruguay and Zimbabwe. Information about these and other developments concerning implementation measures at the level of states can be found in Correspondents' Reports.

8. INTERNATIONAL ORGANISATIONS AND INTERNATIONAL ACTIONS

8.1 United Nations Organisation

The United Nations Security Council has taken note of and called for a cessation of IHL violations in several ongoing conflicts. In other cases, it has condemned violence by the parties to the conflict without alluding directly to IHL. Below we mention just the most recent.

The conflict in Kosovo was first addressed by the UN SC in its resolution 1160 (1998) of 31 March 1998, in which, acting under Chapter VII of the UN Charter, it imposed an arms embargo on the FRY, condemned the use of excess force against civilians by the Serbian police force and acts of terrorism by the Kosovo Liberation Army, called on the parties to seek a peaceful solution through dialogue, confirmed the territorial integrity of the FRY, and urged the Prosecutor of the ICTY to begin gathering information related to the violence in Kosovo. No reference was made to possible IHL violations.

However, on 24 August 1998, the President of the UNSC issued a resolution expressing his concern over reports of 'increasing violations of international humanitarian law in Kosovo', and called for an immediate ceasefire. It stated that the fighting in Kosovo has had a 'devastating impact on the civilian population and greatly increased the numbers of refugees and displaced persons'.[235]

234. See Correspondents' Reports at p. 445 and p. 535 of the Documents section

235. S/PRST/1998/25, 24 August 1998.

In response to the continuing violence and reported atrocities in Kosovo, on 23 September 1998 the SC issued another resolution on Kosovo, acting under Chapter VII of the UN Charter. Resolution 1199 (1998) notes, *inter alia*, that the Prosecutor of the ICTY has indicated that the conflict in Kosovo represents an armed conflict within the terms of the Tribunal's mandate, and expresses concern that increasing violations of IHL have been reported. This was followed by Resolution 1203 on 24 October 1998.

Concerning the conflict in Afghanistan, in its resolution 1193 (1998) of 28 August 1998, the UN SC, *inter alia*, noted and condemned former interference and supply of personnel and *materiel* to all parties to the conflict and called for an end to IHL violations, without naming the party or parties responsible for such violations. In this resolution, three separate references were made to IHL, including a reaffirmation that 'all parties to the conflict are bound to comply with their obligations under international humanitarian law and in particular the Geneva Conventions of 12 August 1949, and that persons who commit or order the commission of grave breaches of the Conventions are individually responsible in respect of such breaches'. An earlier SC resolution concerning Afghanistan of 22 October 1996 made no direct reference to possible breaches of IHL, although it also noted the interference by third parties in the conflict.[236]

Concerning the conflict in the Great Lakes region of Central Africa, the Security Council issued a resolution on 18 February 1997, 'underlining the obligation of all concerned to respect strictly the relevant provisions of international humanitarian law'.[237] Earlier, the SC issued resolution 1080 on 15 November 1996 in which it underlined the obligations of all parties involved in conflicts in the Great Lakes region, particularly Zaire, to respect the relevant provisions of IHL. And in a resolution concerning the conflict in Burundi, the SC noted that all persons who commit or authorize the commission of serious violations of IHL are individually responsible and should be held accountable.[238]

Finally, with regard to the conflict in Sierra Leone, the UN SC, by its resolution 1181 of 13 June 1998, established the United Nations Observer Mission in Sierra Leone (UNOMSIL) with the task of assisting in monitoring respect for IHL, including at disarmament and demobilizations sites, and reporting on IHL violations, *inter alia*. The resolution also demanded that all parties to the conflict in Sierra Leone respect the applicable rules of IHL.

236. S/RES/1076 (1996).
237. S/RES/1097 (1997).
238. S/RES/1072 (1996), 30 August 1996.

8.2 Peacekeeping and Peace Enforcement

The rights and responsibilities of peacekeepers and peace enforcers serving in UN and other international forces has attracted considerable attention over the past few years, as peacekeepers/enforcers are deployed to ever more conflict zones and are increasingly drawn into battle. Currently, peacekeepers and peace enforcers are generally considered to be non-combatants, enjoying the protection of civilians under the Geneva Conventions and Additional Protocols. The protection owing to peacekeepers was enhanced by the 1994 Convention on Safety of UN and Associated Personnel[239], which had 43 signatories and 20 states parties as of September 1998[240], and which has thus not yet entered into force.

However, many commentators believe that IHL can apply to international forces, either of a peacekeeping or peace-enforcing mandate, where they become engaged in combat.[241] However, it is recognized that UN forces involved in peace-enforcement missions are more likely to be drawn into combat situations. It has been suggested that when international forces commit violations of IHL, they could be held responsible under international law.[242]

The question of whether international forces can be held accountable under international law for violations of IHL was considered recently in a couple of cases[243] and in reports issued by committees of enquiry established by several states to investigate allegations of IHL violations committed by their nationals while engaged in UN peacekeeping missions abroad[244]. Without exception, these reports and cases concluded that their national law, not IHL, governs peacekeepers, even when they are serving abroad as part of an international peacekeeping mission, and further, that peacekeepers are not generally to be considered as combatants.[245]

239. Doc. A/49/742 of 2 December 1994. Adopted by the GA on 9 December 1994.

240. Source: ICRC IHL Treaty Database.

241. See Greenwood at p. 3 of this volume; Daphna Shraga, 'The United Nations as an Actor Bound by International Humanitarian Law', 5 *International Peacekeeping* (1998) p. 64; and Paolo Benvenuti, 'The Implementation of International Humanitarian Law in the Framework of United Nations Peace-keeping', in *Law in Humanitarian Crises, supra* n. 2 at p. 83.

242. See, for example, the Simpson study discussed *infra* at p. 365 et seq.

243. Including, De Zaak *Marchal*, Military Court of Belgium, 4 July 1996. For commentary see Cogen in: Correspondents' Reports at p. 413 of this volume.

244. Canada, Belgium and Italy have all issued reports further to national enquiries, and France is currently undertaking an enquiry into the role of its peacekeepers in Rwanda. For details, see under the respective countries in the section Correspondents' Reports.

245. See Judgement of the Belgian Military Court regarding violations of IHL committed in Somalia and Rwanda, Nr. 54 A.R. 1997, 20 November 1997. For commentary, see Cogen in Correspondents' Reports at p. 415; see also *R.* v. *Brocklebank*, Court Martial Appeal Court of Canada, 2 April 1996, Case File No. CMAC-383. Published in 106 *Canadian Criminal Cases* (rd) at p. 234. For commentary see Boustany at p. 371.

The United Nations has long acknowledged that its forces should observe the spirit and basic principle of IHL, although it is unclear whether this amounts to a legal duty or a voluntary undertaking. The greatly increased involvement of UN forces in varying capacities during armed conflicts makes a clarification of the status of these forces all the more urgent.

The UN, with the assistance of the ICRC, is currently attempting to address some of this uncertainty, and has drawn up draft directives for UN forces regarding respect for IHL. These draft directives, which had not been adopted by the GA as of October 1998, address only situations where UN forces are engaged in situations of armed conflicts as combatants, and therefore they do not help to elucidate the rights and responsibilities of forces engaged in peacekeeping missions where the international forces are not drawn into conflict. Moreover, as directives, they shall not be legally binding. However, they will have the merit of clarifying that at least the core principles of IHL apply to UN forces when they are engaged in combat operations.[246]

246. Greenwood discusses the draft directives at p. 29 of this volume.

THE END OF A CULTURE OF IMPUNITY IN RWANDA?
Prosecution of Genocide and War Crimes before Rwandan Courts and the International Criminal Tribunal for Rwanda*

Catherine Cissé**

1. INTRODUCTION

Following the death of Rwandan President Juvénal Habyarimana in a plane crash on 6 April 1994[1], Hutu extremists, members of the Presidential Guard, Rwandan army troops, the *Interhamwe* ('Those who work together') militia affiliated to the ruling party, the M.R.N.D. (Mouvement Révolutionaire National pour la Démocratie) and the *Impuzamugambi* ('Those with a single purpose') militia of the extremist CDR Party (Coalition pour la Défense de la République) began the systematic and widespread killings of Tutsi civilians in the capital Kigali. Hutu moderates were also targeted. Early victims of the violence included Prime Minister Agathe Uwilingiyimana along with ten Belgian soldiers of the United Nations Assistance Mission for Rwanda (UNAMIR). This incident prompted the withdrawal of UNAMIR which left the perpetrators of the genocide a free rein. Ministers and the President of the Constitutional Court were also killed within hours of the plane crash.

** Legal Officer, Office of the Prosecutor, International Criminal Tribunal for Rwanda (ICTR). The views expressed herein are solely those of the author and do not necessarily represent those of the ICTR or the United Nations (UN).

1. President Habyarimana and the President of Burundi, Cyprien Ntaryamira, were returning to Kigali from a regional meeting in Dar es Salaam on peace and security in Rwanda and Burundi when their plane was hit by a rocket. See *The United Nations and Rwanda, 1993-1996* (The United Nations Blue Book Series), Introduction by Boutros Boutros-Ghali (United Nations Department of Public Information, New York 1996) p. 37.

Yearbook of International Humanitarian Law
Volume 1 - 1998 - pp. 161-188

The bloodshed spread quickly throughout the whole country. Within 100 days, the genocide against the Tutsi group[2] and the massacres directed against Hutu moderates resulted in the deaths of an estimated 500,000 to 1 million people.[3] The magnitude and speed with which the massacres were carried out demonstrate that they were planned and organized.

This orchestrated campaign of violence was reinforced by the active role played by government-controlled media such as Radio Rwanda, and above all by Radio Milles Collines, a private radio station allied to the ruling class. Both radio stations broadcast a campaign of incitement to exterminate Tutsis.[4]

By 4 July 1994, however, the Rwandan Patriotic Front (RPF)[5] had captured Kigali, and by 18 July it controlled the entire country and declared a unilateral ceasefire. The RPF established political control on 19 July with the installation of a Government of National Unity.[6]

It appears increasingly obvious that the international community could have prevented or stopped the genocide in Rwanda.[7] It was within the context of a

2. In the Judgement in the case of *Prosecutor* v. *Akayesu*, the Trial Chamber concluded that 'the Tutsis were targeted and killed because of their Tutsi origin'. Case No. ICTR-96-4-T, Judgement of 2 September 1998 at paras. 123-126.

3. For various estimates, see 'Report on the situation of human rights in Rwanda' submitted by René Dégni Ségui, Special Rapporteur of the Commission on Human Rights, under para. 20 of Commission Resolution S-3/1 of 25 May 1994, UN Doc. E/CN.4/1995/7 (1994), 28 June 1994; Final report of the Commission of Experts established pursuant to SC Res. 935 (1994) at para. 57, reproduced in *The UN and Rwanda, supra* n. 1, Doc. 107, p. 415 at 421.

4. See UN Doc. E/CN.4/1995/7, 28 June 1994, para. 26; Final Report of the Commission of Experts, at para. 64. See also Jean Kambanda's guilty plea, case No. ICTR-23-I.

5. The RPF was founded in Kampala, Uganda in 1988 as a political and military movement 'with the stated aims of securing the repatriation of Rwandans in exile and the reform of the Government in Rwanda, including political power-sharing'. Most RPF members were Tutsi refugees, and many had previously served in Ugandan President Yoweri Museveni's National Resistance Army. See *The UN and Rwanda, supra* n. 1, Introduction at p. 12.

6. *The UN and Rwanda, supra* n. 1 at p. 57.

7. Report of the Secretary-General on the situation in Rwanda to the Security Council, reporting on the political mission he sent to Rwanda to move the warring parties towards a ceasefire and recommending that the expanded mandate for UNAMIR be authorized for an initial period of six months. S/1994/640 (1994), 31 May 1994 at para. 43, where he states that the international community 'failed in our response to the agony of Rwanda, and thus have acquiesced in the continued loss of human lives. Our readiness and capacity for action has been demonstrated to be inadequate at best, and deplorable at worst, owing to the absence of the collective political will'. Reproduced in *The UN and Rwanda, supra* n. 1, Document 64, p. 290 at p. 297. See also the conclusions of the report of the Commission of Inquiry on Rwanda of the Belgian Senate, *Commission d'enquête parlementaire concernant les evenements du Rwanda: Rapport fait au nom de la Commission d'enquête par MM. Mahoux et Verhofstadt*. Belgian Senate. Sesssion de 1997-1998. 6 décembre 1997. The former Commander of UNAMIR, General Romeo Dallaire, said in his testimony before the ICTR in the trial of Jean Paul Akayesu that 'the force could have played a

collective feeling of guilt that the United Nations Security Council, acting under powers conferred by Chapter VII of the United Nations Charter[8], on 8 November 1994 established an International Criminal Tribunal for Rwanda to prosecute the persons responsible for the acts of genocide and other serious violations of international humanitarian law (IHL) committed in Rwanda during 1994.[9]

In response to a formal request of the government of Rwanda in September 1994[10], the Tribunal was established. Rwanda invoked four main reasons in support of its establishment: First, 'the genocide committed in Rwanda is a crime against mankind and should be suppressed by the international community as a whole.'[11] Second, international prosecutions would avoid any 'suspicion of its wanting to organise speedy or vengeful justice'. Third, the establishment of the ICTR by the Security Council under Chapter VII of the United Nations Charter would offer the advantage of creating obligations binding on all states, including Rwanda itself, which eventually voted against Resolution 955.[12] It argued that

---

more effective role with adequate equipment and training'. ICTR Press Release, ICTR/INFO-9-2-107, 25 February 1998.

8. The legal basis of the ICTR was unsuccessfully challenged in the case *Prosecutor* v. *Joseph Kanyabashi*, Case No. ICTR-96-15-T, Trial Chamber, Decision on Defence motion on jurisdiction, 28 June 1997. That case and the legal basis of the ICTR generally are discussed in Virginia Morris & Michael P. Scharf, *The International Criminal Tribunal for Rwanda* (Irvington-on-Hudson, New York 1998) Vol. I, pp. 75-115.

9. Eighteen months after the creation by the Security Council of the International Criminal Tribunal for the Former Yugoslavia to prosecute the atrocities committed in the former Yugoslavia (by SC RES/827(1993)), the Council decided to establish a second *ad hoc* Tribunal as an enforcement measure to restore international peace and security, with the mandate to prosecute 'persons responsible for genocide and other serious violations of international humanitarian law committed in the territory of Rwanda and Rwandan citizens responsible for genocide and other such violations committed in the territory of neighbouring States, between 1 January 1994 and 31 December 1994'. Art. 1, Statute of the ICTR, UN Doc. S/RES/955 (1994), in *The UN and Rwanda, supra* n. 1, p. 387. The seat of the ICTR was not indicated in its Statute, the preamble of which states, at para. 6, that the seat would be determined by the SC at a later date, having regard to considerations of justice and fairness, as well as administrative efficiency, *inter alia*. By SC Res. 977 (1995), 22 February 1995, the SC named Arusha, Tanzania as the seat of the Tribunal. In *The UN and Rwanda, supra* n. 1, Document 119 at p. 470.

10. Letter dated 28 September 1994 from the Permanent Representative of Rwanda to the United Nations addressed to the President of the Security Council, transmitting a statement dated 28 September 1994 of the Government of Rwanda on the establishment of an International Tribunal for the prosecution of persons responsible for genocide and other serious violations of international humanitarian law in relation to Rwanda, UN SCOR, 49th Session, UN Doc. S/1994/1115 (1994).

11. S/PV.3453 at p. 14.

12. The government of Rwanda voted against Resolution 955 for the following main reasons: First, Rwanda felt that the ICTR's temporal jurisdiction, which covers the period 1 January to 31 December 1994, was inadequate. It believed that the Tribunal's temporal jurisdiction should extend as far back as 1 October 1990, which it said marked the beginning of the current hostilities, thus

the ICTR is, in particular, an effective instrument to arrest and transfer to the seat of the Tribunal the leaders of the genocide who fled Rwanda in July 1994. It appeared unlikely that the main perpetrators, especially those who had held leadership positions during the massacres and who had left Rwanda, would be extradited back to Rwanda, as many national legal systems prohibit extradition to countries like Rwanda which employ the death penalty. Conversely, the compelling obligation of states to cooperate with the Tribunal is underscored in Article 28[13] of the ICTR Statute, which requires member states of the United Nations to 'comply without undue delay with any request for ... the surrender or transfer of the accused to the International Tribunal for Rwanda'.[14] Fourth, the creation of an International Tribunal would help to achieve a sense of justice necessary for reconciliation and would be an effective deterrent against the perpetration of atrocities.

Despite this call for international justice, the government of Rwanda has always made clear that it would also try persons responsible for genocide before its

---

capturing the planning of the genocide. Second, Rwanda objected to the absence of a provision for capital punishment in the Statute of the ICTR, claiming that this, taken with its provision in the Rwandan penal code, would create the paradoxical effect that the leadership who planned the genocide and who would most likely be tried before the ICTR would face a maximum of life imprisonment whereas low-ranking perpetrators would be subject to the death penalty if tried before Rwandese courts, giving the impression that the main persons responsible for the genocide and who fled the country would receive better treatment than the 'second class planners' who stayed in Rwanda. The Rwandan delegate concluded that such a situation would not be conducive to national reconciliation. Third, the government of Rwanda stressed that the ICTR should be a separate entity, with its own Appeals Chamber and Prosecutor, and not a twin of the ICTY. Fourth, Rwanda argued that the ICTR should only prosecute genocide and crimes against humanity as prosecution of violations of common Art. 3 and Protocol II 'would disperse its energy'. Fifth, Rwanda deplored that persons sentenced by the Tribunal could be imprisoned in third countries. More importantly, Rwanda argued strongly that decisions concerning the pardon and commutation of detainees could not belong to third states. Sixth, the Rwandan delegate to the UN stressed that the seat of the ICTR ought to be in Rwanda, in order to play a preventative and educative role. See Statement of the Permanent Representative of Rwanda following the voting, UNSCOR, 49th session, 3453rd mtg., UN Doc. S/PV.3453 (1994).

13. Art. 28(2)(e).

14. Except in one case, all states have complied with ICTR requests for arrest and transfer of accused. The decision of a US district court judge not to surrender Pastor Elizaphan Ntakirutimana (indicted in ICTR-96-17-I) to the ICTR detention center in Arusha is the only precedent of non-compliance with Resolution 955. See In re *Elizaphan Ntakirutimana,* US District Court for the Southern District of Texas, Laredo Division, 1997 US Dist. LEXIS 20714, 17 December 1997. This decision is reproduced *infra* at p. 607. For commentary on this case see Paust, *infra* p. 205. The US government refiled its request for surrender seeking review by a different judge on 29 January 1998. On 5 August 1998, a Federal Judge ordered the deportation of Elizaphan Ntakirutimana to Arusha. US District Court for the Southern District of Texas, Laredo Division.

national courts.[15] It is noteworthy that the preamble of Security Council Resolution 955 stressed that international cooperation was necessary to strengthen the Rwandese judicial system given the large number of persons to be tried before Rwandan courts. The recognition by the Security Council of the competence of the national jurisdiction of Rwanda to try persons responsible for the genocide delineates the role of the ICTR in relation to domestic courts. Although the Statute provides that the ICTR has primacy over national jurisdictions, it seems that the Tribunal is regarded by the Security Council as a complementary institution to the Rwandese national judicial system and not as a substitute.[16] However, the international community has also recognised the incapacity of Rwandese judicial institutions to prosecute the large number of persons involved in the massacres without the rehabilitation, even the complete reconstruction, of the national judicial system.[17] Aware that this challenging task will be a lengthy process, in February 1995 the Security Council passed a Resolution urging states to arrest and detain, in accordance with their national laws, accused persons pending their prosecution by the ICTR or by the appropriate national authorities.[18]

This article examines the dual prosecution of the genocide in Rwanda by the ICTR and by Rwandan courts. Part 2 provides an overview of the ICTR's subject matter jurisdiction, structure and organisation and briefly reviews its judicial activities. Part 3 looks at the Rwandan legal system and its efforts to rebuild after being devastated by the genocide. It also describes the legislation adopted by Rwanda to prosecute the *génocidaires* and the difficulties it faces in this task.

15. *Rwanda promises fair trials for massacre suspects*, Reuters World Service, 9 August 1994, LEXIS, News library, Curnws file. Rwanda must, of course, respect the principle of *non-bis-in-idem*, as stated in Art. 9 of the ICTR Statute.

16. China stated that 'the establishment of an international tribunal for the prosecution of those who are responsible for crimes that gravely violate international humanitarian law is a special measure taken by the international community to handle certain special problems. It is only a supplement to domestic criminal jurisdiction and the current exercise of universal jurisdiction over certain international crimes.' UN SCOR, 49th session, 3453rd mtg. at 11, UN Doc. S/PV. 3453(1994).

17. See for example 'Letter dated 29 August 1995 from the Secretary-General to the President of the Security Council outlining an approach to improve prison conditions in Rwanda and to help strengthen the justice system,' S/1995/762, 31 August 1995, in *The UN and Rwanda, supra* n. 1, Document 145 and 'Report of the Secretary-General to the General Assembly on emergency international assistance for a solution to the problem of refugees, the restoration of total peace, reconstruction and socio-economic development in Rwanda,' A/50/654, 19 October 1995, in *The UN and Rwanda, supra* n. 1, Document 152 at p. 551.

18. Res. 978 (1995) UN SCOR, 50th session, UN Doc. S/PV.3453 (1994). In *The UN and Rwanda, supra,* n. 1, Document 120 at p. 471.

Finally, Part 4 considers the relationship between these two national and international pillars of justice.

2. OVERVIEW OF THE ICTR'S SUBJECT MATTER JURISDICTION, STRUCTURE, ORGANISATION AND JUDICIAL ACTIVITIES

Despite a few differences, the ICTR's Statute and Rules of Procedure and Evidence are largely inspired by those of the ICTY.[19] However, the fact that Rwanda requested the creation of the Tribunal and was a member of the Security Council at the time of the adoption of the ICTR Statute[20] also influenced the substance of the Statute. The Statute is thus a product of the compromise between Rwanda's conditions and the position of other members of the Security Council on some fundamental issues such as capital punishment and the serving of sentences.

Under Articles 2 to 4 of the Statute, the ICTR has jurisdiction over three categories of crimes: genocide, crimes against humanity and violations of Article 3 common to the 1949 Geneva Conventions and of Additional Protocol II.[21]

The definition of genocide in Article 2 is a verbatim of Articles 2 and 3 of the 1948 Convention on the prevention and punishment of the crime of genocide.[22] In contrast to the ICTY, most of the indictments confirmed by the Tribunal for Rwanda include genocide charges[23], reflecting the widespread feeling that the situation in Rwanda was first and foremost a genocide. Journalists and shareholders of Radio Milles Collines have been charged with direct and public incitement to commit genocide and conspiracy to commit genocide.

19. For an overview of the ICTR and its Statute and Rules, see Daphna Shraga & Ralph Zacklin, 'The International Criminal Tribunal for Rwanda', 7 *European Journal of International Law* (1996) No 4, pp. 501-517 and Morris & Scharf, op. cit. n. 8; Roy S. Lee, 'The Rwanda Tribunal', 9 *Leiden Journal of International Law* (1996) pp. 37-61.

20. Rwanda became a non-permanent member of the Security Council, for two years, on 1 January 1994. *The UN and Rwanda*, *supra* n. 1 at p. 117.

21. See Lee, op. cit. n. 19; Catherine Cissé, 'The International Tribunals for the former Yugoslavia and Rwanda: Some elements of comparison', 7 *Transnational Law & Contemporary Problems* (Spring 1997) pp. 104-117.

22. 78 UNTS 277 (1951).

23. Including the following indictments: Clément Kayishema and Obed Ruzindana, ICTR-95-1-I; Georges Anderson Nderubumwe Rutaganda, ICTR-96-3-I; Jean Paul Akayesu, ICTR-96-4-I; Théoneste Bagosora ICTR-96-7-I; Elie Ndayambaje, ICTR-96-8-I; Ladislas Ntaganzwa, 21 June 1996; Elizaphan Ntakirutimana, Gérard Ntakirutimana, Obed Ruzindana and Charles Sikubwabo, ICTR-96-10-I; André Ntagerura, ICTR-96-10-I; Ferdinand Nahimana, ICTR-11-I; Anatole Nsengiyumva, ICTR-96-12-I; Alfred Musema, ICTR-96-13-I; Eliezer Niyitegeka, ICTR-96-14-I; Joseph Kanyabashi, ICTR-96-15-I.

Crimes against humanity are defined in Article 3 of the Statute.[24] Unlike the ICTY Statute, the ICTR Statute does not require that crimes against humanity be committed during an armed conflict. In contrast to the ICTY Statute, which does not require that act be committed on discriminatory grounds, Article 3 of the ICTR Statute requires that the crimes be committed 'as part of a widespread or systematic attack against any civilian population on national, political, ethnic, racial or religious grounds'.

Article 4 criminalises violations of common Article 3 of the 1949 Geneva Conventions and of Additional Protocol II although these norms have not yet been universally recognised as part of customary international law.[25] By adopting provisions which are exclusively applicable to non-international armed conflicts, the Security Council clearly expanded the boundaries of existing law. The decision on jurisdiction of the ICTY Appeals Chamber in the *Tadić* case, however, explicitly accepted the criminalisation of common Article 3.[26]

The Statute and the Rules of the ICTR are governed by high standards of international criminal justice. Both reflect the international norms on fair trial and due process, in particular those provided under Article 14 of the International Covenant on Civil and Political Rights (ICCPR). Trials *in absentia* are not allowed, although they are permitted under Rwandese legislation.

Unlike Rwandan criminal justice, which is based on the inquisitorial approach of the Civil Law system, the ICTR Statute and Rules are largely based on the

24. Art. 3 states: 'The International Tribunal for Rwanda shall have the power to prosecute persons responsible for the following crimes when committed as part of a widespread or systematic attack against any civilian population on national, political, ethnical, racial or religious grounds: a) murder; b) extermination; c) enslavement; d) deportation; e) imprisonment; f) torture; g) rape; h) persecutions on political, racial and religious grounds; i) other inhumane acts.'

25. See report of the Secretary-General on the Statute of the ICTY, which enumerated those parts of IHL that without a doubt constitute customary international law: the Geneva Conventions; Hague IV and Regulations; the Genocide Convention and the IMT Charter. (S/25704, at p. 9, para. 34). Based on this statement, common Art. 3 of the Geneva Conventions, but not necessarily the two additional Protocols thereto, would form part of customary international law. See also report of the Secretary General pursuant to para. 5 of SC Res. 955 (1994) at p. 2 para. 12 (S/1995/134) which states that 'the Security Council has elected to take a more expansive approach to the choice of the applicable law than the one underlying the statute of the Yugoslav Tribunal, and included within the subject matter jurisdiction of the Rwanda Tribunal international instruments regardless of whether they were considered part of customary international law or whether they have customarily entailed the individual criminal responsibility of the perpetrator of the crime'; See also Theodor Meron, 'International criminalization of internal atrocities', 89 *AJIL* (1995) p. 554; in *Prosecutor* v. *Akayesu*, *supra* n. 2, the Trial Chamber found that under customary international law, breaches of common Art. 3 and Art. 4 of Additional Protocol II entail criminal responsibility for the perpetrator. At paras. 604-610.

26. ICTY Case No. IT-94-1 AR 72. 2 October 1995, at paras. 128-137.

adversarial approach of the Common Law system. However, some elements of the civil law approach can be found in the Rules; for instance, under Rule 85, the Trial Chamber can order the presentation of evidence. The provisions on review proceedings of Article 25 of the Statute and the corresponding Rule 120 are clearly inspired by the Civil Law system. At their last plenary session[27], the Judges, in order to speed up cases before the Tribunal, adopted major amendments allowing them to be more directly involved in controlling the proceedings. The amendments include having pre-trial status conferences which the Judges may order to shorten the examination-in-chief of some witnesses and reduce the number of witnesses.[28]

The Prosecutor and the Defense are on an equal footing, while the Rules (Rule 66) have placed a greater burden of pre-trial disclosure of evidence on the Prosecutor. However, the Trial Chambers have increasingly taken the position that the disclosure obligation applies to the two parties. In the *Akayesu* case, the Trial Chamber ordered the Prosecutor to submit 'all written statements already made available by her to the defence counsel in this case', while stating that such disclosure would not necessarily entail their admissibility as evidence. But at the same time, the Trial Chamber ordered that 'all such statements to which reference has been made by either the Prosecutor or the Defence shall be admitted as evidence and form part of the record.'[29]

The Statute and Rules place special emphasis on the protection of victims and witnesses. The Statute (Art. 21) provides for specific measures such as the conduct of *in camera* proceedings and the protection of the victim's identity. Under the Rules, the Trial Chamber can grant various types of protective measures, including confidentiality, visual distortion of facial image, anonymity, safe conduct and testimony by videolink. The judicial power to provide protection for victims and witnesses has certainly secured the testimony of many witnesses who would otherwise have been reluctant to give evidence in public and open hearings.[30] The giving of testimony by video conference link might be envisaged especially for certain witnesses whose temporary transfer to Arusha from Rwanda would prove particularly traumatic, such as victims of rape and other very vulnerable survivors of the genocide. Video conferencing would also help to

27. Fifth plenary session, 18 June 1998.

28. Rules of Procedure and Evidence adopted on 29 June 1995, as amended on 8 June 1998.

29. *Akayesu* case, ICTR 96-4-T, Decision by the Tribunal on its request to the Prosecutor to submit the written statements, 28 January 1997. The ICTY has taken a similarly broad approach to the disclosure obligations. See for e.g., the *Dokmanović* case, IT-95-13a-PT, written order, 28 November 1997.

30. See for e.g., *The Prosecutor* v. *Rutaganda*, Case No. ITCR-96-3-T, Decision on protective measures for Defence witnesses, 30 June 1998.

avoid an economic disruption for witnesses who cannot afford to leave their farms or shops for several days.

The Statute provides that the determination of a sentence is based on the general practice of the national courts of Rwanda with respect to prison sentences. However, the maximum sentence which the ICTR can hand down is life imprisonment, in contrast with Rwandan law which provides for the death penalty.[31]

The government of Rwanda explained that the exclusion of the death penalty in the Statute was one of the main reasons for its voting against resolution 955 establishing the ICTR. It stated that this disparity in sentencing 'raises serious questions concerning the equality of justice with respect to the crimes committed in Rwanda'.[32] The Statute (Art. 26) provides that the sentences will be served in Rwanda or the state designated by the Tribunal.

In terms of its structure and composition, the ICTR is a separate entity from the ICTY, with its own Trial Judges and Registry and its own seat in Arusha, Tanzania. However, for the sake of consistency, it shares its Chief Prosecutor and Appeals Chamber with the ICTY, both of which are based in the Hague. The Deputy Chief Prosecutor is based with the rest of the Office of the Prosecutor (OTP) in Kigali.

To date, the ICTR has achieved significant results, in particular, the giving of two major decisions – the Judgement in the case of Jean Paul Akayesu and the sentencing of Jean Kambanda. Despite early serious administrative and policy problems[33] and the difficulties of protecting witnesses, 35 persons have been accused in 22 indictments. Twenty-seven accused have been arrested, of whom 26 are in custody in Arusha.[34] The remaining accused is in the USA awaiting surrender to the Tribunal.[35] Significantly, and in contrast to the ICTY, most of the accused fall into the category of persons who held leadership positions.[36] The excellent cooperation of many states, particularly African states such as Cameroon, Benin, Zambia, Kenya, Mali, Togo, Burkina Faso, Côte d'Ivoire and

31. *Code pénal*, Art. 26.

32. Morris & Scharf, op. cit. n. 8 at p. 582.

33. Following the report by the Office of Internal Oversight Services (OIOS) of 6 February 1997, the Deputy Prosecutor, Honoré Rakotomanana and the Registrar, Andronico Adede had to resign. The follow up report of 6 February 1998 stated that 'improvements were observed in virtually every area of the tribunal' and noted that 'substantial changes have occurred in the Tribunal since the review by the OIOS in 1997.'

34. Another five suspects are being held under Rule 40 *bis*, which permits suspects to be held provisionally.

35. See *supra* n. 14.

36. See report of the International Criminal Tribunal for Rwanda, S/1997/868.

Tanzania, facilitated the timely arrest of many high-ranking accused. This focus on the leaders reflects a clear investigation and prosecution strategy, announced in May 1997 in response to strong criticism of the lack of a coherent prosecutorial strategy[37], to only investigate and prosecute the individuals who planned, instigated, ordered and publicly incited the massacres, including perpetrators who might be located in Rwanda. This includes high-ranking administrative, military and political officials. Influential members of the civil society, such as journalists, clergymen and businessmen are also 'targeted'. Prosecution of the leaders by the International Tribunal is necessary primarily because it is considered of the utmost importance that the complex reality of the Rwandan genocide be established, legally and historically, by an international court. Prosecuting the leaders will further that goal and will send a strong signal that political leaders and high-ranking military officers are answerable to the whole international community. Their trials by domestic courts could be seen as politically motivated justice and might therefore prove an obstacle to national reconciliation. As a result of this new strategy, the arrest and transfer of seven high-ranking officials, including the former Prime Minister of the Interim Government, Jean Kambanda, took place during an operation codenamed Naki (Nairobi-Kigali). Operation Naki, of 18 July and 12 August 1997, marked a watershed in the activities of the Tribunal, proving to third states and Rwanda that the ICTR is an efficient institution, able to take into custody people who might otherwise never have been arrested, especially in the absence of an extradition treaty. In June and July 1998, five other senior officials were arrested in West Africa and transferred to Arusha.

On 2 September 1998, the first ever judgement of the crime of genocide by an international court was handed down by the ICTR.[38] The trial of Jean Paul Akayesu, the former bourgmestre of Taba commune, where at least 2,000 people were killed from 7 April to the end of June 1994[39], began on 9 January 1997 and ended on 26 March 1998. Akayesu's trial, the first to begin and conclude before the ICTR, was the first before an international tribunal, indeed, the first such trial in history, of someone on genocide charges. Akayesu also became the first person to be charged by the ICTR with crimes of sexual violence, when, on 17 September 1997, his indictment was amended to include three new counts of sexual violence, crimes against humanity and violations of common Article 3 of the Geneva Conventions and Article 4(2) of Additional Protocol II. During the trial, the Prosecutor presented new evidence of genocide and took the position

37. OIOS Report of 6 February 1997. Position of the government of Rwanda in May 1997. (In the personal files of the author).

38. *The Prosecutor* v. *Jean-Paul Akayesu, supra* n. 2.

39. Ibid. para. 12.

that acts of sexual violence can be genocidal acts within the meaning of Article 2(2) of the Statute. The acts described in the testimonies in the *Akayesu* case that recounted sexual violence committed against Tutsi women in Taba commune by the *Interhamwe* militia and the communal police are considered by the Prosecutor as genocidal acts under Article 2(2)(b) and (c) of the Statute.

The landmark Judgement in the *Akayesu* case, according to the Chief Prosecutor Louise Arbour, 'is a major concrete step in the destruction of the culture of impunity'[40], but it also provides a detailed legal analysis of many legal issues such as the interpretation of the Convention for the Prevention and Punishment of the Crime of Genocide of 1948. The Judgement is also the first to examine the law on sexual violence. First, the Chamber defined rape and sexual violence as acts of a sexual nature, which are committed on a person. The Judges noted that coercive circumstances need not be evidenced by a show of physical force. Second, the Chamber found that sexual violence may constitute a crime against humanity as an inhumane act, or a violation of Article 3 common to the Geneva Conventions and Additional Protocol II as an outrage on personal dignity. Most significantly, the Chamber held that sexual violence and rape constituted serious bodily or mental harm such as to provide the foundation for a conviction for genocide. Akayesu's conviction for sexual violence in part served as the foundation for his conviction for genocide. The Chamber stated that: 'Sexual violence was a step in the process of destruction of the Tutsi group-destruction of the spirit, of the will to live and of life itself.'[41] Third, the Judges found that the participation of the accused in the sexual violence need not be exclusively as a main offender but included ordering, instigating and aiding and abetting the commission of such acts by allowing them to take place (para. 688).

Surprisingly, the Chamber found Akayesu not guilty of violations of common Article 3 and Additional Protocol II on the basis that the Prosecutor failed to prove beyond a reasonable doubt that Akayesu was 'either a member of the armed forces under the military command of either of the belligerent parties, or that he was legitimately mandated and expected, as a public official or agent or person otherwise holding public authority or *de facto* representing the Government, to support or fulfill the war efforts.'[42]

40. See ICTY Press Release CC/PIO/34-E, 4 September 1998.
41. *Supra* n. 2 at para. 732. See also Year in Review at pp. 126-128.
42. *Supra* n. 2 at para. 643.

This contrasts with the Appeals Chamber decision in the Interlocutory Appeal on Jurisdiction before the ICTY[43] which stated that '... beneficiaries of common Article 3 of the Geneva Conventions are those taking no active part in the hostilities'.'[44] The Appeals Chamber held that '[e]ven if substantial clashes were not occurring in the Prejidor region at the time and place the crimes alleged were committed ... international humanitarian law applied. It is sufficient that the alleged crimes were closely related to the hostilities occurring in the other parts of the territories controlled by the parties to the conflict.'[45] This jurisprudence clearly demonstrates that civilians taking no active part in hostilities are protected by common Article 3 and Protocol II, and that the crimes committed by the accused need not be performed on the battlefield.

On 4 September 1998, the former Prime Minister of the Interim Government in Rwanda, Jean Kambanda, was sentenced to life imprisonment – the maximum that can be imposed by the ICTR.[46] It was the first sentence imposed by the ICTR.[47] On 1 May 1998, Kambanda had pleaded guilty to six counts of genocide, conspiracy to commit genocide, direct and public incitement to genocide, complicity in genocide and crimes against humanity at his initial appearance, obviating the need for a trial.[48]

As the first person to enter a guilty plea and the most high-ranking person in the ICTR's custody, Kambanda's confession to genocide and his life sentence have a special significance. His guilty plea is critical to the prosecution being able to establish evidence of a conspiracy to commit genocide between the various layers of power, in particular, the collusion between the government and the military. The sentencing of Kambanda to life imprisonment clearly indicates that state officials, including the highest-ranking ones, are no longer above and beyond the reach of international criminal justice.

In deciding to sentence Kambanda to life imprisonment, the maximum that the Tribunal can impose, the Trial Chamber took into consideration all the submissions presented by the Parties pertaining to the determination of the sentence, from which it could be inferred:

> (A)(i) Jean Kambanda has cooperated and is still willingly cooperating with the Office of the Prosecutor;

43. *Supra* n. 26.
44. Ibid., at para. 69.
45. Ibid., at para. 70.
46. *The Prosecutor* v. *Jean Kambanda*, ICTR-97-23-S, 4 September 1998.
47. On 7 September 1998, Jean Kambanda filed a notice of appeal against the sentence.
48. Rule 62(iv).

(ii) the guilty plea of Jean Kambanda is likely to encourage other individuals to recognize their responsibilities during the tragic events which occured in Rwanda in 1994;
(iii) a guilty plea is generally considered, in most national jurisdictions, including Rwanda, as a mitigating circumstance;

(B) but that, however:
(v)[49] the crimes for which Jean Kambanda is responsible carry an intrinsic gravity; and their widespread, atrocious and systematic character is particularly shocking to the human conscience;
(vi) Jean Kambanda committed the crimes knowingly and with premeditation;
(vii) and, moreover, Jean Kambanda, as Prime Minister of Rwanda, was entrusted with the duty and authority to protect the civilian population and he abused this trust.

The Trial Chamber noted that Kambanda never expressed contrition, regret or sympathy for the victims in Rwanda even when presented with the opportunity to do so.[50]

As of September 1998, it was not known where Kambanda, and Akayesu would serve their sentences. Under the Statute and Rules, convicted persons can serve their sentences in either Rwanda or in any other state designated by the Tribunal from a list of states which have indicated their willingness to accept convicted persons.[51]

The conviction of Jean Paul Akayesu and the sentencing of Jean Kambanda might help to correct the perception of inertia that surrounds the ICTR and hopefully will give the Rwandan victims of the genocide the sense that justice is being done after decades of impunity.

Aside from the cases of Akayesu and Kambanda, two other cases were ongoing at the Tribunal, as of September 1998. One concerns Georges Anderson Rutaganda, the former Vice President of the *Interhamwe* militia[52], the other is a joint trial of two accused, Clement Kayishema, the former Prefect of Kibuye, and Obed Ruzindana, a businessman[53].

Despite this progress and trials of leading members of the establishment, negative comments have been and continue to be directed at the ICTR. Following growing criticism[54] of the slow pace of the proceedings in Arusha, and

49. This is the numbering system adopted in the judgement.
50. *Supra* n. 46, at para. 51
51. Art. 26 of the Statute and Rule 103(A).
52. Case No. ICTR-96-3-T.
53. Case No. ICTR-96-1-T.
54. Amnesty International's report, 'International Criminal Tribunal for Rwanda: Trials and Tribulations', 30 April 1998. AI Index: IOR 40/03/98.

considering the fact that many accused have been in pre-trial detention for more than one year, on 30 April 1998 the Security Council passed a resolution establishing a third Trial Chamber, and to this end amended Articles 10, 11 and 12 of the Statute.[55]

The Prosecutor has also responded to the backlog of cases by unveiling another key aspect of her prosecutorial strategy: the so-called 'mass indictment'. The Prosecutor believes that it presents the dual advantage of a joint trial instead of single trials that could last for several years and reflects more accurately the reality of the genocide. The strategy includes seeking to join more individuals, in cases where conspiracy charges are applicable, into one or more indictments.

In March 1998, the Prosecutor submitted for confirmation the first 'mass indictment' concerning 29 persons.[56] However, the Judge 'dismissed it on the grounds that it was not maintainable in its present form and that, as a single Judge, he lacked the jurisdiction to confirm the indictment with respect to certain individuals who were named therein and who have already been indicted.[57] The prosecutor filed notice of appeal against this decision, which was rejected by the Appeals Chamber on 8 June 1998.[58] Although the Rules do not provide for an appeal against a decision by a confirming judge, the Prosecutor argued that dismissal of the indictment was an obstacle to the achievement of the mandate of the ICTR, and that a broad reading of Article 24 was justified. The Appeals Chamber rejected this argument, stating, '[t]he logical consequence of the interpretation advanced would be that where the Trial or Appeals Chamber refused to grant any relief requested by the Prosecutor, the Chambers would thereby be obstructing her mandate ... The Prosecutor's arguments for a teleological interpretation of the Statute, therefore, do not support such a broad interpretation of Article 24.'[59]

The ICTR has been criticised not only for being slow but also for being remote from the Rwandan population. If the ICTR is to have any sort of significant role in promoting peace and reconciliation in Rwanda and ending the culture of impunity, it is of the utmost importance that the activities of the ICTR be broadly publicized throughout Rwanda. The impact of international criminal justice on

55. (1998) S/RES/1165(1998).

56. Theoneste Bagosora and Others. See ICTR-98-37-I.

57. ICTR Press Release. ICTR/INFO-9-2-115, 1 April 1998. At the request of the Prosecutor, Judge Khan ordered that the unconfirmed indictment not be disclosed, pursuant to Rule 53 of the Rules of Procedure and Evidence.

58. Decision on the Admissibility of the Prosecutor's Appeal from the decision of a Confirming Judge dismissing an indictment against Theoneste Bagasora and 28 others, Case No. ICTR-98-37-A, Appeals Chamber, 8 June 1998.

59. Ibid.

the process of reconciliation in Rwanda can only be significant if Rwandans can follow 'Arusha' justice closely. This notion of 'proximity of justice' still has to become a reality in Rwanda and can be achieved in various ways. Systematic radio broadcast of the trials in Kenyarwanda would certainly be an efficient educational tool. It is worth mentioning that Radio Rwanda, which has a bureau at the Tribunal's seat in Arusha, broadcast simultaneously the court proceedings in which judgement was given in the *Akayesu* case. In addition, hearings could take place in Rwanda itself.[60] Rwandans have also strongly reproved the absence from the ICTR Statute and Rules of provision for victims' representation, in particular, the right to compensation. However, Rule 106 envisages victim compensation indirectly, as the final judgement of the ICTR can serve as the basis for the victims to seek reparations before national courts. Victims could also be given the possibility to appear as *amicus curiae*.

Considering the above-mentioned prosecution strategy to try the leaders, and other factors, such as the limited resources allocated to the Tribunal and its non-permanent character, it is, however, clear that the ICTR will only try a limited number of cases. It will be up to the Rwandan courts to try the bulk of the perpetrators. Its efforts to do so are discussed next.

3. PROSECUTION OF GENOCIDE BEFORE RWANDAN COURTS

The genocide that occurred in Rwanda during the spring of 1994 left the country with no functioning legal system. Rwanda's judicial system, in particular, was decimated. Most judges and lawyers were killed or had fled Rwanda. According to a report of April 1995 issued by the organisations Human Rights Watch and the Fédération Internationale des Droits de l'Homme, the new government was incapable of trying all those accused of killings during the genocide, mainly because it had no resources to implement this objective. The report stated:

> 'The former government had fled with most of the funds and state vehicles. Only 36 judges and 14 prosecutors and assistant prosecutors were available to prosecute and try the accused. All others had been killed, had fled or were themselves implicated in the crimes. Of the 14 ready to carry on the prosecution, only three had formal legal training. To render the judicial system fully functional at all levels, from the communal courts to the Supreme Court, would require nearly 700 magistrates to serve as judges and prosecutors. The prosecutors have been able to call on only 26 judicial police

60. Under Rule 4, 'A Chamber or a Judge may exercise their functions at a place other than the seat of the Tribunal, if so authorised by the President in the interests of justice.'

inspectors (...) An estimated 750 inspectors are needed to investigate the genocide (...).'[61]

In addition to this judicial chaos, the state of the legal system which prevailed before the genocide should be considered. Corruption and a lack of adequate training of a large number of magistrates and prosecutors characterised the judicial system under the Habyarimana regime.[62] According to several experts, if not corrupted by the executive branch, most of the prosecutors, judges and even defense lawyers were either powerless or harassed. The former Prosecutor of Kigali (May 1990-March 1995), Francois-Xavier Nsanzuwera, in his testimony before the ICTR in the *Kayishema* and *Ruzindana* case[63], stated that the executive branch always interfered in the work of the prosecutor and issued injunctions, particularly when civil authorities were involved in the perpetration of crimes. In such circumstances, the prosecutor was merely a cog in the politico-administrative machinery, rather than an independent organ.[64]

In the absence of the rule of law, violations of human rights committed or instigated by Rwandan officials prior to 1994 remained unpunished[65], and as a direct effect of this impunity, the perpetrators of the 1994 massacres were 'boosted' to commit their egregious crimes.

Rather than rebuilding, the government has had to create a judicial system almost from scratch. The construction of an effective and sound judicial system is a long-term objective that will take several years. The most difficult task is not to construct edifices but to train and recruit the first generation of professional prosecutors, police officers and magistrates and to consolidate a Bar Association.

Unlike the building of the judicial system, the challenge of prosecuting genocide is a short term objective. It is of the utmost urgency to prosecute the

61. *Rwanda, the crisis continues* Vol. 7 No. 1, at p. 5, Human Rights Watch and the Fédération Internationale des Droits de l'Homme. UN High Commissioner for Human Rights field operation in Rwanda, 'The administration of justice in post-genocide Rwanda,' at p. 2, para. 11, UN. Doc. HRFOR/JUSTICE/June 1996/E (1996); it is estimated that 90 percent of police officers and prosecutors were either dead or had left Rwanda and only 250 of 719 magistrates survived the genocide. See J.C. McKinley, Jr, '76,000 still in jail in Rwanda awaiting Trial in '94 slayings,' *The New York Times* (24 June 1996).

62. See Frederic Mutagwera, *La justice internationale face au drame rwandais* (Karthala, Paris 1996) pp. 18-19.

63. ICTR-95-I-T.

64. See testimony of the expert witness Francois Xavier Nsansuwera before the ICTR in the *Kayishema* case, on 28 October 1997, ICTR-96-1-T.

65. See the International Commission of Investigation on Human Rights Violations in Rwanda since 1 October 1990, Final Report, 8 March 1993.

perpetrators of the genocide to achieve national reconciliation.[66] Paradoxically, there is a conflict, even a contradiction, between the goal of building the legal system and the goal of prosecuting the genocide. The former, which in theory is the natural means to achieve the latter, cannot in the present circumstances serve this purpose in view of the long but necessary delay to build the judicial system.[67]

The social, political and legal issues related to the Rwandan genocide were discussed at an international conference on genocide held in Kigali in November 1995.[68] One of the main objectives of the conference was, on one hand, to define clear strategies in order to try the large number of persons involved in the massacres and, on the other hand, to analyse alternative forms of justice to the classical judicial system. Major principles emerged from this conference and largely determined the policy of Rwanda on the matter of prosecution of genocide. The necessity to prosecute genocide perpetrators and the exclusion of any amnesty for these criminals were stressed. In the case of Rwanda, it was considered that an amnesty would squarely amount to granting impunity to the perpetrators of the genocide. It was also recognised that alternative forms to prosecution, like the *gacaca*[69], a traditional mechanism of conflict resolution, could apply to offences which are not related with crimes against humanity or genocide. The Conference underscored the need to establish special institutions to prosecute the genocide, such as a Special Prosecution Office, an independent specialised court or specialised chambers within the existing courts.

66. According to William Schabas, the institution of a truth commission in Rwanda was not appropriate 'given the magnitude of the crimes and the scale upon which they were committed', William Schabas, 'Justice, Democracy, and Impunity in post-genocide Rwanda: searching for solutions to impossible problems', 7 *Criminal Law Forum* (1996) p. 529.

67. As suggested by William Schabas, it is therefore 'imperative to separate the goals of rebuilding the judicial system and prosecuting genocide. The two problems should be solved in parallel.' Ibid., at p. 534.

68. *Recommendations of the conference held in Kigali from November 1st to 5th, 1995, on 'genocide, impunity and accountability': Dialogue for a national and international response*. (Office of the President, Rwanda 1995).

69. Charles Ntampaka, 'Le retour à la tradition dans le règlement des différends: le GACACA du Rwanda', *Dialogue* No. 186, pp. 95-104. There are two levels of GACACA. The first level traditionally grouped relatives from the same family and immediate neighbors. Its function is to solve minor conflicts. The second level involves conflicts, including murders, between two non-allied families. Neutral arbitrators are appointed to reconciliate the parties. The author notes that the GACACA now plays a limited role. As a consequence of the genocide, the social fabric has been deeply damaged and it is very difficult to find persons who were not involved in the genocide and who are able to reach a consensus.

Although the pillars of the Rwandan legislation on genocide were adopted in 1996, the categorisation of suspects, the system of plea bargaining and the guilty plea were sensed for the first time at the Kigali conference.

Since the conference, important steps have been taken by Rwanda and by the international community to rehabilitate the Rwandese justice system and allow the prosecution of individuals currently detained in Rwanda. This double challenge of rebuilding the legal system and prosecuting the thousands of detainees suspected of having committed genocide is being carried out following a two-pronged approach.

First, Rwanda has begun to address the material and human 'reconstruction' of the legal system. Intensive training of Rwandan magistrates, prosecutors and judicial police officers began in 1995. The international community has actively participated in the financing and implementing of these training programmes.[70] It is estimated that $18 million has been pledged by donors for building the judicial infrastructure and training.[71] The United Nations has been involved in the rehabilitation of the judicial system[72]; in particular, the Human Rights Field Operation in Rwanda (UNHFOR) played an important role in monitoring national trials. Multilateral donors like the European Union and bilateral donors[73] have also been active parties to the reconstruction of the judicial system.

NGOs have equally demonstrated a desire to support the efforts towards national justice. Training of judicial investigators has been provided, for example, by a Belgian NGO, Citizens Network. The French NGO, Juristes sans frontières and the Canadian Center for Human Rights and Democratic Development have conducted training of Rwandan magistrates and lawyers in the prosecution of genocide. Avocats sans frontières has also provided defense lawyers.

While this assistance serves an importance purpose, as the Special Representative for Rwanda has pointed out, the proliferation of international actors intervening in the process of rehabilitation of the legal system might produce the undesired effect of overlapping and even contradictory and 'competitive' initiatives. He recommended that all interested parties agree on a common list of priority projects with a calendar to implement them and with

70. Res. 114, UN GAOR 51st sess., Supp. No. 49 at 263, UN Doc. A/51/49/1997. The resolution invites all states, United Nations bodies as well as intergovernmental and non-governmental organisations 'to continue and to intensify their contributions of financial and technical support to accelerate the efforts of the government of Rwanda, to *inter alia*, restore the judicial system'.

71. See Samantha Power, 'Life after death', *The New Republic* (6 April 1998) p. 3.

72. UNDP, UNHCR and UNICEF also have programmes of assistance to the Rwandan justice system.

73. Germany; Belgium; Ireland; The Netherlands; United Kingdom and Northern Ireland; Sweden; Canada; USA; and Switzerland.

adequate financing of these projects.[74] It is essential that these external initiatives are not regarded as substitutes for Rwandan initiatives and that they remain under Rwandan control. However, the massive support of the international community to train the legal profession in Rwanda remains unprecedented.

Second, legal reforms aimed at prosecuting the genocide have been enacted since 1996. Most of the reforms were largely inspired by the recommendations of the international conference on genocide held in Kigali.

One of the main perverse characteristics of the Rwandan genocide was the massive participation of civilians in the perpetration of the atrocities. Due to the fact that Rwanda was a very centralised state, the policy of the government to commit the genocide of the Tutsis was carried out rapidly and efficiently by involving a large part of the population in the killings. Moreover, the public incitements to kill Tutsis broadcast by Radio Mille Collines significantly contributed to the massive 'adhesion' of ordinary civilians to the extermination of the Tutsi and the killings of moderate Hutu. In doing so, a large number of the population turned into criminals or *génocidaires*, large numbers of whom have been arrested since the end of the conflict in July 1994. According to UNHFOR, 126,216[75] detainees are currently awaiting prosecution for genocide-related crimes.

Special legislation was necessary for the prosecution of the *génocidaires* and the reorganisation of the judicial system. The new legal framework for the genocide prosecutions is incorporated mainly in four legal reforms adopted by the Transitional National Assembly.

The *Organic Law 8/96 of August 30, 1996 on the organisation of prosecutions for offences constituting the crime of genocide or crimes against humanity since 1 October 1990*[76] entered into force on 1 September 1996. This legislation has two components. First, it fills the legislative *lacunae* regarding penalties for genocide. Second, it provides an original mechanism to ensure speedy trials.

Article 1 defines the crimes of genocide and crimes against humanity in accordance with three conventions ratified by Rwanda: the 1948 Genocide Convention, the 1949 Fourth Geneva Convention and the 1968 Convention on the non-applicability of statutory limitations to war crimes and crimes against

74. Report on the situation on human rights in Rwanda submitted by Mr Michel Moussali, Special Representative of the Commission on Human Rights, under Commission Resolution 1997/66 of 19 February 1998 at paras. 26 and 27.

75. Report of the Special Representative for Rwanda, of 19 February 1998, at para. 22.

76. Published in *Official Journal of the Republic of Rwanda* (1 September 1996). Reproduced at p. 625 of this volume. See also Stefan Vandeginste, 'Poursuite des presumes responsables du genocide et des massacres politiques devant les juridictions rwandaises', *Annuaire 1996-1997 l'Afrique des Grands Lacs* (1997) pp. 93-99.

humanity.[77] While the penal code of Rwanda, adopted on 18 August 1977, does not list the crime of genocide and crimes against humanity, a draft law on the inclusion of the crime of genocide in the penal code is expected to be adopted in the near future.

Temporal jurisdiction under this law, in contrast with the ICTR Statute, starts on 1 October 1990 in order to capture the mass killings of Tutsi which occurred in October 1990, January 1991 and March 1992, and the hate propaganda broadcast by the media since the end of 1990.

One of the main characteristics of this law is the classification of suspects into four categories according to their degrees of culpability in the genocide.

Category 1 encompasses the planners; the instigators; the leaders; the persons who held positions of authority at national and local levels or in political parties, the army, religious groups or militia; notorious murderers; and perpetrators of sexual torture. Category 1 offenders are not entitled to receive a reduced sentence under the system of plea agreement analysed below and are subject to the death penalty. On 30 November 1996, the Procureur General of the Supreme Court, pursuant to Article 9, published a list of 1,946 names belonging to category 1.[78] If, after publication of this list, a person confessed, he would be classified in category 2 even if the crimes he committed would rank him in category 1.

Category 2 includes persons who are 'the perpetrators or accomplices of intentional homicide' or suspected of serious assaults resulting in death. If the perpetrator has confessed and pleaded guilty before prosecution, he will receive a sentence of seven to 11 years imprisonment while, after prosecution, his sentence will be between 12 and 15 years. The sentence is life imprisonment if the perpetrator who refused to confess and plead guilty is convicted at trial.

Category 3 includes persons who committed serious assaults. If they plead guilty before prosecution they will receive a sentence of one third the prison sentence normally applicable. If they plead guilty after prosecution they will receive one half of the normal sentence.

Category 4 encompasses the persons who committed property crimes.

The law opted for a system of confession and guilty plea procedure which is unknown in the ICTR and in civil law systems. Under this plea agreement system, all perpetrators (except those in category 1) who provide an accurate and complete confession of the crimes committed are entitled to a reduced sentence. When a perpetrator has entered a guilty plea agreement, he is requested, pursuant to Article 6(b) of the Genocide law, to apologise to the victims. Such an act of

77. GA Res 2391, 23 UN GAOR supp. No.18 at p. 40, UN Doc. A/7342 & corr. 1 (1968).
78. *Journal Officiel*, special edition, 30 November 1996.

apology must be understood as a full component and condition of national reconciliation.

The system of plea agreement has been established in order to reduce the number of trials of all detainees, except those of category 1, and to bring evidence for other cases.

The Genocide law also established Specialised Chambers[79] within the existing First Instance courts and the military courts with exclusive jurisdiction to prosecute genocide and crimes against humanity. These specialised chambers are composed of three judges, and may 'hear cases as itinerant chambers in any location within its territorial jurisdiction'.[80]

The Military Courts ('Cours Militaires') have exclusive competence to prosecute members of the army with a grade higher than captain who are suspected of having participated in the genocide or having committed crimes against humanity. The lower ranks (ordinary soldiers up to and including captains) are judged by the 'Conseils de Guerre'. Appeals against a decision of a 'Conseil de Guerre' can be initiated before the Military Courts. Military Courts' decisions can be appealed before the Supreme Court ('Cour de Cassation').

The Military Courts as well as the 'Conseil de Guerre' are presided over by a military officer and the Prosecution is done by the Military Auditeur. The suspects are defended by military lawyers.

Articles 24-26 of the Genocide Law establish the conditions of admissibility of appeal and review. Each side has 15 days to appeal a first instance judgement. Appeal of a judgement from the first instance court is admissible only on questions of law or flagrant errors of fact. Appeal is decided by the appellate court on its merits on the basis of the appeal documents. There is no appeal of a decision of the Court of Appeal, except in one case: pursuant to Article 25, the defendant may appeal to the Supreme Court only when the Court of Appeal has found him guilty and sentenced him to death while he was acquitted at first instance.

Pursuant to Article 26, the Prosecutor General may apply for judicial review of a case by the Supreme Court 'on his own initiative and solely in the interests of the law' and on the basis that the decision rendered is contrary to the law.

The rights of the defence are enhanced in the Genocide Law. However, the High Commissioner for Human Rights in Rwanda pointed out a possible

79. Under Art. 20, the Supreme Court plays a vital role in the organisation of the Specialised Chambers. See also the Organic Law No. 07/96 of June 1996 (*Journal Officiel* 10 June 1996) and relating to the organization, working and competence of the Supreme Court.

80. Art. 19, Organic Law, *supra* n. 76.

contradiction between Article 14(3)(d) of the ICCPR[81], ratified by Rwanda, and Article 36 of the Genocide Law. Article 14(3)(d) provides that the accused is entitled to have 'legal assistance, in any case where the interests of justice so require, and without payment by him in any such case if he does not have sufficient means to pay for it'. Article 36 of the Genocide Law provides that the government has no obligation to pay for defence counsel.[82]

The Genocide law allows civil parties to appear in court to obtain compensation for damages resulting from the genocide.[83] Article 32 provides for the right of victims to compensation. The creation of a victims compensation fund, as provided for in the article, is necessary to heal the wounds of the hundreds of thousands of victims of the genocide. In parallel, a law was adopted[84] establishing a national assistance fund for 'needy victims' of genocide and massacres committed in Rwanda between October 1990 and December 31 as envisaged in Article 32 of the Genocide law.

The Genocide Law and the law establishing the fund acknowledge, at both judicial and social levels, the fact that not only individual Rwandans but also the Rwandan nation are victims of the genocide, and that the instigators and directors of the genocide are accountable not only to their direct victims but to all persons affected by their crimes.[85]

Under the Rwandan Code of Criminal Procedure, adopted on 23 February 1963, three legal conditions for arrests and detention are provided: firstly, the arrests are made by Judicial Police Inspectors (JPI), secondly a provisional arrest warrant is issued by an Officer of the Department of Public Prosecution and thirdly, a judge issues a preventive detention order. In fact, most of the arrests and detentions were made by the army, the only functioning institution in a post-genocide context where the legal infrastructure of Rwanda was totally destroyed. For instance, until 1996, it was impossible to issue arrest records, provisional arrest warrants and preventive detention orders in such circumstances.

81. International Covenant on Civil and Political Rights, GA Res. 2200 (XXI), 21 UN GAOR. Supp. (No. 16) 52, UN Doc.A/6316 (1966) (herein after ICCPR).

82. HRFOR/STRPT/59/2/19 December 1997/E, pp. 3-4. See also Amnesty International, *Rwanda. Unfair trials: justice denied,* AFR 47/08/97 (1997) p. 9.

83. Art. 30 makes a distinction between category 1 offenders and other categories. The first are held liable for all damages caused in the country ... while offenders in other categories are liable for damages for the criminal acts they have committed.

84. Law No. 02/98 of 22 January 1998.

85. Under Art. 30(1), 'Convicted persons whose acts place them in Category 1 under Article 2 shall be held jointly and severally liable for all damages caused in the country by their acts of criminal participation, regardless of where the offences were committed', whereas, under subpara. 2, 'Persons whose acts place them within Categories 2, 3 or 4 shall be liable for damages for the criminal acts they have committed.'

The *Law 9/96 of 8 September 1996 relating to provisional modifications to the Criminal Procedure Code* entered into force retroactively, being effective as of 6 April 1994. It authorises the taking into custody of suspects despite the incompleteness or even the absence of the files.

The 9/96 Law is aimed at legalising arrests and pre-trial detentions which were made despite the absence of the three above-mentioned legal requirements. In other words, the Rwandese authorities were obliged to issue arrest records before the end of 1997. The new legislation retroactively regularised arrests and detentions through extending the time prescribed in the Code of Criminal Procedure for every stage of arrest and pre-trial detention.

The Transitional National Assembly adopted on 26 December 1997 a law modifying the 9/96 Law.[86] The new law provides new derogations for arrest and detention. The period to prepare the arrest record of the persons in provisional detention is extended to 31 December 1999 from 31 December 1997. Under this new law, the period within which a suspect must be brought before a judge is also extended to 31 December 1999. This means that a person can be detained for five years without being formally charged. The validity of the preventive detention order is extended to two years from the order of issuance. Moreover, the suspect detained prior to his trial cannot appeal decisions on pre-trial detention.[87]

In 1996, the government of Rwanda established administrative screening commissions ('commissions de triage') to assist the judicial authorities in the preparation of dossiers on detainees and in their release in the case of insufficient evidence against them. It appears that this initiative has been less successful than expected; few releases have occurred.[88] In May 1997, 'Mobile Groups' replaced the screening commissions. These Mobile Groups are composed of investigators who have been assigned to the Prosecutor's office to carry out preliminary investigations in order to immediately release detainees against whom no evidence of their involvement in their genocide can be found. By the end of July 1998, about 3,000 detainees had been released.

The third step was the reestablishment of the Supreme Court, which was abolished in 1978. In accordance with the Arusha Accords, Organic Law No. 07/96 on the Organisation, Functioning and Competence of the Supreme Court

86. Law No. 16/97 of 26/12/1997 modifying Law No. 9/96 of 8 September and relating to provisional modifications to the criminal procedure code. *Journal Officiel* No. SP. of 31/12/1997.

87. Law 9/96 relating to provisional modifications to the criminal procedure code, *Journal Officiel* 1996, No. 18 at p. 8.

88. Stefan Vandeginste, *Justice for Rwanda and international cooperation* (Centre for the study of the Great Lakes Region, Antwerp University September 1996).

was adopted on 6 June 1996.[89] This law was necessary as the Law on Genocide Act of 30 August 1996 gives the Supreme Court a central role in the appointment of judges and the President of the Specialised Chambers. In addition, Law No. 31/96 on the Organisation, Functioning and Competence of the 'Conseil Superieur de la Magistrature, a judicial council, was passed on 29 March 1996.

The last but not least major legislative step taken to reconstruct the rule of Law in Rwanda was achieved through the adoption of *Law No. 03/97 of 19 March 1997* establishing a Bar in Rwanda. Fifty-eight Rwandan lawyers are currently members of the Bar. The law also provides for non-Rwandese lawyers to be admitted to the Bar on the condition that Rwandese lawyers have the right to be admitted to the Bar in the country of origin of the applicant. This condition of reciprocity has, according to the HRFOR Report of December 1997, been met by most European and West African countries, Burundi and the Democratic Republic of Congo. Lawyers from the Madrid and Canadian Bars were not admitted because of the fact that the condition of reciprocity was not met.

The Bar Law also established a consultation and defence bureau 'BCD' to provide assistance to indigents. A legal aid fund will be set up in order to cover the costs of the lawyers defending the suspects. So far, most legal assistance has been assured by the NGO Avocats sans frontières.

Despite the adoption of these new laws, various problems have stymied the prosecution of *génocidaires* in Rwanda.[90]

First, the lack of sufficiently trained judges, prosecutors, policemen and lawyers has not allowed an expeditious pace of the trials.[91] The refusal of the Rwandan government and its National Assembly to allow foreign judges to sit in genocide proceedings, mainly for reasons pertaining to its sovereignty, has also delayed the beginning of the genocide trials in Rwanda. The first national trial for genocide only started on 27 December 1996. As of September 1998, the Specialised Chambers of the Courts of First Instance had handed down judgments in respect of 500 defendants.[92] One hundred and seventeen persons were sentenced to death; 118 to life imprisonment; 29 were acquitted; and 57 entered a guilty plea. Genocide trials were ongoing in most prefectures. In one case, in Byumba Prefecture, 51 defendants were jointly accused.[93]

89. Published in *Journal Officiel*, 10 June 1996.

90. Power, op. cit. n. 71 at pp. 2-3.

91. The Arusha School on international criminal law and human rights established by Avocats sans Frontières in 1995 has only held three sessions since its creation and very few Rwandese lawyers have participated in these sessions.

92. Karin Davies, AP 4 September 1998.

93. UNHFOR: Report on the Human Rights Situation in Rwanda and on the Activities of UNHFOR, March 1998.

On 24 April 1998, 22 persons sentenced to death by Rwandan courts were publicly executed despite several appeals for clemency by the United Nations Secretary-General, and declarations on the lack of due process by the spokesman for the United Nations Human Rights Commission who said that the guilt of the convicted persons had not been proven beyond doubt in the trials in Kigali.[94] According to the Rwandan government, however, these executions served the purpose of national reconciliation. The Minister of Justice of Rwanda said that the public executions would 'show people that justice is really working'.[95] These executions stimulated debate on the *real* nature of the relationship between the ICTR and Rwandan courts and the effectiveness of the complementary processes before Rwandan courts and the ICTR in the promotion of national reconciliation.

Secondly, the problem of (a lack of) security, in particular in the western part of Rwanda, has deterred prosecution witnesses and defence lawyers from appearing. In the absence of a witness protection programme similar to the existing one of the ICTR, it is virtually impossible to ensure that witnesses will appear before Rwandan courts. For similar reasons, sexual crimes have hardly been prosecuted despite the well-known large scale perpetration of those crimes during the genocide.

Thirdly, the procedure of plea agreements has not been used as originally anticipated by the legislators.[96] It is reported by Avocats sans frontières and by UNHFOR that both as a result of lack of knowledge amongst the detainees of this procedure, as well as the absence of separate cells for the suspects who would like to confess on the basis of a plea agreement, and hence the ensuing security risks for those suspects who nevertheless confess, very few plea agreements were entered into. However, following the Spring executions, this trend has been reversed. It is estimated that more than 5,000 accused persons have now confessed or expressed a willingness to confess.[97]

The Rwandan judicial system still remains, after three years of intensive efforts, a fragile institution not yet capable of handling all the cases of people detained. Given factors such as the number of detainees and the limited success of the confession and guilty plea procedure, complementary remedies would perhaps alleviate this painful process. The creation of a non-judicial mechanism

94. Report of the UN High Commissioner for Human Rights, UN Doc. E/CN.4/1998/61. Avocats sans frontières had requested the Rwandan government to allow an individual re-examination of each case. Agence France Presse, 24 April 1998; Deutsche Presse Agentur, 23 April 1998.

95. Deutsche Presse Agentur, 23 April 1998.

96. The confession and guilty procedure has been extended for 18 months from 1 March 1998 by Presidential Order No. 5/01 of 10/03/1998 in *Official Gazette*, 15 March 1998.

97. Figures on file with the author.

such as a truth and reconciliation commission would be conceivable but cannot be a substitute for prosecutions for genocide. In the context of impunity, the establishment of a truth commission could be seen as a provocation to the victims and as a way to deprive them of justice. Moreover, states have a legal obligation under the Genocide Convention to prosecute the crime of genocide. It is too early to analyse the impact on the Rwandan justice system of the newly created National Commission on Human Rights.[98]

4. COOPERATION AND COMPLEMENTARITY BETWEEN THE ICTR AND RWANDAN COURTS

The *ad hoc* Tribunals as unprecedented 'legal events' must be seen as pioneers of a modern transnational criminal justice. Thus, a debate over which is better, the ICTR or the Rwandan system, would be irrelevant. The correct approach is to analyse how these two systems can work together.

The Statute of the ICTR provides that the ICTR has concurrent jurisdiction with national courts, although it affirms its primacy. It is therefore desirable that the Prosecutor of the ICTR adopts a strategy to determine how to divide the caseload between the Tribunal and the national courts. However, this exercise should not compromise the fundamental principle of the independence of the Prosecutor recognised under Article 15(2) of the ICTR Statute. It is difficult for Rwandans to accept that leaders of the massacres tried by the ICTR cannot be sentenced to death, while the perpetrators tried by Rwandan courts do face the death penalty. This difference of treatment will always negatively affect the relationship between the ICTR and Rwandan national courts.

The relationship between the government of Rwanda and the ICTR has also benefitted from the appointment in April 1997 of a new Deputy Prosecutor, Bernard Acho Muna. A liaison officer with the Rwandan Ministery of Justice and Defense has been appointed to channel requests from Rwandan authorities and from the OTP which has increased the level and the quality of exchange of information between the ICTR and Rwanda. The cooperation with Rwandan women's NGOs has also significantly increased following a joint seminar on sexual assaults held under the auspices of the OTP in 3-6 October 1997 and frequent contacts between Tribunal investigators and NGOs.

98. Arrêté présidentiel No. 26/01, 11 November 1997, *Gazette Officielle de la République du Rwanda* (1 December 1997).

Another means to strengthen cooperation between the ICTR and Rwandan courts is the implementation of a 'Rules of the Road', project. Under this project, individuals who are not indicted by the ICTR could not be arrested by the national authorities for serious violations of IHL unless their indictment reviewed by the Prosecutor of the ICTR and deemed consistent with international standards. It is noteworthy that such a project already exists between the ICTY and the three concerned states of the former Yugoslavia.

The implementation of this programme would certainly alleviate the workload of Rwandan courts but could only be achieved if substantial additional resources were given to the OTP, given the very large number of persons already in custody in Rwandan prisons and the current workload of the OTP.

Cooperation between the ICTR and states, including Rwanda, in the taking of evidence was bolstered by the adoption by the Prosecutor on 9 March 1998 of a regulation on the procedure to be adopted following a request by a national authority to take evidence from a person in the custody of the ICTR.[99] Belgium was the first country to require such assistance and sent a magistrate to Arusha to interview detained accused.

Beyond the practical effects for requesting states, this regulation strengthened the complementarity between the ICTR and national jurisdictions. The possibility for states, in particular, Rwanda, to hear ICTR accused as witnesses in their national prosecutions may impact positively on the success of cases tried before Rwandan courts, particularly those involving complex issues such as command responsibility.

Further, ICTR procedures and jurisprudence could provide examples for national legal systems, in particular, for Rwandan courts, provided that its activities are sufficiently publicized. Rwandese lawyers and magistrates should also be given the opportunity to attend the hearings in Arusha. Systematic exchange of information between the ICTR and Rwandese lawyers on technical legal issues and strategies would clearly be conducive to developing a synergy between the two parallel judicial systems.

The coexistence of national and international prosecutions of genocide in Rwanda should not be questioned; both are desirable and necessary to achieve justice. However, a clear mechanism for ensuring an effective complementarity between the International Tribunal and Rwandan courts has still to be established. Otherwise the risk is too high that the aim of national reconciliation and confidence in international justice will never be achieved.

The recent establishment of the International Criminal Court, as stated by the Secretary-General of the United Nations, is 'a gift of hope for future generations,

99. Regulation No. 1 dated 1 March 1998.

and a giant step in the march towards universal human rights and the rule of law'.[100]

Meanwhile, it is important that the international community continues to support the ICTR and the Rwandan domestic judicial system. In a context of recurrent violence in the Great Lakes region, they are the only viable tools, as opposed to military intervention, to put an end to the culture of impunity.

It is time for the international community to systematically integrate a 'judicial approach' in its efforts to restore peace in the Great Lakes Region, exactly as it did in the Balkans.

100. Statement by the United Nations Secretary-General Kofi Annan at the Ceremony held at the Campidoglio Celebrating the Adoption of the Statute of the International Criminal Court, 18 July 1998. Available online at http://www.un.org/icc/speeches/718sg.htm.

THE PRAGMATICS OF PROSECUTING THE KHMER ROUGE*

Balakrishnan Rajagopal**

1. INTRODUCTION

It is generally known that one of the worst acts of mass killings and auto-genocide occurred in Cambodia between 1975-79 during the reign of terror unleashed by the Khmer Rouge (KR) regime. It is estimated that between 1-2 million Cambodians (out of a total population of around 7 million) were killed, starved, or died of malnutrition and disease during this period. The KR regime persecuted religious and ethnic minorities, abolished all religions, private property and money and put the entire population under forced labor. The KR continued such practices in the areas under its control during the 1980s, and conducted a vitriolic and violent campaign against the ethnic Vietnamese in Cambodia until its collapse last year.

Revelations during the last year about the disintegration of the KR in Cambodia have given rise to much excitement about the possibility of prosecuting some of its leaders before an international criminal court. At the request of the Cambodian government[1], a three-member team of experts appointed by the Secretary-General was due to visit Cambodia in November 1998 to assess the factual evidence available in order to make a determination about the establishment of an international criminal tribunal to try the KR. This *modus operandi* is similar to

** Crowe & Dunlevy Visiting International Professor, University of Oklahoma School of Law; SJD candidate, Harvard Law School. The author worked for almost four and a half years with the UN Transitional Authority in Cambodia (UNTAC) and UN High Commissioner for Human Rights, prior to coming to Harvard. This article is based, *inter alia,* on the first-hand information and impressions that he gathered during his work, which included providing legal advice on the issue of bringing the KR to justice. The views expressed herein are strictly those of the author. The author wishes to thank Anthony Anghie, David Ashley, James Gathii, Steve Heder, Peter Krug, Anugraha Palan, and Henry Steiner for their useful comments on earlier drafts.

1. *See infra* n. 9 and the accompanying text.

Yearbook of International Humanitarian Law
Volume 1 - 1998 - pp. 189-204

that seen in the Former Yugoslavia and Rwanda, where teams of experts were appointed prior to the establishment of *ad hoc* tribunals by the Security Council.

This comment describes the events leading up to this and analyzes the options for prosecuting the KR. It will argue that, contrary to the attitude of some people in the US administration and the human rights community, the likelihood of the establishment of an international tribunal, similar to the Rwandan or Former Yugoslavian ones, as well as of its success, are fairly low, and that the best approach for making the KR accountable is a 'mixed' tribunal that has global characteristics while remaining primarily local in nature.

2. EVOLUTION OF EVENTS LEADING UP TO THE CURRENT SITUATION

The international community's apathy towards (indeed, some would say, complicity in) the crimes committed by the KR is well known. Throughout the 1980s, western governments, including the United States and China, and ASEAN propped up the KR and recognized Democratic Kampuchea (DK) as the legitimate state, despite the fact that it controlled very little territory and people compared with the Phnom Penh regime. The DK government was a coalition of forces known as the Coalition Government of Democratic Kampuchea (CGDK), which included the KR as its main component.[2] The KR, through the CGDK, occupied Cambodia's seat at the UN and the UN human rights system maintained a complete silence about the KR's crimes. In the Paris Peace Agreement which established the UN Transitional Authority in Cambodia (UNTAC), there was no mention of the crimes committed by the KR[3] and no provision for the

2. On this well-known aspect of recent Cambodian history, there are numerous studies and books. See e.g., David P. Chandler, *A History of Cambodia*, 2nd ed. (Westview Press 1992); *The Tragedy of Cambodian History: Politics, War and Revolution Since 1945* (Yale University Press 1991); Elizabeth Becker, *When the War Was Over: The Voices of Cambodia's Revolution and Its People* (Simon and Schuster 1986); Nayan Chanda, *Brother Enemy: The War After the War*, (Harcourt Brace Jovanovich 1986).

3. The Agreement called for a non-return to 'the policies and practices of the past' in an indirect reference to the KR crimes, as a result of the opposition by the KR and China to any mention of the word 'genocide', though the US, due to outside pressure from NGOs and activists, made an unsuccessful last-minute attempt to include a reference to genocide in the Agreement. See Agreement on a Comprehensive Political Settlement of the Cambodia Conflict, signed in Paris, 21 October 1991.

investigation of the KR crimes.[4] The KR continued to wage a low-intensity war against the new government after 1993, killing thousands, burning houses and forcibly conscripting peasants. Meanwhile the new government adopted a carrot and stick policy to weaken the KR: a law was adopted in 1994 banning the KR[5] and criminalizing membership in it, while the government aggressively pursued – in violation of that law – an amnesty program for low and middle-ranking defectors from the KR.[6]

Meanwhile, at least since 1993, the West gradually shifted its focus of support from the non-communist members of the CGDK to Hun Sen, the second Prime Minister elected after the 1993 election and the Vice-President of the Cambodian People's Party (CPP) – arch rival of the KR who vilified him as the puppet of the *youn* (a derogatory term for Vietnamese). This shift, pursued by the US and other western countries, reflected the new western strategic thinking towards so-called ex-communist states including Vietnam, which emphasized engagement rather than containment. As part of this strategy, the US passed the Cambodian Genocide Justice Act in 1994[7] which called for US assistance to bring the KR to justice and, for that purpose, provided funding to Yale University in order to compile documentation on the KR crimes. This new strategic policy was strengthened by the fact that it coincided with the moral imperative of bringing the KR to justice, which was seriously pursued by many in the human rights community and the anti-communists in the US administration and Congress itself.

While the carrot and stick policy of the government had a moderate success in attracting the defections of many low-ranking KR, the leadership appeared to be solidly united under the notorious Pol Pot until 1996. In August of that year, Ieng Sary, a senior member of the KR, defected to the government along with a retinue of military commanders, bringing with them a large chunk of territory in the northwest, including the strategically and economically important areas of Pailin and Phnom Malai. Internecine quarrels between the CPP, led by Hun Sen, and FUNCINPEC (French acronym for National United Front for a Neutral,

4. The human rights component of UNTAC had no mandate to investigate KR crimes prior to 1991 and in fact did not investigate any. This continued to be the case even after the KR had flouted the Paris Agreements, attacked and killed UN peacekeepers, and refused to participate in the 1993 election.

5. See Law on the Outlawing of the Khmer Rouge, adopted by the National Assembly of the Kingdom of Cambodia, 1994 (Copy on file with the author).

6. While the law specified that the KR can be granted amnesty for a period of six months after its adoption, the Cambodian government has continued to grant *de facto* amnesties, in violation of the law.

7. Cambodia Genocide Justice Act (11 U.S.C. 2656, Part D, Sections 571 - 574), May 1994. Available online at http://www.yale.edu/cgp/dccam/wwwcgja.txt. The momentum for the Act was provided by some US legislators and academics.

Peaceful and Cooperative Cambodia), led by Prince Norodom Ranariddh, the first Prime Minister who had won the 1993 election, which had been festering at least since late-1994, became much worse with the defection of Ieng Sary, as each side attempted to woo him. Ieng Sary's defection was the spark that ignited all the recent discussions about justice and an international tribunal.

The internal tensions generated by these events resulted, in the course of 1996 and early 1997, in widening the rift between CPP and FUNCINPEC on the one hand, and deepening serious internal divisions within the KR high command, on the other. These developments did not go unnoticed by the UN Centre for Human Rights in Cambodia (as it was known before it was renamed as the High Commissioner for Human Rights)[8] and the SRSGHRC (Special Representative of the UN Secretary-General for Human Rights in Cambodia), Mr. Thomas Hammarberg, both of whom lobbied western governments, Cambodian parties and the UN for a mechanism that would bring the weakened-KR to justice.

Breaking its long silence, in April 1997 the UN Commission on Human Rights (UNCHR) requested the Secretary-General, for the first time since the KR crimes were committed in the 1970s, to 'examine any request by Cambodia for assistance' in relation to past crimes committed by the KR.[9] This was followed by a General Assembly Resolution in November 1997 in which it noted 'with concern that no Khmer Rouge leader has been brought to account for his crimes' and requested the Secretary-General to

> 'examine the request by the Cambodian authorities for assistance in responding to past serious violations of Cambodian and international law, including the possibility of the appointment, by the Secretary-General, of a group of experts to evaluate the existing evidence and propose further measures, as a means of bringing about national reconciliation, strengthening democracy and addressing the issue of individual accountability.'[10]

The co-Prime Ministers of Cambodia wrote a letter on 21 June 1997 to the Secretary-General requesting the UN's assistance in establishing an international tribunal to bring the KR to justice.[11] As it turned out, this was one of the last documents signed jointly by Norodom Ranariddh and Hun Sen, as a violent coup staged by Hun Sen's forces overthrew FUNCINPEC's forces and Ranariddh in

8. It is now known as the Cambodia Office of the High Commissioner for Human Rights

9. See 'Situation of Human Rights in Cambodia', UN Commission on Human Rights Resolution, 1997/49, at para. 12.

10. Situation of Human Rights in Cambodia, A/C.3/52/L.68, 20 November 1997, para. 16.

11. Copy of the letter on file with the author. The letter was actually drafted by the UN Centre for Human Rights.

July 1997. In the weeks preceding this letter, Cambodia had been rife with rumors of Pol Pot's capture, primarily due to serious internal fights within the KR leadership, including the execution of Son Sen, a senior KR leader by forces loyal to Pol Pot, and the resultant weakening of the KR.

During the same period, the human rights community within Cambodia was also actively involved in promoting the idea of prosecuting the KR through active lobbying. Twenty-eight members of the National Assembly belonging to FUNCINPEC and BLDP (Buddhist Liberal Democratic Party), led by Mr. Son Chhay and Mr. Kem Sokha, wrote to the Secretary-General expressing 'complete and unequivocal support' for the 21 June letter of the co-Prime Ministers[12].

This period had also witnessed media zealotry in the US: that it would send in its strike forces, extract Pol Pot from the jungle and have him tried before the courts of a third country such as Canada, relying on universal jurisdiction. However, as then predicted by some observers, these efforts did not come to fruition.[13] Subsequent events showed that the sudden new interest in bringing the KR to justice was grounded in the self-interest of everyone. Prince Ranariddh was interested in keeping the KR under pressure during negotiations for support, while trying to woo certain elements of the KR, by stating that only the 'hard-liners' bore responsibility for the KR crimes. Hun Sen's interest was rooted in the CPP's long-held policy of weakening the KR. The US's aggressive and somewhat rash action for third country prosecution was, it appeared, either ill timed, incompetently handled or deliberately allowed to fail.[14] This was not an isolated incident of missed - or blown - opportunities by the US. A primary objective of US policy towards Cambodia is the establishment of an international tribunal for prosecuting the KR.[15] However, this has hardly been reflected in actual diplomatic practice of the US. For example, very recently the US, somewhat hastily and without consulting any major country or the UN, submitted a draft resolution at the Security Council for the establishment of such a tribunal,

12. Copy of the letter on file with the author.

13. Essentially, the Canadians seemed to have been caught by surprise by the US request, which was publicly made by the US Secretary of State, Ms. Madeline Albright, in June 1997. The Canadians responded by saying that the American request would have to be approved by the UN Security Council, thus effectively ensuring that the request would be vetoed. See *The Times* (London 26 June 1997) p. 15.

14. Perhaps one of the key reasons these efforts failed is that almost no-one was serious about making the KR, as an entity, pay for its crimes: the focus was entirely on a single, one-off trial of the almost-mysterious Pol Pot. This focus on individual leaders could not but reveal itself as ethically unacceptable and practically unsound. I thank David Ashley for pointing out this issue.

15. See US Senate Resolution 124, 24 September 1997. The Senate Resolution states clearly that this is US policy; a policy that was established by the Executive at the time of the Paris Peace Accords.

along with a draft charter.[16] The draft Charter was fundamentally flawed in that it called for the trial of only a small number of 'senior KR leaders'[17] – unlike the tribunals in Former Yugoslavia or Rwanda, for example, whose Statutes do not limit who can be prosecuted, other than in a temporal or geographic sense. However, the ICTR, in practice, has concentrated on prosecution of the leaders. Obviously, the US initiative got nowhere due to lack of consultation with Cambodia, other countries or the UN and due to the lack of any support from the human rights community. Although, this saga of wasted opportunities could be attributed to bureaucratic inefficiency and political confusion in the US administration, one gets the impression that the US is either not serious about the KR crimes or is active in torpedoing any attempt to establish a tribunal. Unfortunately, the intentions of a small number of people are not enough when judging the conduct of nations – the results count.

Subsequently, the KR has almost completely disintegrated as a military-political unit: the notorious Pol Pot was purged, found guilty in a show trial[18] by his erstwhile comrades and is now dead, and a very large number of the senior cadre of the KR have defected to Hun Sen's side. Meanwhile, the UN High Commissioner for Human Rights and Mr. Hammarberg have struggled to keep up the momentum for the prosecution of the KR. As a result, the team of experts would visit Cambodia in November 1998.[19] But the political turbulence during 1996-1997 that brought the prosecution of the KR within the realm of possibility, has all but disappeared. Hun Sen and CPP emerged as the biggest political force in Cambodia from the July 1998 national election and now appear to be firmly in control. Given this political turnaround, it is legitimate to ask: would the effort to establish an international tribunal succeed? The initial indications are that it would be very difficult to establish (more on that later).

In addition, assuming that some mechanism of accountability is politically possible and morally desirable, there are many unanswered questions: Who in the KR should be brought to justice? How wide should the net be cast? Is it

16. Draft resolution dated 28 April 1998. Copy on file with the author. This may seem somewhat puzzling when the US was, at the same time, opposing several key elements of the Rome Charter on the establishment of the permanent International Criminal Court.

17. The US's initiative, which was largely the result of the officials in the State Department who were responsible for human rights, targeted Pol Pot, and later Ta Mok (senior KR military commander known as 'butcher') and Nuon Chea (a senior KR leader).

18. Nate Thayer, 'Pol Pot: The End', *Far Eastern Economic Review* (7 August 1997).

19. The three experts are: Sir Ninian Stephen of Australia, former Judge of the ICTY, who will head the group; Rajsoomer Lallah of Mauritius, currently the Special Rapporteur for Myanmar; and Professor Steven Ratner, an American legal academic who co-wrote a 1995 report for the US State Department on bringing the KR to justice. See 'Legal Experts to Charge Cambodia's Khmer Rouge with Genocide,' (Deutsche Presse-Agentur 13 August 1998).

politically wise and morally acceptable to prosecute a few in return for an amnesty to others who were also part of the KR leadership? What are the options for bringing some of these KR to justice, including in particular, the options for an international tribunal?

3. AN ANALYSIS OF THE POLITICAL, PLANNING AND OPERATIONAL ASPECTS OF PROSECUTION

Many issues emerge from a consideration of the questions posed above. Those issues may usefully be discussed under the following headings.

3.1 The possibility and the desirability of criminal prosecution

Though there have been a few independent judges and prosecutors in Cambodia, historically it has never known an independent judiciary, as an institution. Accountability of public officials has not typically resulted from the rule of law, as it is understood in the west. Instead, the Cambodian political elite has had a purely instrumental view of law, where it is looked upon as either a tool of legitimation or as a method of consolidating power. As a result, trials have traditionally been purely symbolic events intended to affirm the rightfulness of the power-holders. This has been particularly true since 1980 under Vietnamese-trained judges and prosecutors. Not much of this has changed during the last few years under UN tutelage. Indeed, one of the key problems in the administration of justice of Cambodia during the last few years has been that of impunity, resulting from an inability or unwillingness to prosecute.[20] This is a structural problem that has existed in Cambodia since the days of Prince Norodom Sihanouk to the current CPP regime. The impunity of the KR, graver than the rest as it is, fits the pattern of political elites in Cambodia. Given this hard reality, it is somewhat naive to believe, as many apparently do, that criminal prosecutions of the KR, *per se*, will have the same meaning for Cambodians as prosecutions do for westerners. This, however, does not mean that Cambodians do not aspire to justice for the KR crimes – they may just prefer other options that have more meaning for their everyday lives.

As mentioned above, between mid-1996 and mid-1997 there was a reasonable window of political opportunity to bring at least some of the KR to justice. This was made possible by a unique combination of events: Ieng Sary split from the

20. See Basil Fernando, *The Inability to Prosecute: Courts and Human Rights in Cambodia and Sri Lanka* (Future Asia Links, Hong Kong 1993).

KR and was courted by both Hun Sen and Ranariddh; Ranariddh was possibly interested in strengthening the hands of the Ieng Sary faction with whom he was dealing, by pushing for the prosecution of the 'hard-liners' including Ta Mok; Hun Sen was aspiring to deal a final blow to the KR, as he initially saw Ieng Sary's defection as weakening the KR; the UNCHR and Mr. Hammarberg were pushing hard, with the support of other national and international human rights groups, for the prosecution of the KR as they saw this as an opportune moment; and finally, some of the alleged mass killers of the KR, such as Duch[21] and Chan[22], were known to be living in areas that were under the control of Hun Sen's forces, giving rise to expectations that perhaps, with some pressure, they could be captured and turned over.

However, this window of opportunity was closed with the poorly calibrated western response to these events as well as to the July 1997 coup. The Australians, French and the British showed no interest in bringing the KR to justice whereas the Americans made much noise yet showed no real willingness to follow through with their rhetoric. With Hun Sen now firmly in political control, the chances of prosecuting the KR appear to be slim. Hun Sen would see no political benefit in cooperating with a prosecuting body, when he has formed alliances with Ieng Sary, and a large number of senior KR cadre.[23] This is especially so in the aftermath of the 1998 election which the CPP has won. None of the other political players in Cambodia have sufficient power or interest to bring the KR to justice.

Given these realities, it is legitimate to ask: who then has any interest in bringing the KR to justice? First, the international human rights community, consisting of activists, NGOs and interested scholars, has long had an interest in bringing the KR to justice. These individuals and institutions make it rather clear that bringing the KR to justice is an issue that goes beyond Cambodian attitudes towards right and wrong: it is, in the words of *The New York Times*,

21. Kang Kek Ieu, alias Duch, was the director of Office S-21, also known as *santebol* or office of the security police between 1975 and 1979. S-21 was a mass detention, interrogation and extermination facility for ethnic Khmer and some foreigners suspected of espionage, which admitted some 14,000 men, women and children between 1975 and 1979. Of those, only seven are known to have survived. Information from David Chandler. Note on file with the author.

22. Mam Nay, *alias* Chan, was the head of the interrogation unit at S-21 from mid-1976 until 1979. There is documentary evidence of his close association with the tortures and killings at S-21. Information from David Chandler. Note on file with the author.

23. Though Hun Sen may be willing and only too glad to see some of the KR, like Ta Mok and Nuon Chea, brought to trial, he is not likely to sacrifice – or have the capacity to capture – other KR who are close to him, including Ieng Sary.

an issue of 'law and civilization'.[24] To them, bringing the KR to justice would be an important patch on the international normative quilt.

Second, a very sizeable number of Cambodians, both urban and rural, wish to bring the KR to justice. These Cambodians lost their family members during the cataclysm and have suffered greatly, emotionally and materially. To these Cambodians, bringing the KR to justice is a painful but necessary requirement for building a society that is based on respect for human life, individual accountability of power-holders and the rule of law.

Without entirely endorsing the instrumentalist approach of the first group of human rights activists towards the KR, I will note that these two groups of individuals and institutions have established the moral and legal case for bringing the KR to justice and have generated sufficient momentum towards that end.[25] Consequently, any effort to bring the KR to justice, must seek to satisfy the minimum aspirations of both of these constituencies. Such an effort must provide the immediate and contextual basis for building a society that is based on the rule of law, while ensuring the development of the international legal normative framework. Only such a contextual basis will have a chance of promoting the *rule of law for Cambodians,* rather than some mythical rule of law of the purely western variety that assumes, for example, the autonomy of legal outcomes. While there should be no illusions about the capacity of an international effort to transform Cambodia into a just society, there is a role for the international community to act as a catalyst in a complex process of socio-political transformation.

I will argue that the only way of achieving this is by ensuring two conditions: first, any effort to bring the KR to justice must be based in Cambodia; and second, no exceptions must be made unless a legally valid amnesty or immunity has been granted, after a full and public disclosure of the facts surrounding an individual's involvement in any crime. The first condition is essential to ensure that the seeds of accountability are deeply sown among the Cambodian political elite. The second condition is necessary to preclude Hun Sen or other political players from protecting specific KR cadre. Under these two conditions, it would then be possible to consider the other issues as follows.

24. The *Times* noted: 'trying Pol Pot for the crimes he is accused of masterminding would be an extraordinary triumph for law and civilization'. 'A Trial for Pol Pot', Editorial, *The New York Times* (24 June 1997).

25. As a general remark, I should note that pressure exerted from outside by NGOs, activists and academics has been the only reason why the KR crime have received even this much attention. The United States as well as the UN have not historically shown any real interest in the human rights violations committed by the KR starting from 1975. On this issue, see Jamie Metzl, *Western Responses to Human Rights Abuses in Cambodia* (St. Martin's Press, 1996).

3.2 Temporal jurisdiction of the prosecuting body

Who within the KR should be brought to justice depends heavily on the temporal jurisdiction of the prosecuting body; in other words, the period within which the crimes in question were committed. Confining this period to 1975-79 would result in a different outcome as opposed to throwing the door open for prosecuting any KR violation during the last two decades, such as the KR raids on Battambang[26] villages in 1994. For several reasons, the temporal jurisdiction must be as wide open as possible, in order to facilitate the building of evidence, including the planning of crimes such as the forcible transfer of populations in 1975. Otherwise, the prosecuting body will be crippled. The temporal jurisdiction of the Rwanda Tribunal, for example, covers only the period between 1 January 1994 and 31 December 1994, and this was criticized by the Rwandan government as being too restrictive.[27] In addition, the prosecuting body must be able to hear evidence about the political, military and ideological support given to the KR by China, Thailand and the US.[28] Punishing the Cambodians while letting the foreigners off scot free would convey exactly the wrong message about the rule of law that the Cambodians so much want to get across.[29] The one drawback of this expanded temporal jurisdiction is that it would require the tribunal to also prosecute other Cambodians who are guilty of crimes against humanity or the laws of war that were committed during the post-1979 period. Many leaders of the CPP, including Hun Sen, may then also be liable to be prosecuted, although this would depend on the subject-matter jurisdiction of the tribunal. Notwithstanding this difficulty, it is far more sensible, on balance, to allow an expanded temporal jurisdiction for the tribunal.

26. A northwestern province in Cambodia.

27. See Cissé, at p. 163, fn. 12.

28. Former US National Security Adviser Zbigniew Brzezinski is reported to have acknowledged after leaving office: 'I encouraged China to support Pol Pot'. See George Gedda, 'Pol Pot: A "mass murderer" but, for a time, an ally', Associated Press, 20 June 1997. I should also note that the Vietnamese were also responsible for creating the KR, as without Vietnamese assistance, the KR could not have won the 1970-75 war against the US-backed Lon Nol forces. In addition, the UN itself is deeply implicated with the KR: UN 'humanitarian' operations kept the KR alive during the 1980s along the Thai-Cambodian border.

29. I do not mean that it would be possible to find foreign backers of the KR criminally responsible; but if the effort to bring the KR to justice is about establishing the truth (which it is, in the final analysis), then the whole truth must be told. The inescapable part of that truth is the fact that the KR is, to a very significant extent, the creature of the international community.

3.2.1 *Personal jurisdiction*

Given the almost universal revulsion at the crimes committed by the KR, any prosecution must aim at casting the net as wide as possible. Deals such as the *de jure* amnesty granted by Cambodian authorities to Ieng Sary and the *de facto* amnesty granted to other KR cadre such as Kae Pok, do not and cannot prevent an independent prosecuting body such as an international tribunal from indicting them. In other words, no matter what political deals are forged inside Cambodia, any international prosecution process should be open-ended. Legally the deals mean nothing in international law. The targets should include not only the political leadership of the KR in the Central Security Committee, but also the second-rung leadership as well as senior military commanders, commune-level political and military leaders, as well as other individuals against whom there is evidence. This could run into thousands. Those who may claim that it is too dangerous or unrealistic to target so many are in fact morally duplicitous and historically wrong. After all – as in the case of the suspects of the Rwanda genocide (an estimated 126,216 are in Rwandan prisons awaiting trial[30]) – accountability has meant targeting most of the wrongdoers. Selective prosecution is, in other words, not only morally unacceptable and historically unfounded, it is also practically impossible for an independent prosecuting body. The counter-argument, that it would be too expensive or time-consuming to target so many, simply does not work in the Cambodian context, where the purpose of the exercise is to drive home the message of accountability. That message is hardly likely to be sent if only some are held liable.

3.3 **Mechanisms of accountability**

What then are the options for bringing the KR to justice? There appear to be at least four: national prosecution, some sort of a truth commission, third country prosecution and an international tribunal.[31] As the 1995 US State Department study by Steven Ratner and Jason Abrams concluded, national prosecution is not feasible in Cambodia for many reasons. The national judiciary is still a shambles:

30. Report of the Special Rapporteur for Rwanda, of 19 February 1998, at para. 22.

31. There is one more option and that is the possibility of a proceeding before the International Court of Justice, under Art. 36 of its Statute. I am not discussing it here due to the fact that such a measure by any country is highly remote. For a discussion of this option as well as an application under Article IX of the Genocide Convention, see Hurst Hannum, 'International Law and Cambodian Genocide: The Sounds of Silence', 11 *Hum. Rts. Q* (1989) p. 82. Of course, now the Permanent International Criminal Court has also been founded in the Rome Charter, but it has no jurisdiction over past crimes.

the judges and prosecutors are not independent and have a hard time getting their routine orders obeyed by the police; the national police is not well-trained and lacks the expertise or the facilities to conduct investigations into genocide or crimes against humanity; and finally, the judicial process has no credibility in the eyes of the general public.[32]

A truth commission, even one such as in South Africa, which has the option of referring cases for prosecution, stands very little chance of success for many of the same reasons that render national prosecution an impossibility. A key issue here is the absence of nationally respected figures (such as Archbishop Tutu in South Africa), who could provide legitimacy and credibility to the truth commission. The Cambodian political scene is far too fragmented for this option to work. The political divisions between the leading players are so deep that a consensus candidate, let alone a consensus on the method and operation of a truth commission, seem remote at best. This does not mean, however, that recent experiences with truth commissions could not prove useful; for example, the experience of the El Salvadorian truth commission, with local and international personnel, could be studied more closely to assist in establishing the mixed-tribunal that I advocate.[33]

Third country prosecution offers the possibility of prosecution by friendly (and neutral) countries such as Norway or Canada, based on laws that allow prosecutions based on 'universal jurisdiction'; that is, in lay terms, a legal *carte blanche* to prosecute anyone who has committed certain specific crimes, such as genocide, anywhere in the world, since they are *hostis humani generis* (the enemy of all people).[34] This is also undesirable for several reasons. First, it would not satisfy the aspirations of the Cambodians who wish to see the prosecution of the KR lead to a society based on the rule of law, since trials in remote places like Canada would not register on Cambodian public and governmental psyche. Second, third country prosecutions would also suffer from a deep lack of understanding of Cambodian society, culture and government. Third, such prosecutions would find it difficult and expensive to deal with evidence – both testimonies of individuals as well as physical evidence, such

32. See Fernando, *supra* n. 20. See generally the sections on judicial independence and the rule of law in the series of reports submitted by the UNSRSGHRC to the CHR, particularly the 1994 Report: E/CN.4/1994/73; E/CN.4/1995/87; E/CN.4/1996/93; E/CN.4/1997/85.

33. See *infra*. On Truth Commissions, see generally, *Truth Commissions: A Comparative Assessment* (Harvard Law School Human Rights Program, 1997).

34. On universal jurisdiction, *see* generally Kenneth Randall, 'Universal Jurisdiction under International Law', 66 *Texas L Rev*. (1988) p. 785. Third country prosecutions have been termed 'decentralized prosecutions'. See Ruediger Wolfrum, 'The Decentralized Prosecution of International Offences through National Courts', 24 *Israel Y.B. Hum. Rts*. (1995) p. 183.

as bones, which are already decaying. Fourth, only a few individuals who can be taken into physical custody could be prosecuted, thus leaving a large number of guilty individuals beyond accountability. Finally, third country prosecutions would not have the same neutrality, legitimacy and credibility as an international prosecution. These have proved to be important factors in other cases, such as Rwanda.

The final option, and one that has been requested by the Cambodian Government, is an international tribunal. There are at least four ways in which this can be done. First, the subject-matter jurisdiction of the Yugoslav and/or Rwandan tribunal could perhaps be expanded to include offenses committed by the KR in Cambodia. This appears to be politically unlikely at the moment (it was suggested that the Yugoslav tribunal cover Rwanda although this did not succeed) and operationally complex. It also appears to be legally very difficult to accomplish, as it is unlikely that the Security Council would find the situation to be covered by Chapter VII.

Second, the Security Council of the UN could establish a special tribunal by a resolution under Chapter VII of the UN Charter, as it did in the case of Yugoslavia and Rwanda. This also appears politically unlikely as the US recently tried such a measure and failed.[35] The Chinese may veto such a resolution as they may feel uncomfortable at the thought of KR revelations about the extent and the duration of Chinese involvement, in addition to opposing the very idea of international accountability for domestic violations. As above, the Security Council is also unlikely to find that there is a 'threat to the peace, breach of the peace or act of aggression', as required by the UN Charter, in the Cambodian case. It was possible in the case of Yugoslavia and Rwanda (only barely and against some serious opposition) as they were ongoing conflicts.

Third, an 'international penal tribunal' provided for in Article 6 of the Genocide Convention could be established to try the KR. Cambodia is a party to that Convention. This solution is both undesirable and unworkable. If such a tribunal were to be established, its subject-matter jurisdiction would be confined to the crime of genocide; in the case of the KR, that is hardly adequate as they also committed crimes against humanity as well as grave breaches of international humanitarian law, including the 1949 Geneva Conventions. Furthermore, in the almost 40 years since the adoption of the Genocide Convention, such a tribunal has never been established, and in many states, such as the US, the establishment of such a tribunal may once again raise political concerns of the specter of

35. See *supra* nn. 13-14 and the accompanying text.

criminal prosecution of their nationals for acts of genocide against native Americans.[36]

3.4 The Mixed Tribunal: A proposal for a gradualist and minimal justice

Finally, the request by the Cambodian government could be directly acted upon by the SG as a technical assistance request. Under Article 68 of the UN Charter, the UNCHR comes under the Economic and Social Council (ECOSOC). And under Article 98 of the Charter, the SG has to perform any function entrusted to him by the ECOSOC. As the 21 June 1997 letter of the co-Prime Ministers indicates, the April 1997 resolution of the UNCHR requested the SG to 'examine any request by Cambodia for assistance' in relation to past crimes committed by the KR. As a result, there appears to be a legal basis for the SG to respond directly to Cambodia's request, as he has the legal mandate from the UNCHR (and ECOSOC and therefore the Charter) already. Concerning many other such requests, the SG has routinely responded by providing, *inter alia*, assistance in election monitoring. Why not do the same for an international tribunal? All that is needed is the conclusion of a Memorandum of Understanding between Cambodia and the UN to work out the technical details and the adoption of a Charter for the Tribunal.[37]

The SG has taken a first crucial step by appointing the three-member Group of Experts without any endorsement from the Security Council. What is needed now is principled and courageous follow-through by the UN, acting through Mr. Hammarberg, to conclude an MOU with the Cambodian government. The MOU should, ideally speaking, be preceded by a dual effort: one on the part of the western countries, to encourage Hun Sen to agree to this process without preconditions, and two, on the part of the UN to mobilize financial support for the mixed-tribunal, preferably from the Scandinavian countries, the Netherlands and Canada. Many of these countries were recently at the forefront of the battle to conclude the Rome Charter; they should show similar foresight and determination to back this long-overdue effort to bring the KR to justice.

36. See Lawrence J. le Blanc, 'The United States and the Genocide Convention', (Durham N.C., Duke University Press 1991).

37. One variation of this proposal could be the conclusion of a Memorandum of Understanding between Cambodia and interested courts somewhat based on the Nuremburg model. This model has been advocated recently within the UN. I personally believe that the political momentum for such a course of action is fairly limited, unless the UN plays an active coordinating role and involves NGOs.

This solution has several advantages. It fulfils the minimum moral aspirations of both the constituencies of people that I identified above: the foreign human rights community as well as affected Cambodians. It does so by ensuring that the KR is brought to justice inside Cambodia, in a process that significantly contributes to the rebuilding of a society based on the rule of law in which impunity is gradually eliminated. In addition, it has the following practical advantages. First, it avoids the political organs of the UN, such as the Security Council, where any effort to establish yet another criminal court is sure to perish. Second, it reduces the response time drastically, as no formal texts need to be adopted at a multilateral level. Third, it opens the door for additional financing options outside the main UN budgetary channels (and therefore avoids the political wrangling at the Fifth Committee). Fourth, it has very important precedential value, as it demonstrates a way of rendering justice to victims of human rights violations in similar situations, while avoiding becoming embroiled in political imbroglios.

To be effective and credible, such a tribunal should consist of Cambodians and foreigners. Only such a joint composition could ensure that its investigations are effective, and its decisions are credible and locally-rooted. There are such Cambodians, including in the non-governmental sector, and it is only their involvement that can turn this tribunal into an institution that is not merely a foreign imposition. In order to reduce the politicization of the tribunal, relevant international and local NGOs must be consulted by the UN and the countries that are involved while selecting the personnel for the tribunal.[38] There are some disadvantages to this approach as well. The primary disadvantage is that the tribunal may find it difficult to conceal the identities of witnesses and offer them physical protection in the absence of offers from other countries to perform that task. This is necessary to ensure efficient justice. The second disadvantage with the mixed-tribunal is that it may be somewhat removed from the international news media and academic circuits, due to its location. The Rwanda tribunal has been much less in focus than the ICTY, due to these factors, among others.

After a careful evaluation of the advantages and disadvantages, it appears that this solution may present the best option under the present circumstances.

38. For such a suggestion in the case of the permanent International Criminal Court, see, 'International Criminal Court: Making the Right Choice Part II', (AI Index IOR 40/11/97, July 1997).

4. CONCLUSION

While it is unclear whether any senior KR leaders will ever be brought to justice, there must be much advance thinking to prepare the ground for the eventuality of the prosecution of the KR, however slim its chances. This thinking must be guided by an informed understanding of the situation inside Cambodia, as well as a conviction about what is morally warranted. After its multiple moral failures in Cambodia, the international community owes that much to atone for its mistakes. The US and other western countries must shake themselves out of their 'Cambodia fatigue' and cooperate with the international and domestic human rights community to bring the KR to justice. The Scandinavian countries and Canada, in particular, should vigorously pursue the establishment of this mixed tribunal and provide its initial funding. The UN, including Mr. Hammarberg, must not abandon hope at this juncture: any progress towards justice, even if it is minimal and gradualist, is still progress. The SG must show determination and principled courage in taking action upon the Cambodian request, as I advocate above. China must cooperate with the effort, or at least abstain from opposing it, to atone for its support for the KR and to avoid the ignominy of being the KR's lone supporter. Cambodian leaders, including Hun Sen, should actively cooperate with the effort: they have nothing to lose, and much to gain in terms of legitimacy and long-term prospects for establishing the rule of law in Cambodia. Otherwise, the 'tragedy of Cambodian history', to borrow David Chandler's words[39], will forever repeat itself.

39. See *supra* n. 2.

THE FREEING OF NTAKIRUTIMANA IN THE UNITED STATES AND 'EXTRADITION' TO THE ICTR*

Jordan J. Paust**

On 17 December 1997, US magistrate Judge Marcel Notzon ordered the release of Elizaphan Ntakirutimana, who had been held in custody in Texas pending a decision on a request by the United States for his extradition to the International Criminal Tribunal for Rwanda (ICTR).[1]

According to the US magistrate's opinion, Ntakirutimana – who, at the time of the events in question, was the President of the Seventh Day Adventist Church in Rwanda, based in a church complex in Mugonero, Gishyita Commune, Kibuye Prefecture – is accused of 'organizing and leading an attack on his church complex on 16 April 1994, to kill all' the unarmed Tutsi civilians who had gathered there, many allegedly at his instruction.[2] The magistrate's opinion added that '[a]fter the 16 April 1994 attack, the Extraditee is accused of leading armed

** Law Foundation Professor, University of Houston (USA); co-Chair, International Criminal Law Interest Group, American Society of International Law.

1. The US request was made pursuant to a Warrant of Arrest and Order for Surrender, issued by Judge William H. Sekule of the ICTR, on 7 September 1996, and served on the US government on 12 September 1996. The Warrant was accompanied by the two indictments issued against Elizaphan Ntakirutimana by the ICTR: the first, ICTR-96-10-I, of 20 June 1996, charges Elizaphan Ntakirutimana, jointly with Gerard Ntakirutimana, Obed Ruzindana and Charles Sikubwabo, with six counts (1 of genocide; 1 of complicity in genocide; 1 of conspiracy to commit genocide; and 3 of crimes against humanity) for crimes allegedly committed during April 1994 at Mugonero Complex in Gishyita Commune, Kibuye Prefecture, Rwanda. The second, ICTR-96-17-I, of 7 September 1996, charges Elizaphan Ntakirutimana, jointly with Gerard Ntakirutimana, with 7 counts (1 of genocide; 1 of complicity in genocide; 1 of conspiracy to commit genocide; 3 of crimes against humanity and 1 of serious violations of Article 3 common to the Geneva Conventions and of Additional Protocol II) for crimes allegedly committed in Bisesero in Gishyita and Gisovu Communes, Kibuye Prefecture, between April and June 1994.

2. In the Matter of Surrender of Elizaphan Ntakirutimana, 1997 LEXIS 20714 (S.D. Tex., Laredo Div., Dec. 17, 1997). Reprinted at p. 607 of this volume.

Yearbook of International Humanitarian Law
Volume I - 1998 - pp. 205-209

bands of men into the countryside of the Bisesero region of Rwanda in an effort to hunt down and kill those Tutsis who survived the attack at Mugonero.[3]

The two reasons given for the order of release were: 1) that a treaty is required for the United States to extradite a person from US territory and no relevant treaty exists, and 2) that the requesting body [the US government] had not shown probable cause that the crimes charged were committed in view of the nature and credibility of the evidence submitted to support the charges.

With respect to the first issue, the magistrate's opinion stated:

> The Government seeks the surrender of the Extraditee pursuant to the 'Agreement on Surrender of Persons between the Government of the United States and the Tribunal' (Agreement) signed 24 January 1995, and the provisions of Section 1342 of Public Law 104-106. This section makes applicable to the instant case the procedures applicable to international extradition pursuant to 18 USC para. 3184 et seq., and the interpretative case law pertaining to those procedures. Accordingly, Congress has instructed the Court to treat the Agreement as if it were a treaty of extradition negotiated between the United States and some other sovereign country. After much careful consideration, the Court is of the opinion that Congress cannot so instruct the Court and that Public Law 104-106, as it pertains to the Tribunal, is unconstitutional. Accordingly, the Court has no jurisdiction to hear the Government's requests and it will be dismissed.

The opinion also concluded that a review of various cases had demonstrated that, 'contrary to the Government's position, Congress has no independent authority to regulate extradition and that a treaty of extradition is required before extradition can occur'. It added that cases addressing the UN Headquarters Agreement between the US and the UN, which, in domestic parlance, is a treaty-based executive agreement (i.e., an agreement between the US Executive and the UN pursuant to the UN Charter), were distinguishable as the Headquarters Agreement 'was enacted pursuant to a treaty ratified with Senatorial advise and consent' and 'was made to effectuate a validly negotiated, signed and ratified treaty entered into by the United States'. The magistrate considered that '[t]his places it in marked contrast to the Agreement with the Tribunal in the instant case.'

The magistrate, however, was quite mistaken. The executive agreement between the US and the ICTR was also 'enacted pursuant to a treaty' – the United Nations Charter, which set up an institutional process involving the formation of the International Criminal Tribunal through UN Security Council powers and the Tribunal's authority to enter into such agreements for the transfer

3. *Idem.*

of accused to the Tribunal.[4] Clearly, the executive agreement was part of an effort 'to effectuate a validly negotiated and signed and ratified treaty entered into by the United States'. Given the UN Charter treaty-base, the executive agreement was not a sole executive agreement, but at least a treaty-executive agreement with all the constitutional authority in the United States of a treaty.[5]

Further, the magistrate's conclusion directly clashes with the decision of the Eighth Circuit Court of Appeals in *Williams* v. *Rogers*[6], which recognized that a congressional-executive agreement is a sufficient basis for extradition.[7] Extradition of military persons has also occurred between the US and Canada[8] and the US and Taiwan[9] pursuant to executive agreement.

It is also important that the word 'treaty' found in some US statutes has been interpreted to include executive agreements.[10] Sections 3181 and 3184 of the general US extradition statute can be similarly interpreted. Moreover, the US had argued that another statute, Public Law 104-106, Section 1342, allows extradition to the Tribunal because Congress declared that such executive agreements will operate like treaties and that an act of Congress is a sufficient

4. See generally Robert Kushen and Kenneth J. Harris, *Surrender of Fugitives by the United States to the War Crimes Tribunals for Yugoslavia and Rwanda*, 90 *AJIL* (1996) p. 510; Jordan J. Paust, correspondence, 91 *AJIL* (1997) p. 90; Jordan J. Paust, M. Cherif Bassiouni, et al., *International Criminal Law* 76 (letter of ICTY President Cassese), 79 (1996) pp. 403-404 [hereinafter Paust, Bassiouni, et al.]; Ruth Wedgwood, 'Is US Justice Soft on Genocide?', *The Christian Science Monitor* (Feb. 6, 1998), at p. 23. The International Criminal Tribunal for the Former Yugoslavia has already ruled on such general competence under and through the UN Charter and the Security Council. E.g., *The Prosecutor of the Tribunal* v. *Dusko Tadić*, Decision on the Defence Motion on Jurisdiction (10 August 1995), revised and affirmed in part by the Appeals Chamber (2 October 1995), extract reprinted in Paust, Bassiouni, et al., *supra*, at pp. 813-823.

5. See e.g., Restatement of the Foreign Relations Law of the United States para. 115, comment c, and para. 303 (3) and comment f, 3rd edn. (1987) [hereinafter Restatement]; Jordan J. Paust, *International Law as Law of the United States* (1996) pp. 101, 446, 464, 467-468. Section 303, comment f of the Restatement adds: 'An executive agreement may be made by the President pursuant to a treaty ... when the executive agreement can fairly be seen as implementing the treaty ... Such an executive agreement has the same effect and validity as the treaty itself ...' US cases have also recognized that an extradition treaty can be extended or revised by executive agreement. See e.g., *United States* v. *Kin-Hong*, 110 F.3d 103, 111 (1st Cir. 1997); *In re* D'Amico, 117 F. Supp. 648, 652 (SDNY 1959).

6. 449 F.2d 513, 521 (8th Cir. 1971), cert. denied, 405 US 926 (1972).

7. *Idem.* at 521 ('the Agreement, resting as it does on the delegation of legislative authority ... [can] provide such a basis' of authority as that recognized in *Valentine*, addressed *infra* n. 11).

8. See *United States* v. *Salzmann*, 417 F. Supp. 1139, 1157 (EDNY 1976).

9. See *Starks* v. *Seamans*, 334 F. Supp. 1255 (E.D. Wis. 1971).

10. See e.g., Restatement, *supra* n. 5, para. 111, reporters' note 4 and para. 303, reporters' note 1.

basis for extradition.[11] As noted above, the magistrate did not accept this argument, claiming that the US Congress cannot authorize extradition without some treaty base. The better argument would have also stressed that the executive agreement with the ICTR is at least a congressional-executive agreement, sanctified in *Williams* v. *Rogers*, and is actually a treaty-congressional-executive agreement (with even more significant constitutional authority).

The magistrate's opinion also declared that '[t]hroughout the history of this Republic, every extradition from the United States has been accomplished under the terms of a valid treaty of extradition,' but no authority was cited for this viewpoint. Moreover, *Williams* v. *Rogers* and cases involving military personnel, noted above, demonstrate that this statement is erroneous.

The second major rationale for denial of extradition hinged upon review of the evidence presented to support probable cause that the crimes alleged had been committed by the accused.

In support of its application, the US Government presented a 25-page affidavit filed by a Belgian police officer assigned to the ICTR, which provided evidence against the accused. The magistrate pointed to the following deficiencies in the affidavit: it did not identify witnesses other than by letter (e.g., A, B, C, etc.); there was no statement as to the witnesses' reliability; the circumstances and language capabilities of interviewers and witnesses were not indicated; there was no indication that witnesses were under oath while making their statements; only two of twelve witnesses 'claim that they observed the Extraditee during the attacks'; there was 'no mention by any witness that the Extraditee committed a specific act . . . directed the assault or participated in any way other than the

11. The US cited *Grin* v. *Shine*, 187 US 181, 191 (1902) (dictum: 'Congress has a perfect right to provide for the extradition of criminals in its own way, with or without a treaty to that effect, and to declare that foreign criminals shall be surrendered upon such proofs of criminality as it may judge sufficient.'). The magistrate stated that this dictum merely pertained 'to the question of whether Congress could require more or less stringent proofs . . . than those expressly contained in the treaty' in that case. In the landmark case of United States ex rel. *Neidecker* v. *Valentine*, 299 US 5, 8-9 (1936), the Supreme Court declared that the power to extradite 'is not confided to the Executive in the absence of a treaty or legislative provision' and '[i]t must be found that [a] statute or treaty confers the power,' indicating that one or the other might be enough. The court did not decide the question but noted '[w]hatever may be the power of the Congress to provide for extradition independent of treaty, that power has not been exercised save in relation to a foreign country or territory occupied by or under the control of the United States . . .' *Idem* at 9. The fact that Congress could do so regarding occupied or controlled territory should not be viewed as a limiting circumstance because the United States is entirely a creature of the Constitution and has no power or authority to act inconsistent with the Constitution within the US or abroad. See e.g., *Reid* v. *Covert*, 354 US 1, 5-6 (1957); *United States* v. *Tiede*, Crim. Case No. 78-001A (US Ct. for Berlin 1979), extract reprinted in Paust and Bassiouni, et al., op. cit. n. 4, at p. 258; Paust, op. cit. n. 5, at pp. 422-423, 432, et seq.

vague reference that he was "among the attackers",' and so forth. He concluded that 'the possibility for inaccuracy or incredibility in the witnesses' statements is high.'

The magistrate added, incorrectly, that a claim of two witnesses that the accused instructed 'other armed Hutus to take the roof off a church so that it could not be used as a shelter' would not be evidence relevant to genocide, especially an act 'inflicting conditions on *the* Tutsis calculated to bring about *their* physical destruction' [emphasis added]. What was not recognized, however, was the fact that such conduct might have been related to the '[k]illing of members of the group' or '[c]ausing serious bodily or mental harm to members of the group' with genocidal intent, within the meaning of Article 2 of the Genocide Convention.

After consideration of the affidavit, the magistrate found 'that the information contained therein does not rise to the level of probable cause.'

At the time of writing, the US Government had reintroduced a request for extradition. Of course, the United States has a duty under the Statute of the ICTR to cooperate with the Tribunal and to comply without undue delay with any request for assistance, including a request for the surrender or transfer of accused persons to the Tribunal. If the US had not reintroduced a request for extradition, it would not be complying with such duties in good faith.[12]

EDITOR'S NOTE: On 5 August 1988, a Federal Judge ordered the deportation of Ntakirutimana to the ICTR.

12. See e.g., M. Cherif Bassiouni, 2 *International Criminal Law* (1986) pp. 421-422, reprinted in Paust, Bassiouni, et al., *supra* n. 4, at p. 289.

DURESS AS A DEFENCE TO WAR CRIMES AFTER ERDEMOVIĆ: A LABORATORY[1] FOR A PERMANENT COURT?*

Peter Rowe**

1. INTRODUCTION

Dražen Erdemović, a lance corporal in the Bosnian Serb Army, admitted to killing 'from 10 to 100'[2] Bosnian Muslim men by firing squad in July 1995, in and around the area of Srebrenica[3], during which process approximately 1,200

** Professor of Law, University of Lancaster, England; Chairman of the Management Board of the Centre for Defence and International Security Studies, University of Lancaster.

1. The phrase is that of current ICTY President, Judge Gabrielle Kirk McDonald, in a press release of the ICTY of 9 December 1997, CC/PIO/272/E.

2. For the estimated numbers, see The Prosecutor's Brief on Aggravating and Mitigating Factors, *Prosecutor* v. *Dražen Erdemović*, Case No. IT-96-22-T, 11 November 1996, p. 2, fn.8. The Prosecutor estimated that in 'using a Kalashnikov automatic rifle, he might have killed up to a hundred people'. Trial Chamber, *Prosecutor* v. *Dražen Erdemović*, Sentencing Judgment, Case No. IT-96-22-T*bis*, 5 March 1998, para. 15. For the accused's status in the Bosnian Serb Army, see the Prosecutor's Brief on Aggravating and Mitigating Factors, op cit. at para. 17. Erdemović is, in fact, a Bosnian Croat who had earlier served with the Bosnian Government Army and Bosnian Croat Army before joining the Bosnian Serb Army in April 1994. But see letter from Croatian Embassy of 21 November 1996 to foreign-desk editors in which the Croatian authorities state that 'Mr. Erdemović is not a Croat by any recognizable standard'. The letter adds that Mr. Erdemović is 'not a citizen of the Republic of Croatia nor of the Bosnian Croat-Muslim Federation. Nor is he a Croat by his own preferences. (. . .) Finally, from a banal ethnical point of view, he is, coming from a mixed marriage, only "half-Croat".' The letter concludes: 'The description of Mr. Erdemović as a Croat only leads to further muddling of an already very complex problem and to diverting attention of the public from the true identity of the perpetrators of the genocide in Srebrenica.' In the Sentencing Judgment of 5 March, the Trial Chamber stated that 'The possibility of his [sic] being a soldier of fortune has not been suggested by any of the Parties.' op.cit, para. 16.

3. The executions were carried out on or about 16 July 1995 at Pilica collective farm, in the Zvornik Municipality of Bosnia and Herzegovina. The victims were Bosnian Muslim civilian men from Srebrenica who had surrendered to Bosnian Serb military or police personnel. See Indictment, Case No. IT-96-2-I, para. 10.

Yearbook of International Humanitarian Law
Volume I - 1998 - pp. 210-228

unarmed civilians[4] were killed. He expressed a willingness to surrender to the jurisdiction of the International Criminal Tribunal for the Former Yugoslavia (ICTY) and was duly transferred to The Hague from the Federal Republic of Yugoslavia (FRY).[5]

He was charged with a crime against humanity and, in the alternative, with a violation of the laws or customs of war.[6] He pleaded guilty before a Trial Chamber to a crime against humanity and the alternative charge was dismissed by the Trial Chamber.[7] At all times, he expressed remorse for his actions[8] and had told the trial judges that:

> 'I had to do this. If I had refused, I would have been killed together with the victims. When I refused they told me: "If you are sorry for them, stand up, line up with them and we will kill you too." I am not sorry for myself but for my family, my wife and son who then had [sic] nine months, and I could not refuse because then they would have killed me. That is all I wish to add.'[9]

In the first instance, Erdemović was sentenced to ten years imprisonment after the Trial Chamber had taken into account the 'extreme gravity of the offence' and mitigating factors.[10] The mitigating factors included his low rank; his current family situation; the 'lack of danger he presents'[11]; the fact that he 'would serve his sentence in a prison far from his own country'[12]; and his cooperation with the Office of the Prosecutor. In considering these factors, the

4. See para. 8 of the Judgment of the Appeals Chamber in the *Prosecutor* v. *Dražen Erdemović*. Case No. IT-96-22-A, 7 October 1997.

5. Prosecutor's Brief, *supra* n. 2, at p. 4. Erdemović was arrested in the Federal Republic of Yugoslavia (FRY) on 2 March 1996 and transferred to the ICTY on 30 March 1996 for questioning. His case was formally deferred from the FRY to the ICTY following an order for deferral issued by Trial Chamber II. Decision on Deferral Hearing, Case No. IT-96-22-D, 29 May 1996.

6. In an Indictment of 29 May 1996, Case No. IT-96-22-I.

7. During his initial appearance on 31 May 1996.

8. Prosecutor's Brief, *supra* n. 2, p. 6.

9. *The Prosecutor of the Tribunal* v. *Dražen Erdemović*, Case No. IT-96-22-D, Transcript of initial appearance hearing, 31 May 1996, p. 9, lines 7-11.

10. *The Prosecutor* v. *Dražen Erdemović*, Sentencing Judgment, 29 November 1996, Case No. IT-96-22-T. There were a number of features of the procedure adopted by the Trial Chamber which, along with an application to revise the sentence, led to the case being considered by the Appeals Chamber. The accused had, by his statement, set out above, indicated that he might have a defence, such as duress (or compulsion), and, thus, his guilty plea might be considered to have been equivocal.

11. Ibid., at para. 111.

12. Ibid.

Trial Chamber took into account that Erdemović had pleaded guilty to a crime against humanity.

Both the Defence[13] and the Prosecution[14] appealed against this sentence. The Appeals Chamber decided that the guilty plea entered by the accused was uninformed but not equivocal. It remitted the case to a different Trial Chamber in order to give the accused the opportunity to re-plead.[15]

The central issue faced by the Appeals Chamber was whether duress could be a defence where a person was charged with an offence similar to either of those faced by Erdemović. If so, Erdemović's guilty plea was clearly equivocal, as, in his statement he was, in effect, raising duress as a defence. The majority of the Chamber held that duress could not be raised as a complete defence to an offence involving the taking of innocent life.[16] Then-President Cassese and Judge Stephen, however, considered that it could, subject to a number of conditions. These were that an accused must have acted under the threat of imminent harm, both serious and irreparable, to his life or limb (or that of his family); that there was no adequate means of averting such evil; that the crime committed must not have been disproportionate to the evil threatened; and the situation leading to the duress must not have been brought about by the person coerced.[17]

Judges McDonald and Vohrah took the view that, 'No rule may be found in customary international law regarding the availability or the non-availability of duress as a defence to a charge of killing innocent human beings'[18] as did President Cassese[19] (with whom Judge Stephen agreed). Where the majority and minority parted company was in their interpretation of the consequence of this finding. Judges McDonald and Vohrah relied upon the need to 'facilitate the

13. Appeal of the Counsel for the Accused Dražen Erdemović, 23 December 1996, Case No. IT-96-22-A; Appellant's brief, filed on 26 March 1997, Case No. IT-96-22-A; Defence's brief concerning preliminary issues, 16 May 1997.

14. Respondent's brief filed on 28 April 1997. Case No. IT-96-22-A; Respondent's brief on preliminary questions as required by the scheduling order of 5 May 1997, 20 May 1997.

15. *Prosecutor* v. *Dražen Erdemović*, Case No. IT-96-22-A, *supra* n. 4. These issues are not considered further in this article. Erdemović reentered a plea on 14 January 1998, pleading guilty to a breach of the laws or customs of war. The alternative charge of a crime against humanity was withdrawn by the prosecutor.

16. Judges McDonald, Li and Vohrah. *Quaere* as to the significance of the term, 'innocent life'. Civilians who have taken no direct part in the conflict are clearly 'innocent' but so is anyone (including a combatant) against whom an attack is prohibited (i.e., those who have surrendered). The phrase 'innocent life', so crucial to the majority, is, in fact, meaningless.

17. *Supra* n. 4, para. 16 of Separate and Dissenting Opinion of President Cassese.

18. Ibid., at para. 55 of their joint judgment. They also concluded that there was no consistent principle to be derived from the general principles of law recognised by civilised nations (with which Judge Li agreed).

19. Ibid., at para. 40 of his judgment.

development and effectiveness of international humanitarian law'[20] in finding the appropriate rule, whereas President Cassese thought that if customary international law did not preclude duress as a defence it could amount to such, subject to stringent conditions.[21]

All the judges agreed, therefore, that neither customary international law nor the general principles of law recognised by civilised nations provide the answer as to whether duress can be pleaded as a defence to the killing of innocent individuals during an armed conflict. In light of such a gap in the law, what should an international criminal tribunal do? It could seek to determine the matter by resort to policy, as did the majority in their pursuit of the goal of preventing the undermining of international humanitarian law, or it could apply the national law most applicable to the accused.[22] Unfortunately, in neither case is the result satisfactory.

2. AN ASSESSMENT OF THE WORKINGS OF THE APPEALS CHAMBER IN *ERDEMOVIĆ*

The Decision of the Appeals Chamber in *Erdemović* is very disappointing, both in relation to the principal issue before the Chamber, i.e., the applicability of duress as a defence, and in the manner of the operation of the Appeals Chamber itself.

2.1 The defence of duress

It would amount to an injustice to the scholarship of President Cassese's judgement for this author to summarise it. A large number of cases are analysed in great detail to show that the main authorities relied upon by the majority[23] do not accurately reflect the propositions derived from them. Thus, the majority construed the *Stalag Luft III*, the *Feurstein* and *Holzer* cases as supporting the

20. Ibid., at para. 75 of their joint judgment.

21. Ibid., at para. 41 of his judgment.

22. As suggested by President Cassese when he argued that where the majority found a gap in the law, or where the law was genuinely ambiguous, they should have drawn upon the law applicable in the former Yugoslavia. Ibid. at para. 49 of his judgment.

23. *Trial of Max Wielen* et al. *(Stalag Luft III)* XI W.C.R. 31; *Trial of Valentin Fuerstein and others* XV W.C.R. 173; *Trial of Gustav Jepson and others*, XV W.C.R. 172; *Record of Proceedings of the Trial by Canadian Court of Robert Holzer and others*, ibid.; *Trial of Otto Ohlendorf* et al. *(Einsatzgruppen Case)* 4 *Trials of War Criminals* 499.

view of the respective judges-advocate that duress is no defence to a crime involving 'the killing of innocent persons generally, regardless of whether the accused was or was not a soldier'.[24] On the grounds that it had not cited any authority, the majority rejected the view of the United States Military Tribunal in the *Einsatzgruppen* case, which concluded that:

> 'There is no law which requires that an innocent man must forfeit his life or suffer serious harm in order to avoid committing a crime which he condemns. The threat, however, must be imminent, real and inevitable. No court will punish a man who, with a loaded pistol at his head, is compelled to pull a lethal lever.'[25]

President Cassese, however, took the view, after studying the original records of the trials, that *Stalag III* 'left open the possibility that duress could be a defence to an unlawful killing' and that in *Fuerstein* the 'Judge-Advocate's *dictum* on duress was *obiter* since none of the accused raised the defence of duress'.[26] The *Holzer* case was, he argued, one where the *ratio decidendi* supported the proposition that duress could never excuse violations of humanitarian law involving the killing of innocent persons but, in that case, the judge-advocate had 'explicitly stated that the court should apply . . . Canadian law, not international law'.[27] The *Einsatzgruppen* case was explained by the then-President on the ground that it had 'relied upon German law, which recognises duress as a defence to any charges'.[28]

By and large, the modern position of the common law countries is to the effect that duress is not recognised as a defence, at least to crimes involving murder,

24. See Joint separate opinion of Judge McDonald and Judge Vohrah, *supra* fn. 4 at para. 42.

25. *Trial of Otto Ohlendorf et al. (Einsatzgruppen Case) 4 Trials of War Criminals* 480.

26. See *supra* n. 4, at para. 22 of the judgment of President Cassese. The separate trials of *Valentin Feurstein, Jepson* and *Holzer* (see n. 23) are not fully reported and are merely noted at pp. 172 and 173 of Vol. XV of the *War Crimes Reports* (WCR).

27. Ibid., at para. 26.

28. Ibid., at para. 27. Oppenheim's view of this case was that 'there is . . . serious objection to the reasoning of the Tribunal'. *International Law* (London, Longmans 1952) Vol. 2 at p. 572. One reason for this severe criticism may be that the case did not clearly distinguish duress (as understood by all members of the Appeals Chamber in *Erdemović)* from superior orders as a defence. There has also been a tendency to fail to distinguish necessity from both duress and superior orders. There is therefore an obvious danger that if superior orders is rejected as a possible defence (as in Art. 7(4) of the Statute of the International Tribunal for the Former Yugoslavia) necessity and duress, if not properly distinguished, will go the same way. The British *Manual of Military Law (Part III)* (London, H.M.S.O., 1958) at para. 629, n. 1(a) draws attention to the fact that these concepts are 'not easily distinguishable'. A large number of other cases are considered in President Cassese's judgment at paras. 32-39.

while, in civil law counties, no such blanket prohibition of the defence applies.[29] Judges Cassese and Stephen were able, however, to draw attention to the fact that the common law authorities envisaged 'situations where an accused has a choice between his own life and the life of another, as distinct from cases where instead the choice was either death for another or death for both'.[30] Erdemović was in this latter category as his protests could not have saved the lives of the victims and, had he persisted, he would have merely succeeded in joining them. The majority was not prepared to make this distinction. Judges McDonald and Vohrah rejected the '*Masetti* approach'[31] and were not willing to sanction the balancing of harms, preferring instead to lay down a straightforward rule that duress could never justify or excuse the taking of innocent life. Palliating factors could, on this approach, always be considered in mitigation of sentence.

The decision of the majority can, of course, be criticised. President Cassese does this very effectively in his judgment. The major practical difference between the majority and minority judgements is that, on the approach of the former, the actual circumstances of the killing and the pressure put upon an accused to carry it out can only be considered at the sentencing stage of a hearing, whilst on that of the latter, it will be part and parcel of the trial itself. On both views, these circumstances are relevant either to mitigation (majority) or as to a defence to the charge (minority).

How will an accused, who, like Erdemović, pleaded guilty because he was advised that the defence of duress is not available where innocent persons have been killed, raise this issue in mitigation? Will the evidential consequences be the same as if the minority view had prevailed? Had this been the case, the accused would, no doubt, have possessed a burden to raise some evidence that he had been compelled to act and that the four conditions set out by President Cassese were satisfied. It would then be for the prosecution to prove, beyond a reasonable doubt, that he had not, in fact, acted under duress.

29. For the surveys of the law relating to particular states see *Prosecutor's Brief on Aggravating and Mitigating Factors*, *supra* n. 2 at Annex; Judgment of Judges McDonald and Vohrah, see n. 4, at paras. 59-68; Judgment of Judge Li, see n. 4 at para. 3.

30. See *supra* n. 4 at para. 29 of the judgment of President Cassese and para. 47 of the judgment of Judge Stephen. This argument had been advanced by Max Wielen (see n. 23) at p. 39 but it was rejected on the facts by the court.

31. Based on an unpublished decision of the Court of Assize of L'Aquila of 15 June 1948. The Court accepted the defence of duress and explained that 'the possible sacrifice [of their lives] by Masetti and his men [those who comprised the execution squad] would have been in any case to no avail and without any effect in that it would have had no impact whatsoever on the plight of the persons to be shot, who would have been executed anyway even without him [the accused]', set out at para. 79 of the joint judgment of Judges McDonald and Vohrah. Judge Li thought 'the absurdity of this argument is apparent' (para. 16 of his judgment).

On the view that prevailed in the Appeals Chamber, the accused will, in practical terms, have to give evidence himself at the sentencing stage of the trial. He may also be able to call witnesses to show that he faced 'an immediate threat of severe and irreparable harm to life or limb' and there was 'no adequate means of averting such evil'.[32] All this goes to the issue of mitigation after the issue of guilt or innocence has been decided. The burden and standard of proof should not be lower than if the issue of duress was relevant to guilt. It is recognised that a Trial Chamber, as an *international* tribunal, is not a common law nor, indeed, a civil law court but must learn to 'combine and fuse'[33] the two systems. Given that the ICTY will wish to uphold the principles of international humanitarian law, a Trial Chamber should not accept any mitigation where innocent life has been taken without clear and strong evidence. Articles 20 and 21 of the Statute of the Tribunal give the accused his right to a fair trial and they are based solely on the question of culpability and are not concerned with the sentencing stage of a hearing.[34] The Tribunal will have to ensure these same standards as if duress was part and parcel of the issue of guilt or innocence.

2.2 Duress distinguished from superior orders

It is clear that the defence of duress is distinct from superior orders.[35] On both the majority and the minority approaches, it involves proof of an immediate threat of severe and irreparable harm to life or limb, with no adequate means of averting such evil. This is quite different from the fear that a failure to obey a superior's orders may lead to some form of military punishment or unpleasant military duty. All military hierarchies punish in some form those who do not obey a superior's orders. The 'threat' may not be immediate in the same way as the type of threat considered to be sufficient for duress under either the majority or

32. These are two of the conditions set out for the establishment of the defence of duress by President Cassese. It is likely that evidence of fact as to these matters would be required by a trial chamber in considering mitigation.

33. *Per* President Cassese, see *supra* n. 4, at para. 4.

34. Art. 24 requires the Trial Chamber when sentencing to take into account such factors as the gravity of the offence and the individual circumstances of the convicted person. See also Rule 101 of the ICTY's Rules of Procedure and Evidence, where aggravating and mitigating factors must be considered. This is quite different from the enquiry that will need to be conducted if duress is raised as a mitigating factor. Moreover, a reasoned opinion need not be given in relation to the appropriate sentence to be imposed; compare Arts. 23 and 24.

35. See *supra* n. 4, at para. 34 (Joint Opinion of Judges McDonald and Vohrah). Bassiouni, *Crimes Against Humanity in International Criminal Law* (Dordrecht, Martinis Nijhoff 1992) at p. 443 shows how the civil law and common law systems take different views as to whether necessity can be separated from duress.

the minority approaches. A failure to obey a superior's orders may, of course, be converted into duress where there is sufficient evidence that its conditions are satisfied in respect of the accused or, perhaps, his family.[36] Whilst it may be reasonable to stipulate in the Statute[37] of the ICTY that superior orders will not amount to a defence and can only be considered in mitigation, the issue of duress is quite different (although the decision of the majority has made the effects the same). Thus, the duress could come from a person of equal or, indeed, lower rank than the accused.[38] The former ensures that an individual's responsibility to international law prevails over his military obligations, as directed by a superior officer, whilst the latter recognises that international law cannot reasonably expect a soldier to withstand the type of threat imposed upon him in the circumstances, especially if innocent lives would be taken in any event. On either approach adopted by the Appeals Chamber, his sentence will be mitigated (majority) or his conduct excused (minority).

The decision of the majority is therefore unsatisfactory since it offers little guidance in international humanitarian law as to what facts will be sufficient to mitigate substantially the sentence that would otherwise be imposed upon a defendant. It is all left to the Trial Chamber in the sentencing process.[39] By way of example, in its Sentencing Judgment (1998) in *Erdemović*, the Trial Chamber was faced with an accused who decided not to give any oral evidence. It is suggested above that the burden and standard of proof of duress (or superior orders) should be no different where it relates to an issue of mitigation of sentence rather than of guilt.[40] Since he had already raised the circumstances of the killings, it would therefore be the responsibility of the prosecution to prove, beyond reasonable doubt, that Erdemović did not take part in the killings

36. President Cassese was prepared to accept that the risk of the severe and irreparable harm may be to an accused's family, *supra* n. 4, at para. 50 of his separate and dissenting opinion.

37. Art. 7(4).

38. In a non-international armed conflict it may be dangerous to draw illustrations about military hierarchies and rank structures as if they were similar to those in armies engaged in an international armed conflict. For an example of a superior being threatened by a person of lower rank see *Trial of Gozawa Sadaichi* XV *WCR* 175 (note).

39. The common law may not be a good comparator as, in most systems, the penalty for murder is fixed and there is, thus, little scope for a judge to consider mitigation for duress (although it may affect the minimum term an accused will serve).

40. Despite Art. 21(3) of the Statute of the ICTY, which provides that an accused shall be presumed innocent until *proved* guilty. The better view, it is suggested, is that the Appeals Chamber in Erdemović did not intend to cast the burden upon the accused to *prove* these mitigating facts.

for the reasons he gave.[41] The Prosecutor (and, subsequently, the Trial Chamber), however, accepted Erdemović's account of events on that fateful day, that he had 'committed the acts in question pursuant to superior orders and under threat of death'.[42] Had Erdemović given oral evidence, he could have been been cross-examined by the Prosecutor as to the details of the events[43] prior to the killings and his credibility could then have been assessed by the Trial Chamber. None of this was possible in the light of his decision not to give evidence. What then could the Prosecutor do? He could hardly call as witnesses other participants to the killings at Pilica. He might have argued that the brief facts given by Erdemović on arraignment were inherently unlikely, or that there was insufficient evidence to support them – given that Erdemović had not made his statements by way of solemn declaration - and then left it to the Trial Chamber to decide whether the facts were substantiated by way of mitigation.

The Prosecutor had, however, entered into a plea bargain agreement[44] with the accused in which, in return for a plea of guilty to a breach of the laws of customs of war, the Prosecutor would drop the charge of a crime against humanity and would recommend to the Trial Chamber a sentence of seven years imprisonment. The actions of the Prosecutor in agreeing to the version of facts put forward by an accused who does not intend to give evidence and then entering into a plea bargaining agreement with him are fraught with danger. It may well be thought that the court, which is a 'vehicle through which the international community expresses its outrage at the atrocities committed in the former Yugoslavia',[45] requires a prosecution system to prosecute the type of crimes which come before it robustly and not to make concessions.

41. Strictly, since duress is not to be regarded as a defence but merely as grounds for mitigation, use of the term 'duress' is inappropriate. A sentencing judgment can take into account all mitigating facts, whether they would have been relevant to the defence of duress (had the minority view in the Appeals Chamber in Erdemović prevailed) or not.

42. Para. 13 of the Sentencing Judgment, Case No. IT-96-22-T*bis*, 5 March 1998.

43. Questions that might have been relevant here would have been: Would his colleagues on the firing squad have supported him against their superior? How long before the actual killings did he know what was expected of him? Could he have run away? Did Erdemović know before he joined the unit that he might have been expected to carry out such atrocities? Did he believe that his family would also suffer if he had refused, and, if so, how? He had, however, given oral evidence as to his own actions in Rule 61 proceedings in *The Prosecutor* v. *Radovan Karadžić and Ratko Mladić*, IT-96-18-R.61.

44. *Supra* n. 42, para. 18. It is difficult to see why this was necessary given that, after the Appeals Chamber ruling in his case, it was virtually certain that he would subsequently plead guilty to a breach of the laws or customs of war rather than a crime against humanity. The only beneficiary of such an agreement could have been Erdemović in that the Prosecutor would not have challenged his statement about acting under 'duress'.

45. Ibid., para. 21.

Suppose Erdemović was actually telling lies and his, no doubt, strong feelings of guilt had occured subsequent to the killings. He then makes a statement to the court on arraignment indicating that he was threatened with death but does not give oral evidence. Had the minority in the Appeals Chamber in Erdemović prevailed, duress would have been recognised as a defence and it would have been, as shown above, the duty of the Prosecutor to negate it. Since guilt or innocence of an accused is the exclusive function of the Trial Chamber, it is unlikely that the Prosecutor would have agreed that Erdemović did not act under threats of death, especially where he did not give any evidence. The Trial Chamber might then have concluded that Erdemović had not raised *sufficient* evidence (especially as he had not given oral testimony) of duress for it to be a live issue for the Chamber to determine. He would then have been convicted.

Following the majority view of the Appeals Chamber in Erdemović, the possible threat of death may be a factor to be taken into account by way of mitigation. The issue of whether this version of facts is true or not does not, in practice, get tested in the same way before the Trial Chamber since it is mixed in with other facts, such as the accused's age, family circumstances, previous record, whether he has assisted the prosecutor's office, and so on. It is theoretically much easier for an accused charged with a breach of the laws or customs of war (or other relevant charge) merely to say that he was threatened with death and have this considered by way of mitigation (along with other mitigating factors). If he gives every assistance to the Prosecutor's office (as Erdemović had done)[46] and where other mitigating factors come into play, an accused may receive a lighter sentence that he would have done if duress had been a defence although not made out on the facts. In the latter case, the Trial Chamber would be likely to want clear and strong evidence before it would accept that the defence had been made out. Someone who did not give evidence to the Trial Chamber may well then discover that the Tribunal would not be prepared to believe him in the absence of other evidence. In this eventuality, he could expect a very long term of imprisonment for taking part in the killings as Erdemović had done.

Under the majority or the minority view, the Trial Chamber was faced, as we have seen, with an accused who did not give oral evidence in his own defence.[47] This tactic may well occur again and the ICTY may be wise to consider whether

46. '"The collaboration of Dražen Erdemović has been absolutely excellent." These are words rarely spoken by the Prosecution of an accused,' Sentencing Judgment (1998) *supra* n. 42, at para. 16 (iv).

47. See Rule 85 C of the Rules of Procedure and Evidence. Rule 100 provides that the prosecution and defence may submit any relevant information that may assist the Trial Chamber in determining an appropriate sentence.

it is appropriate to amend the Rules of Procedure and Evidence so as to enable a Trial Chamber to draw such inferences as may appear appropriate from the failure of an accused to give evidence.

The Sentencing Judgment took into account a number of aggravating and mitigating factors in arriving at its sentence of five years imprisonment, to run from 28 March 1996 (the date the order for his transfer to the jurisdiction of the ICTY was made). The aggravating factors were the sheer scale of the killings and the suffering of the victims before they were killed. The mitigating factors included Erdemović's age (23 at the time); his family background (he had married someone of a different ethnic background than himself); his character; his admission of guilt; his remorse; his cooperation with the Office of the Prosecutor; and the finding that 'there was a real risk that the accused would have been killed had he disobeyed the order'.[48]

It is, of course, impossible to know which factors weighed in what proportions with the Trial Chamber. No two cases will ever be the same and it will therefore be impossible to predict what the appropriate sentence should be for someone who commits a war crime under threat of death. The decision of the majority in the Appeals Chamber in Erdemović may, ironically, have given greater scope for an accused to raise 'duress' than would have been the case had the minority view prevailed.

Whilst the intention of Judges McDonald and Vohrah, to 'give notice in no uncertain terms that those who kill innocent persons will not be able to take advantage of duress'[49] is laudable, it is unlikely to make any difference to actual conduct on the ground. Had Erdemović known of the majority view at the moment he raised his objection to taking part in the firing squad, it is unlikely that his decision would have been any different. Indeed, international humanitarian law might be placed in a worse position. Knowing that there is no defence of duress, would Erdemović, or someone in his position, then draw the conclusion that 'I might as well kill as many innocent civilians as I like since the law treats me as guilty even when I acted under the greatest compulsion imagineable to take innocent life.' The more discerning Erdemović might wish to rely upon mitigating factors and adhere subsequently to the principles of international humanitarian law but he will, by the very nature of this process, not be able to predict his likely sentence.

48. Sentencing Judgment, *supra* n. 42, at para. 17.
49. *Supra* n. 4, at para. 80.

3. THE OPERATION OF THE APPEALS CHAMBER

The proper role of an *international criminal* court is not, as yet, firmly settled. It cannot merely adopt the procedures of either the common law or the civil law countries. The Statute of the Tribunal and the Rules of Procedure and Evidence made under it draw upon the traditions to be found in various systems of criminal procedure. The lawyers who appear before an international criminal court and its judges are, of course, trained in national legal systems and some transfer of thinking is required before operating within an international court setting. Thus, the simple transplant of national laws or procedures to such a court is inappropriate.[50] Where general principles of law may be discerned, they will be an acceptable source of law. In practice, these may be much easier to discover in relation to the ingredients of an offence than those of a defence.

The Appeals Chamber is, of course, a criminal court. It may therefore seem inappropriate to draw principles from other existing international courts, since these will only be concerned with disputes between states or claims against states by individuals. The responsibility falling upon the Appeals Chamber is all the greater since it will, in the course of its judgements, lay down rules to govern other cases without the guidance of other national or international courts. In doing so, it must not lose sight of the fact that, if guilt is confirmed, an individual will lose his or her liberty for a substantial period given the nature of offences within the jurisdiction of the international tribunal.

An individual charged with an offence before an international criminal tribunal can reasonably expect that his trial will be *fair*. Indeed, the Statutes of the International Tribunals for the Former Yugoslavia and for Rwanda give a defendant this *right*.[51] It would certainly seem that the Rules of Procedure and Evidence are expressly designed to ensure that a defendant receives a fair trial. It may be argued by the national of one state that his state would, because of the Rules of Procedure and Evidence[52] operating there, give him a fairer trial than

50. This point is made forcefully by President Cassese in his judgment. *Supra* n. 4, at para. 3. The difficulty of lawyers facing procedures to which they are unaccustomed is illustrated by Defence Counsel's statement in *Erdemović* that 'the institution of a plea of guilty by an accused ... as formulated in common law systems, is foreign to the procedure applied in the former Yugoslavia as well as to the procedures applied in all the successor states established in the territory of the former Yugoslavia', *Defence Counsel's Brief Concerning Preliminary Issues*, 16 May 1997, para. 2.

51. Art. 21 of the Statute of the International Tribunal for the Former Yugoslavia and Art. 20 of the Statute for the Rwanda International Tribunal. This is similar to the right given in the European Convention on Human Rights 1950 and other human rights treaties.

52. See for example, K. Mann, 'Hearsay Evidence in War Crimes Trials', in Y. Dinstein and M. Tabory, eds., *War Crimes in International Law* (The Hague, Martinus Nijhoff 1996) p. 351 et seq.

could the International Criminal Tribunal but this is to lose sight of the fact that the International Criminal Tribunal is, as its name suggests, an international court. The real issue is not whether the Rules of Procedure and Evidence guarantee an accused a fair trial but whether the law defining criminal liability and the defences to that liability have the potential to *deny* him his right to a fair trial.

Few would have any sympathy for defendants like Tadić or Erdemović, since both were convicted of killing innocent civilians and it is, of course, right for the new[53] President of the Court, Judge Gabrielle Kirk McDonald, to stress that: 'As judges we must not demonise particular indictees.'[54] There is, however, a risk that, at the Tribunal, a defendant may face a criminal justice system lacking in the essential ingredients of any national legal system, namely, clear rules as to criminal liability for principals and secondary parties, along with equally clear rules as to applicable defences.

The decisions of the Appeals Chamber in *Tadić*[55] and *Erdemović* illustrate well the legal difficulties over the extent of individual criminal liability and the scope of a defence. Thus, *Tadić* decided that breaches of the laws or customs of war may be committed in a non-international as well as in an international armed conflict. This was the first time that it had been so held and, it may be argued, the decision was not entirely consistent with the relevant treaty provisions. In particular, Additional Protocol II, applying to non-international armed conflicts, unlike Additional Protocol I, contains no provisions for the trial of grave breaches or indeed, any other breach.[56] In becoming party to both Protocols, states would, no doubt, have taken the view that were an armed conflict to occur in their territory, their own national law would apply and they would have the exclusive right (as against the power of an international court to assume primacy) to try rebels under their own criminal law. Of course, the subtleties of this distinction would be lost on innocent civilian victims (and this may be an overwhelming reason to wish to treat liability as the same) but the distinction was drawn by states themselves. President Cassese stated, however:

53. Elected on 19 November 1997, Press release, CC/PIO/264-E&F.

54. Press release CC/PIO/272-E, 9 December 1997.

55. The Prosecutor v. *Dusko Tadić*. Decision on the Defence Motion for Interlocutory Appeal on Jurisdiction. Case No. IT-94-1-AR72, 2 October 1995.

56. Art. 4 of the Statute of the International Tribunal for Rwanda, however, gave that Tribunal jurisdiction over serious violations of common Art. 3 and of Additional Protocol II. This is not co-extensive with a breach of the laws or customs of war. For an excellent discussion of the arguments for and against Article 4 of the Rwanda Tribunal Statute see T. Meron, 'International Criminalization of Internal Atrocities', 89 *AJIL* (1955) p. 554. See also C. Greenwood, 'International Humanitarian Law and the Tadić Case', 7 *EJIL* (1996) p. 265, at p. 281.

> 'When it decided to establish the International Tribunal, the Security Council did so to put a stop to all serious violations of international humanitarian law occurring in the former Yugoslavia (. . .) the primary purpose of the establishment of the International Tribunal [was] not to leave unpunished any person guilty of any serious violation, whatever the context within which it may have been committed.'[57]

This view has the advantage of simplicity and, in the context of the acts committed in the former Yugoslavia, a certain measure of efficacy. But it creates a number of legal difficulties. Thus, if rebels comply with the laws and customs of war during a non-international armed conflict, are they to be immune from the national criminal law of the territory of the State within which the conflict is taking place?[58] If the answer is in the affirmative, is it not unrealistic to expect States to comply with this and merely treat a rebel, who, for example, has killed a member of the armed forces[59] of that State, as a prisoner of war upon capture? There is no authority for this in common Article 3 or in Protocol II, however commendable it might be. Indeed, Article 6 of the latter provides expressly for the prosecution and punishment of criminal offences related to the armed conflict.[60] If the answer is in the negative, as it appears to be, rebels are in a disadvantageous position compared with members of the armed forces during an international armed conflict, who are not liable for breaches of national law if their acts are in conformity with the laws or customs of war.

Does this lead to the conclusion that rebels should not be liable for breaches of the laws or customs of war before an international tribunal as if they were of the same status as members of the armed forces of a State during an international armed conflict? That was generally considered to be the position before the decision of the Appeals Chamber in *Tadić*.[61] It was therefore appropriate for

57. See n. 55 at para. 92. Emphasis supplied. For a decision that a defendant's actions occurred during an international armed conflict due to the 'significant and continuous military intervention of the Croatian Army', see O. Swaak-Goldman, '*Prosecutor* v. *Rajić*, Review of the Indictment Pursuant to Rule 61 of the Rules of Procedure and Evidence, No. IT-95-12-R61,' 91 *AJIL* (1997) p. 523.

58. During an international armed conflict, it is clear that members of the armed forces of an enemy state are so immune, see *Public Prosecutor* v. *Koi* [1969] 1 *All ER* 419, 427.

59. As opposed to an innocent civilian.

60. Indeed, it envisages the rebels also being able to set up courts for the same purposes.

61. See H.-P. Gasser, 'Armed Conflict within the Territory of a State' in *'Im Dienst an der Gemeinschaft' Festschrift fur Dietrich Schindler zum 65 Geburtstag* (Basel/Frankfurt am Maine, 1989) p. 225 at p. 229; D. Plattner, 'The Penal Repression of Violations of International Humanitarian Law Applicable in Non-International Armed Conflicts', 30 *IRRC* (1990) p. 409, at p. 414; T. Meron, 'War Crimes in Yugoslavia and the Development of International Law', 88 *AJIL* (1994) p. 78 at p. 80; M. Bothe, 'War Crimes in Non-International Armed Conflicts', in Dinstein and Tabory, loc. cit. n. 52, at p. 294. In the Decision on Jurisdiction in the *Tadić* Case, Judge Li quoted the view

Tadić to argue that, although he may be liable under the law of the territory where his offences were committed, he had not committed an offence under *international* law unless the prosecutor could prove that his acts were committed during an international armed conflict.[62]

The majority of the Appeals Chamber in *Tadić* reached their decision that a serious breach of the laws or customs of war may be tried irrespective of the nature of the conflict on the basis of the development of customary international law. Whether this conclusion could properly drawn may be the subject of disagreement[63] and there may also be concern that liability for breaches of the laws or customs of war committed during a non-international armed conflict should be established merely on the basis of customary international law. One effect of the decision is to have rendered *otiose* common Article 3 and Protocol II. Whilst these conventional provisions may dictate that the methods and means of warfare in a non-international armed conflict are not unlimited, they will, in practice, be enforced through the *Tadić* liability of an individual to the international criminal law of breaches of the laws or customs of war which does not require any reference to them.

Judge Li in *Tadić* felt so strongly about this extension of liability that he described it as 'an unwarranted assumption of legislative power which has never been given to this Tribunal by any authority'.[64] These are strong words and they

---

of the ICRC that 'the notion of war crimes is limited to situations of international armed conflict'. Para. 9 of his judgment. See also W. Fenrick, 'International Humanitarian Law and Criminal Trials', 7 *Transnational Law and Contemporary Problems* (1997) p. 23 at pp. 37-41.

62. The argument would not have been based solely upon a lack of *jurisdiction* but upon the non-applicability of *international criminal law* to him for acts committed during a non-international armed conflict.

63. Compare Judge Li at para. 11 of his Separate Opinion with President Cassese at para. 134 of his Separate and Dissenting Opinion. For a disagreement as to whether a rule of customary international law existed in *Erdemović*, see the prosecution argument concerning the status of duress as a defence under customary international law and the view of that taken by President Cassese and in the Separate Opinions of Judges McDonald and Vohrah. The UN SG had concluded that 'the International Tribunal should apply rules of international humanitarian law which are *beyond any doubt part of customary international law*', Report of the Secretary-General Pursuant to para. 2 of SC Res. No. 808 (1993) (Presented 3 May 1993) (S/25704) at para. 34. In ICTY *Basic Documents* 1995 at p. 175, para. 34, reprinted in 32 *ILM* at para. 1170 [emphasis supplied]. The view of the US Ambassador to the UN expressed at the Security Council as to the extent of the laws or customs of war, is, with respect, relied upon too strongly by Meron, loc. cit. n. 56, at p. 560 and by Greenwood, loc.cit. n. 56, at p. 281 as evidence of customary international law.

64. At para. 13 of his judgment. Judge Li was, it is assumed, drawing a clear distinction between the criminality of *Tadić*'s acts and the jurisdiction of the Tribunal. See generally, Meron, loc. cit. n. 56, at p. 561. Judge Li might also have relied upon *SW* v. *United Kingdom* (Series A, No. 355-B); (1996) 21 *EHHR*, 363, which eschewed extensions to criminal liability which did not

illustrate how carefully a judicial body should proceed when considering the question of *criminal* liability. There are other views, of course. President Cassese explained fully his reasoning in the light of the various Security Council resolutions[65] but it was by no means clear from these resolutions that the laws or customs of war would apply (as opposed to crimes against humanity or genocide) during a non-international armed conflict. Indeed, the Statute of the International Tribunal for Rwanda[66] gave that Tribunal jurisdiction over serious breaches of common Article 3 and of Protocol II but no similar reference is made to these conventional provisions in the Statute of the ICTY.[67]

Erdemović also illustrates a further general weakness in international criminal law, namely, uncertainty as to the extent of any defences available to an accused.[68] It is generally not acceptable for a treaty or Security Council resolution to refer only to two possible defences, superior orders and act of state, and to leave the nature and extent of other defences to be worked out from time to time. No modern national legal system would operate on this basis. Defences should not be viewed as somehow less important than establishing the principles of liability since the nature of some defences may affect liability itself. To take an obvious example, a defendant claims that the civilian he has killed was, in fact, a combatant and that he has therefore made a mistake of fact in attacking him. Should an international court accept that he has made a genuine mistake of fact, the result would be that he will lack the necessary *mens rea* and thus no offence will have been committed. Moreover, it may be difficult for a defence counsel to advise properly his client when he or she cannot know whether a particular 'defence' is really a defence or not and, even if it is, what the conditions are for its application. It was precisely this problem that led to Erdemović pleading guilty and then making what might have been an equivocal plea.

---

amount to the 'gradual clarification of the rules of criminal liability through judicial interpretation from case to case' and which were not 'reasonably foreseeable' (at para. 36/34).

65. At para. 74 of his judgment.

66. See SC Res. No. 955, 8 November 1994.

67. Judge Li draws inferences from the absence of jurisdiction over a breach of the laws or customs of war in the Rwanda Tribunal that customary international law had not extended its liability to non-international armed conflicts.

68. See generally, A. Eser '"Defences" in War Crime Trials' in Dinstein and Tabory, eds., loc. cit. n. 52, at p. 251; Bassiouni, loc. cit. n. 35. This is a real issue also at the national level since States Parties to the Geneva Conventions 1949 and Additional Protocol I have a right to try grave breaches of the Conventions or Protocol. They would, presumably, apply their own laws relating to defences to criminal charges. These will vary from state to state and no inter-state consistency could be achieved. Thus, in defence to a charge of a grave breach of the Geneva Conventions, an accused may be able to rely upon the defence of duress in some states but not in others.

It is no real answer to argue that the Nuremberg principles will supply the answer to the scope of defences under international law. The defendants at the International Military Tribunals at Nuremberg and Tokyo were the senior directors of war crimes committed by others. The Hague Tribunal, by way of contrast, is, for the most part, having to deal with the 'small fish' who, in 'armies' with disciplinary systems that would hardly be recognised by senior officers of established state armies and with inadequate training were often as much victims of their own side[69] as were their enemies. Neither are the war crimes tribunals convened by individual states likely to be able to offer much by way of precedent. The treatment by the Appeals Chamber[70] in *Erdemović* of these tribunals, which considered duress in some of its forms, illustrates this.

The relative speed with which the Hague Tribunal was established made it very difficult for its Statute to cover all of the possible defences that might be raised. It was therefore, perhaps, understandable that the Secretary General of the UN should state that: 'The international tribunal will have to decide on various personal defences which may relieve a person of individual criminal responsibility, such as minimum age or mental incapacity, drawing upon the general principles of law recognised by all nations.'[71]

Except for the defence of duress, the Hague Tribunal has not done this. Even then, the result may be considered to be unsatisfactory since the decision of the Appeals Chamber was a bare majority, with extremely cogent arguments being presented by the minority to illustrate how 'wrong' in applying the authorities the majority judges were, and how they had adopted an approach that ran 'contrary to the fundamental customary principle *nullum crimen sine lege*'.[72] When other defences are pleaded, a similar result may occur.

Article 15 of the Statute of the International Tribunal for the Former Yugoslavia directs the 'Judges of the International Tribunal [to] adopt rules of procedure and evidence . . .' It would have been preferable for the Judges also to have considered all the likely defences prior to the trial of any of the defendants. It was foreseeable that possible defences such as minimum age,

69. See the *Defence: Notice of Appeal, Dražen Erdemović* at p. 9 where Erdemović is described as 'an ordinary, used and abused soldier who was driven by the winds of war'.

70. Some tribunals can be ignored on the grounds that they applied *national* law. See for instance, President Cassese at para. 26 of his judgment and Judges McDonald and Vohrah in their joint judgment at para. 52. In any event, the decisions relied upon by the majority and minority would, in common law systems, be considered to be weak authorities since they consisted merely of the summing up of a judge-advocate at first instance.

71. See the Secretary-General's Report, *supra* n. 63, at para. 58.

72. Judge Cassese at para. 11 of his judgment. See also Judge Stephen at para. 24 of his judgment. *Supra* n. 4.

mental capacity, reprisal[73], mistake of fact, mistake of law and self-defence[74] would be raised at trial. At least the general principles might have been established, after debate amongst all the Judges, with the detailed application of each defence being left to be considered when it arose. Had this course been adopted, the conclusions of the Judges could, like the rules of evidence and procedure, have been published prior to any indictment being issued. Although it would not have been possible to exclude entirely the possibility of infringing the principle *nullum crimen sine lege*[75] – as the actions of some of the defendants would have been committed prior to publication of these general principles – this would be preferable to the piecemeal formulation of individual defences when they arise during trials.

It might be argued that for the Judges to have done this would not have been consistent with the normal method of law-making. Certainly in common law countries, the *ratio decidendi* of a case has, depending upon the seniority of the court which decided it, precedential value which will be binding on lower courts. Thus, the approach taken in *Erdemović* of deciding the nature of a possible defence is in keeping with common law traditions. But an international court is not a common law court. Indeed, Article 15 of the Statute is, itself, evidence that this common law approach was not to be the adopted means of establishing the law, since by that article, the Judges, outside the parameters of a particular case, were given power to formulate the Rules of Procedure and Evidence.

The approach taken by the Appeals Chamber of formulating the law through decided cases, both as to the extent of liability and the nature of possible defences, has one further drawback implicit in it. This is the practical difficulty

73. See for example, W. Fenrick, 'Attacking the Enemy as a Punishable Offence', 7 *Duke Journal of Comparative and International law* (1997) p. 539 at pp. 558-559 (and the authorities cited therein); A. Cassese, 'The Status of Rebels under the 1977 Geneva Protocol on Non-International Armed Conflicts', 30 *ICLQ* (1981) pp. 417, 437.

74. Such as where a combatant is attacked by a non-combatant, an event, perhaps, likely in an armed conflict more similar to a non-international than an international armed conflict. Of a similar nature is the issue of whether certain circumstances can mitigate a sentence. Apart from superior orders, this might include action in furtherance of a judicial sentence (although this might be considered to be a mistake of fact) or a mistake of international law.

75. The principle is being used here to refer to uncertainty over the extent of *defences* and not over the otherwise criminal liability of an accused. The UN Secretary-General concluded that the principle '*nullum crimen sine lege* demands that the International Tribunal should apply principles of international humanitarian law which are beyond doubt part of customary law', loc. cit. n. 63 at para. 34. This would meet the concerns of the European Court of Human Rights in interpreting Art. 7 of the Convention, *SW* v. *United Kingdom* (Series A, No. 355-B), (1996) 21 *EHRR* 363, which recognises the need for 'the gradual clarification of the rules of criminal liability through judicial interpretation from case to case', at para. 36/34, but not changes that could not be reasonably foreseen. This same principle may be argued to apply also to the extent of defences.

of changing the law as set down in these cases. In matters of criminal law, it is hardly desirable for one Appeals Chamber to 'overrule' an earlier decision of that Chamber unless it is clearly wrong. Given that the tenure of office of the Judges of The Hague Tribunal is four years[76] it is more likely that, with a fluctuating membership, different views may come to the ascendancy than would be the case in national appeal courts. It is therefore more important for consistency in international criminal law that the decisions of the Appeals Chamber are considered binding unless the law is changed by one of the established sources of international law.[77] In practical terms, this would be very difficult. The Tribunal is now faced with having created precedents which can only be changed with great difficulty and which are binding on all subsequent Trial Chambers and (most likely) on the Appeals Chamber itself.

If President McDonald is right in thinking that The Hague Tribunal is a 'laboratory for the permanent criminal court'[78] lessons will have to be drawn from the experiment. A statute of a permanent court should make clear the basis of criminal liability for acts committed during an armed conflict that cannot unequivocally be described as being of an international character.[79] It should also specify the circumstances under which each of the main defences may apply and those which are ruled out as excusing liability. Were this to be done, a defendant would know that a defence (like duress), which may be open to him if he is tried under the national law of the territory where the act was committed, may not be available to him if he is tried under international law. In addition, the statute should make it clear as to how the *ratio decidendi* of an Appeals Chamber might be overturned should it fail to win the acceptance of the community of states.

The *ad hoc* nature of the former Yugoslavia and the Rwanda Tribunals should relate only to their method of creation and not to the law which they apply. The permanent court must have no element of an *ad hoc* nature about it.

76. Art. 13(4) of the Statute.

77. Art. 38 of the Statute of the International Court of Justice. A decision of the Appeals Chamber might, in theory, be 'overruled' by a Security Council resolution since the Statute of the Tribunal is the product of such a resolution. A multilateral treaty to change a ruling is unlikely and the other sources of international law are also unlikely to be proved.

78. See *supra* n. 1. See also V. Morris and M. Scharf, *An Insider's Guide to the International Criminal Tribunal for the Former Yugoslavia* (New York, Transnational Publishers Inc. 1994) at p. 354, where the authors state, 'whether the international community seizes the opportunity [to establish a permanent criminal court] may depend to a large extent on the success or failure of the international tribunal'.

79. The ICRC now supports the view that 'the international criminal court must have jurisdiction over war crimes committed in international and non-international armed conflicts alike', Statement by the ICRC to the UN General Assembly, 23 October 1997.

A NOTE ON THE JUDGEMENT OF THE APPEALS CHAMBER OF THE INTERNATIONAL CRIMINAL TRIBUNAL FOR THE FORMER YUGOSLAVIA ON THE ISSUANCE OF *SUBPOENAE DUCES TECUM* IN THE *BLAŠKIĆ* CASE*

Peter Malanczuk**

1. INTRODUCTION

On 29 October 1997, the Appeals Chamber of the International Criminal Tribunal for the Former Yugoslavia (ICTY)[1], composed of Judges Antonio Cassese (presiding), Adolphus Karibi-Whyte, Haopei Li, Ninian Stephen and Lal Chand Vohrah, handed down its Judgement[2] in the *Blaškić* case on the appeal filed by the Republic of Croatia against the 'Subpoena Decision' of Trial Chamber II of 18 July 1997.[3] The legal issues raised in this case are complicated, rather new and fundamental from the perspective of international law and the inherent powers of international criminal courts established *ad hoc* by a Security Council resolution under Chapter VII of the United Nations Charter. They concern the authority and power of the Tribunal to issue compulsory orders of this kind to states, to high government officials and other individuals; the question of which remedies are available if there is a failure to comply with such *subpoenae duces*

** Dr. iur., Professor of International Law, Faculty of Law, Erasmus University Rotterdam, Head of Department; Director, Institute of Globalization, International Economic Law and Dispute Settlement; Honorary Guest-Professor, China University of Political Science and Law, Beijing; Member, Tianjin Board of Arbitration, China; Counsel, Lalive & Partners, Geneva.

1. On the ICTY in general, with further references to the literature, see P. Malanczuk, *Akehurst's Modern Introduction to International Law*, 7th edn., 1997, reprinted 1998, p. 355 et seq.

2. *Prosecutor* v. *Tihomir Blaškić* case No. IT-95-14-AR108 *bis*., 29 October 1997 (hereinafter 'Appeals Chamber, *Subpoena* Judgement').

3. Decision on the objection of the Republic of Croatia to the issuance of *supoenae duces tecum*, *Prosecutor* v. *Tihomir Blaškić*, Case No. IT-95-14-PT. Ch. II. 18 July 1997 (hereinafter, '*Subpoena* Decision').

Yearbook of International Humanitarian Law
Volume 1 - 1998 - pp. 229-244

tecum; and other issues, such as how to deal with the problem of the national security interests of sovereign states.

The present author presented oral argument in this case, as one of the *amici curiae* who were invited by the ICTY to submit *amicus curiae* briefs, at a hearing that was held before Trial Chamber II on 16 and 17 April 1997.[4] This note outlines the main findings of the Appeals Chamber Judgement. Within the limited space available, only selected aspects of the reasoning will be addressed in the following.

2. PROCEDURAL BACKGROUND

Very briefly stated, the procedural background is as follows. On 15 January 1997, at the request of the Office of the Prosecutor, Judge Gabrielle Kirk McDonald, as the Judge who confirmed General Blaškić's indictment, issued a *subpoena duces tecum* to Croatia and its Defence Minister, Mr. Gojko Šušak, ordering them to turn over documentary evidence relating to the *Blaškić* Case.[5] At the same time, a *subpoena duces tecum* was also issued to Bosnia and Herzegovina and to the Custodian of the Records of the Central Archive of what was formerly the Ministry of Defence of the Croatian Community of Herceg Bosna.[6] Croatia challenged the legal authority of the ICTY to issue a *subpoena duces tecum* to a sovereign state. It also objected to the naming of a high government official in a request for assistance under Article 29 of the ICTY Statute. Following further procedural steps, including a hearing and the suspension on 20 February 1997 of the *subpoena duces tecum* issued to Croatia and Mr. Šušak, Judge McDonald ordered that all parties file legal briefs addressing the relevant issues and scheduled a hearing for 16 and 17 April 1997. Judge McDonald further ordered that, in view of the importance of the issues,

4. P. Malanczuk, *Amicus Curiae Brief submitted to the International Criminal Tribunal for the former Yugoslavia in the Case Prosecutor v. Tihomir Blaškić (Case No. IT-96-14-PT) on the power of a Judge or Trial Chamber of the International Criminal Tribunal to issue a* subpoena duces tecum *to a sovereign state and questions relating to this issue*, April 1997 [see *International Criminal Tribunal for the Former Yugoslavia Bulletin*, No. 18, 20 June 1997, pp. 10-11.]; P. Malanczuk, The International Criminal Tribunal's Power to issue *subpoena duces tecum*, in Erik Denters/Nico Schrijver, eds., *Reflections on International Law from the Low Countries in Honour of Paul de Waart* (Kluwer Law International, The Hague 1998) pp. 260-277.

5. *Subpoena duces tecum* to the Republic of Croatia and to the Defence Minister Gojko Šušak, 'Subpoena Decision', op. cit. n. 3, Judge McDonald, 15 January 1997.

6. *Subpoena duces tecum* to Bosnia and Herzegovina and the Custodian of the Records of the Central Archive of what was formerly the Ministry of Defence of the Croatian Community of Herceg Bosna, 'Subpoena Decision', op. cit. n. 3, Judge McDonald, 15 January 1997.

Trial Chamber II, composed of herself as Presiding Judge, Judge Elizabeth Odio Benito and Judge Saad Saood Jan, should hear the case. She also invited requests for leave to submit *amicus curiae* briefs.[7]

Following the hearing held on 16 and 17 April, the 'Subpoena Decision' of Trial Chamber II was finally delivered on 18 July 1997. The Chamber upheld the *subpoena duces tecum* issued by Judge McDonald on 15 January 1997 to Croatia and its Defence Minister and reinstated it. Croatia was ordered to comply with its terms within a period of 30 days. The Decision found that a Judge or a Trial Chamber of the ICTY has the power to issue orders such as *subpoenae duces tecum* to states, high government officials and individuals. The reasoning may be briefly summarized as follows: It is up to states to decide how to fulfil their international obligations, but they cannot adopt domestic legislation imposing conditions on the fulfilment of such obligations, in particular, with regard to obligations arising under Chapter VII of the UN Charter from relevant resolutions of the Security Council. States must comply fully with orders of the ICTY and their officials are also bound to comply with orders of *subpoena duces tecum* issued to them in their official capacity. While such officials are subject to orders of the ICTY, states also remain responsible for compliance and for requiring compliance with such orders. Concerning objections against orders of the ICTY raised by states based upon national security considerations, the Chamber held that it is up to the Trial Chamber to decide whether a claim of national security is valid by, for example, holding an *in camera*, *ex parte* hearing to examine the relevant evidence. Finally, the Decision refrained from addressing the issue of which remedies are available in case of failure to comply with such orders because it considered that the issue was not ripe for consideration at that stage.

Croatia appealed against the 'Subpoena Decision' of Trial Chamber II, and, on 29 July 1997, the Appeals Chamber declared Croatia's request for review admissible and stayed the execution of the *subpoena*. The Appeals Chamber invited interested *amici curiae* to submit briefs on the relevant legal issues[8] and,

7. Briefs were submitted by Batram S. Brown; Luigi Condorelli; The Croatian Association of Criminal Science and Practice; Marie-José Domestici-Met; Donald Donavan for the Lawyers Committee for Human Rights; Jochen A. Frowein, Georg Nolte, Karin Oellers-Frahm and Andreas Zimmermann for the Max-Planck-Institute for Comparative Public Law and International Law; Annalisa Ciampi and Giorgio Gaja; Juristes sans frontières and Alain Pellet; Juan-Antonio Carrillo Salcedo; Bruno Simma; Thomas Warrick, Rochelle Stern and J. Stefan Lupp; Ruth Wedgwood; and the present author (see *supra* n. 4).

8. Briefs were submitted by the People's Republic of China; the Government of the Netherlands; The Governments of Canada and New Zealand; the Government of Norway; Ruth Wedgwood; Max Planck Institute for Foreign and International Criminal Law; Juristes sans frontières and Alain Pellet; Carol Elder Bruce; and Herwig Roggemann.

after other procedural steps, held a hearing on the matter on 22 September 1997 and finally delivered its Judgement on 29 October 1997.

3. THE FINDINGS OF THE APPEALS CHAMBER

The Appeals Chamber unanimously decided

> 'to quash the *subpoena duces tecum* issued by Judge McDonald and reinstated by Trial Chamber II addressed to Croatia and the Croatian Defence Minister, Mr. Gojko Šušak, it being understood that the Prosecutor is at liberty to submit to the appropriate Chamber, being Trial Chamber I, a request for a binding order addressed to Croatia alone.'[9]

This decision was based upon four main findings that were also all unanimous, with a Separate Opinion of Judge Karibi-Whyte concerning the modalities envisaged for clarifying whether a claim of a state objecting on grounds of national security to the disclosure of relevant evidence is valid. First, the Appeals Chamber found that the ICTY has the power to issue binding orders and requests to states. States are obliged to comply with such orders and requests under Article 29 of the Statute. In case of non-compliance, a Trial Chamber may make a 'specific judicial finding to this effect' and request the President of the ICTY to transmit it to the UN Security Council.[10] Second, it was found that the ICTY does not have the authority to address binding orders under Article 29 to government officials acting in their official capacity.[11] Third, with regard to individuals acting in their private capacity, the Appeals Chamber held that the ICTY has the power to 'summon, subpoena or address other binding orders' to such individuals. In case of non-compliance, the Judgement envisages two possible avenues. Either the respective state may take enforcement measures as provided for in its domestic law, or the ICTY may instigate contempt proceedings.[12] Fourth, the Appeals Chamber denied states the right, based upon national security interests, 'to withhold documents and other evidentiary material' requested by the ICTY. However, it added that 'practical arrangements may be adopted by a Trial Chamber to make allowance for legitimate and bona fide concerns of *states*'.[13]

9. Disposition, para. (5).
10. Disposition, para. (1).
11. Disposition, para. (2).
12. Disposition, para. (3).
13. Disposition, para. (4).

4. SOME SELECTED ASPECTS OF THE REASONING

4.1 The legal meaning of the term 'subpoena'

As a preliminary question, the Appeals Chamber considered the legal meaning of the term 'subpoena' used in Rule 54 of the ICTY's Rules of Procedure and Evidence.[14] The Trial Chamber had taken the view that the word should simply have the neutral meaning of 'binding order' and left the question open whether or not a penalty (imprisonment or a fine) could be imposed in case of non-compliance with such an order.[15] The Appeals Chamber noted that there is a difference between the English and the French texts of Rule 54. It accepted that in common law jurisdictions the term 'subpoena' is a technical one that 'usually designates compulsory orders issued by courts, the non-compliance with which may be "sanctioned" as contempt of court'.[16] The Appeals Chamber also agreed with the Trial Chamber that the word 'assignation' in the French text of Rule 54 'does not necessarily imply any imposition of penalty'.[17] In an attempt to reconcile the two texts of Rule 54, the Appeals Chamber followed a narrow interpretation offered in the *amicus curiae* brief submitted by Professor Alain Pellet and Juristes sans frontières.[18] It decided to construe both the terms 'subpoena' and 'assignation' 'as referring only and exclusively to binding orders addressed by the International Tribunal, under threat of penalty, to individuals acting in their private capacity'.[19]

The Appeals Chamber arrived at this conclusion by starting from Rule 7 which provides that if there is a discrepancy between the English and French texts of the Rules, 'the version which is more consonant with the spirit of the Statute and the Rules shall prevail'.[20] The Appeals Chamber took into account that Article 29, paragraph 2, of the Statute does not mention 'subpoenas' but only 'orders'

14. Rule 54 ('General Rule') of the Rules of Procedure and Evidence (as amended 3 December 1996), IT/32/Rev. 10, states: 'At the request of either party or *proprio motu*, a Judge or a Trial Chamber may issue such orders, summonses, subpoenas, warrants and transfer orders as may be necessary for the purposes of an investigation or for the preparation or conduct of the trial.'

15. 'Subpoena Decision' op. cit. n. 3, paras. 61-62, 64 and 78.

16. Appeals Chamber, *Subpoena Judgement*, op. cit. n. 2, para. 21.

17. Ibid.

18. Ibid.

19. Ibid.

20. Rule 7 of the Rules, op. cit. n. 14, states: 'The English and French texts of the Rules shall be equally authentic. In case of discrepancy, the version which is more consonant with the spirit of the Statute and the Rules shall prevail.'

and 'requests'.[21] However, the Appeals Chamber wanted to avoid totally ignoring the word 'subpoena' in the English text of Rule 54 by attributing to it merely the neutral meaning of 'binding order'. This would be contrary to the general principle of effectiveness (*principle de l'éffet utile*). This interpretation is based upon the assumption that the Tribunal has no power to issue binding orders under threat of penalty to states or state officials, while it has such power with regard to individuals acting in their private capacity.

4.2 The power of the ICTY to issue binding orders to states

In addressing the power of the Tribunal to issue binding orders to states, at the outset the Appeals Chamber dismissed the view that a 'subpoena', in the sense of an order accompanied by threat of penalty, could be issued to states for two rather briefly stated reasons. First, it noted the Tribunal's lack of any power to take enforcement measures. The Appeals Chamber argued that such a power is not expressly provided for in the Statute and neither does it fall within the scope of the 'inherent powers' of the Tribunal as an international judicial body[22]:

> Under current international law States can only be the subject of countermeasures taken by other States or of sanctions visited upon them by the organized international community, i.e., the United Nations or other intergovernmental organizations.[23]

The second reason emphasized by the Appeals Chamber is that, under international law, 'States, by definition, cannot be the subject of criminal sanctions akin to those provided for in national criminal systems.'[24] Dismissing the view of Croatia, the Appeals Chamber then clearly stated that the Tribunal 'is empowered to issue binding orders and requests to States, which are obliged

21. Art. 29 of the ICTY Statute, in *ICTY Basic Documents* (1995) deals with 'Cooperation and judicial assistance'. It states: 1. States shall cooperate with the International Tribunal in the investigation and prosecution of persons accused of committing serious violations of international humanitarian law. 2. States shall comply without undue delay with any request for assistance or an order issued by a Trial Chamber, including, but not limited to: the identification and location of persons; the taking of testimony and the production of evidence; the service of documents; the arrest or detention of persons; the surrender or the transfer of the accused to the International Tribunal.

22. Para. 25. In note 27, the Appeals Chamber correctly distinguishes between the doctrine of 'inherent powers', as developed in the jurisprudence of the International Court of Justice with regard to its own judicial functions and the doctrine of 'implied powers' which relates to the competences of international organizations. See Manfred Zuleeg, 'International Organizations, Implied Powers', in: R. Bernhardt (ed.), *Encyclopedia of Public International Law*, Vol. II (North Holland/Elsevier, Amsterdam 1995) pp. 1312-1314.

23. Appeals Chamber, Subpoena Judgement, op. cit. n. 2, Para. 25.

24. Ibid.

to comply with them pursuant to Article 29 of the Statute . . .'[25] It noted that the binding force of the obligation of states to cooperate with and lend judicial assistance to the Tribunal derives from Chapter VII and Article 25 of the United Nations Charter and the relevant Security Council resolution adopted in accordance with these provisions. The 'novel and indeed unique power granted to the International Tribunal to issue orders to sovereign States',[26] as recorded by the Appeals Chamber, is based upon the exceptional (as compared to customary law) provision of Article 29 of the Statute.

The obligation upon states under Article 29 of the Statute, in the words of the Appeals Chamber,

> concerns both action that States may take only and exclusively through their organs (this, for instance, happens in case of an order enjoining a State to produce documents in the possession of one of its officials) and also action that States may be requested to take with regard to individuals subject to their jurisdiction (this is the case when the International Tribunal orders that individuals be arrested, or be compelled under a threat of a national penalty to surrender evidence, or be brought to The Hague to testify.'[27]

Clearly, the Appeals Chamber did not view this power to order states to cooperate as an exercise of 'jurisdiction' in the sense of its primary jurisdiction to exercise judicial functions with regard to the prosecution and trial of individuals for certain crimes. With regard to states, the Tribunal's powers are limited to issuing binding orders or requests. The Appeals Chamber therefore discarded the concept of its alleged 'ancillary jurisdiction over States', as suggested by the Prosecutor, and preferred to merely speak of the Tribunal's 'ancillary (or incidental) mandatory powers *vis-à-vis* States'.[28]

In this connection, the Appeals Chamber clarified another important point. The argument had been made by one of the *amici curiae*, Professor Ruth Wedgwood, that Article 29 would only apply to former belligerents, i.e., states or 'entities' of ex-Yugoslavia.[29] In effect, this would mean, for example (to mention two not too far-fetched cases) that relevant and possibly sensitive evidence controlled by the Central Intelligence Agency (CIA) of the United States or by the French military would not be covered by the Tribunal's power to order the production of such evidence. The Appeals Chamber, however, made it clear

25. Ibid., Disposition (1), see also para. 26. For the text of Art. 29 see *supra* n. 21
26. Ibid., para. 26.
27. Ibid., para. 27.
28. Ibid., para 28.
29. Ibid., para. 29.

that the legal obligation stemming from Article 29 applies to *all* UN Member states, disregarding whether or not they are states of the former Yugoslavia.[30]

After further considering the question whether binding orders to states for the production of documents may be broad in scope or must rather be specific in some detail[31], the Judgement turns to the issue of what legal remedies are available to the Tribunal if a state fails to comply with a binding order. The starting point, as noted already above, is the basic legal consideration that the Tribunal has no powers of enforcement and that it is left to the Security Council to adopt measures under Chapter VII of the UN Charter if a state acts in non-compliance with an Order of the Tribunal. The Appeals Chamber, however, confirmed that the Tribunal has two inherent powers in such a situation, as laid down in Rule 7 *bis*.[32] First, it has the power to 'make a judicial finding concerning a state's failure to observe the provisions of the Statute or the Rules'.[33] Second, it has the power to report this judicial finding to the UN Security Council. Reference is then made to five different instances in which the President of the Tribunal informed the Security Council of a failure of a state or entity to comply with Article 29.[34]

The reasoning pays special attention to the illustration of the nature of the judicial finding by the Tribunal that a state has failed to comply with an order or request. This finding is described as being 'totally different from that made, at the request of the Security Council, by a fact-finding body, and *a fortiori* from that undertaken by a political or quasi-political body'.[35] The Appeals Chamber placed strong emphasis on the fact that the Tribunal,

30. On the distinction between 'two modes of interaction with the International Tribunal: the cooperative and the mandatory compliance', with preference given to the first mode, as suggested by the Prosecutor, see para. 31.

31. Appeals Chamber, *Subpoena Judgement*, op. cit. n. 2, para. 32.

32. Rule 7 *bis*, as cited in para. 34 of the Judgement, states: '(A) In addition to cases which Rule 11 [Non-compliance with a Request for Deferral], Rule 13 [Non Bis in Idem], Rule 59 [Failure to Execute a Warrant or Transfer Order] or Rule 61 [Procedure in Case of Failure to Execute a Warrant], applies, where a Trial Chamber or a Judge is satisfied that a State has failed to comply with an obligation under Article 29 of the Statute which relates to any proceedings before that Chamber or Judge, the Chamber or Judge may advise the President, who shall report the matter to the Security Council. (B) If the Prosecutor satisfies the President that a State has failed to comply with an obligation under Article 29 of the Statute in respect of a request by the Prosecutor under Rule 8 [Request for Information], Rule 39 [Conduct of Investigations] or Rule 40 [Provisional Measures], the President shall notify the Security Council thereof.'

33. Appeals Chamber, *Subpoena Judgement*, op. cit. n. 2, para. 33.

34. Ibid., para. 34.

35. Ibid., para. 35.

> engages in a judicial activity proper: acting upon all the principles and rules of judicial propriety, it scrutinises the behaviour of a certain State in order to establish formally whether or not that State has breached its international obligation to cooperate with the International Tribunal.[36]

It is not quite clear exactly which legal consequences follow from such a judicial determination. The reasoning does not explicitly state that such judicial determination is legally binding and the wording 'to establish formally' remains somewhat ambiguous. It is reasonable, however, to assume that a finding by the Tribunal that a state has breached its obligation under Article 29 is legally binding upon that state in terms of establishing its state responsibility under international law for the commission of an internationally wrongful act. This state is thereby legally barred, for example, from invoking any 'circumstance precluding wrongfulness', in the sense of the International Law Commission's draft articles on state responsibility, to justify its failure to comply with a request or order of the Tribunal.[37]

An entirely different matter, however, is the question whether the judicial finding can be equally binding in law upon the Security Council and have some legal effect for other third states. In the case of the Security Council, the difficulty arises that, for political reasons, the Council may have a different view than the Tribunal on whether a state has really failed to comply. One only needs to imagine the hypothetical case that the ICTY would adopt a judicial finding that one of the permanent members of the Security Council has breached its obligation under Article 29 of its Statute. After all, in spite of its judicial functions, the Tribunal remains a subsidiary organ of the Security Council in the 'constitutional' terms of the UN Charter. Ultimately, the Security Council has the legal power to even abolish the ICTY. It may be that it is now factually or politically unlikely that the Security Council would make use of this power; the point made here, however, is a legal one. The ICTY is not in a position comparable to that of the International Court of Justice, which under Article 92 of the UN Charter is directly established as the 'principal judicial organ of the United Nations'.[38] It is noteworthy in this connection that the Appeals Chamber was also very careful to state that 'the finding by the International Tribunal must not include any recommendations or suggestions as to the course of action the Security Council may wish to take as a consequence of that finding' and that it

36. Ibid.

37. On the work of the International Law Commission in codifying state responsibility, see Malanczuk, Akehurst's, op. cit. n. 1, p. 254 et seq.

38. On the relationship between the ICJ and the Security Council see Malanczuk, ibid., p. 292 et seq., with further references to the literature.

'may not encroach upon the sanctionary powers accruing to the Security Council pursuant to Chapter VII of the United Nations Charter'.[39]

The Appeals Chamber also dealt with the right of third states to react against a breach by a non-complying state after such a judicial determination by the Tribunal. In some earlier remarks, the Appeals Chamber asserted that

> [T]he obligation set out – in the clearest of terms – in Article 29 is an obligation which is incumbent on every Member State of the United Nations *vis-à-vis* all other Member States . . . The nature and content of this obligation, as well as the source from which it originates, make it clear that Article 29 does not create bilateral relations. Article 29 imposes an obligation on Member States towards all other Members or, in other words an 'obligation *erga omnes partes*'. By the same token, Article 29 posits a community interest in its observance. In other words, every Member State of the United Nations has a legal interest in the fulfilment of the obligation laid down in Article 2 . . .[40]

Later, the Judgement addressed the specific legal consequences that arise for third states from this qualification of Article 29 as an obligation *erga omnes* after a judicial finding of the Tribunal of a breach of Article 29 has been reported to the Security Council:

> . . . each Member State of the United Nations may act upon the legal interest referred to; consequently it may request the State to terminate its breach of Article 29. In addition to this possible unilateral action, a collective response through other intergovernmental organizations may be envisaged. The fundamental principles of the United Nations Charter and the spirit of the Statute of the International Tribunal aim to limit, as far as possible, the risks of arbitrariness and conflict. They therefore give pride of place to collective or joint action to be taken through an intergovernmental organization. It is appropriate to emphasise that this collective action:
>
> (i) may only be taken after a judicial finding has been made by the International Tribunal; and
> (ii) may take various forms, such as political or moral condemnation, or a collective request to cease the breach, or economic or diplomatic sanctions.
>
> In addition, collective action would be warranted in the case of repeated and blatant breaches of Article 29 by the same state; and provided the Security Council had not

39. Appeals Chamber, *Subpoena Judgement*, op. cit. n. 2, para. 36.
40. Ibid., para. 26.

decided that it enjoyed exclusive powers on the matter, the situation being part of a general condition of threat to the peace.[41]

This reasoning employed in the Appeals Chamber Judgement in the *Blaškić* case is innovative. It is the first detailed explanation, with regard to the legal consequences in a more specific context, given by an international court of the concept of *erga omnes* obligations. This concept has been occupying international law scholars and judges ever since the recognition in an obscure *obiter dictum* of the International Court of Justice in the 1970 *Barcelona Traction* case of the existence of certain norms that are the 'concern of all states'.[42] Obligations *erga omnes* (which are not the same as, albeit connected to, norms of *jus cogens*) are concerned with the enforcibility of norms of international law, the violation of which is deemed to be an offence not only against the state directly affected by the breach, but also against all members of the international community. Under the customary law of reprisals, it is the general rule that only the directly injured state is entitled to act against the breach of an international obligation by another state. The violation of obligations *erga omnes*, it is argued in the literature, entitles all other states to react against the breach. The problem so far has been that the International Court of Justice, although confronted in a number of cases with *erga omnes* obligations, has never addressed the legal consequences of the breach of such an obligation. It also refrained from doing so in the recent *East Timor* case, in which the Court dismissed the claim of Portugal against Australia, but confirmed *in abstracto* that the principle of self-determination was an obligation *erga omnes*.[43]

Similarly, one could point to the difficulties that the International Law Commission is facing in dealing with the legal consequences of the commission of so-called 'international crimes' by states in its draft articles on state responsibility.[44] The Commission adopted a complete set of draft articles in first reading in 1996, including the highly controversial draft Article 19 distinguishing between international 'crimes' and international 'delicts', which is further elaborated in draft Articles 51-53.[45] A discussion of this problem is beyond the

41. Ibid., para. 36.

42. *Barcelona Traction Case, Second Phase*, ICJ Rep. (1970) p. 3 et seq. (paras. 33, 34). See Malanczuk, op. cit. n. 1, pp. 58-60 with extensive references to the literature. See also Jochen Abr. Frowein, 'Obligations erga omnes', in R. Bernhardt, ed., *Encyclopedia of Public International Law*, Vol. III (1997) pp. 757-759 with a bibliography.

43. *East Timor Case (Portugal v. Australia)*, ICJ Rep. (1995) p. 90 et seq. (para. 29). See the Dissenting Opinion by Judge Weeramantry.

44. See Malanczuk, op. cit. n. 1, p. 59 et seq., p. 254 et seq.

45. Text in 37 *ILM* (1998) p. 440 et seq.

scope of the present note. It should only be noted that in its recent comments on the draft articles on state responsibility, the government of the United States still

> strongly opposes the inclusion of distinctions between delicts and so-called 'state crimes', for which there is no support under customary international law and which undermine the effectiveness of the state responsibility regime as a whole.[46]

4.3 The power of the ICTY to issue binding orders to state officials

The Appeals Chamber quite rightly did not find much difficulty in rejecting the contention that state officials could be confronted with a 'subpoena'.[47] State officials act as agents of the state and their acts, at least in principle, if they are acting in their official capacity, are attributed to the state. Customary international law, confirmed by recent cases, is rather clear on this matter, granting state officials 'functional immunity'. The state is an abstract concept and cannot act otherwise than through its officials. If it is inadmissible to issue a 'subpoena' with a threat of penalties to a state, then this can mean nothing else than it is inadmissible to issue such orders to state officials.

A different matter is the question whether the Tribunal may issue binding orders to state officials, as distinct from issuing them to the state as such. As a starting point, the Appeals Chamber rejected in its reasoning what it calls 'the domestic analogy', referring to the power of national courts in many domestic legal systems to issue orders to other state organs or state officials, even those with the highest ranks. Its argument on the structural differences between national legal systems and the international legal system merits full quotation:

> The setting is totally different in the international community. It is known *omnibus lippis et tonsoribus* that the international community lacks any central government with the attendant separation of powers and checks and balances. In particular, international courts, including the International Tribunal, do not make up a judicial branch of a central government. The international community primarily consists of sovereign States; each jealous of its own sovereign attributes and prerogatives, each insisting on its right to equality and demanding full respect, by all other states, for its domestic jurisdiction. Any international body must therefore take into account this basic structure of the international community. It follows from these various factors that international courts do not necessarily possess, *vis-à-vis* organs of sovereign States, the same powers which accrue to national courts in respect of the administrative, legislative and political organs

46. Ibid., p. 468, see also pp. 474-478.
47. Appeals Chamber, *Subpoena Judgement*, op. cit. n. 2, para. 38.

> of the state. Hence, the transposition onto the international community of legal institutions, constructs or approaches prevailing in national law may be a source of great confusion and misapprehension. In addition to causing opposition among States, it could end up blurring the distinctive features of international courts.[48]

The Appeals Chamber then discussed the general principles and rules of customary international law relating to state officials.[49] The general rule is based upon the principle of the sovereign equality of states and says that the internal organization of a state is left to its own discretion. This includes the designation and instruction of certain individuals to act as agents or organs of the state on both the national and international level. Acts performed by a state official in his or her official capacity are therefore attributed to the state and not to the individual state organ, who cannot be held accountable under international law and enjoys functional immunity, except if certain cases are at issue, such as the commission of war crimes, crimes against humanity, genocide or espionage.

The consequence, even under Article 29 of the Statute of the ICTY, is that,

> States, being the addressees of such obligation, have some choice or leeway in identifying the persons responsible for, and the method of, its fulfilment. It is for each such State to determine the internal organs competent to carry out the order. It follows that if a Judge or a Chamber intends to order the production of documents, the seizure of evidence, the arrest of suspects etc., being acts involving action by a State, its organs or officials, they must turn to the relevant State.[50]

In other words:

> Clearly, as State officials are mere instrumentalities in the hands of sovereign States, there is no practical purpose in singling them out and compelling them to produce documents, or in forcing them to appear in court. It is the State which is bound by Article 29 and it is the State for which the official or agent fulfils his functions that constitutes the legitimate interlocutor of the International Tribunal. States shall therefore incur international responsibility for any serious breach of that provision by their officials.[51]

However, this does not exclude the possibility for the Registrar of the ICTY to inform the relevant state officials of an order addressed to the state.[52]

48. Ibid., para. 40.
49. Ibid., para. 41.
50. Ibid., para. 43.
51. Ibid., para. 44.
52. Ibid., para. 45.

4.4 The power of the ICTY to issue binding orders to individuals acting in their private capacity

There is no problem to submit private individuals directly to the authority of the ICTY to issue *subpoena* orders. However, the Judgement also considers the more complicated question whether state officials may receive a *subpoena qua* private individuals.[53] With regard to 'individuals acting in their private capacity', the Chamber sees no difficulties in including state agents who, for example, have witnessed, or have obtained knowledge of, a crime before taking office. The reason is that, in such case, their role in the tasks of the ICTY is unrelated to their current functions as state officials.[54]

A more complicated question arises when a governmental official, while on official duty and exercising official functions, obtains knowledge of a crime. In this case, the Appeals Chamber took the view that the official cannot be subpoenaed because he was acting as a state organ.[55] Again, it is different if the state official has been acting as a member of an international peacekeeping force, like UNPROFOR, IFOR or SFOR, because his mandate stems not from national law, but from a resolution of the Security Council, the same source of law from which the authority of the ICTY derives.

Another scenario addressed in the reasoning is the case where an order has been issued to a state to produce documents in the possession of a state official who refuses to surrender these documents to the ICTY, although requested to do so by the respective state. The Appeals Chamber took the view that such official may be treated like an individual acting in a private capacity, and be subpoenaed and held to be in contempt of court. This would not preclude the possibility of also holding the state responsible for non-compliance.[56]

In addition, the Judgement deals with the question whether the ICTY may enter into direct contact with individuals or is obliged instead to approach the national authorities[57], and with the further question of which legal remedies are available if an individual fails to comply with a *subpoena* or order of the Tribunal[58].

53. Ibid., para. 46.
54. Ibid., para. 49.
55. Ibid., para. 50.
56. Ibid., para. 51.
57. Ibid., paras. 52-56.
58. Ibid., paras. 45-60.

4.5 The problem of national security concerns

With regard to national security claims, the Appeals Chamber confirmed the basic principle asserted by the Trial Chamber that states may not withhold documents because of national security concerns.[59] Legitimate state concerns in this respect should be taken care of, as proposed in the *Subpoena* Decision, by examining the validity of national security claims in *in camera*, *ex parte* proceedings.[60]

However, the Appeals Chamber suggested a number of other practical methods and procedures based upon the following six considerations[61]: First, in raising a national security claim, the state concerned must show that it is acting *bona fide*. Second, the state may be invited to submit the relevant documents to the scrutiny of only one Judge of the Trial Chamber to increase confidentiality. Third, if the documents are in a language other than the two official languages of the ICTY[62], the state should provide certified translations to avoid the involvement of translators of the ICTY. Fourth, the evidence should be reviewed by the Judge *in camera*, in *ex parte* proceedings and no transcripts should be made of the hearing. Fifth, documents which are not relevant to the proceedings or the relevance of which is outweighed by legitimate national security concerns are to be returned to the state without being deposited or filed in the ICTY Registry. Other documents may be edited by blacking out parts, provided that a senior state official submits a signed affidavit explaining the reasons for this. Sixth, in exceptional cases a state may refuse to submit certain documents because of their delicacy, which are at the same time of little relevance to the proceedings. In such a case a signed affidavit of the responsible Minister needs to be submitted

> (i) stating that he has personally examined the document in question;
> (ii) summarily describing the content of the documents;
> (iii) setting out precisely the grounds on which the State considers that the document is not of great relevance to the trial proceedings; and
> (iv) concisely indicating the principal reasons for the desire of the State to withhold those documents.[63]

59. For the argumentation see ibid., paras. 61-66.
60. Ibid., para. 67.
61. Ibid., paras. 68-69.
62. Under Article 33 of the ICTY's Statute, the two working languages of the ICTY are English and French.
63. Appeals Chamber, *Subpoena Judgement*, op. cit. n. 2, para. 68.

Ultimately, however, the control of the matter is vested in the Judge. If the Judge is not content with the arguments put forward by the state, he or she may request the Trial Chamber to make a judicial finding of non-compliance.

A Separate Opinion of Judge Karibi-Whyte basically objects only to the modalities providing for a single Judge to act on behalf of the Trial Chamber. In his view, the Trial Chamber 'is the only body vested with jurisdiction to conduct trial proceeedings'.[64]

5. CONCLUSION

The Appeals Chamber has clarified the limits of the power of the ICTY with regard to the *subpoena* issue and the available remedies for non-compliance by a state in a manner that corresponds to the basic position which the present author has taken in his *amicus curiae* brief and in the hearing before Trial Chamber II.[65] Thus, it is difficult to disagree in this respect. New aspects introduced by the Judgement which will give rise to further discussion in a much more general sense certainly include the parts on obligations *erga omnes*. With regard to national security claims barring the submission of documents, the Appeals Chamber has further refined the procedure to produce a balance between legitimate national security concerns of states and the required effectiveness of the International Tribunal. While this, the most sensitive aspect of the Judgement, needs to be tested in practice, there is no doubt that it is a very important decision, not only in the history of the ICTY. The development of the *subpoena* issue before the ICTY has also been carefully noted by states, which, at the time of writing, were negotiating the establishment of a permanent International Criminal Court. In view of the fundamental and complex issues that need to be addressed with regard to the precise relationship between the International Tribunal, the UN Security Council and states, the Judgement may well turn out to be cited frequently in the future as a landmark decision in the development of general international law and state responsibility.

64. Separate Opinion of Judge Adolphus G. Karibi-Whyte, para. 14.
65. See *supra* n. 4.

NATIONAL IMPLEMENTATION MEASURES OF INTERNATIONAL HUMANITARIAN LAW: SOME PRACTICAL ASPECTS*

María Teresa Dutli**

1. INTRODUCTION

From one perspective, the modern development of international humanitarian law has been a remarkable success. Its rules are among the most detailed and extensive of international law. Its principal treaties enjoy almost universal acceptance. For the other side of the picture, one has only to look at what is happening in most recent armed conflicts to realize that serious violations of humanitarian law are rife all over the world. This leads to the conclusion that it is *compliance* – respect for the rules – which is the major challenge facing humanitarian law today rather than its very existence or the adequacy of its provisions.

Humanitarian law places constraints on the waging of war. Its impact ultimately depends on whether its rules are actually applied in times of conflict. Even in the midst of war, it is still necessary to take measures to ensure respect for the law. However, action which is undertaken only after a conflict breaks out is likely to be too little and too late. The effective application of humanitarian law requires planning and preventive action. In order to forestall and deter violations, humanitarian law prescribes a range of implementation measures which must be taken by all states parties to the humanitarian treaties, and which apply in time of peace as well as in time of war.

** Head of the Advisory Service on International Humanitarian Law, International Committee of the Red Cross (ICRC), Geneva.

Yearbook of International Humanitarian Law
Volume I - 1998 - pp. 245-261

2. NATIONAL IMPLEMENTATION OF HUMANITARIAN LAW

A major part of international humanitarian law is found in the four 1949 Geneva Conventions for the protection of war victims. Nearly every state in the world has agreed to be bound by these treaties[1], which were developed and supplemented by the two Additional Protocols of 1977[2].

This broad participation is unfortunately insufficient to ensure proper application of the humanitarian treaties in all circumstances. Measures have to be taken at the national level to ensure that the rules they contain are fully respected. In particular, these measures are needed to ensure that all individuals, both civilian and military, are familiar with the rules of international humanitarian law; that the structures, administrative arrangements and personnel required for the application of humanitarian law are in place; and that violations of humanitarian law are prevented or, where necessary, punished.

2.1 What does national implementation cover?

In order to pursue the three aims listed above, and, indeed, to achieve the objectives of humanitarian law, the treaties themselves provide for a number of implementation measures.

These can be seen as deriving from the general obligation to 'respect and ensure respect' for humanitarian law in all circumstances.[3] On the basis of this general principle, the lawmakers who drew up the treaties considered it necessary to state more precisely how implementation should be effected and what measures should be taken at the national level in order to ensure respect for the law. Among the most important of these are the following:

- to prepare translations of the Conventions and Protocols in national languages;[4]
- to spread knowledge of the texts of the Conventions and Protocols as widely as possible, both among the armed forces and more generally;[5]

1. 188 States Parties as of 31 January 1998.
2. 150 and 142 States Parties respectively, as of 31 January 1998.
3. This obligation is stated in Article 1 common to the four 1949 Geneva Conventions and, more generally, has been considered by the International Court of Justice to constitute one of the 'general principles of humanitarian law to which the Conventions merely give specific expression'. See Military and Paramilitary Activities in and against Nicaragua (*Nicaragua* v. *United States of America*), Merits, Judgement, ICJ Rep. (1986) p. 114.
4. Arts. 48/49/128/145 of the four Geneva Conventions respectively and Art. 84 of 1977 Additional Protocol I.
5. Arts. 47/48/127/144 of the four Geneva Conventions respectively and Arts. 87 and 19 of Additional Protocols I and II respectively.

— to repress all violations of the Conventions and Protocols, and in particular to adopt national legislation providing for the punishment of war crimes;[6]
— to ensure that persons and places protected by the Conventions and Protocols are properly identified, located and protected;[7]
— to adopt rules to prevent the misuse of the red cross or red crescent emblem and other signs and emblems provided for in the Conventions and Protocols;[8]
— to ensure that fundamental and procedural guarantees are observed in times of armed conflict;[9]
— to provide for the appointment and training of persons qualified in international humanitarian law, including legal advisers within the armed forces;[10]
— to provide for the establishment and/or regulation of National Red Cross and Red Crescent Societies and other voluntary aid societies, civil defence organizations and national information bureaux;[11]
— to take international humanitarian law into account in selecting the location of military sites, and in the development and adoption of weapons and military tactics;[12]
— to provide, as necessary, for the establishment of hospital zones, neutral zones, security zones and demilitarized zones.[13]

Some of these measures require the adoption of legislation or regulations. Others require the development of educational programmes; the recruitment and/or training of personnel; the preparation of identity cards and other materials; the establishment of special structures or units; and the introduction of planning and administrative procedures.

From a purely legal point of view, all these national measures are essential to ensure respect for humanitarian law; there should be no order of importance

6. Arts. 49-50/50-51/129-132/146-149 of the four Geneva Conventions respectively and Arts. 85-91 of Additional Protocol I.

7. Arts. 40 and 41, First Geneva Convention; Art. 42 and Annex, Second Geneva Convention; Arts. 17, 70-71 and 120 and Annex IV, Third Geneva Convention; Arts. 20, 106-107 and Annex III, Fourth Geneva Convention; Arts. 53, 56, 58 and 79, Additional Protocol I.

8. Arts. 44 and 53-54, First Geneva Convention; Arts. 43-45, Second Geneva Convention.

9. Arts. 5, 15-17, 41, 82-90 and 95-108, Third Geneva Convention; Arts. 31-33, 35, 37, 43, 64-78, 99-101 and 117-126, Fourth Geneva Convention; Arts. 11, 44-45, 75-77, Additional Protocol I; and Arts. 4-6, Additional Protocol II.

10. Arts. 6 and 82, Additional Protocol I.

11. *National Societies*: Arts. 26 and 44, First Geneva Convention and Art. 63, Fourth Geneva Convention; Arts. 81 and 18, Additional Protocols I and II respectively; *Civil Defence*: Art. 63, Fourth Geneva Convention and Arts. 61-67, Additional Protocol I; *National Information Bureaux*: Arts. 122-124, Third Geneva Convention and Arts. 136-141, Fourth Geneva Convention.

12. Arts. 36 (weapons), 56 and 58 (military sites), Additional Protocol I.

13. Art. 23 and Annex I, First Geneva Convention; Arts. 14 and 15, Fourth Geneva Convention; Art. 60 and Annex I, Additional Protocol I.

as they are interdependent. It can hardly be said that there has been a grave breach of humanitarian law in the form of an attack on a protected zone, for instance, if the zone or area concerned has not previously been marked by specified signs or emblems.

It would be impossible to give a detailed analysis here of the importance of each such measure, and for the purposes of the present article we have selected a number of substantive matters which appear to be of particular interest and relevance in terms of national implementation. We shall therefore focus on the issues listed below.

— Repression of war crimes

Serious violations of international humanitarian law must be stopped. This will not be possible unless states create at the national level the conditions necessary to bring the culprits to justice.

— Protection of the red cross/red crescent emblem

The red cross or red crescent emblem is the visible sign identifying those assisting victims of armed conflict and entitling them to protection. Respect for the emblem is indispensable on the battlefield, and, to preserve its protective effect, appropriate measures must be taken to avoid misuse of the protected sign.[14]

On the organizational level, we shall discuss the establishment of *committees or other national bodies for the implementation of international humanitarian law* as a mechanism to promote national implementation.

2.1.1 *Repression of war crimes*

States parties to the international humanitarian law treaties are under an obligation to take the legislative measures necessary to impose penalties in the event of the commission of any grave breach designated by these texts.[15]

Grave breaches comprise some of the most flagrant violations of international humanitarian law. They are listed in the Geneva Conventions and Additional Protocol I and include wilful killing; torture or inhumane treatment; wilfully causing great suffering or serious injury to body or health; attacks on the civilian population and indiscriminate attacks; attacks on works and installations contain-

14. On the protection and use of the emblem, see F. Bugnion, 'The red cross and red crescent emblems', 272 *International Review of the Red Cross (IRRC)* (1989) pp. 408-419. See also 'Model law concerning the use and protection of the emblem of the red cross or red crescent', 313 *IRRC* (1996) pp. 486-495.

15. 'The High Contracting Parties undertake to enact any legislation necessary to provide effective penal sanctions for persons committing, or ordering to be committed, any of the grave breaches of the present Convention...' (Arts. 49/40/129/146 of the four Geneva Conventions respectively).

ing dangerous forces and on non-defended localities; perfidious use of the protected emblems; unlawful population transfers; unjustified delay in repatriation of prisoners of war or protected civilians; attacks on historic monuments or places of worship; and denial of judicial guarantees.[16] Grave breaches such as these are regarded as war crimes.[17]

The notion of war crimes is broader than that of grave breaches because it covers, in addition to the acts enumerated above, other serious violations of the rules of international humanitarian law, either customary or treaty-based, regardless of whether such violations are committed in situations of international or of non-international armed conflict.[18]

National criminal legislation adopted to sanction violations of international humanitarian law should, at least:

— establish, in respect of each grave breach covered, the nature and extent of the punishment, with due regard for the principle of proportionality between the penalty imposed and the gravity of the breach committed;
— recognize the individual criminal responsibility not only of persons having committed any of the said breaches, but also of those having ordered the commission thereof; and recognize the individual criminal responsibility of superiors;
— provide, in particular, for the repression of grave breaches which are the result of an omission, where the omission in question is not already punishable under ordinary national law;
— specify that interests and imperatives of a political or military nature, national interests and requirements, and orders issued by superiors do not justify the commission of grave breaches and are not grounds for exemption from punishment;
— have a substantive and personal scope permitting application of the law to any perpetrator of a grave breach, irrespective of his or her nationality or the place where the act was committed;
— give any person prosecuted for committing such a breach the right to a fair trial by an impartial and regularly constituted court and to regular judicial proceedings affording the generally recognized judicial guarantees;

16. Arts. 50/51/129/147 of the four Geneva Conventions respectively and Art. 85 of Additional Protocol I.

17. Art. 85 of Additional Protocol I.

18. See E. David, *Principes du droit des conflits armés* (Brussels, Bruylant 1994) pp. 642-665; T. Meron, 'International criminalization of internal atrocities', 89 *AJIL* (1995) pp. 554-577.

— comply with the obligation to facilitate cooperation with other states in terms of judicial assistance in criminal matters and matters involving extradition.[19]

Moreover, this legislation must be tailored to meet the specific requirements of the legal system of the country in question, so as to resolve any problems involved in providing for the repression of war crimes at the national level.

2.1.2 *Protection of the red cross/red crescent emblem*

The red cross/red crescent emblem is the symbol of impartial humanitarian assistance offered to those in distress. It is often the only means of protection available to persons trying to attenuate the suffering of the victims of armed conflict and the only guarantee that help will reach those victims in time.

It is therefore essential that the significance of the emblem be recognized and respected at all times and in all circumstances. To this effect, every possible form of misuse must be prevented or, if that fails, punished. This issue is dealt with in Articles 53 and 54 of the First Geneva Convention and several provisions of Additional Protocol I.

Generally speaking, misuse of the emblem takes three main forms:

— imitation of the emblem and its use by unauthorized organizations. This gives rise to a risk of confusion as to the purpose of and the protection conferred by the sign;
— misuse of the emblem by doctors, pharmacies or commercial firms, which is in contradiction to the principle of voluntary and disinterested service of those entitled to use it;
— perfidious use of the emblem, a particularly serious offence because it betrays the confidence of the adversary; moreover, it jeopardizes the safety of medical services.

To forestall and prevent misuse of the emblem, states have a duty under the humanitarian treaties to adopt national legislation imposing penalties for such acts. In particular, it is important to:

— draw up legal provisions defining the emblem itself, the persons and objects it protects, lawful and unlawful use, and the persons who are authorized to use the emblem and those who are not;
— designate an authority responsible for monitoring respect for the emblem and for reporting any misuse. This authority may be: (i) as concerns imitations,

19. *National Repression of Violations of International Humanitarian Law: Meeting of Experts* (Geneva, 23-25 September 1997) ICRC Advisory Service on International Humanitarian Law, Introduction to preparatory documents.

misuse for commercial purposes and any other form of misuse in peacetime, the national patent and trademark office, (ii) as concerns perfidious use of the emblem in wartime, the military authority;
- promote knowledge of the rules governing use of the emblem as widely as possible and in peacetime, especially in the context of military exercises;
- prosecute and punish any violation of those rules.[20]

2.2 Committees or other national bodies for international humanitarian law

The measures that must be taken for the implementation of international humanitarian law are complex and involve many spheres of government activity and sectors of public life. Careful coordination and the constant support of all ministries, public administrations, state entities and other institutions are essential. These needs can be met by establishing appropriate mechanisms, particularly bodies set up specifically to address issues relating to the application of international humanitarian law at the national level. The delegates at the 26th International Conference of the Red Cross and Red Crescent, held in Geneva in December 1995, unanimously reaffirmed their support for humanitarian law, while making a commitment to move from law to action'. They undertook to rise to that challenge by taking practical steps to ensure more effective application of and greater respect for international humanitarian law. One of the recommendations adopted by Resolution I of this Conference encouraged states to create national committees 'to advise and assist governments in implementing and disseminating international humanitarian law'.[21]

National committees, interministerial working groups or advisory committees set up by states have thus been created in order to facilitate the process of national implementation of humanitarian law; they have been assigned specific functions to promote humanitarian law and prepare measures for its implementation, with the general objective of supporting governments on matters relating to this body of law.[22] According to information available to the ICRC, more

20. See *supra* n. 15.

21. Recommendation V of the Intergovernmental Group of Experts for the Protection of War Victims (January 1995). See Resolution 1 of the 26th International Conference of the Red Cross and Red Crescent, entitled *International humanitarian law – from law to action. Report on the follow-up to the International Conference for the Protection of War Victims,* in 310 *IRRC* (January-February 1996) p. 58.

22. See C. Pellandini, ed., *Committees or other national bodies for international humanitarian law. Meeting of experts* (Geneva, ICRC Advisory Service on International Humanitarian Law 1997).

than 40 countries had set up committees or working groups dealing with humanitarian law by the end of 1997.[23]

Although there is no legal obligation to set up such bodies and they are not necessarily required if other mechanisms already exist, it may be said that, in countries where they have been established, they have proved to be useful and appropriate means for facilitating the process of adoption of national legislation or its adaptation to bring it in line with humanitarian obligations.

2.3 The Advisory Service on International Humanitarian Law of the International Committee of the Red Cross (ICRC)

The importance and urgency of improving respect for international humanitarian law, including implementation at the national level, have been emphasized at various international meetings during the 1990s. In 1995, the group of experts set up by the International Conference for the Protection of War Victims put forward a series of recommendations aimed at reinforcing respect for humanitarian law. These recommendations included the proposal that the ICRC should increase its technical assistance to states. In response, the ICRC set up a special unit, the Advisory Service on International Humanitarian Law, to advise governments both on adherence to the humanitarian law treaties and on national implementation of humanitarian law. The objectives are clear: to raise governments' awareness of their obligations under humanitarian law and, by offering reliable, relevant advice, to help and encourage them to meet those obligations fully at the national level.

In promoting national implementation, it is essential to take account of local needs and conditions. The structure and working methods of the Advisory Service have therefore been designed to enable it to respond flexibly to specific requirements and opportunities, and to provide advice that is tailored to different political and legal systems.

The ICRC's efforts to promote national implementation measures focus mainly on the provision of accurate, accessible advice. International meetings of experts have been organized by the Advisory Service to draw up authoritative guidelines on issues such as national committees[24] and criminal law. On the first of these issues, pursuant to the meeting of experts on committees or other national bodies for the national implementation of international humanitarian law, held in Geneva on 23-25 October 1996, the Advisory Service drafted some 'Guiding principles

23. *National implementation of international humanitarian law: Annual Report 1996* (Geneva, ICRC Advisory Service on International Humanitarian Law 1997) pp. 78-98.

24. Ibid.

concerning the status and methods of operation of national bodies for the implementation of international humanitarian law'[25], with the aim of encouraging the creation of such bodies, standardizing their modes of operation and facilitating the exchange of information and viewpoints on issues relating to humanitarian law.

A documentation centre has been set up by the Advisory Service to collect information on national implementation measures and to make this information available to governments. The Service has also produced a series of publications and pamphlets explaining humanitarian law issues in clear, non-technical language.[26]

3. EXPERIENCES IN NATIONAL IMPLEMENTATION: A CASE STUDY AND RECENT DEVELOPMENTS

Considerable efforts are being made by governments in the field of national implementation; this is demonstrated by the growing number of states adhering to the humanitarian treaties. International organizations, too, are showing increasing interest and are supporting efforts to establish national structures to promote respect for international humanitarian law.

As for the subject-matter, it is difficult to sum up in a single article the broad range of activities taking place worldwide in the field of national implementation. A choice – arbitrary by definition – must be made to illustrate the current situation in this regard. We shall first offer a case study to show how the process of national implementation may be initiated in a country and how the different players involved in the process interrelate in order to obtain concrete results. We shall then mention some recent developments in the area of national legislation and regulations for the implementation of humanitarian law, referring to activities under way in different regions of the world to deal with the issues identified as priorities for national implementation.

25. These guidelines appear in *National implementation of international humanitarian law: Annual Report 1996*, ibid. pp. 63-68.

26. Ibid. See also 319 *IRRC* (July-August 1997) pp. 456-457.

3.1 A case study: national implementation measures in Zimbabwe

Independent Zimbabwe became a party to the 1949 Geneva Conventions on 7 March 1981 and to the 1977 Additional Protocols on 19 October 1992. Obviously, more has been done to promote implementation of the Conventions than of the Protocols, as the latter were ratified more recently. However, by acceding to the Protocols, Zimbabwe indicated its willingness to be bound by their rules, so no distinction can be drawn between obligations incurred under the Conventions and those incurred under the Protocols. Zimbabwe's performance will be measured by the highest standards of international humanitarian law.

3.1.1 *Implementation mechanisms*

In 1994, the area of competence of the Zimbabwean Interministerial Committee for Human Rights, created one year earlier, was extended and it became the Interministerial Committee for Human Rights and Humanitarian Law.

This Committee facilitates coordination at ministerial level of all matters relating to international humanitarian law. It is composed of representatives of the Ministries of Foreign Affairs, Defence, Home Affairs, Justice and Social Welfare and of the President's Office. Each authority has its own responsibilities and competence within the Committee, whose mandate is to advise on the ratification of new humanitarian law treaties and on national implementation.

Through its representatives, the Committee is also competent to advise on new implementing legislation and to report on progress made in the national implementation of humanitarian law. In this connection, its members have participated in several meetings and fora, sharing their own national expertise and facilitating exchanges of experience on the issue. They have also taken part in the preparation of a study on the degree to which Zimbabwean legislation is compatible with the requirements of international humanitarian law. The recommendations of this document serve as a working basis for the achievement of full national implementation.[27]

3.1.2 *Legal measures*

In Zimbabwe, the Office of the Attorney-General screens all international treaties before adoption so as to identify any rules that are not consistent with Zimbab-

27. E. Kornblum, *Implementation of international humanitarian law. National measures: Zimbabwe*, Internal report (Harare, 8 February 1996). This document can be consulted at the Documentation Centre of the ICRC Advisory Service.

wean law. Should such inconsistencies be observed, either the Zimbabwean law is changed or reservations are made to the international treaty. Once ratified, international treaties do not automatically form part of Zimbabwean law. An Act of Parliament is necessary to allow interpretation of national legislation in accordance with international law.[28]

The four Geneva Conventions were incorporated in Zimbabwean law by the Geneva Conventions Act, 1981. This Act repealed and replaced Chapter 96 of the Statute Laws of Zimbabwe and came into operation on February 1984 through Statutory Instrument No. 30 of 1984. The Additional Protocols were incorporated by the Geneva Conventions Amendment Act, 1996.

By Statutory Instrument No. 68 of 1996, the President assigned to the Minister of Defence responsibility for the administration of the Geneva Conventions Act of 1981.[29]

3.1.2.1 Grave breaches

The Geneva Conventions Act provides in Section 3 for severe penalties for grave breaches of the Conventions. The Amendment Act, 1996, amends this Section in order to include grave breaches of Protocol I. The measures of repression provided for in the Act meet the criteria of universal jurisdiction[30], as it is applicable to both Zimbabweans and foreigners, irrespective of where the crime was committed.[31] Penalties for wilful killing range from the death penalty to imprisonment not exceeding 30 years.[32] For other grave breaches, prison sentences exceeding 14 years may be imposed.[33]

Judicial guarantees in the event of grave breaches are covered in Articles 4-7 of the Act.

There is no reference to the Geneva Conventions Act or the guarantees it contains in the Defence Act or the Defence Regulations. Offences under the Geneva Conventions Act are classified as 'civil offences'. In principle, a military court or a court martial does not have jurisdiction over such cases, unless the violation is also an offence that falls under its jurisdiction.[34]

28. Constitution of Zimbabwe, Section 111B (amended by the Constitution of Zimbabwe Amendment Act, No. 12, 1993).
29. Assignment of Functions (Minister of Defence) (Amendment) Notice, 1996 (No. 1).
30. See Arts. 49/50/129/146 of the four Geneva Conventions respectively.
31. Art. 3, para. 1, of the Geneva Conventions Amendment Act, 1996.
32. Ibid., Art. 3, para. 2(a).
33. Ibid., Art. 3, para. 2(b).
34. Ibid., Section 3(5).

Most 'grave breaches' under the Geneva Conventions and Protocols would probably also be considered grave breaches of common or customary law and could be tried accordingly. Moreover, the Geneva Conventions Act[35] provides that when the Attorney-General does not prosecute a grave breach, anyone can institute a private prosecution for an offence under the general criminal code.[36]

3.1.2.2 Misuse of the emblem and other protected signs

The Geneva Conventions Act[37] protects the red cross and other related emblems and prohibits misuse thereof.

The 1981 Act as amended, in accordance with the Zimbabwe Red Cross Society Act, 1981, requires the authorization of the Ministry of Health for the use of the red cross and red crescent emblems and names.[38] Misuse of the emblem is punishable by a fine not exceeding 2,000 (Zimbabwe) dollars[39], and the forfeiture of any goods or other articles in connection with which the emblem, designation, design or wording was used may be ordered.[40]

The Attorney-General is responsible for prosecuting cases of misuse of the emblem. If the Attorney-General does not prosecute, any person can institute a private prosecution for an offence under common law.[41]

3.1.2.3 Other Acts or regulations relevant to the application of international humanitarian law

The Zimbabwe Red Cross Society Act of 1981 defines the objectives and powers of the National Society. This Act amends the Private Voluntary Organisations Act (Chapter 93) to place the National Society on the list of organizations that are not covered by the latter. This is a very favourable point as organizations covered by the Private Voluntary Organisations Act enjoy very little autonomy, there being tight government control over their budget and fundraising activities.

The Defence Act of 1972, as amended (Chapter 94, Section 4), defines on the national level which persons belong to the armed forces. The Act states that *'the Army and the Air Force shall each consist of a) a Regular Force, and b) a Reserve Force, where such a force has been created'* and includes medical

35. Ibid., Section 3(6).
36. See n. 29.
37. No. 36, 1981, Section 8(3).
38. Ibid., Art. 8, paras 1(a) and 2(a), (b).
39. Ibid., Art. 8, para. 3, as amended by Section 4 of the Amendment Act, 1996.
40. Ibid., Art. 8, para. 4, as amended by Section 4 of the Amendment Act, 1996.
41. Ibid., Section 8(6), which refers to Section 3(6).

officers within these categories. This Act is supplemented by the Defence Forces (Discipline) Regulations, 1978 (amended by the Statutory Instruments on Defence Issues, 1989) and the Police Act, 1995. It is nowhere explicitly stated that the Police Force is part of the Army, even though the two instruments refer to the Regular Forces as comprising both.

The Civil Protection Act, 1989 states the goal of the civil defence corps and defines the situations in which it takes action. The Act places Civil Protection under the responsibility of the Ministry of Local Government, Rural and Urban Development.

3.1.3 *Conclusions on the Zimbabwean experience of national implementation*

The four 1949 Geneva Conventions have been adequately incorporated in Zimbabwean legislation. Since there has not yet been a court case on the basis of the Geneva Conventions Act, it is difficult to assess the extent of the Act's applicability or how workable it is. However, from a formal viewpoint and owing to the important work done by the Interministerial Committee for Human Rights and Humanitarian Law in analysing domestic law and bringing it in line with international standards, most of the requirements of humanitarian law seem to have been met. The Committee played a very important role in the drafting and adoption of the Geneva Conventions Amendment Act, 1996, which incorporated the 1977 Additional Protocols in Zimbabwean law. Furthermore, the Committee has the potential to increase compliance with these international standards even further.

The advantages of having set up a coordinating body is that it has facilitated the distribution of responsibilities among the national authorities as regards national legislation to implement the humanitarian treaties. Each ministry represented on the Committee has a specific area of competence with respect to the application of those treaties. The participation of its representatives in regional and international meetings and seminars has facilitated the exchange of information and experiences and made a contribution to knowledge of the necessary measures and methods at the national level.[42]

42. See G. Chiwese, *Medidas nacionais para a implementação do direito internacional humanitário: apresentaão da experiência do Zimbabwe*, paper submitted for the National Seminar on Implementation of International Humanitarian Law (Maputo, 18-20 March 1997).

3.2 Laws and regulations for the implementation of international humanitarian law: recent developments

3.2.1 *The United States War Crimes Act*

The War Crimes Act of 1996 amended Title 18 of the United States Code by inserting a new Chapter 118 providing for punishment of grave breaches of the Geneva Conventions or any protocol to which the United States is a party, where the person committing such breach or the victim is a member of the United States armed forces or a United States national.[43]

The War Crimes Act 1996 was amended in 1997[44] to extend the range of offences covered to: (i) conduct prohibited by Articles 23, 25, 27 or 28 of the Regulations annexed to Hague Convention IV of 1907 respecting the Laws and Customs of War on Land[45]; (ii) violations of Article 3 common to the Geneva Conventions (or any protocol dealing with non-international armed conflict to which the United States is a party); and (iii) wilfully killing or causing serious injury to civilians in violation of Amended Protocol II (the Mines Protocol) to the 1980 Conventional Weapons Convention (once the United States becomes a party).

The War Crimes Act, as amended, is now one of the few examples of domestic legislation which *expressly* provide for the punishment of violations of common Article 3 and of the Amended Mines Protocol.

However, while the Act bridges a major gap in United States legislation for the national implementation of international humanitarian law, it still requires some modification. To bring it in line with the obligations stemming from humanitarian law, the scope of this instrument, which currently applies only to acts committed by, or against, US nationals or members of the US armed forces, needs to be broadened to provide for universal jurisdiction as required by the Geneva Conventions. This seems particularly important in view of the fact that US courts already have jurisdiction to hear claims by persons who have been victims of torture or human rights abuses committed abroad by foreign nationals.[46]

43. War Crimes Prosecution, SEC 583, Section 2401 of Title 18, United States Code (Public Law 104-192; the War Crimes Act of 1996). Reprinted *infra* at p. 643.

44. [Expanded War Crimes Act] Public Law: 105-119 (11/26/97) (H.R.2159). See *infra* p. 643.

45. Section II, Chapter I: Means of Injuring the Enemy, Sieges and Bombardments.

46. See Alien Tort Claims Act [originally enacted as section 9 of the Judicial Act of 1789] and Torture Victims Protection Act of 1991 (Public Law 102-256 [HR 2092], 106 Stat. 73, approved 12 March 1992.

The Department of State appears committed to expanding the Act to provide for universal jurisdiction as stipulated by the Geneva Conventions.[47] The ICRC and the American Red Cross have expressed their support for war crimes legislation.[48] When signing the 1996 Act into law, President Clinton also spoke in favour of universal jurisdiction.[49]

3.2.2 *The Georgian law for the protection and use of the red cross/red crescent emblem*

A new law for the protection of the emblem entered into force in Georgia on 24 October 1997, the date of its publication in the Official Journal.

Georgia has been a party to the 1949 Geneva Conventions and to the 1977 Additional Protocols since 14 September 1993. Before this new law came into force, the red cross/red crescent emblem enjoyed partial protection under Georgian national law by virtue of a few provisions of Georgian criminal law[50], dealing mainly with the perfidious use of the sign. This protection was nevertheless insufficient.

In late 1996, a draft law on the National Red Cross Society was submitted to Parliament. The draft, which was examined by the Parliamentary Commission for Health and Social Affairs, initially contained a chapter on the protection of the emblem. After various discussions, the draft was separated into two different draft laws, one concerning the National Society and the other concerning protection of the emblem. It was on the basis of the latter that the new law for the protection of the emblem was adopted in October 1997.[51]

Even though the new law is quite comprehensive in defining by whom and in what circumstances the emblem may be used, and how it should be protected, it makes no provision for penalties in the event of misuse. The reason for this is that, in accordance with legislative practice specific to Georgia, the criminal code and the code relating to administrative offences and corresponding penalties

47. 'FYI: The Administration also favours expanding jurisdiction over war criminals who come within US jurisdiction, an approach included in the Senate version of this legislation. We understand that this approach, however, will be considered as a follow-on step after approval of this legislation.' HR 1348 - The Expanded War Crimes Act of 1997.

48. Subcommittee of the Immigration and Claims Committee of the Judiciary, US House of Representatives. Statement of the ICRC, June 1996.

49. '[E]xpansions should address (...) (1) any case in which a person who commits a grave breach of the Geneva Conventions is found within the US ...'. Statement made by President Clinton on signature of the War Crimes Act.

50. Arts. 224 and 283 of the Penal Code of Georgia on the illegal use of the red cross/red crescent emblem.

51. It entered into force on 24 October 1997, the date of its publication.

are regarded as more appropriate instruments for the imposition of penalties. Hence it is essential that both the aforementioned codes, which are still in preparation to replace the criminal legislation in force during the Soviet period, include comprehensive provisions to deal with this issue.

3.2.3 *National bodies for international humanitarian law: the most recent and their common characteristics*

As mentioned above, some states have set up specific bodies to facilitate the national implementation of international humanitarian law at the national level. Known as national committees or interministerial committees, or, less formally, as working groups, some of these bodies have a permanent mandate while others operate on an *ad hoc* basis. Some of them are established as part of their country's National Red Cross or Red Crescent Society, with a mandate from the government. In general, the role of such bodies is to advise governments and provide them with support in matters relating to adherence to the humanitarian treaties, their incorporation in national law, and dissemination of their provisions.

There is a growing trend towards the creation of such bodies and, as in the case of Zimbabwe, a great deal can be done at the national level to ensure respect for and compliance with humanitarian obligations. Between January and December 1997, new national bodies for humanitarian law were set up in Belarus, El Salvador, Ethiopia, Panama, Togo, Portugal and Senegal.[52]

To determine the common characteristics of such national bodies, we should look at their method of constitution, their legal status, their composition and their mandate. Most permanent commissions, committees or working groups are established by law or by executive or presidential decree. They are generally linked in one way or another to the executive authorities and are independent of other state bodies, although they are sometimes requested to report to parliamentary groups. They have only an advisory role, none of them having decision--making or judicial powers. The ministries represented on the committees vary from one country to another, but are most often the Ministries of Foreign Affairs, Defence and Justice.[53]

The fact that most national committees for international humanitarian law are permanent bodies meeting regularly is seen as a considerable advantage. They serve as valuable channels for dialogue between government officials and National Red Cross or Red Crescent Societies, with each side advising the other on new

52. See *Table of national bodies for international humanitarian law*, ICRC internal document (regularly updated) which may be consulted at the Documentation Centre of the ICRC Advisory Service.

53. Ibid.

questions relating to international humanitarian law as they arise. Their sustained contacts with high-level government representatives enable the committees to find the appropriate person to deal with on key issues under debate at the international level, while at the same time ensuring that adequate measures are taken at the national level to meet international obligations.

4. PROSPECTS FOR THE FUTURE

It can be affirmed today that the need to implement humanitarian law at the national level is universally recognized.

The examples given above, coming from different parts of the world, bear witness to the efforts made by states in this field and the importance they attach to the matter.

A great deal remains to be done and, even when national implementation is achieved in formal terms, its success will depend largely on the actual application of the measures taken. The ultimate responsibility to ensure full respect for international humanitarian law rests with governments and individuals. Humanitarian organizations can also play an important role in this regard by helping states to meet their obligations.

A COLOMBIAN VIEW ON PROTOCOL II*

Frits Kalshoven**

Colombia, which never deigned to sign the Additional Protocols of 1977, in 1993 acceded to Protocol I on the protection of victims of international armed conflicts, and in 1996 to Protocol II applicable in situations of non-international (or internal) armed conflict. The latter step was the more remarkable in that Colombia for more than four decades was (and is to the present day) the scene of virulent internal armed conflict.

The accession to the 1977 Protocols was foreshadowed by the adoption of a new Constitution in 1991. This not only provides a full list of human rights, but the section on emergency situations expressly lays down that the rules of international humanitarian law must be respected in all cases.[1]

Another constitutional provision[2] empowers the Constitutional Court to adjudge the constitutionality of treaties the government wishes to ratify. The Court was thus given the opportunity to scrutinise, first, Protocol I[3] and subsequently Protocol II[4]. This note serves, in particular, to highlight some aspects of the latter judgement.

** Formerly, Chair in Public International Law and International Humanitarian Law, Leiden University; Officer with the Royal Netherlands Navy. Currently serving, *inter alia,* as President of the International Humanitarian Fact-Finding Commission.

1. Art. 214, para. 2.
2. Art. 241, para. 10.
3. Judgement of Consitutional Court of 28 October 1992. Sentencia No. C-574/92, Revisión oficiosa del Protocolo Adicional a los Convenios de Ginebra del 12 de agosto de 1949, relativo a la protección de las víctimas de los conflictos armados internacionales (Protocolo I).
4. Judgement of Constitutional Court of 18 May 1995. Sentencia No. C-225/95,Revisión constitucional del 'Protocolo Adicional a los Convenios de Ginebra del 12 de agosto de 1949, relativo a la protección de las víctimas de los conflictos armados sin carácter internacional (Protocolo II)' hecho en Ginebra al 8 de junio de 1977, y de la Ley 171 del 16 de diciembre de 1994, por medio de la cual se apruebra dicho Protocolo.

Yearbook of International Humanitarian Law
Volume I - 1998 - pp. 262-268

The 1995 judgement stands out by the thoroughness and depth of the Court's reasoning. An introductory part sets forth the – largely positive – views of government officials and representatives of social organisations. Thus, a representative of the President recalls a dictum in the Court's 1992 judgement that the Constitution accords the rules of international humanitarian law binding force even without the need for ratification or promulgation of executive orders, and he argues that approval of Protocol II therefore serves solely to give effect to this constitutional rule, incorporate the Protocol into the domestic legislation, and notify the international community of states that Colombia undertakes to respect and ensure respect of its rules.

This official also emphasises the vital importance the government attaches to Protocol II in the Colombian context. Not only do its rules serve to protect the non-combatant population, but by providing a basis for the conclusion of *ad hoc* agreements among the parties for the observation of humanitarian principles, the Protocol may contribute to achieving a negotiated solution of the armed conflict.

Most of the non-governmental voices likewise underscore the binding force of the norms of international humanitarian law and affirm the absence of a need for express ratification of the Protocol as well as its complete concordance with the Constitution. It does not serve the interests of the guerrilla fighters alone nor is its application limited to cases of civil war in the classical sense. Indeed, while the circumstances typifying a conflict as a civil war might induce third states or the international community to recognise a state of belligerency, neither the adoption nor the application of the Protocol entails such a recognition on the part of the government.

How to construe the responsibility of insurgents for violations of international humanitarian law? On this point, a human rights lawyers' group submits the interesting argument that the guerrilla movements are precluded by their own politico-military pretensions from shirking their obligations under customary international humanitarian law as codified in the Protocol.

On a practical level, there is a strong focus on the fate of civilians who do not participate in the hostilities: while according to the applicable law they cannot be attacked, must be protected, and may not be subjected to forced displacement, this is a long way from depicting the actual situation in the country. It is therefore suggested that the Court not confine itself to declaring that Protocol II is in conformity with the Constitution: it should urge the immediate adoption of the necessary legislative and other measures to give effect to its provisions.

One lone dissenting voice denounces three provisions of the Protocol as unconstitutional: Article 1, on scope of application, because, by accepting the existence of internal armed conflicts, it lends legitimacy to irregular armed groups who seek to destroy the democratic system; Article 6, paragraph 5, because its call for amnesty at the end of hostilities entails an unacceptable level of impunity and amounts to a negation of justice; and Article 13, which, although purporting to protect the civilian population, does not require the irregular armed groups to distinguish themselves from civilians, thus enabling them to use the population as a shield and make it suffer the consequences of the confrontation.

The Court begins its own argument by explaining its understanding of the term international humanitarian law: this comprises both the rules for the protection of war victims (the law of Geneva) and the rules on combat or law of The Hague. The term humanitarian law in the Constitution must be interpreted in the same broad sense.

International humanitarian law belongs to the universally accepted customary law of civilised peoples. This, together with the self-evident humanitarian character of its values, underlies its character of *jus cogens*, and its rules are *eo ipso* binding on all belligerent parties. For the Court, this determines why no irregular armed group can consider itself relieved of the obligation to respect the minimum standards of humanity on the mere ground that it is not party to the treaties of humanitarian law. Neither is there room here for a rule of reciprocity: the rules of humanitarian law exist not for the benefit of those taking part in the armed conflict but of the non-combatant population and the victims of the conflict.

Article 214 of the Constitution, paragraph 2, provides (as mentioned above) that the rules of international humanitarian law must be respected at all times. These rules predominate in the internal legal order and form part of a bloc of constitutionality: i.e., those rules which, whether formally articulated in the Constitution or not, are used as parameters to test the constitutionality of laws. Hence the need for the state to adapt its legislation to these rules, so as to enable their actual implementation. A cautious reaction, this, to the point made earlier by a non-governmental representative that the Court should urge the immediate adoption of the necessary legislative and other measures to give effect to the provisions of Protocol II.

The Court emphatically rejects the suggestion that the Protocol violates Colombian sovereignty or implies a recognition of the insurgents as a belligerent party. On the other hand, it wholeheartedly endorses the idea of special agreements between the parties: reinforcing their mutual undertakings, these may result in gradually increased respect of the rules of the Protocol and, it adds, may enable the putting in motion of mechanisms of verification.

The Court emphasises that the purpose of humanising war, which underlies Protocol II and international humanitarian law in general, implies neither a legitimation of internal armed conflicts nor of the recourse to arms by irregular armed groups. The government retains its full responsibility to preserve public order and guarantee the peaceful existence of the population. What humanising the war really refers to, the Court argues, is the special link of humanitarian law with the search for peace. All the more so, then, must Protocol II be seen as in conformity with the Colombian Constitution, Article 22 of which explicitly provides for a fundamental right to peace.

While Protocol II may not have enough to say on the protection of the civilian population or about the conduct of hostilities, the Court rejects the conclusion that whatever is not expressly prohibited is permitted: such a conclusion would go against the Martens clause as included in the Preamble to the Protocol. Indeed, rules in other treaties of humanitarian law that are compatible with the nature of internal armed conflict may be regarded as applicable in such a conflict as well, since, as noted above, they merely give expression to customary norms of *jus cogens,* which are *eo ipso* incorporated in the Colombian legal order.

In a similar vein, and relying on the constitutional rule that international humanitarian law must be respected at all times, the Court holds that application of Protocol II does not require a prior determination that the actual situation meets all the criteria spelled out in Article 1, paragraph 1. Nor can the exception in paragraph 2 of situations of internal disturbances and tensions as not being armed conflicts alter its judgment: while that may be of interest on the international plane in connection with the international responsibilities of Colombia, on the internal plane the constitutional rule predominates.

The Court emphasises the vital importance in the Colombian context of the principles of distinction between combatants and civilians and of protection of the civilian population, if only in view of the alarmingly high number of forcibly displaced persons in the country. Those principles apply in internal armed conflicts in the same fashion and on the same grounds as they do in international ones. It sees the principle of distinction reflected in the first paragraph of Article 4, which guarantees humane treatment in all circumstances to [a]ll persons who do not take a direct part or who have ceased to take part in hostilities.

Admittedly, as noted by the lone dissenter among the non-governmental representatives, Protocol II does not indicate by what means the distinction between combatants and civilians must be made; a silence that had led him to conclude that the Protocol enables the irregular forces to use the population as a shield and make it suffer the consequences of the confrontation. The Court refutes both contentions: on the matter of means of distinction, one may seek guidance in the relevant provisions of Protocol I; and the principles of distinction and protection specifically forbid the parties to the conflict to use the civilian population with a view to obtaining a military advantage.

Article 4, on fundamental guarantees, gives the Court occasion to broach yet another issue of cardinal importance in the Colombian context. The Article prohibits to order that there shall be no survivors[5], as well as acts against the persons mentioned above, such as violence to the life, health and physical or mental well-being of persons[6], acts of terrorism[7], rape[8], and threats to commit such acts[9]. Noting the evident link of these prohibitions with the constitutional values of protection of life and dignity and integrity of persons, the Court concludes that the prohibitions in Article 4 must be deemed to have an impact on the rule on military due obedience. (While Art. 91, para. 1 of the Constitution lays down the general rule that in case of a manifest violation of a constitutional precept to the detriment of any person, a superior order does not exempt the actor from responsibility, para. 2 excepts military personnel in service from this rule, adding that, in their case, responsibility lies solely with the superior who gives the order. Taken together with the fact that military offenders in most cases fall under the jurisdiction of military courts, this special rule in practice has very often resulted in impunity.)

Recalling the distinction it had drawn on an earlier occasion between the obedience a subaltern is due to observe for the sake of discipline, and obedience that exceeds the limits of a reasonable order and hence is tantamount to a blind following of the instructions given by a superior, the Court now draws the conclusion that due military obedience cannot be invoked to justify acts that are manifestly detrimental to human rights, notably the dignity, life and integrity of persons – the bloc of constitutionality, in a word.

A last point concerns the clause on amnesty in Article 6, paragraph 5, of Protocol II; not just because the lone dissenter had listed it among the provisions he regarded as unconstitutional, but in view of its general interest. The Court notes that no comparable provision figures in Protocol I, and for good reason: in an international armed conflict, a soldier who falls into enemy hands may be detained as a prisoner of war but cannot be punished for the fact that he took part in the fighting. In contrast, prisoner-of-war status does not obtain in an internal armed conflict, and captured participants in hostilities may be punished for having taken up arms, specifically, for crimes such as rebellion or insurrection. This explains the suggestion of a broadest possible amnesty, as a measure which, after the cessation of hostilities, may contribute to national reconciliation.

The Court emphasises that the state is under no obligation to grant amnesty, let alone that an amnesty should encompass all crimes committed in the course of the armed conflict. It regards the suggestion of amnesty in Protocol II as

5. Art. 4.1.
6. Art. 4.2 (a).
7. Art. 4.2 (d).
8. Art. 4.2 (e).
9. Art. 4.2 (h).

specifically meant for (pure or relative) political crimes, since those crimes typically are committed for reasons related to the armed conflict. Once the desirability of amnesty is considered, it is for the state to determine which crimes fall under that heading. The Court notes that the option of amnesty for political crimes is perfectly compatible with the Constitution: Article 150, paragraph 17, explicitly empowers Congress to grant amnesty for political crimes. Indeed, the granting of amnesty for political crimes on grounds of public convenience corresponds with a Colombian constitutional tradition that dates back to the Constitution of 1821.

All of this leads the Court to conclude that Protocol II is in conformity with the values, principles, rights and duties enshrined in the Constitution. Accession to the Protocol will be no more than a fulfilment by the authorities involved of their mandates under the Constitution. Yet, as specified in Article 23, the Protocol enters into force as treaty law only six months after its ratification by the President. That does not imply a licence for the parties to the armed conflict in Colombia to disregard their humanitarian obligations in the meantime: the Court reiterates one last time that, as provided in Article 214, paragraph 2, of the Constitution, the rules of international humanitarian law must be respected at all times; and, as it had noted earlier both in its judgment of 1992 and in the present one, the rules of international humanitarian law today are – by virtue of the express will of the Constitutive Assembly – binding norms *per se*, even without ratification or the promulgation of executive orders.

Columbia's declaration under Article 90 of Protocol I

Further steps have followed in Colombia after this judgement and the subsequent accession to Protocol II.[10] In April 1996, the government deposited with the Swiss authorities the declaration, provided for in Article 90 of Protocol I, by which it accepted the competence of the International Humanitarian Fact-Finding Commission. Then, by a letter of December 1997, the Colombian Minister of Foreign Affairs invited the Commission to explore the possibilities for a mission into the country, specifically with a view to its good offices function mentioned in paragraph 2(c)(ii) of that Article. As specified in the letter, the government, in extending the invitation, was well aware that the Commission, although established under Protocol I, regards itself as competent to carry out its functions in internal armed conflicts if parties so request.

10. On 14 August 1995.

Case on due obedience

The Constitutional Court has been given a chance to develop its views on due obedience in a subsequent case, where the underlying issue was the correct interpretation of Article 91, paragraph 2, of the Constitution: does that provision exempt solely legitimate military orders, or simply all orders? Suffice it to relate here the Court's holding that a military order implying the violation of a rule belonging to the bloc of constitutionality cannot be executed and, if it is, cannot be advanced as grounds exempting from responsibility.[11]

Meanwhile, a Bill has been introduced to Congress which seeks to redistribute criminal jurisdiction, effectively removing all crimes allegedly committed by military personnel and involving such bloc of constitutionality rules from the competence of the military courts and leaving them with the ordinary courts.[12] It is too early to predict what the fate of the Bill will be.

11. Sentencia No. C-578/95, Acción de inconstitucionalidad contra el articulo 15 (parcial) del Decreto Ley 85 de 1989.

12. Proyecto de Ley por la cual se asignan competencias para la investigación y el juzgamiento de los miembros de la Fuersza Pública por algunas delitos y se otorgan otras garantías. On 1 January 1998, the bill was pending before the parliament. Although it is impossible to predict with any certainty how the recently elected parliament will react to the bill, it seems a reasonable expectation that it will pass unscathed sometime this year.

THE OTTAWA PROCESS AND THE 1997 MINE BAN TREATY*

Stephen D. Goose**

1. INTRODUCTION

Between 3 and 4 December 1997, 122 governments signed the *Convention on the Prohibition of the Use, Stockpiling, Production and Transfer of Anti-Personnel Mines and On Their Destruction*, marking the first time in history that the international community banned a weapon that is already in widespread use.

Tens of millions of landmines are emplaced in about 70 nations. Another 100-200 million anti-personnel landmines are believed to be in the arsenals of more than 100 governments. Although militaries around the world have used anti-personnel landmines for decades, this treaty banning the weapon was proposed, developed, negotiated and signed in record time in recognition of the humanitarian imperative 'to put an end to the suffering and casualties caused by anti-personnel mines that kill or maim hundreds of people every week, mostly innocent and defenceless civilians and especially children, obstruct economic development and reconstruction, inhibit the repatriation of refugees and internally displaced persons, and have other severe consequences for years after emplacement'.[1]

** Stephen Goose is Program Director of the Arms Division of Human Rights Watch. He serves on the 16-member Coordination Committee of the ICBL and is chairman of its Treaty Working Group. He is also Senior Adviser of the US Campaign to Ban Landmines. He was the deputy head of the official ICBL delegation to the Oslo landmine treaty negotiations in September 1997 and also represented the ICBL at the UN-sponsored negotiations on the Landmines Protocol in 1995 and 1996, as well as the government-sponsored landmine conferences in Ottawa, Vienna, Bonn and Brussels and the treaty-signing conference in Ottawa in December 1997.

1. *Convention on the Prohibition of the Use, Stockpiling, Production and Transfer of Anti-Personnel Mines and On Their Destruction*, Preamble, paragraph one. Reprinted at p. 539.

Yearbook of International Humanitarian Law
Volume 1 - 1998 - pp. 269-291

The Mine Ban Treaty[2] is the result of what has been called the 'Ottawa Process'. Launched by Canada's Foreign Minister Lloyd Axworthy in October 1996 when he challenged governments to conclude a ban treaty by the end of 1997, the Ottawa Process consisted of two parallel tracks: the diplomatic track of developing and negotiating the treaty and the political track of building the will around the globe to support a ban and the treaty. The Ottawa Process has been both praised and vilified for stepping outside of the usual channels of international diplomacy. The Ottawa Process has been different, and historic, for a number of reasons.

It was driven not by the 'big' powers, but rather by small and medium-sized states, who worked together collectively to both set the agenda on this issue, then to carry it out. Canada, Norway, South Africa and Austria were particularly important players, but many others contributed. In the Ottawa Process, and in the actual treaty negotiations, there were no 'blocs', no western Group or Non-Aligned Group. Nations from all regions cooperated towards the common goal. Yet, some regional alliances proved important, especially the solidarity around a ban demonstrated by the Organization of African Unity. And, while participation in the Ottawa Process was in essence 'self-selecting' – a gathering of like-minded governments – it was understood throughout that consensus would be sought, but not required. No one government, or group of governments, would hold the rest of the world hostage. The tyranny of consensus rules would be thwarted. Finally, another key characteristic of the Ottawa Process was the very close cooperation between governments and non-governmental organizations, especially those in the International Campaign to Ban Landmines (ICBL).

The ICBL and its coordinator, Ms. Jody Williams, were jointly awarded the 1997 Nobel Peace Prize for their role in bringing about the treaty and for this new model of conducting international diplomacy.

In announcing the peace prize, the Norwegian Nobel Committee stated: 'The ICBL and Jody Williams started a process which in the space of a few years changed a ban on anti-personnel mines from a vision to a feasible reality. The Convention ... is to a considerable extent a result of their important work ... With the governments of several small and medium-sized countries taking the issue up and taking steps to deal with it, this work has grown into a convincing example of an effective policy for peace ... as a model for similar processes in

2. There is not yet a commonly accepted short title for the treaty. This chapter will use the 'Mine Ban Treaty'. The 'Ottawa Treaty', ' Landmine Convention', and variations thereof are also seen.

the future, it could prove of decisive importance to the international effort for disarmament and peace.[3]

The treaty, negotiated in less than three weeks in Oslo, Norway in September 1997[4], is a rare combination of humanitarian and disarmament law, made all the more remarkable in that the two strands were brought together for the first time to totally ban a weapon in widespread use. Although the treaty contains many elements of disarmament law, the drafters and most of the negotiators were clear that the treaty above all is rooted in humanitarian law. Certainly the impetus behind the treaty arose from humanitarian concerns and not arms control and disarmament concerns. The insistence on addressing the issue primarily as a humanitarian matter was in no small part responsible for the comprehensive nature of the ban and the achievement of a treaty remarkably free of loopholes and exceptions.

At the close of the treaty negotiations in Oslo the ICBL stated: 'We strongly support this treaty. Indeed, we believe it is a gift to the world. Governments have responded to the demands of civil society and have come together with unprecedented speed and produced a treaty that unambiguously bans all antipersonnel landmines ... Together, we have shown that there can be a new way of conducting international diplomacy in the post-Cold War period. This accomplishment is perhaps as important as the treaty itself ...'[5]

The International Committee of the Red Cross (ICRC) and the International Federation of Red Cross and Red Crescent Societies stated that they 'wholeheartedly welcome and endorse the new treaty of international humanitarian law forever banning anti-personnel mines'. Louise Doswald-Beck, head of the ICRC delegation to the negotiations, said, 'This is a victory for humanity. It shows that it is possible, with determination and perseverance, to make significant improvements in international humanitarian law.'[6]

The treaty not only bans the weapon but provides an overall framework for dealing with the landmine crisis, including mine clearance and victim assistance programs, thereby combining hard, binding law with soft law urging cooperation and assistance. It prohibits the use, development, production, transfer and

3. The Nobel Peace Prize for 1997, Announcement by the Norwegian Nobel Committee, 10 October 1997.

4. The formal title is the 'Diplomatic Conference on an International Total Ban on Anti-Personnel Land Mines, Oslo, Norway, 1-18 September, 1997'. Negotiations were based on a draft treaty prepared by Austria. See conference document APL/CRP.3, 1 September 1997.

5. Statement to the Closing Plenary of the Oslo Diplomatic Conference on a Treaty to Ban Antipersonnel Landmines by Jody Williams, Campaign Coordinator, on behalf of the International Campaign to Ban Landmines, 18 September 1997.

6. 'Oslo Conference: Landmines Banned', ICRC Press Release 97/25, 17 September 1997.

stockpiling of anti-personnel mines. It establishes a four-year deadline for destroying stockpiled mines and a ten-year deadline for destroying mines already in the ground. It calls on governments to provide for the care and rehabilitation of victims of landmines.

The treaty is notable in other respects as well. It was negotiated outside of the United Nations framework, yet has enjoyed the strong support of UN agencies and the UN Secretary-General, who is the depositary. NGOs and the ICRC had unprecedented input into the drafting and negotiation of the treaty. Interesting provisions include a 'no withdrawal in wartime' clause, a 'no reservations' clause, and a 'provisional application at ratification' clause. These and other specific articles of the treaty are discussed below in section 4.

2. THE OTTAWA PROCESS

Efforts to regulate the use of anti-personnel landmines began in the 1970s when the ICRC and a handful of NGOs pressed governments to look at weapons that are indiscriminate or cause superfluous injury or unnecessary suffering, leading to the negotiation and conclusion of the Convention on Prohibitions or Restrictions on the Use of Certain Conventional Weapons Which May be Deemed to be Excessively Injurious or to Have Indiscriminate Effect (CCW Convention) and its Landmine Protocol (Protocol II), in 1980.[7] The movement to completely ban anti-personnel mines was originated by the NGO community in the late 1980s and early 1990s, as a number of organizations began to report on the devastating effects of mines and to call for their abolition. The International Campaign to Ban Landmines was formally launched in October 1992 by six NGOs (Handicap International, Human Rights Watch, Medico International, Mines Advisory Group, Physicians for Human Rights and Vietnam Veterans of America Foundation) who called for a total ban on the use, production, trade and stockpiling of anti-personnel mines, as well as for increased resources for mine clearance and victim assistance programs. In 1994, the ICRC also began campaigning for a ban.

7. The Landmines Protocol (Protocol II) is formally the Protocol on Prohibitions or Restrictions on the Use of Mines, Booby Traps and Other Devices. The CCW Convention was negotiated in 1980 and entered into force on 2 December 1983. The official proceedings of the Review Conference are contained in 'The Final Document of the Review Conference of the States Parties to the [CCW], Parts I and II,' United Nations, CCW/CONF.I/16, Geneva, 1996. The CCW negotiations were dominated by attempts by many nations to write in loopholes for particular types of mines or particular means of using mines, with the result a very weak and ineffective treaty.

As part of the ICBL strategy to focus governments' attention on the landmine crisis, Handicap International convinced the French government to call for a review conference of the CCW Convention. This became a more than two year process of expert meetings and negotiating sessions, beginning in February 1994 and ending in May 1996. While a ban was never seriously considered by governments during the CCW Convention review process, the ICBL and ICRC used the review as a platform from which to educate the public and governments alike and to build support for an eventual ban on the weapon. Indeed, at the beginning of the review process, barely a handful of governments lent even rhetorical support for a ban, while at the end, nearly 40 had publicly called for an immediate ban.

Looking to the post-CCW Convention review period, the ICBL, during the January 1996 CCW Convention review session in Geneva, for the first time invited pro-ban governments to meet to discuss a cooperative way forward. Eight governments participated in that first meeting, 14 in a second meeting held at the beginning of the final negotiating session in April, and 11 in a third at the end of the review conference in May. It was out of this series of meetings that the government of Canada offered to host a governmental conference in which pro-ban states would come together to strategize as to how to move forward the ban agenda.

From 3-5 October 1996, the government of Canada sponsored 'Towards a Global Ban on Anti-Personnel Landmines: International Strategy Conference.' This historic conference in Ottawa brought together 50 governments that had pledged support for a total ban on antipersonnel mines, as well as 24 observer states, dozens of NGOs from the International Campaign to Ban Landmines, various United Nations agencies, the International Committee of the Red Cross and other international organizations.

The Ottawa Conference yielded three concrete results: a final declaration agreed to by the 50 participating governments recognizing the urgent need for a ban on antipersonnel mines; the conference Chairman's Agenda for Action; an outline of actions for reaching a ban rapidly; and the stunning announcement by Canada's Foreign Minister Axworthy that Canada was prepared to hold a treaty-signing conference for a total ban in December 1997.

The conference was also notable for the unprecedentedly high level of cooperation with and involvement by NGOs in both the planning and execution of the conference. Between May and October, members of the Canadian government and the ICBL consulted frequently on nearly every aspect of the organization of the conference, and worked together to ensure maximum attendance by governments. The ICBL was given a seat at the table as a full participant in the conference, while those governments unwilling to declare themselves pro-ban sat in the back as observers. Campaigners were actively involved in drafting the precise language of both the final declaration and the action plan, though Mr. Axworthy's announcement took nearly all of them by surprise as well.

This extraordinary level of cooperation continued between October 1996 and December 1997, as the ICBL worked in close partnership with Canada and other pro-ban states to help develop treaty language and to build the political will necessary for a successful treaty signing. It was not clear in the first critical months after that meeting if the Ottawa Process would survive. The Canadian government had to put a lot of diplomatic time, effort and money into making the process work. As the Process moved forward, a 'core group' of pro-ban governments dedicated to the success of the treaty emerged and worked closely with the ICBL. The initial core group included Canada, Norway, Austria, South Africa, Belgium, Mexico, the Philippines, Switzerland and Germany.

For the core group, the Austrian government developed a draft treaty which became the basis for the negotiations in Oslo in September. The draft treaty, with revisions, was circulated to all governments three times for comment during 1997. The ICBL and ICRC were also consulted. Additionally, the ICBL developed its own treaty and members of the ICBL leadership, beginning in January 1997 and several times thereafter, took the treaty to New York to meet with government officials at the United Nations and educate them as to the ICBL's views of the essential aspects of a ban treaty to emerge from the negotiating process.[8] The ICBL's *ad hoc* treaty team pressed strongly throughout the Ottawa process to ensure that the final Mine Ban Treaty would incorporate as much of the ICBL treaty as possible.

The Ottawa Process was comprised of a series of meetings to develop the treaty itself and the political will to sign it. Treaty language was developed at government-sponsored conferences in Vienna, Bonn and Brussels, as well as at smaller meetings of the core group and bilateral government consultations. The ICBL's views on treaty language were sought throughout the process, and the ICBL was an active participant in each of the government conferences. Moreover, pro-ban governments, the ICRC and the ICBL each hosted a number of conferences aimed at ensuring maximum support for the Ottawa Process and the December treaty-signing.

The Austrian government hosted an international conference in Vienna from 12-14 February 1997. At that meeting, the essential components of a treaty to

8. The draft treaty proposed by the ICBL was titled, 'Convention on the Prohibition of the Development, Production, Stockpiling, Transfer and Use of Anti-Personnel Mines and on Their Destruction,' dated January 1997. The text was circulated to governments as a free-standing document. The full-text is reprinted in the ICBL's 'Conference Report: Brussels International Conference for the Total Ban on Anti-Personnel Landmines, 24-27 June 1997, pp. 103-106 (1997).

ban antipersonnel landmines were laid out, using the Austrian draft treaty as a guide. Although the context of the discussion was to be neutral in terms of the appropriate forum for treaty negotiations, significant support for the Ottawa Process was voiced in numerous statements. The number of participants at the meeting was much greater than anyone expected, as 111 countries attended, along with an official delegation of the ICBL, the ICRC, and UN agencies. While their statements indicated that perhaps half of the governments in attendance were not yet ready to ban the weapon, the widespread participation was evidence of the seriousness with which the Ottawa Process was being taken globally. In its closing press statement, the ICBL said, 'The pro-ban nations appear prepared to accept nearly all of the key elements of a ban treaty recommended by the ICBL.'[9]

Although the ICBL was permitted to make statements to the opening and closing plenary sessions of the conference, it was not permitted to attend the working sessions, due to objections from some governments. Nevertheless, communications between numerous pro-ban government representatives and the four ICBL representatives present were nearly constant throughout the conference. The ICBL held press conferences at the opening and the close of the meeting. Notably, governments did not call for their own separate media events. Rather, in a conscious effort to emphasize the collaborative nature of the effort, the ICBL press conferences included the Austrian chairman of the conference, as well as representatives from the Canadian and Belgian governments and the ICRC.

The Vienna conference was followed by a technical meeting held in Bonn in April on verification and compliance measures related to the treaty. As with Vienna, the number of countries which participated (120) was unexpected and again showed the continuing development of momentum of the Process. The ICBL's delegation of two was treated as a full participant in the meeting and was able to attend and make interventions at all sessions. Discussions were based on an options paper developed by the German government, and the majority view that emerged was that a ban treaty is essentially a humanitarian law treaty and as such, should not require stringent and costly verification measures which are more appropriate to arms control treaties. More important, an overwhelming number of speakers reaffirmed the Ottawa Process and the December signing date.

9. 'Mine Ban Closer to Reality', ICBL Press Release, Vienna, Austria, 14 February 1997. The ICBL elucidated the elements as (1) it must be a comprehensive treaty banning use, production, stockpiling and trade of antipersonnel mines; (2) there must be provisions for the destruction of stockpiles in a rapid fashion and a requirement for destruction of emplaced mines; (3) there must be transparency measures requiring reporting of details of stockpiles and minefields.

The midway point between the Ottawa challenge and the treaty-signing in December was the June conference hosted by the Belgian government. The centerpiece of this 'make or break' conference was a declaration that committed governments to the Ottawa Process and to participating in Oslo in the negotiation of a treaty based on the Austrian draft text with a view to signing the treaty in December. Only weeks before the meeting, most observers were estimating that 60 to 75 governments would endorse the Brussels Declaration. By the end of the meeting more than 90 had signed on, and that number subsequently grew to over 100. Among those announcing their support for the ban treaty shortly before or during the conference were major producers, exporters and users of mines, such as France, United Kingdom, Italy, Spain, Czech Republic, Hungary, Bosnia and Angola.

The ICBL coordinator Jody Williams was asked to give one of three keynote speeches to open the conference, along with the Belgian Foreign Minister and the head of the Canadian delegation. During her speech, Ms.Williams coined the refrain that the ICBL used throughout this meeting and the Oslo negotiations – the ICBL demands a comprehensive ban treaty with 'no exceptions, no reservations, no loopholes'. It was picked up as a mantra by many government delegates as well.

Although the Belgian government invited an official ICBL delegation to the conference, it was not permitted to attend meetings the first two days to finalize the Brussels Declaration. As had been the case for mine meetings going back to CCW days, however, there were NGO representatives on many official government delegations, and the Campaign's presence and views were strongly felt throughout. The second two days consisted of panels to raise the profile of the pro-ban movement and the issues that must be grappled with to create a truly mine-free world. The conference ended with a joint press conference by the ICBL, represented by the author and the Belgian Foreign Minister.

The success of the Belgian Conference, which virtually guaranteed that an impressively large number of governments would come to Oslo to negotiate a true ban treaty, indicated that momentum was unstoppable at that point. On the negative side, the ICBL felt compelled to issue a press statement criticizing the United States delegation for 'testing the waters to see how many holes can be shot in the treaty in order to accommodate US policy'.[10] During the Brussels meeting, a senior US official summoned numerous delegations to a hotel to press them regarding their positions on the treaty, the Ottawa process and the preferred

10. 'United States Seeks to Undermine Landmine Ban Treaty', ICBL Press Release, 25 June 1997.

US option of the Conference on Disarmament. The US was pushing for a treaty with an explicit exception for Korea and for 'smart' mines.

In addition to these meetings to develop the treaty text, the ICBL, ICRC and various governments held numerous conferences and seminars throughout 1997 to educate and build political will for signing the ban treaty. These included ICBL regional meetings in Mozambique, Japan, Sweden, Australia, India, Senegal and Yemen, ICRC seminars in Zimbabwe and the Philippines, and governmental meetings in South Africa and Turkmenistan. The ICBL and pro-ban governments also tried to put the mine ban on the agenda of every possible international meeting, be it the G-8 summit in the US, Commonwealth Heads of State meeting in the UK or the Francophonie meeting in Vietnam.

3. THE OSLO NEGOTIATIONS[11]

Eighty-nine governments came to the Oslo negotiations as full participants and another 32 as observers. Based on their commitments made in the Brussels Declaration, nearly all of the 89 were prepared to negotiate a truly comprehensive treaty, based on the Austrian draft, without significant loopholes or exceptions. Indeed, the treaty became stronger over the course of the negotiations, as delegation after delegation sought the best ban treaty possible.

But a handful of nations, most notably the United States, were not of that mind. The US administration, worried about public opinion, at the last moment decided to go to Oslo, not as a 'like-minded' participant in the negotiations but rather to put its full weight behind modifying the treaty in order to accommodate existing US policy. The US decision to go to Oslo under those circumstances – that is, with the intention of weakening the treaty – was not greeted with much enthusiasm in most quarters, and the US presence proved to be the focus of the most significant moments of tension and concern as to the outcome of the negotiations.

Under the rules of procedure for the negotiations, which were agreed to on the first day, the ICBL was invited as an official observer, with the same status as observer governments. This meant that ICBL representatives were permitted to be present at all sessions, including smaller working group sessions, and to make oral interventions at any point. The ICBL could not make formal proposals

11. As of June 1998, official proceedings of the Conference had not been made publicly available. Some of the official documentation, as well as ICBL press releases and newsletters tracking the negotiations, are compiled in the ICBL's 'Report on Activities, Diplomatic Conference on an International Total Ban on Anti-Personnel Landmines, Oslo, Norway, 1-18 September 1997' (November 1997).

for treaty language, but did informally circulate suggested language. The ICBL did not have voting privileges, but, as it turned out, not a single vote was taken. It is believed that this is the first occasion on which NGOs were given official status in international negotiations of an arms control or humanitarian law treaty.

The Campaign's office and meeting rooms were directly opposite the negotiation room itself, providing all campaigners – not just the official ICBL delegation to the negotiations – invaluable contact with government delegates throughout the three weeks of the conference. Landmine exhibits and banners were hung inside and outside the conference site. Regular briefings and press conferences laid out important developments in the negotiations, and government delegations were invited to give their positions to the campaigners as well.

The opening of the treaty negotiations was marked with the death of Diana, Princess of Wales. While this tragedy did not shift the negotiating process or positions of governments in Oslo, it certainly greatly increased media attention to the process unfolding in Oslo. This increased attention might have made it that much more difficult for governments to seriously consider any changes that would affect the integrity of the mine ban treaty.

Another crucial factor in maintaining the strength of the treaty was the decision, agreed to without debate in the Rules of Procedure, to abandon UN-type consensus rules, and to provide for decisions on matters of substance to be taken by a two-thirds majority vote of those present.[12] While no vote was taken, the knowledge that a country would need the support of 59 nations to make a significant or controversial change in the draft treaty undoubtedly discouraged attempts. Many of the negotiators in Oslo had been present during the CCW Convention negotiations, witnessed the 'lowest common denominator' result there, and were determined not to repeat it.

The three-week negotiations were presided over with great skill by South Africa's ambassador to the UN in Geneva, Mr. Jacobo Selebi. Rather than waste significant time with the usual government declarations pontificating great intentions, Selebi immediately opened discussion on core articles of the treaty, forcing sticking points into the open within the first two days of the conference. The US, from the very outset, made a set of interlocking demands that the head of the US delegation told diplomats were, in essence, non-negotiable. The demands included a geographic exception for Korea, a change in definition to exempt certain US 'smart' mines, a nine-year delay in the effective date of the treaty, and deletion of the 'no reservations' and 'no withdrawal during wartime' provisions. The ICBL denounced these demands as measures that would gut the treaty and render it largely meaningless. The campaign produced fact sheets and

12. Rule 35 of the Draft Rules of Procedure, Conference Document APL/CRP.2, p. 10.

newsletters, held briefings and lobbied delegates endlessly to reject the US demands. For its part, the US cajoled and arm-twisted with great vigor. Most dramatic was the US push for a 24-hour delay in the final days of the negotiations, when the conference was on the verge of completing a treaty strongly supported by the ICBL. The 24-hour delay, quite surprisingly supported by the Canadian government, was a period of tremendous tension. While the President and other high officials of the Clinton administration were calling counterparts around the world in their last-ditch effort to find support, the ICBL was holding press conferences to denounce the delay, pressing delegates to hold firm, and engaging in street theater to dramatize the tense hours.

In the face of the tremendous pressure of the US, governments held firm and would not compromise the integrity of the treaty. When the US stood finally to withdraw its demands, and the treaty survived intact and the negotiations were gavelled to a close, the diplomats were cheered, perhaps for the only time in their diplomatic lives. The Campaign representatives in the negotiating room stood and clapped for the treaty and for the process that made it possible. As delegates filed out of the conference, other campaigners were at the door and the cheers and hugs and chants did not end until the last delegate had left the room of the momentous negotiations.

The negotiations and the Ottawa Process overall were historic, for a number of reasons. For the first time, smaller and middle-sized powers had come together, to work in close cooperation with the non-governmental organizations, to negotiate a treaty which would remove from the world's arsenals for the first time a weapon already in widespread use. Smaller and middle-sized powers had not yielded ground to intense pressure from a superpower to weaken the treaty to accommodate the policies of that one country. Negotiations ended with a treaty stronger than the draft on which the negotiations were based. The treaty had not been held hostage to rule by consensus, which would have inevitably resulted in a gutted treaty.

4. TREATY PROVISIONS

4.1 **Preamble**

The humanitarian nature of the treaty is reflected in the Preamble, which begins by declaring that States Parties are '[d]etermined to put an end to the suffering and casualties caused by anti-personnel mines' and concludes with '[b]asing themselves on the principle of international humanitarian law that the right of the parties to an armed conflict to choose methods or means of warfare is not unlimited, on the principle that prohibits the employment in armed conflicts of weapons, projectiles and materials and methods of warfare of a nature to cause superfluous injury or unnecessary suffering and on the principle that a distinction must be made between civilians and combatants'.

The preamble also reflects the high level of government – NGO cooperation in the treaty process by '[s]tressing the role of public conscience in furthering the principles of humanity as evidenced by the call for a total ban of anti-personnel mines and recognizing the efforts to that end undertaken by the International Red Cross and Red Crescent Movement, the International Campaign to Ban Landmines and numerous other non-governmental organizations around the world'. This is the first time that an international humanitarian law treaty or an arms control treaty has explicitly recognized by name an NGO coalition.

4.2 Article 1 – General Obligations

The general obligations of the treaty are contained in Article 1. These obligations constitute a clear, comprehensive ban on anti-personnel mines. The treaty drafters and negotiators took care to try to close potential loopholes, in stark contrast to the negotiations during the Review Conference of the Convention on Conventional Weapons, and its Landmines Protocol, which took place from September 1995 to May 1996.

Each State Party 'undertakes never under any circumstances' to use, develop, produce, acquire, stockpile or transfer 'to anyone, directly or indirectly' anti-personnel mines. The unequivocable nature of the ban is reinforced by a very important, and very broad, additional obligation not '[t]o assist, encourage or induce, in any way, anyone to engage in any activity prohibited to a State Party under this Convention.'[13] The wording is drawn from Article I(1)(a), (b), and (d) of the Chemical Weapons Convention.

The adoption of the broadest possible scope, 'never under any circumstances', was considered essential because landmines have been used so widely in so many different contexts, from major international conflicts, such as the Persian Gulf War and the Afghan War, to internal conflicts such as in Mozambique and Angola, to 'peacetime' uses, such as in Cambodia, where farmers plant landmines to protect their houses. It was decided that, unlike some international humanitarian law conventions, it would be preferable not to have a separate

13. This provision would prohibit, for example, the export of components for use in anti-personnel mines. The ICBL also believes that it prohibits the stockpiling of US anti-personnel mines in States Parties or the transit of US aircraft and ships carrying anti-personnel mines through States Parties. In 1998, the US engaged in bilateral discussions on these matters with Germany, Norway, United Kingdom, Italy, Spain, Greece, and Japan.

article setting out the scope. Without a scope article, the convention is assumed to apply at all times.[14]

In addition to the prohibitions, Article 1 contains a key obligation 'to destroy or ensure the destruction of all anti-personnel mines'. This applies to both stockpiled mines and those already emplaced in or on the ground.

4.3 Article 2 – Definitions

Article 2(1) states, 'Anti-personnel mine means a mine designed to be exploded by the presence, proximity or contact of a person and that will incapacitate, injure, or kill one or more persons.' The most significant aspect of this sentence is the absence of a word 'primarily'. The definition of an anti-personnel mine was a highly contentious issue during the CCW Convention Review talks, because of the addition of the word 'primarily' to the original 1980 definition: '"Anti-personnel mine" means a mine *primarily* designed to be exploded by the presence ...' This addition was seen by the ICBL and the ICRC as a major loophole that seriously damaged the treaty. During the course of 1997, the ICBL and ICRC pressed governments hard not to include that word in the draft ban treaty, and ultimately their view prevailed. Some now see it as problematic that two international instruments governing use of mines have different definitions.

However, the Mine Ban Treaty in Article 2(1) includes new language that mines 'designed to be detonated by the presence, proximity or contact of a vehicle as opposed to a person, that are equipped with anti-handling devices, are not considered anti-personnel mines as a result of being so equipped'. The ICBL opposed this language on anti-vehicle mines with anti-handling devices on the grounds that some such devices will in fact function as anti-personnel mines and pose similar dangers to civilians. While refusing to drop the language, negotiators responded to the ICBL concern in two ways. First, they altered the definition of an anti-handling device to '... a device ... which activates when an attempt is made to tamper with *or otherwise intentionally disturb* the mine'. This establishes that an anti-handling device that activates when a mine is *unintentionally* disturbed is not permissible. Second, it was established for the diplomatic record that an anti-vehicle mine with an anti-handling device that

14. There are precedents for this approach, such as the Genocide Convention and the Convention on Environmental Modification.

explodes from an innocent or unintentional act is to be considered an anti-personnel mine and therefore banned by the treaty.[15]

4.4 Article 3 – Exceptions

A single exception is written into the treaty. States Parties are permitted to retain or transfer anti-personnel mines 'for the development of and training in mine detection, mine clearance, or mine destruction techniques'. While some technical experts believe that live mines are not necessary for those purposes, many governments felt otherwise. In order to prevent governments from using this provision to maintain a stockpile of mines that would be operationally useful, negotiators inserted that the 'amount of such mines shall not exceed the minimum number absolutely necessary for the above-mentioned purposes'. At the urging of the ICBL, a number of governments established for the diplomatic record that 'the minimum number' should be in the hundreds or thousands or less, not the tens of thousands or more.[16] Under Article 7, States Parties are required to report annually on the types and quantities of mines retained or transferred for these training purposes.

4.5 Article 4 – Destruction of Stockpiled Anti-personnel Mines

This article requires States Parties to destroy 'all stockpiled anti-personnel mines it owns or possesses, or that are under its jurisdiction or control, as soon as possible but not later than four years after the entry into force of the Convention for that State Party. The initial time frame for destruction of stocks in the draft treaty was three years, and while the great majority of delegations spoke in favor of that, several governments argued that it would be technically and, more to the point, financially difficult to meet that deadline and argued for five or more

15. This understanding was reached after extensive discussions in the Definitions Working Group during the Oslo negotiations. The representatives from Canada and Australia were most vocal in articulating this clarification. The understanding was then clearly stated by the Chair of the Working Group, Dr. Thomas Hajnoczi of Austria, and agreed to by participants of the Working Group. Dr. Hajnoczi subsequently reported the understanding to the Committee of the Whole, where it was reinforced by the Australian delegation, and met with no objections.

16. Belgium, Canada, Germany and the Netherlands spoke to this point. Subsequently, Austria announced that it will retain for these purposes 58 mines; Canada 1,500; the Czech Republic 3,000; Germany 3,000; Italy 10,000; the Netherlands 2,000; Norway 50; South Africa 5,000; Spain 10,000; the UK 4,000; and Hungary zero.

years.[17] A compromise figure was agreed to of four years. Some governments, such as Ukraine, have cited this as a primary reason for not signing the treaty.[18]

Many view this article as one of the most important in the treaty. By setting a rapid time frame in which governments have to destroy their mine arsenals, the likelihood of future use of mines by governments that now have large stockpiles, a history of extensive use, and the danger of a return to conflict (such as in Cambodia or Angola) decreases dramatically.

4.6 Article 5 – Destruction of Anti-personnel Mines in Mined Areas

Each State Party must destroy mines that have already been laid 'in mined areas under its jurisdiction and control, as soon as possible but not later than ten years' after entry into force. The existence of this article attests to the will of the international community to deal comprehensively with the landmine crisis. Lacking such will, it would not have been difficult for governments to argue that a mine ban treaty should simply prohibit production, trade, and use of the weapon, but set no requirements for the difficult and costly task of removing existing mines from the ground.

A good deal of debate took place over the ten year time frame and over whether or not to make a distinction between mines in identifiable minefields and those outside of identifiable minefields. The draft treaty had two separate articles for mines within and outside minefields, with a ten year deadline for destroying the former and no deadline for the latter. But, after extensive work by a Friends of the Chair group, headed by Ireland's Dr. Darach MacFhionnbhairr, agreement was reached to combine the two into a single article with the ten year deadline.

The ten year period was seen as one that would motivate governments to attempt to deal with humanitarian mine clearance rapidly, but was still attainable for almost everyone. However, it was also recognized that some of the governments of very heavily mined countries, particularly the poor ones such as Cambodia and Mozambique, could not sign a treaty that absolutely required them to demine within ten years. Such governments knew they would have to depend on extensive assistance from others to achieve mine clearance, and could not sign a treaty based on hopes of aid from others.

This led to a provision that allows a State Party to request an extension of the deadline for mine clearance for a period of up to another ten years. The request must be agreed to by a majority of votes of States Parties. At the end of this

17. Among those pushing for a longer time period for destruction were eventual signatories Poland, Brazil, Spain, Italy, Chile, Ecuador, and Croatia, as well as observers Finland and Egypt.

18. Author's meeting with Ukraine Foreign Minister Borys Tarasiuk, Kiev, 25 May 1998.

second ten year period, the State Party may request a renewal of the extension. Thus, a government could have up to thirty years to demine, if it is able to convince a majority of other State Parties that such time is needed.

Article 5 also requires States Parties to 'ensure as soon as possible' that mined areas are perimeter-marked, monitored, and protected by fencing or other means 'to ensure the effective exclusion of civilians'.

4.7 Article 6 – International Cooperation and Assistance

Each State Party 'has the right to seek and receive assistance, where feasible, from other States Parties to the extent possible' in fulfilling its obligations under the treaty. Negotiators made clear that this was not to be considered boilerplate language, and that the success of the treaty would in no small part hinge on the willingness of States Parties with the capability to provide extensive assistance to actually do so. Shortly after the negotiations, Canada pledged $100 million toward treaty implementation (including demining and victim assistance), Norway pledged $120 million, and others announced significant increases in landmine-oriented funding as well.

Article 6(3) was of particular importance to the NGO community. Despite an apparent willingness on the part of some governments, such as South Africa, Norway, and Belgium, during the preparatory meetings to make assistance to mine victims a binding obligation in the treaty, included in Article 1, no government proposed this during the negotiations. However, Article 6(3) states, 'Each State Party in a position to do so shall provide assistance for the care and rehabilitation, and social and economic reintegration, of mine victims and for mine awareness programs.' NGOs insisted on the inclusion of the phrase 'social and economic reintegration' to insure a broad concept and application of victim assistance. NGOs have been pressing governments to take this provision seriously, and the initial responses have been encouraging.

Article 6 also states that assistance for mine clearance and victim assistance may be provided through the UN, international organizations, non-governmental organizations, or on a bilateral basis.

4.8 Article 7 – Transparency Measures

Each State Party is required, within 180 days after entry into force, and annually thereafter, to report to the UN Secretary-General on a wide range of antipersonnel landmine-related matters. This extensive reporting requirement was seen in part as an attempt to address the issues of verification and compliance in the treaty. (See discussion below). The information to be provided includes: national implementation measures; number and types of stockpiled mines; number and types of mines kept or transferred for training purposes; number and types of mines destroyed; location, number, and types of emplaced mines (to the extent possible); status of programs to convert or decommission mine production facilities; measures taken to protect the population from mined areas; and the technical characteristics (to the extent known) of mines produced and currently owned by a State Party, in order to facilitate mine clearance.

The Secretary-General is required only to transmit reports received to States Parties. He is not required to evaluate the information in any way, nor to make it publicly available, though many delegations indicated their desire for this information to be available to all.

4.9 Article 8 – Facilitation and Clarification of Compliance

Entering the negotiations in Oslo, most delegations were clear that they did not believe an overly intrusive, arms control-type verification and compliance regime was necessary or desirable for the Mine Ban Treaty. At a special meeting devoted to verification and compliance in Germany in April 1997, the dominant, but by no means universal, view was that it would be more appropriate to look to human rights or humanitarian treaties for guidance. The result is a treaty that has a 'light' regime in the arms control context, but a 'heavy' regime in the humanitarian context – a compromise between the disarmament model of intrusive verification and the international humanitarian law model of fact-finding.

The key to this article is the provision for fact-finding missions to investigate potential violations of the Convention. A multi-stage system is established. First, one or more State Parties may submit through the Secretary-General a Request for Clarification to another State Party regarding a potential violation. If there is no response or an unsatisfactory response within 28 days, the matter may be taken up at the next regular annual Meeting of States Parties, or a request can be made to hold a Special Meeting of States Parties. If unable to resolve the issue, the Meeting or Special Meeting of States Parties can authorize, by majority vote, a fact-finding mission, carried out by a team of experts from a list maintained by the Secretary-General. (An unusual provision permits the requested State Party – the alleged violator – to invite a fact-finding mission to its territory at any time.) The fact-finding mission must give at least 72 hours notice before its arrival, and may stay up to 14 days. It reports its findings to the Meeting or Special Meeting of States Parties.

The Meeting or Special Meeting of States Parties may then ask the requested State Party to take measures to address the compliance issue within a specified period of time, and may suggest ways and means to resolve the matter, 'including the initiation of appropriate procedures in conformity with international law', by a two-thirds vote if consensus cannot be reached.

4.10 Articles 9 to 22

Article 9 on National Implementation Measures states, 'Each State Party shall take all appropriate legal, administrative and other measures, including the imposition of penal sanctions, to prevent and suppress any activity prohibited to a State Party under this Convention undertaken by persons or on territory under its jurisdiction or control.' The key phrase in this article is the reference to penal sanctions. The wording is similar to Article VII of the Chemical Weapons Convention and Article III of the Comprehensive Test Ban Treaty. An important difference is that the CWC and CTBT assume extraterritorial jurisdiction (states will punish any of their citizens who commit violations of the convention anywhere in the world), while this treaty leaves it to each State Party to decide based on its own practice.

Article 10 states that State Parties shall consult and cooperate with each other to settle disputes regarding application or interpretation of the treaty. This is a fairly standard provision in treaties.

Article 11 requires that the UN Secretary-General convene a meeting of the States Parties within one year after entry into force in order to consider the operation and status of the treaty, and other related matters. The language describing the purpose of the meeting was left deliberately vague, and could include such things as compliance, assistance, ratifications, universalization, and preparations for a future Review Conference. Subsequent meetings are to be convened annually until the first Review Conference, five years after entry into force. This provision was suggested by the ICBL, in order to insure that momentum toward the complete elimination of anti-personnel mines was maintained, and to provide the opportunity to address rapidly any weaknesses in the treaty. The article states that 'relevant non-governmental organizations' may be invited to attend these meetings as observers, as well as governments that are not State Parties, the ICRC, the UN and relevant international organizations.

Article 12 requires the UN Secretary-General to convene a Review Conference five years after entry into force. The ICBL pressed for this as a desirable alternative to the formulation in the CCW Convention which permitted a review conference only after ten years and only if a State Party has requested it. The short time frame for and automaticity of the first review conference were important to those stressing the crisis nature of the landmine problem. Further review conferences of the Mine Ban Treaty can be convened every five years if one or more States Parties requests it. As with the annual meetings, 'relevant' NGOs, non-State Parties, and others may be invited as observers.

Article 13 provides the mechanism for amending the Convention. If any State Party proposes an amendment, the Secretary-General circulates it to all States Parties, and if a majority support further consideration of the proposal, an Amendment Conference will be convened. The Amendment Conference will be held immediately following a Meeting of States Parties or a Review Conference, unless a majority request it to be held earlier. Amendments are adopted by a two-thirds majority of those States Parties present and voting. An amendment does not enter into force until a majority of States Parties have deposited with the UN their instrument of acceptance. Again, 'relevant' NGOs and others may be invited as observers.

Article 14 states that the costs of the annual meetings, review conferences, and amendment conferences shall be borne by the participating States Parties and observer States, in accordance with the UN scale of assessment adjusted appropriately. The costs of any fact-finding mission shall be borne by the States Parties, also according to the UN scale.

Article 15 indicates the treaty opened for signature in Ottawa on 3-4 December 1997, and subsequently at UN Headquarters in New York until entry into force.

Article 16 contains standard language on ratification, acceptance, approval and accession.

Article 17 states that the treaty shall enter into force six months after the fortieth instrument of ratification has been deposited at the UN. For a state which joins the convention after it has entered into force, it will enter into force for that state six months after it deposits its instrument of ratification, acceptance, approval or accession. There was considerable discussion over the number of ratifications required to trigger entry into force. Some pointed to the CCW Convention as a model, which requires only twenty, while others looked at the Chemical Weapons Convention, which requires 65. The ICRC argued that two ratifications would be sufficient, similar to the Geneva Conventions and Additional Protocols. The ICBL felt that some states were pushing for a higher number in order to give themselves additional time to implement the provisions of the treaty, be they the prohibition on use or the requirements to destroy stocks in four years and emplaced mines in ten years after entry into force. Forty was selected as a compromise figure, one that would lend the treaty credibility and demonstrate widespread international support for a ban, but would not be so high as to undercut the urgency of the ban. Both the ICRC and the ICBL, as well as a number of governments, felt that the six month waiting period was unnecessary, or at least too long, but it became part of a compromise package with the number of ratifications.

Article 18, proposed by Belgium, states that any state may at the time of its ratification declare that it will provisionally apply paragraph 1 of Article 1—the basic general obligations not to use, produce, transfer, or stockpile anti-personnel mines—until such time as the treaty formally comes into effect. As of June 1998, the only states known to make such a declaration at the time of ratification were Mauritius and Switzerland. While some felt this might undercut Article 18 of the Vienna Convention on the Law of Treaties obligation that no signatory state shall take an action contrary to the object and purpose of the treaty it has signed, the Belgian delegation argued just the opposite—that it reinforces the tenet that signatories should consider a treaty binding even prior to entry into force. It was agreed to with little formal discussion.

Article 19 states that the treaty articles 'shall not be subject to reservations'. A number of states objected to this, arguing that it was common practice to make reservations to certain provisions of treaties, especially humanitarian law treaties. They also said it would create problems with ratification by some legislatures. However, the view that this must be a comprehensive treaty, without collective or individual loopholes, prevailed. The ICBL's catch-phrase of 'No Exceptions, No Reservations, No Loopholes', coined by its coordinator Jody Williams during the Brussels preparatory meeting, held forth.

Article 20, in fairly standard treaty language, states that the Convention shall be of unlimited duration and that each State Party, 'in exercising its national sovereignty', has the right to withdraw from the Convention, after it has given notice and waited for six months. However, if at the end of the six month period the withdrawing State Party is engaged in armed conflict, it cannot withdraw before the end of the armed conflict. This 'no withdrawal during wartime' clause was strongly opposed by a small number of delegations, most notably the United States. Others argued forcefully that the treaty would mean little if it were perceived as banning mines in peacetime while permitting them in wartime. This was clearly the predominant view, though some concessions were made—some had argued for a longer waiting period after notification, and some had argued that withdrawal should only occur if necessitated by 'supreme national interests'.

Article 21 designates the Secretary-General of the United Nations as the Depositary of the Convention. Although the Convention was conceived, developed and negotiated outside of the U.N. framework, various U.N. agencies (especially UNICEF, but also UNHCR, UNDHA, UNDPKO, and others) were very involved in the ban movement and in the progress of the treaty. Both Kofi Annan and Boutros Boutros-Ghali openly and vocally supported the Ottawa Process. Kofi Annan played a highly visible role in the signing ceremony in Ottawa and the UN appears committed to assisting with the effective implementation of the treaty.

Article 22 contains standard language indicating the original of the Convention, in 'equally authentic' Arabic, Chinese, English, French, Russian and Spanish texts, shall be deposited with the UN Secretary-General.

5. CRITICISMS OF THE MINE BAN TREATY

The treaty has been criticized both for going too far and not far enough. The ICBL has cited four main areas of concern in the treaty.[19] First, the issue of anti-vehicle mines with anti-handling devices (described above under Art. 2). Second, the exception for retention of mines for training purposes (described above under Art. 3). Third, the lack of a binding requirement for provision of assistance to mine victims (described above under Art. 6). Fourth, the failure to include specific language regarding application to non-state actors.[20] The ICBL intends to press governments to improve the treaty in these areas during the annual Meetings of States Parties, the Review Conference and any Amendment Conference.

The specific area of the treaty that has perhaps drawn the most criticism is verification and compliance, but that criticism has come from both sides. Arms controllers tend to think it is too weak in this area, while others fear it may be too strong. The former say that it is an unenforceable treaty without teeth, while the latter say that sensitive states (like India) will stay away because it is overly intrusive and may compromise national sovereignty. The negotiators tried to strike a balance, based on the desire to bring as many countries on board as possible, while still providing meaningful measures to gauge and induce compliance. The final product reflects the widespread view that complete verification of prohibitions on anti-personnel mines is impossible, and therefore an unachievable regime should not be attempted, but that a less ambitious regime

19. See for example, 'Remarks to the Opening Plenary for Mine Action Forum', by Stephen Goose (Human Rights Watch) on behalf of the ICBL, Ottawa, Canada, 2 December 1997.

20. The ICRC, in consultation with the ICBL, had suggested language, but no government formally proposed it.

is acceptable because the anti-personnel mine is not a weapon of mass destruction, unlike nuclear, chemical or biological weapons, where one has to worry about a sudden, devastating militarily significant outbreak.

More generally, the most frequent criticism of the treaty is that it is not 'universal' – that the United States, Russia, China, and India have not signed, and that other major producers and exporters of mines have not signed. This criticism may be heard less frequently now that the US and Russia have both indicated their intention to sign the treaty at some point in the future.[21] Mine Ban Treaty supporters point out that no treaty is born universal, and that 'problem countries' stay outside of virtually every treaty, including those much praised recently, such as the Comprehensive Test Ban Treaty and the Chemical Weapons Convention. For a treaty that was developed and negotiated in such a short period of time, and for an issue that has been prominent for such a short period of time, the number of signatories already achieved can be considered rather remarkable.

And, indeed, it can be argued that, with respect to landmines, those who count the most have signed the treaty. The majority of countries where landmines have been used most frequently, and where the potential for future use is great, have signed; states like Cambodia, Angola, Mozambique, Bosnia and Herzegovina, Croatia, Ethiopia, and Sudan. A majority of the biggest producers and exporters of the past three decades – those largely responsible for feeding today's crises – have signed, such as Belgium, Bulgaria, Czech Republic, France, Hungary, Italy, and the United Kingdom. Every member of the European Union has signed the treaty, except Finland.[22] Every member of NATO has signed (including the three pending members), except the US and Turkey. Every country in the Western Hemisphere has signed, except the US and Cuba. Thirty-nine countries in Africa, the most mined continent, have signed. Key nations in the Asia-Pacific region have signed, such as Japan, Indonesia, Thailand, Cambodia, Philippines, Australia and New Zealand.

Finally, of course, there are those who cling to the notion of the anti-personnel mine as an essential weapon and criticize the treaty because it successfully and totally bans the weapon, rather than merely restricting certain uses of certain types of mines, like the CCW. Those states which favour restrictions rather than

21. The US announcement, made by Secretary of State Madeleine Albright on 21 May 1998, indicated that signature should occur by 2006. Russian officials have stated the intention to sign on several occasions, including at the time of the announcement of the Nobel Peace Prize to the ICBL (Mr. Yeltsin on 10 October 1997), at the treaty signing ceremony in Ottawa in December 1997 and at the ICBL Conference in Moscow in May 1998, using phrases such as 'in due time'. Both countries state the need to develop alternatives to mines before signing.

22. For the Finnish position on landmines, see Hannikainen, *infra* p. 436.

a ban on anti-personnel landmines include such non-signatories as Belarus, China, Cuba, Egypt, India, Israel, North Korea, Pakistan, Sri Lanki and Turkey.

6. CONCLUSION

It has long been the contention of the ICBL that anti-personnel landmines are already illegal under existing customary international humanitarian law, because they are inherently indiscriminate and they fail the proportionality test – the short-term military benefits are far outweighed by the long-term human and socio-economic costs.[23] The Mine Ban Treaty codifies the illegal status of anti-personnel mines and is establishing the new international norm that any use or possession of anti-personnel mines is unacceptable.

As of 11 June 1998, the treaty had been signed by 126 governments, and ratified by nineteen[24] Many other governments were far along in the ratification process, and the government of Canada has estimated that the forty ratifications necessary for entry into force will be achieved by the end of the summer of 1998. If this projection holds, it is believed that the Mine Ban Treaty will enter into force more quickly than any other treaty. The same partners that produced the treaty – key pro-ban governments, the ICBL, and the ICRC – are working together to achieve the earliest possible entry into force, to universalize the treaty, to ensure effective monitoring of implementation and compliance with the treaty, to accelerate the rate of mine clearance and to provide adequate care for the victims of landmines. The treaty is the most crucial step toward, and provides the framework for the complete eradication of the anti-personnel landmine, but a great deal of difficult work lies ahead before millions of civilians around the world can walk in safety.

23. A comprehensive legal analysis of landmines in international humanitarian law appeared in Human Rights Watch and Physicians for Human Rights, *Landmines: A Deadly Legacy* (New York, Human Rights Watch 1993) pp. 261-318.

24. Ratifications include Canada, Ireland, Mauritius, Turkmenistan, Holy See, San Marino., Switzerland, Hungary, Niue, Belize, Trinidad and Tobago, Djibouti, Croatia, Mali, Denmark, Bolivia, Mexico, Fiji, and Peru.

THE 'SANDLINE AFFAIR': PAPUA NEW GUINEA RESORTS TO MERCENARISM TO END THE BOUGAINVILLE CONFLICT*

Tim McCormack**

1. INTRODUCTION

For at least a decade, the Government of Papua New Guinea (PNG) has been engaged in armed efforts to terminate a secessionist movement on the island of Bougainville off the South East coast of the PNG mainland. In late 1996, the government agreed to hire the firm of Sandline International to provide mercenary assistance, in a desperate bid to regain effective control of Bougainville. In an ironical twist to the cycle of violence and missed opportunities for peaceful resolution of the conflict, the controversial decision to engage Sandline proved to be the very catalyst to facilitate a process which appears to offer a real prospect for a negotiated settlement to the dispute.

The public disclosure of the decision of the then-Prime Minister, Sir Julius Chan, to resort to mercenarism was condemned by regional governments and resulted in widespread civil disturbance in PNG. Ultimately, the Chan Government was overthrown in a general election and the new government of Prime Minister Bill Skate has participated in the negotiation of an agreement to establish an independent Truce Monitoring Group and an end to the Bougainville conflict.

2. BACKGROUND

Although the origins of the Bougainville conflict date back many years, key developments occurred in the early 1970s during the final years of Australian administrative control over the trust territory of PNG. Despite the resistance of the indigenous landowners, prospectors had discovered a huge source of copper

** Timothy L.H. McCormack is Australian Red Cross Professor of International Humanitarian Law, University of Melbourne, Australia.

at Panguna on the island of Bougainville. The law in each of the Australian States, which had been inherited from their status as separate colonies of the British Crown, was that ownership of all minerals on and under the land was reserved to the Crown and did not pass with title to land. Consistent with this legal position, various mining ordinances were declared in respect of territory in PNG.

The Conzinc Riotinto Australia (CRA) Company negotiated the first and subsequent Bougainville Copper Agreements with the PNG Administration on the basis of the Administration's title to minerals and in disregard of the wishes of the traditional Panguna landowners. Bougainvilleans were convinced that both the new government of PNG and CRA wanted to exploit them. On the eve of independence for PNG in September 1975, Bougainvilllean leaders unilaterally declared independence from PNG. The PNG government did not accept this declaration and Bougainville remained a part of the newly independent PNG. However, Bougainville was a reluctant constituent member of PNG from the moment of the inception of the newly independent state.

Disputes arose in 1987 about the sufficiency of compensation paid for compulsorily acquired land and about responsibility for environmental damage caused by the Panguna mine. Violence erupted early in 1989 with attacks on the mine's infrastructure, resulting in its closure. The mine had provided the single largest source of revenue to the PNG Government, contributing more than 15 percent of internal revenues.[1] A state of emergency was proclaimed in Bougainville with riot police first reinforced and then replaced by the Papua New Guinea Defence Forces (PNGDF).

In 1990 the 'Bougainville Revolutionary Army' (BRA) took control of the island on a secessionist platform. In response, the PNG Government imposed a trade and transport embargo.This action led to widespread shortages on the island and exacerbated the relatively poor living standards of the estimated population of 180,000 people. After an offensive in 1991, the PNG government claimed to have reasserted control over Bougainville, but fighting continued with increased intensity through 1993. There were several unsuccessful initiatives to negotiate a peaceful settlement to the conflict between 1990 and 1993. However, any demonstrations by Port Moresby of a willingness to negotiate a peaceful resolution were undermined by undisciplined actions of PNGDF personnel in their interventions on Bougainville as well as by a lack of commitment to negotiate on the part of the BRA. While the resolve of the BRA to fight for secession

1. Background Notes 1988 – 1997: Bougainville, *Department of Foreign Affairs and Trade*, http://www.dfat.gov.au/geo/spacific/png/png_bg.html.

increased, a more moderate Bougainvillean leadership emerged calling for concessions in favour of peace.

During 1994, the then-newly elected Prime Minister Chan met with various Bougainvillean groups, including the commander of the BRA, Sam Kauona. As a consequence of the talks, the BRA agreed to a ceasefire and to peace talks in Arawa, Bougainville. The BRA leadership then reneged on the agreement to participate in the talks but the PNG Government agreed on the establishment of the Bougainville Transitional Government (BTG) with a breakaway group of Bougainvillean leaders. The BTG met with the PNG Government in a series of meetings, including the much publicised Cairns talks in December 1995, held under joint UN/Commonwealth Secretariat auspices, and including a BRA delegation. However, the PNGDF attempted to ambush the BRA delegation on its return to Bougainville and this resulted in a fresh outbreak of hostilities.

In March 1996 Prime Minister Chan announced the lifting of the 1994 cease-fire agreement and a new offensive by the PNGDF to regain control over all of Bougainville. This offensive was terminated in July 1996 by the head of the PNGDF, Brigadier General Jerry Singirok, after poor logistic support, ineffective intelligence as to BRA locations, mounting PNGDF casualties and increasing discipline problems among troops combined to prevent a defeat of the BRA.[2] Estimates of the number of lives lost as a direct consequence of the Bougainville conflict range between 10,000 and 20,000 people but, given the living conditions on the island, there is no way of verifying these figures.

3. THE SANDLINE CONTRACT

Early in 1997 the government of Sir Julius Chan contracted the private military consultancy firm, Sandline International, a British-based operation with South African military connections, to equip, train and assist the PNGDF to conduct a special military operation to finally defeat the BRA. Many governments, particularly Australia, New Zealand and others in the region, protested their opposition to the resort to mercenarism as a military solution to the Bougainville conflict. The introduction of mercenaries into the South Pacific was considered to constitute a serious threat to regional stability and a dangerous precedent for other regional governments faced with domestic tensions.[3]

2. See *The Age* [Melbourne] (19 March 1997).
3. *Supra* n. 1.

Sir Julius Chan attempted to portray the engagement of Sandline as a strategy to develop the capabilities of the PNGDF and to force the BRA to negotiate an end to the Bougainville conflict. He argued that Sandline had only been engaged for training purposes and he strenuously refuted the applicability of the 'mercenary' tag to describe the contractual relationship.[4]

However, the actual terms of the contract between PNG and Sandline[5] undermined the Prime Minister's attempts to re-characterise the nature of Sandline's proposed involvement in the conflict. The PNG Government agreed to pay Sandline USD$36 million and to negotiate a joint venture involving Sandline and the PNG Government in relation to the Panguna mine once it was back in operation.[6] In return, Sandline undertook to provide extensive supplies of sophisticated weaponry and ammunition and to 'conduct offensive operations in conjunction with PNG defence forces' in order to quell the BRA and to repossess the Panguna copper mine. Similarly, Port Moresby agreed to 'issu[e] instructions to PNG defence forces personnel to cooperate fully with Sandline commanders and their nominated representatives' and undertook 'to ensure that full cooperation is provided from within its organisation and that of the PNG defence forces'. Responsibilities for initiating planning cooperation between PNG commanders and Sandline commanders were also undertaken by the government.

Although Sandline professes to be available for hire only to recognised governments and to act in accordance with the Geneva Conventions, such claims hardly obscure the nature of the functions Sandline are willing to perform purely for pecuniary gain.[7]

The Sandline Agreement was derailed when Brigadier General Jerry Singirok and other senior officers of the Papua New Guinea Defence Forces eventually refused to cooperate with Sandline staff, publicly condemning the arrangement.[8] Soldiers who had not received pay and adequate equipment for months were unwilling to work with the Sandline staff, particularly once the amounts of money to be paid to Sandline became widely known. The PNGDF made significant allegations of corruption against the government generally, and against Sir Julius

4. Statement by Sir Julius Chan reported in *The Age* (19 March 1997). See also statement by Sandline reported in *Sydney Morning Herald* (27 February 1997).

5. The text of the agreement is available at: http://www.theage.com.au/special/asiaonline/sandline.html.

6. Sir Julius Chan's plan for Bougainville had included a plan for the PNG Government to purchase CRA's controlling share in the Panguna mine and to reopen and operate the mine once the military operation had successfully restored PNGDF control of Bougainville.

7. The Sandline Contract with the PNG government included this claim by Sandline. However, the terms of the contract itself indicate the intention of the parties for Sandline personnel to engage in operational and command activities, not merely in training in the use of particular weaponry.

8. Statement by Sir Julius Chan reported in *The Age* (18 March 1997).

Chan in particular. These allegations were subsequently raised in the PNG Parliament during debate on the motion for the Prime Minister to step down temporarily from office pending the outcome of a judicial inquiry. The Sandline contract was prematurely terminated as a consequence of widespread PNGDF opposition. PNGDF members went as far as to detain some Sandline employees in their barracks at the Sepik army training camp.[9] General Singirok was dismissed by the government for 'gross insubordination bordering on treason',[10] and his acting replacement was ordered to release the Sandline employees. The head of Sandline International and of the PNG operation, Tim Spicer, was arrested on a firearms charge,[11] but charges against him were later dropped.[12]

Although the Australian government supported the right of the democratically elected government of PNG to dismiss Singirok, it continued to make wide ranging criticisms of the contract entered into with Sandline.[13] The sacking of General Singirok provoked a public revolt with thousands of civilians engaged in rioting, looting and protest in the streets of Port Moresby. The PNG government, battered by criticism from outside the country, and from the PNGDF and citizens within the country, announced that the cancellation of the contract with Sandline would be 'considered'.[14] On 18 March 1997, Sandline employees began to leave PNG.[15]

The PNG Parliament voted to institute a formal judicial inquiry into the negotiations and procedures by which Sandline was hired, and the way in which the arrangement was to be financed. The inquiry was headed by the Australian-born judge of the Papua New Guinean Supreme Court, Warwick Andrew.[16] Sir Julius Chan agreed to stand down temporarily as Prime Minister during the inquiry. Sir Julius announced his resumption of the position of Prime Minister on 2 June 1997,[17] claiming exoneration by the inquiry. However, elections were held later that month and, despite the Prime Minister's best efforts to focus the campaign on local issues, the Sandline affair dominated the election. Sir Julius

9. *PNG Post-Courier*, Niuswire (19 March 1997).

10. Statement by Sir Julius Chan reported in *The Age* (19 March 1997).

11. See *Sydney Morning Herald* (1 April 1997).

12. *BBC Online* (19 January 1998).

13. See statements by the Australian Minister for Foreign Affairs and Trade, Mr Downer, reported in *Sydney Morning Herald* (6 June 1997).

14. See *Sydney Morning Herald* (20 March 1997).

15. See *The Age* (18 March 1997).

16. The transcripts of the inquiry are available at: http://www.datec.com.pg/sandline/default.html.

17. See *Sydney Morning Herald* (6 June 1997).

Chan not only lost government but ultimately also the seat which he had held for 29 years.[18]

The crisis focused attention on the *International Convention Against the Recruitment, Use, Financing and Training of Mercenaries,* which was adopted by the General Assembly on 4 December 1989.[19] This treaty is not yet in force; indeed only 16 states have become party since it was opened for signature. Not a single state in the South East Asian or the Pacific regions has signed. Within Australia, for example, this lack of participation in the treaty regime caused some slight embarrassment for the government. After extensive public criticism of PNG's willingness to engage mercenaries, accompanied by the political rhetoric of Australia's long-standing international opposition to mercenarism, the media was quick to point to the lack of Australian support for the principal international treaty regime on the issue. Both Australia and Papua New Guinea[20] stated their intention to become parties to the treaty.[21] The Australian government also discussed possible initiatives to promote participation in the treaty amongst regional states.

4. POST-SANDLINE DEVELOPMENTS

Before the results of the PNG election were known, the New Zealand government hosted a meeting of various Bougainvillean groups at the Burnham Military Camp (near Christchurch, New Zealand) which resulted in agreement to the 'Burnham Declaration' on 18 July 1997. The Declaration announced a new truce on Bougainville and outlined measures to facilitate a peaceful resolution of the conflict – including the possibility of a role for international peacekeepers under UN auspices.[22] After the installation of the new PNG government of Prime Minister Bill Skate, a Minister for Bougainvillean Affairs was appointed and the government indicated that it was willing to negotiate the island's future. A second meeting was held in Burnham, New Zealand in October 1997 and, on this occasion, the PNG government was also represented. At this second meeting, the parties to the discussions agreed to the establishment of a Neutral Regional Truce Monitoring Group (TMG) for deployment on Bougainville and to the

18. *Asia-Pacific News Network* (2 July 1997).

19. 44 UN GAOR, G.A. Res. A/44/341 (1994).

20. See *Sydney Morning Herald* (19 June 1997) which reported the Australian government's intention to participate in the treaty. Australian radio and television reports claimed that the PNG government was also considering acceding to the treaty.

21. As of October 1998, neither state has signed the treaty.

22. *Supra* n. 1.

creation of a Peace Consultative Committee to facilitate negotiations for a final settlement to the conflict.

The TMG, the first indigenous Pacific regional peacekeeping operation, deployed on Bougainville early in December 1997. The Group was primarily constituted by military personnel from New Zealand, Australia, Fiji and Vanuatu. The TMG has been able to carry out its monitoring functions without incident to date and progress towards a peaceful resolution of the conflict has been promising. In January 1998, the parties to the Burnham Declaration met for a new round of talks at Lincoln University, Christchurch, New Zealand where the Lincoln Agreement on Peace, Security and Development on Bougainville[23] was signed by all parties to the meeting. The 'Lincoln Agreement' provided for a 'permanent and irrevocable' ceasefire on Bougainville; a phased withdrawal of the PNGDF from Bougainville subject to restoration of civil authority on the island; a meeting of all parties on Bougainvillle before 30 June 1998 to address the issue of Bougainville's political future; and the holding of elections for a Bougainvillean Reconciliation Government before the end of 1998.

In response to a request from the PNG government to the UN Security Council, the President of the Council issued a statement of support for the Lincoln Agreement and welcomed the establishment of the TMG pursuant to the Agreement.[24] The President's Statement also called on the UN Secretary-General to 'consider the composition and financial modalities' of possible UN involvement in the peaceful resolution of the Bougainville Conflict. The UN Secretary-General has responded to this request and is contemplating sending a small group of 3-5 personnel from the secretariat to observe the implementation of the Lincoln Agreement.[25]

The parties to the Lincoln Agreement met for a public ceremony in Arawa, Bougainville on 30 April 1998 to mark the establishment of the 'permanent and irrevocable ceasefire' provided for in the Lincoln Agreement. At that ceremony, the parties adopted a supplementary 'Agreement Covering Implementation of The Ceasefire'.[26] Pursuant to the supplementary agreement (described as Annex 1 to the Lincoln Agreement) the parties established a new Neutral Regional Peace Monitoring Group (PMG) to continue the mandate of the former TMG. The new PMG is currently constituted by contributions from the four states making up the TMG but the supplementary agreement explicitly invites other regional

23. The full text of the Agreement is available at the following address: http://www.dfat.gov.au/geo/spacific/png/png_lincoln.html.

24. 53 UN SCOR, UN Doc. S/PRST/1998/10 (22 April 1998).

25. Conversation with Australian Foreign Ministry Official.

26. Copy of text on file with author and not publicly available at the time of writing.

governments to participate. Australia has exercised leadership responsibilities for the new group from its inception on 30 April 1998.

In a significant expression of good faith on the part of the PNG government, Prime Minister Bill Skate announced the withdrawal of the PNGDF troops from the Bougainvillean capital of Arawa by 6 June 1998 and the transfer of control to civilian police.[27] The Prime Minister himself characterised this decision as 'the most significant initiative on the ground in Bougainville since the truce was declared last February.[28] The decision enhances the prospects for the current process to lead to a final negotiated settlement and an end to the protracted conflict on Bougainville.

5. CONCLUSIONS

Like solid rain after drought, a peaceful settlement to a protracted armed conflict is always a welcome relief. This is surely as true for Bougainville as for any other conflict. It is disappointing that the balance was only tipped in favour of the political will to finally negotiate a peaceful solution to the conflict by the controversy of resort to mercenarism. Nevertheless, it is encouraging that some good can come from the willingness of a financially stretched PNG government to pay US$36 million to Tim Spicer and Sandline International.

The popular stigma associated with mercenaries was used to strong effect by South Pacific governments and it will be interesting to observe the effects of the Sandline Affair on the status of the 1989 Mercenaries Convention. One suspects that the reticence of the international community to embrace participation in the Convention will continue and that only a few of the states involved in this particular incident will actually ratify or accede to the Convention. However, it is likely that other South Pacific governments will be reluctant to follow a similar strategy to the Chan government in PNG. The incident sparked an interesting public debate in Australia about the specifics of the opprobrium attached to mercenarism. This public debate also exposed telling evidence of involvement in promotion of and support for mercenarism by the growing group of companies engaged in the management of privatised prisons and detention facilities.

One overall reaction to the Bougainville Conflict, however, is to recognise the ongoing problem of the application of international humanitarian law in

27. 'Prime Minister Skate Announces Decision to Withdraw Defence Force and End Call-Out in Arawa', Press Release (2 June 1998). Copy on file with author.

28. Ibid.

internal armed conflicts. PNG has not become a party to either of the Protocols Additional to the Geneva Conventions and is unlikely to do so in the near future. The government of PNG was not keen to expose itself to international scrutiny in relation to the conduct of PNGDF operations on the island and also did not wish in any way to elevate the status of the BRA as a party to the armed conflict. This reluctance has created problems of access to victims for the International Committee of the Red Cross and raised again the weaknesses of enforcement provisions for relevant legal standards.

The lack of capacity to quickly end the fighting on Bougainville and reintegrate the island into the daily political and administrative life of PNG, quite apart from the economic loss associated with the protracted closure of the Panguna Mine, has been a consistent source of frustration for the PNG government. Of course, the whole conflict may have been avoidable in the first place with greater consideration and respect for the rights of the indigenous land owners. The conflict is an interesting case study for the relationship between international humanitarian law and other relevant areas of international law – human rights, including land rights and the right to self-determination; refugee law; and the rights and responsibilities of non-parties to the conflict. It remains to be seen whether the current momentum for peace will translate into a substantive agreement acceptable to all parties.

THE FALL OF SREBRENICA AND THE ATTITUDE OF DUTCHBAT FROM AN INTERNATIONAL LEGAL PERSPECTIVE*

Robert C.R. Siekmann**

1. INTRODUCTION

In the introduction to their book *Srebrenica: Record of a War Crime,* political scientists Jan Willem Honig and Norbert Both write: '"Srebrenica" has become synonymous with such an extraordinarily horrific crime that exceptional explanations have been proposed. Stories of conspiracy and betrayal abound. The most popular theory is that Srebrenica fell as the result of a plot involving senior UN personnel, the French government and the Serbian government. Others place the blame firmly on the Dutch UN soldiers, whom they accuse of cowardice during the Serb offensive against the safe area. We reject these explanations. Conspiracy theories tend to be neatly constructed so that every decision, or failure to decide, seems to stem from sinister ulterior motives. They leave no room for the dilemmas of real life, nor for miscommunication or outright failure. As such, they rarely bring us closer to the truth, and more often create a fertile breeding ground for dangerous stab-in-the-back myths'.[1] Honig and Both claim that final culpability should, without a doubt, be attributed to the highest Serb officials and officers who organised the crime and gave the orders for its perpetration. The systematic manner in which the crime was committed, the evidence that detailed plans had been drawn up and that procedures established earlier had been painstakingly carried out – all this points to the direct responsibility of the Bosnian Serb leadership in Pale. Moreover, the Serbian leadership in Belgrade had given, if not the order, then still its tacit consent. Honig and Both are of the opinion that a moral dilemma lay at the root of the problem: how could ethnic cleansing be effectively resisted and the establishment of safe areas be promoted while at

** Head of Research of the T.M.C. Asser Institute for International Law in The Hague.

1. J.W. Honig and N. Both, *Srebrenica: Record of a War Crime* (Penguin Books, 1996) pp. IX-XX.

the same time there was no willingness to endanger the lives of blue helmets in protecting the safe areas?

Professor Van Staden, Director of the Netherlands Institute for International Relations Clingendael, has examined whether the Dutch soldiers completely discharged themselves of their human duties in the hour of need:
'Admittedly, the circumstances were exceptionally hard and the Dutch soldiers had made obvious efforts to alleviate the population's fate. But why did they not give their all to show the Serbs that Dutchbat would only leave the enclave when *all* Muslims were granted unopposed withdrawal? Should they not have at least more strongly protested the separating of men from women? And the deportation without proper supervision of able and not so able men from the UN compound?'[2]

These questions, Van Staden feels, will probably never entirely fade from the discussion, not least because they pre-eminently concern dilemmas which are morally highly charged. They do not lend themselves to objective answers, free from personal moral standards. Some critics have, after the fact, demanded acts of the Dutchbat soldiers which would, in reality, have amounted to far-reaching self-sacrifice or even martyrdom. Others defend the lack of heroic resistance on the Dutch part by pointing to the suspected futility of such behaviour.

The question I wish to discuss here – and which seems to have been overly neglected, as if the Srebrenica tragedy took place in a legal vacuum – is how the behaviour of Dutchbat may be qualified from a legal perspective. The first question concerns the relationship between the sending state, the Netherlands, and the UN peacekeeping force UNPROFOR, that is, the responsibility of the Dutch government for the acts of Dutchbat in Srebrenica. The second question concerns whether Dutchbat acted in accordance with its mandate: were the powers based on the mandate used or were the obligations arising from it met? In this, two phases may be distinguished: the attack on Srebrenica and the evacuation of its Muslim population. Both questions concern UN law on peacekeeping operations. The third and last question pertains to the witnessing of violations of international humanitarian law by Dutch UN soldiers during the evacuation of the Muslims: does Dutchbat's failure to intervene constitute a punishable act? I have attempted to select the 'facts' which seem most relevant to providing an answer to the legal questions mentioned. The author is fully aware that such a selection is, up to a certain point, inevitably arbitrary. To this it may be added that the developments surrounding the fall of Srebrenica were many and complex.

2. A. Van Staden, *De fuik van Srebrenica – een bijdrage aan nadere oordeelsvorming* [The Srebrenica trap – a contribution to the further formation of judgment] (Nederlands Instituut voor Internationale Betrekkingen 'Clingendael', March 1997) pp. 26-27.

On the other hand, it is not entirely clear which law applies to the 'facts' or in which way the law, if available, should be applied in order to come up with conclusions about the legitimacy of Dutchbat's behaviour in Srebrenica. The following is, in any event, an attempt to provide a legal evaluation. Perhaps the conclusion should be that Dutchbat did, in fact, act wholly or partly inside a legal vacuum.

As far as the descriptions of fact are concerned, they have been based on the very well-documented and, by now, in the Netherlands, authoritative books of Honig/Both and Westerman/Rijs[3] and the parliamentary papers concerning Srebrenica.[4] I have purposely omitted the names of Dutch and UN officials so as to depersonalise the rendition of the facts.

2. UN COMMAND AND INVOLVEMENT OF THE NETHERLANDS

First of all, it needs to be established that Dutchbat was under the operational command of UNPROFOR, which, like all modern UN peacekeeping forces, enjoyed the status of subsidiary organ to the Security Council. This means that the Dutch Government was not entitled to give orders to Dutchbat. The soldiers in UN peacekeeping forces are not endowed with a 'double loyalty' *vis-à-vis* the UN and their own sending state. Dutchbat was not a representative of the Netherlands but instead directly represented the United Nations. If the Netherlands obeyed this fundamental rule, possible wrongful behaviour of Dutchbat during the fall of Srebrenica cannot be legally attributed to the Netherlands.

With regard to contact made by the Netherlands during the crisis in Srebrenica, the Dutch Minister of Defence at the time declared that, in three urgent cases, direct contact had been established with officials who were part of the UN command structure in order to convey the Dutch point of view. In each of these three cases, the UN command structure remained intact. No operational commands were given to the Dutchbat commander from the Netherlands.

The first case concerned the Dutch view that, given the scale of the Bosnian Serb offensive, a battle between Dutchbat and the forces invading the enclave would result in a pointless bloodbath and be coupled with great risk to the civilian population and the UN soldiers involved. The second case entailed a request by the Dutch Minister of Defence to the Special Representative of the UN Secretary-General in the former Yugoslavia to persuade NATO to call off a new air strike

3. *Supra* n. 1 and *infra* n. 5, respectively.

4. Bijl. Hand. II (Annexes to Parliamentary Proceedings) No. 22 181, Nos. 1-181 concerning 'The situation in (former) Yugoslavia'.

at Srebrenica. In the third instance, UN authorities were informed of the Dutch opinion that Dutchbat should in no way cooperate in separating the Srebrenica men from the other refugees during the evacuation.

As a result of a passage in the 1997 book entitled *Srebrenica: het zwartste scenario* [Srebrenica: the bleakest picture] by journalists Frank Westerman and Bart Rijs,[5] doubts had arisen in the Dutch Parliament as to whether the Ministry of Defence had interfered with the UN chain of command during the evacuation of Dutchbat itself. These doubts involved a fax, written in Dutch, containing guidelines for negotiation with the Bosnian Serb general, Ratko Mladić. This fax had been drawn up in the absence of the UNPROFOR commander by the Chief of Staff and his closest associate, two Dutch UN officers at UNPROFOR headquarters in Sarajevo. This explained why the guidelines to the Srebrenica Dutchbat commander had been drawn up in the Dutch language, so the Minister of Defence declared in parliament. The impression had possibly been created that these were national guidelines. The Dutchbat Commander had, however, never received orders from the Netherlands. The UN command structure had at all times been left intact. Written instructions to UN troops were generally given in English. However, communication in one's own language was not at all uncommon within the UN. Dutch UN officers were no exception to this state of affairs. In the hectic circumstances of those days, speedy and efficient communication was of greatest importance. Formally speaking, the text should have been translated into English. In the rush, this had been omitted by those involved.

It was also asked why the Deputy of the absent UNPROFOR Commander had not drawn up the instructions. The answer was that the instructions to Dutchbat had been discussed within the UNPROFOR staff in the presence of the Deputy Commander. It had, at that time, been decided that the (Dutch) UNPROFOR Chief of Staff would formulate the guidelines, after which they would be transmitted by his (Dutch) military assistant to the Dutchbat commander. The instructions to the Dutchbat commander said that, if negotiations came to a halt, immediate referral back to the Chief of Staff at UNPROFOR headquarters in Sarajevo (who was called the 'mandated negotiator on behalf of the Dutch Government and UNPROFOR') should be effected. Parliament asked how this appointment as mandated negotiator on behalf of the Dutch Government related to his international staff function in the UNPROFOR chain of command. The Government replied that there had been no official appointment on behalf of the Dutch government. The Dutch Chief of Staff had, however, been informed by

5. F. Westerman and B. Rijs, *Srebrenica: Het zwartste scenario* [Srebrenica: the bleakest picture] (Amsterdam/Antwerpen, Uitgeverij Atlas 1997) pp. 182-183.

the Government that he could also negotiate on its behalf on the evacuation of Dutchbat. As a UN Commander, he was in a better position to judge the situation on the spot and could more rapidly react to new developments. The UN command structure was thus left intact, according to the Minister of Defence.

This explanation can only be understood if one realises that logistics, personnel and equipment are national responsibilities in the UN context, and that the guidelines for negotiating with General Mladić on the evacuation of Dutchbat – which had been drawn up by the Chief of Staff (in his joint capacity as 'negotiator on behalf of the Dutch Government') for the benefit of the Dutchbat Commander – did, in fact, regard these matters.

Another possible explanation is that evacuation of Dutchbat from Srebrenica implied withdrawal from UNPROFOR. This also meant that the highest authority over the Dutch force would be reallocated to the Dutch government because this would end the participation in UNPROFOR. The UN chain of command had, however, remained intact as it was denied that it had been interfered with by the Netherlands. The evacuation of Dutchbat was, therefore, a 'UN evacuation' and not a Dutch matter, because it was not based on a Dutch decision to withdraw.

In view of the above, the Netherlands cannot be held legally responsible for the acts of Dutchbat in relation to the attack on Srebrenica, nor for the evacuation of the Muslim refugees or that of Dutchbat itself, as a contingent of the UN peacekeeping force UNPROFOR in Srebrenica (which topic is closely related to the other two, although it is, strictly speaking, outside the scope of this contribution). The UN cannot recoup its own responsibility in the matter on the Netherlands, as operational command lay with the UN and it has not been established that the Netherlands issued orders in contravention of it.

3. VIOLATION OF THE UN MANDATE BY DUTCHBAT?

3.1 The Bosnian Serb attack on Srebrenica

According to UN Security Council Resolution 819 of 16 April 1993, the town of Srebrenica and its surroundings formed a 'safe area', which indicated that the area should be free from any armed attack or any other hostile acts. In paragraph 5 of Resolution 836 of 4 June 1993, UN troops were ordered to deter attacks against the safe areas; to monitor the ceasefire; to promote the withdrawal of military and paramilitary units other than those of the government of the Republic of Bosnia and Herzegovina; and to occupy some key points on the ground, in addition to participating in the delivery of humanitarian relief to the population. According to this paragraph, UN troops were only ordered to 'deter' and not to engage in battle. Paragraph 9, however, seemed to go further. This paragraph authorised UNPROFOR, in carrying out the mandate defined in paragraph 5, acting in self-defence, to take the necessary measures, including the use of force, in reply to bombardments against the safe areas by any of the parties or to armed incursion into them, or, in the event of any deliberate obstruction in or around those areas, to the freedom of movement of UNPROFOR or of protected humanitarian convoys. Except for deterring attacks, the UN troops were, thus, also entitled to defend themselves against attack. As a rule, self-defence in UN peacekeeping operations implies that UN troops may use force in return when they are forcefully prevented from carrying out their mandate. Attacks on Srebrenica meant the obstruction of Dutchbat's duties. Therefore, Dutchbat was entitled to react. Moreover, 'in and around the safe areas', the use of air power was permitted.[6] Dutchbat could, if necessary, request air support from NATO. A confidential UNPROFOR Directive[7] provided, however, that 'the execution of the mandate is secondary to the security of UN personnel', and that force could only be used as a last resort. In addition, the military means to ward off an attack were extremely limited. At the moment of the Bosnian Serb attack on Srebrenica at the beginning of July 1995, only 429 Dutch soldiers were still present in the enclave. Only half of them were infantry; the remainder were support and medical troops. Even though they disposed of about 30 YPR armoured infantry battle vehicles, several anti-tank rocket systems and half a dozen 81 mm mortars, they had very little fuel and munitions.

The Bosnian Serb attack on the 'safe area' Srebrenica commenced on 6 July 1995. The Dutchbat commander was faced with an acute dilemma: should fire be answered in a legitimate attempt at self-defence, should he request air support or should he try to allay the crisis through diplomacy? He chose the latter option: the Bosnian Serbs were asked for an explanation. They, in turn, demanded that the Dutch request be entered in writing. On 9 July, Dutchbat received the order to assume 'blocking positions' with all means available to prevent a further breakthrough into and march on Srebrenica by Serbian units of the highest echelons. To support the 'blocking positions', the UNPF (United Nations Peacekeeing Force, of which UNPROFOR was a part) Commander and the Special Representative of the UN Secretary-General in the former Yugoslavia sent the Serbs an ultimatum. If the 'blocking positions' were attacked, use would be made of NATO 'close air support'. In such a case, according to another UNPROFOR Directive[8], UNPROFOR first had to lodge a request with UN Sector North-East in Tuzla. From there, the request had to be sent on to the next link in the chain

6. Para. 10 of Resolution 836.
7. Directive Confidential Commander HQ UNPROFOR Directive 2/95 of 29 May 1995.
8. UNPROFOR Directive OPO 14/94.

of command, UNPROFOR in Sarajevo. If consent was received from there, the request would be transmitted to the highest headquarters of the UN peacekeeping force in the former Yugoslavia in Zagreb. The UNPF Commander would then consult the Special Representative. If they consented, the request would be lodged with NATO (the 'dual-key' formula). On 10 July, the Dutchbat Deputy Commander requested air support when the Bosnian Serbian attack was still in full swing. The UNPF Commander and the Special Representative of the Secretary-General in the end only agreed that, *if* the Dutch were attacked, air strikes could be carried out on actively attacking Serbian forces or 'smoking guns' (firing tanks, mortars and artillery). Dutchbat, however, expected air support to be deployed at the first opportunity that presented itself. UNPF and UNPROFOR, on the other hand, were, in fact, waiting for Dutchbat to contact them as soon as a new Bosnian Serb attack occurred, as was the usual practice regarding air support. After two air strikes had taken place, the Bosnian Serbs sent an ultimatum: if the air strikes would not cease immediately, they would kill the Dutch soldiers who had been taken hostage and open fire on both Dutchbat and the refugees. Thereupon, the air strikes were called off by the Special Representative and the UNPROFOR Commander in Sarajevo.

Did Dutchbat, as part of the UN peacekeeping force in the former Yugoslavia, disregard its obligations under the operation's mandate, i.e., did Dutchbat, in contravention of the law, fail to employ its powers during the Bosnian Serb attack on Srebrenica? Or, more specifically, did Dutchbat disobey or insufficiently obey orders of higher Commanders? After all, it may be that the mandate of a UN peacekeeping force is not binding and it may be that an actual duty to use force to carry out that mandate does not exist (UNPROFOR was merely 'authorized' to use force), but military orders for the implementation of a mandate (in this case, to assume blocking positions) should, of course, be carried out. Still, one cannot reasonably arrive at the conclusion that Dutchbat violated UN law, also considering the fact that the safety of the blue helmets had to prevail over the UNPROFOR mandate (Dutch soldiers were, moreover, being held hostage by the Bosnian Serbs). In addition, one should consider the important fact that due to circumstances, real air support had not been given.

3.2 The evacuation of the Muslims from Srebrenica

On 11 July 1995, Srebrenica fell. The Dutchbat Commander was summoned to Bratunac by General Mladić, as it emerged later from his testimony before the International Criminal Tribunal for the Former Yugoslavia in The Hague. This meant that a Lieutenant-Colonel was to negotiate with a General. His superiors in Sarajevo would have sent the UNPROFOR Chief of Staff with the rank of General by helicopter, but Mladić did not consent to this flight over the territory of the *Republika Srpska.* He wished to do business with Dutchbat directly. To still maintain some control over the course of the meeting, UN command transmitted from its Sarajevo headquarters orders for defence of Dutchbat and protection of refugees in Srebrenica, among which were: 'Enter into local negotiations with BSA [Bosnian Serb Army] forces for immediate ceasefire', 'Take all reasonable measures to protect refugees and civilians in your care' and, 'Continue with all possible means to defend your forces and installations from attack. This is to include the use of close air support if necessary'. In his report of 12 July on the meeting with Mladić, which was, *inter alia*, addressed to the UNPF commander, the Dutchbat commander wrote that he was not able to defend the Muslims nor his own battalion.

On 17 July 1995, a meeting was held in Srebrenica between the new Bosnian Serb 'authorities' of Srebrenica and the UNPROFOR representative, the Dutchbat Deputy Commander. The meeting was also attended by three representatives of the Muslim refugees, who had also been present at meetings with General Mladić on 11 and 12 July. Among other items, the Dutchbat departure from the Dutch compound in Potocari featured on the agenda. At the end of the meeting, the Bosnian Serbs unannouncedly asked the three representatives of the Muslim refugees to sign a 'declaration'. The declaration consisted of two parts. The largest part dealt with what had allegedly been discussed at the meeting of 12 July in Bratunac between the same representatives and General Mladić. At this meeting, the Dutchbat commander had also been present. According to the declaration, it had, at that time, been agreed that the Muslim population would be evacuated 'voluntarily' and under UN military escort.

The declaration did not refer to any differentiation as to groups of refugees. The second part of the text, the actual declaration, established that the evacuation of the refugees had been carried out in a correct manner and in accordance with what had been agreed on 12 July and with due regard to the Geneva Conventions and international humanitarian law. The declaration was signed by one of the representatives of the Muslim refugees, who did not object to its contents, and by the representative of the Bosnian Serbs. The Deputy Commander of Dutchbat was, hereupon, as a representative of UNPROFOR, requested to co-sign the declaration. The declaration, which, at his request, had first been translated into English, could, in his opinion, only refer to convoys which had in reality been escorted by Dutch UN soldiers. He therefore refused to accept the declaration for those convoys which Dutchbat had not or insufficiently been able to supervise; this explains his handwritten (restricting) addition to the text.

Did Dutchbat violate UN law during the evacuation of the Muslims from Srebrenica? The superior orders stipulated the taking of 'all reasonable measures' to protect refugees and civilians after the fall of Srebrenica. This specifically concerned the thousands of people who had fled to Potocari. The guidelines, which prescribed that the safety of Dutch soldiers was to prevail over the mandate, was also in force during this phase. What, given the circumstances, was 'reasonable' in the talks between the Dutchbat commander and Mladić and during the evacuation itself? It was the Dutchbat Commander who had to decide what was 'reasonable', and there are no criteria available to afterwards test his line of action. In any event, reasonableness is a different criterion from moral or ethical ones. From a legal/normative perspective (in the UN context), it cannot be concluded that Dutchbat acted unlawfully during the evacuation of Srebrenica.

4. DUTCHBAT AS A WITNESS OF WAR CRIMES

In the above, I have limited myself to an attempt to apply UN law to the (un)lawfulness of Dutchbat action concerning the fall of Srebrenica and the evacuation of Muslims from that town. The question remains whether, perhaps, other rules of public international law may be held to be applicable in this case. In 1995, Dr. Heike Spieker of the Institute for International Law of Peace and Armed Conflicts of the University of Bochum posed the interesting question whether members of Dutchbat who had witnessed war crimes were not themselves also guilty of war crimes through their passive behaviour:

> The execution of Muslims and the firing at Muslim refugees are in principle to be qualified as serious violations of the Fourth Geneva Convention of 1949 concerning the protection of civilians in times of war and, therefore, as a war crime pursuant to article 147 of the Convention in case the Muslims found themselves in occupied territory. Pursuant to article 146 paragraphs 1 and 2 of the Convention, only the person who commits this serious crime or orders its perpetration is criminally responsible according to public international law. The Dutch soldiers have never been accused of the perpetration of such a crime on their own initiative or the giving out of orders as to its perpetration. The First Additional Protocol of 1977 to the Geneva Conventions does, in fact, in article 85 paragraph 3 contain serious breaches *vis-à-vis* all civilians, but on the condition of a deliberate attack as intended by article 51 of Protocol I in the sense of active doings, so as to preclude public international law responsibility on the part of the Dutch soldiers in that respect as well.

The Statute of the *ad hoc* Tribunal for the former Yugoslavia has extended criminal responsibility based on humanitarian law. It extends to the events mentioned as serious violations of the Geneva Conventions in Article 2 and as genocide in Article 4. Those responsible are persons who, according to these provisions, have committed these acts either in person (Arts. 2 and 4) or who have given orders thereto (Art. 2). Individual responsibility before the Tribunal has been broadened in Article 7 paragraph 1 of the Statute to include the individual responsibility of a person who plans one of the punishable acts mentioned, incites others to their commitment or otherwise facilitates the commitment thereof during the stages of planning, preparation or perpetration of the acts. The Dutch soldiers have, however, not been accused of personally planning or inciting the commitment of the acts mentioned. This leaves the question whether, through aiding and abetting, international legal responsibility has been incurred for the commitment of the acts. Seeing that, up to this time, it does not appear from the coverage in the media that the soldiers in any way through active doings took part in the crimes, only that criminal responsibility remains which springs from not having prevented war crimes, of which omission they may be accused.

In German criminal law, this fits the description of the so-called '*psychische Beihilfe*' [mental assistance], the '*Beihilfe durch Unterlassen*' [assistance by negligence] or the so-called '*Unterlassene Hilfeleistung*) [failed relief]. '*Unterlassene Hilfeleistung*' is described in Article 323(c) of the Criminal Code and concerns the criminal liability of a person who does not render assistance to victims of accidents, even though assistance is obviously necessary and may be demanded of him given the circumstances. It involves a separate punishable act which is used to include certain borderline cases between individual acts and participation in the acts of others.

Neither treaty law nor customary international criminal law nor the Statute of the Tribunal, however, contain a similar provision. The two legal concepts of '*psychische Beihilfe*' and '*Beihilfe durch Unterlassen*' were developed in German case law through interpretation of Article 27 of the Criminal Code, according to which he shall be punished who has assisted another in his act. At the same time, criteria have been elaborated for these constructions which motivate and limit the criminal liability. In principle, Article 7 paragraph 1 of the Statute would also be open to a wider interpretation. For the time being, however, these limiting criteria are not (yet) known in present international criminal law and consequently, these legal concepts are definitely not applicable to the negligence of which the Dutch soldiers may possibly be accused. According to the present state of public international law, the Dutch soldiers have not committed a punishable act.[9]

As far as the question of applicability of international humanitarian law to UN peacekeeping forces is concerned, the UN has always taken the position that it is bound by 'the principles and spirit of the general international Conventions

9. In a BoFax of 31 October 1995 (BoFaxes are analyses of the Institut für Friedenssicherungsrecht und Humanitäres Völkerrecht of the Ruhr-Universität of Bochum and are published by the T.M.C. Asser Institute in the Dutch translation).

applicable to the conduct of military personnel'. In May 1994, Guidelines (later termed Directives) for UN forces regarding respect for international humanitarian law were drawn up in cooperation between the International Committee of the Red Cross and the UN Secretariat. Although these have not yet been formally accepted by the UN, they contain a number of generally accepted points of departure and may, as such, be regarded as a codification of applicable law.

Firstly, they specify the principles and rules of international humanitarian law applicable to UN forces when in situations of armed conflict they are actively engaged as combatants. Secondly, the Directives are applicable to UN forces conducting operations under UN command and control. Thirdly, they are applicable to both peacekeeping and enforcement operations, where the use of force is authorised either in self-defence or in pursuance of a mandate of the Security Council. Fourthly, they are applicable to international and non-international armed conflicts as may be relevant.[10]

Did international humanitarian law apply to Dutchbat? Dutchbat was part of UNPROFOR and UNPROFOR stood under UN command and control. UNPROFOR was, in any case, at least a peacekeeping operation (use of force in self-defence), if not a so-called peace-enforcement operation. The conflict in Bosnia was, in any case, 'at least' a non-international armed conflict in the sense of Article 3 of the Geneva Conventions and Additional Protocol II to these Conventions. Dutchbat itself was not, however, during the evacuation of the Muslim population of Srebrenica, involved in a situation of armed conflict as a combatant. International humanitarian law was, therefore, not applicable to Dutchbat. A '*Beihilfe*' or similar rule as a rule of international criminal law does not (yet) exist. From a UN law perspective, an order had merely been given to take all 'reasonable' measures for the protection of refugees and civilians. I have concluded that the behaviour of Dutchbat during the evacuation of the Muslims may not be qualified as unreasonable and, therefore, unlawful. The same goes for the behaviour in witnessing war crimes committed by the Bosnian Serb forces.

Apart from UN law and the possible applicability of international humanitarian and criminal law, members of UN peacekeeping forces remain subject to the criminal jurisdiction of their respective national states in accordance with the laws and regulations of those states.

Dutch criminal law is applicable to military personnel who are guilty of a criminal offence outside the Netherlands.[11] One of the offences in the Dutch Criminal Code is very similar to the German '*unterlassene Hilfeleistung*': the

10. For a fuller discussion of the international law applicable to UN forces, see Greenwood, *supra* p. 3.

11. Art. 4 of the Military Criminal Code.

violation concerning those in need, i.e., omitting, while being a witness to the immediate life-threatening situation in which the other finds himself, to grant such assistance as can, without reasonable fear of danger to himself or others, be granted, if such person in need does, in fact, die. However, if Dutch soldiers had acted to prevent war crimes, they would undoubtedly have exposed themselves to danger without, moreover, having been able to accomplish much against the Bosnian Serb military dominance.

Generally speaking, one cannot blame, under Dutch criminal law, members of Dutchbat, as witnesses of war crimes, for the death of Muslims during their evacuation from Srebrenica.

5. CONCLUSIONS

- The Dutch government cannot be held responsible for the acts of Dutchbat in respect of the fall of Srebrenica and the evacuation of the Muslims. If Dutchbat's actions were unlawful, then such a legal disqualification is attributable to the UN. It has, in fact, not been established that the Netherlands acted in contravention of the UNPROFOR chain of command.

- Dutchbat did not violate the UNPROFOR mandate or superior orders during the attack on Srebrenica nor during the evacuation of its Muslim population.

- No criminal responsibility of Dutchbat can be established with regard to the witnessing of and not intervening in the commission of war crimes by the Serbs during the evacuation of the Muslim population.

In short, the behaviour of Dutchbat surrounding the fall of Srebrenica can, notwithstanding moral and ethical considerations, stand the test of legal criticism.

THE REVIEW PROCESS OF THE 1954 HAGUE CONVENTION FOR THE PROTECTION OF CULTURAL PROPERTY IN THE EVENT OF ARMED CONFLICT AND ITS IMPACT ON INTERNATIONAL HUMANITARIAN LAW*

Jan Hladik**

The end of the Cold War and the disappearance of bipolarity have resulted in a recrudescence of a number of armed conflicts in the world, in particular in the ex-Yugoslavia and the former Soviet Union. Such conflicts have demonstrated a blatant disregard for the law of armed conflicts and a loss of respect for human lives and cultural heritage. They have also demonstrated deficiencies in the implementation of the 1954 Hague Convention for the Protection of Cultural Property in the Event of Armed Conflict – the only comprehensive international agreement aimed specifically at protecting movable and immovable cultural heritage in the event of armed conflict.

Why has this Convention been unable to deliver on its promise?

First, given the experience of WWII, the Hague Convention was conceived for conditions of a classical war between two or more states, conducted by regular armies over a relatively long period of time. However, the majority of armed conflicts since the end of the Cold War have been non-international.

Second, the control system of the Convention (Commissioners-General and Protecting Powers) is very difficult, if not impossible, to apply in contemporary armed conflicts for several reasons: (i) participation in the Hague Convention is not universal, and therefore states not party to the Convention are not bound by it; (ii) the system is too complex to apply, in particular during a short-term

** Jan Hladik, Assistant Programme Specialist, International Standards Section of the Division of Cultural Heritage, UNESCO, Paris. The author is responsible for the choice of the presentation of the facts contained in this article and for the opinions expressed therein, which are not necessarily those of UNESCO and do not commit the Organization. The article was written in Feb. 1998 and therefore reflects the review process as of that date.

Yearbook of International Humanitarian Law
Volume I - 1998 - pp. 313-322

international armed conflict; and (iii) it is even more difficult to apply in a conflict not of an international character.

Third, the Convention is weak on sanctions for violation of its provisions. Article 28 of the Convention[1] stipulates that States Parties 'undertake to take, within the framework of their ordinary criminal jurisdiction, all necessary steps to prosecute and impose penal or disciplinary sanctions upon those persons, of whatever nationality, who commit or order to be committed a breach of the present Convention'. In other words, it is up to the States Parties to adopt such sanctions if they consider them necessary. Finally, there is no supervisory body of an intergovernmental or non-governmental character which could monitor the implementation of the Convention.

For this reason, at the beginning of the 1990s, the Secretariat of UNESCO initiated a review of the Convention. In particular, it invited a consultant, Professor Patrick Boylan, Vice-Chairperson of the International Council of Museums (ICOM), to prepare a study analysing the implementation of the Convention since 1954 and proposing practical measures addressed to UNESCO; other intergovernmental organizations; States Parties; states which are not party to the Convention; and interested non-governmental organizations. Both English and French editions were published in 1993 and widely disseminated.[2] Finally, an article-by-article commentary on the Convention, written by Professor Jirí Toman, a Geneva-based specialist in international humanitarian law, was published by UNESCO in 1994 in French.[3] The English version was published in 1996.[4]

1. 249 *UNTS* p. 240 et seq.; text available from UNESCO, references in this paper are made to UNESCO publication *Conventions and Recommendations of UNESCO concerning the protection of cultural heritage*, UNESCO (1985) p. 27.

2. Patrick J. Boylan, *Review of the Convention for the Protection of Cultural Property in the Event of Armed Conflict (The Hague Convention of 1954)*, UNESCO Doc. CLT-93/WS/12 (Paris 1993); Patrick J. Boylan, 'Réexamen de la Convention pour la protection des biens culturels en cas de conflit armé (Convention de La Haye de 1954)', UNESCO CLT-93/WS/12, (Paris 1993).

3. Jiří Toman, *La protection des biens culturels en cas de conflit armé* (Commentaire de la Convention et du Protocole de La Haye du 14 mai 1954 pour la protection des biens culturels en cas de conflit armé ainsi que d'autres instruments de droit international relatifs à cette protection) (Paris, Editions UNESCO 1994).

4. Jiří Toman, *The Protection of Cultural Property in the Event of Armed Conflict* (Commentary on the Convention for the Protection of Cultural Property in the Event of Armed Conflict and its Protocol, signed on 14 May 1954 in The Hague, and on other instruments of international law concerning such protection), (Hampshire, Dartmouth Publishing Company Limited and UNESCO 1996).

To date, four expert meetings on the review of the Convention[5] and two meetings of the High Contracting Parties[6] have shown that a majority of UNESCO member states are in favour of improving the implementation of the Convention by adopting a new instrument which should cover the existing loopholes in the Convention. Discussions at these meetings have also revealed a number of important issues which need further clarification. These issues may be summarized as follows.

1. MILITARY NECESSITY

The notion of military necessity is of the greatest importance in international humanitarian law. It may be defined as 'the right to apply that amount and kind of force which is necessary to compel the submission of the enemy with the least possible expenditure of time, life and money'.[7]

It is embodied in the four Geneva Conventions with regard to different aspects of the law of armed conflicts and the First Additional Protocol of 1977 to the Geneva Conventions with regard to the law of armed conflict.[8]

During the drafting of the Convention at the Intergovernmental Conference at The Hague in 1954, two opposing tendencies were evident. Some states wished to exclude the option of military necessity from the Convention, claiming that it would diminish the scope of protection and open the door to abuses, while others insisted on its inclusion, giving various reasons, such as the recognition of this notion by Article 50 of the Geneva Convention for the Amelioration of the Condition of the Wounded and Sick in Armed Forces in the Field (Cuba)[9] or the fact that 'to close the door to those things which were militarily unavoidable in the face of a mission assigned by competent governmental authorities, might have a disastrous effect upon the basic aims of the Convention' (USA).[10]

5. The Hague – July 1993; Lauswolt – February 1994; Paris – November/December 1994; and again Paris – March 1997.

6. Paris, 13 November 1995 and 1997, respectively.

7. Morris Greenspan, *The Modern Law of Land Warfare* (Berkeley and Los Angeles, University of California Press, 1959) pp. 313-314.

8. Arts. 8, 34 and 50 of the First Geneva Convention; Art. 126 of the Third Geneva Convention; Arts. 49, 55, 108 and 143 of the Fourth Geneva Convention; and Arts. 54(5), 62, 67 and 71 of the First Additional Protocol of 1977 to the Geneva Conventions.

9. Records of the Conference convened by the United Nations Educational, Scientific and Cultural Organization held at The Hague from 21 April to 14 May 1954 (published by the Government of the Netherlands, The Hague, Sdu 1961), p. 151.

10. *Records*, ibid., at p. 141.

The Convention employs the notion of military necessity twice; first, with regard to cultural property generally protected[11], second, with respect to cultural property under special protection[12]. In the former case, this notion may be applied to a large amount of cultural property, situated both within the territory of the State Party to the Convention as well within the territory of other States Parties. In the latter case, the reference to military necessity is more limited (in practice, it may be used with respect to six cultural sites currently entered in the International Register of Cultural Property under Special Protection by virtue of Art. 8 of the Convention).

During several expert meetings, some states wished to delete this notion from a future instrument on the protection of cultural heritage during hostilities. The second meeting of the High Contracting Parties to the Convention, held in Paris on 13 November 1995, invited, among others, all those states to submit to the Secretariat written comments on the substantive proposals on improvement of the Convention by 1 September 1996. Countries replying to this point either wished to exclude this notion completely (Croatia, Czech Republic and Slovenia), to modify it (Belgium and an alternative proposal of the Czech Republic), or to reconsider it (Kuwait and Poland).[13]

Finally, during the third meeting of the States Parties to the Convention, held in Paris on 13 November 1997, representatives of several countries (including

11. Art. 4, Respect for cultural property provides:
1. The High Contracting Parties undertake to respect cultural property situated within their own territory as well as within the territory of other High Contracting Parties by refraining from any use of the property and its immediate surroundings or of the appliances in use for its protection for purposes which are likely to expose it to destruction or damage in the event of armed conflicts; and by refraining from any act of hostility directed against such property.
2. The obligations mentioned in paragraph 1 of the present Article may be waived only in cases where military necessity imperatively requires such a waiver.
(. . .)

12. Art. 11, Withdrawal of immunity, provides:
1. If one of the High Contracting Parties commits, in respect of any item of cultural property under special protection, a violation of the obligations under Article 9 [defining the immunity of cultural property under special protection], the opposing Party shall, so long as this violation persists, be released from the obligation to ensure the immunity of the property concerned. Nevertheless, whenever possible, the latter Party shall first request the cessation of such violation within a reasonable time.
2. Apart from the case provided for in paragraph 1 of the present Article, immunity shall be withdrawn from cultural property under special protection only in exceptional cases of unavoidable military necessity, and only for such time as that necessity continues. Such necessity can be established only by the officer commanding a force the equivalent of a division in size or larger. Whenever circumstances permit, the opposing Party shall be notified, a reasonable time in advance, of the decision to withdraw immunity.

13. UNESCO Doc. CLT-96/CONF.603/INF.4 (Paris, December 1996) pp. 2-4.

Argentina, Austria, France and Israel) defended the value of the concept of military necessity, asserting that it is one of the basic rules of international humanitarian law. However, they favoured defining it more precisely and narrowly.

It will be for further meeting(s) of governmental experts and a Diplomatic Conference to judge the relevance of the notion of 'military necessity' to the present day and/or to define it in such a way that it will exclude abuses.

2. INDIVIDUAL CRIMINAL RESPONSIBILITY

As mentioned above, Article 28 of the Convention is very general and gives States Parties leeway as to the adoption and enactment of the necessary penal and administrative measures punishing violations of the Convention. This situation is far from satisfactory, because – in accordance with information provided by the States Parties and published by the Secretariat in periodic reports on the implementation of the Convention under Article 26(2) of the Convention – to date, only 15 states[14] of the current 90 States Parties have done so, although there may be some states which have passed legislation but not reported.

For this reason, the drafters of the Lauswolt document, and subsequently the drafting group at the March 1997 meeting, decided to include a separate Article on this subject-matter. This draft Article[15] is, in principle, exclusively based on

14. Austria; Belarus; Belgium; the former Czechoslovakia; India; the Federal Republic of Germany; Hungary; the Islamic Republic of Iran; Italy; Mexico; Netherlands; Poland; Slovenia; Ukraine; and Yugoslavia.

15. Art. 9, Individual criminal responsibility, of the new draft provides:

1. The commission of any violation of a provision of this instrument entails individual criminal responsibility.
2. A person who planned, instigated, ordered, committed or otherwise aided and abetted in the planning, preparation or execution of a grave breach [any violation of] this instrument, shall be individually responsible.
3. Any attempt in respect of acts referred to in paras. (1) and (2) of this Article entails individual criminal responsibility.
4. The official position of any accused person, whether as Head of State or Government or as a responsible Government official, shall not relieve that person of criminal responsibility nor mitigate punishment for any grave breach under this instrument.
5. The commission of any act prohibited under this instrument by a subordinate shall not relieve a superior of criminal responsibility if the superior knew or had reason to know that the subordinate was about to commit the act or had done so and the superior failed to take the necessary and reasonable measures to prevent the act or to punish the perpetrators.
6. The fact that an accused person acted pursuant to an order of a Government or of a superior shall not relieve that person of criminal responsibility but may be considered in mitigation of punishment.

Article 7 of the Statutes of the International Tribunal for the Prosecution of Persons Responsible for Serious Violations of International Humanitarian Law Committed in the Territory of the Former Yugoslavia since 1991.[16] (Issues put into square brackets are subject to further discussions.)

To summarize its content, the draft article reiterates basic principles of international criminal law, such as the causal link between the commission of a crime against cultural property and individual responsibility and the impossibility of avoiding responsibility by referring to orders from a superior or by referring to one's official position of head of state, head of government or position in the bureaucracy, or by invoking internal orders of one's own government.

3. RESPONSIBILITY OF STATES

A three-paragraph draft Article[17] reconfirms one of the basic rules of international law, namely, state responsibility for wrongful acts and states' obligation to provide full reparation. In particular, paragraph 3 of this draft Article complements Article 91[18] of Additional Protocol I of 1977 to the four Geneva Conventions of 1949. Again, issues put into square brackets are subject to further discussions.

7. Prosecution of an individual for [a grave breach] [an act] under Article [s] [....] of this instrument shall not relieve a State Party of any responsibility under international law for an act or omission attributable to it. Draft provisions for the revision of the 1954 Hague Convention and commentary from the UNESCO Secretariat, UNESCO Doc.CLT-97/CONF.208/2 (Paris, October 1997), p. 12.

16. *Report of the Secretary-General pursuant to paragraph 2 of Security Council Resolution 808 (1993)*, UN Doc. S/25704 of 3 May 1993, p. 15.

17. Art. 8, Responsibility of States, provides:
1. States Parties are responsible for any violation of their obligations under this instrument.
2. States Parties are responsible for any [serious] violation of a provision of this instrument which is attributable to a State under international law.
[3. This responsibility entails the duty to provide reparation in accordance with international law, including i.a. compensation and restitution, as the case may be.]
Draft provisions for the revision of the 1954 Hague Convention and commentary from the UNESCO Secretariat, UNESCO Doc. CLT-97/CONF.208/2 (Paris, October 1997) p. 11.

18. Art. 91, Responsibility, provides:
'A Party to the conflict which violates the provisions of the Conventions or of this Protocol shall, if the case demands, be liable to pay compensation. It shall be responsible for all acts committed by persons forming part of its armed forces.' In *International Red Cross Handbook,* 12th edn. (Geneva, July 1983) p. 269.

4. JURISDICTION

This draft Article[19] codifies the obligation of states to take the necessary penal measures against individuals responsible for, or accused of, crimes against cultural property. Paragraph 3, concerning the competence of an international tribunal, was inspired by the experience of the International Tribunal for the Prosecution of Persons Responsible for Serious Violations of International Humanitarian Law Committed in the Territory of the Former Yugoslavia since 1991, as well as the UN Preparatory Committee on the Establishment of an International Criminal Court. Paragraph 4 states that the principle *aut dedere aut judicare* applies to grave breaches of this instrument. As in previous cases, issues put into square brackets are subject to further discussions.

Both the March 1997 meeting of experts and the third meeting of States Parties revealed that the issues of jurisdiction and responsibility will be certainly subject to further discussion. Not all States Parties are in favour of universal jurisdiction in this area, and some of them preferred to await the results of the UN Preparatory Committee on the Establishment of an International Criminal Court.

5. SUPERVISORY BODY

This issue has been as widely discussed as the notion of military necessity since the Intergovernmental Conference held at The Hague in 1954. However, neither The Hague Conference, expert meetings nor governmental meetings held to date have reached consensus on this point. The ongoing discussions since 1954 have revealed two tendencies: one for an Intergovernmental Committee and the other for an expert non-governmental body, perhaps coordinated with a very small group of representative States Parties.

19. Art. 10, Jurisdiction, provides:
1. States Parties undertake to prosecute, bring to trial and punish persons present in their territory responsible for, or accused of, [the acts] defined in Article[s] [....] of this instrument.
2. To that end States Parties shall adopt, whenever necessary, appropriate legislative and administrative measures.
3. Persons charged with [the acts] enumerated in Article [s] [....] of this instrument may be tried by a competent court of any State Party which may acquire jurisdiction over the accused or by any international tribunal which may have jurisdiction. This does not preclude the jurisdiction of any international tribunal which may be established.
4. A State Party in whose territory a person alleged to have committed a grave breach under Article[s] [....] of this instrument is present shall either try or extradite that person.
Draft provisions for the revision of the 1954 Hague Convention and commentary from the UNESCO Secretariat, UNESCO Doc. CLT-97/CONF.208/2 (Paris, October 1997) p. 14.

During the Lauswolt meeting, the drafters included a whole chapter on an intergovernmental organ, enumerating its functions and responsibilities. This notion was further elaborated in the draft provisions for the revision of the 1954 Hague Convention (Option I, draft Art. 14[20]) to include tasks such as identification and formulation of criteria for special protection; technical assistance; elaboration and implementation of projects and programmes of international assistance; and the regime of special protection (Option I, draft Art. 17[21]). The

20. Art. 14 (Option I), Committee, provides:
1. A Committee is hereby established within UNESCO. It shall be composed of [...] States Parties to this instrument which shall be elected by the States Parties during the ordinary session of the General Conference of UNESCO in accordance with the Rules of Procedure as referred to in Article [...] of this instrument.
2. Election of members of the Committee shall ensure an equitable representation of the different regions and cultures of the world.
[3. States members of the Committee shall choose as their representatives persons qualified in the fields of defence, international law or culture.]
4. Representatives of intergovernmental or non-governmental organizations may attend the meeting of the Committee in an advisory capacity upon invitation of the Committee.
Draft provisions for the revision of the 1954 Hague Convention and commentary from the UNESCO Secretariat, UNESCO Doc. CLT-97/CONF.208/2 (Paris, October 1997) p. 18.

21. Art. 17 (Option I), Functions, provides:
1. The Committee shall have the following functions and tasks without limiting UNESCO's competence to offer its services under Article 19 of the Convention and to initiate proposals under Article 23 of the Convention:
(a) to identify and formulate criteria on the basis of which cultural property will be specially protected;
(b) to receive requests from States Parties for the entry into the Register established in accordance with Article (....) of this instrument of cultural property (protected by the Convention) (as defined in Article 1 of the Convention), situated in its territory and suitable for inclusion in the Register provided for in Article (...) of this instrument. This request shall include information and documentation about the exact location, significance and nature of the cultural property;
(c) to establish, keep up to date, publish and distribute every two years the Register;
(d) to monitor and supervise the implementation of this instrument;
(e) to cooperate with the Director-General of UNESCO in fulfilling the functions provided for in Article (...) of this instrument and in his performance of the mission of control according to the Regulations for the Execution of the Convention;
[(f) to decide on the use of the resources of the [Fund] established in accordance with Article (17A) of this instrument;]
(g) to perform any other function which may be attributed to it under this instrument or by States Parties;
[(h) to receive and study requests for international assistance formulated by States Parties under Article (...) of this draft with respect to ....];
[(i) to decide on the action to be taken with regard to requests for international assistance under Article (...) of this instrument, determine where appropriate, the nature and extent of its assistance, and authorize the conclusion, on its behalf, of the necessary arrangements with the government

drafting group also put into square brackets a second sub-paragraph concerning the participation of the International Committee of the Blue Shield, a coordinating body created in 1996 by the International Council of Museums (ICOM), the International Council on Monuments and Sites (ICOMOS), the International Council on Archives (ICA) and the International Federation of Library Associations and Institutions (IFLA), in the sessions of the Committee.

Option II of the above draft provisions provided in draft Article 14[22] for a creation of a six-member Bureau, elected by a meeting of States Parties on the occasion of the General Conference of UNESCO. While this Bureau would meet normally at least once a year, it might be convened by the Director-General at any other time, as necessary. It may also be supported in its work by the International Committee of the Blue Shield, which would act in an advisory capacity. The draft provisions stipulate that in either case the supervisory body would be serviced by UNESCO.

---

concerned;]

[(j) to draw up, keep up to date and publicize a list of projects and programmes under Article (....) of this instrument for which international assistance has been granted;]

[(k) to define the procedure by which requests to it for international assistance shall be considered;]

(l) to submit to the General Conference of UNESCO at each of the ordinary sessions a report on its activities;

2. The Committee shall cooperate with international and national governmental and non-governmental organizations having objectives similar to those of the Convention, its 1954 Protocol and this instrument and also may call upon individual experts.

[2. Representatives of the International Committee of the Blue Shield (ICBS) shall attend the Committee in an advisory capacity. A representative of the International Centre for the Study of the Preservation and Restoration of Cultural Property (Rome Centre) (ICCROM) shall also be invited to attend.].

Draft provisions for the revision of the 1954 Hague Convention and commentary from the UNESCO Secretariat, UNESCO Doc. CLT-97/CONF.208/2 (Paris, October 1997) pp. 19-20.

22. Art. 14 (Option II), Bureau, provides:

(a) The Director-General will call a meeting of States Parties to the Convention to be held at the same time as the General Conference of UNESCO.

(b) The meeting shall elect a Bureau, consisting of 6 States party to the Convention, with due regard to equitable representation of the different regions and cultures of the world. It shall elect a President and Rapporteur.

(c) The Bureau shall hold office for two years and shall hold at least one meeting each year. The Director-General of UNESCO may call the Bureau into session at any other time as he considers necessary.

(d) The Bureau shall adopt its own rules of procedure.

(e) Representatives of the International Committee of the Blue Shield (ICBS) shall attend the Bureau in an advisory capacity. A representative of the International Centre for the Study of the Preservation and Restoration of Cultural Property (Rome Centre) (ICCROM) shall be also invited to attend.

Draft provisions for the revision of the 1954 Hague Convention and commentary from the UNESCO Secretariat, UNESCO Doc. CLT-97/CONF.208/2 (Paris, October 1997) p. 23.

When comparing the advantages and disadvantages of both Options, the argument has been made that Option I, if adopted and if the Committee were composed of states having significant influence on international affairs, would largely enhance the protection of cultural heritage during hostilities, provided that states were willing to take the necessary administrative, legal and financial measures for the protection of cultural property in the event of armed conflict. It could result in systematic implementation of the Convention and the new provisions and reinvigorate the Convention. However, other views see drawbacks in this Option, suggesting that it would lead to an establishment of a new intergovernmental structure during a period of criticism of the United Nations and its Agencies and an effort to contract the international bureaucracy. It would be costly and put a new burden on an already understaffed Secretariat. Finally, it is suggested that conflict often involves many states indirectly and this could affect the efficiency of the Committee at the time when its advice is most necessary. A smaller advisory unit may be less subject to the tides of international politics, and a smaller group of states would be less expensive. States Parties at the forthcoming expert meeting(s) will have to decide between these arguments.[23]

23. The most recent meeting of the governmental experts on the revision of the Convention was held in Vienna from 11-13 May 1998. See Year in Review pp. 135-136.

THE ITALIAN LAW FOR THE BAN OF ANTI-PERSONNEL LANDMINES*

Pietro Gargiulo**

1. The adoption by the Italian parliament of Law No. 374 on 29 October 1997[1], entitled *Rules for the ban of anti-personnel land-mines,* formalizes the transformation of Italy from one of the major producers of such mines to one of the leaders of national and international initiatives for the ban of anti-personnel landmines.[2]

** Lecturer of International Organization – University of Teramo, Italy.

1. Hereafter, Law 374/1997. The Law is reproduced *infra* at p. 563. Law 374/1997 is the result of a legislative course that started with the introduction of four bills regarding a ban on anti-personnel mines at the Chamber of Deputies during the 13th Parliament. These bills were submitted for first consideration to the III Committee-Foreign and Community Affairs (hereafter III Committee), acting in a reporting capacity. The III Committee decided (17 December 1996) to establish an *ad hoc* Subcommittee, which was entrusted with the detailed analysis. The Committee held its last session on 8 May 1997, approving a consolidated draft bill accepted by the III Committee on 28 May 1997, in plenary meeting. On 31 July 1997, the III Committee, acting in a legislative capacity, unanimously approved the consolidated draft bill. The text was then transmitted to the Senate and assigned to the Defence Committee. On 24 September 1997, this Committee unanimously approved the consolidated draft bill, with only a few modifications. The text was then returned to the Chamber of Deputies, as modified by the Senate, and definitely adopted by a majority of votes, yet with a significant number of abstentions. The latter were mainly due to the weakening of the Law as a consequence of the changes introduced by the Senate (see *infra,* paragraphs 7 and 10). Cf. the texts of the various bills, the text of the consolidated draft bill approved by the Committee and the discussions at the Foreign Affairs Committee of the Chamber of Deputies and at the Defence Committee of the Senate, in Camera dei Deputati - Servizio Studi (Chamber of Deputies - Research Department), *Messa al bando delle mine antipersona* (Ban of Anti-Personnel mines), Dossier Provvedimento nn. 151/3 e 151/4, III Legislatura (Dossier Provision 151/3 and 151/4, 13th Parliament) giugno 1997 e ottobre 1997 (June 1997 and October 1997).

2. A few countries have adopted specific rules for the ban of anti-personnel mines, including Belgium (Law 9 March 1995, regarding anti-personnel mines, booby traps or similar devices) and Austria (Federal Law on the ban of anti-personnel mines, 1 January 1997. See the text in the English translation in UNGA, 52nd Session, Doc. A/52/91, 17 March 1997). The Austrian Law is

Yearbook of International Humanitarian Law
Volume 1 - 1998 - pp. 323-332

Since 1994, both the Italian government and parliament have been seized of this matter. On 2 August 1994, the Senate carried a motion according to which the government was invited to: ratify the Protocol on Prohibitions or Restrictions on the Use of Mines, Booby-Traps and Other Devices (hereafter, Protocol II) of the United Nations Convention on Prohibitions or Restrictions on the use of Certain Conventional Weapons Which May Be Deemed to Be Excessively Injurious or to Have Indiscriminate Effects[3] (hereinafter, 1980 Convention); provide adequate legal instruments to adopt a moratorium on the export of anti-personnel mines; stop production of those mines by any Italian company or companies operating in Italy and support the reconversion of workers in that sector; and promote demining in countries contaminated with anti-personnel mines. During the Senate debate, the government representative noted that export authorizations for anti-personnel mines had not been issued since November 1993, and that the government intended to observe a unilateral moratorium on the sale of anti-personnel mines to other countries and also wanted to adopt the necessary legal instruments for stopping production of such devices by any Italian company or companies operating on Italian territory.

After the ratification of the 1980 Convention on 3 October 1995, the Senate Defence Committee unanimously approved a resolution, accepted by the government, that committed the latter to promote, during the revision of the Convention, a total ban on anti-personnel mines, including those with self-neutralization mechanisms. Moreover, the government agreed to promote the extension and implementation of the Convention to non-international armed conflicts. Last but not least, it committed itself to introduce in Italy, notwithstanding the results of the revision Conference, a set of rules to prohibit production; stockpiling; research; exportation; selling; and use of mines.

Furthermore, during the LI Session of the United Nations General Assembly (26 September 1996), the Minister of Foreign Affairs, Lamberto Dini, stated that

---

reproduced *infra* at p. 561. However, a significant number of countries have adopted global moratoria on the production, selling and exportation of mines. See J. Williams, 'National Initiatives and Legislation to Limit and Restrict the Production, Use and Transfer of Land Mines', 28/29 *UNIDIR Newsletter*, (December 1994/May 1995) pp. 11-12. See also the reports of the Secretary-General of the United Nations, Doc. A/49/275 and Add.1, A/50/701 and A/51/313.

3. Italy signed the 1980 Convention on 10 April 1981 and inserted a declaration expressing great regret for the absence in the text of the Convention 'of an article on the establishment of a consultative committee of experts competent to verify facts which might be alleged and which might constitute violations of the undertakings subscribed to'. See United Nations, *Status of Multilateral Arms Regulation and Disarmament Agreement*, 4th edn., 1992, Vol. 1 (New York 1993) p. 263. Italy then ratified the 1980 Convention and the three annexed Protocols on 20 January 1995 (by Law No. 715, 14 December 1994). See Nations Unies, *Traités multilateraux déposés auprès du Secrétaire Général. Etat au 31 décembre 1996* (New York 1997) pp. 929-936.

'[t]he Italian government pledges to renounce, once and for all, the production and export of anti-personnel land-mines. We will also initiate the destruction of existing devices and promote further restrictions, in the hope that such measures will contribute to reaching a solid international understanding and a definitive ban'[4].

The commitment of the Italian government, both at the national and international level, to interrupt the production of mines, had already yielded satisfactory results before Law 374/1997 was introduced, if we only consider that the latter had no need to include any refund or financial support for the industrial reorganization of companies of the sector. Between 1994 and 1996, the largest Italian mine-manufacturing companies were enabled to gain access to the national and European instruments devised to protect occupation and support industrial reorganization. Therefore, before the discussion on new rules for the ban of anti-personnel landmines ended, those companies had just completed the industrial reorganization process.[5]

The parliamentary proceedings concerning Law 374/1997 coincided with the emergence, at an international level, of increased awareness of and attention to the problems caused by landmines, especially in the aftermath of conflicts, and an increase in efforts to reform existing international law in order to limit the production and indiscriminate use of those weapons.[6]

4. See UNGA, Fifty-first Session, 10th Plenary meeting, 26 September 1996, Doc. A/51/PV. 10.

5. Nearly all the bills introduced to the Chamber of Deputies comprised references to financial support for the industrial reconversion of the Italian mine-manufacturing companies. By the time of the consideration and drafting of the consolidated draft bill in the III Committee of the Chamber of Deputies, these provisions had become redundant. See the documents cited *supra* at n. 1.

6. The development of adequate international rules began with the revision of the 1980 Convention and its Protocol II and continued with the adoption in Oslo on 18 September 1997 of the Convention on the Prohibition of the Use, Stockpiling, Production and Transfer of Anti-personnel Mines and on Their Destruction (hereafter Oslo Convention). For a discussion of this process, see Goose, *supra* p. 269. For the text of the Oslo Convention see *infra* p. 539. The Review Conference of the States Parties to the 1980 Convention was held in Vienna from 25 September to 13 October 1995, and in Geneva, from 15 to 19 January 1996, and from 22 April to 3 May 1996. The Final Report, Documents and Summary Records of the Conference are reproduced in CCW/CONF. I/16 (Part. I) and (Part II), Geneva, 1996. For a recent analysis of the international law on mines, see J.E. Lord, 'Legal Restraints in the Use of Landmines: Humanitarian and Environmental Crisis', 25 *California Western International Law Journal* (1995) pp. 311-355; A. H. Petrarca, 'An Impetus of Human Wreckage?: The 1996 Amended Landmine Protocol', 27 *California Western International Law Journal* (1996) pp. 205-239; M. A. Ferrer, 'Affirming Our Common Humanity: Regulating Landmines to Protect Civilians and Children in the Developing World', 20 *Hastings International and Comparative Law Review* (1996) pp. 135-182; M. Bettati, 'L'interdiction ou la limitation d'emploi des mines (Le Protocole de Genève du 3 mai 1996)', XLII *AFDI* (1996) pp. 187-205; V. A. Bogomolov, 'Some Legal Aspects of Landmine Prohibition or Limitation'. *International Law*

An intense and unremitting international campaign, conducted by hundreds of NGOs, managed to awaken vast sectors of public opinion, as well as to press a significant number of governments to adopt concrete measures to ban anti-personnel landmines.[7]

2. The Italian Law for the ban of anti-personnel landmines was inspired, in part, by humanitarian considerations arising from the dissemination and use of mines.[8] The most reliable assessments consider that currently about 110 million landmines have been sown in 64 countries, two thirds in the last two decades. These weapons kill an estimated 10,000 people per year, more than 90 percent of whom are civilians, and maim or injure more than 10,000 others.[9] These data clearly show that landmines are one of the most widespread, lethal, and long-lasting means of combat, with a devastating impact on civilian populations.

Another consideration was the great costs/benefits disproportion related to the production of mines. From this perspective, landmines do not represent a very advantageous business for arms manufacturers. Most landmines are very inexpensive and very easy to produce, with little profits for manufacturers. On the other hand, the life cycle costs of landmines, that is, the cost of their removal and of the long-term socio-economic problems they create, is extremely high.[10] Altogether, the low costs of landmines generate scarce benefits for companies that produce and sell mines, while the burden of their indiscriminate use weighs on the international community as a whole.[11]

Bulletin (Russia and CIS), (1/1997) pp. 26-27.

7. The coalition of more than 1,000 NGOs played a very important role that was also internationally recognized in 1997, when the Nobel Peace Prize was awarded to the International Campaign to Ban Landmines and formally to its coordinator, Jody Williams.

8. There is a long list of papers on this issue. Following are only some of the most important: Human Rights Watch Arms Project and Physicians for Human Rights, *Landmines: A Deadly Legacy* (Human Rights Watch and Physicians for Human Rights, USA, 1993); U.S. Department of State, *Hidden Killers: The Global Landmines Crisis* (1994); Handicap International, *Mines antipersonnel, la guerre en temps de paix* (Éd. Complexe, Paris 1996).

9. See D. Gowdey, 'The Land Mines Crisis: The Humanitarian Dimension', 28/29 *UNIDIR Newsletter* (December 1994/May 1995) pp. 17-19.

10. See S. Goose, 'The Economics of Land Mines', 28/29 *UNIDIR Newsletter* (December 1994/May 1995) pp. 13-16.

11. The United Nations estimated that in 1993 the international community spent about $70 million to clear roughly 100,000 landmines. In 1994 the UN Secretary-General underlined that $60-100 million will be necessary to expand existing demining operations and start new ones in other countries. See UNGA, *Assistance in mine clearance*, Report of the Secretary-General, A/49/357, 6 September 1997.

Finally, a further element that has weighed is the insignificant tactical value of these weapons, compared to the damage they cause. During the parliamentary debates, an important study by the ICRC was frequently quoted to demonstrate the negligible military usefulness of landmines, while a more effective tactical defence system could be achieved through alternative means – often even more useful for tactical-strategic purposes – such as fencings, barrages, better observation technologies and intelligence.[12]

3. The primary objective of Law 374/1997 is to provide an effective legal framework for the ban of anti-personnel mines, as well as to restrict all those activities connected with mine production which had actually weakened the political commitment undertaken with the 1994 moratorium on production and exportation.

Article 1(1) and (2) of the Law not only prohibits the use of antipersonnel mines but also restricts technological research; manufacturing; selling; transfer; export; import; and stockpiling of any type and composition of these weapons or their components. The sole exception to the use of landmines permits a fixed quantity for exclusive use in demining operations training.[13]
Moreover, paragraph 3 prohibits the use and transfer of patent rights for the manufacture of anti-personnel mines or their components, as well as the technologies suitable to the production of such weapons.

4. Article 2 of Law 374/1997 defines *anti-personnel mine*. An anti-personnel mine is to be considered any means, munition or device placed on, under, inside or near the ground or any surface area, which is designed to explode or to release incapacitating substances as a consequences of the presence, proximity or contact of a person. This definition also includes devices which release incapacitating substances other than explosives.

The disposition does not refer to anti-tank mines explicitly. It may be useful to remember that the consolidated draft bill on this matter, which was adopted by the *ad hoc* Subcommittee of the Chamber of Deputies' Foreign Affairs Committee, referred directly to anti-tank mines as an example of devices suitable to explode consequent to the presence, proximity or contact of a person.[14] We do not consider the missing explicit reference to anti-tank mines in Law 374/1997

12. See International Committee of the Red Cross, *Anti-Personnel Landmines - friend or Foe? A Study of the Military Use and Effectiveness of Anti-Personnel Mines* (International Committee of Red Cross, Geneva, 1996). See also S.D. Biddle and J. Klare, 'Military Utility and the Control of Land Mines', 28/29 *UNIDIR Newsletter* (December 1994/May 1995) pp. 22-24.

13. See *infra* section 6.

14. For the consolidated draft bill, see the documents cited *supra* at n. 1.

as a limitation on its definition of anti-personnel mines. Actually, the Law states that anti-personnel mines are to be considered 'any munition or device...designed or *adaptable* – by means of specific mechanisms – so as to explode...' [emphasis added]. It is, therefore, necessary to interpret Article 2 as comprising also those anti-tank mines that by means of mechanical or other devices may be calibrated to explode under a minimum pressure and weight.[15]

This represents a very significant aspect of Law 374/1997, because so many anti-tank mines are easily convertible into anti-personnel mines. The exclusion of those mines would have been a substantial limitation on a new and up-to-date set of rules on the ban of these weapons.

5. Articles 3 and 4 establish specific obligations for possessors of mines, patent rights and technologies necessary to manufacture anti-personnel landmines. Those who hold mines are compelled to report and disclose the number of mines and their components to the competent local authorities, and to deliver them all to appropriate sites as indicated by the competent authorities. In accordance with Article 5, all devices handed over by producing companies and other possessors are to be destroyed within five years from the entry into force of the Law.

Those who hold patent rights and technologies necessary to produce mines and their components are obliged to report the fact to the Ministry of Industry and Trade.

6. As for the mines held or stocked by the Armed Forces, the first paragraph of Article 5 provides for their destruction within five years of the entry into force of the Law, excepting a limited amount not exceeding 10,000 units, to be used exclusively for demining operations training.

The same article, derogating from Article 1(2), provides for the integration with new mines imported from abroad of the stockpiles used for training.

At first, the bill approved by the III Committee of the Chamber of Deputies established that the amount of mines held for demining operations training was

15. We believe that the interpretation given to this text is confirmed by Parliament's proceedings regarding Law 374/1997. See the Dossier Provvedimento (Dossier Provision) No. 151/3 cited *supra* at n. 1, pp. 24-55. A confirmation of the correct interpretation derives from the authoritative statement of Hon. Achille Occhetto, President of the III Committee of the Chamber of Deputies: 'The scope of the definition is so extensive, as to include all sort of anti-handling and other mechanical devices – *as well as those anti-tank mines that can be easily adjusted to explode under the weight of a child...*' [emphasis added] in the introduction of Law 374/1977 to the Conference of Ottawa (3-4 December 1997). See Rules for the Ban of Anti-Personnel Mines, Italian Law No. 374, 29 October 1997, with Foreword by Achille Occhetto, Chairman of the Foreign Affairs Committee, Italian Chamber of Deputies, document prepared by the Italian Society for International Organization (Rome, 1997) p. 3.

to be 'limited' and 'not renewable', and in any case not more than 200,000 units. The Senate modified the provision on this particular point, reducing the Armed Forces' fixed stock to 10,000 mines, but making it renewable through importation.

The change introduced by the Senate was the subject of a lively discussion during its review by the Chamber of Deputies. In particular, if, on the one hand, the speakers generally appreciated the reduction in the number of mines for training activities, on the other hand, they noted that the amount still exceeded that indicated by the Oslo Convention.[16] Moreover, many criticized the fact that it had become possible to renew the stock through importation, thus derogating from Article 1(2).[17]

Although approved by the Chamber of Deputies with the changes introduced by the Senate, the question of stockpiles for demining operations training, together with other matters[18], was the subject of a recommendation, approved contextually with the Law. This states that the Chamber of Deputies commits the government to interpret the indication of a maximum of 10,000 mines in Article 5 in the most restrictive terms, and to evaluate the opportunity of keeping no more than 3,000 units in accordance with the provisions of the Oslo Convention.[19] Furthermore, the recommendation approved by the III Committee commits the government to interpret the possibility of renewing the stock of mines to be used for training activities in the most restrictive terms, excluding the possibility of exceeding the limit of 500 new mines per year.

Article 6, which is related to Article 5, provides for the issuance, within six months, of a decree by the Ministry of Defence outlining the rules for the destruction of the stockpiles, taking into account the environment protection exigencies.

This decree should select the structures, be they military or private, where the destruction of the mines should take place. It should also determine the Ministry of Defence's Office responsible for recording quantity and types of mines held by the Armed Forces and those handed over in accordance with Article 3, as well as the dates and means of their destruction.

16. Art. 3 of the Oslo Convention states that the amount of anti-personnel mines for the development of and training in mine detection, mine clearance or mine destruction techniques, shall not exceed the *minimum number absolutely necessary* for those purposes. During negotiations, there were different opinions concerning the exact amount, but all well below 10,000 units: Germany proposed 3,000 mines, while Canada and Belgium proposed 1,500.

17. See Camera dei Deputati, XIII Legislatura, III Commissione-Affari Esteri e Comunitari, Seduta del 22 ottobre 1997 [Chamber of Deputies, 13th Parliament, III Committee-Foreign and Community Affairs, sitting of 22 October 1997].

18. See *infra* section 9.

19. See the document cited *supra* at n. 17.

The same Office must register the data, as provided for by Article 4, concerning patent rights and technologies.

7. Non-compliance with the prohibitions and obligations set by Law 374/1997 is sanctioned by Article 7 with utmost severity: three to twelve years of imprisonment and fines from 200 to 500 million Italian lira for those unobservant of the prohibition to produce, sell, transfer, export or import anti-personnel mines or their components, as well as the use or transfer of patent rights or technologies for their production, and three to six years of imprisonment and fines from 200 to 500 million lira for non-compliance with obligations set by Articles 3 and 4, concerning possessors of mines or patent rights and technologies necessary to manufacture such devices. The sanctions of Article 7 have been tightened up and integrated in the final text through the determination, in paragraph 2, of an additional sanction that bans guilty parties from all public contracts for a period ranging from five to ten years. This could be a particularly effective deterrent for the companies of the sector.

8. Article 8 is significant as it supports anti-personnel mines victims through compensation, assistance and rehabilitation programmes. These activities are part of Italy's Cooperation for Development policy. This explains the editing of Article 8, which is actually a modification of the Italian Law for Cooperation with Developing Countries and an integration of the current cooperation activities, which now also comprise assistance to victims of anti-personnel mines.[20]

To be precise, this form was meant to avoid the indication of a specific allocation of funds in Law 374/1997, which, in consideration of the present lack of financial resources allocated for Cooperation with Developing Countries, would have been surely inadequate for the exigencies of anti-personnel mines victims. Article 8 instead makes it possible to evaluate and finance the activities in favour of these victims in the context of the reform proposals of the entire Cooperation sector.

9. As to the measures to control the implementation of Law 374/1997, therein including the connected destruction of stockpiles, Article 9 provides for coordination between the competent Ministries (Foreign Affairs, Defence, Industry and Trade). In particular, these Ministries will report to the competent

20. Art. 8 of Law 374/1997 integrates Art. 2(3) of Law No. 49, 26 February 1997, adding to the existing Cooperation activities 'support in favour of anti-personnel mines victims through compensation, assistance and rehabilitation programmes'.

Parliamentary Committees every six months on the state of implementation of the Law.

Moreover, Article 8 obliges the Ministry of Defence to provide a yearly account of the ongoing destruction of stockpiles and related expenses and budget.

As to the control mechanisms, one should note that the first bill approved by the III Committee of the Chamber of Deputies established a Parliamentary Committee, in order to control, set guidelines and verify the correct implementation of the Law. This Committee would have had particular inspection powers in: examining register activities of military arsenals and of other mine-holders; examining destruction procedures; verifying, in the same plants of mine manufacturing companies or elsewhere, compliance with the Law; controlling the correct use of financial resources devoted to the specific finalities set by the Law. The Committee would also have had particular powers otherwise reserved to commissions of inquiry, such as the cooperation of the criminal investigation police employed in a judicial function. The establishment of a Committee of this kind followed the model of control and verification mechanisms of the Convention on Chemical Weapons, that, because of its different systems of inspection, is commonly acknowledged as the most advanced international instrument as to verification mechanisms.

The elimination from the Law of this Committee was decided by the Senate. The clear intention was to avoid the proliferation of bicameral organs that subtract competence from Standing Committees and infer the Parliament's functionality. During the final vote by the Chamber of Deputies on the Law, this change was loudly criticized and ultimately included in the above-mentioned recommendation.[21] The latter asks the competent Ministers to provide updated and precise information – especially concerning mine-destruction activities – to the Standing Parliamentary Committees, when reporting every six months.

10. The Law ends with Article 10, which is of great importance in consideration of military and security questions related to anti-personnel mines. This article excludes absolutely the application of the Laws on State Secrets and on Military Secrets[22] from the discipline of this Law for the Ban of Anti-Personnel Mines.

21. See *supra* section 6.

22. State Secrets are regulated by Law No. 801, 24 October 1977 and by No. 202 and 256 of the Code of Criminal Procedure; Military Secrets are regulated by the Royal Decree No. 1161, 11 July 1941.

11. As already mentioned above[23], when the Law was definitely adopted, it had lost the unanimous consent that characterized its process. This was mainly due to the weakening of the Law that some Members of the Chamber of Deputies ascribed, on one hand, to the failure to establish a steering and implementation control committee and, on the other hand, the derogation, provided for by Article 5, from the prohibition to import mines for demining operations training. In particular, the latter seems to conflict with the main objective of the Law, that is, to guarantee the ban of anti-personnel mines – not only in Italy, but worldwide – because, even if it serves the need to practice demining, it legitimates the production of these weapons in other countries.

These aspects are only relatively mitigated by the recommendation of the Chamber of Deputies that commits the government to interpret the indications on importation in the most restrictive terms and guarantee maximum information on the implementation of the Law to the Standing Parliamentary Committees. It is, in any case, a political and not a juridical commitment.

Notwithstanding these few points, the parliament's initiative must be judged positively. Law 374/1997 represents a relevant model for other countries to follow in order to ban anti-personnel mines and make humanitarian exigencies prevail over military needs.

23. See *supra* n. 1.

COMMENTARY ON PROTOCOL IV ON BLINDING LASER WEAPONS*

Markus C. Zöckler**

1. INTRODUCTION

On the modern battlefield, lasers are employed for a variety of military tasks, including rangefinding, target designation, jamming or destruction of optical or electro-optical systems.[1] Sweden and the ICRC, in particular, alerted the international community to the fact that many existing and currently developed laser systems might well be used to blind enemy combatants. They argued that intentional blinding causes unnecessary suffering and pushed for an international agreement which would explicitly prohibit the use of lasers for blinding as a method of warfare.[2] More than 20 years after the first discussions about regulation of laser weapons, the Review Conference of States Parties to the UN Conventional Weapons Convention adopted Protocol IV on Blinding Laser Weapons on 13 October 1995.[3]

** Wissenschaftlicher Assistant, Institüt für Völkerrecht, Universität München, BRD.

1. For an overview of such laser employments, see M. Hewish, 'Battlefield Lasers', 2 *International Defense Review* (1995) pp. 39-44; J. Hecht, *Beam Weapons - The Next Arms Race* (1984); B. Anderberg & M. Wolbarsht, *Laser Weapons - The Dawn of a New Military Age* (1992); A. O'Leary, ed., *Jane's Electro-Optic Systems*, 3rd edn., 1997.

2. L. Doswald-Beck, ed., *Blinding Weapons* - Reports of the Meetings of Experts Convened by the International Committee of the Red Cross on Battlefield Laser Weapons 1989-1991 (1993); Human Rights Watch Arms Project, 'Blinding Laser Weapons - The Need to Ban a Cruel and Inhumane Weapon' (September 1995).

3. For the text of Protocol IV, see *infra* p. 594.

Yearbook of International Humanitarian Law
Volume 1 - 1998 - pp. 333-340

2. PROTOCOL ON BLINDING LASER WEAPONS

The negotiations on blinding lasers at the Preparatory Conference of Government Experts[4] and the Vienna Session of the Review Conference[5] were dominated by two distinct approaches towards regulation of laser systems: Whereas Sweden and the ICRC advocated a ban on blinding as a method of warfare, other states (in particular, the US) lobbied for a narrow definition of prohibited blinding laser systems which would exempt legitimate employments of lasers for, *inter alia*, rangefinding, target designation or attacks on optical or electro-optical systems.

The Blinding Laser Weapons Protocol adopted at the Vienna session of the Review Conference[6] constitutes a compromise between these two approaches: Article 1 establishes a general prohibition on the use of a specifically defined type of laser system and Article 3 serves as a corollary exemption for legitimate employments of lasers; the obligation to take precautions to avoid blinding, demanded by Article 2, on the other hand, seems to presuppose a ban on anti-personnel uses of lasers.

2.1 The Definition of Blindness (Article 4)

Laser radiation with a wavelength of 400-1400 nm ('retinal hazard zone') will result in dazzling and, above certain thresholds, in retinal lesions and possibly haemorrhages. Laser beams operating in the ultraviolet or far infra-red parts of the electromagnetic spectrum can damage lens and/or cornea. Whereas deep corneal damage and cataracts can be treated, any destruction of the retina is irreversible, uncorrectable and permanent.[7]

In order to meet the interest (especially of the US) in ideally quantifiable criteria, the term 'seriously disabling' has been defined by adopting the WHO definition of blindness. However, the Snellen test used in the WHO definition measures contrast sensitivity whereas laser injuries lead to a complete loss of

4. The Preparatory Conference held four sessions between February 1994 and January 1995. See Final Report of the Group of Governmental Experts to Prepare the Review Conference, Doc. CCW/CONF.I/GE/23.

5. On the Vienna Conference, see the partially diverging accounts of these negotiations by W. Hays Parks, '*Travaux Préparatoires* and Legal Analysis of Blinding Laser Weapons Protocol', *The Army Lawyer* (June 1997) pp. 33-41; L. Doswald-Beck, 'Le nouveau Protocole sur les armes à laser aveuglantes', *RICR* (1996) pp. 289-321.

6. The Protocol entered into force on 30 July 1998 in accordance with Article 2 of the Additional Protocol.

7. On the ophthalmological aspects of laser radiation see e.g., B. Stuck & M. Belkin, eds., 'Laser-Inflicted Eye Injuries' (SPIE-Proceedings Vol. 2674, 1996); B. Stuck & A. Katzir, eds., 'Laser and Noncoherent Ocular Effects' (SPIE-Proceedings Vol. 2974, 1997).

vision in the affected portions of the retina. The degree of visual impairment depends on the location of these blind spots. Major retinal lesions in the fovea or macula will not allow a person to read, drive a car etc.; a visual impairment which may be regarded as equivalent to a visual acuity of 20/200 Snellen.[8]

2.2 Prohibited Laser Systems (Article 1)

The term 'weapon' might have been deliberately chosen to exclude such lasers which were not designed for anti-matériel or anti-personnel uses. At the same time, participants at the Vienna Conference were well aware that a variety of other laser systems primarily employed in auxiliary functions such as rangefinding or target designation are quite often also capable of producing permanent blindness in the sense of Article 4.[9] This dual capacity is explicitly acknowledged in Article 1 in the phrase 'as one of their combat functions'.

As the Vienna Conference was unable to reach an agreement on a specific definition[10], the term 'weapon' must be interpreted within the systematic context of general humanitarian law. Under the general law of warfare, however, a prohibtion of use is based on the unlawful effects of a means or method of warfare regardless of whether a weapon is employed or something else is used 'as a weapon'.[11]

Any such laser weapon must be capable of producing 'permanent blindness' to unenhanced vision, i.e., the respective laser should at least have sufficient power to produce serious retinal lesions in the unaided (and unprotected) eye at ordinary battlefield distances and atmospheric conditions. These are objective criteria which can be assessed for every laser system on the basis of its technical parameters. Those laser systems which are designed *exclusively* for the purpose of blinding could be identified because they lack certain components or the emitted laser beam shows characteristics which are inadequate for the performance of any other legitimate military function.

For laser systems with a potential dual capacity for blinding and some other legitimate military purpose, some commentators interpret the phrase 'specifically

8. Cf. testimony of the ophthalmologist Prof. Marshall at the Vienna Review Conference, see L. Doswald-Beck, op. cit. n. 5, at p. 315 et seq.

9. On the ocular hazards of existing laser systems, see J. Wolfe, 'Laser Retinal Injury', 150 *Military Medicine* (1985) pp. 177-185; J. Mellerio et al., 'Battlefield laser weapons: an assessment of systems, hazards, injuries and ophthalmic resources required for treatment', 4 *Laser and Light in Ophthalmology* (1991) pp. 41-67.

10. Only the Austrian delegation had proposed an explicit definition of the term 'weapon'. See Doc. CCW/CONF.I/MCIII/WP.2 (26 September 1995), Art. 2.

11. C. Greenwood, 'Battlefield laser weapons in the context of the law on conventional weapons', in Doswald-Beck, op. cit. n. 2, p. 71, at p. 73.

designed' to require an intentional element, i.e., blinding must be one of the intended combat functions of such a system.[12] Such an interpretive approach leaves important questions unanswered: Whose intentions are relevant – those of the designer, the state organs responsible for the appropriation of the system or even the potential users? What kind of *mens rea* would be required? Most important from a humanitarian perspective, as the relevant intentions can only be proved on the basis of documents and pronouncements of state organs on a suspect laser system, a meaningful implementation of Article 1 (including the prohibition of transfer!) would entirely depend on good faith attitudes of the states parties.[13]

However, a grammatical interpretation of 'specifically designed' does not necessarily require an element of intent. For example, even the formula 'calculated to cause', in the unfortunate English translation of Article 23(e) of the Hague Regulations Respecting the Laws and Customs of War on Land (1907) has been interpreted as equivalent to the expression 'of a nature to cause'. Hence, the expression 'specifically designed' might well be interpreted in an objective way, i.e., the specific design enables a laser systems to be used in combat for the purpose of blinding. On the basis of a broad conception of 'weapon' in the context of general humanitarian law and the suggested objective interpretation of 'specifically designed', all laser systems with a capacity for blinding would be covered by the prohibition of use in Article 1. This approach could thus escape the pitfalls of the notion of intent which would relegate the observance of Article 1 entirely to the uncontrollable auto-interpretation of the states parties.

2.3 Legitimate Employments of Laser Systems (Article 3)

The suggested interpretation of Article 1 would not ignore the intention of those drafters of the Protocol who wanted to allow the use of lasers for purposes such as rangefinding, jamming, target designation, etc., since Article 3 still explicitly exempts such legitimate employments of laser systems, including attacks on optical and electro-optical systems.

12. See e.g., Hays Parks, loc. cit. n. 5, at p. 37.

13. So far only China North Industries Corp. has publicly advertised that one of the major applications of its ZM-87 laser system would be 'by high power laser pulses, to injure or dizzy the eyes of an enemy combatant', see Cook, 'Chinese laser "blinder" weapon for export', 23 *Jane's Defence Weekly* (27 May 1995) at p. 3. Even more disturbing than this anouncement as such is the prediction 'now that an international standard against deliberate blinding has been adopted, such advertising can be expected to cease', B. Carnahan & M. Robertson, 'The Protocol on "Blinding Laser Weapons"', 90 *AJIL* (1996) p. 484 (at p. 489).

As the Protocol itself does not present a definition of 'legitimate' employment, this term may reasonably be interpreted as a direct reference to general standards of international humanitarian law on the uses of laser systems (see *infra* section 3). From the systematic context of Article 3 with the general prohibition of blinding lasers (Art. 1) and the obligation to take precautions to avoid the incidence of blinding (Art. 2), one can infer that blinding of combatants as the primary purpose of a use of lasers is regarded as illegitimate.[14]

The terms 'incidental' or 'collateral' presuppose that there must be a main purpose for a specific use of a weapon the realization of which will, on occasion or even inevitably, cause blindness as an unintended side effect. Hence, any legitimate use requires, first, that the weapon system in question must at least be capable of achieving its main purpose and, secondly, is indeed employed for the realization of this main purpose. From this follows, for the critical issue of the use of lasers against optics, that anti-optic lasers may only be legitimately employed if they have sufficient energy to destroy or incapacitate the targeted optical system. In those cases of an anti-optical use, however, where the laser beam leaves the optical system intact, merely passes through the respective optical train and injures the eye behind the optics, blinding is not an incidental or collateral but the main and only possible effect.[15]

2.4 Precautions for the Employment of Laser Systems (Article 2)

The negotiations on Article 2 were particularly complicated because many delegations favoured an explicit prohibition of blinding as a method of warfare whereas others opposed the allegedly ambiguous phrase 'method of warfare' and feared unpredictable war crimes charges against soldiers using laser systems.[16] The present version, adopted at the final meeting of Committee III, places an obligation on the States Parties to avoid the incidence of blinding, which includes education and training of military personnel. In essence, Article 2 contains an

14. In a letter to Congressman Evans, US Secretary of Defence Perry confirmed that '. . . [u]nder both the CCW and DoD policy, laser weapons designed specifically to cause permanent blindness may not be used against an individual enemy combatant', Letter of 8 May 1996 (on file at Human Rights Watch, Washington, D.C). See also Memorandum from the Secretary of Defence, dated 17 January 1997, prohibiting the use of laser weapons 'specificially designed to cause permanent blindness', *infra* p. 595.

15. Such lasers do not qualify as anti-optic lasers but are in fact anti-personnel lasers. Other commentators seem to reject any anti-optical use of lasers and do not exempt lasers capable of incapacitating optical systems, cf. A. Peters, 'Blinding Laser Weapons', 18 *Loy. L.A. Int'l & Comp. L.J.* (1996) p. 733 (at p. 757 et seq.); Doswald-Beck, loc. cit. n. 5, at p. 314.

16. See the report of the negotiations in Doswald-Beck, loc. cit. n. 5, at p. 316 et seq.

implicit recognition that blinding of individual combatants is an illegitimate use of laser systems.

Within the systematic context of Articles 1 and 3, this obligation applies only to 'legitimate' employments of lasers, not targeting the eyesight of individual combatants. The structure of Article 2 *mutatis mutandis* shows significant parallels with the precautions required in performing attacks against military targets with collateral effects on civilian people and objects.[17]

Although no specific examples were given, 'other practical measures' might include an obligation of states to develop or acquire eye-safe laser systems for military tasks which do not require lasers operating in the retinal hazard zone.[18]

2.5 Prohibited Transfers of Laser Systems (Article 1)

The prohibition of transfer *prima facie* hinges entirely on the definition of the prohibited laser system in the first sentence of Article 1 and poses no difficulties with regard to lasers exclusively designed for blinding. For lasers with a dual capacity, however, Article 3 states that certain legitimate employments are not 'covered by the prohibition [singular!] of this Protocol', although Article 1 contains an explicit prohibition not only of the use but also of the transfer of blinding lasers. If such laser systems with a dual capacity are excluded from the prohibition of use in Article 1, it seems reaonable to conclude that these systems are also excluded from the prohibition of transfer since they perform legitimate military functions.

2.6 The Scope of Protocol IV

At the Vienna Conference, many states seemed to be willing to apply the Laser Protocol in all kinds of armed conflicts or even all circumstances. The issue was postponed to the follow-up meeting in Geneva where the revised mines protocol was extended to all armed conflicts, but negotiations on the scope of the laser protocol were not reopened. Hence, the scope of the Laser Protocol is defined *de lege lata* by Article 1 of the 1981 Convention on Prohibitions or Restrictions of Certain Conventional Weapons Which May be Deemed to be Excessively Injurious or to Have Indiscriminate Effects. Upon signature or ratification, however, some states declared unilaterally that they would apply the protocol

17. See Art. 57 et seq. and Art. 85 et seq. of Additional Protocol I on precautionary measures and criminal charges for violations of these provisions.

18. 'Where there is an eye-safe solution available today it should replace any older, unsafe system. Not only would this guarantee compliance with the protocol, it would also represent the best practice the industry offers,' A. O'Leary, *Jane's Electro-optic Systems*, 3rd edn. (1997) p. 11.

in all armed conflicts or in all circumstances or even asserted that the subject matter of the protocol required such broader application.[19] These statements confirm a growing *opinio juris* that prohibitions of means or methods of warfare must be observed in all types of armed conflict including civil disturbances: '[E]lementary considerations of humanity and common sense make it preposterous that the use by States of weapons prohibited in armed conflicts between themselves be allowed when States try to put down rebellion by their own nationals on their own territory.'[20]

3. PROTOCOL IV AND GENERAL HUMANITARIAN LAW

Many voices have argued that blinding with lasers constitutes a violation of the general principle prohibiting unnecessary suffering.[21] Even after the entry into force of the Laser Protocol, a review of laser systems under legal rules of general humanitarian law will remain critical for several reasons: Universal acceptance of the Protocol cannot be expected; major states with advanced capabilities in military laser research and development (e.g., USA, Russia, Israel, China etc.) have not yet ratified the Protocol; and, most important, the phrase 'legitimate' employment in Article 3 must interpreted in the broader context of general humanitarian law.

A broad consensus exists that the application of the general prohibition of unnecessary suffering requires a balancing of military and humanitarian interests.[22] Under closer scrutiny, the past interpretative practice reveals that

19. For example, the declarations of Australia, Germany, Greece, Ireland, Liechtenstein, Sweden and Switzerland.

20. ICTY, Appeals Chamber, *Tadić* Case (No. IT-94-1-AR72), Decision on the defence motion for interlocutory appeal on jurisdiction (2 October 1995), reprinted in 16 *HRLJ* (1995), p. 437 (at 462, para. 119). See also Turku-Declaration of Minimum Humanitarian Standards, reprinted in Report of the Sub-Commission on Prevention of Discrimination and Protection of Minorities on its 45th Session, Commission on Human Rights, 51st Sess., Provisional Agenda Item 19, p. 4, UN-Doc. E/CN.4/1995/116 (1995).

21. See e.g., A. Cassese, 'Weapons Causing Unnecessary Suffering: Are They Prohibited?', *Rivista di Diritto Internazionale* (1975) p. 12 (at p. 40); L. Hannikainen, *Peremptory Norms* (1988) p. 701 et seq.; E. David, *Principes de droit des conflits armés* (1994) p. 273 et seq.; B. Anderberg & O. Bring, 'Battlefield Laser Weapons and International Law', 57 *Nordic Journal of International Law* (1988) pp. 457-469.

22. For a more detailed analysis of the prohibition of unnecessary suffering as applied to the use of laser systems see M. Zöckler, *Das Verbot unnötiger Leiden und der Einsatz personenschädigender Lasersysteme* (forthcoming).

humanitarian interests had a much stronger weight in this equation whenever human beings were the targets of a new weapon as opposed to anti-matériel weapons.[23] As regards the anti-personnel use of laser systems, the probability of permanent disablement and the severity of blindness will most likely outweigh the marginal advantages of laser systems as compared to other options of putting enemy combatants *hors de combat*. In short, plausible arguments have been presented that the intentional blinding of individual combatants violates the prohibition of unnecessary suffering of general humanitarian law.

23. This distinction has been reaffirmed in the discussions on blinding laser weapons. See 'Blinding Weapons under the Laws on Armed Conflict. Working Paper Submitted by the Netherlands', Doc. CCW/CONF.I/MCIII/WP.1, at p. 6 et seq.

THE *PRIEBKE* EXTRADITION CASE BEFORE THE ARGENTINE SUPREME COURT*

José Alejandro Consigli**

In early 1995, Italy ordered the extradition from Argentina to Italy of Erich Priebke.[1] The request was made on the basis of an arrest petition against Priebke issued by the Judge in charge of the preliminary investigation before the Military Justice of Rome. Priebke was accused of 'having been a member of the German Army, an enemy of the Italian State, in cooperation with . . . other German soldiers, with . . . executive action of . . . criminal design and acting with cruelty on people . . . causing the death of 335 people most of them Italian citizens, military men and civilian people who were not taking part in military operations, and premeditated shooting some shots against them, in "Cave Ardeatine", Rome, on 24 March 1944 during the time of the war between Italy and Germany.'[2]

The Court of First Instance allowed the extradition.

On Appeal, the Appeals Court rejected it, finding that the charge of homicide was prescripted and did not meet the dual requirements of the crime: that it be a crime under the law of both the requesting and requested state.

On 2 November 1995, the Argentine Supreme Court approved the extradition (5 for; 3 against).[3]

One of the votes in favour, signed by Judges Boggiano and López, considered that the fact that Priebke was required for trial in Italy established *prima facie* the crime of genocide 'for killing 75 Jews of out 335 dead'. It stated that the criminal qualification of crimes against humanity does not depend on the will

** Assistant Professor of Public International Law, University of Buenos Aires and a member of the Institute of International Law of the Argentine Counsel for International Relations.

1. By Order No. XXX.

2. Arrest petition signed by Judge Giusseppe Mazzi, Rome, 9 May 1994.

3. Sentence of the Argentine Supreme Court on Erich Priebke's Extradition Request. Case 16.063/94, 2 November 1995. For details, see *infra* p. 404.

Yearbook of International Humanitarian Law
Volume I - 1998 - pp. 341-343

of states, but on the principle of *jus cogens*, and there is no prescription of these kind of crimes.

Another vote in favour, signed by Judges Nazareno and Moliné O'Connor, considered that the qualification of the crime as homocide by the Italian Judge does not limit the possibility of it being regarded by the required state just *nomem juris* (a name of the law; a technical legal term) and, thus, the required state can go to the substance of the infraction. With this proposition, they left aside the rules of the Argentine Penal and Military Codes, and they put the crimes committed by Priebke under Articles 129 and 130 of the Third Geneva Convention of 1949, Articles 146 and 147 of the Fourth Geneva Convention and Article 75 of Protocol I Additional to the Geneva Conventions. The Judges regarded these crimes as serious infractions of these conventions and as war crimes (in accordance with Art. 85(5) of Protocol I) (*'without prejudice to the application of the Conventions and of this Protocol, grave breaches of these instruments shall be regarded as war crimes'*).

The Judges asserted that there was a concurrence of crimes against humanity, because of the level of cruelty shown by Priebke, and especially that it was genocide, because people from the Jewish community were especially selected. This showed a racial or religious hatred on the execution of the reprisal. At the date of the sentence, the Argentine Republic had not ratified the Convention on war crimes and crimes against humanity[4], so the Judges relied on international custom and norms of *jus cogens* to assert that at that moment those crimes were imprescriptible and had to be respected by Argentina.

Judges Nazareno and O'Connor rejected the argument that extradition should be denied since the charges laid against Priebke did not have a definite punishment. They argued that the *bona fides* principle, which should regulate the application of treaties between Argentina and Italy, also implied respecting the *principle of useful effect*. Otherwise, an extradition because of lesser crimes could be approved while the punishment of more serious crimes (whose prohibition, but not penalty is included in the *jus gentium*) would not be permitted, and this would be absurd.

Judge Bossert, voting in favour of extradition, stated that the only way for states to secure the protection of essential values and to avoid excesses on the part of the state relies precisely on the principles and practices created by the juridical common conscience. These principles and practices have been developed

4. By Law number 24.584, on 1 November 1995, the Argentine Congress approved the Convention on the Imprescriptibility of War Crimes and Crimes against Humanity (Convención sobre la Imprescriptibilidad de los Crimenes de Guerra y de los Crimenes de lesa Humanidad.) On 23 November 1995, the President of Argentina promulgated the law. Argentina ratified the Convention without any reservations.

during the formulation of general international law. The Judge highlighted the fact that the purpose of modern humanitarian treaties was to avoid states reciprocally conceding one another rights and duties with the aim of serving national interests. The purpose was to establish a common public order with the aim of safeguarding their heritage of political customs, ideas and legal regimes. He asserted that the Geneva Conventions are not only conventional but customary. Judge Bossert rejected regarding Priebke's conduct as strictly military behaviour as his actions, because of their cruelty and immorality, were clearly against the common feeling of civilized peoples. He also relied on customary international law and general principles of law to account for the imprescriptibility of these crimes. Another reason that customary international law applied was that many states have adjusted their internal legislation to incorporate the Convention on the Imprescriptibility of war crimes and crimes against humanity. Although Argentina had not yet done so, it undoubtedly respected it.[5]

The votes against extradition have two different basis. Judges Belluscio and Levene asserted that if the charges brought against Priebke were considered war crimes, then there would be neither an international law to punish them nor a definite penalty. Besides, neither Argentine nor Italian legislation penalises war crimes differently than ordinary homicide, nor does it regulate their prescriptibility or imprescriptibility.

They also rejected considering the charges brought against Priebke as crimes against humanity. All in all, however terrible the criminal offences committed by Priebke may have been, there could be no excuse for departure from the principle *nulla poene sine lege* on a customary law which is not imperative. These offences could only be considered as homicides, which are proscribed in the Argentine legal system.

Judge Petracchi's vote said that even if we can affirm that Argentine Law must assert that war crimes and crimes against humanity are against the law, because their sources are treaties, and Argentina is a party, they are not autonomously punishable. This requirement is included in the extradition treaty between Argentina and Italy.

The arguments used to arrive at the different conclusions illustrate the convenience of having an International Penal Code which would contain definitions and prescribe punishments for crimes like these. It would be a way of joining legal certainty and justice.

5. Argentina adopted a law to incorporate the Convention on 1 November 1995. See *infra* p. 401.

THE *PRIEBKE* CASE BEFORE THE ITALIAN MILITARY TRIBUNALS: A REAFFIRMATION OF THE PRINCIPLE OF NON-APPLICABILITY OF STATUTORY LIMITATIONS TO WAR CRIMES AND CRIMES AGAINST HUMANITY*

Sergio Marchisio**

1. The complex case of Erich Priebke can be analysed through two different phases. The first runs from the massacre of 335 Italian citizens at the Ardeatine Caves in Rome in 1944 to the conviction of Herbert Kappler and other Nazi officers involved in that shooting on 20 July 1948. During this four-year period, Priebke became untraceable and escaped justice. The second phase starts when the former SS officer was detected in Argentina in May 1994 and, following extradition proceedings there[1], was extradited to Italy, where he underwent two criminal trials in front of the Italian military jurisdiction.

Priebke's first trial in Italy ended on 1 August 1996 with a decision that found the defendant guilty of the crime of violence with multiple murder against Italian citizens with aggravating circumstances, as described in Articles 13 and 185 of the 1941 Military Penal Code of War, but which nonetheless ordered his release because of the expiration of the statutory limitations on the charge on 25 November 1966. This decision, which aroused very negative public reactions[2], was quashed in September 1996 by the Court of Cassation, which accepted a petition for exception to the President of the Military Court filed by the aggrieved parties.

A second trial against Priebke and a second Nazi officer, Karl Hass, began in April 1997. This time, the Military Court, by a decision of 22 July 1997,

** Professor of International Law, University of Perugia; Part-time Professor of Law of the European Union, LUISS, Rome; Director of the Institute for Legal Studies on the International Community, National Research Council, Rome.

1. For a consideration of the Argentine leg of the case, see Consigli, p. 341.

2. Cf., C. Bohlen, 'Italian Court Throws Out Case in 1944 Rome Massacre', *The New York Times*, (2 August 1996) p. A3.

deemed that the existence of aggravating circumstances (premeditation and cruelty) had prevented the expiration of the statutory limitations on the charge. It thus condemned the accused to a custodial sentence. The crime foreseen in Articles 13 and 185 of the Military Penal Code of War is normally punished with life sentence. The Military Court, however, in consideration of some mitigating circumstances (both defendants being well-on in years and, as for Hass, the limited participation in the organisation and the enactment of the crime) sentenced Priebke to 15 years imprisonment and Hass to 10 years and 8 months.[3]

It must be stressed that the judgement of July 1997 clearly defines the massacre at the Ardeatine Caves as a war crime and a crime against humanity, although it does not consider this argument decisive in view of the non-applicability of statutory limitations on the crime.

Both the Public Prosecutor and the counsels for the defence appealed against the judgement to the Appellate Military Court; the first requesting reform of the section concerning the existence of mitigation and commuting of the imprisonment term, the second asking instead, on the basis of a number of considerations, for the acquittal of both condemned. The Appellate Court rendered its judgement on 7 March 1998, by which, after declaring the reasons of the defence groundless, it granted the request of the Public Prosecutor and followed with condemning the defendants to life sentences.

The judgement is at date *res iudicata* on the merits, save for the possibility to appeal to the Court of Cassation on issues of law.

The *Priebke* case as a whole contributes to the consolidation of the principle of non-applicability of statutory limitations on war crimes as a peremptory norm of general international law.

2. The Ardeatine Caves massacre of 1944 was perpetrated during the German occupation of central and northern Italy, which was affected after the 8 September 1943 Armistice of Cassibile. At the time, clandestine paramilitary groups belonging to the Resistenza were actively combatting the occupation through acts of sabotage and surprise attacks.[4] On 24 March 1944, a group of partisans staged an attack in Via Rasella in Rome where 26 soldiers of the Bozen contingent were

3. For both defendants, a ten year-imprisonment was pardoned because of post-1945 amnesties, which entailed the immediate release of Hass.

4. On the juridical status of partisans, see R. Bierzanek, *Le status juridique des partisans et des mouvements de résistance armée: évolution historique et aspects actuels, Mélanges offerts a Juraj Andrassy* (The Hague 1968) pp. 54-77.

killed; the casualties rose to 32 the following day when some of the wounded died.[5]

As a reprisal, the Commandant of the German Military Police, Lieutenant-Colonel Herbert Kappler, was ordered by Field Marshal Kesserling, the Commander of Army Group C in Italy, through various intermediaries, to execute 10 Italians for every one German soldier killed. The order, which came from Hitler himself, was to be carried out within 24 hours. Two lists were drawn up, comprising a total of 320 people, including both soldiers and civilians – some Jewish and some minors. After another wounded German died, another ten names were added. Eventually, a total of 335 persons were killed, five more than was foreseen, due to bad accounting. The victims were executed in a partic'ılarly atrocious way inside the caves; divided into groups of five, on their knees, with a single-shot to the back of the head from close range.

Erich Priebke, as Captain of the SS under Kappler, had major organisational tasks in the preparation of the massacre. He participated in forming the groups of victims, checked their arrival and directly executed two of them. The massacre perpetrated, dynamite was used to hide the entrance to the caves.[6]

On 25 November 1946, Italian military judicial authorities notified the Allied Military Authority on Italian territory of a warrant of arrest against Herbert Kappler and a number of other officers acting on his orders, including Priebke, in respect of the Ardeatine Caves massacre.[7] They were indicted for crimes foreseen in Articles 13 and 185 of the Military Penal Code of War, approved by Royal Decree on 20 February 1941 and still in force today. Article 185 of Title IV, on crimes against laws and usages of war, relates to violence by Italian soldiers against enemy citizens. Article 13 (Title I) extends the application of the

5. Cf., D. Peretti-Griva, 'L'attentato di via Rasella e la responsabilità per l'eccidio delle Fosse Ardeatine', *Giurisprudenza italiana*, Vol. CII (1950) pp. 577-580, commenting on the Judgement of 9 June 1950, issued by *Tribunale di Roma* in *Lidomici ed altri v. Bentivegna ed altri*. Relatives of some victims of the Ardeatine massacre brought a civil action against the authors of the attack in via Rasella, alleging the illegitimacy of the attack. The Court stated that recovery of damages could not be granted, since the attack in via Rasella was an act of war framed within the Partisan war, and, as such, not subject to the control of the judicial authority.

6. In late 1997, Wilheim Schuberning, the former SS lieutenant who exploded the charge, was traced to Veit an der Glan in Carinthia.

7. On 6 May 1946, the British Military Court sitting in Venice had declared Marshal Kesselring guilty of ordering the massacre at the Ardeatine caves in violation of the laws of war. See *Annual Digest of International Law Cases* (1946) p. 258 et seq. See also the judgement of condemnation against General von Machensen issued by the British Military Court of Rome on 30 November 1946, ibid. Von Machensen was part of the chain of command that communicated the order from Hitler via Field Marshal Kesselring, General Von Machensen, and General Maelzer to Lieutenant-Colonel Kappler.

above rule to crimes perpetrated by enemy soldiers against Italian citizens. Kappler and other Nazi officers were thus consigned to the Italian authorities so that criminal proceedings against them could be held. However, Priebke, being untraceable, could not be tried.

A first judgement was issued by the Military Court of Rome in the case of Kappler on 20 July 1948.[8] As this judgement – which was confirmed by the Military Supreme Court on 25 October 1952 – has served as a precedent for the recent proceedings against Priebke, it seems convenient to briefly evaluate its essential elements.

The first point to be made concerns the legal classification of the attack in via Rasella and of the German reaction. The partisan action was defined as an illegitimate act of war, as it had been carried out by a group of partisans which did not meet the conditions foreseen in Article 1 of the Regulations Respecting the Laws and Customs of War on Land annexed to the Hague Convention IV of 18 October 1907 to be considered 'volunteer corps' and, hence, legitimate belligerents. However, the Court deemed that the group should have been regarded as a *de facto* organ of the legitimate Government of the Kingdom of Italy, operating in south Italy. The international responsibility of the attack in via Rasella was thus to be attributed to the Italian State[9], whilst Germany, as the occupying power, had the right of reprisal. However, following the court, the reprisal had to be considered illegitimate as it lacked the necessary requisites of proportionality and necessity: the Ardeatine execution was, in fact, enormously disproportionate both as regards the number of victims and the damage entailed.

The judgement did not refer to the notion of a war crime, since it defined the Ardeatine Caves massacre as a multiple murder. It made only superficial reference to the limits that international law imposes on belligerents in case of reprisals. After the condemnation of *Kappler* and other Nazi officers, the register concerning Priekbe stayed officially open until 14 February 1962, when the military authorities decided to close the file on the case.

3. The more recent phase of the *Priebke* case commenced in 1994 when, on 5 May, a journalist of the US broadcasting network ABC interviewed the former German SS Captain in San Carlos de Bariloche, Argentina, where he had lived for many years. Three days later, Italy presented, through Interpol, a request for the provisional arrest of Priebke, stressing that a warrant of arrest against

8. *Il Foro Italiano* (1949) II, pp. 160-168. See also F. Capotorti, *Qualificazione giuridica dell'eccido delle Fosse Ardeatine Rassegna di diritto pubblico* (1949) II, pp. 170-192.

9. Text of the Judgment in Rivista di diritto internazionale, 1953, p. 193 et seq. The final judgement on the *Kappler* case reversed the argument of the *de facto* organ, stating that there was no legal link between the group and the Italian state. See also R. Ago, ibid., pp. 200-206.

him had been issued by the military judicial authority in Rome for the crime of multiple murder of Italian citizens, under Articles 13 and 185 of the Military Penal Code of War, as in the *Kappler* case. The extradition request was founded on Article 15 of the Italo-Argentinean Convention of Extradition, signed in Rome on 9 December 1987 and entered into force on 1 December 1992, stating that, each Party can request, in case of urgency, the provisional arrest of an individual whose extradition it intends to request. At the same time, Italy requested Argentina to extradite Erich Priebke for the above offence.

The Argentinean Supreme Court, in a judgement issued on 2 November 1995, granted the extradition on the grounds that the murder of 75 members of the Jewish community in Rome among the victims of the Ardeatine Caves constituted, *prima facie*, a case of genocide. On 16 November 1995, Priebke was extradited to Italy where he was detained in the military prison of Forte Boccea in Rome.[10]

4. Following the preliminary investigation activities, the Military Prosecutor requested that the military judicial authority proceed with the committal for trial of Erich Priebke for the offences against Articles 13 and 185 of the 1941 Military Penal Code. Meanwhile, the Public Prosecutor took similar steps with regard to the ordinary judicial authority for the crimes of slaughter and persistent homicide with aggravating circumstances, as foreseen in the Penal Code. With the judgement on this point pending, the ordinary judicial authority *re melius perpensa* concluded that the indictment crime was not that of slaughter as in the Penal Code, but the crime described in Articles 13 and 185 of the Military Penal Code of War, it having been perpetrated by German soldiers in time of war. By consequence, it declared himself incompetent. At this point, the Court of Cassation, acknowledging the disclaimer of competence by the ordinary judicial authority and the subsequent non-existence of a conflict among judges, confirmed the competence of the military judicial authority.[11]

This decision, however, was challenged by the aggrieved parties, who filed a preliminary objection to the jurisdiction of the military judge, asserting that the accused were to be judged for the crime of genocide – referred to by the Argentinean Supreme Court when granting the extradition to Italy – and thus in front of the ordinary judicial authority. The Military Court in Rome twice rejected such a plea; on 8 May 1996 (first trial) and on 24 April 1997 (second trial). Both times, it gave identical grounds: Priebke could not be judged for genocide because the crime of genocide was introduced into the Italian system

11. *Il Foro Italiano* (1996) II, pp. 558-562.

by Law no. 962 of 9 October 1967, that is, 23 years after the crime, whereas Article 25 of the Italian Constitution upholds the principle of *nulla poena sine lege previa.*

Two remarks should be made here. First, the subsequent judicial decisions on the *Priebke* case have excluded, consistent with this approach, any reference to the crime of genocide. The second judgement of 22 July 1997 defines the crime as a *reato di lesa umanità,* in a general sense, and as a war crime *stricto sensu.* Second, it is true that although Italy ratified the Convention on the Prevention and Punishment of the Crime of Genocide of 1948 on 4 June 1952, the full and effective implementation of the Convention into the Italian legal system was delayed until the adoption of the 'necessary legislation' provided for in Article V of the same Convention.[12] It is only with Constitutional Law no. 1 of 21 June 1967 and with Law no. 962 of 9 October 1967, which introduced and even expanded the categories of crimes identified by the Genocide Convention with their penalties, that the applicability of punishment to genocide became fully effective. Therefore, in order to prosecute Priebke for the crime of genocide, it should have been demonstrated that the latter was considered a crime under Italian law in 1944 and that the defendant could be judged in 1997 without violating the principle *nulla poena sine lege previa.* It is then understandable why the solution of military jurisdiction was followed, excluding all reference to the crime of genocide, which nonetheless had been the keystone for the extradition of Priebke from Argentina.

5. The first trial against Priebke commenced on 8 May 1996. Relatives and friends of the victims were permitted to participate in all phases of the proceedings as aggrieved parties.[13] At this stage, the climate of the proceedings deteriorated. In particular, rumours circulated that the President of the Military Court had underrated the importance of witnesses against Priebke and revealed an intention to acquit the defendant. The first judgement of the *Priebke* case was issued on 1 August 1996 and was entered on 30 September.[14]

12. See Law no. 153 of 11 March 1952. Reference is made, in particular, to the legislation necessary to secure effective penalties for persons guilty of genocide. See R. Barsotti, *Genocidio, Codice internazionale dei diritti umani*, E. Vitta et al., ed., (Grementieri, Milan 1981) pp. 229-232.

13. In the judgement of 29 February 1996, the Constitutional Court had declared the constitutional illegitimacy of Article 270 of the Military Penal Code of Peace for that part that does not foresee the possibility of the participation of aggrieved parties to the proceeding in front of the military judge and calls upon the military judge himself to fix compensation damages for the victims following possible condemnation.

14. No. 305 of 1996.

The judgement partly includes the argument of the 1948 judgement against Kappler, recognising that the attack in via Rasella was an illegitimate act of war attributable to the Italian state. The judgement thus defines the massacre at the Ardeatine Caves as a war crime, specifically, multiple murder against civilians in occupied territories, perpetrated beyond the limits set by customary international law on reprisals, provided for by Article 50 of the Hague Regulations relating to collective punishments.

As to the issue of the non-applicability of statutory limitations to the crime, Article 157 of the Italian Penal Code states that statutory limitations shall not be applied to crimes punishable with life imprisonment. However, the judgement refused to admit the above after comparing the aggravating circumstances (the atrociousness of the massacre) with the mitigating circumstances, both specific (the obedience to a superior order) and general, granted to all defendants worthy of mercy. Hence, the crime had to be considered, in the Court's view, as statutorily limited, it being 'a war crime which cannot be classified as a crime against humanity with the sole end of transforming it into a crime to which statutory limitations are not applicable'.[15] It is clear that, with these arguments, the Military Court tended to detract from the gravity of war crimes, affirming that they are subject to a *minus quam* legal regime than crimes against humanity.

On the contrary, according to international law, the arguments in favour of the non-applicability of statutory limitations to crimes against humanity, like genocide, are the same that support the non-applicability of statutory limitations to war crimes.

After the judgement was declared, ordering the immediate release of the defendant, relatives of the victims protested vigorously and blockaded the courtroom with the defendant, his lawyer and the whole of the Court inside. At 2 a.m. on 2 August 1996, however, Priebke was arrested a second time under Articles 715 and 716 of the Code of Criminal Procedure relating to peril of escape, and on the grounds of a request for provisional arrest filed on 16 July 1996 by judicial authorities in Dortmund as a precursor to a further request of extradition from Germany.[16]

On 15 October 1996, the Court of Cassation granted the plea of exception to the President of the Military Court, who was found to have made, prior to the commencement of the trial, declarations indicating a preconceived opinion on

15. Non-official translation of the relevant part of the as yet unpublished judgement, that reads as follows: 'Quello addebitato al Priebke, infatti, almeno formalmente, è un crimine di guerra e non può essere definito un "crimine contro l'umanità" al solo fine di renderlo imprescrittibile . . .'

16. On 5 September 1996, the Court of Cassation stated that Priebke's arrest was legitimate. *Il Foro Italiano* (1996) II, pp. 537-541.

his part concerning, in particular, the legal classification of the facts of indictment.[17] Consequently, the whole first trial was cancelled and the judgement declared void and without effect. The proceeding against Priebke would be undertaken again in front of the same military judicial authority, in consolidation with the action against Karl Hass, meanwhile accused of the same crime.[18]

6. The second judgement of the Military Court of Rome was rendered on 22 July 1997.[19] Only in part does it innovate in respect of the 1948 judgement against Kappler and the 1996 judgement against Priekbe that was later quashed by the Court of Cassation. In fact, the judgement first revisits the questioned legitimacy of the Ardeatine reprisal to definitively exclude it. It also excludes that the applicability of punishment to Priebke and Hass be denied because they acted in obedience to a superior order, as the criminality of the order was patent.[20] Finally, it affirms the responsibility of the defendants for perpetrating the crime against the laws and usages of war foreseen in Articles 13 and 185 of the 1941 Military Penal Code of War – violence with multiple murder against Italian citizens, with the aggravating circumstances of premeditation, for Priekbe, and cruelty towards individuals, for both defendants.

Two truly innovative elements of the judgement must be noted. The Court interpreted the principle that war crimes perpetrated during warfare are always punished according to the punitive system set by the wartime military criminal code in force at the time of the *commissi delicti*, as implying the prevalence of the aggravating circumstances over the mitigating ones. Consequently, the indictment crime can be punished with a life sentence and thus, consistent with Article 157 of the Penal Code, is not subject to the application of statutory limitations. Having established that the crime is to be deemed as not subject to

17. See *Il Foro Italiano* (1997) II, pp. 6-17. The Military Court had instead expressed a contrary opinion with regard to two pleas of exception previously filed by, respectively, the Military Prosecutor and one of the aggrieved parties. The pleas were dismissed by the Court by Order no. 69 of 23 July 1996 and Order no. 117 of 29 July 1996. In both cases, the Court deemed that the declarations of the President of the Military Court were of a merely declaratory character of part of public opinion.

18. With the judgement of 10 February 1997, the Court of Cassation decided once again that the military court had jurisdiction and rejected the decision of the Military Court of Rome of 4 December 1996 in which the Court had declared its own lack of jurisdiction. *Il Foro Italiano* (1997) II, pp. 137-143.

19. No. 322 of 22 July 1997, filed on 13 September 1997.

20. See G. Sacerdoti, *A proposito del caso* Priebke: *la responsabilità per l'esecuzione di ordini illegittimi costituenti crimini di guerra* (Rivista di diritto internazionale 1997) pp. 130-151. The author illustrates how the order to commit the massacre could also be considered illegitimate under German law at the time, in light of the international law of warfare.

statutory limitations on the grounds of the applicable rules of municipal law, the Court granted, *ad abundantiam* and not as a decisive element, the argument that the Ardeatine crime was not statutorily limited as it is a war crime and a crime against humanity under international law.

This is, indeed, the most interesting part of the decision and would certainly have merited a more in-depth analysis and precision in the context of the grounds of the judgement. Nonetheless, it has to be positively regarded that, for the first time in the long-lasting juridical case of the Ardeatine Caves, a judicial authority affirmed without any incertitude that the offence is a 'war crime and a crime against humanity' and, as such, is not subject to statutory limitations.[21] Following the Court, in fact, the logical premise is that, amongst the norms of international law generally recognised, there is also one establishing the obligation of states to punish war crimes and declare the non-applicability of statutory limitations to them. All norms of municipal law inconsistent with the above are thus non-applicable.

In the Court's view, the principle of non-applicability of statutory limitations results from a slow evolution of international law resulting in the Convention on the Non-Applicability of Statutory Limitations to War Crimes and Crimes Against Humanity, opened for signature on 16 December 1968 and entered into force on 11 November 1970.[22] The Court stated clearly and unequivocally that the principle of non-applicability of statutory limitations to war crimes and crimes against humanity has the status of *jus cogens*, set, as it is, for the protection of the general interests of the international community and, thus, not subject to derogation by way of agreement. Based on the above considerations, we arrive at the double conclusion that: a) the principle of non-applicability of statutory limitations is effective in the Italian legal system since 1968 by virtue of Article 10(1) of the Constitution; b) the crime of the Ardeatine Caves was not statutorily limited at the time because of the judgement rendered on 25 October 1952 by the Supreme Military Court in the *Kappler* case, that applied to all those who had perpetrated the crime (Article 161(1) of the Penal Code), *ex quibus* Erich Priebke.

The judgement thus clarifies that the Ardeatine massacre should be considered as not subject to statutory limitations according to the Italian criminal law applicable at the time of the crime, interpreted in light of the norms of international law on war crimes and crimes against humanity. From this

21. As for non-applicability of statutory limitations to crimes against humanity, see also the Judgements of 6 October 1983 and 26 January 1984 by the French Court of Cassation in the case of *Barbie*, *ILR* (1988) pp. 125-148.

22. The Convention was adopted by the UN General Assembly at its 23rd session on 26 November 1968, *ILM* (1969) pp. 68-72.

perspective, it also helps to clarify that not only genocide but also war crimes and other crimes against humanity are not subject to statutory limitations.

If the decision of the Military Court can be faulted, it is for not having reconstructed with more coherence the situation regarding the international laws of warfare, both written and unwritten, applicable at the time of the Ardeatine massacre. There is only a vague reference to the preparatory works of the 1941 Military Penal Code of War on crimes and customs of war. As for post-World War II developments, the judgement mentions acts of differing legal significance: the Statute of the Nuremberg Tribunal; UNGA resolution 95 (I) of 11 December 1946; the Fourth Geneva Convention of 1949; and the text adopted in 1950 by the International Law Commission on principles of international law recognised at Nuremberg.

More precision by the Military Court, avoiding any terminological vagueness, on the question of the international norms applicable in 1944, would have been greatly appreciated.

Notwithstanding the above, the *Priebke* case shows once again the need for clearly reaffirming the paramount necessity of judging war criminals and the non-applicability of statutory limitations to war crimes perpetrated.

THE DEFENCES OF REPRISALS, SUPERIOR ORDERS AND DURESS IN THE *PRIEBKE* CASE BEFORE THE ITALIAN MILITARY TRIBUNAL*

Francesca Martines**

1. INTRODUCTION

The aim of this article is to discuss the three defences raised by Erich Priebke for his participation in the killing of 335 civilians at the Ardeatine Caves which took place on 24 March 1944, and for which Priebke was tried by the Italian Military Tribunal which rendered its second judgement on 22 July 1997.[1] The defences were: (1) the characterisation of the shootings at the Ardeatine Caves as lawful belligerent reprisals, (2) the defence of superior orders, and (3) duress.

2. REPRISALS

First, the Military Tribunal considered whether the killings could be considered as legitimate belligerent reprisals.[2]

** Dr. Francisca Martines is a researcher at the International Law Chair, University of Florence.

1. For background to the case see S. Marchisio, *supra*, p. 344. The sentence of the Military Tribunal was appealed by the General Military Prosecutor and by the Military Prosecutor of Rome. The final judgment was rendered on 7 March 1998 by the Military Court of Appeal (Corte Militare di Appello).

2. The question was also dealt with at length by the Military Tribunal which tried Kappler in 1948. See F. Capotorti, "'Rappresaglie" esercitate dall'occupante per atti ostili della popolazione nemica in *Foro Penale'* (1949) p. 112.

Yearbook of International Humanitarian Law
Volume 1 - 1998 - pp. 354-361

It seems clear that the Germans were permitted to have recourse to reprisals[3] only if the attack on via Rasella was an illegitimate act of warfare, meaning that, a) the act was imputable to the Italian State (that is, the partisans who carried out the attack were organs of the state (Italy) (subjective element of the international illegal act), and b) the attack against the German soldiers infringed the laws of war in force at that time (objective element of the international illegal act). The Tribunal chose not to deal with the question of the qualification of the attack by the partisans in via Rasella, as this was not decisive for the judgement.[4] Even if the killings at the Ardeatine Caves could have been considered belligerent reprisals[5], they were illegitimate because the requisites of proportionality (between the injury suffered – the death of 33 German soldiers – and the injury caused – the death of 335 innocent persons) and of necessity (the German authorities did not make any serious attempt to identify and to arrest the persons responsible for the attack in via Rasella) were lacking. According to the Tribunal, in fact, '[i]t is obvious that with the shooting at the Ardeatine caves – as a reaction of the German state to the attack in via Rasella – an unacceptable disproportion between the death of 33 Germans and the killing of 335 persons was committed.'[6] Therefore, the killings – at least that part exceeding the proportionality – could be considered as serious violations of the laws of war.

One could also consider whether the killing of defenceless civilians could be considered a further argument against the legitimate character of the Ardeatine shootings, although one not dealt with by the Tribunal. It should be noted that reprisals against civilian populations were not prohibited at the time of the event.[7] Although the Hague Convention of 1907 included the well-known

3. Belligerent reprisals are a category of international reprisals (or counter-measures according to a more common terminology) which are defined as violations of the laws of war committed by one belligerent against another belligerent who committed a previous violation of the laws of war. See generally F. Kalshoven, *Belligerent Reprisals* (Leiden, Sijthoff 1971).

4. 'Thus, if neither of the two defenses (reprisals and collective punishment) for the Ardeatine caves shooting can be accepted, it is obvious that the legal qualification of the attack made by partisans in via Rasella is unimportant, if not even potentially misleading' (Unofficial translation). See p. 31 of the typewritten text of the judgement of the Military Tribunal.

5. This could be maintained if one considers that the partisans were *de facto* organs and that they infringed Art. 23 (which prohibits the treacherous killing and wounding of enemies) in connection with Art. 1 of the Regulation (which lays down the requisites of legitimate combatants) annexed to the IV Hague Convention of 1907. The text of the Regulation is reported in D. Schindler, J. Toman, *Droit des conflits armès,* (Institut Henry-Dunant, Genève 1996) p. 65 et seq.

6. Unofficial translation. See p. 28 of the typewritten text of the judgement of the Military Tribunal. These conclusions are shared by the Military Court of Appeal, at p. 127 of the typewritten text of the judgement.

7. These became the object of an express prohibition only after 1949, under Art. 33 of the IV Geneva Convention.

Martens clause[8], it is rather difficult to affirm that the humanitarian law in force at the time expressly prohibited the killing of civilians, even if Article 46 of the Hague regulations required the respect of the life of the civilian population by the occupying state.

The Tribunal also excluded the possibility that the shootings could be justified as measures of collective punishment as provided by Article 50 of the Hague Regulations (annexed to the IV Hague Convention of 1907).[9] Once a strict connection is established between the civilian population and the authors of an illegal act who cannot be identified, this provision allows the occupying Power to adopt measures against that population. However, according to the Military Tribunal, these measures may affect only collective property and cannot infringe the right to life of civilians.[10]

3. SUPERIOR ORDERS

It was sustained on Priebke's behalf that he ought not to be punished since he took part in the killing of the 335 people at the Ardeatine Caves in pursuance of an order given by one of his superiors. The Tribunal applied Article 40 of the Italian military criminal code in time of peace and in force at the time of facts.[11] According to this provision, criminal responsibility is attributed to the person who issued the order; however, if the given order is manifestly illegal, the subordinate does not escape liability even if acting in pursuance of a command.

One of the most problematic questions arising in connection with the application of this rule is in establishing when an order is 'manifestly' illegal. In other

8. 'Dans les cas non compris dans les dispositions réglementaires adoptées par (les Hautes Parties contractantes), les populations et les belligérants restent sous la sauvergarde et sous l'empire des principes du droit des gens, tels qu'ils resultent des usages ètablis entre nations civilisées, des lois de l'humanité et des exigences de la conscience publique'. Sulla Clausola Martens vedi P. Benvenuti, 'La Clausola Martens e la tradizione classica del diritto naturale nella codificazione del diritto dei conflitti armati', in *Scritti in memoria di Giuseppe Barile* (Cedam, 1996) p. 173 et seq.

9. According to this provision, no general penalty, pecuniary or otherwise, shall be inflicted upon the population on account of the acts of individuals for which they cannot be regarded as jointly and severally responsible.

10. 'The Tribunal notes that, according to the doctrine, collective punishment can affect only a community and not individuals: in that sense a classical example of collective punishment is the requisition of properties of the state such as libraries, museums, etc.' At p. 31 of the typewritten text of the judgement of the Military Tribunal.

11. This article has been repealed by Art. 22 of Italian Statute 11 July 1978, no. 382, but has rightly been considered still applicable by the Tribunal, being substantive and not procedural law. See p. 49 of the typewritten text of the judgement of the Military Tribunal.

words, one should ask whether a tribunal should apply an objective or a subjective test. On the basis of an objective test, the order should appear illegitimate to the common military person. The subjective test takes into consideration the knowledge of the actor and implies an investigation into the existence of the requisite *mens rea.*[12]

According to the Military Tribunal, one should apply the objective criterion considered together with the subjective one. However, when the subjective test clearly shows that the subordinate was aware of the illegal character of the act performed, it will not be necessary to apply the objective criterion. In the case of the killing at the Ardeatine Caves, the Tribunal considered that the plea of superior orders could not be invoked[13] since Priebke was 'indifferent to the criminal character of the order'[14] and, therefore, the superior order could not be considered as a complete defence. The Tribunal, however, considered the plea of superior orders as an attenuating circumstance.[15]

The conclusion was significant because it reversed the approach taken by the Military Tribunal which had tried Kappler in 1948 in relation to the same massacre.[16] The Tribunal in 1948 had accepted that the defence of superior

12. T. Padovani, 'Ordine criminoso e obbedienza gerarchica nel diritto penale italiano', in *Dei delitti e delle pene* (1987) pp. 477 et seq.; R. Venditti, *Il diritto penale militare nel sistema penale italiano* (Giuffrè 1992) pp. 181 et seq.; Y. Dinstein, *The Defence of 'Obedience to Superior orders' in International law* (Leiden 1965) pp. 10 et seq.; A. Cassese, 'Abramo, Antigone ed il conflitto tra imperativi' in A. Cassese, *Violenza e diritto nell'era nucleare* (Laterza 1986) p. 109 et seq.

13. Very often, in criminal proceedings against war criminals, superior order has been invoked as a defence in connection with duress. The defendants often argued that they obeyed an order even if it was illegitimate because they were threatened with execution in case of disobedience. The two defenses are, of course, to be distinguished. Superior orders can exist without duress and duress without superior orders. The order does not constitute duress even if an element of coercion were present, not as a direct threat but as a form of pressure on the subordinate because of the implied sanction which accompanies disobedience.

14. Military Tribunal, p. 51 of the type written text of the judgment. According to the Military Court of Appeal, this defence cannot be invoked in the specific case since 'the defendant(s) completely adhered to the order received without being subject to any coercion'; the Court considers that in that case there was not a conflict of duties, no conflict between the order and (the defendant's) conscience was present", see p. 134 and 135 of the typewritten text of the judgment (unofficial translation).

15. 'In the case under consideration [the Tribunal considers that] the defendant had been led to commit the crime by ... Kappler', p. 81 of the typewritten text of the judgement of the Miliary Tribunal (unofficial translation).

16. Kappler was prosecuted in Italy in 1948 for the killings in the Ardeatine caves. He was tried by the Military Tribunal of Rome in 1948 and by the Supreme Military Tribunal in 1952. The 1948 judgement can be read in *Foro Penale* 1948, p. 604. The judgement of the Supreme Military Tribunal of 1952 is reported in *Rivista di Diritto inernazionale* (1953) p. 193 et seq. with comment by R. Ago.

orders could cover the killing of the first 320 persons (10 people killed for every German soldier killed in Via Rasella) and, in fact, condemned Kappler for the killing of the other 15 (10 of whom had been added to the list on the initiative of Kappler himself after the death of a German soldier in hospital; the remaining five were added to the list by mistake, but were killed all the same although it appeared that the Nazis were aware of the mistake). The other officials involved in the killing were all acquitted because the Tribunal accepted the plea of superior orders.

4. DURESS

The final prong of Priebke's defence was that he had acted under duress. According to the plea of duress, a person threatened with severe and irremediable harm to life or limb can invoke duress to avoid criminal responsibility.[17]

Priebke claimed that he participated in the killings at the Ardeatine Caves under threat of being court-marshalled and sentenced to death. The Military Tribunal rejected this version of the facts, denying that such a threat had ever been made.[18] The threat of being brought before the SS Court cannot in fact be considered an immediate and serious threat of death, which is one of the applicable conditions for this defence.

The presumed threat made by Captain Schutz to kill those subordinate officers who refused to participate in the execution was also rejected by the Tribunal as the danger of being killed was not realistic because of the equal position of Captain Schutz in the military hierarchy with Priebke.

Moreover, according to the Tribunal, 'the defendant's statement, according to which he was implicitly threatened by the structure of the SS, was unreasonable. It was, in fact, well-known that Priebke had voluntarily joined the SS and had reached a position of high authority within that organisation.'[19] It seems, therefore, for the Tribunal, that the condition according to which duress can actually be invoked as a defence only if the danger is not voluntarily caused by

17. According to Art. 54 of the Italian criminal code, 'Anyone who has committed an act having been compelled to do so by the necessity of saving himself or others from the present danger of serious bodily harm, a danger not voluntary caused by him, nor otherwise avoidable, shall not be punishable, provided the act is proportionate to the danger ... The provision of the first paragraph ... shall apply even if the state of necessity is caused by the threats of others ...'

18. This conclusion was shared by the Military Court of Appeal : 'Kappler did not make any threat regarding the life and physical integrity (of the defendant) ... because there was no need ...' see p. 146 of the typewritten text of the judgment. Non-official translation.

19. Unofficial translation, p. 57 of the typewritten text of the judgement of the Military Tribunal.

the defendant (situation of duress not self-induced) was lacking in the case of Priebke who voluntarily joined the SS.

However, it should be noted that, even if this had not been the case, duress could not have been invoked. The Tribunal could not, in fact, accept this plea because of the 'lack of proportionality between the danger hypothetically threatening the defendant and the acts that he was allegedly obliged to commit'.[20] It is clear that the condition of proportionality would not have been met if one compared the life of the defendant and the life of 335 people.[21] However, the defence argued that the circumstances which the Tribunal should have considered were much more complex as the (possible) sacrifice of the defendant's life would have been without effect, because the prisoners would have been killed anyway.

The Tribunal rejected this argument, affirming that, '[t]his argument ... according to which the possible disobedience of the defendant could not have prevented the event ... is not founded since the duty to disobey a manifestly illegal order exists independently from the fact that the subordinate who disobeys could prevent the commission of the crime.'[22]

In the Italian legal system, duress can only be invoked when the threat to the life of the defendant is unequivocally proved (which was not the case for Priebke), while it seems that there is no room for other considerations such as the fact that his refusal could have saved the life of another person.

However, moving to international law, one should consider that different solutions are adopted in the legal systems of the member states of the international community. In common and civil law systems, the requirement of an immediate and effective threat are not considered sufficient for the application of this defence.

The Appeals Judges of the International Criminal Tribunal for the Former Yugoslavia in the *Erdemović* case excluded that duress could be invoked as a defence to a charge of killing of innocent people.[23] However, in his dissenting

20. See p. 57 of the typewritten text of the judgement of the Military Tribunal.

21. See p. 28 of the typewritten text of the judgement of the Military Tribunal. As underlined by Judge Cassese in his dissenting opinion to the Appeals judgment in the case of *Erdemović* before the International Criminal Tribunal for the Former Yugoslavia, 7 October 1997, Case No. IT-96-22-A, it is not clear whether the lack of proportionality refers to 'the possible death (...) of the defendants on the one side, and their participation in the execution, on the other' or 'to the fear by the defendants to be court-martialled by an SS Court, on the one side, and their participation in the execution, on the other' (fn. 69, pp. 33-34 at p. 34 of the typewritten text of the dissenting opinion annexed to the judgment). I would say that the first hypothesis should be preferred since it was not proved that Priebke would have been sentenced to death by the SS military court.

22. See p. 53 of the typewritten text of the judgment of the Military Tribunal.

23. For an analysis of this decision, see Rowe, *supra* p. 210.

opinion to the judgement, Judge Cassese concluded that international criminal law does not exclude the defence of duress, even in the case of the killing of innocent persons, provided that the severe conditions of the rule are respected. In evaluating the requisite of proportionality, great emphasis was given by Judge Cassese to the inevitable death of the innocent person. According to Judge Cassese, the 'criterion [of] proportionality (meaning that the remedy should not be disproportionate to the evil or that the lesser of two evils should be chosen) ... [p]erhaps ... will never be satisfied where the accused is saving his own life at the expense of his victim, since there are enormous, perhaps insurmountable, philosophical, moral and legal difficulties in putting one life in the balance against that of others ... Conversely, ... where it is not a case of a direct choice between the life of the person acting under duress and the life of the victim – in situations ... where there is a high probability that the person under duress will not be able to save the life of the victims whatever he does – then duress may succeed as a defence.'

5. THE JUDGEMENT AND SENTENCE

Priebke was found guilty. The Tribunal considered his participation[24] in the killings at the Ardeatine Caves to have been covered by Article 185 of the Italian military criminal code applicable in times of war, which punishes murder committed by Italian or enemy militaries without necessity or justification for causes not unrelated to the war.

The sentence of life imprisonment was, however, reduced to 21 years in consideration of ordinary extenuating circumstances, as provided in Article 62 *bis* of the Italian criminal code.[25] In this case, these were, in particular, the age of the defendants and their behaviour subsequent to the crime. The penalty was further reduced to 14 years because of the application of the extenuating circumstance as provided in Article 59(1) (superior orders) and an increase of one year for the continuous character of the crime. A 10-year reduction of sentence was granted as pardon (*condono*) by the Tribunal.

On appeal, the Military Court of Appeal, on 7 March 1998, rejected all the attenuating circumstances granted by the Military Tribunal and applied the aggravating circumstances of premeditation (for both Priebke and Haas) and of having acted with cruelty.

24. Priebke was involved in the preparation of the list of prisoners to be killed at the caves and in the actual killing of some of the prisoners.

25. '... the judge may take into account various other circumstances regard for which justifies a reduction of punishment.'

Therefore, the existence of aggravating circumstances and the absence of any attenuating circumstances led the Military Court of Appeal to pronounce a sentence condemning the two defendants to life imprisonment.

IHL AND PEACE OPERATIONS: Sharing Canada's lessons learned from Somalia*

Robert M. Young and Maria Molina**

1. INTRODUCTION

This note briefly reviews certain aspects of international humanitarian law (IHL) arising from the civilian Commission of Inquiry established in Canada on 20 March 1995[1] to investigate the role of Canadian forces during the multinational peace operation in Somalia in 1992 and 1993.

After some background information, we focus on two key issues concerning IHL arising from the Commission's work:

(1) The applicability of IHL to a peace operation such as the Canadian deployment to Somalia; and

(2) Canada's obligation to provide IHL training to the members of its armed forces.[2]

We conclude with some observations on the Commission's impact, including the responses of the Canadian government and the Canadian Forces.

** Robert M. Young, Barrister & Solicitor, Ottawa, Ontario, Canada, B.A. (Queen's University, Kingston, 1985)dd LL.B (University of Ottawa, 1993) was a Research Consultant for the Somalia Inquiry, and contributed to the Report and to the Simpson study, referred to at length in this note. He has been active as a volunteer and a staff member with the Canadian Red Cross, with a particular interest in IHL. He is a co-author of *On the Front Line: Uprising in Enclavia*, an IHL training simulation activity created by the Ottawa-Carleton Red Cross Branch.

Maria Molina, LL.M. (University of Ottawa), D.E.A. (Université Aix-Marseille III) is the International Humanitarian Law Coordinator, IHL National Training Unit, Canadian Red Cross. She was a Researcher for Canada for the ICRC's Customary International Humanitarian Law Study (1997), and was an Intern in the ICRC's Legal Department in 1996-1997.

The authors would like to acknowledge the assistance of David Goetz and Avril McDonald.

1. By Order-in-Council,PC 1995-442, 20 March 1995, pursuant to the federal Inquiries Act.

2. Please note that the expression 'Law of Armed Conflict' (LOAC) is used by the members of the Canadian National Defence Forces as referring to International Humanitarian Law.

Yearbook of International Humanitarian Law
Volume 1 - 1998 - pp. 362-370

2. BACKGROUND

In 1992, the world was shaken by images of the civil war, drought and famine in Somalia. Acting through the United Nations, many states agreed to take part in a mission designated 'Operation Cordon' (United Nations Operation in Somalia (UNOSOM)), authorized under Chapter VI of the UN Charter.[3] Canada was one such state, and through the late summer and fall, the Canadian Forces (CF) designated personnel and equipment and prepared to deploy on a peacekeeping mission to Somalia. During this time, however, conditions in Somalia began to deteriorate, raising questions about the nature of the mission.

On 3 December 1992, the UN Security Council approved, by its Resolution 794, the establishment of the Unified Task Force (UNITAF). The mission known as 'Operation Deliverance' was a so-called 'peace enforcement' mission, with authorization to use force in self-defence. It had two main goals:

– to establish a secure environment for the delivery of humanitarian aid by non-governmental organizations (NGOs); and

– to assist in the rebuilding of essential civilian infrastructure to ensure that progress was sustained by the Somali population once UNITAF forces departed.

Canada, already committed to the Chapter VI mission planned for Somalia, continued with its plan to take part in the multinational effort. The CF contingent was based around the Canadian Airborne Regiment (CAR). The CAR, which had earlier seen its planned deployment to the Western Sahara cancelled because of delays in the referendum process, was eager to undertake the Somalia mission. It and the other elements of the Canadian contingent worked hard, under strict time constraints and with limited information, to prepare for the Somalia deployment.

Sadly, the deployment proved a wrenching experience for the CAR, for Canada, and for numerous other states that took part in the mission. The CAR was later disbanded under a cloud of controversy. For Canada, the Somalia mission battered the nation's considerable pride in its long-standing participation in UN peace operations. Other states suffered the loss of lives of members of their military contingents.

The now-infamous events in Somalia with which Canada is associated included the beating death of Shidane Arone, a Somali teenager in the custody of CF soldiers; an apparent suicide attempt by one of those soldiers; the shooting of Somali intruders at the CF compound in Belet Huen; and allegations of a 'cover-up' in Somalia and back in Canada. These events led to a military Board of Inquiry, several Courts Martial (and appeals from these), and then to the

3. Established by UN SC Res. 751, 24 April 1992.

civilian Commission of Inquiry into the Deployment of Canadian Forces to Somalia (the Commission).[4] Further litigation over the Commission's activities and especially its Report, including actions to strike out the Commission's findings, continues.

The Commission's mandate, established by the Canadian government, was broad, involving an investigation into and a report on the chain of command system, leadership, discipline, actions and decisions of the Canadian Forces as well as the actions and decisions of the Department of National Defence in respect of the Canadian Forces' 1992-1993 deployment to Somalia.

3. THE APPLICABILITY OF IHL TO THE CANADIAN DEPLOYMENT TO SOMALIA

The Commission's Report[5] discusses in several places the applicability of IHL, and specifically the Geneva Conventions and the Protocols, to the CF deployment to Somalia. Yet, curiously, the Report itself does not appear to reach any definitive conclusions on this issue, arguably one of the most important questions arising from Canada's experience in Somalia. However, a Research Study prepared for the Commission and published with the Report, entitled *Law applicable to Canadian Forces in Somalia 1992/1993*[6] (the 'Simpson Study'), sheds some light on the matter, as discussed below.

As noted above, litigation has been ongoing since almost the start of the Commission's mandate. This created an interesting situation in terms of legal proceedings: in several cases, the Commission had the benefit of reviewing, before it released its final report, some of the decisions in the various legal proceedings.

4. See *Dishonoured Legacy, Report of the Commission of Inquiry into the Deployment of Canadian Forces to Somalia* (Canadian Government Publishing, 1997).

5. The entire report of the Commission of Inquiry into the Deployment of Canadian Forces to Somalia is available in a bilingual French and English CD-ROM format. The CD-ROM is entitled 'Information Legacy' and contains: the Commission's Report, the Research Studies, the Hearing Transcripts of the Inquiry, Evidentiary Exhibits, Transcripts of the Courts Martial, Transcripts of the Board of Inquiry, Written Submissions and Historical Documents of the Somalia Inquiry. Parts of the Report are also available at the website of the Department of National Defence of Canada at: www.dnd.ca.somaliae.htm (for the English version) and at: www.dnd.ca.somaliaf.htm (for the French version).

6. James M. Simpson, *Law Applicable to the Canadian Deployment in Somalia 1992/1993*, Study prepared for the Commission of Inquiry into the Deployment of Canadian Forces to Somalia, (Canadian Government Publishing, 1997).

The question of the applicability of IHL to the Canadian forces deployment to Somalia was raised by the Court Martial Appeal Court (CMAC) in the *Brocklebank* decision of 1996.[7] Private David John Brocklebank was arrested for aiding and abetting the torture of Shidane Arone, the Somali teenager who entered the CF compound and was tortured and beaten to death while in custody.

Charges against Private Brocklebank included negligent performance of a military duty imposed on him by the National Defence Act[8], the duty being the obligation, according to the Fourth Geneva Convention, to ensure safety to civilian prisoners. The CMAC held that Brocklebank did not participate actively in the torture of Shidane Arone in custody, but failed to intervene to stop his mistreatment.

The Court considered the applicability of the Geneva Conventions and the Additional Protocols. The Court held that Private Brocklebank had no legal obligation to ensure the safety of the prisoner because neither the Geneva Conventions nor Additional Protocol II applied to the CF in Somalia. The Court found that there was no evidence of an armed conflict in Somalia, and further, that the Geneva Conventions and Additional Protocols did not apply to peace operations.

The *Brocklebank* decision was questioned in the Simpson Study. Its principal author, BGen (ret.) James M. Simpson, was eminently qualified to prepare the study: a WWII veteran, a former Judge Advocate General of the Canadian Forces, former Senior Legal Officer for the UN, and a member at that time of the International Humanitarian Fact-Finding Commission established under the First Additional Protocol to the Geneva Conventions.

The Simpson Study questions the Court's finding in *Brocklebank* that the Geneva Conventions were not applicable to the CF in Somalia, identifying three questionable bases for the Court's conclusions.

The first is the Court's finding that there was no 'armed conflict' in Somalia in 1992-1993. The Simpson Study analyses the situation in the following manner:

> In the common ordinary meaning of the expression, there surely was available information – although apparently not presented in evidence – of 'armed conflict' in Somalia at the relevant time. Not only was it noted in reports of the Secretary General of the UN to the Security Council in 1992 and 1993, but hundreds of shooting deaths of members of other contingents of UNITAF and Somalis attested to serious and persistent armed conflict.[9]

7. *Her Majesty the Queen* v. *Private D.J. Brocklebank*, Court Martial Appeal Court of Canada, April 2, 1996. For an analysis of this decision, see Boustany, *infra*, p. 371.
8. R.S.C., 1985, N-5, section 124.
9. Simpson Study, *supra* n. 6, at p. 28.

The second basis for questioning the Court's decision relates to the mandate or nature of the deployment, or more precisely, to the characterization of the Canadian deployment as being part of a peacekeeping mission:

> It is well established that what started out as the UNOSOM peacekeeping mission under Chapter VI of the UN Charter was transformed into a national (albeit a coalition of nations) UNITAF peace-making or peace-enforcing mission authorized by the Security Council under Chapter VII of the UN Charter. The conduct in question of Pte. Brocklebank occurred when his unit was part of the UNITAF mission or operation.[10]

Further, the Simpson Study suggested that the Court's findings were based on a consideration of the incorrect provisions of the Fourth Geneva Convention. The CMAC may have failed to properly consider the relevance of Articles 4 and 27 of the Fourth Geneva Convention.The CF may arguably have been 'a party to the conflict' or 'occupying' part of Somalia within the meaning of the Fourth Convention. If so, this would create a group of 'protected persons' that the Court failed to recognize.

Finally, the majority's finding in the Court Martial Appeal Court that the Geneva Conventions did not apply to the CF is questioned in the Simpson Study.

The Commission of Inquiry, in the Simpson Study, advances what can only be called a common sense approach to this question of applicable norms:

> Even if Governments question the applicability of common Article 3 and Protocol II to specific situations of non-international armed conflicts, they are nonetheless bound by some fundamental principles of humanity, such as those proclaimed by the Universal Declaration of Human Rights and other human rights instruments, where they are applicable and for those States who have ratified them.[11]

Further,

> They are also bound by the Martens Clause, to which Protocol 11 also refers in its Preamble, and which is a principle of customary law.[12]

On the question of applicability, the Simpson Study observes:

> In any event, it is illogical that combatants who are trying to kill each other in an armed conflict are subject to the LOAC when they are acting as members of national armed forces, whereas members of armed forces in the same armed conflict acting

10. Ibid.
11. Ibid., at p. 18.
12. Ibid.

as UN peacekeepers are exempt from the obligation to respect the rights of protected persons.[13]

The Simpson Study relied on learned authors and International Committee of the Red Cross (ICRC) opinion to conclude that the minimum standards of conduct which now arguably comprise customary law – for example, the prohibition against torture and other harming of those *hors de combat* – should bind peacekeepers.

To sum up, it appears that the Commission made no conclusive pronouncement on the applicability of the Geneva Conventions and Protocols to the CF deployment to Somalia. Nonetheless, the Commission concluded that the CF in Somalia were bound by minimum humanitarian standards.

It is interesting to note that numerous senior CF officers gave evidence before the Commission that they believed that the LOAC, or at a minimum, the principles of the Geneva Conventions, applied to the CF deployment in Somalia.[14]

4. CANADA'S OBLIGATION TO PROVIDE TRAINING IN IHL TO MEMBERS OF ITS ARMED FORCES

Concerning Canada's obligations to provide IHL training to its armed forces, some of the findings of the Report were strongly worded:

> The CF is obliged under international law to provide training in the LOAC. We have determined that the insufficient knowledge of the Law of Armed Conflict on the part of the CAR members was in the first instance the result of weaknesses in training in the LOAC that existed in the CF more generally.[15]

According to the Commission's Report, the training plan for the original Ch. VI peacekeeping mission Operation Cordon (UNOSOM), did not adequately provide for sufficient and appropriate training in relation to several non-combat skills that are essential for peacekeeping, including the nature of UN peacekeeping and the role of the peacekeeper; the Law of Armed Conflict, including arrest and detention procedures; training in use of force policies, including mission-specific rules of engagement; conflict resolution and negotiation skills development; inter-cultural relations and the culture, history and politics

13. Ibid., at p. 24.
14. Ibid., at p. 27.
15. Ibid., at p. 613.

of the environment; and psychological preparation and stress management. The failure of the training plan to provide adequately for these non-combat skills was found by the Commission to have arisen primarily from the lack of any doctrine recognizing the need for such training, and the lack of supporting training materials and standards.

A number of the Commission's Findings concerning training were overturned, in respect of one senior officer, by a 1998 Federal Court of Canada decision.[16] Other senior officers have launched similar challenges. Whatever conclusions are ultimately reached about responsibility for training deficiencies concerning IHL, these deficiencies are striking. Some of the testimony from CF members before the Commission raises grave concerns about the soldiers' understanding of the basics of the LOAC.

It is clear from the testimony before the various courts-martial that there was no uniform understanding of how detainees should be treated. Several witnesses stated that they believed detainees were to be made uncomfortable in order to deter them from coming back. This was interpreted differently by various soldiers: some thought it meant keeping detainees awake all night and not giving them food or water, while others had the incredible notion that they were to keep detainees awake and uncomfortable by pouring cold water over their heads and not feeding them.[17]

The Commission was also very concerned with the development and content of the Rules of Engagement (ROE), and with the training of CF members about the ROE. There was extensive and at times painstaking examination and cross-examination of witnesses on these questions. The Commission's Recommendations's on IHL training included the following:

– Legal officers should receive increased training in matters of international law, including the Law of Armed Conflict;
– Legal officers providing advisory services should be deployed on training missions as well as actual operations;
– Legal officers should provide an advisory services guide commanding officers and troops on legal issues arising from all aspects of operations, including Rules of Engagement, the Law of Armed Conflict, Canadian Forces Organization Orders and Ministerial Organization Orders;
– A Law of Armed Conflict section of legal officers should be established and staffed as soon as possible within the office of the Judge Advocate General and

16. See *Morneault* v. *Canada* [*Attorney General*] 1998 F.C.J, No. 501, 27 April 1998.
17. See Report, Vol. 2, Ch. 21, fnn. 373-375, and related text.

moved to the office of the Director General of Military Legal Services once that office is established;

– Legal officers providing advisory services should educate Canadian Forces members before and during deployment on local law, the Law of Armed Conflict, and Rules of Engagement; and

– The Chief of the Defence Staff should oversee the development of specialist expertise within the Canadian Forces in training in the Law of Armed Conflict and the Rules of Engagement, and in intercultural and intergroup relations, negotiation and conflict resolution; and ensure continuing training in these skills for all members of the Canadian Forces.

These recommendations are noteworthy in three ways. First, they emphasise the need for more training in the LOAC at all stages of a deployment. Second, they call for an integration of legal expertise and legal experts into operations. Finally, they focus on extra-legal aspects - such an intercultural relations and conflict resolution skills - that can help prevent the escalation of tensions and the use of force. These recommendations reflect a innovative and broad-minded approach to Canada's obligations to ensure compliance with the law of armed conflict.

5. CONSEQUENCES AND RESPONSES

In October 1997, Canada's Minister of Defence officially responded to the Commission's Report.[18] In a paper over 100 pages long, the Minister reported that the government supported 83 percent of the Commission's Recommendations, and provided details on their implementation. The Minister also established a committee of eight prominent Canadians (the Monitoring Committee on Change) which for two years will study and report directly to Parliament on the process of implementing change at Canada's Department of National Defence and the CF.

Even before the release of the Commission's Report, many actions were taken by the Department of National Defence to increase IHL training of its members.

Today, increased resources have been committed to ensuring that CF members receive adequate training in IHL, and it can be said that IHL training has become a priority for Canada's Department of National Defence.

18. A commitment to change. Published by Canada's Department of National Defence, October 1997. Available on the national Defence website: www.dnd.ca.

6. CONCLUSIONS

The Commission's Report, released in June 1997, received extensive media coverage and much public comment. The government was widely criticized for cutting the Commission's mandate prematurely, but its actions withstood judicial challenge and to some degree fell largely from the headlines.

Two key observations arise from Canada's Somalia experience: first, the critical question of the applicability of IHL to CF members on UN peace operations remains unclear. This is a cause for concern, given Canada's desire to remain active in UN peace operations. This, of course, only serves to underline the need for IHL training based on universally recognized minimum humanitarian standards of protection.

Second, despite the trauma and unanswered questions arising from Canada's Somalia deployment, there is little doubt that the Commission identified a serious need for enhanced IHL training, and for resources to do this properly.

The Somalian experience still evokes strong reactions from many Canadians, civilians and members of the armed forces alike. While this file is far from being closed, what cannot be disputed is that the experience of the CF in Somalia produced an intense reflexion on Canadians' expectations from members of the armed forces.

In concluding, it is to be hoped that the 'lessons learned' from Canada's deployment to Somalia in 1992 and 1993 will be studied and widely assimilated by armed forces around the world. This would help ensure that the many tragedies of the Somalia deployment are not repeated. It would also help ensure that IHL is fully respected by those who must face the difficult challenges implicit in complex UN peace operations.

BROCKLEBANK: A QUESTIONABLE DECISION OF THE COURT MARTIAL APPEAL COURT OF CANADA*

Katia Boustany**

During the Canadian mission in Somalia pursuant to resolution 794 (1992) of the Security Council, a stunning incident occurred involving some Canadian soldiers who tortured to death a sixteen-year-old unarmed Somali civilian. The victim was captured during the night of 16 March 1993 while attempting an intrusion into the camp of Belet Huen. Shidane Arone did not offer any resistance and was entrusted to chief corporal Matchee to be kept in custody in a bunker designed for this purpose. This is where the unfortunate Somali had to endure frightful ill-treatment, mainly at Matchee's hands.

Soldier Brocklebank himself did not actually participate in acts of torture; however, that night, while performing his guard duty, he discovered what was taking place in the bunker but did not attempt to put an end to it by reporting it to a superior of Matchee.[1] Therefore, he was charged under section 269.1 of the Criminal Code of Canada (1985) with the offense of aiding and abetting in the commission of torture.

While this accusation was dismissed for lack of evidence 'beyond reasonable doubt that Brocklebank, a) did or omitted to do something, b) for the purpose of aiding Matchee in the commission of the offense of torture'[2], it remains striking that the Court did not retain the Prosecution's allegation of negligent performance of a military duty.

** Professor of International Law at the Department of Legal Studies of the University of Quebec, Montreal.

1. *Dishonoured Legacy,* Report of the Commission of Inquiry into the Deployment of Canadian Forces to Somalia (Canadian Government Publishing, 1997) vol. 1, pp. 351-363.

2. *Her Majesty the Queen* v. *Private D.J. Brocklebank,* Court Martial Appeal Court of Canada, 2 April 1996, hereafter cited as *The Queen* v. Brocklebank.

The core of the subject matter in this respect was the applicability to the case of the Unit Guide to the Geneva Conventions[3], which 'imposes on a member of the Canadian Forces, at all times including in peacetime, a duty to safeguard civilians in Canadian Forces custody whether or not these civilians are in that member's custody'.[4] But, in the view of the Court, there was no declared war nor armed conflict in Somalia; and, as the Canadian Forces deployed in that country were performing a peacekeeping mission, they were not engaged in any conflict. Therefore, the Geneva Conventions, and, in particular, the Civilian Convention, were not applicable to this situation, nor was the Unit Guide.[5]

Such an analysis of the Canadian involvement in Somalia completely omits to take into consideration the nature of the operation at this very stage of the whole process, which led the Security Council to adopt various steps aimed at securing the safe conduct of humanitarian relief to the long-starving population of this battered and fractured country.

Actually, the torture episode took place while Canadian Forces were acting within UNITAF (United Nations Task Force), a *peace enforcement* operation authorized by the executive organ of the United Nations under Chapter VII of the Charter and entrusted to American command. The wording of Security Council resolution 794 meant clearly, as per UN jargon, that recourse to armed force would not be merely for self-defence, as is usually the case in peacekeeping missions, but was intended to be coercive in order to achieve the objectives assigned to this action, which was distinct and different from the Organization's ailing operation in Somalia, UNOSOM. Resolution 794 also condemned vigorously all violations of international humanitarian law committed in Somalia, meaning implicitly but clearly that there was a warfare state. And what would a peacekeeping operation be meant for otherwise; let alone the characterization of the UNITAF mission as one of peace enforcement?

On the other hand, the Canadian Rules of Engagement (ROE) specifically set for the forces sent to Somalia dealt explicitly with hostile acts, hostile intention, hostile force and terrorist attacks by armed civilians, military or paramilitary groups, and allowed a response using all necessary force, including deadly force. Moreover, the document itself directed that the precepts and ROE contained in it must be implemented according to domestic law and international law.

In this respect, customary international law had already been acknowledged by Canadian doctrine as becoming 'part of domestic law without the necessity

3. The Unit Guide to the Geneva Conventions was issued by the Chief of Defense Staff on 15 June 1973. It is a manual aimed at acquainting all ranks of the Canadian Forces with the principles of the Geneva Conventions.

4. Ibid.

5. *The Queen* v. *Brocklebank*, op. cit. n. 2.

of implementing legislation'[6]; thus, the Martens clause should have been given consideration as it imposes at all times the minimal, but overriding, obligation to act according to 'the laws of humanity and the dictates of public conscience'. This clause had previously been recognized by a Canadian Court as proof that 'under international law, war did not totally negate the legal protection accorded to civilian population'.[7] Further, in the *Nicaragua* case[8], the ICJ referred to the terms of the Martens clause as corresponding to what it had earlier identified under 'elementary considerations of humanity, even more exacting in peace than in war'.[9]

From this perspective, no matter what qualification may be given to the situation in Somalia, Brocklebank had, in fact, failed to fulfill a duty incumbent upon any military in all circumstances. Therefore, the Court's elaboration of the standard of care appears completely inopportune, particularly the idea applied to the matter under consideration that, in the context of a military operation, the standard of care will vary considerably in relation to the degree of responsibility exercised by the accused, the nature and purpose of the operation, and the exigencies of a particular situation.[10]

No relativity is admissible concerning the performance of obligations under the Martens clause and their enforcement. However, as to the partial discharge of the Court Martial Appeal Court, it appears quite likely that the prosecution did not submit appropriate legal evidence – mainly resolution 794 of the Security Council and the Rules of Engagement of Canadian Forces in Somalia – nor did it invoke the Martens clause as a binding norm of customary international humanitarian law. And in this respect, the prosecution's preparation of the case is also questionable.

Nevertheless, the main problem raised by the *Brocklebank* decision results from the Court's assumption that IHL would not be applicable to peacekeeping operations. Although a domestic court may well question whether what is known as the law of armed conflicts applies to actions where military forces from various countries are not engaged in hostilities, *stricto sensu,* the answer could have been found in the United Nations' long-established practice – pursuant to constant pledges from the International Committee of the Red Cross. According to this, a standard clause is included in the Agreements between the UN and Member States contributing military forces to a given peacekeeping operation 'whereby

6. Honourable Jules Deschênes, Commissioner, Commission of Inquiry on War Criminals, Part 1: Public (Canadian Government Publishing Center, 30 December 1986) p. 128.

7. *Finta* case, Canada High Court of Justice, 10 July 1989, *ILR* 82, p. 435.

8. *Nicaragua* v. *USA, ICJ Rep.* 1986, Para. 218.

9. *The Corfu Channel* case (Merits), *ICJ Rep.* (1949) p. 22.

10. *The Queen* v. *Brocklebank*, op. cit. n. 2.

the United Nations peace-keeping mission or operation undertakes to observe and respect the principles and spirit of the general conventions applicable to the conduct of military personnel, and the participating State undertakes to ensure that the members of its national contingent are fully acquainted with the principles and spirit of said conventions'.[11]

It might then be assumed that Canada's involvement in so many UN peacekeeping operations since the inception of this mechanism with the creation of UNEF (United Nations Emergency Force) in 1956[12] has been governed by such a practice, at least with regard to the Canadian Government's international obligations in this respect. However, technically speaking, UNITAF was not a UN peacekeeping operation: it was a Coalition action authorized by a Security Council resolution; therefore, no agreement was entered into between acting states and the UN under which the applicability of IHL to the conduct of military personnel would have been reasserted. Thus, the matter was left to each Government's decision and policy; and, apparently, the issue of IHL applicability to Canadian Forces deployed in Somalia was not a major concern at the time.

In fact, Coalition operations raise once more the broader question of the applicability of IHL to actions undertaken within the framework of peacekeeping, whether that kind of military activity is undertaken within the framework of an interstate or intrastate conflict, and whether it is decided by the UN itself or by a regional organization.

Obviously, the *Brocklebank* decision proves that it cannot and should not be relied solely upon states to draw the policy line concerning the applicability of IHL to any type of peacekeeping action. Whenever an organization, be it the UN or a regional one, adopts a resolution creating or authorizing any such operation, notwithstanding its specific nature and structure, it has the responsibility to ensure that so-called peace troops are subject in their behaviour to the rules of IHL, and therefore to define, within the very same resolution or another appropriate instrument, participating Governments' obligations to secure the same.

Otherwise, there would remain a gap between the implementation of international law through peace action and the conduct of the latter. Citizens and populations, who are not aware of the would-be subtleties of law but are nevertheless regularly overwhelmed by demagogic governments' rhetoric about enforcement of international law, cannot understand that peace operations escape from the appropriate instruments of the same international law.

11. Daphna Shraga, 'The United Nations as an actor bound by international humanitarian law,' in Luigi Condorelli, Anne-Marie La Rosa, Sylvie Scherrer, eds., *The United Nations and International Humanitarian Law* (Pedone, Paris 1996) pp. 315-338 at p. 324.

12. The UNEF remained in the Sinai until 1967.

REPORT BY THE ENQUIRY COMMISSION ON THE BEHAVIOUR OF ITALIAN PEACE-KEEPING TROOPS IN SOMALIA*

Natalia Lupi**

Following the collapse of Somalia into a state of general anarchy after the fall of Siad Barre's regime, the UN Security Council, on 24 April 1992, adopted Resolution 751 with which, under the direction of the Secretary-General, it created the UNOSOM (United Nations Operation in Somalia) mission. The duty of UNOSOM was to supervise both the ceasefire between the fighting factions and the distribution of humanitarian aid.[1]

When the situation worsened, the Security Council adopted Resolution 794 on 3 December 1992 under Chapter VII of the UN Charter, authorizing the creation of UNITAF (Unified Task Force) under the command of the United States. UNITAF's mandate was to create a safe environment for humanitarian aid and for reconstruction. With Resolution 814 of 16 March 1993, the Security Council entrusted the UN Secretary-General with the command of operation UNOSOM II, which took over from the international task force directed by the United States and concluded its mandate in 1994.[2]

By means of Security Council Resolutions 794 and 814, Italy collaborated in the operations in Somalia with its own contingent (Operation IBIS-ITALFOR), which participated in both UNITAF and UNOSOM II consistent with Law-Decree

** Consultant at the Institute for Legal Studies on the International Community, Rome.

1. Following the initiative of the Secretary-General of the United Nations to restore peace in Somalia, on 3 March 1992, Interim President Ali Mahdi and General Aidid signed an 'Agreement on the Implementation of a Cease-fire'. See *The United Nations and the Situation in Somalia,* Reference Paper (United Nations Department of Information, New York May 1995) p. 2.

2. On the United Nations operation in Somalia, see *The Blue Helmets, A Review of the United Nations Peacekeeping Operations*, 3rd edn. (United Nations Department of Public Information, New York 1996) p. 285 et seq.

Yearbook of International Humanitarian Law
Volume 1 - 1998 - pp. 375-379

No. 21 of 1 February 1993 and subsequent legislation.[3] Overall, the role of the Italian contingent was appreciated, in particular for the humanitarian initiatives performed in a situation of chaos and widespread violence.

Therefore, the publication in the weekly magazine *Panorama*[4] of some photographs concerning presumed maltreatment and violence to Somali citizens by Italian soldiers aroused considerable amazement amongst public opinion.

Consequently, both the competent military and ordinary judicial authorities commenced investigations.[5] (Further episodes of violence were reported by Somali citizens to the Fact-Finding Commission later established by the Italian Government. As will be seen below, the Commission considered only one of these subsequent episodes as reliable.)

Some considerations must be expressed at this stage. Firstly, a specific legal regime for operations of the kind under examination does not exist in Italy. Secondly, under Article 9 of the Military Penal Code of War [Codice Penale Militare di Guerra-c.p.m.g.], provisions of the Code are extended to Italian military contingents abroad. However, the Code has not been deemed applicable to this specific case. The c.p.m.g contains a Title which also deals with crimes committed by military persons against civilian and military enemies. The crimes of violation, torture and maltreatment against civilians are not provided for by the Military Penal Code of Peace, which was actually applied in the case under examination).[6]

It is, however, true that this norm appears inadequate to operations like the one in Somalia for several reasons: a) the Code entered into force in 1941 and is thus suspected not to be respondent to the needs of such situations, b) the operations directed or promoted by the UN cannot be easily framed within the outlines of the Italian law of war.

3. Italian participation in Operations in Somalia was regulated by a number of law-decrees: D.L. [Law-Decree] no. 21 of 1 February 1993, in *Gazzetta Ufficiale* [Official Journal] no. 25 of 1 February 1993; D.L. no. 56 of 10 March 1993, in *G.U.* no. 58 of 11 March 1993, later reiterated and converted in Law no. 125 of 22 February 1994, in *G.U.* no 47 of 26 February 1994; D.L. no. 16 of 11 January 1994, in *G.U.* no. 8 of 12 January 1994, converted in Law no. 151 of 22 February 1994, in *G.U.* no. 54 of 7 March 1994; D.L. no. 11 of 17 January 1995, in *G.U.* no. 13 o f 17 January 1995, later reiterated and converted in Law no. 285 of 13 July 1995, in *G.U.* no. 167 of 19 July 1995.

4. *Panorama*, no. 24, 19 June 1997, p. 42.

5. The military judicial authority has normally competence concerning violations foreseen in the Military Penal Codes, which, however, do not automatically limit the competence of the ordinary judicial authority on common crimes although perpetrated by military persons. As a matter of fact, investigations in front of both authorities are still pending.

6. Both Codes were adopted by Royal Decree no. 303 of 20 February 1941 and published in *Codici penali militari e norme complementari*, edited by Mazzi, Brunelli, Milan, 1995.

Taking into account the above, the Italian regulation stated, at Article 1, paragraph 5 of Law-Decree no. 21, that the Italian contingent in Somalia be subject to the Military Penal Code of Peace [Codice Penale Militare di Pace-c.p.m.p.], derogating from the above-mentioned Article 9, c.p.m.g.

If, on the one hand, the regulation adopted solves the problems illustrated, on the other hand, it raises new worries. According to Italian law, in fact, military offences are normally judged by the military jurisdiction on the basis of military laws. C.p.m.p., however, does not deal with common offences; thus, a military person responsible for an offence not foreseen by military regulation must be judged by the ordinary jurisdiction. In this legal context, both the military and ordinary judicial authorities can commence investigations, each on the basis of its own competence. The above does not necessarily yield a conflict amongst judges.

The ascertaining of possible disciplinary infractions is still the subject of an internal administrative investigation under Military Authorities. The investigation is still pending and it is as yet unclear when it will be terminated and whether the result will be made public.

For a preliminary verification that the events concerning the reported episodes actually took place, the Italian government established a Government Fact-Finding Commission by a Decree of the Ministry of Defense on 16 June 1997. It is composed of five members: three civilians, one of whom is the president[7], and two military.

The Commission is charged with ascertaining whether the illegal events reported are founded and verifying any malfunctions in the management of the mission which could have undermined its humanitarian aims. The Commission can submit reports to the competent judicial authorities to identify evidence relevant to ongoing trials. To this end, the Commission is empowered to carry out inspections and interrogations, collect information and request documentation from the administrative authorities.

On 8 August 1997, the Commission, although still on mandate[8], presented the 'Conclusive Report on the Events [which] Occurred in Somalia'. It expressed appreciation for the overall work of the Italian contingent, in particular for being successful in creating a climate of trust with the local population in spite of

7. The president of the commission is Prof. Ettore Gallo, former President of the Italian Constitutional Court.

8. The Decree establishing the Commission did not fix any expiry date for the Commission's mandate, the existence of which is thus subject to the evaluation of the Minister of Defense.

recourse, in some cases, to the use of force for self-defense[9] and for ensuring humanitarian operations management.

In this context, the Report asserted the 'absolutely individual' nature of the episodes of maltreatment reported. It also stressed that those episodes presented a character of 'exceptional gravity'.

The Commission examined eight episodes of alleged violations of human rights, recognizing as founded charges in only three cases which are currently under investigation by judicial authorities. In particular, all responsibility was excluded for events concerning Somali prisoners 'hooded and bound' during patrols, in that such treatment is allowed by military law for transferring individuals whose freedom must be restricted.

The first episode where the Commission verified that the accusation was founded took place on 9 April 1993 in the Johar camp[10], while the Italian contingent was part of UNITAF, and concerns the interrogation of a Somali citizen where a telephone wire was used to cause electric shocks, the photographs of which were published in *Panorama*, above mentioned. Since it was not possible to question the victim, the Commission based its conclusions upon a witness of one of the two soldiers involved and of his accused superior who is still under investigation by the judicial authority. The Commission concluded on the occurence of the fact, but not on any ascertained responsibility.

The other two cases took place during the course of the UNOSOM II operation. The first concerns the rape of a Somali female citizen perpetrated around 14-15 June 1993 at the Mogadishu port. On this occasion, the victim reported that she was compelled into a container by a junior officer and there raped by a group of soldiers. The Commission based its conclusions on the evidence of the woman and on that of the accused officer, who denied all accusations. It found that the incidence alleged occured but did not draw any conclusions on the question of responsibility.

The last episode took place between 17-19 November 1993 at a checkpoint controlled by the Italian contingent. Here also a Somali woman alleged that she was raped with a rifle flare. Verification is based on photographic documentation and on some depositions of soldiers present, since it was not possible to verify the identity of the victim nor of the authors.

The Commission concluded as in the previous cases.

The Commission did not consider the other five reports credible. The unreliability of the witnesses, the contradictions in depositions and the lack of objective

9. On this point, see S. Marchisio, *The Use of Force by Peace-keeping Forces for the Implementation of Their Mandate: Recent Cases and New Problems, Italian and German Participation in Peace-keeping: From Dual Approaches to Co-operation* (Pisa 1997) pp. 75-84.

10. The Johar Camp was situated North-West of Mogadishu.

evidence of the events reported were decisive elements in concluding that the facts were unfounded.

At the end of the investigation, the Commission reached the conclusion that the responsibilities ascertained were circumscribed to the lower levels of the military hierarchy, including non-commissioned officers and subordinate officers who were responsible for illicit tolerance or omission of control, contributing to causing the events. In the Commission's view, the patronizing attitude of subordinate officers apparently determined their failure to report the events to superior officers, whose responsibility in the events, either direct or indirect, was thus absolutely excluded.

The Report concludes by recognizing the necessity for teaching tolerance to military personnel engaged abroad and hopes that, along with more efficient controls, magistrates and human rights experts will be present on missions of an international nature.

The report from the Commission, which had a restricted mandate, merits observations on some interesting aspects. A first question concerns the applicability of international humanitarian law. It appears evident from the Report that it is truly difficult to ascertain whether the events reported can be set within a legal context of war or within that of a police operation aiming at restoring public order. Therefore, the Commission failed to express any legal evaluation of the facts, particularly from the perspective of international humanitarian law.

The Somali case thus highlights the urgent need to find a solution to the controversial question of the applicability of humanitarian law to operations with humanitarian aims in situations of internal conflict, instituted under Chapter VII of the UN Charter.[11]

The second aspect concerns the identification of the competent judge for the alleged episodes of maltreatment. As already noted, Italian soldiers in Somalia were subject to the c.p.m.p. not dealing with war-related crimes. The above entailed that a number of trials were initiated in front of the ordinary Italian judge for offences actually committed by military persons in a war context.

11. See P. Benvenuti, 'The Implementation of International Humanitarian Law in the Framework of United Nations Peace-keeping Operations', *Law in Humanitarian Crises* (Office for Official Publications of the European Communities, Luxembourg 1995) Vol. I, pp. 83-120. Also L. Condorelli, A. La Rosa and, S. Scherrer, *Les Nations Unies et le droit international humanitaire, Actes du colloque international à l'occasion du cinquantième anniversaire de l'ONU* (Paris, 1995).

SOME ASPECTS OF GERMAN STATE PRACTICE CONCERNING IHL*

Horst Fischer**

1. RECENT DEVELOPMENTS CONCERNING THE PUNISHMENT OF INTERNATIONAL CRIMES RELATED TO ARMED CONFLICT

Germany is one of only a few countries to have prosecuted and convicted persons for international crimes related to the conflicts in the former Yugoslavia. Three trial procedures were held between 1994 and 1998.[1] Proceedings in a fourth case were due to commence in the fall of 1998. Two defendants were convicted, and their sentences are currently under appeal on questions of law.[2]

The judgments of the courts in Munich and Düsseldorf in the cases of *Novislav Djajić* and *Nikola Jorgić* are interesting from many perspectives though, due to the appeals, they have not yet been officially published and it will be interesting to see how the German High Court will decide. Some general observations might help to explain the judicial system with regard to war crimes in a country which has a specific history of dealing with war crimes committed during the Second

** Professor Dr. Horst Fischer is Professor of International Humanitarian Law at the University of Leiden, the Netherlands; Academic Director of the Institute for International Law of Peace and Armed Conflict (IFHV), Ruhr-Universität, Bochum, Germany; and General Editor of the *Yearbook of International Humanitarian Law*.

1. Concerning *Dusko Tadić*, whose case was later deferred to the ICTY, *Novislav Djajić* and *Nikola Jorgić*.

2. According to the German Criminal Procedure Law (StPO), two types of appeal are admittable. An appeal on questions of fact is permissible from judgements only from certain courts (§312 StPO) and it can also include questions of law. An appeal on law does not allow a reexamination of the facts, but is restricted to a determination of whether the law has been correctly applied and whether the judgement is based on a correct application of the procedural rules (§338 StPO). Published in *BGBl.* (1998) I, p. 164 et seq.

Yearbook of International Humanitarian Law
Volume 1 - 1998 - pp. 380-392

World War.[3] In particular, it might be helpful to compare the basic preconditions for punishing war crimes as expressed in the recent war crimes cases with the position of the German Government expressed in the years 1997 and 1998 during the preparatory phase for the establishment of the International Criminal Court (ICC) to be able to ascertain how far the applicable German law must be changed in order to fully implement the Statute of the ICC.

1.1 Jurisdiction to Prosecute International Crimes before German Courts

There is no all-inclusive German code dealing with international crimes. Plans to develop a specific code for war crimes and related crimes have never been implemented.[4] The most important rules on jurisdiction and substance are included in the German Penal Code (StGB). Rules of other codes relate in particular to acts and omissions of German nationals.[5]

Jurisdiction under German law is primarily based on geographical and functional criteria. Which court has jurisdiction in any particular case can only be determined by an application of three codes, all of which have recently been amended: the GVG[6], the StGB[7] and the StPO[8].

The StGB includes in sections 3-5 the common jurisdictional clauses governing acts of nationals at home and abroad, acts committed abroad against Germans and specific rights of German nationals or the German state. According to section 5(1), planning a war of aggression is prohibited, irrespective of the law applicable in the place of the act.

3. For an evaluation of the practice of German courts see H. Ostendorf, 'Die -widersprüchlichen - Auswirkungen der Nürnberger Prozesse auf die westdeutsche Justiz', G. Hankel & G. Stuby, eds., *Strafgerichte gegen Menschheitsverbrechen: Zum Völkerstrafrecht 50 Jahre nach den Nürnberger Prozessen* (Hamburg 1995) pp. 73-98.

4. For an early comprehensive overview see G. Dahm, *Zur Problematik des Völkerstrafrechts* (Göttingen 1956).

5. Other laws with recent amendments: The War Weapons Control Act (*Kriegswaffenkontrollgesetz, BGBl.* (1997) I, p. 1059); the Foreign Trade and Payments Act (*Außenwirtschaftsgesetz, BGBl.* (1997) I, pp. 1439); the Legal Status of Military Personnel Act (*Soldatengesetz, BGBl.* (1997) I, p. 2042); the Military Penal Code (*Wehrstrafgesetz, BGBl.* (1974) I, p. 1213); the Code for Military Discipline (*Wehrdisziplinarordnung, BGBl.* (1997) I, p 2042); and the Law of International Assistance in Criminal Matters (*Gesetz über die Internationale Rechtshilfe in Strafsachen, BGBl.* (1994) I, p. 1537).

6. The law on the unification of the court system, *Gerichtsverfassungsgesetz, BGBl.* (1998) I, p. 1580 et seq.

7. The penal code, *Strafgesetzbuch, BGBl.* (1998) I, p. 164 et seq.

8. The penal procedural code, *Strafprozeßordnung, BGBl.* (1998) I, p. 164 et seq.

For the prosecution of crimes committed abroad against internationally protected legal rights, sections 6 and 7 determine the jurisdiction of German courts. Three different types of jurisdictional clauses are embodied in these two sections. Under section 6(1), jurisdiction is explicitly given for genocide. However, no reference is made in this paragraph to the Genocide Convention and its jurisdictional clauses. Under section 6(9), jurisdiction is also given for acts which Germany has agreed to prosecute in intergovernmental agreements, even if the acts were committed abroad. Finally, a third and very broad clause in section 7 of the Penal Code provides jurisdiction over specific cases not involving German nationals, in which the act was punishable in the place where it was committed if the place of the act is not subject to any punitive power. If in such cases a person who was a foreigner at the time of the act is caught in Germany, jurisdiction is given provided that extradition is not requested, a request for extradition is rejected or extradition is not feasible.

While the jurisdictional clause with regard to genocide is specific and clear – although as already mentioned, its relation to Article 5 of the Genocide Convention is not explained in the law – the latter two paragraphs are not easy to apply as they refer on the one hand to Germany's international obligations without specifying the different treaty rules, and on the other hand they link the law applicable in the country[9] where the act was committed with extradition preconditions and decisions. Nonetheless, in recent years the clause dealing with Germany's international obligations has always been understood as embodying the Geneva Conventions and the Additional Protocols.

1.2 The Penal Code and International Crimes

Excepting genocide[10] and preparation for aggression[11], none of the acts today described as the 'core international crimes' are expressly dealt with in the German penal code.[12] Neither war crimes in the traditional sense, including grave breaches of the Geneva Conventions and violations of the laws and customs of war, nor crimes against humanity have been specified as crimes under German penal law. Despite some judgements referring to crimes committed in the Second World War, no specific new laws have been inserted into the penal code to deal with the particularities of a war situation. Consequently, if jurisdiction is given in cases of the acts described above, the German penal code applies in full,

9. As provided in section 7.

10. Section 220a of the Penal Code.

11. Section 80.

12. For a general overview see L.C. Green, 'Die Bundesrepublik Deutschland und die Ausübung der Strafgerichtsbarkeit', 5 *Humanitäres Völkerrecht* (1992) p. 32 et seq.

including its definitions of crimes, rules about attempt, participation, justification and mitigating circumstances.[13] German law and not international law forms the basis for a judgement, as is made clear by the introductory sentence of sections 3-7 stating that 'German criminal law applies'. The current prosecution of the so-called core international crimes is therefore framed by specific aspects of the section of the penal code in question, be it murder, taking of hostages or damage to property.

It is clear from the foregoing observation that, under the existing German penal code, IHL does not define the crimes. Still, it plays an important role which is not defined in any of the written penal codes. As German criminal law applies to all acts, even if committed in war, IHL comes into play as a justifying element. Killing a soldier of an enemy army can be an act of manslaughter or may even amount to murder, but, according to the accepted rules on justification, it may be justified as a lawful act of war and therefore would not result in punishment.

For several years, there have been discussions about whether, according to the obligations embodied in the Geneva Conventions, a specific German law on international crimes is necessary. A draft law prepared for this purpose was discussed in the relevant ministries but did not reach the level of serious parliamentary consideration. For the past decades, Germany could live with this situation, not being compelled by overwhelming incidents or political pressure to deal with war crimes committed on foreign territory by non-Germans, despite some recent attempts to change the law within Germany.

1.3 Actual Cases

With the establishment of the International Tribunals for the former Yugoslavia (ICTY) and Rwanda (ICTR) and, in particular, with the recent war crimes cases in Germany, the peculiar legal situation was perceived by many as being no longer appropriate.[14] The *Tadić* case prompted a discussion about the appropri-

13. For the specific problem of rape see H. Fischer, 'Grundlagen der völkerstrafrechtlichen Verfolgung von Vergewaltigungen im bosnischen Krieg', 11 *Sicherheit und Frieden* (1993) p. 71 et seq.; more generally see B. Wentzek, 'Zur Geltung des deutschen Strafrechts im Ausland', 39 Neue Zeitschrift für Wehrrecht (1997) p. 25 et seq.

14. For a general overview see H. Fischer and S. Lüder, eds., *Völkerrechtliche Verbrechen vor dem Jugoslawien-Tribunal, nationalen Gerichten und dem Internationalen Strafgerichtshof: Beiträge zur Entwicklung einer effektiven internationalen Strafgerichtsbarkeit* (forthcoming); D. Füth, 'Die Verfolgung von Kriegsverbrechen durch deutsche Gerichte aufgrund des Weltrechtspflegeprinzips', 10 *Humanitäres Völkerrecht* (1997) p. 38 et seq.

ateness of the German legal situation, though he was later deferred to the ICTY.[15] Dusko Tadić was taken into custody in Munich in February 1994 after he was discovered by survivors of one of the concentration camps where he was alleged to have committed several severe crimes. He was brought to The Hague in April 1994 to be put on trial before the ICTY.[16]

The trial against *Novislav Djajić* opened before the Bavarian High Court in February 1997 and the judgement was announced three months later on 23 May 1997. The hearings against *Nikola Jorgić* also began in February 1997 and lasted until September 1997. The District Court in Düsseldorf announced its judgement on 26 September 1997.

The charges against both defendants were based on acts committed in Bosnia and Herzegovina in 1992, and were similar, though the cases differed in substance. Djajić was charged with genocide, murder and deprivation of liberty, according to sections 211, 220a, and 239 of the German penal code, which define the crimes, and section 6(9), dealing with jurisdiction, in connection with Articles 3, 146 and 147 of the Fourth Geneva Convention. The same and additional charges were brought forward against Jorgić, who was charged with genocide, murder and deprivation of liberty, bodily injury, robbery and receiving stolen goods, according to sections 211, 220a, 223, 223a and 239, 249, 250 and 255 and section 6(9) of the German penal code concerning Articles 3, 146 and 147 of the Fourth Geneva Convention.

In both cases, the question of jurisdiction was crucial. According to the general situation outlined above, from the outset jurisdiction was undisputedly given in both cases with regard to the genocide charge,[17] while for the other charges it was important to decide whether section 6(9) or section 7 would be applicable. According to the general understanding of section 6(9), the treaties mentioned therein do not refer to crimes committed in a non-international armed conflict and they do not refer at all to crimes against humanity. Both courts seem to have

15. See Application for Deferral by the Federal Republic of Germany in the Matter of Duško Tadić also known by the names Dusan 'Dule' Tadić, Case No. 1 of 1994; Decision of the Trial Chamber on the Application by the Prosecutor for a Formal Request for Deferral to the Competence of the International Criminal Tribunal for the Former Yugoslavia in the Matter of Duško Tadić (pursuant to Rules 9 and 10 of the Rules of Procedure and Evidence.' Case No. IT-94-1-D.

16. For a analysis of the German law relating to cooperation with the Tribunal for the Former Yugoslavia see C. Kreß, 'Strafen, Strafvollstreckung und internationale Zusammenarbeit im Statut des Internationalen Strafgerichtshofes', 11 *Humanitäres Völkerrecht* (1998) p. 151 et seq.; K. Oellers-Frahm, 'Zusammenarbeit der Staaten mit dem Internationalen Strafgerichtshof für das ehemalige Jugoslawien nach Art. 29 des Statuts - Durchführungsregelung Italiens', 7 *Humanitäres Völkerrecht* (1994) p. 60 et seq.

17. See also D. Oehler, 'Verfolgung von Völkermord im Ausland', 14 *Neue Strafrechts-Zeitschrift* (1994) p. 485 et seq.

applied in their respective judgements both sections of the German penal code, assuming that the charged acts were committed in an international armed conflict environment. It was also important for the judgements in both cases to decide whether, under the circumstances, jurisdiction is given generally or whether additional circumstances must be proved to establish jurisdiction. One element of such specific circumstances was identified by the German High Court in *Tadić*[18] in the specific link of the accused with Germany created by his permanent residence in Germany. Another element mentioned in the literature and which was taken into account by both courts is the interest of Germany and the international community in the prosecution of these crimes.

Djajić was sentenced to five years imprisonment. The judgement as reported was generally based on aiding and abetting murder. Jorgić was convicted to life imprisonment based on the charges, including genocide. His judgement was the first of a national or international court dealing with crimes committed in the former Yugoslavia to rule on a charge of genocide.

To classify the acts committed, all specific elements of the German penal code had to be applied to every single act in both cases. The killing of unarmed persons as alleged by the prosecutors could have been classified as manslaughter according to section 212 of the penal code or as murder according to section 211 of the code. Classification of an act as murder according to section 211 requires the fulfilment of certain criteria such as 'avarice or base motives'. The courts were expected to make certain that such motives were present in carrying out the accused acts. The overall political situation in the area, the aims of the action in question and the personal motives and expectations of the accused were prominent elements in deciding whether the specific criteria to establish murder under section 211 were satisfied.

Before deciding on the specific justification grounds according to the German penal code, such as self-defence and state of emergency, the courts had to characterize the act in question as being a violation of the laws of war. According to newspaper reports about the judgement, the killings of the civilians or prisoners had not been accepted as lawful behaviour in war despite the fact that reasons to justify the actions as reprisals were put forward by the defence.[19]

These short remarks demonstrate the interrelation between the German penal code and the rules on war crimes in Additional Protocol I as well as the grave breaches provisions of the Geneva Conventions. Despite the fact that IHL is not explicitly mentioned in the penal code, the written and unwritten rules about lawful and unlawful behaviour in war are essential to any judgement based on

18. Procedural Decision in the *Tadić* case.

19. Mitigating circumstances were only discussed in the *Djajić* case.

the jurisdictional clauses of sections 6 and 7 of the penal code. The application of the German penal code to situations of non-international armed conflicts can only be based on the rapidly changing international environment accepting the notion of war crimes for such cases.

1.4 The Governmental Position with Regard to the Prosecution of International Crimes

Since the early 1990s, German governmental representatives within the United Nations and the European Union stressed on several occasions the need to establish a permanent ICC.[20] Germany participated actively in the preparatory phase for the establishment of the ICC.[21] In particular, in 1997 a paper was produced which reflected in detail the position of several states, including Germany, with regard to the core crimes.[22] This reference paper on war crimes, as it was called, was used to prepare the German and like-minded positions for the international conference in Rome.[23] The paper included a detailed list of war crimes committed in international as well as non-international armed conflicts. It is interesting to note that, in addition to this broad approach, this paper referred to war crimes which up to 1997 were not regarded as grave breaches of the Geneva Conventions or as crimes under the old Hague law. Its reference to intentionally using starvation of civilians as a method of warfare is one example of the advanced character of the paper; forcing children under the age of 15 years to take a direct part in hostilities is another. Although, as with all the other documents prepared before the Rome conference, the reference paper did operate with so-called 'options', it is obvious what repercussions one should expect from this position paper on the German penal code when the Court is actually established.

20. K. Kinkel, 'Für einen funktionsfähigen Weltstrafgerichtshof', 50 *Neue Juristische Wochenschrift* (1997) p. 2860 et seq.

21. See also A. Zimmermann, 'Die Schaffung eines ständigen Internationalen Strafgerichtshofes: Perspektiven und Probleme vor der Staatenkonferenz in Rom', 58 *Zeitschrift für ausländisches Öffentliches Recht und Völkerrecht* (1998) p. 47 et seq.; B.B. Ferencz, 'Von Nürnberg nach Rom: Auf dem Weg zu einem Internationalen Strafgerichtshof', 11 *Humanitäres Völkerrecht* (1998) p. 80 et seq.

22. UN Doc. A/AC.249/1997/WG.1/DP.23. Rev. 1 (12 December 1997). Also published in *Humanitäres Völkerrecht* 11 (1998), issue 2, p. 90.

23. See in particular for the negotiating process H.-P. Kaul, 'Towards a Permanent International Criminal Court: Some Observations of a Negotiator', 18 *Human Rights Law Journal* (1997) p. 169 et seq.

In an overall evaluation of the Rome conference one has to accept the importance of the so-called 'main building blocks' strategy of several states to overcome difficulties in agreeing about the format and the content of the Statute of the ICC. Five main building blocks were proposed: the core crimes, jurisdiction, complementarity, the competence of the prosecutor, and the role of the Security Council. The overall German attitude in this regard had been demonstrated by what the paper explicitly called 'the German position' which, in its introductory sentence, stated that 'Germany is in favour of an effective, functioning, independent and thus credible international criminal court ...'[24] Nevertheless, the building blocks also made clear that the establishment of the ICC would necessitate a thorough evaluation of the national system for prosecution of war crimes.

It has been accepted by all states that, with regard to the role of national courts, the building blocks of complementarity and jurisdiction were most important. During the preparatory phase and later at the Rome conference, the specific aim of the German delegation was to strengthen the ICC but also to accept the principle of complementarity, which gives national courts an important role with regard to the core crimes. From the outset, therefore, one had to consider the possible result of the Rome conference and its implications for the German penal code.

1.5 Implementing the Rome Statute and the Need for a Thorough Reform

There is no doubt that, taking into account the particular role played by Germany in developing the Statute[25] for the ICC, the *Bundestag* (lower house of Parliament) will soon take the necessary steps for ratification.[26] Taking into account Germany's above-described interest in developing the international treaty rules dealing with the core crimes, it must be asked how far the present internal law situation is affected by the Statute.[27] There is one general observation which has

24. *Supra* n. 22.

25. See H.-P. Kaul, 'Der Internationale Strafgerichtshof: Das Ringen um seine Zuständigkeit und Reichweite', 11 *Humanitäres Völkerrecht* (1998) p. 138 et seq.

26. For an evaluation of the Rome statute see C. Tomuschat, 'Das Statut von Rom für den Internationalen Strafgerichtshof', 73 *Die Friedens-Warte* (1998) p. 335 et seq.

27. For a preliminary analysis see S. Rolf Lüder, 'Zur Inkorporierung eines Statuts für einen Ständigen Internationalen Strafgerichtshof in das deutsche und englische Recht', 11 *Humanitäres Völkerrecht* (1998) p. 59 et seq.

not yet been discussed sufficiently in Parliament and literature.[28] The present structure, in particular the complementarity between jurisdiction at the international and national levels, will require a preparation of national law systems to fulfill the function foreseen for them in the Statute.

The Statute of the new ICC is more specific and precise than the old Geneva treaty rules of 1949 and 1977. In particular, it refers to crimes committed in non-international armed conflicts. Such crimes can only be prosecuted under German law, as already pointed out, if one interprets the jurisdictional clauses in the light of the recent developments on the international agenda. It would be a rather strange situation if Germany contributed to the clarification of such rules at the international level while refraining from adapting its national law to integrate the international law developments. The penal code or an entirely new code (*Völkerstrafrechtsgesetz)* must be based on the same presumptions as used in the ICC Statute and therefore be more explicit than it is now.

Furthermore, with regard to the jurisdictional clauses, Parliament might feel compelled to state more explicitly, in an amendment to the already existing jurisdiction clauses, under what circumstances German courts should deal with war crimes in non-international armed conflicts if the ICC does not have jurisdiction under the terms of its Statute.

In addition to these and other general questions, the ICC Statute has reaffirmed the need to deal with more specific questions relating to the content of the crimes. According to the existing German penal code, every single act in war can be perceived as a war crime if the preconditions of the different sections are fulfilled independently of the acts of others. The policy of one of the parties to the conflict might be taken into account, for example in the genocide charge, but generally it is not decisive for the determination of an act as a crime under the code. Article 8 of the Rome Statute (War Crimes) is more limited with its reference to crimes 'committed as a part of a plan or policy or as a part of a large-scale commission of such crimes'. Whether, in the future, Germany wants to retain its broad attitude towards the definition of crimes committed in war situations or whether it would apply the more limited approach of the Rome Statute must be decided upon by Parliament. One could follow Article 8 of the Rome Statute or define jurisdiction as applicable in cases of single acts. Neither option would be easy to implement as such law would also apply to Germans involved in armed conflicts. The application of the sections on murder and manslaughter cannot be

28. For the question of deferral of German nationals see C. Rinio, 'Die Auslieferung eigener Staatsangehöriger: Historische Entwicklung und neuere Tendenzen', 108 *Zeitschrift für die gesamte Strafrechtswissenschaft* (1998) p. 356 et seq.; B. Schöbener & W. Bausback, 'Verfassungs- und völkerrechtliche Grenzen der "Überstellung" mutmaßlicher Kriegsverbrecher an den Jugoslawien-Strafgerichtshof', 49 *Die öffentliche Verwaltung* (1996) p. 621 et seq.

made dependent on the overall policy of a party to the armed conflict. If it is at all possible, a distinction between ordinary crimes and war crimes must be apparent.

Several of the definitions in Article 8 of the Rome Statute are difficult to include under sections of the German penal code.[29] Either the definitions in the Rome Statute have no obvious counterparts in the German penal code or justifications that are accepted under IHL cannot be applied without creating problems with the German penal code [just to mention a few critical cases of a long list of questions resulting from a comparison between the new Statute and the German penal code sections]. Examples are the following crimes listed in Article 8 of the Rome Statute: extensive destruction and appropriation of property, not justified by military necessity and carried out unlawfully and wantonly; attacking or bombarding by whatever means, towns, villages, dwellings or buildings which are undefended and which are not military objectives; making improper use of a flag of truce, of the flag or of the military insignia and uniform of the enemy or of the United Nations, as well as of the distinctive emblems of the Geneva Conventions, resulting in death or serious personal injury; declaring that no quarter will be given; intentionally using starvation of civilians as a method of warfare by depriving them of objects indispensable to their survival, including wilfully impeding relief supplies as provided for under the Geneva Conventions.

It is obvious that specific problems are caused by the so-called Hague rules if converted into a national penal law system, in particular when the Constitution requires that an act can only be punished if it was defined as a punishable offense by law before the crimes was committed[30] and if the legal consequences were provided for by the Statute.[31] For the application of the German penal code, it will be difficult to refer to the elements of a crime which is to a large extent not embodied in the written law and instead can only be found in an international treaty. However, it has been done with regard to implementing international treaties dealing with international crimes not related to armed conflicts, such as attacks on air traffic. Though it will be a difficult process and it will take a long time to define which adjustments are necessary or how a new law should look, for the sake of clarity the discussion process must be started as soon as possible. The prospects are quite good because in the recent past Germany has changed its position regarding IHL, as is made clear in the following section.

29. Wilkitzki in 1987 did not see the need to adopt German penal law to the Geneva Conventions and Additional Protocol rules on grave breaches and war crimes. P. Wilkitzki, 'Die völkerrechtlichen Verbrechen und das staatliche Strafrecht (Bundesrepublik Deutschland)', 99 *Zeitschrift für die gesamte Strafrechtswissenschaft* (1987) p. 455 et seq.

30. Art. 103 para. 2 of the Basic German Law (*Grundgesetz*).

31. Art. 104 para. 2 of the Basic German Law (*Grundgesetz*).

2. IMPLEMENTATION OF TREATY LAW

Germany needed 14 years from 1977 to 1991 to ratify both Additional Protocols to the Geneva Conventions. It is remarkable that the ratification of the four major treaties negotiated between 1993 and 1997[32] was achieved much more rapidly, with the explicit intention to make them applicable as soon as possible.

A second general remark concerns Germany's role in the negotiating process of these four treaties. After Germany had participated in UNOSOM (United Nations Operation in Somalia) II, the need for specifically protective rules for peacekeepers was more obvious to the German public than ever before. In particular, from the practice shown during the engagement of German Armed Forces in the Former Yugoslavia, it can be safely concluded that, for Germany, even under customary law there exists a special protection for United Nations and humanitarian assistance personnel.[33] It was therefore not difficult for Germany to actively participate in the negotiation process and to demand ratification of the new 1994 Convention on the Safety of United Nations and Associated Personnel by all states. Before ratifying the Convention, Germany repeatedly referred in international fora to the obligation to protect United Nations and Humanitarian Assistance Personnel.[34] It nevertheless took roughly two years to conclude the ratification process in the parliament.[35] The support given to the negotiation process in the United Nations and the statements by German authorities after adoption of the Convention showed that Germany wanted

32. The Convention on the Safety of United Nations and Associated Personnel of 1994; Protocol IV of the UN Conventional Weapons Convention (Blinding Laser Weapons) of 1995; amended Protocol II of 1996 of the UN Conventional Weapons Convention (Landmines); and the Landmines Convention of 1997. Germany also amended its law ratifying Protocol I concerning identification measures [Additional Protocol I to the Geneva Conventions of 12 August 1949, and Relating to the Protection of Victims of International Armed Conflicts of 12 December 1977 (Zusatzprotokoll zu den Genfer Abkommen vom 12. August 1949 über den Schutz der Opfer internationaler bewaffneter Konflikte [Protokoll I] vom 12. Dezember 1977) Änderungsgesetz vom 17. Juli 1997, *BGBl.* 1997 II, S. 1366].

33. Economic and Social Council, draft res., 2 March 1995, E/CN.4/1995/L.88, p. 5.

34. The most explicit statement was made by Germany's representative to the UN, Ambassador Eitel, in 1996. He called upon all parties to the Afghan civil war not to hamper humanitarian assistance and to provide for the safety and full freedom of movement of the United Nations personnel and other international personnel as well as for the security of their premises. Statement by Ambassador Eitel, Permanent Representative of Germany to the United Nations to the United Nations' 51st General Assembly, 13 December 1996, p. 2.

35. Convention on the Safety of United Nations and Associated Personnel of 15 December 1994 (Übereinkommen vom 15. Dezember 1994 über die Sicherheit von Personal der Vereinten Nationen und beigeordnetem Personal) Gesetz vom 5. Februar 1997, *BGBl.* (1997) II, p. 230.

to play a more active and visible role in the process of developing humanitarian law-related treaties.

Germany's position with regard to international treaties since the Second World had always been based on consensus with its NATO allies. The long period between signing and ratifying the Additional Protocols to the Geneva Conventions has always been explained by the need to forge a consensus with the Allies to harmonize the understanding of the reaffirmed and new rules in the Protocols.

During the international discussion about a new Anti-Personnel Landmines Protocol, however, it became clear that this attitude had changed and that additional parameters were used by the German Government to decide about its political support for proposals to develop humanitarian law treaties. In the initial phase of governmental discourse about the outdated UN-Weapons Convention of 1981 [the UN Conventional Weapons Convention], between 1993 and 1995, the German Government refrained from presenting its own position, either in public or in discussions with the German Red Cross or other non-governmental organizations. A new approach first became apparent in 1995 *vis-à-vis* the initiative of the ICRC started at the Montreux meeting on the prohibition of anti-personnel landmines in 1993. With growing public support for a revised Protocol II dealing with landmines, in 1996 the Government slowly but steadily developed its own and more visible position compared with the allied NATO countries.

During the various meetings negotiating the revised Protocol II on Prohibitions or Restrictions on the Use of Mines, Booby-Traps and Other Devices, specific contributions made by the German delegation illustrated this problem-orientated approach.[36] Moreover, the political support given in 1997 by the German

36. Germany ratified amended Protocol II by the law entitled Protokoll über das Verbot oder die Beschränkung des Einsatzes von Minen, Sprengfallen und anderen Vorrichtungen in der am 3. Mai 1996 geänderten Fassung [Protokoll II in der am 3. Mai 1996 geänderten Fassung] zu dem Übereinkommen vom 10. Oktober 1980 über das Verbot oder die Beschränkung des Einsatzes bestimmter konventioneller Waffen, die übermäßige Leiden verursachen oder unterschiedslos wirken können. Gesetz vom 18. April 1997, *BGBl.* (1997) II, p. 806. During the negotiations, the German state secretary (Staatsminister) Schäfer argued in favour of a protocol encompassing non-international armed conflicts and peace-time situations (Statement by Mr. Schäfer at the Vienna Review Conference on the UN Weapons Convention, 29 September 1995, CCW/Conf.I/SR.2, p. 8.). In January 1996 the government declared an unlimited extension of the export moratorium of anti-personnel landmines, later to be complemented by the declaration that all anti-personnel landmines in German possession would be destroyed by the end of 1997.

Germany ratified Protocol IV to the UN Conventional Weapons Convention (Blinding Laser Weapons) by the law entitled Protokoll vom 13. Oktober 1995 über blindmachende Laserwaffen [Protokoll IV] zu dem Übereinkommen vom 10. Oktober 1980 über das Verbot oder die Beschränkung des Einsatzes bestimmter konventioneller Waffen, die übermäßige Leiden verursachen oder unterschiedslos wirken können. Gesetz vom 18. April 1997, *BGBl.* (1997) II, p. 806.

authorities – including both the Foreign Ministry and the Ministry of Defence – to the development of the Ottawa process leading to the adoption of the Landmines Convention[37], despite different positions by other major NATO-allies, reaffirmed this new and extraordinarily active humanitarian policy.

The short period between adoption and ratification of the Landmines Convention is easy to understand taking into account the preparatory steps accomplished in Germany and on the international level. The international efforts to prohibit anti-personnel landmines completely was already supported by the so-called seven points programme of Foreign Minister Kinkel of July 1996 in which he called for a total and global ban on all anti-personnel mines.[38] The German Parliament reacted to the limited success of the revised protocol by adopting a resolution in January 1997 calling for a complete ban on all Anti-personnel landmines.[39]

This more active approach culminated in Germany's assumption of a leadership role that was recognized by many countries and non-governmental organizations before and at the Rome conference on the establishment of a permanent criminal court in 1998. It is to be expected that the new Government will continue this policy as, during the most recent negotiations, the then-opposition party supported the general policy line and indeed actively contributed its own initiatives in the parliament.

In an answer to a Parliamentary motion, the German Government in November 1995 reaffirmed its support shown during the Vienna negotiations that year (Statement by Mr. Schäfer at the Vienna Review Conference on the UN Weapons Convention, 29 September 1995, CCW/Conf.I/SR.2, p. 8.) to prohibit laser weapons that have a lasting effect on the human eye and that the mere production of these weapons should also be prohibited (Antwort der Bundesregierung vom 14 November 1995, Überprüfung des VN-Waffenübereinkommens (Wien 1995) BT.-Drs. 13/2998, p. 2.).

37. Convention on the Prohibition of the Use, Stockpiling, Production and Transfer of Anti-Personnel Mines and on Their Destruction of 3 December 1997 (*Übereinkommen über das Verbot des Einsatzes, der Lagerung, der Herstellung und der Weitergabe von Antipersonenminen und über deren Vernichtung vom 3. Dezember 1997*) Gesetz vom 11. Mai 1998, *BGBl.* (1998) II, p. 778.

38. Auswärtiges Amt (Hg.), Weltweite Ächtung von Antipersonenminen, Das 7-Punkte Aktionsprogramm des Bundesministers des Auswärtigen Dr. K. Kinkel (pp. 5, 8, 9, 19).

39. Beschlußempfehlung und Bericht des Auswärtigen Ausschusses vom 26.2. 1997, Anti-Personen-Minen, VN-Waffenübereinkommen, M (Sprengkörper), BT.-Drs. 13/7068, p. 2. (Annex 35) "The German Parliament appeals to the German Government to actively participate in the adoption of an international agreement on the complete prohibition of all anti-personnel landmines". United Nations General Assembly Resolutions 51/45 entitled 'An international agreement to ban anti-personnel land mines' and UN-Resolution 51/49 which requested a strengthening of the revised Protocol II to the UN-Weapons Convention was co-sponsored by Germany.

CORRESPONDENTS' REPORTS

A guide to state practice concerning International Humanitarian Law

CORRESPONDENTS' REPORTS[1]

A Guide to State Practice Concerning IHL

1. Correspondents' Reports is compiled and edited by the Managing Editor, Ms. Avril McDonald, primarily from information provided to the *YIHL* by its correspondents but also drawing on other sources. It does not purport to be a fully inclusive compilation of all IHL-related developments in every state; reflecting, in this volume, recent developments that have come to the Yearbook's attention. In future volumes, a single year will be covered. While the *YIHL* apologises for any omissions, it does not accept responsibility for them. Readers are kindly invited to send relevant information to the Managing Editor for inclusion in this section, with a view to promoting its inclusiveness. Where citations or dates have not been provided, they were not available or obtainable.

Yearbook of International Humanitarian Law
Volume 1 - 1998 - pp. 395-527

A NOTE ON SOURCES AND ABBREVIATIONS REGARDING TREATIES

☛ All information regarding signings, ratifications, accessions and reservations to the treaties mentioned herein has been obtained from the UN Treaty Series and, concerning most recent information, from the IHL Treaty Database maintained by the International Committee of the Red Cross which provides current information on and the full text of 91 IHL treaties.
The database can be accessed at
http://www.icrc.org (English language) and
http://www.cicr.org (French language).

☛ The following abbreviations have been used concerning the named treaties:
- The United Nations Convention on the Prevention and Punishment of the Crime of Genocide, 1948 (Genocide Convention)
- The four Geneva Conventions of 12 August 1949 (Geneva Conventions)
- The Hague Convention for the Protection of Cultural Property in Times of Armed Conflict, 1954 (Cultural Property Convention)
- Convention on the Non-Applicability of Statutory Limitations to War Crimes and Crimes Against Humanity, 26 November 1968 (Convention on the Non-Applicability of Statutory Limitations)
- Convention on the Prohibition of the Development, Production and Stockpiling of Bacteriological (Biological) and Toxin Weapons and on their Destruction, 1972 (Biological Weapons Convention)
- 1977 Geneva Protocols I + II Additional to the Geneva Conventions of 12 August 1949 (Additional Protocols of 1977)
- United Nations Convention on Prohibitions or Restrictions on the Use of Certain Conventional Weapons Which May be Deemed to be Excessively Injurious or to Have Indiscriminate Effects and its Protocols I, II, and III 1980 (CCW) Convention and its amended Protocol II of 1996 and Protocol IV of 1995
- Convention on the Rights of the Child, 1989 (CRC)
- International Convention Against the Recruitment, Use, Financing and Training of Mercenaries of 1989 (Mercenaries Convention)
- Convention on the Prohibition of the Development, Prohibition, Stockpiling and Use of Chemical Weapons and on Their Destruction, 1993 (CWC)
- Convention on the Prohibition of the Use, Stockpiling Production and Transfer of Anti-Personnel Mines and on Their Destruction 1997 (Landmines Treaty).

☛ Information regarding States Signatories and Parties to the Statute of the International Criminal Court of 1998 was not available at presstime. It will be included in volume 2.

AFGHANISTAN

Signings, Ratifications, Accessions, Successions, Denounciations, Reservations, etc.

☛ Afghanistan signed the CWC on 14 January 1993

ALBANIA[2]

Multinational Military Intervention Force

☛ Law No. 8203 of 30 March 1997 of the Republic of Albania People's Assembly for the Acceptance in Albania of a Multinational Military Force Supporting Humanitarian Operations. Published in *La Comunita Internazionale*, 1, 1997, p. 15

☛ Agreement between the Government of the Republic of Albania and the Governments of the Nations contributing to the multinational protection force bearing on the status of the said force, 21 April 1997. Published in *La Comunita Internazionale*, 1, 1997, pp. 34-41

Implementation

☛ An interministerial Commission of International Humanitarian Law was established in March 1994 with the task of ensuring the implementation of IHL including arranging for studies and formulating proposals on means of disseminating and implementing IHL and preparing draft legislation. It is comprised of representatives of the Ministries of Foreign Affairs, Justice, Defence and Health, the University of Tirana and the Albanian Red Cross.[3]

Signings, Ratifications, Accessions, Successions, Denounciations, Reservations, etc.

☛ Albania signed the CWC on 14 January 1993 and ratified it on 11 May 1994

ALGERIA

Signings, Ratifications, Accessions, Successions, Denounciations, Reservations, etc.

☛ Algeria signed the CWC on 14 January 1993 and ratified it on 14 August 1995

☛ On 3 December 1997, Algeria signed the Landmines Treaty

2. Information provided by Professor Sergio Marchisio, Director, Instituto Di Studi Giuridici Sulla Comunita Internazionale, Rome.

3. See 'Table of National Bodies for International Humanitarian Law,' in 'National Implementation of International Humanitarian Law,' Annual Report 1996, Advisory Service on International Humanitarian Law, International Committee of the Red Cross (Geneva 1997) p. 78.

ANDORRA

Signings, Ratifications, Accessions, Successions, Denounciations, Reservations, etc.

☛ Andorra signed the CRC on 2 October 1995 and ratified it with reservations on 2 January 1996

☛ Andorra signed the Landmines Treaty on 3 December 1997 and ratified it on 29 June 1998

ANGOLA

Peace Process (Amnesty)

☛ Law No. 96, Law of Amnesty, 8 May 1996. Annex to Letter dated 8 May 1996 from the Permanent Representative of Angola to the United Nations Addressed to the President of the Security Council, S/1996/340, 8 May 1996

Signings, Ratifications, Accessions, Successions, Denounciations, Reservations, etc.

☛ Angola signed the Landmines Treaty on 4 December 1997

ANTIGUA and BARBUDA

Signings, Ratifications, Accessions, Successions, Denounciations, Reservations, etc.

☛ Antigua and Barbuda signed the Landmines Treaty on 3 December 1997

ARGENTINA[4]

War Crimes and Crimes against Humanity

☛ Law N° 24/517 concerning the National Commission to Investigate War Crimes, created by the Ministry of Defence, 5 July 1995 [Ley 24.517 apruébase Comisión Nacional Investigadora de Crimenes de Guerra - Creación en el ámbito del Ministerio de Defensa - Funciones, 5 julio 1995]. Promulgated/promulgada 28 July/julio 1995. Published in *Boletín Oficial de la República Argentina,* 3 August 1995

COMMENT BY J.A. CONSIGLI

'The Commission's purpose is to elucidate the facts related to the possible commission of war crimes during the war in the South Atlantic in 1982 (the Falklands/Malvinas War).'

4. Information provided by Professor José Alejandro Consigli, Assistant Professor of Public International Law, University of Buenos Aires, Member of the Institute of International Law of the Argentine Council for International Relations, and Gabriel Valladares, Assistant Professor of International Humanitarian Law, Buenos Aires University, Member of the Institute of International Law of the Argentine Council for International Relations.

☛ Law N° 24-584 concerning the imprescriptibility of war crimes and crimes against humanity, adopted 1 November 1995; promulgated 23 November 1995 [Ley 24.584 apruébase la 'Convención sobre la imprescriptibilidad de los crimenes de guerra y de los crimenes de lesa humanidad', Sancionada: 1 noviembre 1995; Promulgada: 23 noviembre 1995]. Published in *Boletín Oficial de la República Argentina*, 29 November 1995

COMMENT BY J.A. CONSIGLI
'On 1 November 1995, the Argentine Congress approved by law N° 24.584 the Convention on the Non-Applicability of Statutory Limitations to War Crimes and Crimes against Humanity. On 23 November, the President of Argentina promulgated the law. Argentina ratified the Convention without reservations.'

☛ Constitution of the City of Buenos Aires, 1 October 1996, Article 104, para. 18

COMMENT BY J.A. CONSIGLI
'This article describes the powers of the Chief of the City Government. Under para. 18, he can pardon and commute breaches and penal interdictions of the Constitution, except in cases of crimes against humanity.'

☛ Law, N° 24.767 concerning cooperation in extradition and penal matters. 18 December 1996; Promulgated 13 January 1997 [Ley de Cooperacion internacional en materia penal - Extradicion - Código de Procedimientos en Materia Penal (ley 2372) - Modificación - Derogacón de la ley 1612 (18 diciembre 1996. Promulgado 13 enero 1997)]. Published in *Boletín Oficial de la República Argentina*, 16 January 1997

COMMENT BY GABRIEL VALLADARES
'Law 24.767 "International Cooperation in Criminal Affairs. Extradition" does not allude to extradition to face charges of war crimes. But Article 9(a) affirms that war crimes and crimes against humanity are not to be considered as political crimes, in respect of which there is no extradition.'

Disappearances

☛ Law N° 24.820 concerning the constitutional hierarchy of the Convention on Forced Disappearances of Persons. Approved by the Congress on 30 April 1997 and promulgated on 26 May 1997 [Provides for constitutional hierarchy of the Inter-American Convention on the Forced Disappearance of Persons, approved at the 24th General Assembly of the Organisation of American States]. [Ley 24.820 Otórgase dicho carácter a la Convención Interamericana sobre Desaparición Forzada de Personas, aprobada por la Vigésima Cuarta Asamblea General de la Organización de los Estados Americanos (OEA), registrada bajo Ley 24.556, publicada en la edición del 18 de octubre de 1995. Sancionada: 3 abril 1997; Promulgada de Hecho: mayo 26 de 1997]. Published in *Boletín Oficial de la República Argentina*, 29 May 1997 (N° 28.657)

Chemical Weapons

- Presidential Decree 920/97 creating the Inter-Ministerial Commission for the Prohibition of Chemical Weapons within the under-department of politics for Europe, North America, Africa, Asia, Oceana, international organisations and special affairs. The competence, functions and personnel involved in this Commission are explained in the Decree. [Créase la Comisión Interministerial para la prohibición de Armas Químicas, en el ámbito de la Subsecretaria de Politica para Europa, America del Norte, Africa, Asia, Oceanía, organizaciones interacionales y temas especiales]. Published in *Boletín Oficial de la República Argentina*, 1 September 1997
- Conjoint Resolutions 125/98, 2097/98 and 41/98 of the Ministries of Defense, External Affairs and Economics [These Interministerial resolutions modified the list of chemical substances under the government exportation control, taking into account the list of chemical substances prohibited under the Chemical Weapons Convention] [Modifícase el decreto 603/92 en relación al listado de substancias quimicas sujetas a control de exportacion por parte del gobierno nacional y el listado de substancias químicas a que se refiere la Convención sobre la Prohibición del desarrollo, la producción, el almacenamiento y el empleo de Armas Quimícas y sobre su destrucción]. Published in *Boletín Oficial de la República Argentina,* 4 March 1998

Landmines and Blinding Laser Weapons

- Executive Decree 485/95 [Article 2 suspends for five years the export, sale and transfer of antipersonnel landmines]. Published in *Boletín Oficial de la República Argentina,* 3 April 1995.
- Law 24974 approving amended Protocol II to the CCW Convention (concerning landmines) and Protocol IV (concerning blinding laser weapons) [Apruébase el Protocolo sobre Prohibiciones o Restricciones del empleo de Minas, Armas Trampa y otros Artefactos (Protocolo II según fue enmendado e 3 de mayo de 1996), anexo a la Convención sobre Prohibiciones y Restricciones del Empleo de Ciertas Armas Convencionales que puedan considerarse excesivamente novivas o de efectos indiscriminados, y el protocolo sobre armas láser cegadoras (Protocolo IV) adicional a la Convención sobre Prohibiciones o Restricciones del Empleo de ciertas Armas Convencionales que puedan considerarse excesivamente nocivas o de efectos indiscriminados]. Published in *Boletín Oficial de la República Argentina*, 26 June 1998

Anti-Nazi Activity[5]

- Presidential Decree No. 390/97 creating the Commission of Enquiry into Activities of Nazism in Argentina [Comisión para el Esclarecimiento de las Actividades del Nazismo en la Argentina (CEANA)], May 1997
- On 9 March 1998 Argentina published its first comprehensive governmental report on Nazi activity in Argentina which stated that many infamous ex-Nazis were suspected to be hiding out in Argentina, including Erich Mueller and Friedrich Rauch. In early May 1998, the government announced that it would establish a Nazi-hunting office to chase down those suspected former war criminals still at large.[6] On 1 July 1998, Argentina announced that it had signed agreements with Germany, Israel and the United States to share information on fugitive Nazis and neo-Nazi activity.[7] In 1995 and 1998, Argentina cooperated with the Italian and Croatian authorities in the extradition of suspected Nazi war criminals, Erich Priebke and Dinko Sakić, as noted below.

Implementation

- Presidential Directive 933/94 for the Creation of the Commission for the Application of IHL, 16 June 1994 [Decreto 933/94 Créase la Comisión de Aplicación de Derecho Internacional Humanitario. Integración, 16 junio 1994]. Published in *Boletín Oficial de la República Argentina*, 27 June 1994 (N° 27.919)

COMMENT BY GABRIEL VALLADARES

'The Commission's objective is to study and promote measures for the application and diffusion of IHL in Argentina. It is composed of two representatives of the Foreign Office, two representatives of the Defence Ministry, and two of the Internal Affairs Ministry. Since 1995, the Commission has been working on several legal projects concerning IHL.'

- Law N° 24.668 recognising the competence of the International Committee of Inquiry under Clause 90 of Additional Protocol I, 3 July 1996. Promulgated 29 July 1996 [Ley 24.668 reconócese la competencia de la Comisión Internacional de Encuesta en los términos del artículo 90 del Protocolo Adicional a los Convenios de Ginebra, del 12 de agosto de 1949, relativo a la protección de las víctimas de los conflictos armados internacionales. Sancionada: 3 julio 1996; Promulgada de Hecho: 29 julio 1996]. Published in *Boletín Oficial de la República Argentina*, 6 August 1996 [Argentina

5. The Anti-Nazi Commission of the Argentine Government maintains a website at http://www.ceana.org.ar (Spanish only).

6. See 'Extradition – to a Hero's Welcome? World War II Camp Chief May be Greeted Warmly in Croatia', *Washington Post* (6 May 1998) p. A21.

7. 'Argentina signs Nazi-Hunting Accord', Associated Press (1 July 1998).

formally recognised the competence of the Fact-Finding Commission on 11 October 1997]

Cases

- Decision of the Argentine Supreme Court on *Priebke, Erich's* extradition request, Case 16.063/94, 2 November 1995. Published as Priebke, Erich, about extradition. Sentence of the Supreme Court, Vol. 318/3, pp. 2148-2228 [Priebke Erich/s Extradicción. *Fallos de la Corte Supreme de Justicia.* Tomo 318/3. Pags. 2148-2228][8]
- Decision of Federal Judge on the extradition request of Croatia in respect of *Dinko Sakić*[9] [Case 1279 of Dolores Federal Court/Tribunal Federal de la ciudad de Dolores], 5 May 1998 (unpublished) [Sakić was extradited to Croatia further to Decree 583/98, which allowed the extradition and immediate sending of an Argentine citizen to the Republic of Croatia/Concédese la extradiccion y autorízase la entrega inmediata a la República de Croacia de un ciudadano argentino naturalizado]. Published in *Boletín Oficial de la República Argentina,* 19 May 1998

COMMENT BY GABRIEL VALLADARES

'On 5 May 1998, Judge Hernan Bernasconi ruled that Sakić could be extradited to Croatia for crimes allegedly carried out while he was commander of Jasenovac concentration camp in the former Yugoslavia during the Ustashe regime of WWII. The Argentine Government allowed the Sakić extradition to Croatia by Executive Decree number 583, dated 15 May 1998. Previously, Sakić did not appeal the Judge's sentence because he wanted to be extradited to Croatia and judged there. Before Sakić flew to Croatia on 18 June 1998, Judge Bernasconi rejected an extradition request from Yugoslavia' [Presidential Decree 619/98 denied the extradition of Sakić to the Federal Republic of Yugoslavia/Deniégase la extradicción de un ciudadano argentino naturalizado requerida por la República Federal de Yugoslavia]. Published in *Boletín Oficial de la República Argentina*, 10 June 1998.

- On 23 July 1998, *Esperanza Sakić* (aka, Nada Lububrić), was arrested and detained by the Argentine authorities, further to a petition of provisional detention requested by the Federal Republic of Yugoslavia, which accused her of crimes against humanity, genocide and other international crimes, such as war crimes against the civilian population. Croatia also requested her extradition. During a hearing on 29 August 1998 before the Federal Court of Dolores, Mrs. Sakić maintained her innocence and told Judge Bernasconi that she wished to be judged by Croatian authorities. Presidential Decree 980/98 (published in *Boletín Oficial de la República Argentina*, 24 August 1998) determined that both the Croatian and Yugoslav petitions should be decided

8. For commentary on this case, see Consigli, at p. 341.
9. See *infra*, p. 429.

by the Judge of the Federal Court of Dolores. The Argentine Ministry of External Affairs stated that Croatia should have preference.

Signings, Ratifications, Accessions, Successions, Denounciations, Reservations, etc.

- Argentina signed the CWC on 13 January 1993 and ratified it on 2 October 1995
- Argentina signed the Safety Convention on 15 December 1994 and ratified it on 6 January 1997
- On 2 October 1995, Argentina ratified the CCW Convention (Protocols I, II and III)
- Argentina signed the Landmines Treaty on 4 December 1997

Pending Projects (before the Argentine Parliament)[10]

- Draft for the reform of the Code of Military Justice to include rules of IHL [Anteproyecto de Reforma al Código de Justicia Militar] (Unpublished). [The General Staff of the Army has prepared a draft for the reform of the Code of Military Justice that is currently being studied. This draft incorporates the specific criminal characterisation of serious violations of IHL]
- Obligatory instruction of IHL to the Armed Forces
- The emblem [Proposal before Argentine Parliament to replace Law 2976 of 21 September 1993 in order to better safeguard the emblem]
- Prohibition of the use, warehousing and production of anti-personnel landmines [This is a law to implement the Landmines Treaty]

ARMENIA[11]

The Emblem, the National Society and the ICRC

- The Decree of the President of the Republic of Armenia No. 262 on the Recognition of the National Society of the Red Cross, 26 September 1993
- Bilateral Agreement between the Government of Armenia and the ICRC on the Status of the ICRC in Armenia, 5 November 1993
- The Resolution of the Republic of Armenia Government No. 41 on the Use of the Emblem of the Armenian Red Cross Society, 19 January 1994, *Official Bulletin of the Government of Armenia*; also available in online legal library IRTEK.
- The Resolutions of the Ministry of Justice No. 51/2-3 and No. 3/1-7 on the Registration and Amendments to the Statute of the Armenian Red Cross Society, 31 October 1995 and 24 January 1997. Available from Ministry of Justice, Registration Dept.

10. There is no guarantee that these projects will become law.

11. Information provided by Mr. Shahen Avakian, Director of Legal Department, and Mr. David Akakessian, LL.M., Head of International Law Section, Ministry for Foreign Affairs, Republic of Armenia. All of these laws and agreements can be obtained from the Ministry of Foreign Affairs of the Republic of Armenia, Government House, 2 Republic Square, Yerevan, Armenia.

- 'Memorandum of Understanding', signed between the Ministry of Defence, the Ministry of National Security, the Prosecutor's General Office and the ICRC on 9 January 1996[12] concerning ICRC visits to persons in detention in Armenia
- Accord Between the Minister of Education and of Science of the Republic of Armenia and the Delegation of the International Committee of the Red Cross, 11 December 1996[13]
- The Law on Goods and Services, Trademarks and Origin of Goods and the Register of Protected Trademarks, 9 June 1997 [Concerning the emblem]
- Information Note on ICRC Memorandum on issues relating to search for and exchange of information on persons missing or imprisoned in the Nagorno-Karabakh conflict, sent to ICRC on 10 January 1996

Signings, Ratifications, Accessions, Successions, Denounciations, Reservations, etc.

- Armenia signed the CWC on 19 January 1993 and ratified it on 27 May 1995
- Armenia ratified the Biological Weapons Convention on 7 June 1994

AUSTRALIA[14]

International Criminal Tribunals

- International War Crimes Tribunals Act, 1995, No. 18 of 1995, *Acts of the Parliament of the Commonwealth of Australia 1995*, Vol. 1, p. 439. Australian Government Publishing Service, Canberra 1996 [http://www.austlii.edu.au/do/disp.pl/au/legis/cth/consol_act/iwcta1995367?query=title]
- International War Crimes Tribunals Regulations, Statutory Rules Made Under *Acts of the Parliament of the Commonwealth of Australia 1995*, No. 250 of 1995, Vol. 2, p. 1879. Australian Government Publishing Service, Canberra 1996 [http://www.austlii.edu.au/do/]

COMMENT BY TIM MCCORMACK

'The legislation and regulations permit Australian courts to extradite indicted individuals from Australia to either of the two *ad hoc* Tribunals. The legislation implements Australia's UN Charter obligations to cooperate with binding Security Council resolutions.'

12. Copy on file with the Yearbook.
13. Copy on file with the Yearbook.
14. Information provided by Professor Tim McCormack, Australian Red Cross Professor of International Humanitarian Law, University of Melbourne; member of the Board of Editors, *Yearbook of International Humanitarian Law*.

Nuclear Weapons

☛ Report of the Canberra Commission on the Elimination of Nuclear Weapons, Department of Foreign Affairs and Trade, Canberra, August 1996

COMMENT BY TIM MCCORMACK

'The Canberra Commission was established as an independent Commission of Experts by Australia in late-1995 to propose practical steps towards a nuclear weapons-free world. The report of the Commission was presented to the Prime Minister of Australia on 14 August 1996, in time to be tabled at the 51st session of the United Nations General Assembly. Between the initiation of the Commission and the tabling of the Report, Australia experienced a change of Government. Unfortunately, the new Government chose not to promote the recommendations of the Report and, although the Report was widely circulated, it did not receive the support it warranted.'

Blinding Laser Weapons and Landmines

☛ Restrictions on the Use of Blinding Laser Weapons and Landmines. 5th Report. The Parliament of the Commonwealth of Australia, Joint Standing Committee on Treaties, February 1997, Australian Government Publishing Services, February 1997[15]

COMMENT BY TIM MCCORMACK

'The new Protocol IV (on Blinding Laser Weapons) to the CCW Convention was adopted by a Review Conference of States Parties to the Convention, including Australia, on 13 October 1995. The newly-amended Protocol II (on Landmines) to this Convention was adopted by the Review Conference on 3 May 1996. On 15 April 1996, the Australian Government announced that Australia would support a global ban on the production, stockpiling, use and transfer of anti-personnel landmines and declared a moratorium on the use of such landmines by the Australian Defence Forces.[16] However, the Australian Government announced its intention to maintain its stockpile of anti-personnel landmines for use in demining training and also indicated that it would not discount the need to renounce its moratorium on use if Australia's national security required a change of policy. The Joint Parliamentary Standing Committee on Treaties has the responsibility to review all

15. The full-text of the report is available online at http://www.aph.gov.au/house/committee/jsct/reports/report50/start.htm/.

16. See 'Australia pledges support for a global ban on anti-personnel landmines; unilaterally suspends use.' Media Release of the Department of Foreign Affairs and Trade, Australia, FA22 (15 April 1996).

proposed treaty action by Australia. The report reflects the Committee's view that Australia should ratify its signature of Revised Protocol II and Protocol IV to the CCW Convention but includes a recommendation that the Australian Government destroy its stockpile of anti-personnel landmines. This recommendation, made in February 1997, represented a significant advance on official Australian policy at the time it was made. The Australian Government deposited its instrument of ratification for amended Protocol II and for Protocol IV in August 1997.'

Mercenaries

☛ Joint Statement by the Minister for Foreign Affairs, Alexander Downer MP and the Attorney-General, Daryl Williams AM QC MP, 14 July 1997: 'Government Announces Move to Accede to the International Mercenaries Convention'

Signings, Ratifications, Accessions, Successions, Denounciations, Reservations, etc.

☛ Australia signed the CWC on 13 January 1993 and ratified it on 6 May 1995
☛ Australia signed the Safety Convention on 22 December 1995
☛ Australia ratified Protocol IV (on Blinding Laser Weapons) and amended Protocol II (on Landmines) of the CCW Convention on 22 August 1997
☛ Australia signed the Landmines Treaty on 3 December 1997

AUSTRIA[17]

International Criminal Tribunals

☛ Draft Text and Explanatory Memorandum on the Government Bill 'Federal Law on Cooperation with the International Tribunals' [Regierungsvorlage: Bundesgesetz über die Zusammenarbeit mit den internationalen Gerichten]. Published 8 May 1996, RV 102 *BlgNR* [*Beilagen zu den Stenographischen Protokollen des Nationalrates*] 20.GP
☛ Federal Law on Cooperation with the International Tribunals [Bundesgesetz über die Zusammenarbeit mit den internationalen Gerichten] (entered into force 1 July 1996) Published 13 June 1996 in *BGBl* [Bundesgesetzblatt] Nr. 263/1996

COMMENT BY THOMAS DESCH and PETER KUSTOR

'The Federal Law implements the obligations under Security Council Resolutions 827 (1993) and 955 (1994) concerning the International Tribunals for the former Yugoslavia and for Rwanda, in particular, to grant judicial assistance and to surrender the accused to the International Tribunals. The first part of the law contains provisions on the basic relationship between the Austrian Courts, the Public Prosecutor's Office, the penal authorities and the security services with the

17. Information provided by Dr. Thomas Desch, Federal Ministry of Defence, and Mag. Peter Kustor, Federal Chancellery, Vienna.

International Tribunals as well as provisions on the applicable procedural law. The second part relates to issues of a more specific character, such as letters of request; judicial assistance; searches and handing over; assistance in law enforcement; procedures for the inspection of files; or independent investigations and proceedings by the International Tribunals on Austrian Territory. Due to Austria's proximity to the territory of the former Yugoslavia, the law also contains provisions concerning the transfer and through-transportation and the safe conduct of persons who are summoned by the International Tribunals.'

Chemical Weapons

☛ Draft text and Explanatory Memorandum on the Government Bill 'Federal Law on the Implementation of the Convention on the Prohibition of the Development, Production, Stockpiling and Use of Chemical Weapons and on Their Destruction of 13 January 1993' [Regierungsvorlage: Bundesgesetz zur Durchführung des Übereinkommens vom 13. Jänner 1993 über das Verbot der Entwicklung, Herstellung, Lagerung und des Einsatzes chemischer Waffen und über die Vernichtung solcher Waffen (Chemiewaffenkonvention - Durchführungsgesetz - CWKG)]. Published 31 May 1995 in RV 193 *BlgNR* 19.GP

☛ Federal Law on the Implementation of the Convention on the Prohibition of the Development, Production, Stockpiling and Use of Chemical Weapons and on Their Destruction of 13 January 1993 [Bundesgesetz zur Durchführung des Übereinkommens vom 13. Jänner 1993 über das Verbot der Entwicklung, Herstellung, Lagerung und des Einsatzes chemischer Waffen und über die Vernichtung solcher Waffen (Chemiewaffenkonvention-Durchführungsgesetz - CWKG)] (in force since 29 April 1997). Published 14 March 1997 in *BGBl.* I Nr. 24/1997

COMMENT BY THOMAS DESCH AND PETER KUSTOR

'This law provides for an obligation to submit the development, production, acquisition, stockpiling, retention and transfer of chemicals contained in schedules 1 and 2 annexed to the CWC to the authorization of the Federal Minister of Economic Affairs, who is also designated as the "national authority" responsible for the execution of the specific obligations under the CWC. Furthermore, the law provides for a registration duty with regard to the production, acquisition, stockpiling and retention of chemicals contained in schedule 3 annexed to the CWC as well as of certain other chemicals. The law also provides for the inspection of facilities in order to monitor compliance with the Convention.'

☛ Regulation on the Implementation of the Federal Law on the Implementation of the Convention on the Prohibition of the Development, Production, Stockpiling and Use of Chemical Weapons and on Their Destruction of 13 January 1993 [Verordnung des Bundesministers für wirtschaftliche Angelegenheiten zur Durchführung des

Bundesgesetzes zur Durchführung des Übereinkommens vom 13. Jänner 1993 über das Verbot der Entwicklung, Herstellung, Lagerung und des Einsatzes chemischer Waffen und über die Vernichtung solcher Waffen (Chemiewaffenverordnung - CWKG-VO)]. Published 4 June 1997 in *BGBl.* II Nr. 145/1997

Landmines

- Common action of the European Union on anti-personnel mines [Gemeinsame Aktion der Europäischen Union über Antipersonenminen], Brüssel, am 1. Oktober 1996 (*ABl.* [*Amtsblatt*/Official Journal (of the EU)] Nr. L 260. Published 12 October 1996) [ÖAD] [Österreichische Außenpolitische Dokumentation] 1997/1
- Draft text with explanations concerning a Federal Law on the prohibition of anti-personnel mines [Antrag (IA 163/A) der Abgeordneten Dr. Irmtraut Karlsson, Werner Amon und Genossen betreffend ein Bundesgesetz über das Verbot von Anti-Personen-Minen] (proposed on 19 April 1996). Published in *AB* [Ausschußbericht] 540 *BlgNR* 20.GP
- Federal Law on the prohibition of anti-personnel mines [Bundesgesetz über das Verbot von Anti-Personen-Minen] (entered into force 1 January 1997). Published 10 January 1997 in *BGBl.* I Nr. 13/1997[18]

COMMENT BY THOMAS DESCH AND PETER KUSTOR

'This law prohibits the production, acquisition, sale, procurement, import, export, transit, use and possession of anti-personnel mines as well as of anti-detection mechanisms, and provides for their destruction. Austria was among the first states to completely ban anti-personnel mines by law, thereby supporting the international efforts in the framework of the so-called Ottawa process to achieve a global and comprehensive ban of anti-personnel landmines. Meanwhile, the law sets a standard for the implementation of the Convention on the Prohibition of the Use, Stockpiling, Production and Transfer of Anti-Personnel Mines and on Their Destruction, which was signed in Ottawa on 3-4 December 1997.'

Blinding Laser Weapons

- Draft text with explanations concerning a Federal Law on the Prohibition of Blinding Laser Weapons [Antrag (IA 563/A) der Abgeordneten Dr. Peter Kostelka, Dr. Andreas Khol und Genossen betreffend ein Bundesgesetz über das Verbot von blindmachenden Laserwaffen] (18 September 1997). Published in *AB* 985 *BlgNR* 20.GP
- Federal Law on the Prohibition of Blinding Laser Weapons [Bundesgesetz über das Verbot von blindmachenden Laserwaffen] (entered into force 1 January 1998) Published 15 January 1998 in *BGBl.* I Nr. 4/1998

18. Reproduced at p. 561.

COMMENT BY THOMAS DESCH AND PETER KUSTOR

'Whereas the Protocol on Blinding Laser Weapons of 1995 (Protocol IV) to the CCW Convention only interdicts the use of blinding laser weapons, this law also prohibits the acquisition, possession, carrying, development, production, sale, procurement, import, export and transit of blinding laser weapons as well as of specific parts thereof.'

Signings, Ratifications, Accessions, Successions, Denounciations, Reservations, etc.

- ☛ Austria signed the CWC on 13 January 1993 and ratified it on 17 August 1995
- ☛ Austria signed the Landmines Treaty on 3 December 1997 and ratified it on 29 June 1998
- ☛ Austria ratified Protocol IV and amended Protocol II of the CCW Convention on 27 July 1998

AZERBAIJAN

Signings, Ratifications, Accessions, Successions, Denounciations, Reservations, etc.

- ☛ Azerbaijan signed the CWC on 13 January 1993
- ☛ On 4 December 1997, Azerbaijan acceded to the Mercenaries Convention without making any declarations or reservations
- ☛ Azerbaijan ratified the Convention on the Non-Applicability of Statutory Limitations on 16 August 1996

BAHAMAS

Signings, Ratifications, Accessions, Successions, Denounciations, Reservations, etc.

- ☛ Bahamas signed the CWC on 19 January 1993 and ratified it on 27 May 1995
- ☛ Bahamas signed the Landmines Treaty on 3 December 1997 and ratified it on 31 July 1998

BAHRAIN

Signings, Ratifications, Accessions, Successions, Denounciations, Reservations, etc.

- ☛ Bahrain signed the CWC on 19 January 1993 and ratified it on 27 May 1995

BANGLADESH

Signings, Ratifications, Accessions, Successions, Denounciations, Reservations, etc.

- ☛ Bangladesh signed the CWC on 14 January 1993 and ratified it on 15 April 1997
- ☛ Bangladesh signed the Safety Convention on 21 December 1994
- ☛ Bangladesh signed the Landmines Treaty on 7 May 1998

BARBADOS

Signings, Ratifications, Accessions, Successions, Denounciations, Reservations, etc.
- Barbados signed the Landmines Treaty on 3 December 1997

BELARUS

Implementation
- Council of Ministers Order No. 1242 of 19 September 1997

The Order established a National Committee for the Implementation of IHL in Belarus, whose mandate is to fulfill Belarus' obligations arising from the Geneva Conventions and their Additional Protocols and to harmonise proposals for national legislation to implement IHL.[19]

Signings, Ratifications, Accessions, Successions, Denounciations, Reservations, etc.
- Belarus signed the CWC on 14 January 1993 and ratified it on 11 July 1996
- Belarus signed the Safety Convention on 23 October 1995
- On 28 May 1997 Belarus ratified the Mercenaries Convention without making any declarations or reservations. Belarus signed the Treaty on 13 December 1990

BELGIUM[20]

War Crimes (Geneva Conventions)
- Law of 16 June 1993 concerning represssion of grave infractions of the Geneva Conventions of 12 August 1949 and their Additional Protocols I and II of 8 June 1977, entered into force, 5 August 1993 [Loi du 16 juin 1993 relative à la repression des infractions graves aux Conventions internationales de Genève du 12 août 1949 et aux Protocoles I et II du 8 juin 1977, additionnels a ces Conventions, 5 août 1993]. Published in *Moniteur belge,* 5 August 1993

International Criminal Tribunals
- Law concerning the recognition of the International Tribunal for the Former Yugoslavia and the International Tribunal for Rwanda, and cooperation with these Tribunals, 22 March 1996 [Loi relativé à la reconaissance du Tribunal international pour l'ex-

19. Source: Table of National Bodies for International Humanitarian Law, Advisory Service on International Humanitarian Law, ICRC, as of 31 March, 1998. Thanks to Monika Cometti, Documentalist, Advisory Service on IHL, for supplying this information.

20. Information provided by Professor Marc Cogen, International and European Research Unit, University of Gent, and Professor Eric David, Centre de droit international, Institut de Sociologie, Brussels.

Yougoslavie et du Tribunal international pour le Ruanda, et à la cooperation avec ces Tribunaux, 22 mars 1996]. Published in *Moniteur belge*, 27 April 1996

Parliament (Enquiry into Belgian peacekeepers in Rwanda)

- ☛ Parliamentary Commission of Inquiry concerning the Events in Rwanda: Report of the Commission of Inquiry by Messers Mahoux and Verhofstadt [Commission d'enquête parlementaire concernant les évenéments du Ruanda: Rapport fait au nom de la Commission d'enquête par MM. Mahoux et Verhofstadt. Belgian Senate. Sesssion de 1997-1998] 6 December/décembre 1997. Published in *Documents parlementaires/Parliamentary Documents*, Sénat de Belgique/Belgian Senate, session 1997/8, nos. 611/7, 611/8, 611/9, 611/10, 611/11/, 611/12, 611/13, 611/14 et 611/15
- ☛ Debates of the Belgian Senate on the 'Rapport de la Commission d'enquête parlementaire concernant les événements du Ruanda', 17 December 1997. Published in *Annales parlementaires*/Parliamentary Records, Sénat de Belgique/Belgian Senate, 1997/98, 17 December/décembre 1997, pp. 4001-4045
- ☛ Vote of the Belgian Senate on the 'Rapport de la Commission d'enquête parlementaire concernant les événements du Ruanda', 18 December/décembre 1997. Published in *Annales parlementaires*/Parliamentary Records, Sénat de Belgique/Belgian Senate, 1997/98, 17 December/décembre 1997, pp. 4105-4110 [The vote followed the debate in the senate]

Cases

- ☛ The case of *Marchal*, Military Court of Belgium, 4 July 1996 [Militaire Strafrechtspraak België, De Zaak *Marchal*: vrijspraak van dood door schuld, Arrest van het Belgische Militair Gerechtshof van 4 juli 1996] (The English translation is published in the *Military Law and Law of War Review*, XXXVI, 1-2 (1997), pp. 85-100) [Involving the trial on charges of lack of caution or precaution of Colonel Marchal, commander of ten Belgian members of the United Nations Assistance Mission for Rwanda (UNAMIR) who were killed during the genocide in Rwanda]

COMMENT BY MARC COGEN

'Ten Belgian blue helmets were escorting the Rwandan Prime Minister, Ms. Agathe Uwilingiyimana, during the peacekeeping mission UNAMIR when they were taken prisoner by Rwandan soldiers and subsequently killed on 7 April 1994 in Kigali. Their commander, Colonel Luc Marie Ghislain Marcel Marchal, was indicted for their death on the ground of lack of caution or precaution. According to the act of indictment, he had not prepared a timely contingency plan to guarantee the safety of the soldiers in case the situation would rapidly turn into an armed conflict, nor had he taken into account the well-known fact that members of the *Interhamwe* ('Those who work together') militia wanted the departure of the Belgian troops in order to carry out the planned genocide. Colonel Marchal was acquitted on all charges. A couple of points of the Court's judgement merit comment.

First, criminal jurisdiction and immunities. Belgian law is applicable to Belgian soldiers while they are on mission abroad, even when they are serving in a UN peacekeeping mission. Colonel Marchal could be indicted by a Belgian prosecutor because of the personal jurisdiction principle mentioned in Article 10 *bis* of the Preliminary Title of the Belgian Code of Penal Prosecution.[21] The order to escort the Rwandan Prime Minister was given by the UNAMIR commander, the Canadian General Romeo Dallaire. Although the Court mentioned Dallaire's order, no further attention was paid to his views or his responsibility. This follows from the fact that General Dallaire enjoyed diplomatic immunities on the basis of the Agreement between the United Nations and the Government of the Republic of Rwanda on the Status of the United Nations Assistance Mission for Rwanda of 3 November 1993 and the Convention on the Privileges and Immunities of the United Nations of 1946. Although concluded between the UN and Rwanda, the Belgian authorities recognised General Dallaire's immunities under this agreement. This was also what happened at the Belgian Senate hearing on the tragedy in Rwanda. As a result, the Court could not hear Dallaire as a witness. Moreover, the UN Secretary-General did not permit Dallaire to act as a witness at the trial. It is regrettable that diplomatic immunities are fully and indiscriminately granted in the framework of UN peacekeeping operations, preventing judicial authorities from carrying out their duties and establishing the truth in a particular case. It also demonstrates a shortcoming in balancing the need for protection against political interference and the interest of criminal justice. This shortcoming foreshadows, in a sense, what can happen at other tribunals, such as the Tribunal for the Former Yugoslavia or the newly established International Criminal Court. It can only be remedied by specifying and limiting the immunities enjoyed by commanders and personnel of UN peacekeeping operations, a task which falls upon the UN itself.

Second, guilt and negligence in carrying out peacekeeping operations. The Court stated that a contingency plan existed, consisting of three progressive stages. The Belgian commanders were facing the difficulty that they did not know exactly where the ten Belgian soldiers had been taken and they were misled by the fact that a high-ranking Rwandan officer had taken charge of the 'safety' of the Belgian soldiers. No contingency plan could give an adequate solution to this particular problem. However, according to Belgian penal law, a foreigner can be brought before a Belgian tribunal for crimes committed against Belgian citizens in a foreign country if the acts are also punishable under the *lex loci*. More important is the

21. Art. 10 *bis* has been inserted by Art. 1 of the Belgian Law of 14 July 1951, published in *Moniteur belge*/Belgian Official Journal of 9 August 1951.

question of the light weapons carried by the Belgian soldiers and the Court's conclusion that the responsibility for an appropriate level of armament in the first place belongs to the unit officer carrying out the operation, and in the second place, to the higher ranking commander who gives the order to the unit. Another question arises from the first but has not been answered explicitly: can a unit officer refuse to carry out a particular operation because the appropriate armament is not available at the time of the operation itself? The logic of the Court's legal reasoning seems to indicate that he can refuse because he should also protect the safety of his soldiers on duty; if not, he can be brought to Court for negligence and found guilty.

For the first time in Belgian military history, an officer has been indicted as a result of casualties in the performance of his duties. It provoked some unrest in the Belgian military establishment. The reasons for this precedent must be sought in Belgian public opinion. The death of the ten Belgian soldiers during a UN peacekeeping operation came as a shock, and raised questions about the role of political and military leaders in this tragedy. Public transparency and accountability in this case became an important national issue. The Belgian Senate not only started a debate and published a report on the events, but the military tribunal also investigated the question whether irregularities had occurred.'

☛ Judgement of the Belgian Military Court regarding violations of IHL committed in Somalia and Rwanda, Nr. 54 A.R. 1997, 20 November 1997. Published in *Journal des tribunaux*, 24 April/avril 1998, pp. 286-289 (French language)

COMMENT BY MARC COGEN

'The Prosecutor and the Centre for Equal Opportunites and Combat of Racism were the plaintiffs in this case against two Belgian soldiers, B and C. The Military Court, acting as the Court of Appeals, confirmed the acquittal of the two defendants as pronounced by the Military Tribunal in its judgement of 30 June 1997. The two Belgian soldiers had been indicted for injuries and threats made against the civilian population when they took part in the UNOSOM (United Nations Operation in Somalia) II peacekeeping operation in Somalia. The Court came to the conclusion that the four Geneva Conventions of 1949 and their two Additional Protocols of 1977 were not applicable to the armed conflict in Somalia. The protection of the civilian population could not be granted on the basis of these Conventions or Protocols. Even common Article 3 of the Geneva Conventions could not be applied as the militia did not have an organised military structure, a responsible leadership or exercise authority over a specific part of territory. Consequently, the Belgian law of 16 July 1993 implementing the four Geneva Conventions and the two Additional Protocols of 1977 (see above) was not applicable either. Finally, members of UNOSOM II could not be considered as 'combatants' since their primary task was not to fight against any of the factions, nor could they be considered as an 'occupying force'.'[22]

Signings, Ratifications, Accessions, Successions, Denounciations, Reservations, etc.

- ☛ Belgium signed the CWC on 13 January 1993 and ratified it on 27 January 1997
- ☛ Belgium acceded to the CCW Convention (Protocols I, II and III) on 7 February 1995
- ☛ Belgium signed the Safety Convention on 21 December 1995
- ☛ Belgium signed the Landmines Treaty on 3 December 1997

BELIZE

Signings, Ratifications, Accessions, Successions, Denounciations, Reservations, etc.

- ☛ Belize signed the Landmines Treaty on 27 February 1998 and ratified it on 23 April 1998
- ☛ Belize ratified the Genocide Convention on 10 March 1998

BENIN

Signings, Ratifications, Accessions, Successions, Denounciations, Reservations, etc.

- ☛ Benin signed the CWC on 14 January 1993 and ratified it on 14 May 1998
- ☛ Benin signed the Landmines Treaty on 3 December 1997

BHUTAN

Signings, Ratifications, Accessions, Successions, Denounciations, Reservations, etc.

- ☛ Bhutan signed the CWC on 14 January 1993

BOLIVIA

Signings, Ratifications, Accessions, Successions, Denounciations, Reservations, etc.

- ☛ Bolivia signed the CWC on 14 January 1993, ratified it on 14 August 1998 and became a state party on 13 September 1998
- ☛ Bolivia signed the Safety Convention on 17 August 1995

22. For an analysis of the findings of a case concerning Canadian peacekeepers in Somalia, see the commentary of Boustany on the *Brocklebank* case, at p. 371. Investigations concerning the activities of peacekeeping contingents in Somalia have also been concluded by Canada and Italy. For commentary on the Canadian report into the behaviour of Canadian peacekeepers in Somalia, see Young and Molina, at p. 362; for commentary on the report of the Commission of Enquiry into the behaviour of Italian peacekeepers in Somalia, see Lupi, at p. 376. France is also currently undertaking an investigation into the role of its troops in Somalia. For a general discussion of the rights and responsibilities of peacekeepers, see Greenwood, at p. 3.

- Bolivia signed the Landmines Treaty on 3 December 1997 and ratified it on 9 June 1998

BOSNIA AND HERZEGOVINA

International Criminal Tribunal

- Decree with Force of Law on Deferral upon Request by the International Tribunal, 10 April 1995, *Official Gazette of the Republic of Bosnia and Herzegovina*, No. 12, page 317 (applicable to the Yugoslav Tribunal only)

Cases

- The trial of *Goran Vasić* opened before the High Council of the Sarajevo canton court, chaired by Judge Amira Rizvić, on 31 August 1998. Vasić, a former member of Bosnian-Serb paramilitary forces, was arrested in February 1998 and charged with the murder of Bosnia's vice-premier, Dr. Hakija Turajlić, who was shot in 1993 in the presence of French peacekeepers, and other war crimes against civilians and prisoners of war.[23]

Signings, Ratifications, Accessions, Successions, Denounciations, Reservations, etc.

- Bosnia and Herzegovina ratified the Biological Weapons Convention on 15 August 1994
- Bosnia and Herzegovina signed the CWC on 16 January 1997 and ratified it on 25 February 1997
- Bosnia and Herzegovina signed the Landmines Treaty on 3 December 1997

BOTSWANA

Signings, Ratifications, Accessions, Successions, Denounciations, Reservations, etc.

- Botswana ratified the CRC on 14 March 1995 with reservations
- Botswana signed the Landmines Treaty on 3 December 1997
- Botswana acceded to the CWC on 31 August 1998 and became a party on 30 September 1998

BRAZIL

Signings, Ratifications, Accessions, Successions, Denounciations, Reservations, etc.

- Brazil signed the CWC on 13 January 1993 and ratified it on 13 March 1996
- Brazil signed the Safety Convention on 3 February 1995
- Brazil acceded to the CCW Convention (Protocols I, II and III) on 3 October 1995
- Brazil signed the Landmines Treaty on 3 December 1997

23. Source Radio BiH, 31 August 1998.

BRUNEI DARUSSALAM

Signings, Ratifications, Accessions, Successions, Denounciations, Reservations, etc.

- Brunei Darussalam signed the CWC on 13 January 1993 and ratified it on 28 July 1997
- Brunei Darussalam ratified the CRC on 27 December 1995 with reservations
- Brunei Darussalam signed the Landmines Treaty on 4 December 1997

BULGARIA

Signings, Ratifications, Accessions, Successions, Denounciations, Reservations, etc.

- Bulgaria signed the CWC on 13 January 1993 and ratified it on 10 August 1994
- On 9 May 1994, Bulgaria made a declaration under Article 90 of Additional Protocol I to the Geneva Conventions of 1949 recognising the competence of the International Fact-Finding Commission
- Bulgaria signed the Landmines Treaty on 3 December 1997
- Bulgaria acceded to the Safety Convention on 4 June 1998

BURKINA FASO

Signings, Ratifications, Accessions, Successions, Denounciations, Reservations, etc.

- Burkina Faso signed the CWC on 14 January 1993 and ratified it on 8 July 1997
- Burkina Faso signed the Landmines Treaty on 3 December 1997 and ratified it on 16 September 1998, becoming the 40th state to do so and thus triggering the entry into force of the Convention. The Landmines Treaty will enter into force on 1 March 1999

BURUNDI

Signings, Ratifications, Accessions, Successions, Denounciations, Reservations, etc.

- Burundi signed the CWC on 15 January 1993 and ratified it on 4 September 1998
- Burundi ratified the Genocide Convention on 6 January 1997
- Burundi signed the Landmines Treaty on 3 December 1997

CAMBODIA

Implementation

- Joint National Committee for the Implementation of International Humanitarian Law [Commission nationale mixte pour responsables de la mise en oeuvre du droit international humanitaire] 17 October 1996

'The committee comprises representatives of various ministries, and one representative each of the Council of Ministers, the Cambodian Mines Action Centre, and the Cambodian Red Cross Society. Its terms of reference have yet to be defined.'[24]

Signings, Ratifications, Accessions, Successions, Denounciations, Reservations, etc.

- ☛ Cambodia signed the CWC on 15 January 1993
- ☛ Cambodia signed the Landmines Treaty on 3 December 1997
- ☛ Cambodia acceded to the CCW Convention (Protocols I, II and III, amended Protocol II and Protocol IV) on 25 March 1997
- ☛ On 14 January 1998, Cambodia acceded to the Additional Protocols of 1977 without making any declaration or reservations. The Protocols entered into force in Cambodia on 14 July 1998

CAMEROON

The Emblem

- ☛ Law No. 97-2 on the protection of the emblem and the name 'Red Cross'. Published in the *Official Journal of the Republic of Cameroon*, 47th year, No. 2, 1 February 1997[25]

Signings, Ratifications, Accessions, Successions, Denounciations, Reservations, etc.

- ☛ Cameroon signed the CWC on 14 January 1993 and ratified it on 16 September 1996
- ☛ On 26 January 1996, Cameroon ratified the Mercenaries Convention. It signed the Treaty on 21 December 1990
- ☛ Cameroon signed the Landmines Treaty on 3 December 1997

CANADA[26]

Canadian Peacekeeping Mission to Somalia

- ☛ *Dishonoured Legacy, Report of the Commission of Inquiry into the Deployment of Canadian Forces to Somalia*, Canadian Government Publishing, 1997[27]
- ☛ *Regina* v. *Brocklebank,* Court Martial Appeal Court of Canada, 2 April 1996 (Court File No. CMAC-383) Published in 106 *Canadian Criminal Cases* (3d) at p. 234[28]

24. *Supra* n. 3 at p. 51.
25. *Supra* n. 3 at p. 31.
26. Information provided by Professor René Provost, Faculty of Law, McGill University, Montreal; and Katia Boustany, Professor of International Law at the Department of Legal Studies of the University of Quebec, Montreal.
27. For commentary, see Young and Molina, *supra* p. 362.
28. For commentary see Boustany at p. 371.

In which case, concerning a Canadian soldier accused of torture and negligent performance of a military duty in respect of acts committed while he was serving on a peacekeeping mission in Somalia, the Court Martial Appeals Court held that there was no evidence that Brocklebank had formed the necessary *mens rea* to commit the offence with which he was charged. The Court found further that no armed conflict existed in Somalia at the relevant time, nor were the Canadian forces to be considered as a party to a conflict, as they were engaged in a peacekeeping mission. Therefore, neither the Geneva Conventions nor the Unit Guide to the Geneva Conventions were applicable.

Signings, Ratifications, Accessions, Successions, Denounciations, Reservations, etc.
- ☛ Canada signed the CWC on 13 January 1993 and ratified it on 26 September 1995
- ☛ Canada signed the Safety Convention on 15 December 1994
- ☛ Canada signed and ratified the Landmines Treaty on 3 December 1997
- ☛ Canada acceded to the CCW Convention (Protocols I, II and III) on 24 June 1994, and ratified Protocol IV and amended Protocol II on 5 January 1998

CAPE VERDE

Signings, Ratifications, Accessions, Successions, Denounciations, Reservations, etc.
- ☛ Cape Verde signed the CWC on 15 January 1993
- ☛ On 16 March 1995, Cape Verde acceded to the Additional Protocols of 1977
- ☛ On 16 March 1995, Cape Verde made a declaration under Article 90 of Additional Protocol I to the Geneva Conventions of 1949 recognising the competence of the International Fact-Finding Commission
- ☛ Cape Verde acceded to the CCW Convention (Protocols I, II and III) on 16 September 1997, and to Protocol IV and amended Protocol II on the same day
- ☛ Cape Verde signed the Landmines Treaty on 4 December 1997

CHAD

Signings, Ratifications, Accessions, Successions, Denounciations, Reservations, etc.
- ☛ Chad signed the CWC on 11 October 1994
- ☛ On 17 January 1997, Chad acceded to Protocols I and II of 1977
- ☛ Chad signed the Landmines Treaty on 6 July 1998

CHILE

Signings, Ratifications, Accessions, Successions, Denounciations, Reservations, etc.
- ☛ Chile signed the CWC on 14 January 1993 and ratified it on 12 July 1996
- ☛ Chile acceded to the Safety Convention on 27 August 1977
- ☛ Chile signed the Landmines Treaty on 3 December 1997

(PEOPLE'S REPUBLIC OF) CHINA[29]

National Defence Law

☛ National Defence Law of the People's Republic of China. Entered into force 14 March 1997. Published in the *Gazette of the Standing Committee of the National People's Congress of the People's Republic of China*. No. 11, 1997, 9 April 1997

COMMENT BY ZHANG YONG[30]

'No precise definition of combatants and civilians can be found in regulations and written documents in China's practice in the field of IHL, and consequently there is no clear distinction between them.[31] The National Defence Law of the People's Republic of China uses the term 'armed forces' instead of the term 'combatant'. The armed forces of the PRC comprises the People's Liberation Army (PLA) in active service, the PLA in reserve service, the Chinese People's Armed Police Force and the People's Militia. The PLA in active service is the regular army of the country with the primary function of defence and military operations and assistance in the maintenance of public order in accordance with the law where necessary. The PLA in reserve service is normally required to undergo regular training, to assist in the maintenance of public order in accordance with the law where necessary and to be incorporated into the active service force according to the mobilization order of the country in times of war. Under the leadership of the State Council and of the Central Military Commission, the Chinese People's Armed Police Force is tasked to safeguard national security and maintain social order. Under the command of military authorities, the People's Militia carries out the duty of assisting with the preparatory work for military operations, participating in defence and military operations, and assisting in the maintenance of social order.[32] The provisions of this law regarding soldiers shall also apply to those serving in the Chinese People's Armed Police Force.[33] According to the law, the state applies a military ranking

29. Information provided by Professor Zhang Yong, Professor of International Law, Faculty of International Law, University of Nankai, People's Republic of China; member of the Board of Editors, *Yearbook of International Humanitarian Law*.

30. Ibid.

31. The term 'combatant' is used by the author in this study in conformity with the Geneva Conventions and IHL.

32. Art. 22, the National Defence Law of the People's Republic of China, passed by the 8th National People's Congress on 14 March 1997.

33. Ibid., Art. 68.

system to the PLA in active service and in reserve service alike.[34] However, in spite of the fact that the PLA in reserve service also uses the military ranking system, before being incorporated into the active service they shall not be regarded as combatants. Civilians and organizations shall support the construction of national defence, provide conveniences and other help to the military training of the armed forces, logistic duties for combat readiness, defence and military operations.[35] The fact that civilians and organizations become involved in these activities as such does not deprive them of the right of protection attaching to civilians and non-military objects.

Article 67 of the National Defence Law of the People's Republic of China stipulates that the People's Republic of China observes the relevant treaties and protocols she has concluded with foreign countries, joined or accepted in foreign military relations. The relevant regulations and orders of the army all provide that the officers and soldiers shall be organized to study international law and the Geneva Conventions and shall be familiar with the principles and rules of the Geneva Conventions and shall respect as well as observe IHL.

The PLA pays great attention to the dissemination of humanitarian law in the army and has conducted education of the army concerning IHL through various measures. As early as 1954, the Secretariat of the General Political Department of the PLA compiled and publicized *Collections of Main International Treaties on the Law of War*, which was handed out to the army for study. In 1985, the PLA Press published *Collection of Documents on the Law of War*, which has become a necessary manual for military officers. In 1993, the PLA Military Science Press published *Chinese Military Encyclopaedia - International Military Treaties and Conventions*. In 1994, the Shenyang Military Court of the PLA compiled the *Selected Materials on the Law of War*, in which 56 important international documents, including international conventions and treaties regarding the law of war and armed conflict and IHL since 1865 are included. The publication of these documents and books on IHL has played an important role in the dissemination and implementation of IHL in the PLA. The PLA has also sent representatives on many occasions to attend training courses on IHL organized by the ICRC.

The PLA, with the help of the ICRC, has systematically educated its soldiers. During this education, the distinction between international and non-international armed conflict is not made. The PLA considers that there is no necessity to make such a distinction, and regards the humanitarian rules to reduce the effects of armed conflicts and to guide the conduct of the armed forces as applicable whether a conflict is international or internal.'

34. Ibid., Art. 24. The Art. uses the term 'armed forces' instead of the term 'combatants'.
35. Ibid., Art. 53.

Criminal Law

☛ Criminal Law of the PRC, entered into force 1 October 1997. Published in the *Gazette of the Standing Committee of the National People's Congress of the People's Republic of China*. No. 2, 1997, 30 March 1997

COMMENT BY ZHANG YONG

'When defining the crimes committed by military personnel, the Chinese Criminal Law stipulates the notion of military personnel as including PLA officers and its non-military officials; PLA soldiers in active service; military college students with formal registration; police officers and nonmilitary police officials; soldiers of the Chinese People's Armed Police Force in active service; public security college students with formal registration; other PLA soldiers in reserve service and other individuals carrying out military missions.[36] That is to say, the reserve force of the PLA shall not under normal conditions (before being incorporated into the active service force, according to the mobilization order of the country in times of war) be regarded as combatants. The stipulation equally means that the reserve force of the PLA and even civilians will lose their status as civilians and become combatants when they get involved in military activities, and consequently lose the protection for civilians. Article 446 of the Chinese Criminal Law stipulates that, during armed conflicts and in the area of military operations, cruelly injuring innocent civilians and looting the property of innocent civilians constitutes the crime of cruelly injuring innocent civilians and looting the property of innocent civilians, for which convicted persons shall serve imprisonment of less than five years; for serious offences, those convicted shall be jailed for between five to ten years; for the most serious offences, convicted persons shall serve imprisonment of from ten years up to life imprisonment, or shall receive the death penalty.[37] The present Chinese Criminal Law provides that those who are directly responsible for the deliberate abandonment of the wounded and sick in the battlefield, if the matter is serious, shall be sentenced to imprisonment of less than five years.'[38]

☛ Explanation of the Draft Revision of the Criminal Law of the PRC by the Deputy Chairman of the National People's Congress, Wang Hanbin, 6 March 1997, at the Fifth Session of the Eighth National People's Congress

36. The Criminal Law of the People's Republic of China, Art. 450.

37. Ibid., Art. 446. There has not yet been any official comment or elaboration on the Act, and it has not yet been used.

38. Ibid., Art. 444.

Export of Nuclear Weapons and Military Products

- Regulations of the People's Republic of China on Nuclear Export Control. Decree no. 230, passed on 1 August 1997. Published in the *Gazette of the Standing Committee of the National People's Congress of the People's Republic of China*, No. 29, 1997, 29 September 1997
- Circular of the State Council on Issues Related to Strictly Implementing the Nuclear Export Policy of China. Issued on 27 May 1997. Published in the *Gazette of the Standing Committee of the National People's Congress of the People's Republic of China*, No. 18, 1997, 19 June 1997; entered into force 1 January 1998

COMMENT BY ZHANG YONG

'The Circular indicates China's stand that the possessing of nuclear weapons as a means of defence and deterrence is legally permissible, but their proliferation is forbidden. Even the export of such materials or skills as might be used to produce nuclear weapons shall be under strict control. China includes nuclear weapons in the notion of inhumane weapons. It is in favour of a total ban on weapons of this kind, with the exception of nuclear weapons, for which it supports further restrictions. The conditions for the use of such weapons, according to China, are: as a method of defence, as a last resort and against a prior use. This has long been the attitude of the Chinese Government towards these kind of weapons. On 13 July 1952, the People's Republic of China acknowledged its acceptance of the 1925 Geneva Protocol for the Prohibition of the Use in War of Asphyxiating, Poisonous or Other Gases, and of Bacteriological Methods of Warfare, and became a party to the Protocol. In fact, the Nationalist Government joined the Protocol in 1929. But after the coming to power of the Communist Government, all the treaties ratified by the Nationalist Government were not automatically succeeded to and therefore the status of the treaties was uncertain. According to Article 55 of the Common Guiding Principles of the Chinese People's Political Consultative Conference, the Central Government of the People's Republic of China shall examine all the treaties made between the Kuomintang Government and foreign countries and determine whether to accept, terminate, revise or reject them, according to their contents. After careful examination, considering that the Geneva Protocol of 1925 is of a nature favourable to the consolidation of international peace and security, and is in conformity with humanitarian principles, the Communist Government decided to accept and strictly implement it on the condition of mutual performance.'

- Regulations of the PRC Governing the Export of Military Products. Entered into force 1 January 1998. Published in the *Gazette of the State Council of the People's Republic of China,* No. 33 of 1997, 18 November 1997

Bilateral Treaties and Agreements

- Agreement Between the Government of the PRC and the Government of the Republic of India on the Measures for Building up Trust in the Military Field Along the Boundaries of Actual Control Between China and India. Ratified on 9 May 1997. Published in the *Gazette of the Standing Committee of the National People's Congress of the People's Republic of China*, No. 3, 1997, 30 May 1997

Signings, Ratifications, Accessions, Successions, Denounciations, Reservations, etc.

- China signed the CWC on 13 January 1993 and ratified it on 25 April 1997

COLOMBIA[39]

Implementation

- Presidential Decree No. 1863 of 11 October 1996 establishing a Governmental Commission for the Humanisation of Armed Conflict and the Application of International Humanitarian Law [Comisión Gubernamental para la humanización del conflicto amado interno y la aplicación del Derecho Internacional Humanitario]

'The Committee's tasks are to prepare measures for promoting the humanization of armed conflict and the implementation of IHL, for coordinating the activities of the various government departments involved in this sphere, to draw up annual plans of action to this end, and to advise ... national and regional authorities on IHL. The Committee comprises representatives of the principal ministries, the Director of the Presidential Programme for the Defence of Individual Freedom, the High Commissioner for Peace, and the Presidential Advisor on Security and on Human Rights. Observers may be invited to its working sessions.'[40]

- Presidential Decree, 1997, recognising the competence of the International Fact-Finding Commission under Article 90 of Protocol I of 1977, 8 April 1996 [Colombia officially recognised the Fact-Finding Commission on 17 April 1996]

Cases

- Judgement of Constitutional Court of 18 May 1995. Sentencia No. C-225/95, Revisión constitucional del 'Protocolo Adicional a los Convenios de Ginebra del 12 de agosto

39. Information provided by Professor Frits Kalshoven, formerly, Chair in Public International Law and International Humanitarian Law, Leiden University; Officer with the Royal Navy. Currently serving, *inter alia*, as President of the International Humanitarian Find-Finding Commission; member of the Board of Recommendation, *Yearbook of International Humanitarian Law*.

40. *Supra* n. 3 at p. 51.

de 1949, relativo a la protección de las víctimas de los conflictos armados sin carácter internacional (Protocolo II)' hecho en Ginebra al 8 de junio de 1977, y de la Ley 171 del 16 de diciembre de 1994, por medio de la cual se apruebra dicho Protocolo (unpublished).[41]

Signings, Ratifications, Accessions, Successions, Denounciations, Reservations, etc.
☛ Colombia signed the CWC on 13 January 1993
☛ Colombia signed the Landmines Treaty on 3 December 1997

COMOROS

Signings, Ratifications, Accessions, Successions, Denounciations, Reservations, etc.
☛ Comoros signed the CWC on 13 January 1993

CONGO

Signings, Ratifications, Accessions, Successions, Denounciations, Reservations, etc.
☛ Congo signed the CWC on 15 January 1993

COOK ISLANDS

Signings, Ratifications, Accessions, Successions, Denounciations, Reservations, etc.
☛ The Cook Islands signed the CWC on 14 January 1993 and ratified it on 15 July 1994
☛ The Cook Islands ratified the CRC on 6 June 1997 with reservations
☛ The Cook Islands signed the Landmines Treaty on 3 December 1997

COSTA RICA

Signings, Ratifications, Accessions, Successions, Denounciations, Reservations, etc.
☛ Costa Rica signed the CWC on 14 January 1993 and ratified it on 31 May 1996
☛ Costa Rica signed the Landmines Treaty on 3 December 1997

CÔTE d'IVOIRE

Implementation
☛ Decree No. 96-853 of 25 October 1996 establishing a National Interministerial Committee for the Implementation of International Humanitarian Law [Commission Interministérielle Nationale pour la mise en oeuvre du droit international humanitaire]

41. For commentary, see Kalshoven at p. 262.

'By decree No. 96-853 of 25 October 1996, the Ivorian authorities set up a National Interministerial Committee for the Implementation of International Humanitarian Law. This body is responsible for monitoring respect for IHL and its implementation, studying and preparing the law and regulations required to bridge gaps in national legislation, guaranteeing the application of IHL in the country, and encouraging its promotion, dissemination and teachings. The Committee's inaugural session was held on 27 December 1996 under the auspices of the Ministries of Foreign Affairs and Justice and Public Liberty. Its members include two representatives of each of the ministries concerned, two members of the Bar Association, a representative of the ICRC regional delegation, and a representative of the Red Cross Society of Côte d'Ivoire.'[42]

Signings, Ratifications, Accessions, Successions, Denounciations, Reservations, etc.

- ☛ Cote d'Ivoire signed the CWC on 13 January 1993 and ratified it on 18 December 1995
- ☛ Cote d'Ivoire signed the Landmines Treaty on 3 December 1997

CROATIA[43]

War Crimes and Amnesties

- ☛ Decision about founding a war crimes commission, 5 December 1996. Published in *Narodne novine*, no. 28/1995
- ☛ Law on General Amnesty, 20 September 1996. Published in *Narodne novine*, no. 27/1996

COMMENT BY MAJA SERŠIĆ

'The 1996 Law on General Amnesty proclaimed the abolition of and pardon for all acts related to aggression, rebellion and armed conflicts committed on the territory of the Republic of Croatia from 17 August 1990 to 23 August 1996 (Articles 1 and 2). Under Article 3 of the same Law, amnesty cannot be granted to persons who have been found guilty of committing acts constituting war crimes (under Arts. 120-122 of the 1993 Criminal Code), genocide (under Art. 119 of the 1993 Criminal Code) and any other act constituting a violation of the laws and customs of war according to the 1993 Criminal Code. The former Abolition Law of 1992, as amended in 1995, contained similar provisions. During the armed conflict in the Republic of Croatia, the captured combatants of the adverse party to the conflict who were not on the list of persons suspected of having committed crimes which exclude the application of the Abolition Law were released, and were allowed either to stay in the Republic of Croatia or to leave the country.'

42. *Supra*. n. 3 at pp. 51-52.

43. Information provided by Professor Maja Seršić and Professor Ivo Josipovic, Faculty of Law, University of Zagreb.

International Criminal Tribunal

- Decision about an observer of the Republic of Croatia at the International Criminal Tribunal for proceedings against persons responsible for serious violations of humanitarian law committed in the area of former Yugoslavia since 1991, taken by the Government of the Republic of Croatia on 20 April 1995 on the basis of Article 36(1) of the Government of the Republic of Croatia Law. Published in *Narodne novine*, no. 61/1996
- Constitutional Law concerning the Cooperation of the Republic of Croatia with the International Criminal Tribunal, 1996. Adopted on 19 April 1996. Published in *Narodne novine*, no. 32/1996, 26 April 1996. Entered into force the date of its publication
- Order about an Office for Cooperation with the International Criminal Tribunal, 4 July 1996. Published in *Narodne novine*, no. 103/1996

COMMENT BY MAJA SERŠIĆ

'The 1957 European Convention on Extradition, to which Croatia is a party, allows its contracting parties to refuse the extradition of their nationals (Art. 1(a)). The Constitution of the Republic of Croatia (Art. 9(2)) prohibits extradition of a Croatian citizen to another state. The Code of Criminal Procedure of 19 September 1997[44] repeats this prohibition. Consequently, there is a ban on the extradition of Croatian nationals, regardless of the crime they are suspected of having committed. An exception has been made in the case of the surrender of a suspect of Croatian nationality to the ICTY. This exception has been made on the basis of the theory that such surrender is not to be considered as an extradition in the classical sense, because it concerns extradition to an international court rather than to another state. Cooperation of the Republic of Croatia with the ICTY is regulated by the 1996 Constitutional Law concerning the cooperation of the Republic of Croatia with the International Criminal Tribunal. On the basis of the said law, the Government of the Republic of Croatia passed the Order about the Office for Cooperation with the International Criminal Tribunal; the Decision on Founding a War Crimes Commission; and the Decision about the Observer of the Republic of Croatia at the International Criminal Tribunal for Proceedings against Persons Responsible for Serious Violations of Humanitarian Law Committed in the Area of Former Yugoslavia since 1991.'

44. Published in *Narodne novine*, no. 110/1997.

Signings, Ratifications, Accessions, Successions, Denouncations, Reservations, etc.[45]

- On 2 December 1993, Croatia acceded to the CCW Convention (Protocols I, II and III)
- Croatia signed the CWC on 13 January 1993 and ratified it on 23 May 1995
- On 5 May 1996, Croatia accepted amended Protocol II (Landmines) to the CCW Convention following the issuance on 19 April 1996 of a Joint Statement on the Moratorium on the Use, Production, Stockpiling, Import and Export of Antipersonnel Landmines, Booby-Traps and Remotely Delivered Antipersonnel Mines by the Ministers of Foreign Affairs and Defence of the Republic of Croatia
- Croatia signed the Landmines Treaty on 4 December 1997 and ratified it on 20 May 1998

Pending: (war crimes prosecutions)

- The Case of *Dinko Sakić*

As the Yearbook went to press, Dinko Sakić, the former Commander of the Jasenovac concentration camp in Croatia during WWII, had been extradited from Argentina to Croatia to face trial on war crimes charges, and was awaiting trial. Sakić, a former Captain during the Ustashe regime of Ante Pavelić in Croatia, is accused of having participated in the murder and ill treatment of Jews, Serbs, Muslims and Gypsies at Jasenovac, where up to 600,000 died. Sakić fled to Argentina in 1947. In 1997, he gave an interview to Argentine TV, prompting calls for his arrest. A *subpoena* issued in April 1998 by a court in Croatia accused him of committing 'grave and fatal' criminal acts. On 1 May 1998, Argentine police arrested Sakić, and on 5 May, a Judge in Argentina ordered his extradition to Croatia on a request of the Croatian government which was not contested by Sakić.[46]

After Croatia's national archives were unable to locate the government's documentation on the Jasenovac camp, the US Government, on 1 May 1998, produced a top-secret December 1943 German Wehrmacht report on senior officers of the Ustashe, from its State Department archives.[47]

Sakić arrived in Zagreb on 18 June 1998. Charges against him must be brought within six months. Any trial of Sakić in Croatia is expected to be very politically divisive.[48]

45. The provisions of the treaties to which the Republic of Croatia is a party are directly applicable in the Republic of Croatia. Under Art. 134 of the Croatian Constitution, treaties duly concluded and ratified in accordance with the Constitution and published are part of the domestic legal system and overrule municipal statutory law.

46. See *supra*, p. 404.

47. 'Details of Death Camp in Document', Roy Gutman, *New York Newsday* (2 May 1998) p. A07.

48. See 'War Crimes Horrors Revive as Croat Faces Possible Trial', Chris Hedges, *The New York Times* (2 May 1998); 'World War II crimes suspect arrives home for trial', Snjezana Vukić, Associated Press (18 June 1998).

On 29 April 1998, a Yugoslav federal court council decided to institute criminal proceedings against Sakić for committing acts of genocide. Although the crimes of which Sakić is suspected were committed on territory that is now outside the jurisdiction of the Federal Republic of Yugoslavia (FRY), under the criminal law of the FRY, Yugoslav criminal legislation applies to foreigners who have committed crimes abroad (Art. 107(1)).[49] However, on 5 May 1998, an Argentine Federal Judge rejected the request of FRY for the extradition of Sakić.[50] As of September 1998, Sakić's wife, Esperanza, was awaiting extradition from Argentina and was also expected to face criminal prosecution in Croatia.[51]

CUBA

Signings, Ratifications, Accessions, Successions, Denounciations, Reservations, etc.

- ☛ Cuba signed the CWC on 13 January 1993 and ratified it on 29 April 1997

CYPRUS

Signings, Ratifications, Accessions, Successions, Denounciations, Reservations, etc.

- ☛ Cyprus signed the CWC on 13 January 1993, ratified it on 28 August 1998 and became a state party on 27 September 1998
- ☛ Cyprus became a party to Additional Protocol II of 1977 on 18 March 1996
- ☛ Cyrpus signed the Landmines Treaty on 4 December 1997 and ratified it on 20 May 1998

CZECH REPUBLIC

Signings, Ratifications, Accessions, Successions, Denounciations, Reservations, etc.

- ☛ The Czech Republic signed the CWC on 14 January 1993 and ratified it on 6 March 1996
- ☛ On 2 May 1995, the Czech Republic made a declaration under Article 90 of Additional Protocol I to the Geneva Conventions of 1949 recognising the competence of the International Fact-Finding Commission
- ☛ The Czech Republic signed the Safety Convention on 27 December 1995 and ratified it on 13 June 1997
- ☛ The Czech Republic signed the Landmines Treaty on 3 December 1997
- ☛ On 30 April 1998, the Czech Republic ratified amended Protocol II and Protocol IV of the CCW Convention, following on its accession to the Convention on 22 February 1993

49. 'Belgrade Court initiates proceedings against Croatian World War II war crimes suspect,' Tanjug (29 April 1998).

50. *Supra* p. 404.

51. Ibid.

DENMARK

International Tribunals

- Act on Criminal Proceedings before the International Tribunal for the Prosecution of Persons Responsible for War Crimes Committed in the Territory of Former Yugoslavia, Act No. 1099 of 21 December 1994 (extended to Rwanda Tribunal by order of the Minister of Justice pursuant to Article 6 of this act)

Cases (repression of breaches)

- *The Director of Public Prosecutions* vs. *T.* Sentence passed by the Eastern High Court (3rd Division) on 22 November 1994 (unpublished)

In which case, concerning an accused charged under Article 8(5) of the Danish Penal Code, cf. Articles 129 and 130 and Articles 146 and 147, respectively, of the Third and Fourth Geneva Conventions of 1949, for crimes committed against persons detained in the Croatian POW camp of Dretelj during the wars in Bosnia and Herzegovina in 1993, the Court stated: '[T]aking account of the fact that the large number of offences – of which several are very grave – were committed in quite uniform circumstances, the Supreme Court finds that all counts related to the Conventions shall be considered as a whole. This approach, which is considered to conform most appropriately to the objectives of the Conventions, implies that the requirements set out in the Conventions as to "grave breaches" have been met in the case of all counts of the indictment. Consequently, the Court cannot find for the claim of acquittal of the accused on the grounds of non-applicability of Danish criminal jurisdiction.'

Signings, Ratifications, Accessions, Successions, Denounciations, Reservations, etc.

- Denmark signed the CWC on 14 January 1993 and ratified it on 13 July 1995
- Denmark signed the Safety Convention on 15 December 1994 and ratified it on 11 April 1995
- On 30 April 1997, Denmark ratified amended Protocol II and Protocol IV of the CCW Convention
- Denmark signed the Landmines Treaty on 4 December 1997 and ratified it on 8 June 1998

DJIBOUTI

Signings, Ratifications, Accessions, Successions, Denounciations, Reservations, etc.

- Djibouti signed the CWC on 28 September 1993
- On 29 July 1996, Djibouti acceded to the CCW Convention (Protocols I, II and III)
- Djibouti signed the Landmines Treaty on 3 December 1997 and ratified it on 8 June 1998

DOMINICA

Signings, Ratifications, Accessions, Successions, Denounciations, Reservations, etc.

- ☛ Dominica signed the CWC on 2 August 1993
- ☛ On 25 April 1996, Dominica acceded to Additional Protocols I and II of 1977
- ☛ Dominica signed the Landmines Treaty on 3 December 1997

DOMINICAN REPUBLIC

Implementation

- ☛ Interministerial Commission for the implementation and application of International Humanitarian Law [Comisión Interministerial para el seguimiento y la aplicación del derecho internacional humanitario] established on 4 November 1995

The Commission is composed of representatives of the Ministries of Foreign Affairs; Defence; Education; Arts and Culture; Public Health and Social Welfare; the National Police; Civil Defence; Legal Office of the Executive; Office of the State Prosecutor; the Supreme Court and the National Commission for Disaster Relief.[52]

Signings, Ratifications, Accessions, Successions, Denounciations, Reservations, etc.

- ☛ Dominican Republic signed the CWC on 13 January 1993
- ☛ On 26 May 1994, the Dominican Republic acceded to Additional Protocols I and II of 1977
- ☛ Dominican Republic signed the Landmines Treaty on 3 December 1997

ECUADOR

Signings, Ratifications, Accessions, Successions, Denounciations, Reservations, etc.

- ☛ Ecuador signed the CWC on 14 January 1993 and ratified it on 6 September 1995
- ☛ Ecuador signed the Landmines Treaty on 4 December 1997

EL SALVADOR

Implementation

- ☛ Executive Presidential Decree No. 118 of 4 November 1997, formally establishing the Interinstitutional Committee for IHL [Comité Interinstitucional de Derecho Internacional Humanitario (CIDIH-ES)][53]

52. See Table of National Bodies for International Humanitarian Law, Advisory Service on International Humanitarian Law, ICRC, as of 31 March 1998. Provided by the Advisory Service, p.7.

53. The Committee was first established on an *ad hoc* basis in May 1997. Ibid., p. 8. Provided by the Advisory Service.

The Committee is composed of representatives of the Ministries of Foreign Affairs; the Interior; Public Security; Justice; Education; Defence; Public Health and Social Welfare; the Attorney-General for the Defence of Human Rights; and the Salvadorean Red Cross Society. Its chair is the Deputy Minister for Foreign Affairs. Thus far, the Committee has established three sub-committees, each of which is charged with studying and preparing one of three priority areas, which have been identified as:
– the adoption of a law protecting the use of the emblem (the sub-committee on the law relating to the emblem, chaired by the Salvadoren Red Cross Society);
– repression of grave breaches (the sub-committee on Legislation, represented by the Ministry of Defence); and
– the preparation of a dissemination and education programme (the sub-committee on dissemination and education, chaired and represented by the Ministry of Education).

Signings, Ratifications, Accessions, Successions, Denounciations, Reservations, etc.
☛ El Salvador signed the CWC on 14 January 1993 and ratified it on 30 October 1995
☛ El Salvador signed the Landmines Treaty on 4 December 1997

EQUATORIAL GUINEA

Signings, Ratifications, Accessions, Successions, Denounciations, Reservations, etc.
☛ Equatorial Guinea signed the CWC on 14 January 1993 and ratified it on 25 April 1997

ERITREA

Signings, Ratifications, Accessions, Successions, Denounciations, Reservations, etc.
☛ Eritrea ratified the CRC on 3 August 1994

ESTONIA[54]

Criminal Code
☛ Criminal Code. Adopted by the Riigikogu (Parliament) on 7 May 1992. Published in *Riigi Teataja* (National Gazette) 1992, 20, 287, 29 May 1992. Chapter I (concerning liability for crimes against humanity) was adopted on 9 November 1994. Published in *Riigi Teataja* I 1994, 83, 1447, 439. [The Criminal Code has been amended and changed several times. The final amendments are published in *Riigi Teataja* I 1997, 21/22, 353, 21 March 1997]

54. Information provided by Tanel Kerikmäe, lecturer in International Law, Tartu University, Estonia. Laws mentioned regarding Estonia enter into force nine days after their publication in *Riigi Teataja*, if no other specific date is mentioned in the law.

COMMENT BY TANEL KERIKMÄE

'In Estonia, the Criminal Code is the sole source of criminal law, applying both to civilians and the military. The special part concerning crimes against humanity and war crimes (Chapter I of the Special Part of the Criminal Code) was introduced in November 1994. Article 61 §1 of the Criminal Code prescribes criminal liability for crimes against humanity. Article 61 § 2 - § 4 prescribes liability for war crimes, such as aggression against the civilian population in an active war zone, violation of the legal rights of prisoners of war, use or command to use prohibited means or methods of war. However, the issue of omission to prevent war crimes is not regulated. Also, the Code does not mention clearly the case of war crimes being committed upon superior orders. However, by Article 37 § 1 p. 3, the commission of an offence upon a threat, coercion or material, service or other dependency is a mitigating factor to be considered when awarding punishment. The Estonian legislation in force contains no specific provision concerning compensation to victims of war crimes.'

Wartime National Defence Law

☛ Wartime National Defence Law, adopted by the Riigikogu on 28 September 1994. Published in *Riigi Teataja* I, 1994, 69/1194, 21 October 1994

Peacetime National Defence Law

☛ Peacetime National Defence Law, adopted by the Riigikogu on 6 February 1995. Published in *Riigi Teataja* I 1995, 18, 240, 1 March 1995. Changed by law of amendments, adopted 2 April 1996. Published in *Riigi Teataja* I 1996, 25/519, 12 April 1996. Entered into force the day after its publication

National Defence Policy and Defence Forces

☛ Approval of the Guidelines of the National Defence Policy of the Estonian State (decision of the Riigikogu), adopted on 7 May 1996. Published in *Riigi Teataja* 1996, 33, 684, 16 May 1996. Entered into force the day following its publication.

☛ Law on disciplinary punishments in national defence forces, adopted by Riigikogu on 3 December 1997. Published in *Riigi Teataja* I, 1997, 95/96, 1575, 31 December 1997. Entered into force the day following its publication

COMMENT BY TANEL KERIKMÄE

'Until recently, disciplinary punishment connected with deprivation of liberty in Estonian military service was regulated by the Government Decree of Military Service Disciplinary Punishments of 2 April 1930. Today, a new law on disciplinary punishments in defence forces has been adopted (December 1997) and is in force. However, the new law seems to contain some contradictions, and conflicts with the Estonian Constitution; for example, it does not leave room for courts to review whether there has been a disciplinary offence. If the disciplinary punishment is disputed, the court (by the new law) has only the right to control the "technical" side of the appointed punishment.'

- The Implementation of Humanitarian Law in National Defence Forces, Regulation of Defence Minister Andrus Oeoevel No. 2 of 10 July 1998. Published in *Riigi Teataja* annex 1998, 238/239, 1000, 30 July 1998

Signings, Ratifications, Accessions, Successions, Denounciations, Reservations, etc.

- Estonia signed the CWC on 14 January 1993
- Estonia ratified the Cultural Property Convention on 4 April 1995

ETHIOPIA

Implementation

- General Information on Measures Taken at a National Level to Implement IHL in Ethiopia. Report of Ministry of Foreign Affairs, Addis Ababa, November 1996
- Report of National Seminar on the Implementation of International Humanitarian Law in Ethiopia (Organised by the International Committee of the Red Cross in cooperation with the Ethiopian Red Cross Society, held in Addis Ababa, 28-29 November 1996), Addis Ababa, January 1997
- Advisory Committee on the Implementation of International Humanitarian Law, February 1997

The Advisory Committee was formally established in February 1997 under the auspices of the Ministry of Foreign Affairs, by decision of the Minister of Foreign Affairs. It is composed of representatives of the Ministries of Foreign Affairs; Defence; Justice; Information and Culture; Health; Education; Parliament; University Law Faculty; Civil Service; College Law Faculty; and the Ethiopian Red Cross Society. It is chaired by the Vice-Minister of Foreign Affairs. Its mandate is to advise the government on the full range of measures concerning national implementation of IHL.[55]

Signings, Ratifications, Accessions, Successions, Denounciations, Reservations, etc.

- Ethiopia signed the CWC on 14 January 1993 and ratified it on 13 May 1996
- On 8 April 1994, Ethiopia acceded to Additional Protocols I and II of 1977
- Ethiopia signed the Landmines Treaty on 3 December 1997

55. See *supra* n. 52 at p. 9.

FIJI

Signings, Ratifications, Accessions, Successions, Denounciations, Reservations, etc.

- Fiji signed the CWC on 14 January 1993 and ratified it on 20 January 1993
- Fiji signed the Safety Convention on 25 October 1994
- Fiji signed the Landmines Treaty on 3 December 1997 and ratified it on 10 June 1998

FINLAND[56]

War Crimes and Crimes Against Humanity

- Chapter 11 of the revised Penal Code dealing with War Crimes and Crimes against Humanity, 21 April 1995.[57] Published in *Finnish Law Gazette* [Suomen säädöskokoelman sopimussarja] 1995/587

International Criminal Tribunal

- Act on the Jurisdiction of the International Tribunal for the Prosecution of Persons Responsible for Crimes Committed in the Territory of the Former Yugoslavia and on Legal Assistance to the International Tribunal, 5 January 1994. Published in *Finnish Law Gazette* [Suomen säädöskokoelman sopimussarja] 1994/12

Landmines

- Finland's Position on Anti-Personnel Landmines: Fact Sheet of the Finnish Ministry for Foreign Affairs, Political Department, 26 August 1997[58]

COMMENT BY LAURI HANNIKAINEN

'When the Convention on the Prohibition of the Use, Stockpiling, Production and Transfer of Anti-Personnel Landmines was opened for signature in December 1997 in Ottawa, Finland was the only EU Member not to sign it. The Finnish Government had not expected that as many as 122 states would immediately sign the Convention. Politically, the matter is difficult for Finland. Finland wants to be a responsible member of the international community but anti-personnel landmines have been vital for its defense. These mines played an important role in Finland's defense against the Soviet Union during World War II (the Russo-Finnish boundary is over 1,000 km long).

Although 122 states signed the Ottawa Convention, this is still far from universal acceptance. A number of militarily strong and populous states, including Russia,

56. Information provided by Professor Lauri Hannikainen, Professor of International Law, Turku Law School, University of Turku and Mr. Juhani Parkkari, Secretary, Finnish Society of Humanitarian Law.

57. Reprinted at p. 619.

58. Reprinted at p. 562.

China, India and Pakistan, have not signed. Those states produce and export large quantities of anti-personnel landmines. In the opinion of Finland, for the ban on anti-personnel landmines to be effective, it is essential that all or nearly all militarily strong states commit themselves. A less widely accepted ban could prove to be harmful to the security of small states. The worst scenario for Finland would be to commit itself to a convention, 1) which prohibits defensive anti-personnel landmines but, 2) outside of which a number of militarily strong states decide to remain, and 3) which does not prohibit technologically advanced, remotely delivered mines, capable of being used for aggressive purposes. A Fact-Sheet issued by Finland's Foreign Ministry on September 1997 states as follows:

> APLs are an integral part of the Finnish territorial defense doctrine. They would only be used in response to armed aggression against Finland. Given their importance to Finland's defense, any decision to destroy APLs and to bear the considerable cost of providing the same defensive impact with other means would have to be made in the context of such a total ban that Finland regards as responding to the global landmine crisis.

Because the Finnish Government understands that the current situation puts it in a politically uncomfortable position, it has taken efforts to clarify in what ways Finland could replace anti-personnel mines in its defense arsenal. According to a press release of the Finnish Foreign Ministry on this matter, a task force of officials estimates that Finland could replace anti-personnel mines over a ten-year period, although it would be very expensive.[59] Finnish public opinion is divided on the question of landmines. Humanitarian and some other organizations call upon Finland to commit itself to, and to join the advocates of, the total ban. In leading circles, it is believed that it would cost too much to replace anti-personnel landmines in Finland's defence strategy. However, it is recognized that if the number of states committing themselves to the Landmines Convention grows and includes militarily strong states close to Finland - or such a result is accomplished in the Geneva Conference on Disarmament[60] - Finland should give up its anti-personnel mines and bear the necessary costs. The Government Bill proposing Finland's ratification of amended Protocol II of the CCW Convention was presented to Parliament in late 1997. It is expected that Finland will ratify the amended Protocol during 1998. The Convention and its Protocols are in force in Finland's legal system at the level

59. See report of Task Force and Press Release of Foreign Ministry thereon, *infra*, p. 438.
60. Ibid.

of a presidential decree.[61] Ratification of the amended Protocol II would lead to certain changes in the Manual on Obstacle Employment of the Finnish Defence Forces, for example, regarding the marking and reporting of minefields, etc.'

☛ Report of the Task Force on Landmines, 16 December 1997 (Jalkaväkimiinatyöryhmän Raportti, Ulkoavirinministeriön julkaisuja, 1/1998 (Finnish language)) [on 16 December 1997, the Ministry issued press release No. 352 on the Report with an enclosure on the recommendations of the Task Force, English, unofficial translation]

Bilateral Treaties

☛ Treaty on Cooperation for the Commemoration of the Deceased in War in Tartu between Finland and Estonia, 16 August 1997 (Finnish Treaty Series 74/1997). Entered into force 1 November 1997

COMMENT BY JUHANI PARKKARI

'This treaty follows a similar bilateral Treaty with Russia, signed in Helsinki on 11 July 1992.[62] Altogether, 666 deceased soldiers from the Second World War have been found in Russia, unburied or in unmarked graves. In addition, a search revealed war grave sites where over 1,000 deceased soldiers had been laid to rest. Memorials have been erected on seven such field cemeteries. From 1993 to 1997 altogether 127 identified and 438 unidentified deceased Finnish soldiers have been reburied in Finnish cemeteries. The forensic research into 88 deceased has not yet been completed. The remains of 13 deceased await reburial. In addition, a significant number of deceased Russian (Soviet) soldiers have been found, information about which has been forwarded to the Russian authorities. Cooperation between the Finnish and Russian search parties has been constant. The search has been conducted on major battlefields and places where men have been reported missing on the Isthmuses of Karelia, Olonets and Masaelkä and north of Lake Ladoga, and also on the Rūkajärvi and Kiestinki areas, so that few unburied Finnish soldiers can be expected to be found. The nationality of those found on the field has been established with the help of military equipment, clothing and military records. Identification is based on military diaries and medical data, and in some cases, on identification tags and DNA methods. The Association Cherishing the Memory of the Dead of War has been established and registered according to the Finnish Associations Act of 26 May 1989.'

61. See the Chapter on the status of IHL in Finland, in Lauri Hannikainen, Raija Hanski and Allan Rosas, *Implementing Humanitarian Law Applicable in Armed Conflicts: The case of Finland* (Martinus Nijhoff, Dordrecht 1992) pp. 109-113.

62. Finnish Treaty Series 95/1992.

The National Society

- ☛ Decree on the Finnish Red Cross, enacted 28 November 1997; entered into force 1 January 1998. Published in *Finnish Law Gazette* [Suomen säädöskokoelman sopimussarja] 1997/1065

COMMENT BY JUHANI PARKKARI

'The Finnish National Red Cross Society celebrated its 120th anniversary on 7 May 1997. The Society is, according to Section 2(2) of the Finnish Associations Act of 26 May 1989 (503/1989) a corporation which has been founded by statute for a special purpose. Therefore, the Associations Act shall not apply to the Red Cross Society. The new Decree of 28 November 1997 is more comprehensive than the previous one, taking into consideration the requirements of the Statutes of the International Red Cross and Red Crescent Movement. The main purpose of the new Decree is to increase internal democracy by giving the local branches of the Finnish Red Cross Society power to elect their representatives to the General Assembly of the Society that is to be held every three years. Earlier representatives were elected by the Districts of the Society; the General Assembly was held every second year.'

IHL Education in Finland

COMMENT BY JUHANI PARKKARI

'Yearly, the Finnish National Red Cross Society is organizing two courses on IHL for officers and military lawyers of the Finnish Defence Forces. Finnish officers and military lawyers frequently take part in the military courses organised by the International Institute of Humanitarian Law at San Remo, Italy. The Legal Department of the Finnish Military Headquarters that was established in November 1996 during the reorganisation of the Headquarters is also organising an annual comprehensive legal course for officers and military lawyers, which deals, *inter alia*, with IHL. The Finnish Defence Academy has made a contract of legal cooperation with the Erik Castrén International Law Institute of the University of Helsinki (established in late 1997) and the Legal Department of the Finnish Military Headquarters. Humanitarian law issues will be taken into consideration in the activities of this cooperation in the near future. The Finnish Society for Military Law and the Law of War was established in 1990 and registered according to the Finnish Associations Act of 26 May 1989. It has 50 members who have given lectures on IHL to local branches of the Finnish Red Cross Society, to local Societies of the National Finnish Rescue Federation and to local Branches of the Finnish Voluntary Defence Organization. The Legal Department of the Finnish Ministry for Foreign Affairs published in November 1997 in the Finnish language the second and enlarged edition of the compilation of conventions dealing with IHL that are legally binding on Finland.[63] It is much more comprehensive than its predecessor of 1981, containing almost all internationally legally binding conventions, including the full text of the 1981 UN Weapons Convention and amended Protocol II dealing with landmines.'

Signings, Ratifications, Accessions, Successions, Denounciations, Reservations, etc.

- Finland signed the CWC on 14 January 1993 and ratified it 7 February 1995
- Finland ratified the Cultural Property Convention on 16 September 1994
- Finland signed the Safety Convention on 15 December 1994
- On 11 January 1996, Finland ratified Protocol IV to the CCW Convention and on 3 April 1998 it ratified its amended Protocol II

Pending (Code of Conduct)

- Codes of Conduct and Training of Humanitarian Law in the Finnish Defence Forces [awaits acceptance by the Parliament]

FORMER YUGOSLAV REPUBLIC OF MACEDONIA

Signings, Ratifications, Accessions, Successions, Denounciations, Reservations, etc.

- The Former Yugoslav Republic of Macedonia ratified the Genocide Convention on 18 January 1994
- The Former Yugoslav Republic of Macedonia ratified the Convention on the Non-Applicability of Statutory Limitations on 18 February 1994
- On 30 December 1996, the Former Yugoslav Republic of Macedonia ratified the CCW Convention (Protocols I, II and III) of 1980
- The Former Yugoslav Republic of Macedonia ratified the Cultural Property Convention on 30 April 1997
- The Former Yugoslav Republic of Macedonia acceded to the Chemical Weapons Convention on 20 June 1997

FRANCE[64]

International Criminal Tribunals

- Act N° 95-1 of 2 January 1995 adapting French legislation to the provisions of United Nations Security Council resolution 827 establishing an international criminal tribunal to prosecute persons responsible for serious violations of international humanitarian law committed in the territory of the former Yugoslavia since 1991 [Loi N° 95-1 du 2 janvier 1995 portant adaption de la législation française aux dispositions de la

63. *Sodan Oikeussäännöt* (Helsinki 1997).

64. Information provided by Professor Paul Tavernier, Centre de Recherches et D'Etudes Sur les Droits de l'Homme et le Droit Humanitaire (CREDHO), Faculté Jean Monet, Université de Paris-Sud.

résolution 827 du Conseil de sécurité des Nations Unies instituant un tribunal international en vue de juger les personnes présumées responsables de violations graves du droit international humanitaire commises sur le territoire de l'Ex-Yougoslavie depuis 1991]. Published in *Journal Officiel de la République Française*, 3 January/janvier 1995

- Law N° 96-432 of 22 May 1996 concerning the adaption of French legislation to the provisions of United Nations Security Council resolution 955 establishing an international criminal tribunal to prosecute persons presumed responsible for acts of genocide and other serious violations of international humanitarian law committed in 1994 on the territory of Rwanda and concerning Rwandese on the territory of neighbouring states [Loi N° 96-432 du 22 mai 1996 portant adaption de la legislation française aux dispositions de la resolution 955 du Conseil de sécurité des nations unies instituant un tribunal international e vue de juger des personnes presumees responsables d'actes de genocide ou de'autres violations graves du droit international humanitaire commis en 1994 sur le territoire du Rwanda et, s'agissant des rwandais, sur les territoroire d'etats voisons]. Published in *Journal Officiel de la République Française*, 23 May/mai 1996

Circulaires du Ministère de la Justice

- Circulaire of 10 February 1995 concerning law N° 95-1 of 2 January 1995 concerning French cooperation with the ICTY. Published in *Journal Officiel de la République Française*, 21 February/février 1995
- Circulaire of 22 July 1996 concerning law N° 96-432 of 22 May 1996 concerning French legislation to cooperate with the ICTR. Published in *Journal Officiel de la République Française*, 31 August/août 1996

Advisory Opinions of the National Consultative Commission on Human Rights[65]

- Advisory Opinion concerning the Creation of an International Criminal Court, 16 January 1997 [Avis sur la creation d'une Cour criminelle internationale, adopté le 16 janvier 1997]
- Advisory Opinion on the implementation of the introduction of a total ban of antipersonnel landmines, adopted by the plenary assembly on 1 October 1997 [Avis sur la mise en oeuvre nationale de l'introduction totale des mines anti-personnel, adopté par l'assemblée plénière du 1er octobre 1997]
- Opinion (statement) of the French National Advisory Commission on Human Rights concerning the relationship between French Federal Authorities and the Yugoslav Tribunal, 8 January 1998 [Avis sur la cooperation avec les jurisdiction penales internationales, adopté en assemblée plénière du 8 janvier 1998]
- Advisory opinion on the requirements of human rights and humanitarian action taking into consideration the international embargo, adopted in plenary session of 8 January

65. Not yet published.

1998 [Avis sur les exigences des droits de l'homme et de l'action humanitaire a prendre en consideration dans l'embargo international, adopté en séance plénière le 8 janvier 1998]

- Advisory opinion on the ratification by France of Protocol I Additional to the Geneva Conventions of 1998, adopted in Plenary session on 8 January 1998 [Avis sur la ratification par la France du protocole I additionnel aux conventions de Genève, adopté en séance plénière le 8 janvier 1998][66]
- Advisory Opinion on the Adaption of the French Legal Order to the Conventions of Humanitarian Law, adopted by the plenary assembly of 16 February 1998 [Avis sur l'adaptation de l'ordre juridique français aux conventions de droit humanitaire, adopté par l'assemblée plénière du 16 février 1998][67]

Cases

- *Javor* e.a., (JCP 1996, IV 1392) Cour de Cassation, crim., 26 March/mars 1996. Published in *Revue générale de droit international public*, 1996 p. 1083. (*Droit Pénal*, June/juin 1996), chr. 131, 'note' (comment) by J.H. Robert

Concerning a complaint brought before the Examining Magistrate of Paris by Bosnian subjects against an unnamed person for crimes of war, torture, genocide and crimes against humanity committed against the plaintiffs in Bosnia and Herzegovina in 1992. In which judgement the court found that the legal grounds could not be considered as, despite the fact that the victims were present in France, the offender was not. Under the regulations of Articles 1 and 2 of the law of 2 January 1995 adapting French legislation to the regulations of resolution 827 of the UN Security Council establishing the ICTY, applicable to the parties in court, the French judicial powers can prosecute and judge only when the offenders or accomplices of crimes or offences defined by French law which constitute, according to Articles 2 to 5 of the Statute of the International Tribunal, grave breaches of the Geneva Conventions, violations of the laws or customs of war, genocide or crimes against humanity, have been found in France. In this case, the presence of the victims of such violations in France could not in itself justify a public action, as the offenders or accomplices suspected of these violations had not been found on French territory.

- *Munyeshyaka.* (JCP 1998, IV 2025) Cour de Cassation, crim., 6 January/janvier 1998 (quashing two judgements of the Nimes Appeals court).[68] Published in *Droit Pénal*, May/mai 1998 (n° 5) Chr. 70 'note' (comment) by J.H. Robert; comment by Dintilhac (Jean-Pierre), *Revue de science criminelle et de droit pénal comparé*, N° 2, avril-juin 1998, pp. 348-350

66. Reprinted at p. 616.
67. Reprinted at p. 615.
68. Reprinted at p. 598.

Concerning a complaint brought by several persons against Father Wenceslas Munyeshayaka concerning crimes allegedly committed by the defendant in Rwanda in April and May 1994. In which case the Cour de Cassation, crim., found that the French jurisdiction is competent to examine an offence committed in a foreign country, by a foreigner, if it covers fact which, under a different qualification, would come under its competence [the case was referred to the Chambre d'Accusation of the Cour d'Appel of Paris].

☛ *Maurice Papon*. Sentence of 2 April 1998. Cour d'Assises de la Gironede, sitting at Bordeaux (unpublished)

Implementation

☛ 'Pursuant to the Prime Minister's decree of 11 September 1996, the National Advisory Committee on Human Rights (CNCDH) was officially recognized as competent, within its terms of reference, to address all questions relating to humanitarian emergencies, and to promote and ensure the implementation of IHL. To help the Committee perform its new tasks as effectively as possible, a Humanitarian Law and Action Sub-committee was established on 10 December 1996, and the CNCDH was expanded to include experts on IHL and humanitarian activities.'[69]

Signings, Ratifications, Accessions, Successions, Denounciations, Reservations, etc.

☛ France signed the CWC on 13 January 1993 and ratified it on 2 March 1995

☛ France signed the Safety Convention on 12 January 1995

☛ France signed the Landmines Treaty on 3 December 1997 and ratified it on 27 July 1998

☛ On 30 June 1998, France ratified Protocol IV to the CCW Convention, and on 23 July 1998 it ratified its amended Protocol II

Pending Ratifications

☛ During a visit to the ICRC on 17 March 1998, French Prime Minister, Lionel Jospin, declared France's intention to ratify Additional Protocol I of 1977. France's accession to Protocol I would leave the USA and Turkey as the only NATO states not to be party to this Protocol. France ratified Additional Protocol II of 1977 in 1984.

69. *Supra* n. 3 at p. 53.

GABON

Signings, Ratifications, Accessions, Successions, Denunciations, Reservations, etc.

- Gabon signed the CWC on 13 January 1993
- Gabon ratified the CRC on 9 February 1994
- Gabon signed the Landmines Treaty on 3 December 1997

GAMBIA

Signings, Ratifications, Accessions, Successions, Denunciations, Reservations, etc.

- Gambia signed the CWC on 13 January 1993 and ratified it on 19 May 1998
- Gambia signed the Landmines Treaty on 4 December 1997

GEORGIA

The Emblem

- Law for the Protection and Use of the Red Cross/Red Crescent Emblem, entered into force, 24 October 1997[70]

Signings, Ratifications, Accessions, Successions, Denunciations, Reservations, etc.

- Georgia signed the CWC on 14 January 1993 and ratified it on 27 November 1995
- Georgia ratified the CRC on 2 June 1994
- Georgia ratified the Convention on the Non-Applicability of Statutory Limitations on 31 March 1995
- On 8 June 1995, Georgia acceded to the Mercenaries Convention without making any declarations or reservations
- On 29 April 1996, Georgia acceded to the CCW Convention (Protocols I, II and III)
- On 22 May 1996, Georgia ratified the Biological Weapons Convention

GERMANY[71]

Signings, Ratifications, Accessions, Successions, Denunciations, Reservations, etc.

- Germany signed the CWC on 13 January 1993 and ratified it on 12 August 1994
- Germany signed the Safety Convention on 1 February 1995 and ratified it on 22 April 1997
- On 27 June 1997, Germany ratified Protocol IV of the CCW Convention, and on 2 May 1997, it ratified its amended Protocol II. Germany became a party to the Convention on 25 November 1992
- Germany signed the Landmines Treaty on 3 December 1997 and ratified it on 23 July 1998

70. See Dutli, *supra* at p. 259 .
71. German state practice is discussed by Fisher at p. 380.

GHANA

Signings, Ratifications, Accessions, Successions, Denounciations, Reservations, etc.

- Ghana signed the CWC on 14 January 1993 and ratified it on 9 July 1997
- Ghana signed the Landmines Treaty on 4 December 1997

GREECE[72]

Military Criminal Code

- Military Criminal Code, Law 2287/1995 (*Government Gazette* A 20/1-2-1995), in force since 1 August 1995[73] [in particular, Chapter 8 dealing with crimes committed by and against prisoners of war and non-combatants]

COMMENT BY MARIA GAVOUNELI

'In the Greek legal order, the treatment of prisoners of war is traditionally regulated in the Military Criminal Code (MCC), the provisions of which reflect the developments of international law in this respect. Thus, the current Code, promulgated by Law 2287/1995, devotes Chapter 8 to crimes committed by and against prisoners of war and non-combatants, in application of the obligations undertaken by the Greek State when it signed and ratified the Third Geneva Convention of 1949 (GC III) relative to the treatment of prisoners of war[74] and the 1977 Protocol I Additional to the Geneva Conventions of 12 August 1949 and relating to the protection of victims of international armed conflicts.[75] The prohibition of physical or psychological violence against prisoners of war stipulated in Articles 156-157 and 160-161 MCC clearly implements the obligation undertaken by the detaining power in Article 3(1)(a)(c) common to all four Geneva Conventions to refrain from any act of violence to the life and person of prisoners of war, in particular, murder, cruel treatment and torture, as well as from outrages upon their personal dignity, in particular humiliating and degrading treatment. As a specific manifestation of the latter must also be considered any theft from a prisoner of war, although the right to booty was traditionally an important component of the law of war. Article 18 GC III contains detailed provisions on the use, rather than the actual ownership, of personal items, taking due account of the security interests of the detaining power. Thus, according to Article 18(3) GC III, items of personal and sentimental value are not to be confiscated unless they are essential to an attempted escape and replaceable by other objects provided by the detaining authorities (e.g., wedding

72. Information provided by Dr. Maria Gavouneli, Hellenic Institute of International and Foreign Law, Greece.

73. Chapter Eight of the Military Criminal Code, Law 2287/1995, is reprinted at p. 535.

74. By Law 348/1956.

75. By Law 1786/1988.

rings cannot be confiscated).[76] No such distinctions are made in Article 160 MCC; instead emphasis is put on the special duty of care the detaining authorities have towards their prisoners. Theft committed by military personnel under such circumstances is treated as an instance of aggravated theft and is punishable by a graver penalty than that applicable to common theft.[77] The prohibition of interference with the religious observances of a prisoner of war set out in Article 158 MCC corresponds to the 'complete latitude' required by Article 34 GC III, including the condition that such observances comply with the disciplinary routine prescribed by the military authorities. Article 159 MCC comprises several obligations of the detaining power in a single phrase: prohibition of coercion in order to obtain information under Article 17 GC III; prohibition of forced labour of a military character under Article 50 GC III; or in breach of 'the international conventions' in general. Both the right of the detaining power to question the prisoner and the obligation placed upon the latter by his own national legislation to refrain from providing any information relevant to the war effort are essential components of all war situations and constitute the core of the protection afforded to prisoners of war. On the one hand, in perhaps the best known of all GC provisions, a prisoner of war is entitled, when questioned, only to give his name, rank, date of birth, regiment and serial number, thus permitting the detaining power to identify him and pass on information about him to the Official Information Bureau in accordance with Article 122 GC III. On the other hand, the prisoner is subject to punishment by his army (and probably his colleagues in captivity) if any other information is disclosed: e.g., under Article 144 of the Greek Criminal Code (GrCC), anyone who, with respect to war or imminent war against the Greek State, acts unlawfully and knowingly in a manner which may support the enemy forces of war or cause harm to the Greek or allied forces of war is punishable by death or life imprisonment. The first section of Article 159 MCC purports therefore to delineate the means available to the detaining power for the questioning of prisoners of war; such questioning being at all times allowed in principle.[78] The second prohibition indicated in Article 159 MCC relates to the entitlement[79] of the detaining power to make use

76. H. Fischer, 'Protection of prisoners of war' in Dieter Fleck, ed., *The Handbook of Humanitarian Law in Armed Conflicts* (Oxford 1995) pp. 321-367 at pp. 337-338.

77. According to Art. 372 of the Greek Criminal Code (GrCC), the offence of theft is punishable by incarceration for a period of at least three months.

78. Fischer, op. cit. n. 74, pp. 345-347.

79. It has been argued that, in view of the general obligation of the detaining power to maintain the prisoners of war in a good state of physical and mental health in conjunction with the prohibition of employing them on labour of an unhealthy or hazardous nature (Art. 52 GC III), one may deduce a right of prisoners to work. Nevertheless, the language used in Art. 49 GC III, 'The detaining power *may* utilise the labour of prisoners of war', testifies to the contrary.

of the labour of prisoners of war for non-military purposes. Such non-military tasks are restrictively enumerated in Article 50 GC III, to which Article 159 MCC clearly refers. Of particular importance is the general reference in the same article to any action in breach of 'the international conventions', without any further specification of such documents. It is, however, clearly understood that the legislator had in mind not only the 1949 Geneva Conventions and the 1977 Protocols Additional thereto but also the whole corpus of IHL as occasionally expanded and amended. General rules of international law thus directly become the applicable domestic rule, the breach of which entails criminal sanctions for the perpetrator. Important as it may be, this express reference to international regulations in the Code itself is indeed superfluous as, pursuant to Article 28 of the Greek Constitution, international treaties duly ratified by the Greek Parliament form part of the law of the land superseding any contrary statutory provision.[80] A second category of prohibitions in Articles 162-166 MCC refers to penal and disciplinary sanctions imposed on prisoners of war in case of breach of the laws, regulations and orders in force in the armed forces of the detaining power. Article 82 GC III accepts in principle the jurisdiction of the detaining power to take such measures, provided that they are punishable under the same terms and conditions as they would have been if committed by a member of the detaining forces; it is further stated, however, that they shall be applied with the greatest leniency, with preference shown for disciplinary rather than judicial measures (Article 83 GC III).

The offences of disobedience, riot and mass insubordination by prisoners of war punishable under Articles 162-166 MCC relate to the common offences of disobedience (Article 169 GrCC), riot (Article 170 GrCC) and riot of prisoners (Article 174 (GrCC), punishable by imprisonment ranging between at least six months and a maximum of two years. In the latter case, the penalty imposed will be served once the period of imprisonment to which the prisoners involved were initially convicted has been served. It is also worth mentioning that although Greece has finally decided to abolish the death penalty, and thus was able to sign and ratify by Law 2462/1997 the Second Optional Protocol to the 1966 International Covenant on Civil and Political Rights on the Abolition of the Death Penalty, she nevertheless reserved[81] her right to impose this ultimate sanction in case of war and only

80. For a brief overview of the status of international law in the Greek legal order, see M. Gavouneli, 'The jurisprudence of Greek Courts on public international law', *Revue hellénique de droit international* 48 (1995) pp. 351-391 at pp. 351-355.

81. The reservation to Art. 2(1) of the Second Optional Protocol is contained in Art. 2 of Law 2462/1997. The 1966 International Covenant on Civil and Political Rights, the Optional Protocol thereto and the Second Optional Protocol thereto on the Abolition of the Death Penalty came into force in Greece on 5 August 1997; Ministry of Foreign Affairs communiqué Ö.0546/63/ÁÓ292/M.2870 dated 7/16.5.1997.

following a conviction for an extremely grave offence of a military nature: the general understanding is that the case applies more to instances of high treason than offences committed by prisoners of war. As a general rule, a prisoner of war is tried by a military court; Article 84 GC IV, however, is very precise and clear in the absolute prohibition it establishes: 'In no circumstances whatsoever shall a prisoner of war be tried by a court of any kind which does not offer the essential guarantees of independence and impartiality as generally recognised.' According to Article 167 MCC, criminal justice in the army is dispensed by military courts assembled by military judges enjoying guarantees of personal and institutional independence who issue fully and specifically reasoned decisions. Elementary as they seem to be, these standard guarantees constitute an innovation when compared with the previously applicable Military Code. Indeed, in spite of the express provisions set out in Article 96(5) of the Constitution[82] safeguarding the independence of the judiciary and demanding that court decisions should be fully and specifically reasoned, military judges were considered to be first and foremost officers bound by their disciplinary duties to decide on grounds of national security. Consequently, any lack of reasoning in their decisions did not constitute grounds for cassation, as clearly was the case with the civilian courts. Indeed, in a long series of decisions[83] Areios Pagos, the (civilian and military) Supreme Court, held that such lack of a full and specific reasoning was not contrary to either Article 96(5) of the Constitution or Article 6 of the European Convention on Human Rights (ECHR).[84] It is true that the obligation for a fair and public hearing by an independent and impartial tribunal established by law, set out in Article 6 of the European Convention on Human Rights, also does not require a court to give full reasons for its decision. However, the European Commission on Human Rights has consistently

82. The same article further stated that for the implementation of the relevant guarantees of judicial independence to military courts, an Act of Parliament was necessary: the new Military Criminal Code came into force a few months after the 20th anniversary of the Constitution.

83. For example, *Full Bench of Areios Pagos 169/1984, NoB* 32 (1984) 539-541; *Full Bench of Areios Pagos 464/1992, NoB* 40 (1992) 915; *Areios Pagos 882/1995, NoB* 44 (1996) 261-262.

84. Greece ratified the European Convention first by Law 2329/1953 and again, in a symbolic fashion after the brief interlude of the *affaire grecque*, by Legislative Decree 53/1974; Ph. Vegleris & A. Kiss, 'L'affaire grecque devant le Conseil de l'Europe et la Commission européenne des droits de l'homme', *AFDI* (1971) pp. 890-931. For the current status of the Convention in the Greek legal order see Krateros M. Ioannou, 'The application of the European Convention on Human Rights in the Greek legal order', *Revue hellénique de droit européen* (1996) p. 223 et seq. at 236-237; Gavouneli, op cit. n. 78, at pp. 375-376.

held that, should a court have ignored a fundamental defence clearly put before it and which, if successful, could have discharged the applicant wholly or partially from liability, the presumption of a fair hearing would be rebutted and a breach of Article 6 of the ECHR could be ascertained.[85] It was generally accepted that the Military Criminal Code, as it stands today, fully conforms with the requirements of the Constitution and the international obligations undertaken by Greece.[86] In a surprise reversal, however, the Special Court on Miscarriages of Justice held recently in DAK 31/1997 that the guarantees of personal and institutional independence accorded to military judges by the Constitution and the new Military Criminal Code cannot elevate them to the status of a true civilian judge and thus they are not to be held liable for a miscarriage of justice according to Article 99 of the Constitution. The question therefore as to the real status of military judges in domestic law remains open. However, the guarantees of personal and institutional independence and impartiality which they are endowed with by the Constitution clearly meet the minimum standards required by the III Geneva Convention.'

Signings, Ratifications, Accessions, Successions, Denounciations, Reservations, etc.[87]

- ☛ Greece signed the CWC on 13 January 1993 and ratified it on 22 December 1994 (by virtue of Law 2254/1994 of 18 November 1994)
- ☛ On 5 August 1997, Greece ratified Protocol IV of the CCW Convention. Greece became a party to the CCW Convention on 28 January 1992
- ☛ On 3 December 1997, Greece signed the Landmines Treaty
- ☛ On 4 February 1998, Greece made a declaration accepting the competence of the International Fact-Finding Commission, in accordance with Article 90(2)(a) of Additional Protocol I of 1977

85. *Firestone Tyre & Rubber Co. Ltd. and International Synthetic Rubber Co. Ltd.* v. *United Kingdom*, case 5460/1972, *Collection of Decisions* 43, 99; see also Paul Sieghart, *The International Law of Human Rights* (Oxford 1983) pp. 284-285.

86. Note, however, the critique on the broad language used in Art. 74 MCrC which was, nevertheless, found by the European Court of Human Rights to meet the standard of foreseeability required by the 'prescribed by law' formula in Art. 10 ECHR; *Grigoriades v. Greece*, Judgment of 25 November 1997, paras. 34-38.

87. Greece has ratified and thus incorporated into domestic law, with force superior to that of a common Statute (according to Art. 28 of the Constitution), most of the treaties pertaining to either Hague or Geneva Law. Some of the older Conventions have remained without ratification but, to the extent that they have acquired customary law status, they have also become part of the law of the land applicable by the courts and administrative authorities alike.

GRENADA

Signings, Ratifications, Accessions, Successions, Denounciations, Reservations, etc.

- ☛ Grenada signed the CWC on 9 April 1997
- ☛ Grenada signed the Landmines Treaty on 3 December 1997

GUATEMALA

Peace Agreement

- ☛ Guatemala-Unidad Revolucionaria Nacional Guatemalteca: Agreement on a Firm and Lasting Peace, (29 December 1996) and the 10 Integral Agreements Covering Human Rights Resettlement, Human Rights Violations, Indigenous Peoples, Social and Economic Issues, Civilian Power and the Armed Forces, Definitive Ceasefire, Constitutional and Electoral Reforms, the Legal Integration of URNG, and Implementation, Compliance and Verification, published in 36 *ILM* 258 (1997)

Signings, Ratifications, Accessions, Successions, Denounciations, Reservations, etc.

- ☛ Guatemala signed the CWC on 14 January 1993
- ☛ Guatemala signed the Landmines Treaty on 3 December 1997

GUINEA

Signings, Ratifications, Accessions, Successions, Denounciations, Reservations, etc.

- ☛ Guinea signed the CWC on 14 January 1993 and ratified it on 9 June 1997
- ☛ Guinea signed the Landmines Treaty on 4 December 1997

GUINEA-BISSAU

Signings, Ratifications, Accessions, Successions, Denounciations, Reservations, etc.

- ☛ Guinea-Bissau signed the CWC on 14 January 1993
- ☛ Guinea-Bissau signed the Landmines Treaty on 3 December 1997

GUYANA

Signings, Ratifications, Accessions, Successions, Denounciations, Reservations, etc.

- ☛ Guyana signed the CWC on 6 October 1993 and ratified it on 12 September 1997
- ☛ Guyana signed the Landmines Treaty on 4 December 1997

HAITI

Signings, Ratifications, Accessions, Successions, Denounciations, Reservations, etc.

- ☛ Haiti signed the CWC on 14 January 1993
- ☛ Haiti signed the Safety Convention on 19 December 1994
- ☛ Haiti ratified the CRC on 8 August 1995
- ☛ Haiti signed the Landmines Treaty on 3 December 1997

(THE) HOLY SEE

Signings, Ratifications, Accessions, Successions, Denounciations, Reservations, etc.

- The Holy See signed the CWC on 14 January 1993
- On 22 July 1997, the Holy See ratified Protocols I, II, III and IV of the CCW Convention
- The Holy See signed the Landmines Treaty on 4 December 1997 and ratified it on 17 February 1998

HONDURAS

Signings, Ratifications, Accessions, Successions, Denounciations, Reservations, etc

- Honduras signed the CWC on 13 January 1993
- On 16 February 1995, Honduras ratified Additional Protocols I and II of 1977
- Honduras signed the Safety Convention on 17 May 1995
- Honduras signed the Landmines Treaty on 3 December 1997

HUNGARY[88]

International Criminal Tribunal

- Act xxxix of 1996 on the fulfillment of obligations deriving from the Statute of the International Criminal Tribunal established for punishing the serious violations of international humanitarian law committed in the territory of the former Yugoslavia, May 1996

Cases

- Decision of the Constitutional Court on the direct applicability of the Geneva Conventions [Alkotmánybíróság 36/1996 (IX.4.) *AB határozata* (Magyar Közlöny:-1996/75 pp. 4673-4675) Decision N° 36/1996 (IX.4) AB of the Constitutional Court (*Official Journal*: 1996/75 pp. 4673-4675)]

COMMENT BY PÉTER KOVÁCS

'The Decision of the Hungarian Constitutional Court concerning the direct applicability of the Geneva Conventions is the last in the series of jurisprudential decisions linked to the so-called "historical justice policy"[89]. Attempts to prosecute those implicated in criminality during the totalitarian regimes were complicated, however,

88. Information provided by Péter Kovács, Professor of International Law, Péter Pázmány Catholic University of Budapest and Miskolc University. Unofficial translations by Prof. Kovacs.

89. By this I understand, a) the laws giving partly symbolic, partly monetary satisfaction to the victims of the totalitarian regimes in Hungary, and b) the legal and political efforts to judge the collaborators of those regimes (especially the Hungarian collaborators with the Soviet invasion of 1956) even if their crimes (like murder) had been covered by the rule of prescription

by the fact that murder, as such, was covered by the rule of prescription stipulated in the criminal code (Act IV of 1978).[90]

The first attempt to provide a legal basis for prosecuting persons for violations was the so-called Lex Zétényi-Takàcs[91], stipulating that, in the case of high treason, murder with premeditation and death caused by corporal violations committed between December 1944 and May 1990, the delay of prescription, as stipulated in the criminal code for the different crimes, restarts if the governments deliberately and manifestly because of political motives did not pursue the offenders.

Acting on a motion of the President of the Republic[92], the Constitutional Court declared the Lex Zétényi-Takàcs unconstitutional in all respects and declared that a "rule of law" state cannot use unconstitutional means in the administration of justice: in the eyes of the Constitutional Court, prescription has an objective nature and no reason can be admitted for the reopening of the delay.[93]

The second attempt of the 1990-1994 Parliament to prosecute offenders was the adoption of a Bill entitled "the procedure to follow in case of certain crimes committed during the freedom fight and revolution of 1956".[94] In this Bill, the legislator wanted to base the state's competence of penal prosecution on Geneva law (and especially on Article 3(1) of the Third Geneva Convention on Prisoners of War as well as on Articles 3(1) and 147 of the Fourth Geneva Convention on the protection of the civilian population) because war crimes and crimes against humanity are imprescriptible.

The Constitutional Court, again on the request of the President of the Republic, in a decision in 1993 declared one article absolutely unconstitutional[95] and developed a series of arguments about how the legislator should take care to ensure harmony between the contracted commitments and the national law.[96] It emphasized that the

90. '833:1) The punishability is prevented by the prescription: a) after 20 years if the crime can be punished also by capital punishment; b) in other cases, by the respective maximum time of the confinement but at least 3 years.
2) There is no prescription if the crime is a war crime under Act VII of 1945 or a crime against humanity.'

91. The Bill is named for the MPs who submitted it. The Bill was adopted by the Parliament on 4 November 1991 under the title, 'About the punishability of serious crimes committed between the 21st December 1944 and the 2nd of May 1990, if they were not prosecuted because of political reasons.'

92. Filed on 16 November 1991.

93. Decision N° 11/1992 (III.5) *AB*.

94. Adopted on 16 February 1993.

95. Art. 1 referring to Act VII of 1945 on the procedure of the people's court (for war crimes of World War II).

96. Alkotmánybiróság 53/1993(X.13) *AB határozata* (Magyar Közlöny: 1993/147 pp. 8793-8801) Decision N° 53/1993 (X.13.) *AB* (*Official Journal*): 1993/147 pp. 8793-8801.

Constitution and the national law should be interpreted in such a way that general or particular international commitments would be executed effectively.[97] It did not pronounce explicitly on the unconstitutionality of other articles.

It emphasized, however, that "war crimes and crimes against humanity are undoubtedly part of international custom: they are recognized as general principles by the community of nations, that's why they should be seen as 'generally accepted rules of international law'. These rules are adopted by the Hungarian law according to Article 7(1) [of the Hungarian Constitution], that's why they belong to the 'assumed international legal obligations' whose harmony with the domestic law is also ordered by the above-mentioned constitutional paragraph. The international obligation to punish war crimes and crimes against humanity concerns the whole international legal material of the *jus cogens*."[98]

It is worth emphasizing that it was not entirely clear whether the Constitutional Court referred to *jus cogens* as international lawyers do (i.e., as a norm of international law that is peremptory over simple international legal norms) or as constitutional or civil lawyers do (i.e., as international legal commitments versus national legislative freedom).

The Court added that:

> ... these 'generally accepted rules' are without any further transformation part of the Hungarian law. The transformation was done by the Constitution itself. (...) This does not exclude that certain 'generally accepted rules' would be defined by special conventions subject to special transformation ...[99]

On the basis of this decision and taking account of the unconstitutionality of the first article, the Parliament made certain stylistic changes to the law, omitting the unconstitutional first article and renumerating the other articles of the law which then entered into force as Act XC of 1993. However, this Act, in its first article, made a reference not only to common Article 3 but also to Article 147 of the first Geneva Convention. As a result, problems arose during criminal proceedings initiated by the prosecutors: the judiciary had to consider whether 1956 was an international armed conflict or an internationalized civil war. In the procedures concerning the mass shootings in the towns of Salgótarjàn and Mosonmagyaróvàr, the two competent courts decided differently: the first in favour of the international conflict option, the second for the civil war option, so, in 1996, the President of

97. Ibid., at p. 8795 (Part III: § a and b).
98. See decision N° 53/1993 - *Official Journal* 1993/147 p. 8798 (Part V, § 1).
99. See decision N° 53/1993 - *Official Journal* 1993/147 p. 8795 (Part III: § a).

the Supreme Court, together with the Chief Attorney General, submitted a motion to the Constitutional Court to deal once again with the Act.

An interesting issue was raised at that time in the scientific literature: in 1954, when Hungary followed the classical dualistic approach, the Geneva Conventions were promulgated in the *Hungarian Official Journal* in a very strange way. The promulgatory phrase was pronounced in the bylaw with the following: "the text will be in due time subject to publication". In fact, the text of the Convention was distributed within the Army and different explanatory leaflets were also circulated but the internal applicability of an imperfect ratification was considered doubtful - also by the defence counsels in the above cases.

It is necessary to take note of the status of international law within domestic law. The comprehensive constitutional reform of 1989 also concerned the relationship of national and international law, and since then Article 7(1) of the Hungarian Constitution states: 'The legal system of the Republic of Hungary shall adopt the generally accepted rules of international law and shall ensure harmony between the assumed international law obligations and domestic law.' This wording, showing certain similarities with the German *Grundgesetz*, was formerly interpreted by the Constitutional Court in 1993[100] in a style very close to that which is considered in the German legal literature as Adoption or General Transformation.

On 4 November 1996, however, the Constitutional Court arrived at the following conclusions:

– the Act XC of 1993 is void in its totality because it has established such cross-references as do not exist in the Geneva Conventions,[101] but

– 'with the nullification of the law there is no obstacle preventing the state from pursuing the offender of war crimes and crimes against humanity as defined by international law. (...) It is the international law itself which defines the crimes to be persecuted and to be punished as well as all the conditions of their punishableness.'[102]

100. Ibid.

101. The Constitutional Court pointed out that the grave violations referred to in Art. 147 of the IV Geneva Convention concern only Art. 2 but not common Art. 3. See decision N° 36/1996 *Official Journal*: 1996/75 p. 4674 (Part II: §1).

102. See decision N° 36/1996 *Official Journal:* 1996/75 pp. 4674-4675 (Part. II: §2). A trial of two persons accused of the shootings of Tiszakécske on 27 October 1956 opened in the Military Chamber of the District Court of Csongrád on 9 June 1998. The facts of the case are alleged as followed: 'After having received a false piece of news about an alleged pogrom against local politicians, the commandant of the 3rd Division gave an order to the commandant of the air brigade at Keeskemét to fly over Tiszakécske in order to shoot on the masses (...) 12 people were reported to have died and 102 were injured. The first indictee, the vice-colonel Török, tried to convince his superior of the unlawfulness of the order but he was threatened to be put before a war court so he

This means that the Constitutional Court interpreted the Hungarian legal system in rather a monist way by the stipulation of the direct applicability or self-executing nature of the Geneva Conventions. It is certainly true that it could refer back to its previous argumentation based on the relationship of customary law and *jus cogens*.'

Signings, Ratifications, Accessions, Successions, Denounciations, Reservations, etc.

☛ Hungary signed the CWC on 13 January 1993 and ratified it on 31 October 1996

☛ Hungary signed the Landmines Treaty on 3 December 1997 and ratified it on 6 April 1998

☛ On 30 January 1998, Hungary ratified Protocol IV and amended Protocol II of the CCW Convention

ICELAND

International Criminal Tribunal

☛ A Bill on Legal Aid to the International Tribunal for Trial of War Crimes in Former Yugoslavia, submitted to the Althing (Parliament) at its 117th legislative session, 1994, adopted without any changes by the Althing on 28 April 1994 as Law N° 49, 1994. Published in the *Official Gazette* on 9 May 1994

transmitted the order to commandant Korbély (second indictee) who ordered the pilot to [carry out] the executions. The accusation is based on [a] crime against humanity running counter [to] the Geneva Conventions. The pronouncement of the verdict is scheduled for mid-July.' See *Magyar Nemzet* of 9 June 1998.

This accusation may seem strange, given that the Geneva Conventions are not concerned with crimes against humanity. The reason for any confusion resides in the bad structure of the Hungarian Criminal Code (Act IV of 1978). Its Chapter XI is entitled: Crimes against humanity. Its first title: Crimes against peace § 153 War Propaganda, § 154: Crime against freedom of peoples, § 155: genocide, § 156: crime against national, racial or religious groups, § 157: racial discrimination. Second title: War crimes § 158: duress against civilian population, § 159: Pillage of the civilian population, § 160: Criminal warfare § 161: pillage on the battlefield, § 162: violation of armistice § 163: duress against truce-bearer, § 164: perfidy (abuse of Red Cross, Red Crescent etc., symbols) § 165: other war crimes (with a very complicated formulation it concerns the war crimes committed during WWII).

From the point of view of the relationship of humanitarian law and crimes against humanity, this structure is very problematic, even erroneous, but this is the positive law. The two indictees in the Tiszakécske case are charged under § 160: criminal warfare, which provides: 'Any commandant, who – in violation of the international legal rules of warfare: a) performs any military activity, causing serious harm to health or patrimony of the civilian population, to internationally protected cultural objects or to buildings containing dangerous substances, or b) launches an attack against non-defended or weaponless zones, commits a crime, subject to imprisonment for 10-15 years or for perpetuity.' (Unofficial translation by Dr. Kovács.)

Signings, Ratifications, Accessions, Successions, Denounciations, Reservations, etc.

- ☛ Iceland signed the CWC on 13 January 1993 and ratified it on 28 April 1997
- ☛ Iceland signed the Landmines Treaty on 4 December 1997

INDIA

Signings, Ratifications, Accessions, Successions, Denounciations, Reservations, etc.

- ☛ India signed the CWC on 14 January 1993 and ratified it on 3 September 1996

INDONESIA[103]

Armed Forces

- ☛ Extract Law N° 26 of 1997 regarding the Law of Discipline for Members of the Indonesian Armed Forces (promulgated on 3 October 1997) [This law is not publicly available as the subject is classified]

COMMENT BY FADILLAH AGUS

'This law replaces the Law on Discipline for members of Indonesian Armed Forces which was regulated by the *Wetboek van Krijgstucht voor Nederlands Indie*[104], as changed by the Law N° 40 of 1947, which were no longer appropriate considering the development of the state's infrastructure and the growth of the Indonesian Armed Forces. The Military Discipline Code Book, as regulated by Law number 40 of 1947, with the promulgation of this new law is no longer in force.

The substance of Law N° 26 of 1997 consists of six chapters and 40 articles and governs the procedures and the forms of sanctions for violation of the disciplinary regulations for the Indonesia Armed Forces. The said disciplinary regulations consist of the laws and norms as decreed by the Commander-in-Chief of the Indonesian Armed Forces. Members of Indonesia's Armed Forces who violate the disciplinary regulations can be punished by his/her competent superior.[105] The forms of punishment are: (a) a warning; (b) light detention for a maxium of 14 days; and (c) grave detention for a maximum of 21 days. In particular circumstances, the form of punishment provided for in Article 8(b) and (c) could be extended by a maximum of seven days.[106] The particular circumstances are (a) a state of emergency; (b) during a military operation; in a unit that is in a stage of preparedness; and (d) if the soldier had been punished more than twice during a

103. Information provided by Mr. Fadillah Agus, Secretary, The Centre Study on International Humanitarian Law, Faculty of Law at Trisakti University, Jakarta.

104. *Staatsblad* 1934 no. 168.

105. Under Art. 7.

106. Under Art. 5.

six-month period. Those who violate the disciplinary regulation, according to this Law, can also receive physical punishment.[107]

In addition to governing the procedures for the settlement of the discipline's violation, this law also governs the right of the superior to punish his/her subordinate for violating the discipline. It also governs the rules for the investigation; administrative matters; and the execution of the disciplinary sanction. This law consists, also, of some rules related to appeal of punishment, such as procedural matters and the implications of the acceptance or of the refusal of the said appeal.

While the law does not touch on the question of superior orders, some articles deal with superiors with the legal authority to impose a disciplinary sanction (namely, the authorized superior). In this regard, Chapter III Articles 10 to 12 governs superiors with the legal authority to punish soldiers, *inter alia*, to order investigations into the conduct of soldiers under their command; to punish a breach of discipline and to postpone the execution of the disciplinary sanction.'

Military Court

☛ Extract Law N° 31 of 1997 regarding the Military Court (promulgated on 15 October 1997) [Not publicly available; classified]

COMMENT BY FADILLAH AGUS

'This Law, consisting of eight chapters and 353 articles, primarily governs the organization and the procedural rules of the Indonesia military court. As mentioned in the Law concerning the Authority of Justice[108] and the Law regarding the State Defense and Security[109], the military has its own judicial institutions. The main reason for promulgating this Law was that the regulations regarding the military court and military attorney, governed by some old laws[110], are no longer relevant to the development of national law.

Under this Law, Indonesia's military court system consists of four courts: Military Court, High Military Court, Primary Military Court and Military Court in War Territory (Art. 12). The organization and the procedural rules of the military courts are governed by the Government Regulation (Art. 13). Several articles of this Law regulate the authority of each military court. For example, a military court

107. Under Art. 7(2).
108. Law N° 14 of 1970.
109. Law N° 20 of 1982.
110. Such as Law N° 5 of 1950; Law N° 5 pnps of 1965, and Law N° 3 pnps of 1965.

in war territory is competent to judge any criminal case which occurs within the territory of the war. The judgement of this court is final and binding [there is no possibility of an appeal to a higher court]. The military court has jurisdiction over: a) soldiers; (b) persons who, based on this law, are treated as equal to soliders; (c) members of a group or institution who, based on this law, are treated as equal to soldiers; and (d) persons not included in (a), (b) or (c) but who, by the decision of the Chief Commander of the Indonesian Armed Forces, with the approval of the Minister of Justice, should come within the jurisdiction of the military court.[111]

This Law also governs, through some articles, the structure and competency of Indonesia's military attorney. Regarding to this Law, the structure of Indonesia's military attorney system consists of a Military Attorney, a High Military Attorney, an Attorney General, and a Military Attorney in War Territory.[112] The organization and procedural rules of the military attorneys are governed by the Decree of the Chief Commander of the Indonesian Armed Forces.'[113]

Implementation

COMMENT BY FADILLAH AGUS

Indonesia ratified the Geneva Conventions of 1949 on 10 September 1958, without any reservations or unilateral declarations. Some steps have been taken to implement specific aspects of the Convention. For example, the formation of national societies of the Red Cross (under Art. 26 of Convention I) and the establishment of fixed and mobile medical units (as governed in Art. 19 of Convention I) have been undertaken by Indonesia.[114]

In addition, Law N° 20 of 1982[115] concerning the Principles of State Defense and Security is closely related with the implementation of IHL, in particular, regarding the principle of distinction, with which Indonesia's Total Defence System might conflict. In addition, Law N° 26 of 1997 regarding the law of discipline for the members of armed forces, and Law N° 31 of 1997 concerning the Military Court (see *supra)* are part of national implementation of the Geneva Conventions of 1949.

Some specific regulations closely related to military activities have also been promulgated further to the implementation of the Geneva Conventions by Indonesia.

111. Under Art. 9.

112. Under Art. 49.

113. Under Art. 50.

114. The legal basis for the formation of the Indonesian Red Cross Society is Presidential Decree N° 25 of 1950 and Presidential Decree N° 246 of 1963 concerning the Indonesian Red Cross Society.

115. Promulgated on 19 September 1982.

Particularly relevant are the internal regulations for the members of armed forces. For example, the Ministry of Defence has issued a decree on the operational guidance for the treatment of prisoners of war[116], which implements the relevant clauses of the third Geneva Convention, including relating to subjects who could be classified as prisoners of war, information bureaux and an office for prisoner information; the Protecting Power; the treatment of prisoners of war; rights and duties of a POW; the planning and organization as well as the administrative coordination of the POW camp, and the duties and functions of military police.

Unfortunately, the promulgation of some important and necessary national legislation, as mentioned in the Conventions, such as legislation relating to the punishment of grave breaches (under Article 146 of Geneva IV) and regulations concerning the protection of the Red Cross emblem, has not yet occurred. Regarding the emblem, a draft law has been prepared and is currently before the Ministries of Justice and Defence. It is expected to be promulgated by next year.

On 18 July 1998, the Indonesian Government and Parliament agreed to ratify the CWC. A law for the ratification of the said Convention is expected to appear shortly.

Finally, on 15 August 1998, the Government of Indonesia promulgated Presidential Decree No. 129 of 1998 concerning the Indonesia Plan of Action on Human Rights. This plan has four main aspects: (a) preparation for ratification of international human rights instruments; (b) dissemination of information and education on human rights; implementation of priority on human rights and (d) implementation of the international human rights instruments that have been ratified by Indonesia.

This Plan of Action also includes the intention to ratify and disseminate the IHL instruments. It is stipulated that it is intended to ratify the Additional Protocols to the Geneva Conventions by the end of 1999. Some programs of study and dissemination of information on IHL are also mentioned in the national Plan of Action.'

☛ 'By a decision of the Minister of Justice of 24 July 1996, the Indonesian authorities renewed the mandate of the Permanent Committee on Humanitarian Law, which was established in 1980. The Committee comprises representatives of the principal ministries concerned, the armed forces and the Indonesian Red Cross Society, and its members are assisted by three expert advisers. The Committee's primary function is to promote the dissemination of IHL and encourage research on its implementation.'[117]

116. Manual no. LB-164-STRATOPS of 1979.
117. *Supra* n. 3, at p. 53.

Signings, Ratifications, Accessions, Successions, Denounciations, Reservations, etc.
- Indonesia signed the CWC on 13 January 1993
- Indonesia signed the Landmines Treaty on 4 December 1997

(ISLAMIC REPUBLIC OF) IRAN

Signings, Ratifications, Accessions, Successions, Denounciations, Reservations, etc.
- Iran ratified the CRC on 13 July 1994 with reservations
- Iran signed the CWC on 13 January 1993 and ratified it on 3 November 1997

IRAQ

Amnesty
- Resolution No. (97) of 11 September 1996 (28th Rabia Al-Thani, 1417 H.) concerning a full amnesty for all Iraqi Kurd citizens from any legal procedures for previous acts (Published in the *Alwaqai Aliraqiya Ar.* Edit. No. (3637) of 30 September 1996)

Signings, Ratifications, Accessions, Successions, Denounciations, Reservations, etc.
- Iraq ratified the CRC on 15 June 1996 with reservations

IRELAND[118]

Chemical Weapons
- Chemical Weapons Act 1997 (1997 No. 28). Published in *Irish Current Law Statutes Annotated*, Dublin, Round Hall/Sweet & Maxwell

COMMENT BY RAY MURPHY AND COLM CAMPBELL[119]

'The Chemical Weapons Convention was signed by Ireland on 13 January 1993 and ratified on 13 June 1996. Because of the dualist nature of Ireland's legal system, national implementation measures were required to give effect to its provisions. Thus, on 23 April 1997, the Chemical Weapons Bill was introduced to incorporate the Convention into Irish law. The Act came into effect on 1 July 1997.[120] Section 1(2) states that the Act will come into effect on such day as the Minister for Enterprise and Employment shall by order appoint. This responsibility has been delegated to the Minister for Enterprise and Employment owing to his/her overall responsibility for dangerous substances within the state.

118. Information provided by Mr. Ray Murphy, University College Galway and Professor Colm Campbell, Dean of the Law School, University College Galway, Republic of Ireland.

119. Ibid.

120. Statutory Instrument 269/1997 signed by the Minister for Enterprise and Employment.

Section 2, defining chemical weapons, is the most important definition in the Act, and is based on the definition contained in the Convention.[121] The term covers toxic and precursor chemicals, except where intended for peaceful purposes or purposes relating to protection against toxic chemicals[122], as long as the types and quantities are consistent with such purposes; it also covers any equipment specifically designed for direct uses in the employment of such munitions and devices. The term applies to them separately and together. In this way, the key element in the definition is that of intent to abuse. A weapon is usually considered to be the entirety of its components and defined according to objective criteria. The definition in the Act and the Convention allows for a broad and expansive interpretation of what constitutes a chemical weapon, something not usually found in treaty or statute law. Thus all toxic chemicals and their precursor chemicals are covered by the Act, and the criterion for determining whether such chemicals constitute weapons depends upon their intended purpose. "Precursor" is also defined under the Act, and must be read in conjunction with the definition of chemical weapon. They are chemical reactants which take part at any stage and by whatever method in the production of a toxic chemical. Again, the element of intent or purpose is crucial to the interpretation of this open-ended definition. A precursor is prohibited only if it has been manufactured or stored for chemical weapons purposes. This is important for a country like Ireland with a relatively large chemical industry, as so-called "dual use chemicals", i.e., chemicals which may be used for legitimate and prohibited purposes, come within the terms of the Act. Any toxic or precursor chemical is *prima facie* a chemical weapon, unless developed, produced, stored or used for purposes not prohibited. Furthermore, types and quantities must be consistent with the stated intent and purpose.

The term "toxic chemical" is also defined. This too must be read in conjunction with other definitions to interpret the full implications of the Act. The distinguishing feature of a toxic chemical for the purposes of the Act is its toxicity to humankind and animals, and not plant life. There is no dosage requirement, and the use of the phrase "can cause" as opposed to "cause" is significant here. A chemical comes within this definition if it has the potential to cause death, temporary incapacitation or permanent harm. This definition is of particular relevance to Ireland as stocks of certain riot control agents are retained by the state. Though they may only cause

121. Art. II: Definitions and Criteria, Paragraph 1 of the Convention.

122. Art. X(2) of the Convention states that 'Nothing in this Convention shall be interpreted as impeding the right of any State Party to conduct research into, develop, produce, acquire, transfer or use means of protection against chemical weapons, for purposes not prohibited under this Convention.'

temporary incapacitation, they nonetheless constitute toxic chemicals under the Act and are prohibited unless retained for "peaceful purposes".

As virtually all armed forces, including the Irish Defence Forces, possess weapons with a chemical content, distinguishing these from "chemical weapons" prohibited under the Act is of practical relevance. Technically, a round fired from any weapon has a chemical component; this is so for small arms and for artillery/mortar shells. However, it is only when a weapon is intended to utilise the toxicity of a chemical as the predominant weapons effect that it comes within the definition of "chemical weapon". So-called conventional weapons can be modified to carry toxic chemicals, but the scope to do so is reduced significantly when the Act and the Convention are implemented in their entirety.

The National Authority for Occupational Safety and Health (the HSA) is defined as the National Authority for the purposes of the Convention. The role and mandate of the National Authority is not clear under the Act. The Convention states that the purpose of the Authority is to "serve as the national focal point for effective liaison with the Organisation [for the Prohibition of Chemical Weapons (OPCW)] and other States Parties".[123] The general purpose of the National Authority is to ensure that Ireland can provide evidence to the OPCW or other states parties that it is in full compliance with the obligations under the Convention. An important "function of the Authority will be as a focus for the communication of information-instructions from the organisation to Irish industry and accompanying the international inspectors on their inspections to Irish firms".[124] In order to do this effectively, secondary legislation in the form of regulations by the Minister are required. The HSA was the logical national body in Ireland to carry out this function, having been established under the Health, Safety and Welfare at Work Act 1989. The Environmental Protection Agency might also have been a suitable designated National Authority, in particular as it operates a licensing system for dangerous substances. The HSA was chosen as it has the necessary scientific and technical background to carry out its function as National Authority; it also has a good track record and the benefit of being regionally based.

Chemical Weapons and Chemicals for Permitted Purposes: Section 3 prohibits the production, development, use, retention or transfer of chemical weapons. This is the core provision of the Act reflected in the fact that it is from this section that the title is taken. The wording here is somewhat different than that contained in Article 1(1) of the Convention, but the intention and purpose is the same. The

123. Art. VII: National implementation measures, para. 4 of the Convention.

124. Statement by Minister for State, Ms. E. Fitzgerald, *Dail Debates*, Vol. 478, (23 April 1997) p. 256.

prohibitions contained in Section 3 constitute a comprehensive ban on all activities connected with the acquisition and keeping of chemical weapons. The paramount prohibition is that relating to the actual use of chemical weapons, reflected in the Preamble to the Convention. However, the prohibition on production and development is of more immediate relevance to a small political power like Ireland, which remains committed to military neutrality but whose economic policy is dependent on investment by multinational companies with research and development facilities. The monitoring of research that could be used for legitimate and prohibited purposes will be especially problematic. The use of premises or equipment for the production and development, *inter alia,* of chemical weapons is also prohibited.

Section 3(2) states that, in determining whether a toxic chemical or precursor is a chemical weapon, the type and quantities of each shall be taken into account. This is a common sense provision which may shift the burden of proof to persons in possession or otherwise of types and quantities of toxic chemicals or precursors inconsistent with their stated purpose. The maximum penalty for the contravention of this section is life imprisonment.

Section 4 places restrictions on the use of certain toxic chemicals or precursors listed in the First Schedule to the Act, and it must be read in conjunction with the First Schedule below. It is prohibited to produce, use, acquire or possess listed substances without authorisation under Section 12 of the Act. This facilitates commercial and non-prohibited usage, while at the same time putting in place a regulatory framework to comply with the verification requirements of the Convention. However, this is not a definitive list, as any toxic chemical or precursor coming within the terms of the definition contained in Section 2 is *prima facie* prohibited, except where intended for non-prohibited purposes under the Act.

Sections 5 to 8 are concerned with inspection and enforcement procedures and arise from the general obligation to undertake all the necessary measures to implement the Convention.[125] States Parties are required to adopt appropriate legislation and administrative measures to establish or designate organs to oversee the implementation of the prohibitions, exchanges of information and data, and other "necessary measures" to ensure full compliance with the obligations undertaken under the Convention. In particular, the Convention obliges Ireland to permit inspectors of the OPCW to enter Ireland and carry out independent inspections. The National Authority, in this instance the HSA, is central to the enforcement and inspection provisions envisaged under the Convention. There is already in existence a considerable body of regulations associated with the chemical industry which governs the production, storage and handling of chemical products. The specific

125. Art. VII, National Implementation Measures, the Convention.

information required by the implementation process is one of the most important confidence-building tools and it allows States Parties to demonstrate compliance in the early days after ratification. Though Ireland could not be said to have posed a chemical weapons threat to any other state, it was nonetheless essential to put in place effective and transparent implementation measures to conform to the international standards and norms required by the Convention. Section 5 gives such inspectors the same powers as an inspector of the HSA.

Sections 6 governs the appointment of authorised officers by the National Authority, at present the HSA. In practice, authorised officers will probably be persons authorised to be inspectors under the Safety Heath and Welfare at Work Act 1989.[126] Authorised officers must be in possession of a warrant and produce it if and when requested to do so.

Section 7: In order to ensure compliance with the provisions of the Act, an authorised officer is given extensive powers under this section to enter, inspect, examine, take samples and/or photographs, remove, retain or copy records, install monitoring equipment, etc. Where entry to a place is denied, a warrant may be obtained from a District Court, but this is not necessary under Section 7(9) if by reason of "exigent circumstances", it would not be practical. The extent of the powers granted to ensure compliance are such that it is difficult to envisage how compliance could be improved by any further powers. The only apparent fetter on these powers is the requirement that a warrant be obtained to enter a private dwelling when permission is not forthcoming.

Section 8 gives to a member of the *Garda Síochána* [the police] the same powers of an inspector under the Act in addition to his or her own powers.

Sections 9, 10 and 11 are concerned with the information needed by the National Authority to comply with the Convention. Companies which produce, possess, consume or transfer the chemicals or precursors listed in Schedule 2 and Schedule 3 of the Act must provide information and keep records in accordance with the requirements of the HSA. This is one area where the specific provisions of the Act are too general. There is a need for more detailed regulations to be made pursuant to Section 12 below. Any information obtained pursuant to the Act or the Convention is privileged in accordance with Section 11. Section 9(d) requires, *inter alia*, any person who holds a riot control agent for riot control purposes to provide the necessary information and keep appropriate records. This is binding on relevant Government ministers, e.g., the Minister for Defence, as the person with primary responsibility for all matters relating to the Defence Forces and their equipment.

126. Section 33.

Section 12 provides powers to the Minster to make regulations to give effect to the provisions of the Act and the Convention. No regulations have yet been made, but this is an important provision in the Act, as more detailed secondary legislation is required governing reporting, recording, inventories etc., in order to render some of the more general provisions of the Act effective.

Section 13 outlines the penalties for offences under the Act. These range from a fine not exceeding IR £1,500 or imprisonment for a term not exceeding 12 months on summary conviction to a fine not exceeding IR £100,000 or imprisonment for a term not exceeding two years, or both, on conviction on indictment.

Section 13(3) is one of the potentially more important provisions for personnel working in the chemical industry in Ireland. Where an offence is committed by a body corporate or any person working on behalf of a body corporate, and it is proven to have been committed with the consent, connivance or approval of, or to have been attributable to any neglect on behalf of any person who was an officer of the body corporate at the time, that person shall be guilty of an offence. This means that an offence under this section does not require wilful intent or recklessness; negligence alone will suffice to render a director, manager, secretary or similar officer guilty of an offence under the Act.

Section 14 provides for the forfeiture and destruction of chemical weapons seized by the authorities as required by the Convention. An appeals procedure against forfeiture is provided.

Section 15 states that prosecutions may be brought by the HSA.

First Schedule: This contains a schedule of certain toxic chemicals and precursors. This should be read in conjunction with Sections 2(3)(c) and 4 of the Act. The Convention obliges States Parties to comply with certain prohibitions and restrictions, in particular, with regard to the amount of Schedule 1 chemicals they can annually produce or possess at any given time.[127] The chemicals listed are those that pose the highest risk to the purposes and objectives of the Convention, and they are the same as those listed in the Schedules of Chemicals set out in the Annex on Chemicals in the Convention (Section 2(3)(c) of the Act). Owing to the nature of the chemicals listed, i.e., super-toxic lethal chemicals usable for chemical weapons purposes as well as major key-precursors for chemical weapons, it is assumed that their production will be a rare event in the Irish chemical industry.

Second Schedule[128]: This is also a list of toxic chemicals and precursors which were perceived during the Convention negotiations as potentially posing a particular risk to the objective and purpose of the Convention, given their chemical closeness

127. Part VI, Verification Annex, the Convention.
128. Part VII, Verification Annex, the Convention.

to Schedule 1 chemicals. This Schedule should be read in conjunction with Sections 2(3)(c) and 9(b) above.

This provides for a more onerous regime than for Schedule 1 substances, as the chemicals listed are more likely to be used in the civilian chemical industry.

Third Schedule: This sets out an identical regime to that in existence for Schedule 2 chemicals and precursors. Under the Convention, the regime governing Schedule 3 chemicals is, in fact, less stringent than that for those listed in Schedule 2.[129] The chemicals and precursors listed are dual purpose, produced in large quantities and which could be used for chemical weapons purposes.'

Education and Training of the Defence Forces:
Courses: All basic officer courses in the Military College include lectures by Defence Forces legal officers on IHL. In addition, a day-long seminar/exercise on IHL is conducted for the Command and Staff course. This is the course undertaken by officers who wish to qualify for promotion to senior rank, i.e., Lieutenant Colonel and above. Non-Commissioned Officers (NCOs) and private soldiers are instructed in the ten basic rules regarding the protection of war victims, and it is planned to develop practical exercises in this area for incorporation into recruit and NCO training in the future.
Courses abroad: Since the 1970s, officers of the Permanent Defence Forces have been attending the International Military Law course on the Law of Armed Conflict at the International Institute of Humanitarian Law, San Remo, Italy. A number of line officers and all current officers have completed this course. Since 1990, the Defence Forces have been making officers available as members of the teaching staff at the Institute. Lieutenant Colonel W. Nott is currently a Course Director and Commandant D. Hogan an instructor.
Briefings for UN and Similar Missions: All officers and some NCOs proceeding on what the Defence Forces refer to a 'overseas' missions receive briefings on IHL and Human Rights law at the United Nations Training School in the Curragh Training Camp.
Support for the ICRC: Defence Forces legal officers have been involved with the ICRC in the development of training programmes on IHL for armed forces and the police. At least three former army officers are currently engaged as delegates by the ICRC to armed forces in Africa, Central America and countries of the former Soviet Union. Their function is to assist the armed forces in these countries in the dissemination of IHL.

129. Part VIII sets forth the regime of declarations, State Party obligations and verification pursuant to para. 5 of Art. VI, relating to Schedule 3 chemicals and to facilities which produce such chemicals above a certain threshold.

The above indicates that there is a policy of support for the principles of IHL within the Defence Forces, and this is particularly evident in its formal incorporation into military training and briefings. A genuine effort is made to disseminate information regarding these principles. However, there seems to be little or no recent material on Humanitarian Law published by the Defence Forces or Department of Defence which is accessible and useful to ordinary serving personnel.

Peace Process

- ☛ Stormont Agreement [Agreement reached in the Multi-Party Negotiation], 10 April 1998. Published in 37 *IML* July 1998, p. 751. Full text also available online at http://BRITAIN-INFO.ORG/bis/nireland/nireland.htm

Signings, Ratifications, Accessions, Successions, Denounciations, Reservations, etc.

- ☛ Ireland signed the CWC on 14 January 1993 and ratified it on 24 June 1996
- ☛ On 26 March 1997, Ireland ratified Protocol IV and amended Protocol II to the CCW Convention, following its accession to the CCW Convention on 13 March 1995
- ☛ Ireland signed and ratified the Landmines Treaty on 3 December 1997

Pending (legislation)

- ☛ International War Crimes Tribunals Bill, 1997. Published by the Stationary Office
- ☛ Geneva Conventions (Amendment) Bill, 7 April 1997. Published by the Stationary Office

COMMENT BY RAY MURPHY AND COLM CAMPBELL

'The Bill has been debated in the Dáil (lower house of Parliament) and Seanad (Senate). Although passed by the Dáil, it must still go through some further stages before being signed by the President. It is expected that the Bill will become law before the end of the year.'

ISRAEL[130]

Peace Process

- ☛ (Israel) Summit of Peacemakers. Sharm el-Sheikh, Final Statement. 13 March 1996
- ☛ Text of cease-fire 'understanding' reached on Friday 26 April 1996 between Israel and Lebanon. Available at http://www.israel-mfa.gov.il/ceasefir/html
- ☛ Text of the Protocol on the Work of the Monitoring Group
- ☛ Protocol Concerning the Redeployment in Hebron, 17 January 1997. Available at http://www.israel-mfa.gov.il/peace/hebronpt.html

130. Information provided by Professor Eyal Benvenisti, Faculty of Law, Hebrew University of Jerusalem, Israel and Professor Ruth Lapidoth, Faculty of Law, Hebrew University of Jerusalem, Israel. Official citations for these materials could not be found.

- Note for the Record on the Agreement Between the Sides on Non-Hebron Issues. Main Points

Cases

- *Bilbeisi* Case, 11/1/96, HCJ-VR 336/96 (HCJ 7964/95)
  Concerning request by respondent, the General Security Service, for a lifting of an interim injunction against the use of physical force during administrative detention of a 'self-confessed' suicide bomber. Request granted. Available at http://www. btselem. org/reports/ 1997/jan_2.htm
- *Hamdan* Case, 14/11/96, HCJ 804/96
  Concerning request by respondent, the General Security Service, for a lifting of an interim injunction against the use of physical force during administrative detention of a member of Islamic Jihad. Request granted. Available at http://www.btselem. netgate/met/reports.1997/jan_3.htm)
- *Mubarak* Case, 17/11/96. HCJ 3124/96
  In which case the High Court of Justice (HCJ) rejected an appeal to issue an order *nisi* and an interim injunction against the use of interrogation methods not involving the use of direct violence; the HCJ, however, found that painful shackling is a prohibited act. Available at http://www.btselem.org/reports/1997/jan_4.htm
- AAD (Appeal on Administrative Detention) 10/94, *John Doe* v. *Minister of Defence*
  In which the continued detention of Lebanese citizens abducted from south Lebanon was approved, as their detention may help in obtaining information on Israeli soldiers missing in action. The decision is pending rehearing (13/11/97)

Signings, Ratifications, Accessions, Successions, Denounciations, Reservations, etc.

- Israel signed the CWC on 13 January 1993
- On 22 March 1995, Israel acceded to Protocols I and II of the CCW Convention

ITALY[131]

International Criminal Tribunal

- Provisions on Co-operation with the International Criminal Tribunal for the Prosecution of Serious Violations of International Humanitarian Law Committed in the Territory of the Former Yugoslavia (Decree-Law No. 544 of 28 December 1993)
- Act No. 120 of 14 February 1994 on cooperation with the ICTY. Published in *Gazetta Ufficiale*, no. 43, 22 February 1994

131. Information provided by Professor Sergio Marchisio, Director, Instituto di Studi Giuridici Sulla Comunita' Internazionale, Rome and Professor Paolo Benvenuti, Chair of International Law, Facolta di Scienze Politiche, Universita di Firenza; Presidente della Commissione Nazionale CRI per la Diffusione del diritto umanitario.

- Agreement between the Government of Italy and the United Nations on Enforcement of Sentences of the International Criminal Tribunal for the Former Yugoslavia, 6 February 1997
- Law of 9 September 1997, as presented to the Senate, on the ratification by the Italian Government of the UN Agreement on the Execution of Judgements rendered by the ICTY

Chemical Weapons

- Law for the Implementation of the Convention on Chemical Weapons, n. 496, 18 November 1995 [Legge 18 Novembre 1995, n. 496. Ratifica ed esecuzione della convenzione sulla proibizione dello sviluppo, produzione, immagazzinaggio ed uso di armi chimiche e sulla loro distruzione, con annessi, fatta a Parigi il 13 gennaio 1993]. Published in *Supplemento ordinario alla Gazetta Ufficiale*, series generale, n. 276, 25 November 1995

Landmines

- Law n. 374 of 29 October 1997, banning anti-personnel mines [Leggi, Decreti e Ordinanze Presidenziali, Norme per la messa al bando delle mine antipersona][132] Published in *Supplemento ordinario alla Gazetta Ufficiale*, series generale, n. 256, 3 November 1997

Mercenaries

- Law No. 210 of 12 May 1995 concerning the Ratification and Implementation of the Convention against the Recruitment, Use and Financing of Mercenaries of 4 December 1989 [Ratifica ed esecuzione della convenzione internazionale contro il reclutamento, l'utilizzazione, il finanziamento e l'istruzione di mercenari, adottato dall'Assemblea generale delle Nazioni Unite a New York il 4 dicembre 1989]. Published in *Supplemento ordinario alla Gazetta Ufficiale*, series generale n. 126, 1 June 1995

Concerning the Italian Military Mission to Somalia

- Resolution adopted by the Council of Ministers on 13 June 1997 establishing the Governmental Inquiry Committee on the Italian Military Mission to Somalia (Communiqué no. 74) (unpublished)
- Executive Decree from the Minister of Defence of 16 June 1997 establishing the Governmental Inquiry Committee on the mission (unpublished)
- Report of 8 August 1997 adopted by the Enquiry Commission on the behaviour of Italian Peacekeeping troops in Somalia [Relazione conclusiva sui fatti di Somalia][133]

132. For commentary, see Gargiulo, p. 323.
133. The report is analysed by Lupi at p. 375.

- Final (supplementary) Report of the Governmental Enquiry Commission on the Behaviour of the Italian Peacekeeping troops in Somalia, 26 May 1998

Italian Military Mission to Albania

- Letter of 27 March 1997 to the Permanent Representative of Italy by the UN Secretary General
- Decree No. 108 of 24 April 1997 on the Italian contribution to the international initiatives in favour of Albania [Decreto-Legge 24 aprile 1997, n. 108, Partecipazione italiana alle iniziative internazionali in favore dell'Albania]. Published in *Gazetta Ufficiale*, series generale, n. 95 of 24 April 1997

Italian Involvement in Peacekeeping in the Former Yugoslavia

- Decree No. 319 of 14 June 1996 on urgent interventions in social and humanitarian affairs. Published in *Gazetta Ufficiale*, no. 139, 15 June 1996
- Act No. 428 of 8 August 1996 on Italian participation in the peacekeeping mission in Bosnia. Published in *Gazetta Ufficiale*, no. 193, 19 August 1996
- Act No. 239 of 25 July 1997 authorising Italian participation in an international peace force in Bosnia. Published in *Gazetta Ufficiale*, series generale, no. 174, 28 July 1997

Cases

- In re. *Karl Hass* and *Erich Priebke*. Judgement (sentence) of the Military Tribunal of Rome, 1 August 1996. Date of deposit, 30 September 1996. Sentence N° 305
- In re. *Karl Hass* and *Erich Priebke*. Judgement (sentence) of the Military Tribunal of Rome, 22 July 1997. Date of deposit, 13 September 1997. Sentence N° 322
- In re. *Karl Haas* and *Erich Priebke*, Judgement of the Corte Militare di Appello of 7 March 1998. Date of deposit,15 April 1998. Sentence N° 24[134]

Implementation

- A Ministerial Decree of 16 February 1998 reconfirmed the mandate of the National Interministerial Commission for the Implementation of International Humanitarian Law, which was set up in 1988[135]

Signings, Ratifications, Accessions, Successions, Denounciations, Reservations, etc.

- Italy signed the CWC on 13 January 1993 and ratified it on 8 December 1995
- Italy signed the Safety Convention on 16 December 1994
- On 20 January 1995, Italy acceded to the CCW Convention (Protocols I, II and III)
- On 21 August 1995, Italy ratified the Mercenaries Convention without making any declarations or reservations. Italy signed the Convention on 5 February 1990

134. The Priebke case is considered by Professor Sergio Marchisio and Dr. Francesca Martines at pp. 344 + 354 respectively.

135. Source: Advisory Service on International Humanitarian Law, ICRC.

☛ Italy signed the Landmines Treaty on 3 December 1997

JAMAICA

Signings, Ratifications, Accessions, Successions, Denounciations, Reservations, etc.

☛ Jamaica signed the CWC on 18 April 1997

☛ Jamaica signed the Landmines Treaty on 3 December 1997 and ratified it on 17 July 1998

JAPAN

Depositions (war crimes)

The May 1998 issue of the Japanese magazine *Sekai* published the depositions given by senior Japanese military officials during war crimes trials in China in 1956, which provided detailed admissions of biological warfare, poison gas attacks and sexual slavery during WWII. In one account, Major General Masaru Uesaka described a May 1942 poison gas attack that killed more than 1,000 Chinese soldiers and civilians in China's northern Hebai province, and in another, Lieutenant General Hiraku Suzuki described ordering the abduction of Chinese and Korean women to serve in front-line military brothels and the use of cholera as a biological warfare agent.[136]

Signings, Ratifications, Accessions, Successions, Denounciations, Reservations, etc.

☛ Japan signed the CWC on 13 January 1993 and ratified it on 15 September 1995

☛ Japan ratified the CRC on 22 April 1994 with reservations

☛ Japan signed the Safety Convention on 6 June 1995

☛ On 10 June 1997, Japan ratified Protocol IV and amended Protocol II of the CCW Convention. Japan ratified its Protocols I, II and III on 9 June 1982

☛ Japan signed the Landmines Treaty on 3 December 1997

JORDAN

Signings, Ratifications, Accessions, Successions, Denounciations, Reservations, etc.

☛ Jordan signed the CWC on 29 October 1997

☛ On 19 October 1995, Jordan acceded to Protocols I and III of the CCW Convention

KAZAKHSTAN

Signings, Ratifications, Accessions, Successions, Denounciations, Reservations, etc.

☛ Kazakhstan signed the CWC on 14 January 1993

136. See 'Magazine to Print Japan War Stories', Associated Press (6 April 1998).

- Kazakhstan ratified the CRC on 12 August 1994
- Kazakhstan ratified the Cultural Property Convention on 14 March 1997

KENYA

Signings, Ratifications, Accessions, Successions, Denounciations, Reservations, etc.

- Kenya signed the CWC on 15 January 1993 and ratified it on 25 April 1997
- Kenya signed the Landmines Treaty on 5 December 1997

KIRIBATI

Signings, Ratifications, Accessions, Successions, Denounciations, Reservations, etc.

- Kiribati signed the CRC on 11 December 1995 with reservations

(REPUBLIC OF) KOREA[137]

Operational and Military Law Manuals

- Operational Law Manual, 1996, published 5 September 1996 by the Division of Legal Affairs of the Korean Air Force

COMMENT BY JAE HO SUNG

'*Duty to give quarter*: Chapter 4, section 4.7 stipulates that combatants who are unwilling to fight or express an intention to surrender shall not be attacked. Combatants who are disabled shall not be attacked. These two practices show that the duty to give quarter during armed conflicts is *opinio juris* of the Republic of Korea.

Protection of works and installations containing dangerous forces: Chapter 5, Section 4.2 provides that dams and nuclear power plants cannot be attacked. Attacks on dams and nuclear power plants are prohibited when the attacks will cause severe damage to civilians.

Protection of civilians against starvation: The 1996 Operational Law Manual states in Chapter 5, Section 4.2 that it shall be prohibited to use starvation of the civilian population as a means of warfare. Protection of the civilian population against starvation can be regarded as an established rule of customary international law in the Republic of Korea.

Definition of combatants: Chapter 5 Combat Rules, Section 4.5 of the 1996 Operational Law Manual states that regular army, reserve forces, militia corps and

137. Information provided by Professor Jae Ho Sung, Professor of International Law, Sung Kyun Kwan University, Republic of Korea. The comments are drawn from a longer study of customary international law in the Republic of Korea, prepared by Professor Sung for the ICRC study on customary international humanitarian law.

combatant police can be regarded as combatants, and persons who are not participating in combat but supporting military operations (other than medical personnel, chaplains and sick persons) are considered to be combatants.

Duty to disobey an order to commit a violation of international humanitarian law: Chapter 9, Section 1.2.3 provides that soldiers who follow an illegal order of their commander are not exempt from responsibility.

Weapons of a nature to cause unnecessary suffering or superfluous injury: The 1996 Operational Law Manual states in Chapter 9, Section 1.4.1 and 1.4.2 that weapons of a nature to cause unnecessary suffering are prohibited. The *opinio juris* of the Republic of Korea is that prohibiting these kind of weapons is a part of customary international law.

Protection of the environment: The 1996 Operational Law Manual states in Chapter 9, Section 1.4.4 that it is a principle not to use weapons that injure the natural environment.

Weapons that are by nature indiscriminate: Chapter 9, Section 2.3.2 of the 1996 Operational Law Manual requires that weapons that are by nature indiscriminate shall be prohibited. Prohibiting these kind of weapons is established as a part of customary international law in the Republic of Korea.

Protection from attack of medical and religious personnel and medical objects: The 1996 Operational Law Manual indicates in Chapter 9, Section 2.4.4 that medical and religious personnel and facilities shall be protected. The *opinio juris* of the Republic of Korea shows that the protection from attack of medical and religious personnel and medical objects is required under international law.

Ruses, perfidy and treachery: The 1996 Operational Law Manual indicates in Chapter 9, Section 2.5.3 that perfidy against humanitarian principles is not permitted. Korean practice regarding ruses of war, perfidy and treachery follows the Geneva Conventions.

Identification: The 1996 Operational Law Manual indicates in Chapter 9, Section 4.3.6 that the emblem of medical organisations is a red cross on a white background. The Red Crescent, Red Lion or Sun are equivalent emblems to the Red Cross. Misuse of the Red Cross emblems is prohibited. This means that Korean practice regarding the identification follows the Geneva Conventions of 1949.

Respect for human rights in occupied areas: The 1996 Operational Law Manual indicates in Chapter 9, Section 6.3.1 that occupying forces should respect the human rights of the inhabitants within their occupied areas. These statements are evidence of the *opinio juris* of the Republic of Korea that human rights should be respected during armed conflicts.'

Negotiations with the enemy: Chapter 9, Section 7.3.1 provides that it is the expression of surrender for one soldier or a platoon to raise a white flag. A white flag, generally, was used for starting negotiations. Instead of white flags, radio

communications or messages dropped from aircraft can be used. The *opinio juris* of the Republic of Korea is that the use of white flags to indicate the opening of negotiations with the enemy is a part of customary international law.
Duty to try or extradite under the principle of universal jurisdiction; duty to try or extradite own nationals for crimes occurring on own territory: Chapter 9, Section 9.4.2 stipulates that war criminals who have committed grave breaches of international humanitarian law shall be tried or extradited. Contracting parties shall cooperate in extraditions. This duty is customary in the Republic of Korea.

☛ Military Law Manual [used to teach officers and soldiers], published 23 January 1996 by the Division of Legal Affairs of the Korean Air Force

COMMENT BY JAE HO SUNG
Principle of proportionality in attack: Unnecessary destruction shall be avoided, under Chapter 6, Section 1.3. The *opinio juris* of the Republic of Korea is that the principle of proportionality in attack is required under international law.
Distinction between civilian and military objectives: The 1996 Military Law Manual provides in Chapter 6 Laws of War, Section 2.1.1 that killing combatants and destroying military objectives only are admissible, and further, in Chapter 6, Section 2.1.1.2, that railways, airports, ports, highways, transmission towers and electronic communication facilities used for military operations can be regarded as military objectives.
Protection of cultural and religious objects: The 1996 Military Law Manual stresses in Chapter 6, Section 2.1.1.2 that special attention shall be paid to cultural property during armed conflicts. The 1996 Operational Law Manual indicates that marked cultural property shall be respected as far as possible. This kind of protection is customary in the Republic of Korea.
Protection of the Environment: The 1996 Military Law Manual explains in Chapter 6, Section 2.1.2.3 that the UN Convention on the Prohibition of Military or Any Other Hostile Use of Environmental Modification Techniques, which prohibits weapons and actions changing the environment, applies only to contracting parties. This means that protection of the environment is enforced only *vis-à-vis* states that are party to the treaty concerned.
Ruses of war, perfidy and treachery: The 1996 Military Law Manual states at Chapter 6, Section 2.1.2.4 that ruses such as camouflage, decoys and misinformation are permitted. This Manual explains that distributing misinformation during some landing operations was proved to be permitted, but resort to perfidy is prohibited.
Improper use of the emblem/enemy uniforms: Improper use of the Red Cross emblem and of the enemy's uniform is prohibited under Chapter 6, Section 2.1.2.4.

Direct attacks on civilians and the notion of military attacks: The 1996 Military Law Manual states in Chapter 6, Section 2.2.1 that direct attacks on civilians are against international law.

Human rights law practice relating to the treatment of persons in armed conflict: The 1996 Military Law Manual requires in Chapter 6, Section 2.2.2.3 that humanitarian treatment should be given to refugees and that refugees cannot be regarded as war prisoners.

Prohibition of pillage: The Manual provides at Chapter 6, Section 2.3.1 that commanders are responsible for their soldiers' pillage.

International responsibility of states for violations of international humanitarian law: A reservation to Protocol I provides that a party to the conflict which violates the provisions of the Conventions or this Protocol shall take responsibility for paying compensation to the party affected. The 1996 Military Law Manual for soldiers indicates in Chapter 6, Section 2.3.2 that any party injured through violations of the laws of war by an enemy party can request remedies. This shows that international responsibility of states for violations of international humanitarian law has become customary in Korean practice.

Chemical Weapons

☛ The White Paper of the Korean Ministry of National Defense of 1997, ROK. Published by the Division of Legal Affairs of the Korean Ministry of National Defense

COMMENT BY J.H. SUNG

'The White Paper states that the CWC was ratified by the ROK National Assembly in July 1996. The *opinio juris* of the Republic of Korea is that prohibiting these kinds of weapons is a part of customary international law.'

Cases

☛ *The North Korean Submarine Infiltration case*, 17 September 1996 [This case was not decided by a court but by the Government of the ROK. This is found in the Official Statement of the Spokesman of the Korean Ministry of National Defense. Some comments were found in the Opinion Paper – which was not publicised – submitted by the legal adviser of the Korean Ministry of Foreign Affairs]

COMMENT BY J.H. SUNG

'In mid-December 1996, a North Korean submarine, which had reconnoitred South Korea, was run aground on a rock near 'KangNeung' beach. The submarine crew landed on 'KangNeung' and killed a few civilians while trying to transgress the ceasefire line between North and South Korea. Some of them then killed themselves and the others fled.

The opinion of the legal adviser of the Korean Ministry of Foreign Affairs, in the *North Korean Submarine Infiltration case*, indicates that commandos are considered to be combatants, and further that a captured spy who is a member of an enemy party's armed forces cannot be classified as a war prisoner and punished under national law.'

Signings, Ratifications, Accessions, Successions, Denouncications, Reservations, etc.
- Republic of Korea signed the CWC on 14 January 1993 and ratified it on 28 April 1997

KUWAIT

Signings, Ratifications, Accessions, Successions, Denounciations, Reservations, etc.
- Kuwait signed the CWC on 27 January 1993 and ratified it on 28 May 1997
- Kuwait ratified the Convention on the Non-Applicability of Statutory Limitations on 7 March 1995
- Kuwait ratified the Genocide Convention on 7 March 1998

KYRGYZSTAN

Signings, Ratifications, Accessions, Successions, Denounciations, Reservations, etc.
- Kyrgyzstan signed the CWC on 22 February 1993
- Kyrgyzstan ratified the CRC on 7 October 1994
- Kyrgyzstan ratified the Genocide Convention on 5 December 1997

LAOS

Signings, Ratifications, Accessions, Successions, Denounciations, Reservations, etc.
- Laos signed the CWC on 13 May 1993 and ratified it on 25 February 1997
- On 30 January 1998, Laos made a declaration accepting the competence of the International Fact-Finding Commision, in accordance with Article 90(2)(a) of Additional Protocol I of 1977

LATVIA

Implementation

'A National Working Group for the Implementation of International Humanitarian Law was set up and was scheduled to become an interministerial committee. The group, which comprises representatives of the principal ministries, the National Human Rights Office and the Latvian Red Cross was requested to prepare a document on means of bringing Latvian national law in line with IHL.'[138]

138. *Supra* n. 3, at p. 52.

Signings, Ratifications, Accessions, Successions, Denounciations, Reservations, etc.

- Latvia signed the CWC on 6 May 1993 and ratified it on 23 July 1996

LEBANON

Signings, Ratifications, Accessions, Successions, Denounciations, Reservations, etc.

- On 23 July 1997, Lebanon acceded to Additional Protocols I and II of 1977
- On 11 March 1998, Latvia ratified Protocol IV of the CCW Convention. Latvia acceded to its Protocols I, II and III on 4 January 1993

LESOTHO

Signings, Ratifications, Accessions, Successions, Denounciations, Reservations, etc.

- Lesotho signed and ratified the CWC on 7 December 1994
- On 20 May 1994, Lesotho acceded to Additional Protocols I and II of 1977
- Lesotho signed the Landmines Treaty on 4 December 1997

LIBERIA

Signings, Ratifications, Accessions, Successions, Denounciations, Reservations, etc.

- Liberia signed and ratified the CWC on 15 January 1993

LIECHTENSTEIN

Signings, Ratifications, Accessions, Successions, Denounciations, Reservations, etc.

- Liechtenstein signed the CWC on 21 July 1993
- Liechtenstein ratified the Genocide Convention on 24 March 1994
- Liechtenstein signed the Safety Convention on 16 October 1995
- Liechtenstein ratified the CRC on 22 December 1995 with reservations
- On 19 November 1997, Liechtenstein ratified Protocol IV and amended Protocol II of the CCW Convention. Liechtenstein became a party to its Protocols I, II and III on 16 August 1989
- Liechenstein signed the Landmines Treaty on 3 December 1997

LITHUANIA

Implementation

- 'In 1996 the Lithuanian government set up a Working Group to coordinate the national implementation of IHL and to advise the authorities on the subject. It was anticipated that the group, whose members are representatives of the government departments concerned, will become an interministerial committee.'[139]

Cases

- *Aleksandras Likeikis* (pending)
  Likeikis is the first person from the Baltic States to be tried for war crimes. He is accused of having handed Jews over to Nazi death squads while he was head of the Saugamus, the Nazi-sponsored Lithuanian security police. He is being tried *in absentia*, after suffering a stroke. His trial began on 4 March 1998 but was adjourned after only one day. In May, it was postponed for a second time. Under Lithuania's criminal code, the penalty for genocide is five to 15 years in prison.[140]
- *Gimzauskas Kazys* (pending)
  As the Yearbook went to press, Lithuania was pressing charges against a second suspected war criminal. Kazys is accused of giving orders to arrest, imprison and execute Jews while he was deputy chief of the Nazi-sponsored Lithuanian secret police between 1941 and 1944.[141]

Signings, Ratifications, Accessions, Successions, Denounciations, Reservations, etc.

- Lithuania signed the CWC on 13 January 1993 and ratified it on 15 April 1998
- Lithuania ratified the Genocide Convention on 1 February 1996
- Lithuania ratified the Convention on the Non-Applicability of Statutory Limitations on 1 February 1996
- Lithuania became a party to the Geneva Conventions of 1949 on 3 October 1996
- On 3 June 1998, Lithuania acceded to Protocols I, III, IV and amended Protocol II of the CCW Convention

LUXEMBOURG

Signings, Ratifications, Accessions, Successions, Denounciations, Reservations, etc.

- Luxembourg signed the CWC on 13 January 1993 and ratified it on 15 April 1997
- Luxembourg ratified the CRC on 7 March 1994 with reservations
- Luxembourg signed the Safety Convention on 31 May 1995

139. *Supra* n. 3, at p. 52.

140. See 'Lawyer for alleged war criminal asked that charges be dismissed,' Lev Krichevsky, JTA (Jewish Telegraphic Agency) (4 March 1998); 'Lithuanian Judge delays trial of alleged Nazi war criminal,' Lev Krichevsky, JTA (18 May 1998).

141. See 'Second alleged war criminal faces prosecution in Lithuania,' JTA (1 March 1998).

- On 23 May 1996, Luxembourg acceded to Protocols I, II and III of the CCW Convention
- Luxembourg signed the Landmines Treaty on 4 December 1997

MADAGASCAR

Signings, Ratifications, Accessions, Successions, Denounciations, Reservations, etc.

- Madagascar signed the CWC on 15 January 1993
- Madagascar signed the Landmines Treaty on 4 December 1997

MALAWI

Signings, Ratifications, Accessions, Successions, Denounciations, Reservations, etc.

- Malawi signed the CWC on 14 January 1993 and ratified it on 11 June 1998
- Malawi signed the Landmines Treaty on 4 December 1997 and ratified it on 18 August 1998

MALAYSIA

Signings, Ratifications, Accessions, Successions, Denounciations, Reservations, etc.

- Malaysia signed and ratified the CWC on 13 January 1993
- Malaysia ratified the Genocide Convention on 20 December 1994 with reservations
- Malaysia ratified the CRC on 17 February 1995 with reservations
- Malaysia signed the Landmines Treaty on 3 December 1997

MALI

Signings, Ratifications, Accessions, Successions, Denounciations, Reservations, etc.

- Mali signed the CWC on 13 January 1993 and ratified it on 28 April 1997
- Mali signed the Landmines Treaty on 3 December 1997 and ratified it on 2 June 1998

MALTA

Signings, Ratifications, Accessions, Successions, Denounciations, Reservations, etc.

- Malta signed the CWC on 13 January 1993 and ratified it on 28 April 1997
- Malta signed the Safety Convention on 16 March 1995
- On 26 June 1995, Malta acceded to Protocols I, II and III of the CCW Convention

MARSHALL ISLANDS

Signings, Ratifications, Accessions, Successions, Denounciations, Reservations, etc.

- Marshall Islands signed and ratified the CWC on 13 January 1993
- Marshall Islands signed the Landmines Treaty on 4 December 1997

MAURITANIA

Signings, Ratifications, Accessions, Successions, Denounciations, Reservations, etc.

- Mauritania signed the CWC on 13 January 1993 and ratified it on 9 February 1998
- Mauritania signed the Landmines Treaty on 3 December 1997
- On 9 February 1998, Mauritania acceded to the Mercenaries Convention without making any reservations or ratifications

MAURITIUS

Signings, Ratifications, Accessions, Successions, Denounciations, Reservations, etc.

- Mauritius signed the CWC on 14 January 1993 and ratified it on 9 February 1993
- On 6 May 1996, Mauritius acceded to Protocols I, II and III of the CCW Convention
- Mauritius signed and ratified the Landmines Treaty on 4 December 1997

MEXICO

Signings, Ratifications, Accessions, Successions, Denounciations, Reservations, etc.

- Mexico signed the CWC on 13 January 1993 and ratified it on 29 August 1994
- Mexico signed the Landmines Treaty on 3 December 1997 and ratified it on 9 June 1998
- On 10 March 1998, Mexico ratified amended Protocol II of the CCW Convention

MICRONESIA

Signings, Ratifications, Accessions, Successions, Denounciations, Reservations, etc.

- Micronesia signed the CWC on 13 January 1993
- On 19 September 1995, Micronesia acceded to Additional Protocols I and II of 1977

(REPUBLIC OF) MOLDOVA

Implementation

- Presidential Decree No. 382 of 9 September 1996 establishing a National Committee on Consultation and Coordination of implementation of international humanitarian law[142]

Signings, Ratifications, Accessions, Successions, Denounciations, Reservations, etc.

- Moldova signed the CWC on 13 January 1993 and ratified it on 8 July 1996
- Moldova signed the Landmines Treaty on 3 December 1997

142. *Supra* n. 3, at p. 52.

MONACO

Signings, Ratifications, Accessions, Successions, Denounciations, Reservations, etc.

- Monaco signed the CWC on 13 January 1993 and ratified it on 1 June 1995
- On 4 May 1997, Monaco ratified amended Protocol II of the CCW Convention and became a party to its Protocol I on 12 August 1997
- Monaco signed the Landmines Treaty on 4 December 1997

MONGOLIA

Signings, Ratifications, Accessions, Successions, Denounciations, Reservations, etc.

- Mongolia signed the CWC on 14 January 1993 and ratified it on 17 January 1995
- On 6 December 1995, Mongolia made a declaration under Article 90 of Additional Protocol I of 1977 recognising the competence of the International Fact-Finding Commission
- On 6 December 1995, Mongolia ratified Additional Protocols I and II of 1977

MOROCCO

Signings, Ratifications, Accessions, Successions, Denounciations, Reservations, etc.

- Morocco signed the CWC on 13 January 1993 and ratified it on 28 December 1995

MOZAMBIQUE

Signings, Ratifications, Accessions, Successions, Denounciations, Reservations, etc.

- Mozambique ratified the CRC on 26 April 1994
- Mozambique signed the Landmines Treaty on 4 December 1997

MYANMAR

Signings, Ratifications, Accessions, Successions, Denounciations, Reservations, etc.

- Myanmar signed the CWC on 14 January 1993

NAMIBIA

Implementation

- An Interministerial Technical Committee on Human Rights and Humanitarian Law was established at the end of 1995. It is composed of the relevant government ministries and the Namibian Red Cross. No internal regulations have yet been adopted.[143]

Signings, Ratifications, Accessions, Successions, Denounciations, Reservations, etc.

- Namibia signed the CWC on 13 January 1993 and ratified it on 27 November 1995
- On 17 June 1994, Nambia acceded to Additional Protocol II of 1977 and on 21 July 1994 to Additional Protocol I[144]
- On 21 July 1994, Namibia made a declaration under Article 90 of Additional Protocol I of 1977 recognising the competence of the International Fact-Finding Commission
- Namibia signed the Landmines Treaty on 3 December 1997

NAURU

Signings, Ratifications, Accessions, Successions, Denounciations, Reservations, etc.

- Nauru signed the CWC on 13 January 1993
- Nauru ratified the CRC on 27 July 1994

NEPAL

Signings, Ratifications, Accessions, Successions, Denounciations, Reservations, etc.

- Nepal signed the CWC on 19 January 1993 and ratified it on 18 November 1997

THE NETHERLANDS[145]

International Criminal Tribunals

- Act of 21 April 1994 containing provisions relating to the establishment of the International Tribunal for the prosecution of persons responsible for serious violations of international humanitarian law committed in the former Yugoslavia since 1991. Published in *Staatsblad* (1994) 308
- Act of 18 December 1997 containing provisions relating to the establishment of the International Tribunal for the prosecution of persons responsible for genocide and other serious violations of IHL committed in the territory of Rwanda and of Rwandan citizens responsible for genocide and other such violations, committed in the territory of neighbouring States, between 1 January 1994 and 31 December 1994. This Act entered into force 30 December 1997. Published in *Staatsblad* (1997) 754

143. *Supra* n. 3, at p. 94.

144. *IRRC* No. 322, March 1998, p. 184.

145. Information provided by Professor Nico Keijzer, Professor of International Criminal Law, Catholic University of Brabant.

COMMENT BY NICO KEIJZER

'It is noteworthy that the Rwanda Tribunal Implementation Act does not refer to extradition but uses the word "surrender". The Explanatory Memorandum related to this Act contains, *inter alia*, the following phrase:

> "It is in the present context self-evident that, unlike extradition in the traditional sense, the mode of international legal cooperation provided for under subsection 1 is the transfer of a requested person to an international body, which has been established by a United Nations Security Council Resolution, instead of to a sovereign state as usual. This justifies a separate regulation, as proposed in the present Bill."

Accordingly, the traditional exceptions of extradition law, such as the nationality exception and the political offence exception, do not apply.'

Cases

☛ Supreme Court of the Netherlands (De Hoge Raad der Nederlanden). Decision No. 3717, 11 November 1997. Published in *Nederlandse Jurisprudentie* (NJ) 1998, 463, (with annotations by Professor 't Hart); and *Militair Rechtelijk Tijdschrift* (MRT) 1998, p. 198 (with annotations by H. van der Wilt)

COMMENT BY NICO KEIJZER

'On 11 November 1997, the Supreme Court of the Netherlands rendered an important decision in the field of international humanitarian law.[146] By clarifying an obscurity in the War Crimes Act of 1952 [Wet Oorlogsstrafrecht, 10 July 1952], it opened the way for violations of the laws and customs of war, allegedly committed by foreigners on foreign territory, to be tried before Dutch courts.

Article 8 of the War Crimes Act of 1952 makes punishable, *inter alia*, any violation of the laws and customs of war (without restriction to the grave breaches of the Geneva Conventions and their Additional Protocol I). Article 3 of the Act establishes criminal jurisdiction in this respect over any person who has allegedly committed such an offence anywhere in the world.

The problem was caused by the rather cryptic wording of Article 1 of the Act, which states, *inter alia*, that - unless in relation to peacekeeping activities, an Order in Council were passed to the contrary - the provisions of the Act only apply during a state of war (including civil war). The preparatory documents indicate that the framers of the Act used the term "war" in the sense of a war to which the Netherlands is a party. (The War Crimes Act, promulgated only a few years after World

146. Decision 3717 of 11 November 1997. Reprinted *infra* at p. 600.

War II, was basically designed for the better organisation of future post-war justice for traitors and collaborators with the enemy, such as had then recently taken place.) If the Act were construed along these lines, it would - in the absence of such an Order in Council - not provide for universal jurisdiction regarding war crimes unless the Netherlands was itself at war. This would imply that the obligation to establish universal jurisdiction, which the Netherlands has assumed by ratifying the Geneva Conventions of 1949 and their Additional Protocol I of 1977, would not be met.

The Dutch prosecution service instituted a test case, in the context of which the Supreme Court was asked to rule on a preliminary motion and clarify this matter.

In its decision 3717 of 11 November 1997, the Supreme Court ruled that, in spite of the wording of its Article 1, the Act must, in light of the Geneva Conventions and their Additional Protocol I, be construed in such a way that its Article 3 establishes universal jurisdiction for violations of the laws and customs of war, including when the Netherlands is not at war.

The ruling also decided that cases of this kind come under the competence of the same courts which deal with crimes committed by Dutch military persons. These are special branches of the District Court and the Appeals Court, in which two of the three judges (excepting the president) are military lawyers.'

Signings, Ratifications, Accessions, Successions, Denounciations, Reservations, etc.

- ☛ The Netherlands signed the CWC on 14 January 1993 and ratified it on 30 June 1995
- ☛ The Netherlands ratified the CRC on 6 February 1995 with reservations
- ☛ The Netherlands signed the Safety Convention on 22 December 1995
- ☛ The Netherlands signed the Landmines Treaty on 3 December 1997

NEW ZEALAND[147]

International Criminal Tribunals

- ☛ International War Crimes Tribunals Act 1995 (short title), No. 27, *The Statues of New Zealand 1995*, Volume 1, p. 207, Government of New Zealand, Wellington 1996 [http://www.knowledge-basket.co.nz/gpprint/acts/public/text/1995/an/027.html]

Chemical Weapons

- ☛ Chemical Weapons (Prohibition) Act 1996, No. 37, *The Statutes of New Zealand 1996,* Volume 2, p. 1044, Government of New Zealand, Wellington 1997 [http://www.knowledge-basket.co.nz/gpprint/acts/public/text/1996/an/037.html]

147. Information provided by Prof. Tim McCormack, *supra* n. 14.

COMMENT BY TIM MCCORMACK

'The Chemical Weapons (Prohibition) Act formally passed into law on 24 June 1996. Its stated purpose is to implement New Zealand's obligations as a state party to the CWC.

The application of the Act extends beyond the territory of New Zealand to acts done, or omitted to be done, by: (i) New Zealand citizens or residents; or (ii) any person aboard New Zealand ships or planes.

There are 31 articles in the Chemical Weapons (Prohibition) Act 1996, with the CWC being attached as a schedule and constituting by far the bulk of the Act.

Part II of the Act lists the offences which are committed under New Zealand domestic law in respect of the production, stockpiling and trading in chemical weapons. Part III of the Act provides that information on chemicals to which the provisions of Parts VI and X of the Verification Annex of the CWC applies must be reported to authorities and may be transmitted to the CWC Secretariat.

Part IV of the Act allows and facilitates inspections of premises in accordance with the CWC and allows New Zealand authorities to participate in inspections. The application of the Act has been extended to the territory of Tokelau under Article 30.'

Signings, Ratifications, Accessions, Successions, Denounciations, Reservations, etc.

- New Zealand signed the CWC on 14 January 1993 and ratified it on 15 July 1996
- New Zealand signed the Safety Convention on 15 December 1994
- New Zealand signed the Landmines Treaty on 3 December 1997
- On 8 January 1998, New Zealand ratified Protocol IV and amended Protocol II of the CCW Convention. New Zealand became a party to its Protocols I, II and III on 18 October 1993

NICARAGUA

Penal Code

- Penal Code of the Republic of Nicaragua [Ley de Código Penal de la República de Nicaragua] 1996, Bibliografías Técnicas, 1997[148]

148. '*Under the heading, "Delitos de carácter intenacional"*, Art. 551 of the Nicaraguan penal code adopts a very comprehensive approach to the prosecution of any violation of humanitarian law, whether committed in time of international or civil war. Art. 16, para. 3(f), of the code gives Nicaraguan courts jurisdiction over offences included under this heading, irrespective of who committed them and where.' Thomas Graditzky, 'International criminal responsibility for violations of international humanitarian law committed in non-international armed conflicts.' *IRRC* No. 322, March 1998, p. 29 at 41.

Signings, Ratifications, Accessions, Successions, Denounciations, Reservations, etc.

- ☛ Nicaragua signed the CWC on 9 January 1993
- ☛ Nicaragua signed the Landmines Treaty on 4 December 1997

NIGER

Signings, Ratifications, Accessions, Successions, Denounciations, Reservations, etc.

- ☛ Niger signed the CWC on 14 January 1993 and ratified it on 9 April 1997
- ☛ Niger signed the Landmines Treaty on 4 December 1997

NIGERIA[149]

Teaching of IHL

- ☛ Final document of the national workshop on the teaching of IHL in Nigerian Universities, Abuja, 23-24 April 1997

A two-day workshop on the teaching of IHL was jointly organised in Abuja on 23 and 24 April 1997 by the ICRC, the Nigerian Institute of International Affairs and the Nigerian Red Cross Society. This followed up a National Seminar on the Implementation of IHL in Nigeria, held in Lagos on 13 and 14 August 1996. At the latter, it was resolved, *inter alia*, that: 'Teaching of IHL at university level should be systematised and developed in all the Nigerian universities and other higher education institutions in the country. For that purpose, the ICRC Legal Advisory Services has produced a plan for IHL courses which can be used by professors and lecturers...' At the Abuja meeting, attended by academics and government representatives, scientific presentations were given on the following subjects: background to IHL: history, definition, fundamental principles, scope and recent developments; the role and importance of the teaching of IHL today; the new ICRC plan for teaching IHL at university level; how to develop, systematise and/or improve the teaching of IHL in Nigerian Universities; customary international law in the teaching of IHL in Nigeria; and the ICRC and the teaching of IHL to Nigerian armed forces. In view of 'the imperative necessity to disseminate IHL principles and Red Cross ideals, particularly in the context of persistent conflict situations in Africa', the participants came to the conclusion that there is an overwhelming need for university-based IHL programmes. The workshop recommended, *inter alia,* that the National Universities Commission should include a course of IHL in the list of General Studies courses which must be offered and passed by all undergraduates in the universities before they can be awarded a degree, and that the Federal Government should increase its support to Universities to promote the teaching of IHL. Further, that Nigeria should establish a National Committee for the Implementation of IHL, with responsibility for coordinating

149. Information provided by Mr. Michael Ibanga, Faculty of Law, University of Calabar Calabar - Cross River State, Nigeria.

efforts and advising the Federal Government and Institutions on the development of the teaching of IHL, and that Nigeria should incorporate the two Additional Protocols of 1977 into its domestic law.

Signings, Ratifications, Accessions, Successions, Denounciations, Reservations, etc.

- Nigeria signed the CWC on 13 January 1993

NIUE

Signings, Ratifications, Accessions, Successions, Denounciations, Reservations, etc.

- Niue ratified the CRC on 20 December 1995
- Niue signed the Landmines Treaty on 3 December 1997 and ratified it on 15 April 1998

NORWAY

International Criminal Tribunals

- Act No. 38 of 24 June 1994 relating to the incorporation into Norwegian Law of the UN Security Council Regulation on the establishment of international tribunals for crimes committed in the former Yugoslavia and Rwanda

Signings, Ratifications, Accessions, Successions, Denounciations, Reservations, etc.

- Norway signed the CWC on 13 January 1993 and ratified it on 7 April 1994
- Norway made a reservation to the CRC on 25 October 1994. She signed it on 8 January 1991
- Norway signed the Safety Convention on 15 December 1994 and ratified it on 3 July 1995
- Norway signed the Landmines Treaty on 3 December 1997 and ratified it on 9 July 1998
- On 20 April 1998, Norway ratified Protocol IV and amended Protocol II of the CCW Convention. Norway became a party to the Convention on 7 June 1983

OMAN

Signings, Ratifications, Accessions, Successions, Denounciations, Reservations, etc.

- Oman signed the CWC on 2 February 1993 and ratified it on 2 February 1995
- Oman ratified the CRC on 9 December 1996 with reservations

PAKISTAN

Signings, Ratifications, Accessions, Successions, Denounciations, Reservations, etc.

- Pakistan signed the CWC on 13 January 1993 and ratified it on 28 October 1997
- Pakistan signed the Safety Convention on 8 March 1995

PALAU

Signings, Ratifications, Accessions, Successions, Denounciations, Reservations, etc.

- On 25 June 1996, the Republic of Palau acceded to the Geneva Conventions of 1949 and their Additional Protocols without making any declarations or reservations.

PANAMA

Implementation

- The Inter-institutional Committee for the Application of International Humanitarian Law [Comité interinstitucional de aplicación del Derecho Internacional Humanitario] held its first meeting on 9 July 1996

The Commission is composed of representatives of the Ministries of Foreign Relations, Justice, Health, the Interior, Education and Defence. The Commission's mandate is the implementation and application of IHL and its primary aim is to help draft a law on the prevention and repression of misuse of the Emblem.[150]

Signings, Ratifications, Accessions, Successions, Denounciations, Reservations, etc.

- Panama signed the CWC on 16 June 1993
- Panama signed the Safety Convention on 15 December 1994 and ratified it on 4 April 1996
- On 26 March 1997, Panama acceded to Protocols I, II, III and IV of the CCW Convention
- Panama signed the Landmines Treaty on 4 December 1997

PAPUA NEW GUINEA[151]

Mercenary Support to the Armed Forces

- Sandline Document: Agreement for the Provision of Military Assistance Dated 31 Day of January 1997 Between the Independent State of Papua New Guinea and Sandline International [http://www.theage.com.au/special/asiaonline/sandline/htm][152]
- The Burnham Declaration by Bougainville Leaders on the Re-Establishment of a Process for Lasting Peace and Justice on Bougainville, dated 18 July 1997 [http://www.dfat.gov.au/geo/spacific/png/png_burn_dec.html]

COMMENT BY TIM MCCORMACK

'Despite numerous unsuccessful joint declarations and statements by various parties to the Bougainville conflict in the past, the Burnham Declaration was the first

150. *Supra* n. 3, at pp. 52-53
151. Ibid.
152. For commentary on this agreement, see McCormack, at p. 292 .

agreement after the Sandline Affair in PNG and has proved to be the initiation of a serious attempt to negotiate an end to the Bougainville Conflict. In this particular Declaration, the parties to the talks agreed to the establishment of a clear process for a negotiated settlement which included proposals for a ceasefire; the establishment of a neutral peacekeeping force, the demilitarisation of Bougainville; and a commitment to provide Bougainvilleans with a free and democratic choice about their political future.'

- The Burnham Truce, dated 10 October 1997
- The Cairns Commitment on Implementation of the Agreement Concerning the Neutral Regional Truce Monitoring Group (TMG) for Bougainville, dated 24 November 1997 [http://www.dfat.gov.au/geo/spacific/png/cairns.html]

COMMENT BY TIM MCCORMACK

'This particular agreement, signed by all relevant parties to the conflict on Bougainville, guarantees protection for the members of the Truce Monitoring Group (TMG) and respect for the inviolability of their premises, equipment, supplies and lines of communication. The agreement also established the Peace Consultative Committee to act as the principal liaison between the parties to the conflict and the TMG.'

- Agreement Between Papua New Guinea, Australia, Fiji and Vanuatu Concerning the Neutral Truce Monitoring Group for Bougainville, dated 5 December 1997. *Australian Treaties Series 1997,* No. 30. Australian Government Publishing Service, Canberra 1998 [http://www.austlii.edu.au/do/disp.pl/au/other/dfat/treaties/]

COMMENT BY TIM MCCORMACK

'The Agreement constitutes the first establishment of an exclusively South Pacific Regional Truce Monitoring Group (TMG) and is the legally binding agreement between PNG and the participating states for the implementation of the Burnham Agreement and the Burnham Truce. The Agreement includes the details of the mandate of the TMG, and issues such as jurisdiction over and discipline of members, inviolability of premises, uniforms and emblems, and liability for loss of property etc., that often appear in Status of Forces Agreements. Eighty-five members of the group were deployed on Bougainville pursuant to the Agreement on 6 December 1997.'[153]

153. See Joint Statement by the Minister for Foreign Affairs, Alexander Downer MP and the Minister for Defence, Ian McLaughlin AO, MP, 5 December 1997: 'Bougainville Truce Monitoring Group'. Text of the release available online at www.dfat.gov.au/pmb/releases/fa/ fa149_97.html.

☛ Lincoln Agreement on Peace, Security and Development on Bougainville, dated 23 January 1998 [http://www.dfat.gov.au/geo/spacific/png/png_lincoln.html]

COMMENT BY TIM MCCORMACK
'The Lincoln Agreement builds on the earlier Burnham Declaration and Burnham Truce by providing some of the details for the "in principle" agreements in those earlier instruments. Specifically, the Lincoln Agreement commits all the parties to "a permanent and irrevocable ceasefire" to commence at midnight on 30 April 1998; to a phased withdrawal of PNGDF troops from Bougainville subject to the restoration of civil authority; to conclude the arrangements for deployment of the Peace Monitoring Group (to replace the Truce Monitoring Group) once the ceasefire takes effect; to cooperation in the restoration and development of Bougainville; and to free and democratic elections on Bougainville before the end of 1998.'

☛ Agreement Covering Implementation of the Ceasefire (described as 'Annex 1 to the Lincoln Agreement'), dated 30 April 1998

COMMENT BY TIM MCCORMACK
'The Agreement provides the details for the implementation of the Lincoln Agreement and, in particular, obligates the PNG government to invite the governments of Australia, Fiji, New Zealand and Vanuatu to participate in the new Peace Monitoring Group (PMG) once the ceasefire takes effect and to negotiate an agreement to that effect. The Agreement sets out the mandate of the PMG and the functions of the Peace Consultative Committee. The PNG government is also obligated to request the UN Security Council to endorse the PMG and to invite the UN Secretary-General to send a UN observer mission to Bougainville.'

☛ Protocol Concerning the Peace Monitoring Group Made Pursuant to the Agreement Between Papua New Guinea, Australia, Fiji, New Zealand and Vanuatu Concerning the Neutral Truce Monitoring Group for Bougainville. Done at Port Moresby on 5 December 1997, dated 29 April 1998 [The Protocol will appear in the Australian Treaty Series 1998, which had not been published at the time of writing. Meanwhile, the text of the Protocol and accompanying National Interest Analysis have been tabled before the Joint Parliamentary Standing Committee on Treaties and the text of the Analysis is available online at: http://www.austlii.edu.au/do/disp.pl/au/other/dfat/nia]

COMMENT BY TIM MCCORMACK
'The Protocol constitutes the legally binding agreement between PNG and the states participating in the Peace Monitoring Group explicitly referred to in the Agreement Covering Implementation of the Ceasefire (described as 'Annex 1 to the Lincoln Agreement'), dated 30 April 1998 as outlined above.'

Signings, Ratifications, Accessions, Successions, Denounciations, Reservations, etc.

- Papua New Guinea signed the CWC on 14 January 1993 and ratified it on 17 April 1996

PARAGUAY[154]

Penal Code

- Law N° 1160/97 Penal Code of the Republic of Paraguay, 16 October 1997. Entered into force, November 1998[155] [Código Penal de la República del Paraguay]. Published in Instituto de Ciencias Penales del Paraguay, Colección Legislación Paraguaya Edición: 1998 (Intercontinental Editora, Asunción, Paraguay, 1998)

COMMENT BY ALFONSO VELÁSQUEZ

'On 16 October 1997, the Paraguayan Congress passed Law N° 1160/97, by which the new Penal Code of the Republic of Paraguay was adopted. The Executive Power, on 26 November 1997, promulgated the said law, which entered into force in November 1998.

The previous Paraguayan criminal legislation was in force since the nineteenth century. Indeed, the Criminal Procedural Code was enacted in 1890 and the Penal Code in 1914. Both laws were severely criticised as obsolete and inadequate. The new legislation seeks to incorporate new developments in the field of criminal law, to protect fundamental rights guaranteed under the Constitution and to effectively repress violations of these rights. However, implementation of the new Penal Code will require the enactment of new procedural legislation, and a new Procedural Penal Code is currently under analysis by the Congress.

Regarding IHL it is noteworthy that the new Penal Code sets forth the principle that Paraguayan penal laws shall be applied to acts against universally protected interests committed in a foreign country.[156] Furthermore, the above-mentioned legislation contains a separate section for the so-called "acts against the peoples", in particular genocide and war crimes. Article 319 of the Code represses the crime of genocide, and its wording is based, with some differences, upon Article II of the 1948 Convention on the Prevention and Punishment of the Crime of Genocide, to which Paraguay is a contracting party. Article 320 of the Code represses war crimes. It is noteworthy that the article refers to the violations of the norms of international law applicable in times of war and also includes armed conflicts and military occupations. Moreover, the said article enumerates the acts that are

154. Information provided by Professor Alfonso Velásquez, Professor of International Law, Catholic University of Asunción.

155. Reproduced in part at p. 621.

156. Art. 8, Title 1, Chapter II, Application of the Law.

considered as war crimes. Paraguay being a contracting party to the Geneva Conventions of 1949 and their two Additional Protocols of 1977, it would have been more effective to refer to the Conventions or to expressly add that war crimes also include any other violation of those instruments. As far as punishment is concerned, the Code sets forth a minimum of five years imprisonment for both genocide and war crimes.

With respect to human rights, the Code represses the crime of torture. This is a significant development in Paraguay, considering that the existing Paraguayan Penal Code does not punish the crime of torture. Indeed, nowadays, in order to investigate, prosecute and punish cases of torture, Paraguayan lawyers, judges and victims have to resort to other criminal offences, such as personal injury, abduction, abuse of authority, legal imprisonment or murder. Thus, except in cases where murder was committed, many criminals receive a rather light sentence, corresponding to personal injury. The lack of specific regulation of the crime of torture contributed to a great deal of impunity in cases committed during the regime of President Alfredo Stroessner.'

Implementation

☛ Presidential Decree N° 8802 establishing an Interministerial Commission for the Application of IHL [Comision Interministerial de Aplicacion del Derecho Internacional Humanitario]. It is composed of representatives of the Ministries of Foreign Affairs, Defence, the Interior, Justice and Labour, Education and Worship, Health and Social Welfare. Its mandate is to implement and disseminate IHL.[157]

Cases

☛ The *Napoleon Ortigosa* case, Supreme Court of Justice, Asunción, 31 December 1996

COMMENT BY ALFONSO VELÁSQUEZ

'Napoleon Ortigoza is a military officer who, during the dictatorship of General Alfredo Stroessner, was accused of murdering a soldier named Benitez. Apparently, Benitez's death was used by the Stroessner regime to inculpate Ortigoza, who at that time was a captain of the army, and who was supposedly conspiring against Stroessner and preparing a coup. Ortigoza was found guilty of Benitez's death and was held in prison for 25 years. The Paraguayan Supreme Court, by Sentence Number 585, dated 31 December 1996, decided to nullify the process against Ortigoza. In the reasoning of this sentence, the Court acknowledged that crimes against humanity (*lesa humanidad*) are not subject to the Statute of Limitations.'

157. Table of National Bodies for Implementation of International Humanitarian Law, Advisory Service on International Humanitarian Law, ICRC, as of 31 March 1998, p. 13.

Signings, Ratifications, Accessions, Successions, Denounciations, Reservations, etc.

- ☛ Paraguay signed the CWC on 14 January 1993 and ratified it on 1 December 1994
- ☛ Paraguay signed the Landmines Treaty on 4 December 1997
- ☛ On 30 January 1998, the Republic of Paraguay made a declaration accepting the competence of the International Fact-Finding Commission, in accordance with Art. 90 (2)(a) of Protocol I of 1977

PERU[158]

Penal Code (crimes against humanity)

- ☛ Law N° 29626 Amending Certain Articles of the Penal Code and Incorporating Section XIV-A Concerning Crimes Against Humanity, 30 January 1998[159]. Published in *El Puruano* (diario oficial/official gazette), section 'Normas Legales', Lima 21 February 1998, No. 6450, p. 157575

Signings, Ratifications, Accessions, Successions, Denounciations, Reservations, etc.

- ☛ Peru signed the CWC on 14 January 1993 and ratified it on 20 July 1995
- ☛ On 3 March 1997, Peru acceded to Protocols I, III, IV and amended Protocol II of the CCW Convention
- ☛ Peru signed the Landmines Treaty on 3 December 1997 and ratified it on 17 June 1998

THE PHILIPPINES

Signings, Ratifications, Accessions, Successions, Denounciations, Reservations, etc.

- ☛ The Philippines signed the CWC on 13 January 1993 and ratified it on 11 December 1996
- ☛ The Philippines signed the Safety Convention on 27 February 1995 and ratified it on 17 June 1997
- ☛ On 12 June 1997, the Philippines ratified Protocol IV and amended Protocol II of the CCW Convention, following its accession to its Protocols I, II and III on 15 July 1996
- ☛ The Philippines signed the Landmines Treaty on 3 December 1997

158. Information provided by Professor Raul Vinuesa, Professor of International Law and Human Rights, Faculty of Law, University of Buenos Aires.

159. Reprinted *infra* at p. 623.

POLAND[160]

Military Service and Military Discipline

- Order of the Minister of National Defence dated 19 December 1996 on military service of regular soldiers. *Journal of Laws* 1997, No. 7, item 38 [Rozporządzenie Ministra Obrony Narodowej zdnia 19 grudnia 1996 r. w sprawie służby wojskowej żołnierzy zawodowych, Dziennik Ustaw 1997 r. Nr 7 poz. 38]
- Act on military discipline from 4 September 1997. *Journal of Laws* 1997, No. 141, item 944, amendments: *Journal of Laws* 1997, No. 160, item 1083 [Ustawa z dnia 4 września 1997 r. Odyscplinie Wojskowej Dziennik Ustaw 1997r. Nr 141 poz944 zmiany: Dziennik Ustaw 1997 r. Nr 160 poz. 1083]

State Security and Defence

- Order of the Council of Ministers dated 13 January 1998 on determining types of real property considered indispensable for the state defence and security purposes. *Journal of Laws* 1998, No. 9, item 31 [Rozporządzenie Rady Ministrów z dnia 13 stycznia 1998 r. w sprawie określenia rodzajów ieruchomości uznawanych za niezbędne na cele obronności i bezpieczeństwa państwa. Dziennik Ustaw 1998 r. Nr 9 poz. 31]

Signings, Ratifications, Accessions, Successions, Denounciations, Reservations, etc.

- Poland signed the CWC on 13 January 1993 and ratified it on 23 August 1995
- Poland signed the Safety Convention on 17 March 1995
- Poland signed the Landmines Treaty on 4 December 1997

PORTUGAL

Penal Code

- Portuguese Penal Code [Código Penal Portugués] 1996[161]

Implementation

- The Commission for International Humanitarian Law was established in 1997. It is composed of representatives of various ministries and the Portuguese Red Cross.[162]

160. Information provided by Professor Jerzy Menkes, Professor at the University of Commerce and Law, Warsaw.

161. 'Generally applicable in time of war, armed conflict, and occupation, Arts. 241 and 242 of the Portuguese penal code covers some aspects of humanitarian law (war crimes against civilians and the destruction of monuments, respectively). However, Art. 5 extends jurisdiction beyond the national territory and to non-nationals only in certain specified cases, which, curiously enough, include only the second of the above-mentioned articles, or when such jurisdiction is imposed by international treaty provisions.' Thomas Graditzky, 'International criminal responsibility for violations of international humanitarian law committed in non-international armed conflicts,' *IRRC* No. 322 (March 1998) p. 29 at p. 43.

162. *Supra* n. 52.

Signings, Ratifications, Accessions, Successions, Denounciations, Reservations, etc.

- Portugal signed the CWC on 13 January 1993 and ratified it on 10 September 1996
- On 1 July 1994, Portugal made a declaration under Article 90 of Additional Protocol I of 1977 recognising the competence of the International Fact-Finding Commission
- On 4 April 1997, Portugal acceded to Protocols I, II and III of the CCW Convention
- Portugal signed the Landmines Treaty on 3 December 1997

QUATAR

Signings, Ratifications, Accessions, Successions, Denounciations, Reservations, etc.

- Quatar signed the CWC on 1 February 1993 and ratified it on 3 September 1997
- Quatar ratified the CRC on 3 April 1995
- Quatar signed the Landmines Treaty on 4 December 1997

ROMANIA

Signings, Ratifications, Accessions, Successions, Denounciations, Reservations, etc.

- Romania signed the CWC on 13 January 1993 and ratified it on 15 February 1995
- On 31 May 1995, Romania made a declaration under Article 90(2)(a) of Additional Protocol I of 1977 recognising the competence of the International Fact-Finding Commission
- On 26 July 1995, Romania acceded to Protocols I, II and III of the CCW Convention
- Romania signed the Safety Convention on 27 September 1995 and ratified it on 29 December 1997
- Romania signed the Landmines Treaty on 3 December 1997

RUSSIAN FEDERATION[163]

Amnesty (Chechyna)

- Declaration of Amnesty for persons who have committed socially dangerous acts relating to the armed conflict in the Republic of Chechyna, 15 March 1997
- The execution of the Decree of the State Duma of the Federal Assembly of the Russian Federation 'Declaration of Amnesty for persons who have committed socially dangerous acts relating to the armed conflict in the Republic of Chechyna', 12 March 1997

Cases

- Presidential Decrees and Federal Government's Resolution on the Situation in Chechyna. Constitutional Court of the Russian Federation, Moscow. Judgement of

163. Information provided by Professor Igor Blischchenko, Professor of International Law, Russian University of Friendship, Moscow.

31 July 1995 [recognising the applicability of Protocol II]. Published in *Human Rights Law Journal*, Vol. 17, No. 3-6, p. 133

Signings, Ratifications, Accessions, Successions, Denounciations, Reservations, etc.

- The Russian Federation signed the CWC on 13 January 1993 and ratified it on 5 November 1997

RWANDA[164]

Genocide and Crimes against Humanity

- The Organic Law 8/96 of 30 August 1996 on the organisation of prosecutions for offences constituting the crime of genocide or crimes against humanity since 1 October 1990 (entered into force 1 September 1996)[165]. Published in 'The Genocide and the Crimes against Humanity in Rwanda Law', Brussels, Editions ASSEPAC, 1996
- The Law 9/96 of 8 September 1996 relating to provisional modifications to the Criminal Procedure Code (entered into force retroactively, being effective as of 6 April 1994). *Journal Official*, 1996, No. 18 at p. 8
- Law N° 16/97 of 26 December 1997 modifying the law 9/96 of 8 September and relating to provisional modifications to the criminal procedure code [extending permissible period that can be spent in detention on remand]. *Journal Officiel* N° SP. of 31 December 1997

Signings, Ratifications, Accessions, Successions, Denounciations, Reservations, etc.

- Rwanda signed the CWC on 17 May 1993
- Rwanda signed the Landmines Treaty on 3 December 1997

SAINT KITTS AND NEVIS

Signings, Ratifications, Accessions, Successions, Denounciations, Reservations, etc.

- Saint Kitts and Nevis signed the CWC on 16 March 1994
- Saint Kitts and Nevis signed the Landmines Treaty on 3 December 1997

SAINT LUCIA

Signings, Ratifications, Accessions, Successions, Denounciations, Reservations, etc.

- Saint Lucia signed the CWC on 29 March 1993 and ratified it on 9 April 1997
- Saint Lucia signed the Landmines Treaty on 3 December 1997

164. Information provided by Ms. Catherine Cissé, Legal Advisor to the Chief Prosecutor, International Criminal Tribunal for Rwanda.

165. Reprinted at p. 625.

SAINT VINCENT AND THE GRENADINES

Signings, Ratifications, Accessions, Successions, Denounciations, Reservations, etc.

- Saint Vincent and the Grenadines signed the CWC on 20 September 1993
- Saint Vincent and the Grenadines signed the Landmines Treaty on 3 December 1997

SAMOA

Signings, Ratifications, Accessions, Successions, Denounciations, Reservations, etc.

- Samoa signed the CWC on 14 January 1993
- Samoa ratified the CRC on 29 November 1994 with reservations
- Samoa signed the Safety Convention on 16 January 1995

SAN MARINO

Signings, Ratifications, Accessions, Successions, Denounciations, Reservations, etc.

- San Marino signed the CWC on 13 January 1993
- On 5 April 1994, San Marino ratified Additional Protocols I and II of 1977
- San Marino signed the Landmines Treaty on 3 December 1997 and ratified it on 18 March 1998

SAO TOME and PRINCIPE

Signings, Ratifications, Accessions, Successions, Denounciations, Reservations, etc.

- On 5 July 1996, the Democratic Republic of Sao Tome and Principe acceded to Additional Protocols I and II of 1977 without making any declaration or reservations.
- Sao Tome and Principe signed the Landmines Treaty on 4 December 1997

SAUDI ARABIA

Signings, Ratifications, Accessions, Successions, Denounciations, Reservations, etc.

- Saudi Arabia signed the CWC on 20 January 1993 and ratified it on 9 August 1996
- Saudi Arabia ratified the CRC on 26 January 1996 with reservations
- On 14 April 1997, Saudi Arabia acceded to the Mercenaries Convention with a reservation in respect of Article 17(1) by which Saudi Arabia does not consider itself bound

SENEGAL

Implementation

- Decree No. 97.674 establishing the Interministerial Committee on Human Rights and International Humanitarian Law [Comité interministériel des droits de l'homme et du droit international humanitaire] on 2 July 1997

The Interministerial Committee includes representatives of the Ministries of Foreign Affairs, Justice, the Interior, the Armed Forces, Finance, the Modernisation of the State, National Education, Communications, Children and Family Welfare, and the University of Dakar. It is charged with drawing up, presenting and following up periodic reports to international bodies dealing with human rights and with coordinating and following up all administrative measures relating to human rights and IHL. It shall oversee the adaption of laws and regulations in force relating to human rights and international humanitarian law.[166]

Signings, Ratifications, Accessions, Successions, Denounciations, Reservations, etc.
- ☛ Senegal signed the CWC on 13 January 1993 and ratified it on 20 July 1998
- ☛ Senegal signed the Safety Convention on 21 February 1995
- ☛ Senegal signed the Landmines Treaty on 3 December 1997

SEYCHELLES

Signings, Ratifications, Accessions, Successions, Denounciations, Reservations, etc.
- ☛ Seychelles signed the CWC on 15 January 1993 and ratified it on 7 April 1993
- ☛ Seychelles signed the Landmines Treaty on 3 December 1997

SIERRA LEONE

Signings, Ratifications, Accessions, Successions, Denounciations, Reservations, etc.
- ☛ Sierra Leone signed the CWC on 15 January 1993
- ☛ Sierra Leone signed the Safety Convention on 13 February 1995
- ☛ Sierra Leone signed the Landmines Treaty on 29 July 1998

SINGAPORE

Signings, Ratifications, Accessions, Successions, Denounciations, Reservations, etc.
- ☛ Singapore signed the CWC on 14 January 1993 and ratified it on 21 May 1997
- ☛ Singapore ratified the Genocide Convention on 18 October 1995
- ☛ Singapore acceded to the Safety Convention on 26 March 1996
- ☛ Singapore ratified the CRC on 5 October 1997 with reservations

SLOVAKIA

Signings, Ratifications, Accessions, Successions, Denounciations, Reservations, etc.
- ☛ Slovakia signed the CWC on 14 January 1993 and ratified it on 27 October 1997

166. *Supra* n. 52.

- On 13 March 1995, Slovakia made a declaration under Article 90(2)(a) of Additional Protocol I of 1977 recognising the competence of the International Fact-Finding Commission
- Slovakia signed the Safety Convention on 28 December 1995 and ratified it on 26 June 1996
- Slovakia signed the Landmines Treaty on 3 December 1997

SLOVENIA

Penal Code (Crimes against Humanity)

- Slovene Penal Code, Chapter 35, Criminal Offences Against Humanity and International Law. Published in the *Official Gazette of the Republic of Slovenia* No. 63 on 13 October 1994 [Kazenski zakonik Republike Slovenije (Penal Code); Uradni list Republike Slovenije stevilka (No.): 63/94]. Entered into force 1 January 1995[167]

Signings, Ratifications, Accessions, Successions, Denounciations, Reservations, etc.

- Slovenia signed the CWC on 14 January 1993 and ratified it on 11 June 1997

SOLOMON ISLANDS

Signings, Ratifications, Accessions, Successions, Denounciations, Reservations, etc.

- Solomon Islands ratified the CRC on 10 April 1995
- Solomon Islands signed the Landmines Treaty on 4 December 1997

SOMALIA

Peace Agreement

- Somalia Political Leaders: Cairo Declaration on Somalia [aimed at achieving national reconciliation and the formation of a national government in Somalia]. Published as annex to Letter dated 22 December 1997 from the Permanent Representative of Egypt to the United Nations Addressed to the President of the Security Council, UN Doc. S/1997/1000, 29 December 1997. Also published in 37 *ILM* (July 1998) p. 780

SOUTH AFRICA[168]

Truth and Reconciliation

- Promotion of National Unity and Reconciliation Act, 1995. Act No. 34, 1995. Published in the *Republic of South Africa Government Gazette* (Capetown, 26 July 1995). No. 16579. Vol. 361

167. Information provided by Grega Peljhan, Attorney at Aleš Rojs, Ljubljana, Slovenia.

168. Information provided by Professor Michael Cowling, School of Law, University of Natal, Pietermaritzburg, South Africa.

Landmines

- ☛ Memorandum on Cooperation on Disarmament between South Africa and New Zealand, 8 August 1996
- ☛ Fact Sheet - South Africa's Initiatives on Banning Anti-Personnel Mines, February 1997
- ☛ Press statement by the Minister of Defence: SA Government Policy on Anti-Personnel Landmines. Parliament, 20 February 1997

COMMENT BY M.G. COWLING

'South Africa acceded to the 1980 Convention on Prohibitions or Restrictions on the Use of Certain Conventional Weapons which may be Deemed to be Excessively Injurious or have Indiscriminate Effects (and its Protocols) on 13 September 1995 and became a State Party to the Convention on 13 March 1996.

South Africa attended the first two sessions of the Review Conference of the CCW Convention (from 25 September to 13 October 1995 in Vienna and 15 to 19 January 1996 in Geneva) as an observer, and the final session (22 April to 3 May 1996 in Geneva) as a State Party. The South African Government regarded the amendments to Protocol II of the Convention (on Prohibitions or Restrictions on Mines, Booby-traps, etc.) that were adopted at the final session of the Review Conference as part of a process toward the achievement of the ultimate goal of the eventual elimination of landmines. This was followed by the signing of a Memorandum of Cooperation by President Mandela (South Africa) and Prime Minister Bolger (New Zealand) on 8 August 1996 in which the worldwide elimination of anti-personnel landmines was called for in view of the 'suffering and casualities caused by landmines to civilians'.

In addition, South Africa was one of 50 states that actively participated in the International Strategy Conference 'Towards a Global Ban on Anti-personnel Mines', held from 3-5 October 1996, which committed participants to ensure 'the earliest possible conclusion of a legally binding international agreement to ban anti-personnel land-mines'.

South Africa also co-sponsored the 1994 and 1995 UN GA Resolutions on the Moratorium on the Export of Anti-Personnel Landmines' which called for 'further immediate efforts to seek solutions to the problems caused by anti-personnel landmines with a view to their eventual elimination' as well as the 1996 GA Resolution titled 'An International Agreement to ban Anti-personnel Landmines' which urges states to pursue vigorously an effective, legally binding and international agreement to ban the use, stockpiling, production and transfer of anti-personnel landmines with a view to completing the negotiations as soon as possible.

This resulted in the Minister of Defence making a pronouncement before Parliament on 20 February 1997 to the effect that the use, development, production and stockpiling of anti-personnel mines in South Africa has been banned with immediate effect.

This pronouncement was accompanied by an endorsement of one of the ICRC's fundamental humanitarian principles to the effect that the "limited military utility of anti-personnel mines is far outweighed by the appalling humanitarian consequences of their use in actual conflicts. On this basis, their prohibition and elimination should be pursued as a matter of utmost urgency by governments and the entire international community."

This statement further announces that, as a result of this endorsement, the South African Government (through the Ministry of Foreign Affairs) reinforced efforts to bring about a universal ban on landmines and their complete elimination. To this extent, the Government undertakes to do everything possible to encourage and influence governments and international institutions to adopt this position.

In order to give internal effect to this undertaking, the Government has pledged to destroy its existing stockpile of 160,000 landmines as well as to undertake demining activities in neighbouring states such as Mozambique and Angola.'

Implemention (Humanitarian Affairs Committee)

☛ A National Committee on Humanitarian Affairs was established on 21 June 1995 with representatives of the Ministry of Foreign Affairs, the South African Defence Force and the South African Red Cross Society[169]

Implementation (Protocols I and II Additional to the Geneva Conventions of 1949)

☛ White Paper on Defence: Defence in Democracy: Department of Defence, May 1996

☛ Department of Defence: Civic Education Manual, September 1997

COMMENT BY M.G. COWLING

'As a result of the South African Government's accession to Geneva Protocols I and II (1977) in November 1995, the Department of Defence prepared two policy papers in order to ensure that the rules and principles contained in the Protocols as well as the fundamental principles of IHL are incorporated into South African law and may therefore be properly enforced. The White Paper on Defence states that IHL will enjoy primary consideration in the preparation and execution of military operations. As a result, the South African Defence Force, together with the ICRC, is currently developing a comprehensive curriculum on IHL.'

169. *Supra* n. 3 at p. 95.

Cases

- ☛ *The Azanian Peoples Organization (Azapo),* et al v. *The President of the Republic of South Africa,* et al. Constitutional Court of South Africa, Case CCT 17/96, 25 July 1996

Signings, Ratifications, Accessions, Successions, Denounciations, Reservations, etc.

- ☛ South Africa signed the CWC on 14 January 1993 and ratified it on 13 September 1995
- ☛ South Africa signed the Landmines Treaty on 3 December 1997 and ratified it on 26 June 1998
- ☛ On 26 June 1998, South Africa ratified Protocol IV and amended Protocol II of the CCW Convention, following its accession to its Protocols I, II and III on 13 September 1995

SPAIN[170]

Penal Code

- ☛ Organic Law [Ley Orgánica] of Parliament 10/95 of 23 November 1995. Entered into force 24 May 1996 [introducing new penal code][171]

COMMENT BY ANTONI PIGRAU SOLÉ

'The Ley Orgánica [Organic Act] of Parliament 10/95 of 23 November 1995, which introduced a new penal code (hereinafter, NPC) to Spain and which has been in force since 24 May 1996, is a landmark that concludes a long process which began after the passing of the Spanish Constitution in 1978. Over a period of almost twenty years, there were a variety of drafts and bills for the penal code, and many partial reforms of the code that had been in force since 1973[172] and whose basic structure can, in fact, be traced back to 1848.

The text of the penal code in force up to the Act of Parliament of 1995 did not explicitly deal with crimes of humanitarian international law, which were limited to military legislation.[173] In fact, the only internationally important crimes included in the old penal code were in the First Title of Book II. Under the inadequate rubric of "Crimes against the overseas safety of the State", "crimes of treason" (chapter 1), "crimes which threaten the peace or independence of the State" (chapter 2) and

170. Information provided by Antoni Pigrau i Solé, Vice-rector D'Estudiants i Docència, Professor of Public International law, Rovira i Virgili University (Tarragona), Spain.

171. Title XXIV of the New Penal Code, dealing with Crimes against the International Community, is reproduced at p. 636.

172. Act 55/71 of 15 November 1971 and Decree 3096/1973 of 15 September 1973.

173. Spain acceded to the four Geneva Conventions of 12 August 1949 on 4 August 1952 and the Convention for the Protection of Cultural Property in the Event of Armed Conflict of 14 May 1954 on 7 July 1960. Spain acceded to the two Additional Protocols of 1977 on 11 April 1989.

"crimes relative to national defence" (chapter 2A) were mixed in "crimes against the *ius gentium*" (chapter 3) which typified the crimes against internationally protected people, in accordance with the Convention of 14 December 1973[174] (violation of the personal immunity of the Head of another state or of an internationally protected person)[175] and the crime of genocide, in accordance with the Convention of 9 December 1948.[176] Also mixed in with all the above were the crimes of piracy (chapter 4), in accordance with the Convention on the High Seas of 29 April 1958. In particular, Articles 136 and 137, which dealt with the *ius gentium*, had been introduced by the Act of Parliament 8/1983 of 25 June 1983 and Article 137A (the crime of genocide) by Act 44/71 of 15 November 1971, which contained the recast text of the penal code.

Title XXIV of the NPC is entitled "Crimes against the International Community", which supposes from the outset that there is a new juridic asset deserving protection that goes beyond the scope of the state and beyond the viewpoint that justified protecting those interests that affected the state, to assume the protection of the interests of the International Community, as have been formulated in the relevant international agreements.[177]

Title XXIV is divided into four chapters: crimes against the *ius gentium*, genocide crimes, crimes against protected people and property in the event of armed conflict and the common provisions for them all.[178]

The first chapter deals with crimes against the *ius gentium*. Articles 605 and 606 describe the crimes typified in the former Articles 136 and 137: causing death or other injuries or committing any other crime against a foreign Head of State or other internationally protected person, as well as crimes against local officials and the private residences or means of transport of such people, and violating their personal immunity. In both cases, the condition of reciprocity is upheld although the wording in the case of Article 606 makes it practically inoperative.[179]

174. Spain acceded to the Convention on 8 August 1985.

175. Spain acceded to the Vienna Convention on Diplomatic Relations of 18 April 1961 on 21 November 1967 and the Vienna Convention on Consular Relations of 24 April 1963 on 3 February 1970.

176. Spain acceded to this Convention on 13 September 1968.

177. See D. López Garrido and M. García Arán, *El Código penal de 1995 y la voluntad del legislador* [The Penal Code of 1995 and the will of the legislator] (Madrid, 1996) pp. 208-209.

178. The crime of piracy disappears from the penal code but, however, is still typified in the special penal laws: Arts. 9 and 10 of the Penal Act of the Merchant Navy [Ley Penal de la Marina Mercante] and Arts. 39 and 40 of the Penal and Procedural Act of Aerial Navigation [Ley Penal y Procesal de la Navegación Aérea].

179. See G. Quintero Olivares et al., *Comentarios a la Parte Especial del Derecho Penal* [Comments on the Special Part of the Penal Law] (Pamplona, Aranzadi, 1996) pp. 1637-1638.

The second chapter deals with the crime of genocide. The text of Article 607 corresponds, generally speaking, to the former Article 137A, although there are important modifications in the following aspects:
1) the placement of a comma between the terms "ethnic" and "national" in the first paragraph, thus making the description of those groups likely to suffer genocide coincide more exactly with the terms of the 1948 Convention;[180] 2) the inclusion of sexual aggression among those acts that constitute genocide, a direct result of the armed conflict in the former Yugoslavia which signified an extension of the concept contained in the Convention of 1948; 3) the greater grading of the penalties according to the gravity of the different acts that constitute genocide. It is noteworthy that the penalties for diffusing the ideas or doctrines which condone or justify acts of genocide or which attempt to rehabilitate regimes or institutions that defend such crimes are typified separately in paragraph 2. This had been introduced in the previous penal code by the Act of Parliament 4/95 of 11 May 1995, although it is no longer described as an apologia.[181]

Finally, it should be pointed out that, according to Article 131(4) of the NPC, genocide is the only crime in the penal code that is imprescriptible. The third chapter includes, for the first time in a Spanish penal code, crimes against protected people and property in the event of armed conflict. Until now, and only since the Act of Parliament 13/1985 of 9 December 1985, these crimes were provided for in the military penal code, although only partially, because it was applicable exclusively to military personnel. Since the NPC came into force, two parallel systems of provision have been applied[182] (although they do not totally coincide substantively or as far as the technique for determining penalties is concerned) in which the

180. In the first text of 1971, the term 'social' was used instead of the term 'racial'. The modification in 1983 substituted the term 'social' for 'racial' although there was no separation between the term 'ethnic' and the term 'national'. That is to say, it spoke of the 'racial, religious or ethnic national group'.

181. For a critique of this option, see G. Quintero Olivares et al., op. cit. n.179, at pp. 1640-1642.

182. From a substantial approach, while the Spanish Military Criminal Code does not include any type of crime to protect cultural goods, the NPC does. Looking at it from the point of view of the penal technique, the Military Criminal Code follows the criterion of aggravating common crimes when they take place during an armed conflict; and the new Criminal Code prefers the confluence of crimes, adding to the breaches of IHL - for which a less grevious penalty is foreseen - the punishment derived from the concrete attack on protected persons or goods.

military or civilian status of the perpetrator of the crime means applying the military penal code or the common NPC.[183]

The third chapter of the NPC includes Articles 608 to 614. These articles comprise the serious offences committed against protected people and property contained in the Geneva Conventions of 1949, the two Additional Protocols of 1977, and even regulations derived from the 1954 Hague Convention for the Protection of Cultural Property in Armed Conflict.

An important aspect is that the penalties established in these articles for violating the regulations of international humanitarian law are to be added to those penalties which derive from the nature of the specific results produced (injuries or others). That is the meaning of the repeated sentence "notwithstanding the penalty that might correspond for the result produced". So, for instance, an act of violence against a protected person might mean imprisonment for four to eight years, according to Article 609, and also the penalty typified in the Criminal Code for those crimes against persons, depending on the resulting outcomes (injuries, death, etc.). Another striking aspect is that these articles, do not explicitly mention crimes of a sexual nature other than enforced prostitution in Article 612(3), unlike the aforementioned case of genocide.

The fourth chapter is made up of Articles 615 and 616 and contains the common provisions for the previous chapters. The acts of provocation, conspiracy and proposition to commit the crimes established are stipulated and sanctions of disqualification for such crimes are envisaged.

In short, the NPC is a very positive qualitative step towards integrating the interests of the international community in the Spanish penal code. The relevant crimes are more systematized, although there is still room for improvement in some of the specific solutions adopted.'

International Tribunal

☛ Organisation Act 15/1994 of 1 June 1994 on Co-operation with the International Tribunal for the Prosecution of Persons Responsible for Serious Violations of International Humanitarian Law committed in the Territory of the Former Yugoslavia

183. For a commentary on the regulations of the military penal code, see J. M. Silva Sánchez, 'Represión de los crímenes de guerra y crímenes internacionales en el Derecho penal español' [Repression of War Crimes and International Crimes in Spanish Criminal Law], in V. Abellán Honrubia, ed., *La regulación jurídica internacional de los conflictos armados* [International Legal Regulation of Armed Conflicts] (Barcelona, Cruz Roja Cataluña, 1992) pp. 182-185

Ongoing Cases (concerning human rights violations in Argentina and Chile during the military Juntas)

COMMENT BY ANTONI PIGRAU I SOLÉ

'Different accusations brought by the Association of Progressive Prosecutors Union (Unión Progresista de Fiscales) became, in June 1996 and February 1997, the beginning of two proceedings at the Audiencia Nacional – a nationwide special court for certain crimes – against, respectively, those responsible for serious breaches of human rights in Argentina (between 1976 and 1983) and Chile (between 1973 and 1990), whom they accuse of genocide and terrorism. Both proceedings are now in the instruction phase, and the judges in charge – those in the central instructing courts (Juzgados centrales de instrucción) N° 5 and 6 – have issued orders deciding that Spanish courts are competent to deal with those crimes (against the opinion of the prosecutors that have asked for the proceedings to be filed) and have also issued citations for those accused to appear in front of them, and have even put some of them in prison. The last of these judicial decrees was issued by the central instructing court N° 5 on 25 March 1998 (case 19/97).'

Signings, Ratifications, Accessions, Successions, Denounciations, Reservations, etc.

- ☛ Spain signed the Safety Convention on 19 December 1994 and ratified it on 13 January 1998
- ☛ Spain signed the Landmines Treaty on 3 December 1997
- ☛ On 19 January 1998, Spain ratified Protocol IV of the CCW Convention, and on 27 January 1998 it ratified its amended Protocol II. Spain became a party to the CCW Convention on 29 December 1993

SRI LANKA

Signings, Ratifications, Accessions, Successions, Denounciations, Reservations, etc.

- ☛ Sri Lanka signed the CWC on 14 January 1993 and ratified it on 19 August 1994

SUDAN

Signings, Ratifications, Accessions, Successions, Denounciations, Reservations, etc.

- ☛ Sudan signed the Landmines Treaty on 4 December 1997

SURINAME

Signings, Ratifications, Accessions, Successions, Denounciations, Reservations, etc.

- ☛ Suriname signed the CWC on 28 April 1997 and ratified it on 28 April 1997
- ☛ Suriname signed the Landmines Treaty on 4 December 1997

SWAZILAND

Signings, Ratifications, Accessions, Successions, Denounciations, Reservations, etc.

- Swaziland ratified the CRC on 7 September 1995 with reservations
- Swaziland signed the CWC on 23 September 1993 and ratified it on 20 November 1996
- On 2 November 1995, Swaziland acceded to Additional Protocols I and II of 1977
- Swaziland signed the Landmines Treaty on 4 December 1997

SWEDEN

International Criminal Tribunal

- Act relating to the Establishment of an International Tribunal for Trial of Crimes Committed in former Yugoslavia, SFS 1994:569, 13 June 1994
- Act amending the Act relating to the Establishment of an International Tribunal for Trial of Crimes Committed in former Yugoslavia, issued on 7 December 1995, entered into force 1 January 1996 (extending application to Rwanda Tribunal)

Implementation

- An Advisory Council on International Law, with emphasis on IHL, was set up in 1995 by the Ministry for Foreign Affairs. It is composed of legal, technical, military and medical experts and members of the Ministries of Foreign Affairs and Defence and is under the Chairmanship of the Ministry of Defence. Its mandate is to advise the Ministry of Foreign Affairs on international law in general and on IHL in particular.[184]

Signings, Ratifications, Accessions, Successions, Denounciations, Reservations, etc.

- Sweden signed the CWC on 13 January 1993 and ratified it on 17 June 1993
- Sweden signed the Safety Convention on 15 December 1994 and ratified it on 25 June 1996
- On 15 January 1997, Sweden ratified Protocol IV and on 16 July 1997 it ratified amended Protocol II of the CCW Convention.
- Sweden signed the Landmines Treaty on 4 December 1997

SWITZERLAND[185]

International Criminal Tribunals

- Message of the Federal Council to the Federal Assembly dated 18 October 1995 concerning cooperation with the International Tribunals for the Prosecution of Persons Responsible for Serious Violations of International Humanitarian Law [Message concernant l'arrêté fédéral relatif à la coopération avec les tribunaux

184. *Supra* n. 3 at p. 96.

185. Information provided by Anne-Marie La Rosa, International Labour Office, Freedom of Association Branch, Geneva and A.D. Henchoz, Swiss Department of Foreign Affairs, Bern.

internationaux chargés de poursuivre les violations graves du droit international humanitaire, en date du 18 octobre 1995]. Published in *Feuille fédérale* IV 1065

☛ Federal Decree on the cooperation with the International Tribunals for the Prosecution of Persons Responsible for Serious Violations of International Humanitarian Law, dated 21 December 1995 [Arrêté fédéral relatif à la coopération avec les tribunaux internationaux chargés de poursuivre les violations graves du droit international humanitaire, en date du 21 décembre 1995]. Published in *Recueil systématique du droit fédéral* 351.20

COMMENT BY A.D. HENCHOZ AND A.-M. LA ROSA

'A Federal Decree was adopted by Switzerland on 21 December 1995 organising cooperation with the International Tribunal for the Prosecution of Persons Responsible for Serious Violations of International Humanitarian Law committed in the Territory of the former Yugoslavia since 1991 (hereinafter, ICTY) and the International Tribunal to Prosecute Those Responsible for Genocide and Other Serious Violations of International Humanitarian Law committed in Rwanda between 1 January 1994 and 31 December 1994 (hereinafter, ICTR).

Before December 1995, Switzerland had already enacted, on 20 March 1981, federal legislation on international cooperation in criminal matters.[186] The 1981 law applies to interstate cooperation in the field of criminal matters generally and cannot be directly used for regulating relations with international tribunals. However, its provisions could be referred to *mutatis mutandis* in order to put into place the various means of cooperation required by the Security Council resolutions establishing the ICTY and ICTR.

It should be observed that the Swiss Federal Decree provides *inter alia* for the suppression of recourse at the cantonal level[187]; the spontaneous transmission of relevant information and evidence to the international tribunals; the deferral of Swiss courts to the competence of the International Tribunals; and the transfer of Swiss citizens to the International Tribunals on condition that they will be returned to Switzerland at the end of the procedure. The provisions of the Federal Decree cover cooperation with the ICTY and the ICTR only and should not be understood as regulating the relationship with the permanent international criminal court. However, the scope of the Decree could be extended to similar *ad hoc* international criminal tribunals established by Security Council resolutions pursuant to Chapter VII of

186. Loi fédérale sur l'entraide internationale en materière pénale, RS 351.1.

187. In order to avoid unnecessary delay. Recourse may, however, be made to the Federal Tribunal against a decision of a first instance authority competent to deal with the International Tribunal's requests.

the United Nations Charter. The Swiss Decree will remain in effect until 31 December 2003.'

Chemical Weapons

- Message of the Federal Council to the Federal Assembly dated 20 April 1994 concerning the Convention on the Prohibition of the Development, Production, Stockpiling and Use of Chemical Weapons and on their Destruction [Message, en date du 20 avril 1994, concernant la Convention sur l'interdiction de la mise au point, de la fabrication, du stockage et de l'emploi des armes chimiques et sur leur destruction]. Published in *Feuille fédérale* 1994 III 1
- Federal Decree concerning the Convention on the Prohibition of the Development, Production, Stockpiling and Use of Chemical Weapons and on their Destruction, dated 7 October 1994 [Arrêté fédéral concernant la Convention sur l'interdiction de la mise au point, de la fabrication, du stockage et de l'emploi des armes chimiques et sur leur destruction, en date du 7 octobre 1994] [authorising the ratification of the Convention]. Published in *Recueil officiel des lois fédérales* 1998 334
- Federal Decree concerning the Execution of the CWC, dated 7 October 1994. Entered into force 1 January 1997 [Arrêté fédéral concernant l'exécution de la Convention sur les armes chimiques, en date du 7 octobre 1994 et entré en vigueur le 1 janvier 1997]. Published in *Recueil systematique du droit fédéral* 515.08

COMMENT BY A.D. HENCHOZ AND A.-M. LA ROSA

'The Convention on the Prohibition of the Development, Production, Stockpiling and Use of Chemical Weapons and on their Destruction (hereinafter, the CWC) was signed by Switzerland on 14 January 1995 and ratified on 10 March 1995. Dated 7 October 1994, the Federal Decree implementing the Convention at the national level entered into force 1 January 1997.

In its message of 20 April 1994 to the Federal Assembly, the Federal Council stated that the CWC was the first international agreement on global disarmament which comprised a verification mechanism prohibiting a whole category of weapons of mass destruction. It recalled that Switzerland did not possess any weapons of mass destruction. With the Treaty on the Non-Proliferation of Nuclear Weapons of 1968 (entered into force in 1970), the CWC represents the most important multilateral agreement from a security policy point of view, aiming at the complete destruction of chemical weapons. The support given by the Swiss chemical industry to the ratification of the Convention was essential as its efficient implementation involves regular inspections in this sector.'

Conventional Weapons Convention

- Statement of Ambassador Lucius Caflisch, Legal Adviser to the Swiss Ministry of Foreign Affairs, dated 3 May 1996 [Déclaration prononcée le 3 mai 1996 par l'Ambassadeur Lucius Caflisch, Jurisconsulte du Département fédéral des affaires étrangères, Chef de la délégation suisse. Annexed to the Message mentioned above and reproduced in *Feuille fédérale* 1997 IV 32
- Federal Law on War Equipment dated 13 December 1996, entered into force 1 April 1998 [Loi fédérale sur le matériel de guerre du 13 décembre 1996, entrée en vigeur le 1er avril 1998.] *Recueil systematique du droit fédéral* 514.51
- Message of the Federal Council to the Federal Assembly dated 14 May 1997 on the revised Protocol on Prohibitions or Restrictions on the Use of Mines, Booby-traps and Other Devices (Protocol II as modified) and the Additional Protocol on Blinding Laser Weapons (Protocol IV) to the 1980 Convention on Prohibitions or Restrictions on the Use of Certain Conventional Weapons which may be Deemed to be Excessively Injurious or to have Indiscriminate Effects [Message du 14 mai 1997 concernant le Protocole II révisé et le Protocole IV joints à la Convention de 1980 sur les armes conventionnelles]. *Feuille fédérale* 1997 IV 1
- Federal Decree approving Revised Protocol II and Protocol IV Additional to the 1980 Convention on Conventional Weapons, dated 8 December 1997 [Arrêté fédéral approuvant le Protocole II révisé et le Protocole IV joints à la Convention de 1980 sur les armes conventionnelles, en date du 8 décembre 1997]

COMMENT BY A.D. HENCHOZ AND A.-M. LA ROSA

'The 1980 Convention on Prohibitions or Restrictions on the Use of Certain Conventional Weapons which may be Deemed to be Excessively Injurious or to have Indiscriminate Effects (and its Protocols) was ratified by Switzerland on 20 August 1982. Pursuant to Article 5(1) of the Convention, it entered into force 2 December 1983.

The Review Conference of the State Parties to the 1980 Convention resulted in the revision of Protocol II and the adoption of a new text on blinding laser weapons (Protocol IV), prohibiting recourse to weapons which are specifically conceived to induce blindness.[188]

In its message to the Federal Assembly of 14 May 1997, the Federal Council observed that the protection granted to combatants by Protocol IV was substantial but not complete since the use of (laser) weapons which did not entail blindness remained legal. It nevertheless marked significant progress in the field of international humanitarian law. On the other hand, revised Protocol II was not entirely satisfactory. Only a complete prohibition on the use, production and transfer of

188. At its 8th plenary meeting, on 13 October 1995, the Review Conference, by consensus, adopted the text of the Protocol on Blinding Laser Weapons (Protocol IV) (CCW/CONF.I/7). On

anti-personnel mines – as provided by the Swiss legislation on war equipment adopted on 13 December 1996 – would make it possible to control or ban the indiscriminate use of such a weapon. In this regard, it should be recalled that, on 24 November 1995, the Swiss Federal Military Department announced that it renounced totally the possession and use of anti-personnel mines. The destruction of the last stocks of this ammunition was completed on 2 December 1997. Humanitarian considerations led Switzerland to accept revised Protocol II, since it introduced certain improvements which it felt should be encouraged. Therefore, Switzerland signified its consent to be bound by revised Protocol II and Protocol IV on 24 March 1998. Revised Protocol II was approved with an interpretative declaration concerning anti-personnel mines as defined in Article 2(3) of the Protocol.[189] Regarding Protocol IV, Switzerland stated that its provisions would be applied in all circumstances thus covering, *inter alia*, both international and non-international armed conflicts.'

Landmines

☛ Message of the Federal Council to the Federal Assembly dated 19 January 1998 on the Convention on the Prohibition of the Use, Stockpiling, Production and Transfer of Anti-Personnel Mines and on their Destruction [Message concernant la Convention sur l'interdiction de l'emploi, du stockage, de la production et du transfert des mines antipersonnel et sur leur destruction, en date du 19 janvier 1998]. *Feuille fédérale* 1998 537

COMMENT BY A.D. HENCHOZ AND A.-M. LA ROSA

'In its message to the Federal Assembly, the Federal Council stated that the Convention represented an entirely new text and was an opening with regard to international humanitarian law. Contrary to existing instruments, the Convention not only restricted the use of anti-personnel mines but envisaged a complete

12 December 1995, the UN SG circulated Protocol IV to all states. At its 14th plenary meeting, on 3 May 1996, the Conference adopted by consensus the amended Protocol II on Prohibitions or Restrictions on the Use of Mines, Booby-traps and Other Devices. See Final Report of the Review Conference of the States Parties to the Convention on Prohibitions or Restrictions on the Use of Certain Conventional Weapons Which May be Deemed to be Excessively Injurious or to have Indiscriminate Effects.' Geneva 1996 (GE.96-61703) CCW.CONF.I/16 (Part I), paras. 36-37. For the text of Protocol IV, see p. 594; for the text of amended Protocol II, see p. XX. For commentary on Protocol IV, see Zöckler, p. 333.

189. Art. 2 (3) defines anti-personnel mines, for the purposes of the Protocol, as 'a mine primarily designed to be exploded by the presence, proximity or contact of a person and that will incapacitate, injure or kill one or more persons'. In its interpretative declaration, Switzerland specified that it interprets the definition of anti-personnel mines as excluding all mines designed to be exploded by the presence, proximity or contact of a vehicle, when equipped with an anti-manipulation device.

prohibition of this ammunition in banning the use, stockpiling, production and transfer of anti-personnel mines. Also, the scope and extent of international cooperation and assistance which were essential to efficient implementation of the Convention were extensively covered by its provisions.

In March 1998, the definition of anti-personnel mines found in the Swiss legislation on war equipment, mentioned above, was revised to take into account the definition now found in the Convention.'

Cases

☛ *In re.* G. First Division Military Tribunal, Lausanne. Hearings held from 14 to 18 April 1997. Decision: 18 April 1997. Except for the evaluation of moral damages incurred by the accused, the decision was confirmed by the Appeal Military Tribunal [Tribunal militaire de Cassation]. Moral damages were reduced from 70 000 SF to 50 000 SF by a military appeals court

COMMENT BY A.D. HENCHOZ AND A.-M. LA ROSA

'Hearings were held from 14 to 18 April 1997 before a bench comprised of one President and three Judges. G. was accused of having committed violations of the laws and customs of war pursuant to Article 109 of the Swiss military penal code[190]. It was alleged *inter alia* that in May, July and August 1992, the accused participated in the beatings of prisoners at Keraterm and Omarska camps in the Prijedor area of Bosnia and Herzegovina, causing injury to their bodily or mental health. G. was also accused of having committed outrages upon personal dignity by forcing one prisoner to lick the boots of a person in uniform who was accompanying him. After consideration by the Tribunal, the accused was acquitted, having successfully raised a doubt regarding his effective presence in the territory of Bosnia and Herzegovina when the crimes were allegedly committed.

With regard to the nature of the armed conflict in Bosnia and Herzegovina in 1992, the Tribunal considered that:

> the conflict in the former Yugoslavia shall be considered and qualified globally as an international conflict. The armed conflict in the former Yugoslavia between the armed forces of the Federal Republic of Yugoslavia and the armed forces

190. Art. 109 reads as follows: Violations of the Laws of War (violations des lois de la guerre):
(1) Whoever acts contrary to the provisions of any international agreement governing the laws of war or the protection of persons and property, or whoever acts in violation of any other recognized law or custom of war shall be punished with imprisonment except in cases where other provisions involving more severe sanctions are applicable. For offences of high gravity, the penalty is penal servitude.
(2) For offences of little gravity, the punishment can consist of a disciplinary sanction.

of Slovenia and Croatia started soon after their declaration of independence on 25 June 1991. This armed conflict shall be considered as internal since the declarations of independence were suspended for three months at the request of the European Community. At the expiration of this period, on 7 October 1991, Slovenia proclaimed its independence with effect on that date and Croatia followed with effect on 9 October 1991. Therefore, starting on 8 October 1991, the armed conflict in the former Yugoslavia shall be qualified as international since these two States were independent. All States had adhered to the Geneva Conventions.[191]'

Signings, Ratifications, Accessions, Successions, Denounciations, Reservations, etc.
- Switzerland signed the CWC on 14 January 1993 and ratified it on 10 March 1995
- Switzerland ratified the CRC on 24 February 1997
- On 24 March 1998, Switzerland ratified Protocol IV and amended Protocol II of the CCW Convention.
- Switzerland signed the Landmines Treaty on 3 December 1997 and ratified it on 24 March 1998

Pending (ratifications):
- Switzerland is now examining the possibility of acceding to the Genocide Convention

TAJIKISTAN

Peace Agreement and National Reconciliation
- Letter dated 24 December 1996 from the Permanent Representative of the Russian Federation to the United Nations Addressed to the Secretary-General. S/1996/1070, Annex I: Agreement between the President of the Republic of Tajikistan, E. S. Rakhmonov, and the leader of the United Tajik Opposition, S.A. Nuri, on the results of the meeting held in Moscow on 23 December; Annex II: Protocol on the main functions of the Commission on National Reconcilation
- Protocol on the main functions and powers of the Commission on National Reconciliation. S/1996/1070, Annex II, 27 December 1996

Signings, Ratifications, Accessions, Successions, Denounciations, Reservations, etc.
- Tajikistan signed the CWC on 14 January 1993 and ratified it on 11 January 1995

191. Judgement, pp. 8-9. For further commentary on this case, see Andreas R. Ziegler in 92 *AJIL*, (January 1998) p. 78. For a contrary finding on the character of the conflict, see the opinion of the majority in *Prosecutor* v. *Tadić*, Opinion and Judgment, Case No. IT-94-1-T, 7 May 1997, paras. 577-608. See Year in Review at pp. 139-141.

- On 10 September 1997, Tajikistan agreed to accept the competence of the International Humanitarian Fact-Finding Commission under Article 90(2)(a) of Additional Protocol I

TANZANIA

Signings, Ratifications, Accessions, Successions, Denounciations, Reservations, etc.

- Tanzania signed the CWC on 25 February 1994 and ratified it on 25 June 1998
- Tanzania signed the Landmines Treaty on 3 December 1997

THAILAND

Signings, Ratifications, Accessions, Successions, Denounciations, Reservations, etc.

- Thailand signed the CWC on 14 January 1993
- Thailand signed the Landmines Treaty on 3 December 1997

TOGO

Implementation

- Interministerial Order No. 97-031 of 11 June 1997 establishing the Interministerial Commission for the application of International Humanitarian Law [Commission interministérielle de mise en oeuvre du droit international humanitaire]

Signings, Ratifications, Accessions, Successions, Denounciations, Reservations, etc.

- Togo signed the CWC on 13 January 1993 and ratified it on 23 April 1997
- On 4 December 1995, Togo acceded to Protocols I, II and III of the CCW Convention
- Togo signed the Safety Convention on 22 December 1995
- Togo signed the Landmines Treaty on 4 December 1997

TONGA

Signings, Ratifications, Accessions, Successions, Denounciations, Reservations, etc.

- Tonga ratified the CRC on 6 November 1995

TRINIDAD and TOBAGO

Signings, Ratifications, Accessions, Successions, Denounciations, Reservations, etc.

- Trinidad and Tobago acceded to the CWC on 24 June 1997
- Trinidad and Tobago signed the Landmines Treaty on 4 December 1997 and ratified it on 27 April 1998

TUNISIA

Signings, Ratifications, Accessions, Successions, Denounciations, Reservations, etc.

- Tunisia signed the CWC on 13 January 1993 and ratified it on 15 April 1997

- Tunisia signed the Safety Convention on 22 February 1995
- Tunisia signed the Landmines Treaty on 4 December 1997

TURKEY

Signings, Ratifications, Accessions, Successions, Denounciations, Reservations, etc.

- Turkey signed the CWC on 14 January 1993 and ratified it on 12 May 1997
- Turkey ratified the CRC on 4 April 1995 with reservations

TURKMENISTAN

Signings, Ratifications, Accessions, Successions, Denounciations, Reservations, etc.

- Turkmenistan signed the CWC on 12 October 1993 and ratified it on 29 September 1994
- On 18 September 1996, Turkmenistan acceded to the Mercenaries Convention without making any declarations or reservations
- Turkmenistan signed the Landmines Treaty on 3 December 1997 and ratified it on 19 January 1998

TUVALU

Signings, Ratifications, Accessions, Successions, Denounciations, Reservations, etc.

- Tuvalu ratifed the CRC on 22 September 1995

UGANDA

Signings, Ratifications, Accessions, Successions, Denounciations, Reservations, etc.

- Uganda signed the CWC on 14 January 1993
- On 14 November 1995, Uganda acceded to Protocols I, II and III of the CCW Convention
- Uganda signed the Landmines Treaty on 3 December 1997

UKRAINE

Signings, Ratifications, Accessions, Successions, Denounciations, Reservations, etc.

- Ukraine signed the CWC on 13 January 1993

UNITED ARAB EMIRATES

Signings, Ratifications, Accessions, Successions, Denounciations, Reservations, etc.

- United Arab Emirates signed the CWC on 2 February 1993
- United Arab Emirates ratified the CRC on 3 January 1997 with reservations

UNITED KINGDOM[192]

International Criminal Tribunals

- The United Nations (International Tribunal) (Former Yugoslavia) Order 1996. Enacted on 13 March 1996, entered into force 15 March 1996. *Statutory Instruments* 1996 No. 716
- The Joint Committee on Statutory Instruments, The United Nations (International Tribunal) (Former Yugoslavia) Order 1996. *Statutory Instruments* 1996 No. 716, Memorandum by the Foreign Office, 27 March 1996
- The United Nations (International Tribunal) (Rwanda) Order 1996. Enacted on 15 May 1996, entered into force 17 May 1996. *Statutory Instruments* 1996 No. 1296
- The United Nations (International Tribunal) (Former Yugoslavia) (Amendment) Order 1997. Enacted on 22 July 1997, entered into force 1 October 1997. *Statutory Instruments* 1997 No. 1752
- The United Nations (International Tribunal) (Rwanda) (Amendment) Order 1997. Enacted on 22 July 1997, entered into force 1 October 1997. *Statutory Instruments* 1997 No. 1751
- The United Nations (International Tribunals) (Former Yugoslavia and Rwanda) (Amendment) Order 1998. Enacted on 21 July 1998, entered into force 23 July 1998. *Statutory Instruments* 1998 No. 1755

Landmines

- Landmines Act 1998, 1998 Chapter 33. Enacted 28 July 1998
- Foreign and Commonwealth Office Explanatory Memorandum for the Ottawa Convention
- Letter of 29 July 1998 from Sir Jeremy Greenstock, United Kingdom Mission to the United Nations New York to Mr. Kofi Annan, UN Secretary-General enclosing Instrument of Ratification by the UK Government of the Landmines Treaty and containing statement in respect of that ratification[193]

192. Information provided by Professor Françoise Hampson, Dean of the School of Law, University of Essex. Thanks to Mr. Paul Berman, Assistant Legal Adviser, Foreign and Commonwealth Office, London, and Dr. Danesh Sarooshi, Lecturer in Public International Law, University College London, University of London.

193. The statement reads as follows: 'It is the understanding of the Government of the United Kingdom that the mere participation in the planning or execution of operations, exercises or other military planning activity by the United Kingdom's Armed Forces, or individual United Kingdom nationals, conducted in combination with the armed forces of States not party to the Convention on the Prohibition of the Use, Stockpiling, Production and Transfer of Anti-personnel Mines and of their Destruction, opened for signature at Ottawa on 3 December 1997, which engage in activity prohibited under that Convention, is not, by itself, assistance, encouragement or inducement for the purposes of Art. 1, paragraph 1 (c) of the Convention.'

Ratification of the Additional Protocols

- Letter to His Excellency, Mr. Flavio Cotti, Federal Councillor, President of the Swiss Confederation, 28 January 1998, enclosing the Instruments of Ratification of the United Kingdom of Additional Protocols I and II of 1977 to the Geneva Conventions of 1949 and containing the UK's statements regarding the Protocols. The Protocols came into force in the United Kingdom on 28 July 1998
- Statement by Mr. Tony Lloyd, Secretary of State for Foreign and Commonwealth Affairs, concerning the ratification of the Additional Protocols, Hansard, Written Answers, 28 January 1998, p. 270
- Geneva Conventions (Amendment) Act, 1995 [amending Geneva Conventions Act of 1957 to enable effect to be given to the Additional Protocols of 1977], Chapter 27, 19 July 1995
- The Geneva Conventions Act (First Protocol) Order 1998. Enacted on 21 July 1998, entered into force 28 July 1998. Statutory Instruments 1998 No. 1754. The Schedule to the Order contains the statements made by the United Kingdom when depositing its Instrument of Ratification of Protocol I[194]

UN Personnel

- United Nations Personnel Act, 1997 [to enable effect to be given to certain provisions of the Convention on the Safety of United Nations and Associated Personnel adopted by the GA on 9 December 1994] Ch. 13. Enacted 27 February 1997.

Pending (war crimes prosecutions):

- On 29 May 1998, a London magistrate ordered the trial on war crimes charges of *Andrzej Sawoniuk*, who is suspected of murdering Jews in Nazi-occupied Belarus during WWII. Sawoniuk will face four charges of killing two women and two men in the town of Domachevo between September and December 1942. Sawoniuk is the second person to be charged under Britain's 1991 War Crimes Act[195]. Four others are currently under investigation by Scotland Yard. The other person charged, Szymon Serafinowicz, who was accused of murdering three Jews while working as a senior policeman in Belarus during WWII, died in August 1997, six months after a jury ruled that he was not fit to stand trial.

Signings, Ratifications, Accessions, Successions, Denounciations, Reservations, etc.

- The United Kingdom signed the CWC on 13 Jan. 1993 and ratified it on 13 May 1996
- On 13 February 1995, the United Kingdom ratified Protocols I, II and III of the CCW Convention

194. Reprinted at p. 640.

195. War Crimes Act 1991, 1991 Chapter 13. Enacted 9 May 1991. The Act gives UK courts jurisdiction 'in respect of certain grave violations of the laws and customs of war committed in German-held territory during the Second World War and for connected purposes'.

- ☛ The United Kingdom signed the Landmines Treaty on 3 December 1997 and ratified it on 31 July 1998
- ☛ On 28 January 1998, the United Kingdom ratified Additional Protocols I and II of 1977
- ☛ On 6 May 1998, the United Kingdom ratified the Safety Convention.

UNITED STATES OF AMERICA[196]

War Crimes

- ☛ Cambodia Genocide Justice Act (11 U.S.C. 2656, Part D, Sections 571 - 574), May 1994. Available online at http://www.yale.edu/cgp/dccam/wwwcgja.txt
- ☛ United States War Crimes Act of 1996 (Public Law 104-192, 110 Stat. 2104, 18 U.S.C. 2401)[197]

COMMENT BY BURRUS CARNAHAN

'The War Crimes Act of 1996 for the first time grants penal jurisdiction over grave breaches of the 1949 Geneva Conventions to US Federal civilian courts. When the US ratified the 1949 Conventions in 1956, it was assumed, on the basis of the post-World War II war crimes trials, that grave breaches would generally be tried by US military courts (General Courts-Martial or Military Commissions). Since then, however, a number of decisions of the US Supreme Court have raised doubts as to the constitutionality of any trial of a civilian, including a former member of the US armed forces, by a military court. It should be noted that the War Crimes Act of 1996 bases its extra-territorial jurisdiction on the active and passive personality principles (i.e., either the victim or the defendant must be a US national or a member of the US armed forces), rather than on the principle of universal jurisdiction over war crimes. (United States legislation implementing the UN Convention on Torture, by comparison, does apply the principle of universal jurisdiction.[198]) Although the wording of the statute is not completely clear, it appears that the victim or defendant must have been a national of the United States at the time the grave breach was committed, and not merely at the time of trial.'

- ☛ Expanded War Crimes Act of 1997.[199] Section 583 of Foreign Operations, Export Financing, and Related Programs Appropriations Act, 1998 (Public Law: 105-118

196. Information provided by Mr. Burrus Carnahan, Senior Analyst, Science Applications International Corp., McClean, Va.; Lt. Colonel, USAF (ret); Commander Ron Neubauer, US Department of Defense, Office of General Counsel, Member of the Board of Recommendation,*YIHL*; and Professor em. Howard Levie, St. Louis University Law School.

197. Reprinted at p. 643.

198. See, Title 18 US Code section 2340A.

199. Reprinted at p. 643.

(11/26/97) (H.R.2159))

- Statement by Mr. Jenkins, Honorable Representative of Tennessee, regarding the Expanded War Crimes Act of 1997, House of Representatives, 28 July 1997, *Congressional Record* Page: H5865

COMMENT BY BURRUS CARNAHAN

'This legislation extends the 1996 War Crimes Act to certain violations of the 1907 Hague Regulations on Land Warfare, and to violations of common Article 3 of the Geneva Conventions. When the US becomes a party to the Protocol on Mines, Booby-Traps and Other Devices, as amended on 3 May 1996, wilful killing or injury to civilians in violation of the Protocol will also be punishable under this legislation. The Expanded War Crimes Act passed the lower house (House of Representatives) by a vote of 391 to 32 on 28 July 1997 and was referred to the upper house (Senate). In late 1997, the President signed it into law, as section 583 of a Foreign Appropriations Bill.'

International Criminal Tribunals

- Agreement on Surrender of Persons between the Government of the United States and the International Tribunal for the Prosecutions of Persons Responsible for Serious Violations of International Humanitarian Law in the Territory of the Former Yugoslavia, 5 October 1994
- Agreement on Surrender of Persons between the Government of the United States and the International Tribunal for the Prosecutions of Persons Responsible for Serious Violations of International Humanitarian Law in the Territory of Rwanda, 24 January 1995
- Judicial Assistance to the International Tribunal for Yugoslavia and to the International Tribunal for Rwanda, Pub. L. 104-106. Div/ A. Title XIII. Sec/ 1342, 10 February 1996. 110 Stat. 486

Nuclear Weapons and Belligerent Reprisals (White House)

- Press Briefing by Mike McCurry and Robert Bell, Special Assistant to the President and Senior Director for Defense Policy and Arms Control, National Security Council, 11 April 1996 on the subject of the African Nuclear Weapons-Free Zone Treaty

COMMENT BY BURRUS CARNAHAN

'Mr. Bell's statement has humanitarian law significance because he specifically noted that while Protocol I of the African Nuclear Weapons-Free Zone (Anfz) Treaty (Treaty of Pelindaba) would obligate the United States not to use or threaten to use nuclear weapons against any state party to the Treaty, this obligation would not limit the options available to the US in response to an attack using "weapons of mass destruction" (commonly understood to mean nuclear, chemical, biological and radiological weapons). During a meeting on 9 June 1997, Mr. Bell made it clear that his earlier remarks were intended to refer to the doctrine of belligerent reprisals. Taken together, Mr. Bell's statements are a high-level endorsement of the continued legality of belligerent reprisals in the United States. It should also be noted that the US regards nuclear weapons as lawful in principle, and that the doctrine of belligerent reprisals would only be relevant to their use where the US had accepted a legally binding non-use obligation, such as that in Protocol I to the African Nuclear Weapons Free Zone Treaty.'

Chemical Weapons

☛ Message from the Office of the Press Secretary to the Congress of the United States concerning the Convention on the Prohibition of the Development, Production, Stockpiling and Use of Chemical Weapons and on Their Destruction, 24 April 1997[200]

Landmines

(i) Department of Defense

☛ Memorandum from the Secretary of Defense, dated 17 June 1996, implementing the President's Decision on anti-personnel landmines[201]

COMMENT BY BURRUS CARNAHAN

'Implicit in the memorandum is the legal position that while the US will, in principle, support a ban on anti-personnel landmines as *lex ferenda*, it does not regard all use of such mines as prohibited by customary international law.'

(ii) White House

☛ Fact Sheet from the Office of the Press Secretary concerning the banning of Anti-Personnel Landmines, 16 May 1997

Landmines and Laser Weapons (Office of the President)

☛ Message dated 7 January 1997 from the President of the US to the US Senate submitting three Protocols to the UN Convention on Certain Conventional Weapons: Amended Protocol II on Mines, Booby-Traps and Other Devices, adopted on 3 May 1996; the 1980 Protocol III on Incendiary Weapons and the Protocol IV on Blinding Laser Weapons adopted on 13 October 1995[202]

200. Reprinted at p. 595.
201. Reprinted at p. 592.
202. Reprinted at p. 566.

COMMENT BY BURRUS CARNAHAN

'Under the US Constitution, the Senate must "advise and consent" to the ratification of any treaty by the President. The Protocols submitted for advice and consent were the Amended Protocol (II) on Mines, Booby-Traps and Other Devices, adopted on 3 May 1996; the 1980 Protocol (III) on Incendiary Weapons and the Protocol (IV) on Blinding Laser Weapons adopted on 13 October 1995. The message contains a detailed discussion of the provisions of the Protocols, including official interpretations of their provisions. Particular note should be paid to the reservation that the US intends to make in regard to Article 2(2) of Protocol III. This provision prohibits the use of air-delivered incendiary munitions against military targets located in a concentration of civilians. Military experts within the US Government argued that this provision was ill-conceived, as in some circumstances incendiary weapons could pose less risk of collateral injury to civilians than alternative munitions. A reservation to that effect will therefore be taken to Protocol II after the Senate advises and consents to its ratification.'

Laser Weapons (Department of Defense)

☛ Memorandum from the Secretary of Defense, dated 17 January 1997, prohibiting the use of laser weapons 'specifically designed to cause permanent blindness'[203]

COMMENT BY BURRUS CARNAHAN

'This policy goes beyond the provisions of Protocol IV on Blinding Laser Weapons, adopted on 13 October 1995, which prohibits weapons specifically designed to cause permanent blindness to "unenhanced vision". The Department of Defense appears to have concluded that any laser specifically designed to cause permanent blindness, even to a person with enhanced vision (e.g., using binoculars or an electro-optical sight), would produce unnecessary suffering or superfluous injury, as temporary blindness would be sufficient to place the person *hors de combat.*'

Legality of Defence Acquisitions vis-à-vis *IHL*

(i) Department of Defense

☛ Directive, Number 5000.1, 15 March 1996. Subject: Defence Acquisition. extract: Subparagraph D.2.j, dealing with compatibility of defense acquisitions with IHL

COMMENT BY BURRUS CARNAHAN

'This Directive covers many aspects of Defense Department research, development and purchasing policy. Only subparagraph D.2.j. pertains to IHL. It requires legal review of all weapons being considered for purchase by the US military to ensure

203. Reprinted at p. 595.

compliance with the laws of war. The requirement for legal review of US weapons was first established on 16 October 1974 by Department of Defense Instruction 5500.15, which has now been superseded by the new Directive. The new Directive goes beyond the old Instruction in that it encourages (but does not require) "legal reviews of new, advanced or emerging technologies which may lead to the development of weapons or weapons systems".'

(ii) Department of the Army

Hollow-Point Ammunition

- ☛ Memorandum (legal review) for the Staff Judge Advocate by W. Hays Parks, Special Assistant for Law of War Matters, 27 March 1996. Subject: Special Operations Forces Use of Hollow-Point Handgun Ammunition

COMMENT BY BURRUS CARNAHAN

'This opinion was precipitated by a 1993 opinion that had found the use of hollow-point ammunition in a Special Forces offensive handgun to be lawful in the specific contexts in which that weapons is intended to be used, primarily hostage situations and similar extreme situations.'

- ☛ Memorandum (legal review) for Commander, Crane Division, Naval Surface Warfare Centre by William Hays Parks on the subject of the legality of the Fabrique Nationale 5.7 x 28 mm Weapon System (a French handgun and ammunition) being considered for purchase by the US military (DAJA-IO (27-1a)), 13 May 1996
- ☛ Memorandum (legal review) by Parks reviewing the legality of a Swedish Cannister munition loaded with flechettes which the US military was considering to purchase, 25 July 1997

Application of IHL

- ☛ International Operational Law Note (When Does the Law of War Apply: Analysis of Department of Defence Policy on Application of The Law of War). Published in *The Army Lawyer*, Dept. of the Army pamphlet 27-50-307 (June 1998) Reprinted at p. 617.

Cases (under Alien Tort Crimes Act and Torture Victims' Protection Act)

- ☛ *S. Kadić* v. *Radovan Karadžić*; *Jane Doe* v. *Radovan Karadžić*. US District Court for the Southern District of NY, 23 September 1993
- ☛ *Jane Doe* et al. v. *Karadžić*; *Kadić* et al v. *Karadžić*. 93 Civ. 0878 (PKL), 93 Civ. 1163 (PKL). US District Court for the Southern District of New York. 866 F. Supp. 734, 1994 US Dist. LEXIS 12599, 7 September 1994
- ☛ *Kadić* et al v. *Karadžić*; *Jane Doe* et al. v. *Karadžić*. Docket Nos. 94-9035, 94-9069. US Court of Appeals for the Second Circuit. 70 F.3d 232; 1995 US App. LEXIS 28826, 13 October 1995

- *Jane Doe* et al. v. *Karadžić; Kadić* et al v. *Karadžić* 93 Civ. 0878 (PKL), 93 Civ. 1163 (PKL) US District Court for the Southern District of New York. 1996 US Dist. LEXIS 5291. 22 April 1996
- *Jane Doe* et al. v. *Kadić* et al v. *Karadžić*. 93 Civ. 0878 (PKL), 93 Civ. 1163 (PKL). US District Court for the Southern District of New York. 1997 US Dist. LEXIS 1073, 3 February 1997
- *Jane Doe* et al. v. *Karadžić*. 93 Civ. 0878 (PKL). US District Court for the Southern District of New York. 176 F.R.D. 458, 1997 US Dist. LEXIS 19160, 2 December 1997

COMMENT BY RONALD D. NEUBAUER

'Plaintiffs are Croat and Muslim citizens of Bosnia and Herzegovina who allege that they are victims and/or survivors of victims of a campaign of ethnic cleansing directed by Defendant Radovan Karadžić, a Bosnian-Serb, to rid the *Republika Srpska* of non-Serbs. The Second Circuit Court of Appeals ordered the suit to proceed in the District Court, finding personal and subject matter jurisdiction over Karadžić and holding that acts of genocide are actionable under the Alien Tort Crimes Act (ATCA),whether or not committed by a state. The ATCA proscribes "violation[s] of the law of nations", that is, acts which are prohibited under universally accepted norms of international law, and includes acts of genocide.

The District Court then ordered Karadžić to respond more thoroughly to Plaintiffs' written requests for information and to appear for deposition in New York. Karadžić informed the court that he did not have the financial resources to defend himself in US courts. Given that Plaintiffs were likely to be successful in obtaining a judgment against an uncontesting Defendant and that such judgment was likely to exhaust the Defendant's limited financial resources, the court certified a class of plaintiffs in December 1997. Class certification ensures that if judgment is obtained against the Defendant, his limited financial resources will be distributed equitably among the named Plaintiffs as well as the thousands of future plaintiffs who have identical claims against the Defendant. The certified class of Plaintiffs consists of all people who suffered injury as a result of rape, genocide, summary execution, arbitrary detention, disappearance, torture or other cruel, inhuman or degrading treatment inflicted by Bosnian-Serb forces under the command and control of Defendant between April 1992 and the present, and will be represented in this suit by the original named individual Plaintiffs.'

- *Louise Mushikiwabo*, et al., v. *Jean Bosco Barayagwiza*. 94 Civ. 3627 (JSM), US District Court for the Southern District of New York. 1996 US Dist. LEXIS 4409. 8 April 1996

COMMENT BY RONALD D. NEUBAUER

'Five plaintiffs sued on behalf of Tutsi relatives murdered in a genocidal campaign orchestrated by the Hutu Defendant. The District Court found personal jurisdiction over the Defendant on the basis that he was served with a summons and complaint while in the country to attend a UN session. The Defendant did not appear personally in court, and default judgment was entered against him on the basis of the facts contained in Plaintiffs' affidavits. Liability was found under the Alien Tort Crimes Act (ATCA) for nearly $100 million in damages. The ATCA applied because the Defendant committed genocide and acted under color of state law, as his actions were part of a coordinated effort with officials of the Rwandan government. The ATCA covers "violations of the laws of nations", which includes genocide whether or not committed by a state, and torture and summary execution when committed by state officials or under color of law.'

☛ *Humberto Alvarez-Machain*, et al v. *USA*. No. 95-55464; No. 95-55768; No. 95-56121. US Court of Appeals for the Ninth Circuit. 107 F. 3d 696, 1996 US App. LEXIS 37014, 24 September 1996 (filed), as amended 19 February 1997

COMMENT BY RONALD D. NEUBAUER

'A Mexican citizen filed suit against agents of the US Drug Enforcement Agency for torturing and falsely extraditing him on allegations that he killed an agent. He claimed a violation of the Torture Victims' Protection Act (TVPA), which establishes liability for acts of torture committed under color of law. The District Court's decision not to apply the TVPA because it was enacted subsequent to the relevant events was overturned on appeal. The Ninth Circuit Court of Appeals reasoned that the TVPA does not have prohibitively retroactive effects because it does not impose new duties or liabilities on defendants. International law and the Alien Tort Crimes Act (ATCA) have long condemned and prohibited torture. The Court of Appeals rejected the Defendants' argument that the ATCA confers only jurisdictional authority and reasoned that the ATCA confers substantive legal rights as well.'

☛ *Weinberg Hirsh, Henry Eisler, Theodore Hilsenrath, Benzion Berkowitz, and Others* v. *State of Israel and State of Germany* 95 Civ. 9460 (JFK). US District Court for the Southern District of New York. 962 F. Supp. 377, 1997 US Dist. LEXIS 4406, 7 April 1997; aff'd without opinion, US Court of Appeals for the Second Circuit, 1997 US App. LEXIS 36435, 31 December 1997

COMMENT BY RONALD D. NEUBAUER

'The Plaintiff Holocaust victims attempted to sue the states of Israel and Germany for insufficient payment of war retributions. The Plaintiffs claimed first that Israel (and Germany as Israel's principal with respect to Holocaust payments) grossly mismanaged or embezzled the funds provided by the former West Germany and second, that Germany owed additional compensation on behalf of the former East Germany, which allegedly never paid reparations to Holocaust victims. The court dismissed the suit for lack of subject matter jurisdiction. The Plaintiffs had tried to invoke the Alien Tort Crimes Act (ATCA) which prohibits "violations of the law of nations", but the ATCA does not provide a basis for jurisdiction over a foreign sovereign. The Foreign Sovereign Immunities Act (FSIA) provides the exclusive source of subject matter jurisdiction over suits against foreign states brought in US courts and provides immunity from suit except in certain circumstances. The Plaintiffs failed to establish that any of the exceptions to immunity listed in the FSIA were applicable to the Defendants. Moreover, neither Defendant waived its immunity, either explicitly or implicitly. Specifically, a violation of *jus cogens* (i.e., fundamental norms of international law) does not constitute an implied waiver under the FSIA.'

ICTR

- In re. *Elizaphan Ntakirutimana. US District Court for the Southern District of Texas*, Laredo Division. 988 F. Supp. 1038, 1997 US Dist. LEXIS 20714, 17 December 1997 [204]

Signings, Ratifications, Accessions, Successions, Denounciations, Reservations, etc.

- The USA signed the CWC on 13 January 1993 and ratified it on 25 April 1997
- On 24 March 1995, the US ratified Protocols I and II of the CCW Convention

URUGUAY

Implementation

- Decree of 24 March 1994, following up Decree No. 966/992, created the National Commission for International Humanitarian Law [Comisión nacional de Derecho Internacional Humanitario]. It is composed of representatives of the Ministries of Foreign Relations, National Defence, the Interior, Education and Culture, Health, the Supreme Court, the Faculty of Law of the University of the Republic and of the Catholic University of Uruguay, and the Uruguay Red Cross. Its mandate is to study and propose recommendations with regard to dissemination of IHL at all levels of public and private education and the implementation and practical application of IHL through legislative provisions, regulations and other measures[205]

Signings, Ratifications, Accessions, Successions, Denounciations, Reservations, etc.

- Uruguay signed the CWC on 15 January 1993 and ratified it on 6 October 1994

204. Reprinted at p. 607. For commentary, see Paust, p. 205.
205. *Supra* n. 52, at p. 16.

- On 6 October 1994, Uruguay acceded to Protocols I, II and III of the CCW Convention
- Uruguay signed the Landmines Treaty on 3 December 1997

UZBEKISTAN

Signings, Ratifications, Accessions, Successions, Denounciations, Reservations, etc.

- Uzbekistan ratified the CRC on 29 June 1994
- Uzbekistan ratified the Cultural Property Convention on 21 February 1996
- Uzbekistan signed the CWC on 24 November 1995 and ratified it on 23 July 1996
- On 29 September 1997, Uzbekistan acceded to Protocols I, II, III, and IV of the CCW Convention
- On 19 January 1998, Uzbekistan acceded to the Mercenaries Convention without making any declarations or reservations

VANUATU

Signings, Ratifications, Accessions, Successions, Denounciations, Reservations, etc.

- Vanuatu signed the Landmines Treaty on 4 December 1997

VENEZUELA

Signings, Ratifications, Accessions, Successions, Denounciations, Reservations, etc.

- Venezuela signed the CWC on 14 January 1993 and ratified it on 3 December 1997
- Venezuela signed the Landmines Treaty on 3 December 1997
- Venezuela acceded to Additional Protocols I + II of 1977 on 23 July 1998
- On 23 July 1998, Venezuela made a declaration under Art. 90(2)(a) of Protocol I recognising the competence of the International Fact-Finding Commission

VIETNAM

Signings, Ratifications, Accessions, Successions, Denounciations, Reservations, etc.

- Vietnam signed the CWC on 13 January 1993

YEMEN

Signings, Ratifications, Accessions, Successions, Denounciations, Reservations, etc.

- Yemen signed the CWC on 8 February 1993
- Yemen signed the Landmines Treaty on 4 December 1997

ZAMBIA

Signings, Ratifications, Accessions, Successions, Denounciations, Reservations, etc.

- Zambia signed the CWC on 13 January 1993
- On 4 May 1995, Zambia acceded to Additional Protocols I and II of 1977
- Zambia signed the Landmines Treaty on 12 December 1997

ZIMBABWE

Implementation

- ☛ Geneva Conventions Amendment Act, 1996 [incorporating the Additional Protocols of 1977 into Zimbabwean law. Amends the Geneva Conventions Act of 1981 incorporating the Geneva Conventions into Zimbabwean law, to include the grave breaches provisions of Protocol I]
- ☛ Statutory Instrument No. 68 of 1996 [Assignment of Functions (Minister of Defence) (Amendment) Notice, 1996 (No. 1) in which the President assigns to the Minister of Defence responsibility for the administration of the Geneva Conventions Act of 1981][206]
- ☛ In 1994, the competence of the Zimbabwean Interministerial Committee for Human Rights, created in 1993, was extended and it became the Interministerial Committee for Human Rights and Humanitarian Law.[207] Amongst its responsibilities are advising on implementing legislation and studying the extent to which Zimbabwean legislation is compatible with IHL. The Committee played an important role in drafting the Geneva Conventions Amendment Act

Signings, Ratifications, Accessions, Successions, Denounciations, Reservations, etc.

- ☛ Zimbabwe signed the CWC on 13 January 1993 and ratified it on 25 April 1997
- ☛ Zimbabwe signed the Landmines Treaty on 4 December 1997 and ratified it on 18 June 1998

206. *See Dutli* at p. 255.
207. *See Dutli* at p. 254.

DOCUMENTATION

The Documentation section is compiled and edited by the Managing Editor, Ms. Avril McDonald, from materials provided to the *YIHL* by its correspondents, *inter alia*. Restricted space forces us to be selective in the documents we print. Our general policy is to prefer documents to which access might otherwise be difficult, in particular regarding state practice. In general, we will tend not to publish documents that are easily and widely available, such as UN Documents or jurisprudence of the *ad hoc* Tribunals, although we may make exceptions. Readers are invited to send documents to the Managing Editor for inclusion in this section. Please note that, in order to save space, documents may appear in a more condensed format than the original, and some changes may have been made to the form, though not the content, in order to conform with the Yearbook's house style.

CLASSIFICATION OF DOCUMENTS

1.	**One:**	**SOURCES AND GENERAL PRINCIPLES**
1.1	I	SOURCES
1.11		A. Pre-Hague
1.12		B. Hague Law
1.13		C. Geneva Law
1.14		D. Post-1977 Developments
1.15		E. Customary Law
1.2	II	GENERAL PRINCIPLES
1.21		A. Martens Clause
1.22		B. Superfluous Injury and Unnecessary Suffering
1.23		C. Principle of Distinction
1.24		D. Principle of Proportionality
1.25		E. Military Necessity
2.	**Two:**	**CONFLICTS, ARMED FORCES AND COMBATANTS**
2.1	I	TYPES OF CONFLICTS
2.11		A. International
2.12		B. Non-international
2.13		C. Other
2.2	II	TYPES OF ACTOR(S)
2.21		A. Armed Forces and Combatant Status
2.22		B. Non-State Actors
2.23		C. Specific Groups
2.231		1.Mercenaries
2.232		2.Spies
2.233		3.Other
3.	**Three:**	**PROTECTED PERSONS**
3.1	I	TYPES OF PROTECTED PERSONS
3.11		A. Wounded, Sick and Shipwrecked
3.12		B. Prisoners of War
3.13		C. Civilian Population
3.131		1.Civilians Generally
3.132		2.Women and Children
3.133		3.Medical Personnel and Religious Personnel
3.134		4.Journalists
3.135		5.Other

3.2	II	SPECIFIC SITUATIONS AND PROHIBITIONS
3.21		A. Internment
3.22		B. Occupation
3.23		C. Prohibition of Collective Punishment
3.24		D. Prohibition of Deportation and Transfer
3.25		E. Reprisals
4.	**Four:**	**METHODS, MEANS AND TYPES OF WARFARE**
4.1	I	METHODS AND MEANS OF WARFARE
4.11		A. Basic Rules
4.111		1. Existing Weapons
4.1111		a. Conventional Weapons
4.11111		i. mines
4.11112		ii. small weapons and others
4.1112		b. Weapons of Mass Destruction
4.11121		i. nuclear weapons
4.11122		ii. chemical and biological weapons
4.112		2. New Weapons
4.113		3. Prohibition of Perfidy
4.114		4. Emblems and Safeguards of Persons *hors de combat*
4.12		B. Direct and Indiscriminate Attacks
4.13		C. Precautionary Measures
4.14		D. Protection of Civilian and Other Specified Objects and Actions
4.141		1. Specifically Protected Objects
4.142		2. Cultural Property and Places of Worship
4.143		3. Works and Installations Containing Dangerous Forces
4.144		4. The Natural Environment
4.145		5. Localities and Zones
4.146		6. Civil Defence
4.15		E. Medical Assistance
41.6		F. Humanitarian Assistance Operations
4.2	II	SPECIFIC TYPES OF WARFARE
4.21		A. Land Warfare
4.22		B. Air and Missile Warfare
4.23		C. Naval Warfare

5.	**Five:**	**TERMINATION OF ARMED CONFLICTS**
5.1	I	CEASEFIRE, ARMISTICES AND PEACE AGREEMENTS
5.2	II	WAR CRIMES COMMISSIONS
5.3	III	AMNESTIES, TRUTH AND RECONCILIATION COMMISSIONS
5.4	IV	REPARATIONS/COMPENSATION
6.	**Six:**	**PROSECUTION OF IHL VIOLATIONS**
6.1	I	THE ELEMENTS OF THE CRIMES
6.2	II	DEFENCES
6.3	III	REPRESSION OF BREACHES
6.31		A. International Courts
6.32		B. Regional Courts
6.33		C. National Courts
7.	**Seven:**	**IMPLEMENTATION OF IHL**
7.1	I	NATIONAL POLICY STATEMENTS
7.2	II	NATIONAL LAW
7.21		A. Legislation to Implement IHL Treaties
7.22		B. Legislation to Implement Obligations *vis-à-vis* the International Court and Tribunals
7.23		C. Military Manuals/National Instructions/Codes of Conduct
7.24		D. Role of Defence Force Legal Advisers
7.3	III	PROTECTING POWERS
7.4	IV	ICRC
7.5	V	FACT-FINDING, INCLUDING THE INTERNATIONAL FACT-FINDING COMMISSION
7.6	VI	DISSEMINATION
8.	**Eight:**	**THE LAW OF NEUTRALITY**
8.1	I	THE RIGHTS AND DUTIES OF NATIONALS
8.2	II	WAR ON LAND
8.3	III	NAVAL WARFARE
8.4	IV	AERIAL WARFARE
9.	**Nine:**	**INTERNATIONAL ORGANISATIONS AND INTERNATIONAL ACTIONS**
9.1	I	INTERNATIONAL ORGANISATIONS
9.11		A. United Nations Organisation
9.12		B. Other

NOTE

Many international and national documents related to international humanitarian law are available on the internet through an on-line access to the ICRC IHL database (ICRC website: http://www.icrc.org). This database now contains 91 treaties and texts on the conduct of hostilities and the protection of victims of war (dating from 1856 to the present); the commentaries on the four Geneva Conventions and their Additional Protocols; an up-to-date list of signatures, ratifications, accessions or successions to IHL treaties; and, the full text of reservations. Constantly updated, this data is also regularly replicated on a CD-ROM that can be obtained from the ICRC (Public Information Division, 19, av. de la Paix, CH-1202 GENEVA; e-mail; webmaster.gva@icrc.org; Fax: ++ 41 22 733 20 57; CHF 49.- or USD 39,-). National implementating legislation (Geneva Conventions Acts, extracts from Penal Codes, laws related to the protection of the emblem, laws on cooperation with the international Tribunals, etc.) and jurisprudence are also available for an increasing number of countries. This data will be integrated in the next version of the CD-ROM, which will be available in the course of 1999.

DOCUMENTS

3.12.B PRISONERS OF WAR

☛ GREECE: Military Criminal Code
Law 2287/1995[1] (Government Gazette A 20/1-2-1995, in force 1 August 1995)

EIGHTH CHAPTER
PRISONERS OF WAR – NON COMBATANTS

Article 156 – Insults, threats or violence against a prisoner of war
1. Military personnel who insults or threatens a prisoner of war or performs acts of violence against him is punishable by incarceration for a period of at least three months.
2. The provision of the previous paragraph is also applicable if the act specified therein has been committed against a prisoner of war by another prisoner of war, appointed by the Greek Military Authority in charge of prisoners of war in the course of their service.

Article 157 – Outrages against a prisoner of war
Military personnel who inflicts torture or other outrages upon the human dignity of a prisoner of war is punishable by imprisonment for a period of up to ten years, unless the offence is subject to greater punishment under another statutory provision.

Article 158 – Insults against the religion of a prisoner of war
Military personnel who arbitrarily hinders the reasonable, within the limits of the specific public order provisions stipulated by the Military Authority, exercise of the religious duties of a prisoner of war or insults his religion in his presence is punishable by incarceration for a period of at least one month.

Article 159 – Coercion of a prisoner of war into providing information
Military personnel who uses physical violence or threatens to use physical violence in order to coerce a prisoner of war into providing information prejudicial to the interests of his country or labour directly related to war operations or prohibited by the international conventions is punishable by incarceration for a period of at least six months, unless the offence is subject to greater punishment under another statutory provision.

1. Unofficial translation provided by Dr. Maria Gavouneli, the Hellenic Institute of International and Foreign Law, Greece. For commentary thereon see Gavouneli, *supra*, p. 445 et seq.

Article 160 - Theft against a prisoner of war
Military personnel who commits theft against a prisoner of war under his supervision is punishable by incarceration for a period of at least one year, unless the offence is subject to greater punishment under another statutory provision.

Article 161 - Violence against non-combatants
Military personnel who without provocation or necessity performs acts of violence against non-combatant citizens of the enemy state or places under arrest such persons as hostages is punishable by incarceration for a period of up to two years, unless the offence is subject to greater punishment under another statutory provision.

Article 162 - Insults, threats or violence by a prisoner of war
1. A prisoner of war who insults or threatens or performs acts of violence against Greek military personnel is punishable by incarceration for a period of at least one year, unless the offence is subject to greater punishment under another statutory provision.
2. The provision of the previous paragraph is also applicable if the offence specified therein has been committed against a prisoner of war by another prisoner of war, appointed by the Greek Military Authority in charge of prisoners of war in the course of their service.

Article 163 - Disobedience by a prisoner of war
1. A prisoner of war who does not obey a lawful and conforming to the international conventions order by the military personnel charged with his supervision is punishable by incarceration for a period of at least three months.
2. The provision of the previous paragraph is also applicable if the offence specified therein has been committed by a prisoner of war regarding an order issued by another prisoner of war, appointed by the Greek Military Authority in charge of prisoners of war in the course of their service.

Article 164 - Riot by prisoners of war
1. Prisoners of war who, in groups of three or more, commit the offence of disobedience by a prisoner of war or perform acts of violence against persons or proceed to destroy things are deemed to be in sedition.
2. The instigators and the persons in charge of sedition as well as the participating commissioned and non-commissioned officers are punishable by death or life imprisonment and all others by incarceration.
3. If for any reason whatsoever the act had not been carried through, the instigators are punishable by incarceration for a period of at least three months and those who accepted their call by incarceration for a period of up to one year.

Article 165 - Mass insubordination by prisoners of war
1. Prisoners of war who, except in the case of article 164, in groups of three or more:
   a) insist on the submission of a group complaint, petition or report, oral or in writing;
   b) submit on an individual basis but following prior agreement the same complaint, petition or report.

2. Instigators are punishable by imprisonment for a period of up to ten years and the others by incarceration.[2]
3. The instigators to mass insubordination by prisoners of war that was not carried through are punishable by incarceration for a period of at least three months.

Article 166 - Disobedience to the orders of the Commander-in-Chief
Whoever disobeys the general orders of the Commander-in-Chief of the Greek armed forces operating in foreign territory under occupation or of the Commander appointed by him is punishable by incarceration.

3.22 OCCUPATION

☛ The League of Arab States and the Applicability of the Fourth Geneva Convention to the Occupied Territories, including the Golan Heights and Jerusalem[1]

In 1997, the Council of the League of Arab States (LAS)[2] adopted the following resolutions related to the rules of IHL, namely:

A) Resolution No. 5676/B (21 September 1997).
Para. 4 of that resolution reads:
'The League Council calls upon States signatories of the Fourth Geneva Convention of 1949 to exert pressure upon Israel for the sake of applying the provisions of that Convention on occupied Palestinian territories, including Jerusalem.'[3]
B) Resolution No. 5678, adopted on 21 September 1997, provides in para. 3:

2. According to Article 52 of the Greek Criminal Code, imprisonment may be imposed for life or for a period of no less than five and no more than twenty years. Incarceration, on the other hand, imposed for lighter offences, cannot extend to less than 10 days or more than five years (Art. 53).

1. Prepared and annotated by Professor Ahmed Abou-El-Wafa, Professor at the Faculty of Law, Cairo University.

2. The machinery of the League, as expressly embodied in the Pact, includes three principal organs, namely: the Council, Special Committees and the Secretariat General. The League Council is the plenary organ of the organization i.e., it is composed of representatives of all member states (Art. 3 of the Pact). Thus, all members are represented in the Council on an equal footing. The Council meets at the level of foreign ministers, their representatives or permanent delegates. The League Council is the supreme organ within the organization. It is the main policy-making body. See Ahmed Abou-El-Wafa: *A manual on the law of international organizations: an analysis of some international organizations*, dar Al-Nahda Al-Arabia, Cairo, 1998, pp 174-175.

3. Cf, Resolutions of the Council of the LAS in its ordinary session 108, LAS - The Secretariat General, Cairo, September 1997, p. 6 (in Arabic). This is not the first time that the League Council refers to the Fourth Geneva Convention relative to the protection of civilian persons in time of war. In fact, such reference has been contained in many resolutions of the Council, the most important of which are the following: Res. 1595 (7/9/1959); Res. 2456 (3/9/1968); Res. 3618 (6/9/1977); Res. 5366 (27/3/1994); and Res. 5628 (31/3/1997).

'The League Council decides, Settlement activities constitute a violation of the Geneva conventions, the Madrid framework and the peace process.'[4]

C) Resolution No. 5681, adopted the same day, states in para. 5 that:
'The League Council, Calls upon the Arab Group in the United Nations, in response to the message of the Swiss Government in which it demands the best ways to follow up General Assembly Resolution No. 10/3 of 15/7/1997, to take speedy action for the convocation of a conference on the measures to implement the Fourth Geneva Convention in occupied Palestinian territories, including Jerusalem, and to ensure its respect in pursuance of Article 1, in accordance with General Assembly resolution No. 10/3 of 15/7/1997.'[5]

D) Resolution No. 5682, adopted on 21 September 1997, which states, in part:
'The League Council,
3 - Reaffirms the application of the Fourth Geneva Convention of 1949, to the citizens of the occupied Syrian Arab Golan.
6 - Considers that the establishment of settlements and the coming of settlers constitute a breach of the Geneva Conventions, the Madrid framework and an obstacle to the peace process.'[6]

E) Resolution No. 5684, adopted on 21 September 1997, which states:
'The League Council,
1 - Condemns continuous Israeli violations of human rights in the occupied area of South Lebanon and Western Bika'a.
2 - Calls upon the international community particularly the United Nations Organization, to take necessary measures to deter Israel from committing such violations.
3 - Calls upon the international community, to adopt necessary measures *vis-à-vis* Israel, in order to immediately release all Lebanese prisoners and hostages detained in Israeli prisons and places of detention controlled by its forces, in violation of rules of international law, the Fourth Geneva Convention of 1949 and the Hague Convention of 1907.
4 - Incites Member States to call on international organizations to take all measures *vis-à-vis* the Israeli Government, in order to enable the International Red Cross and other humanitarian organizations, to regularly and systematically visit the detainees in Al-Khayam and Margueioun

4. Ibid, p. 16.

5. Ibid, p. 22. During its Tenth Extraordinary Session, the General Assembly of the United Nations adopted Resolution 10/3 on 10 July 1997 which provides that the General Assembly: 'Recommends that the High Contracting Parties to the Geneva Convention relative to the protection of civilian persons in time of war convene a conference on measures to enforce the Convention in the occupied Palestinian territory, including Jerusalem, and to ensure its respect, in accordance with common article 1, and requests the Secretary-General to present a report on the matter within three months'.

6. Ibid., p. 25. On the same subject, the League Council previously adopted similar resolutions. See e.g., Resolutions 5633 (31/3/1997); 5585 (15/9/1996); 5542 (21/3/1996); 5493 (21/9/1995); 5323 (21/9/1993); 5168 (27/4/1992); and 4126 (13/1/1982).

prisons, to investigate their status, to grant them humanitarian and health care and to allow their relatives to continuously visit them.
5 - Requests to proceed to enquiries imposed by international conventions about Lebanese detainees who died in Israeli prisons and to pay damages to injured persons resulting therefrom, according to applicable international laws.[7]

F) Finally, the problem of 'the Kuwaiti prisoners and missing persons and others in Iraq' is still generating considerable discussion within the League despite the passage of more than seven years from the end of the Second Gulf War and the occupation of Kuwait by Iraq. In this respect, in his last report, the Secretary-General of the League, said: 'The topic of Kuwaiti prisoners and missing persons and others in Iraq is still constituting an Arab concern, because of its humanitarian nature and the painful feelings of relatives of those missing persons and prisoners.... I have treated of that subject with all the Kuwaiti and Iraqi persons responsible .... I hope that this case will be settled soon, because of its humanitarian dimension and its positive impact on the purification of the Arab atmosphere.'[8]

4.11111 LANDMINES

☛ Convention on the Prohibition of the Use, Stockpiling, Production and Transfer of Anti-personnel Mines and on Their Destruction, 18 September 1997

Preamble
The States Parties,
Determined to put an end to the suffering and casualties caused by antipersonnel mines, that kill or maim hundreds of people every week, mostly innocent and defenceless civilians and especially children, obstruct economic development and reconstruction, inhibit the repatriation of refugees and internally displaced persons, and have other severe consequences for years after emplacement,
Believing it necessary to do their utmost to contribute in an efficient and coordinated manner to face the challenge of removing anti-personnel mines placed throughout the world, and to assure their destruction,
Wishing to do their utmost in providing assistance for the care and rehabilitation, including the social and economic reintegration of mine victims,
Recognizing that a total ban of anti-personnel mines would also be an important confidence-building measure,
Welcoming the adoption of the Protocol on Prohibitions or Restrictions on the Use of Mines, Booby-Traps and Other Devices, as amended on 3 May 1996, annexed to the Convention on Prohibitions or Restrictions on the Use of Certain Conventional Weapons Which May Be Deemed

7. Ibid., p. 29.
8. Cf, Report of the Secretary-General between the two sessions of the Council 107-108, The Secretariat-General, LAS, Cairo, September 1997, p. 23 (in Arabic).

to Be Excessively Injurious or to Have Indiscriminate Effects, and calling for the early ratification of this Protocol by all States which have not yet done so,
Welcoming also United Nations General Assembly Resolution 51/45 S of 10 December 1996 urging all States to pursue vigorously an effective, legally-binding international agreement to ban the use, stockpiling, production and transfer of antipersonnel landmines,
Welcoming furthermore the measures taken over the past years, both unilaterally and multilaterally, aiming at prohibiting, restricting or suspending the use, stockpiling, production and transfer of anti-personnel mines,
Stressing the role of public conscience in furthering the principles of humanity as evidenced by the call for a total ban of anti-personnel mines and recognizing the efforts to that end undertaken by the International Red Cross and Red Crescent Movement, the International Campaign to Ban Landmines and numerous other nongovernmental organizations around the world,
Recalling the Ottawa Declaration of 5 October 1996 and the Brussels Declaration of 27 June 1997 urging the international community to negotiate an international and legally binding agreement prohibiting the use, stockpiling, production and transfer of anti-personnel mines,
Emphasizing the desirability of attracting the adherence of all States to this Convention, and determined to work strenuously towards the promotion of its universalization in all relevant fora including, *inter alia*, the United Nations, the Conference on Disarmament, regional organizations, and groupings, and review conferences of the Convention on Prohibitions or Restrictions on the Use of Certain Conventional Weapons Which May Be Deemed to Be Excessively Injurious or to Have Indiscriminate Effects,
Basing themselves on the principle of international humanitarian law that the right of the parties to an armed conflict to choose methods or means of warfare is not unlimited, on the principle that prohibits the employment in armed conflicts of weapons, projectiles and materials and methods of warfare of a nature to cause superfluous injury or unnecessary suffering and on the principle that a distinction must be made between civilians and combatants,

Have agreed as follows:
Article 1 (General obligations)
1. Each State Party undertakes never under any circumstances
   a) To use anti-personnel mines;
   b) To develop, produce, otherwise acquire, stockpile, retain or transfer to anyone, directly or indirectly, anti-personnel mines;
   c) To assist, encourage or induce, in any way, anyone to engage in any activity prohibited to a State Party under this Convention.
2. Each State Party undertakes to destroy or ensure the destruction of all antipersonnel mines in accordance with the provisions of this Convention.

Article 2 (Definitions)
1. 'Anti-personnel mine' means a mine designed to be exploded by the presence, proximity or contact of a person and that will incapacitate, injure or kill one or more persons. Mines designed to be detonated by the presence, proximity or contact of a vehicle as opposed to a person, that are equipped with anti-handling devices, are not considered anti-personnel mines as a result of being so equipped.

2. 'Mine' means a munition designed to be placed under, on or near the ground or other surface area and to be exploded by the presence, proximity or contact of a person or a vehicle.
3. 'Anti-handling device' means a device intended to protect a mine and which is part of, linked to, attached to or placed under the mine and which activates when an attempt is made to tamper with or otherwise intentionally disturb the mine.
4. 'Transfer' involves, in addition to the physical movement of anti-personnel mines into or from national territory, the transfer of title to and control over the mines, but does not involve the transfer of territory containing emplaced anti-personnel mines.
5. 'Mined area' means an area which is dangerous due to the presence or suspected presence of mines.

Article 3 (Exceptions)
1. Notwithstanding the general obligations under Article 1, the retention or transfer of a number of anti-personnel mines for the development of and training in mine detection, mine clearance, or mine destruction techniques is permitted. The amount of such mines shall not exceed the minimum number absolutely necessary for the above-mentioned purposes.
2. The transfer of anti-personnel mines for the purpose of destruction is permitted.

Article 4 (Destruction of stockpiled anti-personnel mines)
Except as provided for in Article 3, each State Party undertakes to destroy or ensure the destruction of all stockpiled anti-personnel mines it owns or possesses, or that are under its jurisdiction or control, as soon as possible but not later than four years after the entry into force of this Convention for that State Party.

Article 5 (Destruction of anti-personnel mines in mined areas)
1. Each State Party undertakes to destroy or ensure the destruction of all antipersonnel mines in mined areas under its jurisdiction or control, as soon as possible but not later than ten years after the entry into force of this Convention for that State Party.
2. Each State Party shall make every effort to identify all areas under its jurisdiction or control in which anti-personnel mines are known or suspected to be emplaced and shall ensure as soon as possible that all anti-personnel mines in mined areas under its jurisdiction or control are perimeter-marked, monitored and protected by fencing or other means, to ensure the effective exclusion of civilians, until all antipersonnel mines contained therein have been destroyed. The marking shall at least be to the standards set out in the Protocol on Prohibitions or Restrictions on the Use of Mines, Booby-Traps and Other Devices, as amended on 3 May 1996, annexed to the Convention on Prohibitions or Restrictions on the Use of Certain Conventional Weapons Which May Be Deemed to Be Excessively Injurious or to Have Indiscriminate Effects.
3. If a State Party believes that it will be unable to destroy or ensure the destruction of all anti-personnel mines referred to in paragraph 1 within that time period, it may submit a request to a Meeting of the States Parties or a Review Conference for an extension of the deadline for completing the destruction of such anti-personnel mines, for a period of up to ten years.
4. Each request shall contain:
   a) The duration of the proposed extension;

b) A detailed explanation of the reasons for the proposed extension, including:

(i) The preparation and status of work conducted under national demining programs;

(ii) The financial and technical means available to the State Party for the destruction of all the anti-personnel mines; and

(iii) Circumstances which impede the ability of the State Party to destroy all the anti-personnel mines in mined areas;

c) The humanitarian, social, economic, and environmental implications of the extension; and

d) Any other information relevant to the request for the proposed extension.

5. The Meeting of the States Parties or the Review Conference shall, taking into consideration the factors contained in paragraph 4, assess the request and decide by a majority of votes of States Parties present and voting whether to grant the request for an extension period.

6. Such an extension may be renewed upon the submission of a new request in accordance with paragraphs 3, 4 and 5 of this Article. In requesting a further extension period a State Party shall submit relevant additional information on what has been undertaken in the previous extension period pursuant to this Article.

Article 6 (International cooperation and assistance)

1. In fulfilling its obligations under this Convention each State Party has the right to seek and receive assistance, where feasible, from other States Parties to the extent possible.

2. Each State Party undertakes to facilitate and shall have the right to participate in the fullest possible exchange of equipment, material and scientific and technological information concerning the implementation of this Convention. The States Parties shall not impose undue restrictions on the provision of mine clearance equipment and related technological information for humanitarian purposes.

3. Each State Party in a position to do so shall provide assistance for the care and rehabilitation, and social and economic reintegration, of mine victims and for mine awareness programs. Such assistance may be provided, *inter alia*, through the United Nations system, international, regional or national organizations or institutions, the International Committee of the Red Cross, national Red Cross and Red Crescent societies and their International Federation, non-governmental organizations, or on a bilateral basis.

4. Each State Party in a position to do so shall provide assistance for mine clearance and related activities. Such assistance may be provided, *inter alia*, through the United Nations system, international or regional organizations or institutions, nongovernmental organizations or institutions, or on a bilateral basis, or by contributing to the United Nations Voluntary Trust Fund for Assistance in Mine Clearance, or other regional funds that deal with demining.

5. Each State Party in a position to do so shall provide assistance for the destruction of stockpiled anti-personnel mines.

6. Each State Party undertakes to provide information to the database on mine clearance established within the United Nations system, especially information concerning various means and technologies of mine clearance, and lists of experts, expert agencies or national points of contact on mine clearance.

7. States Parties may request the United Nations, regional organizations, other States Parties or other competent intergovernmental or non-governmental fora to assist its authorities in the elaboration of a national demining program to determine, *inter alia*:

a) The extent and scope of the anti-personnel mine problem;

b) The financial, technological and human resources that are required for the implementation of the program;

c) The estimated number of years necessary to destroy all anti-personnel mines in mined areas under the jurisdiction or control of the concerned State Party;

d) Mine awareness activities to reduce the incidence of mine-related injuries or deaths;

e) Assistance to mine victims;

f) The relationship between the Government of the concerned State Party and the relevant governmental, inter-governmental or non-governmental entities that will work in the implementation of the program.

8. Each State Party giving and receiving assistance under the provisions of this Article shall cooperate with a view to ensuring the full and prompt implementation of agreed assistance programs.

Article 7 (Transparency measures)

1. Each State Party shall report to the Secretary-General of the United Nations as soon as practicable, and in any event not later than 180 days after the entry into force of this Convention for that State Party on:

a) The national implementation measures referred to in Article 9;

b) The total of all stockpiled anti-personnel mines owned or possessed by it, or under its jurisdiction or control, to include a breakdown of the type, quantity and, if possible lot numbers of each type of anti-personnel mine stockpiled;

c) To the extent possible, the location of all mined areas that contain, or are suspected to contain, anti-personnel mines under its jurisdiction or control, to include as much detail as possible regarding the type and quantity of each type of antipersonnel mine in each mined area and when they were emplaced;

d) The types, quantities and, if possible, lot numbers of all anti-personnel mines retained or transferred for the development of and training in mine detection, mine clearance or mine destruction techniques, or transferred for the purpose of destruction, as well as the institutions authorized by a State Party to retain or transfer antipersonnel mines, in accordance with Article 3;

e) The status of programs for the conversion or de-commissioning of antipersonnel mine production facilities;

f) The status of programs for the destruction of anti-personnel mines in accordance with Articles 4 and 5, including details of the methods which will be used in destruction, the location of all destruction sites and the applicable safety and environmental standards to be observed;

g) The types and quantities of all anti-personnel mines destroyed after the entry into force of this Convention for that State Party, to include a breakdown of the quantity of each type of anti-personnel mine destroyed, in accordance with Articles 4 and 5, respectively, along with, if possible, the lot numbers of each type of antipersonnel mine in the case of destruction in accordance with Article 4;

h) The technical characteristics of each type of anti-personnel mine produced, to the extent known, and those currently owned or possessed by a State Party, giving, where reasonably possible, such categories of information as may facilitate identification and clearance of anti-personnel mines; at a minimum, this information shall include the dimensions, fusing, explosive content, metallic content, colour photographs and other information which may facilitate mine clearance; and

i) The measures taken to provide an immediate and effective warning to the population in relation to all areas identified under paragraph 2 of Article 5.

2. The information provided in accordance with this Article shall be updated by the States Parties annually, covering the last calendar year, and reported to the Secretary-General of the United Nations not later than 30 April of each year.

3. The Secretary-General of the United Nations shall transmit all such reports received to the States Parties.

Article 8 (Facilitation and clarification of compliance)

The States Parties agree to consult and cooperate with each other regarding the implementation of the provisions of this Convention, and to work together in a spirit of cooperation to facilitate compliance by States Parties with their obligations under this Convention.

2. If one or more States Parties wish to clarify and seek to resolve questions relating to compliance with the provisions of this Convention by another State Party, it may submit, through the Secretary-General of the United Nations, a Request for Clarification of that matter to that State Party. Such a request shall be accompanied by all appropriate information. Each State Party shall refrain from unfounded Requests for Clarification, care being taken to avoid abuse. A State Party that receives a Request for Clarification shall provide, through the Secretary-General of the United Nations, within 28 days to the requesting State Party all information which would assist in clarifying this matter.

3. If the requesting State Party does not receive a response through the Secretary-General of the United Nations within that time period, or deems the response to the Request for Clarification to be unsatisfactory, it may submit the matter through the Secretary-General of the United Nations to the next Meeting of the States Parties. The Secretary-General of the United Nations shall transmit the submission, accompanied by all appropriate information pertaining to the Request for Clarification, to all States Parties. All such information shall be presented to the requested State Party which shall have the right to respond.

4. Pending the convening of any meeting of the States Parties, any of the States Parties concerned may request the Secretary-General of the United Nations to exercise his or her good offices to facilitate the clarification requested.

5. The requesting State Party may propose through the Secretary-General of the United Nations the convening of a Special Meeting of the States Parties to consider the matter. The Secretary-General of the United Nations shall thereupon communicate this proposal and all information submitted by the States Parties concerned, to all States Parties with a request that they indicate whether they favour a Special Meeting of the States Parties, for the purpose of considering the matter. In the event that within 14 days from the date of such communication, at least one-third of the States Parties favors such a Special Meeting, the Secretary-General of

the United Nations shall convene this Special Meeting of the States Parties within a further 14 days. A quorum for this Meeting shall consist of a majority of States Parties.

6. The Meeting of the States Parties or the Special Meeting of the States Parties, as the case may be, shall first determine whether to consider the matter further, taking into account all information submitted by the States Parties concerned. The Meeting of the States Parties or the Special Meeting of the States Parties shall make every effort to reach a decision by consensus. If despite all efforts to that end no agreement has been reached, it shall take this decision by a majority of States Parties present and voting.

7. All States Parties shall cooperate fully with the Meeting of the States Parties or the Special Meeting of the States Parties in the fulfilment of its review of the matter, including any fact-finding missions that are authorized in accordance with paragraph 8.

8. If further clarification is required, the Meeting of the States Parties or the Special Meeting of the States Parties shall authorize a fact-finding mission and decide on its mandate by a majority of States Parties present and voting. At any time the requested State Party may invite a fact-finding mission to its territory. Such a mission shall take place without a decision by a Meeting of the States Parties or a Special Meeting of the States Parties to authorize such a mission. The mission, consisting of up to 9 experts, designated and approved in accordance with paragraphs 9 and 10, may collect additional information on the spot or in other places directly related to the alleged compliance issue under the jurisdiction or control of the requested State Party.

9. The Secretary-General of the United Nations shall prepare and update a list of the names, nationalities and other relevant data of qualified experts provided by States Parties and communicate it to all States Parties. Any expert included on this list shall be regarded as designated for all fact-finding missions unless a State Party declares its non-acceptance in writing. In the event of non-acceptance, the expert shall not participate in fact-finding missions on the territory or any other place under the jurisdiction or control of the objecting State Party, if the non-acceptance was declared prior to the appointment of the expert to such missions.

10. Upon receiving a request from the Meeting of the States Parties or a Special Meeting of the States Parties, the Secretary-General of the United Nations shall, after consultations with the requested State Party, appoint the members of the mission, including its leader. Nationals of States Parties requesting the fact-finding mission or directly affected by it shall not be appointed to the mission. The members of the fact-finding mission shall enjoy privileges and immunities under Article VI of the Convention on the Privileges and Immunities of the United Nations, adopted on 13 February 1946.

11. Upon at least 72 hours notice, the members of the fact-finding mission shall arrive in the territory of the requested State Party at the earliest opportunity. The requested State Party shall take the necessary administrative measures to receive, transport and accommodate the mission, and shall be responsible for ensuring the security of the mission to the maximum extent possible while they are on territory under its control.

12. Without prejudice to the sovereignty of the requested State Party, the fact-finding mission may bring into the territory of the requested State Party the necessary equipment which shall be used exclusively for gathering information on the alleged compliance issue. Prior to its arrival, the mission will advise the requested State Party of the equipment that it intends to utilize in the course of its fact-finding mission.

13. The requested State Party shall make all efforts to ensure that the fact-finding mission is given the opportunity to speak with all relevant persons who may be able to provide information related to the alleged compliance issue.
14. The requested State Party shall grant access for the fact-finding mission to all areas and installations under its control where facts relevant to the compliance issue could be expected to be collected. This shall be subject to any arrangements that the requested State Party considers necessary for:
  a) The protection of sensitive equipment, information and areas;
  b) The protection of any constitutional obligations the requested State Party may have with regard to proprietary rights, searches and seizures, or other constitutional rights; or
  c) The physical protection and safety of the members of the fact-finding mission. In the event that the requested State Party makes such arrangements, it shall make every reasonable effort to demonstrate through alternative means its compliance with this Convention.
15. The fact-finding mission may remain in the territory of the State Party concerned for no more than 14 days, and at any particular site no more than 7 days, unless otherwise agreed.
16. All information provided in confidence and not related to the subject matter of the fact-finding mission shall be treated on a confidential basis.
17. The fact-finding mission shall report, through the Secretary-General of the United Nations, to the Meeting of the States Parties or the Special Meeting of the States Parties the results of its findings.
18. The Meeting of the States Parties or the Special Meeting of the States Parties shall consider all relevant information, including the report submitted by the fact-finding mission, and may request the requested State Party to take measures to address the compliance issue within a specified period of time. The requested State Party shall report on all measures taken in response to this request.
19. The Meeting of the States Parties or the Special Meeting of the States Parties may suggest to the States Parties concerned ways and means to further clarify or resolve the matter under consideration, including the initiation of appropriate procedures in conformity with international law. In circumstances where the issue at hand is determined to be due to circumstances beyond the control of the requested State Party, the Meeting of the States Parties or the Special Meeting of the States Parties may recommend appropriate measures, including the use of cooperative measures referred to in Article 6.
20. The Meeting of the States Parties or the Special Meeting of the States Parties shall make every effort to reach its decisions referred to in paragraphs 18 and 19 by consensus, otherwise by a two-thirds majority of States Parties present and voting.

Article 9 (National implementation measures)
Each State Party shall take all appropriate legal, administrative and other measures, including the imposition of penal sanctions, to prevent and suppress any activity prohibited to a State Party under this Convention undertaken by persons or on territory under its jurisdiction or control.

Article 10 (Settlement of disputes)

1.The States Parties shall consult and cooperate with each other to settle any dispute that may arise with regard to the application or the interpretation of this Convention. Each State Party may bring any such dispute before the Meeting of the States Parties.

2. The Meeting of the States Parties may contribute to the settlement of the dispute by whatever means it deems appropriate, including offering its good offices, calling upon the States parties to a dispute to start the settlement procedure of their choice and recommending a time-limit for any agreed procedure.

3. This Article is without prejudice to the provisions of this Convention on facilitation and clarification of compliance.

Article 11 (Meetings of the States Parties)

1. The States Parties shall meet regularly in order to consider any matter with regard to the application or implementation of this Convention, including:

a) The operation and status of this Convention;

b) Matters arising from the reports submitted under the provisions of this Convention;

c) International cooperation and assistance in accordance with Article 6;

d) The development of technologies to clear anti-personnel mines;

e) Submissions of States Parties under Article 8; and

f) Decisions relating to submissions of States Parties as provided for in Article 5.

2. The First Meeting of the States Parties shall be convened by the Secretary-General of the United Nations within one year after the entry into force of this Convention. The subsequent meetings shall be convened by the Secretary-General of the United Nations annually until the first Review Conference.

3. Under the conditions set out in Article 8, the Secretary-General of the United Nations shall convene a Special Meeting of the States Parties.

4. States not parties to this Convention, as well as the United Nations, other relevant international organizations or institutions, regional organizations, the International Committee of the Red Cross and relevant non-governmental organizations may be invited to attend these meetings as observers in accordance with the agreed Rules of Procedure.

Article 12 (Review Conferences)

1. A Review Conference shall be convened by the Secretary-General of the United Nations five years after the entry into force of this Convention. Further Review Conferences shall be convened by the Secretary-General of the United Nations if so requested by one or more States Parties, provided that the interval between Review Conferences shall in no case be less than five years. All States Parties to this Convention shall be invited to each Review Conference.

2. The purpose of the Review Conference shall be:

a) To review the operation and status of this Convention;

b) To consider the need for and the interval between further Meetings of the States Parties referred to in paragraph 2 of Article 11;

c) To take decisions on submissions of States Parties as provided for in Article 5; and

d) To adopt, if necessary, in its final report conclusions related to the implementation of this Convention.

3. States not parties to this Convention, as well as the United Nations, other relevant international organizations or institutions, regional organizations, the International Committee of the Red Cross and relevant non-governmental organizations may be invited to attend each Review Conference as observers in accordance with the agreed Rules of Procedure.

Article 13 (Amendments)

1. At any time after the entry into force of this Convention any State Party may propose amendments to this Convention. Any proposal for an amendment shall be communicated to the Depository, who shall circulate it to all States Parties and shall seek their views on whether an Amendment Conference should be convened to consider the proposal. If a majority of the States Parties notify the Depository no later than 30 days after its circulation that they support further consideration of the proposal, the Depository shall convene an Amendment Conference to which all States Parties shall be invited.
2. States not parties to this Convention, as well as the United Nations, other relevant international organizations or institutions, regional organizations, the International Committee of the Red Cross and relevant non-governmental organizations may be invited to attend each Amendment Conference as observers in accordance with the agreed Rules of Procedure.
3. The Amendment Conference shall be held immediately following a Meeting of the States Parties or a Review Conference unless a majority of the States Parties request that it be held earlier.
4. Any amendment to this Convention shall be adopted by a majority of two-thirds of the States Parties present and voting at the Amendment Conference. The Depository shall communicate any amendment so adopted to the States Parties.
5. An amendment to this Convention shall enter into force for all States Parties to this Convention which have accepted it, upon the deposit with the Depositary of instruments of acceptance by a majority of States Parties. Thereafter it shall enter into force for any remaining State Party on the date of deposit of its instrument of acceptance.

Article 14 (Costs)

1. The costs of the Meetings of the States Parties, the Special Meetings of the States Parties, the Review Conferences and the Amendment Conferences shall be borne by the States Parties and States not parties to this Convention participating therein, in accordance with the United Nations scale of assessment adjusted appropriately.
2. The costs incurred by the Secretary-General of the United Nations under Articles 7 and 8 and the costs of any fact-finding mission shall be borne by the States Parties in accordance with the United Nations scale of assessment adjusted appropriately.

Article 15 (Signature)

This Convention, done at Oslo, Norway, on 18 September 1997, shall be open for signature at Ottawa, Canada, by all States from 3 December 1997 until 4 December 1997, and at the United Nations Headquarters in New York from 5 December 1997 until its entry into force.

Article 16 (Ratification, acceptance, approval or accession)
1. This Convention is subject to ratification, acceptance or approval of the Signatories.
2. It shall be open for accession by any State which has not signed the Convention.
3. The instruments of ratification, acceptance, approval or accession shall be deposited with the Depositary.

Article 17 (Entry into force)
1. This Convention shall enter into force on the first day of the sixth month after the month in which the 40th instrument of ratification, acceptance, approval or accession has been deposited.
2. For any State which deposits its instrument of ratification, acceptance, approval or accession after the date of the deposit of the 40th instrument of ratification, acceptance, approval or accession, this Convention shall enter into force on the first day of the sixth month after the date on which that State has deposited its instrument of ratification, acceptance, approval or accession.

Article 18 (Provisional application)
Any State may at the time of its ratification, acceptance, approval or accession, declare that it will apply provisionally paragraph 1 of Article 1 of this Convention pending its entry into force.

Article 19 (Reservations)
The Articles of this Convention shall not be subject to reservations.

Article 20 (Duration and withdrawal)
1. This Convention shall be of unlimited duration.
2. Each State Party shall, in exercising its national sovereignty, have the right to withdraw from this Convention. It shall give notice of such withdrawal to all other States Parties, to the Depositary and to the United Nations Security Council. Such instrument of withdrawal shall include a full explanation of the reasons motivating this withdrawal.
3. Such withdrawal shall only take effect six months after the receipt of the instrument of withdrawal by the Depositary. If, however, on the expiry of that six month period, the withdrawing State Party is engaged in an armed conflict, the withdrawal shall not take effect before the end of the armed conflict.
4. The withdrawal of a State Party from this Convention shall not in any way affect the duty of States to continue fulfilling the obligations assumed under any relevant rules of international law.

Article 21 (Depositary)
The Secretary-General of the United Nations is hereby designated as the Depositary of this Convention.

Article 22 (Authentic texts)
The original of this Convention, of which the Arabic, Chinese, English, French, Russian and Spanish texts are equally authentic, shall be deposited with the Secretary-General of the United Nations.

☛ **Amended Protocol II of the United Nations Convention on Prohibitions or Restrictions on the Use of Certain Conventional Weapons Which May Be Deemed to Be Excessively**

Injurious or to Have Indiscriminate Effects (Amended Protocol on Prohibitions or Restrictions on the Use of Mines, Booby-traps and Other Devices), 3 May 1996

Article 1 - Scope of application

1. This Protocol relates to the use on land of the mines, booby-traps and other devices, defined herein, including mines laid to interdict beaches, waterway crossings or river crossings, but does not apply to the use of anti-ship mines at sea or in inland waterways.

2. This Protocol shall apply, in addition to situations referred to in Article 1 of this Convention, to situations referred to in Article 3 common to the Geneva Conventions of 12 August 1949. This Protocol shall not apply to situations of internal disturbances and tensions, such as riots, isolated and sporadic acts of violence and other acts of a similar nature, as not being armed conflicts.

3. In case of armed conflicts not of an international character occurring in the territory of one of the High Contracting Parties, each party to the conflict shall be bound to apply the prohibitions and restrictions of this Protocol.

4. Nothing in this Protocol shall be invoked for the purpose of affecting the sovereignty of a State or the responsibility of the Government, by all legitimate means, to maintain or re-establish law and order in the State or to defend the national unity and territorial integrity of the State.

5. Nothing in this Protocol shall be invoked as a justification for intervening, directly or indirectly, for any reason whatever, in the armed conflict or in the internal or external affairs of the High Contracting Party in the territory of which that conflict occurs.

6. The application of the provisions of this Protocol to parties to a conflict, which are not High Contracting Parties that have accepted this Protocol, shall not change their legal status or the legal status of a disputed territory, either explicitly or implicitly.

Article 2 - Definitions

For the purpose of this Protocol:

1. 'Mine' means a munition placed under, on or near the ground or other surface area and designed to be exploded by the presence, proximity or contact of a person or vehicle.

2. 'Remotely delivered mine' means a mine not directly emplaced but delivered by artillery, missile, rocket, mortar, or similar means, or dropped from an aircraft. Mines delivered from a land-based system from less than 500 metres are not considered to be 'remotely delivered', provided that they are used in accordance with Article 5 and other relevant Articles of this Protocol.

3. Anti-personnel mine' means a mine primarily designed to be exploded by the presence, proximity or contact of a person and that will incapacitate, injure or kill one or more persons.

4. 'Booby-trap' means any device or material which is designed, constructed, or adapted to kill or injure, and which functions unexpectedly when a person disturbs or approaches an apparently harmless object or performs an apparently safe act.

5. 'Other devices' means manually emplaced munitions and devices including improvised explosive devices designed to kill, injure or damage and which are actuated manually, by remote control or automatically after a lapse of time.

6. 'Military objective' means, so far as objects are concerned, any object which by its nature, location, purpose or use makes an effective contribution to military action and whose total or

partial destruction, capture or neutralization, in the circumstances ruling at the time, offers a definite military advantage.

7. 'Civilian objects' are all objects which are not military objectives as defined in paragraph 6 of this Article.

8. 'Minefield' is a defined area in which mines have been emplaced and 'mined area' is an area which is dangerous due to the presence of mines. 'Phoney minefield' means an area free of mines that simulates a minefield. The term 'minefield' includes phoney minefields.

9. 'Recording' means a physical, administrative and technical operation designed to obtain, for the purpose of registration in official records, all available information facilitating the location of minefields, mined areas, mines, booby-traps and other devices.

10. 'Self-destruction mechanism' means an incorporated or externally attached automatically functioning mechanism which secures the destruction of the munition into which it is incorporated or to which it is attached.

11. 'Self-neutralization mechanism' means an incorporated automatically functioning mechanism which renders inoperable the munition into which it is incorporated.

12. 'Self-deactivating' means automatically rendering a munition inoperable by means of the irreversible exhaustion of a component, for example, a battery, that is essential to the operation of the munition.

13. 'Remote control' means control by commands from a distance.

14. 'Anti-handling device' means a device intended to protect a mine and which is part of, linked to, attached to or placed under the mine and which activates when an attempt is made to tamper with the mine.

15. 'Transfer' involves, in addition to the physical movement of mines into or from national territory, the transfer of title to and control over the mines, but does not involve the transfer of territory containing emplaced mines.

Article 3 - General restrictions on the use of mines/booby-traps and other devices

1. This Article applies to:
   (a) mines;
   (b) booby-traps; and
   (c) other devices.

2. Each High Contracting Party or party to a conflict is, in accordance with the provisions of this Protocol, responsible for all mines, booby-traps, and other devices employed by it and undertakes to clear, remove, destroy or maintain them as specified in Article 10 of this Protocol.

3. It is prohibited in all circumstances to use any mine, booby-trap or other device which is designed or of a nature to cause superfluous injury or unnecessary suffering.

4. Weapons to which this Article applies shall strictly comply with the standards and limitations specified in the Technical Annex with respect to each particular category.

5. It is prohibited to use mines, booby-traps, and other devices which employ a mechanism or device which is specifically designed to detonate the munition by the presence of commonly available mine detectors as a result of their magnetic or other non-contact influence during normal use in detection operations.

6. It is prohibited to use a self-deactivating mine equipped with an anti-handling device that is designed in such a manner that the anti-handling device is capable of functioning after the mine has ceased to be capable of functioning.
7. It is prohibited in all circumstances to direct weapons to which this Article applies, either in offence, defence or by way of reprisals, against the civilian population as such or against individual civilians or civilian objects.
8. The indiscriminate use of weapons to which this Article applies is prohibited. Indiscriminate use is any placement of such weapons:
   (a) which is not on, or directed against, a military objective. In case of doubt as to whether an object which is normally dedicated to civilian purposes, such as a place of worship, a house or other dwelling or a school, is being used to make an effective contribution to military action, it shall be presumed not to be so used;
   (b) which employs a method or means of delivery which cannot be directed at a specific military objective;
   (c) which may be expected to cause incidental loss of civilian life, injury to civilians, damage to civilian objects, or a combination thereof, which would be excessive in relation to the concrete and direct military advantage anticipated.
9. Several clearly separated and distinct military objectives located in a city, town, village or other area containing a similar concentration of civilians or civilian objects are not to be treated as a single military objective.
10. All feasible precautions shall be taken to protect civilians from the effects of weapons to which this Article applies. Feasible precautions are those precautions which are practicable or practically possible taking into account all circumstances ruling at the time, including humanitarian and military considerations. These circumstances include, but are not limited to:
   (a) the short- and long-term effect of mines upon the local civilian population for the duration of the minefield;
   (b) possible measures to protect civilians (for example, fencing, signs, warning and monitoring);
   (c) the availability and feasibility of using alternatives; and
   (d) the short- and long-term requirements for a minefield.
11. Effective advance warning shall be given of any emplacement of mines, booby-traps and other devices which may affect the civilian population, unless circumstances do not permit.

Article 4 - Restrictions on the use of anti-personnel mines
It is prohibited to use anti-personnel mines which are not detectable, as specified in paragraph 2 of the Technical Annex.

Article 5 - Restrictions on the use of anti-personnel mines other than remotely delivered mines
1. This Article applies to anti-personnel mines other than remotely-delivered mines.
2. It is prohibited to use weapons to which this Article applies which are not in compliance with the provisions on self-destruction and self-deactivation in the Technical Annex, unless:
   (a) such weapons are placed within a perimeter-marked area which is monitored by military personnel and protected by fencing or other means, to ensure the effective exclusion of civilians from the area. The marking must be of a distinct and durable character and must at least be visible to a person who is about to enter the perimeter-marked area; and

(b) such weapons are cleared before the area is abandoned unless the area is turned over to the forces of another State which accept responsibility for the maintenance of the protections required by this Article and the subsequent clearance of those weapons.

3. A party to a conflict is relieved from further compliance with the provisions of sub-paragraphs 2 (a) and 2 (b) of this Article only if such compliance is not feasible due to forcible loss of control of the area as a result of enemy military action, including situations where direct military action makes it impossible to comply. If that party regains control of the area, it shall resume compliance with the provisions of sub-paragraphs 2 (a) and 2 (b) of this Article.

4. If the forces of a party to a conflict gain control of an area in which weapons to which this Article applies have been laid, such forces shall, to the maximum extent feasible, maintain and, if necessary, establish the protections required by this Article until such weapons have been cleared.

5. All feasible measures shall be taken to prevent the unauthorized removal, defacement, destruction or concealment of any device, system or material used to establish the perimeter of a perimeter-marked area.

6. Weapons to which this Article applies which propel fragments in a horizontal arc of less than 90 degrees and which are placed on or above the ground may be used without the measures provided for in sub-paragraph 2 (a) of this Article for a maximum period of 72 hours, if:

(a) they are located in immediate proximity to the military unit that emplaced them; and

(b) the area is monitored by military personnel to ensure the effective exclusion of civilians.

Article 6 - Restrictions on the use of remotely-delivered mines

1. It is prohibited to use remotely-delivered mines unless they are recorded in accordance with sub-paragraph 1 (b) of the Technical Annex.

2. It is prohibited to use remotely delivered anti-personnel mines which are not in compliance with the provisions on self-destruction and self-deactivation in the Technical Annex.

3. It is prohibited to use remotely delivered mines other than anti-personnel mines, unless, to the extent feasible, they are equipped with an effective self-destruction or self-neutralization mechanism and have a back-up self-deactivation feature, which is designed so that the mine will no longer function as a mine when the mine no longer serves the military purpose for which it was placed in position.

4. Effective advance warning shall be given of any delivery or dropping of remotely delivered mines which may affect the civilian population, unless circumstances do not permit.

Article 7 - Prohibitions on the use of booby-traps and other devices

1. Without prejudice to the rules of international law applicable in armed conflict relating to treachery and perfidy, it is prohibited in all circumstances to use booby-traps and other devices which are in any way attached to or associated with:

(a) internationally recognized protective emblems, signs or signals;

(b) sick, wounded or dead persons;

(c) burial or cremation sites or graves;

(d) medical facilities, medical equipment, medical supplies or medical transportation:

(e) children's toys or other portable objects or products specially designed for the feeding, health, hygiene, clothing or education of children;
(f) food or drink;
(g) kitchen utensils or appliances except in military establishments, military locations or military supply depots;
(h) objects clearly of a religious nature;
(i) historic monuments, works of art or places of worship which constitute the cultural or spiritual heritage of peoples; or
(j) animals or their carcasses.

2. It is prohibited to use booby-traps and other devices in the form of apparently harmless portable objects which are specifically designed and constructed to contain explosive material.
3. Without prejudice to the provisions of Article 3, it is prohibited to use weapons to which this Article applies in any city, town, village or other area containing a similar concentration of civilians in which combat between ground forces is not taking place or does not appear to be imminent, unless either:
(a) they are placed on or in the close vicinity of a military objective; or
(b) measures are take to protect civilians from their effects, for example. the posting of warning sentries, the issuing of warnings or the provision of fences.

Article 8 - Transfers

1. In order to promote the purposes of this Protocol, each High Contracting Party
(a) undertakes not to transfer any mine the use of which is prohibited by this Protocol;
(b) undertakes not to transfer any mine to any recipient other than a State or a State agency authorized to receive such transfers;
(c) undertakes to exercise restraint in the transfer of any mine the use of which is restricted by this Protocol. In particular, each High Contracting Party undertakes not to transfer an anti-personnel mines to States which are not bound by this Protocol, unless the recipient State agrees to apply this Protocol; and
(d) undertakes to ensure that any transfer in accordance with this Article takes place in full compliance, by both the transferring and the recipient State, with the relevant provisions of this Protocol and the applicable norms of international humanitarian law.

2. In the event that a High Contracting Party declares that it will defer compliance with specific provisions on the use of certain mines, as provided for in the Technical Annex, sub-paragraph 1 (a) of this Article shall however apply to such mines.
3. All High Contracting Parties, pending the entry into force of this Protocol, will refrain from any actions which would be inconsistent with sub-paragraph 1 (a) of this Article.

Article 9 - Recording and use of information on minefields, mined areas, mines, booby-traps and other devices

1. All information concerning minefields, mined areas, mines, booby-traps and other devices shall be recorded in accordance with the provisions of the Technical Annex.
2. All such records shall be retained by the parties to a conflict, who shall, without delay after the cessation of active hostilities, take all necessary and appropriate measures, including the use of such information, to protect civilians from the effects of minefields, mined areas, mines,

boobytraps and other devices in areas under their control. At the same time, they shall also make available to the other party or parties to the conflict and to the Secretary-General of the United Nations all such information in their possession concerning minefields, mined areas, mines, booby-traps and other devices laid by them in areas no longer under their control; provided, however, subject to reciprocity, where the forces of a party to a conflict are in the territory of an adverse party, either party may withhold such information from the Secretary-General and the other party, to the extent that security interests require such withholding, until neither party is in the territory of the other. In the latter case, the information withheld shall be disclosed as soon as those security interests permit. Wherever possible, the parties to the conflict shall seek, by mutual agreement, to provide for the release of such information at the earliest possible time in a manner consistent with the security interests of each party.
3. This Article is without prejudice to the provisions of Articles 10 and 12 of this Protocol.

Article 10 - Removal of minefields, mined areas, mines, booby-traps and other devices and international cooperation
1. Without delay after the cessation of active hostilities, all minefields, mined areas, mines, booby-traps and other devices shall be cleared, removed, destroyed or maintained in accordance with Article 3 and paragraph 2 of Article 5 of this Protocol.
2. High Contracting Parties and parties to a conflict bear such responsibility with respect to minefields, mined areas, mines, booby-traps and other devices in areas under their control.
3. With respect to minefields, mined areas, mines, booby-traps and other devices laid by a party in areas over which it no longer exercises control, such party shall provide to the party in control of the area pursuant to paragraph 2 of this Article, to the extent permitted by such party, technical and material assistance necessary to fulfil such responsibility.
4. At all times necessary, the parties shall endeavour to reach such agreement, both among themselves and, where appropriate, with other States and with international organizations, on the provision of technical and material assistance, including, in appropriate circumstances, the undertaking of joint operations necessary to fulfil such responsibilities.

Article 11 - Technological cooperation and assistance
1. Each High Contracting Party undertakes to facilitate and shall have the right to participate in the fullest possible exchange of equipment, material and scientific and technological information concerning the implementation of this Protocol and means of mine clearance. In particular, High Contracting Parties shall not impose undue restrictions on the provision of mine-clearance equipment and related technological information for humanitarian purposes.
2. Each High Contracting Party undertakes to provide information to the database on mine clearance established within the United Nations System, especially information concerning various means and technologies of mine clearance, and lists of experts, expert agencies or national points of contact on mine clearance.
3. Each High Contracting Party in a position to do so shall provide assistance for mine clearance through the United Nations System, other international bodies or on a bilateral basis, or contribute to the United Nations Voluntary Trust Fund for Assistance in Mine Clearance.
4. Requests by High Contracting Parties for assistance, substantiated by relevant information, may be submitted to the United Nations, to other appropriate bodies or to other States. These

requests may be submitted to the Secretary-General of the United Nations, who shall transmit them to all High Contracting Parties and to relevant international organizations.
5. In the case of requests to the United Nations, the Secretary-General of the United Nations, within the resources available to the Secretary-General of the United Nations, may take appropriate steps to assess the situation and, in cooperation with the requesting High Contracting Party, determine the appropriate provision of assistance in mine clearance or implementation of the Protocol. The Secretary-General may also report to High Contracting Parties on any such assessment as well as on the type and scope of assistance required.
6. Without prejudice to their constitutional and other legal provisions, the High Contracting Parties undertake to cooperate and transfer technology to facilitate the implementation of the relevant prohibitions and restrictions set out in this Protocol.
7. Each High Contracting Party has the right to seek and receive technical assistance, where appropriate, from another High Contracting Party on specific relevant technology, other than weapons technology, as necessary and feasible, with a view to reducing any period of deferral for which provision is made in the Technical Annex.

Article 12 - Protection from the effects of minefields, mined areas, mines, booby-traps and other devices

1. Application
   (a) With the exception of the forces and missions referred to in sub-paragraph 2 (a) (i) of this Article, this Article applies only to missions which are performing functions in an area with the consent of the High Contracting Party on whose territory the functions are performed.
   (b) The application of the provisions of this Article to parties to a conflict which are not High Contracting Parties shall not change their legal status or the legal status of a disputed territory, either explicitly or implicitly.
   (c) The provisions of this Article are without prejudice to existing international humanitarian law, or other international instruments as applicable, or decisions by the Security Council of the United Nations, which provide for a higher level of protection to personnel functioning in accordance with this Article.
2. Peace-keeping and certain other forces and missions
   (a) This paragraph applies to:
      (i) any United Nations force or mission performing peace-keeping, observation or similar functions in any area in accordance with the Charter of the United Nations;
      (ii) any mission established pursuant to Chapter VIII of the Charter of the United Nations and performing its functions in the area of a conflict.
   (b) Each High Contracting Party or party to a conflict, if so requested by the head of a force or mission to which this paragraph applies, shall:
      (i) so far as it is able, take such measures as are necessary to protect the force or mission from the effects of mines, booby-traps and other devices in any area under its control;
      (ii) if necessary in order effectively to protect such personnel, remove or render harmless, so far as it is able, all mines, booby-traps and other devices in that area; and
      (iii) inform the head of the force or mission of the location of all known minefields, mined areas, mines, booby-traps and other devices in the area in which the force or mission is

performing its functions and, so far as is feasible, make available to the head of the force or mission all information in its possession concerning such minefields, mined areas, mines, booby-traps and other devices.

3. Humanitarian and fact-finding missions of the United Nations System

(a) This paragraph applies to any humanitarian and fact-finding missions of the United Nations System.

(b) Each High Contracting Party or party to a conflict, if so requested by the head of a force or mission to which this paragraph applies, shall:

(i) provide the personnel of the mission with the protections set out in sub-paragraph 2 (b) (i) of this Article; and

(ii) if access to or through any place under its control is necessary for the performance of the mission's functions and in order to provide the personnel of that mission with safe passage to or through that place:

(aa) unless on-going hostilities prevent, inform the head of the mission of a safe route to that place if such information is available; or

(bb) if information identifying a safe route is not provided in accordance with subparagraph (aa), so far as is necessary and feasible, clear a lane through minefields

4. Missions of the International Committee of the Red Cross

(a) This paragraph applies to any mission of the International Committee of the Red Cross performing functions with the consent of the host State or States as provided for by the Geneva Conventions of 12 August 1949 and, where applicable, their Additional Protocols.

(b) Each High Contracting Party or party to a conflict, if so requested by the head of a force or mission to which this paragraph applies, shall:

(i) provide the personnel of the mission with the protections set out in sub-paragraph 2 (b) (I) of this Article; and

(ii) take the measures set out in sub-paragraph 3 (b) (ii) of this Article.

5. Other humanitarian missions and missions of enquiry

(a) Insofar as paragraphs 2, 3 and 4 above do not apply to them, this paragraph applies to the following missions when they are performing functions in the area of a conflict or to assist the victims of a conflict:

(i) any humanitarian mission of a national Red Cross or Red Crescent society or of their International Federation;

(ii) any mission of an impartial humanitarian Organization, including any impartial humanitarian demining mission; and

(iii) any mission of enquiry established pursuant to the provisions of the Geneva Conventions of 12 August 1949 and, where applicable, their Additional Protocols.

(b) Each High Contracting Party or party to a conflict, if so requested by the head of a force or mission to which this paragraph applies, shall:

(i) provide the personnel of the mission with the protections set out in sub-paragraph 2 (b) (I) of this Article; and

(ii) take the measures set out in sub-paragraph 3 (b) (ii) of this Article.

6. Confidentiality
All information provided in confidence pursuant to this Article shall be treated by the recipient in strict confidence and shall not be released outside the force or mission concerned without the express authorization of the provider of the information. Without prejudice to such privileges and immunities as they may enjoy or to the requirements of their duties, personnel participating in the forces and missions referred to in this Article shall:

(a) respect the laws and regulations of the host State; and

(b) refrain from any action or activity incompatible with the impartial and international nature of their duties.

Article 13 - Consultations of High Contracting Parties

1. The High Contracting Parties undertake to consult and cooperate with each other on all issues related to the operation of this Protocol. For this purpose, a conference of High Contracting Parties shall be held annually.
2. Participation in the annual conferences shall be determined by their agreed Rules of Procedure.
3. The work of the conference shall include:

(a) review of the operation and status of this Protocol;

(b) consideration of matters arising from reports by High Contracting Parties according to paragraph 4 of this Article;

(c) preparation for review conferences; and

(d) consideration of the development of technologies to protect civilians against indiscriminate effects of mines.

4. The High Contracting Parties shall provide annual reports to the Depositary, who shall circulate them to all High Contracting Parties in advance of the Conference, on any of the following matters:

(a) dissemination of information on this Protocol to their armed forces and to the civilian population;

(b) mine clearance and rehabilitation programmes;

(c) steps taken to meet technical requirements of this Protocol and any other relevant information pertaining thereto;

(d) legislation related to this Protocol;

(e) measures taken on international technical information exchange, on international cooperation on mine clearance, and on technical cooperation and assistance; and

(f) other relevant matters.

5. The cost of the Conference of High Contracting Parties shall be borne by the High Contracting Parties and States not parties participating in the work of the Conference, in accordance with the United Nations scale of assessment adjusted appropriately.

Article 14 - Compliance

1. Each High Contracting Party shall take all appropriate steps, including legislative and other measures, to prevent and suppress violations of this Protocol by persons or on territory under its jurisdiction or control.
2. The measures envisaged in paragraph 1 of this Article include appropriate measures to ensure the imposition of penal sanctions against persons who, in relation to an armed conflict and contrary

to the provisions of this Protocol, wilfully kill or cause serious injury to civilians and to bring such persons to justice.
3. Each High Contracting Party shall also require that its armed forces issue relevant military instructions and operating procedures and that armed forces personnel receive training commensurate with their duties and responsibilities to comply with the provisions of this Protocol.
4. The High Contracting Parties undertake to consult each other and to cooperate with each other bilaterally, through the Secretary-General of the United Nations or through other appropriate international procedures, to resolve any problems that may arise with regard to the interpretation and application of the provisions of this Protocol.

Technical Annex
1. Recording
(a) Recording of the location of mines other than remotely delivered mines, minefields, mined areas, booby-traps and other devices shall be carried out in accordance with the following provisions:
(i) the location of the minefields, mined areas, booby-traps and other devices shall be specified accurately by relation to the coordinates of at least two reference points and the estimated dimensions of the area containing these weapons in relation to those reference points;
(ii) maps, diagrams or other records shall be made in such a way as to indicate the location of minefields, mined areas, booby-traps and other devices in relation to reference points, and these records shall also indicate their perimeters and extent; and
(iii) for purposes of detection and clearance of mines, booby-traps and other devices, maps, diagrams or other records shall contain complete information on the type, number, emplacing method, type of fuse and life time, date and time of laying, anti-handling devices (if any) and other relevant information on all these weapons laid. Whenever feasible the minefield record shall show the exact location of every mine, except in row minefields where the row location is sufficient. The precise location and operating mechanism of each booby-trap laid shall be individually recorded.
(b) The estimated location and area of remotely delivered mines shall be specified by coordinates of reference points (normally corner points) and shall be ascertained and when feasible marked on the ground at the earliest opportunity. The total number and type of mines laid, the date and time of laying and the self-destruction time periods shall also be recorded.
(c) Copies of records shall be held at a level of command sufficient to guarantee their safety as far as possible.
(d) The use of mines produced after the entry into force of this Protocol is prohibited unless they are marked in English or in the respective national language or languages with the following information:
(i) name of the country of origin;
(ii) month and year of production; and
(iii) serial number or lot number.

The marking should be visible, legible, durable and resistant to environmental effects, as far as possible.

2. Specifications on detectability

(a) With respect to anti-personnel mines produced after 1 January 1997, such mines shall incorporate in their construction a material or device that enables the mine to be detected by commonly available technical mine detection equipment and provides a response signal equivalent to a signal from 8 grammes or more of iron in a single coherent mass.

(b) With respect to anti-personnel mines produced before 1 January 1997, such mines shall either incorporate in their construction, or have attached prior to their emplacement, in a manner not easily removable, a material or device that enables the mine to be detected by commonly available technical mine-detection equipment and provides a response signal equivalent to a signal from 8 grammes or more of iron in a single coherent mass.

(c) In the event that a High Contracting Party determines that it cannot immediately comply with sub-paragraph (b), it may declare at the time of its notification of consent to be bound by this Protocol, that it will defer compliance with sub-paragraph (b) for a period not to exceed 9 years from the entry into force of this Protocol. In the meantime it shall, to the extent feasible, minimize the use of anti-personnel mines that do not so comply.

3. Specifications on self-destruction and self-deactivation

(a) All remotely delivered anti-personnel mines shall be designed and constructed so that not more than 10 percent of activated mines will fail to self-destruct within 30 days after emplacement, and each mine shall have a back-up self-deactivation feature designed and constructed so that, in combination with the self-destruction mechanism, no more than one in one thousand activated mines will function as a mine 120 days after emplacement.

(b) All non-remotely delivered anti-personnel mines, used outside marked areas, as defined in Article 5 of this Protocol, shall comply with the requirements for self-destruction and self-deactivation stated in sub-paragraph (a).

(c) In the event that a High Contracting Party determines that it cannot immediately comply with sub-paragraphs (a) and/or (b), it may declare at the time of its notification of consent to be bound by this Protocol, that it will, with respect to mines produced prior to the entry into force of this Protocol defer compliance with sub-paragraphs (a) and/or (b) for a period not to exceed 9 years from the entry into force of this Protocol. During this period of deferral, the High Contracting Party shall:

(i) undertake to minimize, to the extent feasible, the use of anti-personnel mines that do not so comply, and

(ii) with respect to remotely delivered anti-personnel mines, comply with either the requirements for self-destruction or the requirements for self-deactivation and, with respect to other anti-personnel mines comply with at least the requirements for self-deactivation.

4. International signs for minefields and mined areas

Signs similar to the example attached on following page and as specified below shall be utilized in the marking of minefields and mined areas to ensure their visibility and recognition by the civilian population:

(a) size and shape: a triangle or square no smaller than 28 centimetres (11 inches) by 20 centimetres (7.9 inches) for a triangle, and 15 centimetres (6 inches) per side for a square;

(b) colour: red or orange with a yellow reflecting border;
(c) symbol: the symbol illustrated in the Attachment, or an alternative readily recognizable in the area in which the sign is to be displayed as identifying a dangerous area;
(d) language: the sign should contain the word 'mines' in one of the six official languages of the Convention (Arabic, Chinese, English, French, Russian and Spanish) and the language or languages prevalent in that area; and
(e) spacing: signs should be placed around the minefield or mined area at a distance sufficient to ensure their visibility at any point by a civilian approaching the area.

☛ **AUSTRIA: Federal Law on the Ban of Anti-Personnel Mines**[1]

Article 1 - Definitions
In the context of this Federal Law: (...)
1. 'Anti-personnel mine', a means of combat designed to be placed under, on or near the ground or other surface area and designed to detonate or explode by the presence, proximity or contact of persons.
2. 'Anti-detection mechanism', a device designed to bring an anti-personnel mine to explosion or detonation by the use of a mine-detecting device.

Article 2 - Prohibitions
The production, acquisition, sale, procurement, import, export, transit, use and possession of anti-personnel mines as well as of anti-detection mechanisms shall be prohibited.

Article 3 - Restrictions
1. Mines earmarked exclusively for training purposes within the Federal Army or the Mine Clearance Service or the Explosives Disposal Service are not subject to the prohibition set out in Article 2.
2. The import, possession and the stockpiling of anti-personnel mines for the purpose of immediate delaboration [sic] or other ways of destruction are not subject to the prohibition set out in Article 2.

Article 4 - Destruction of Existing Stockpiles
Existing stockpiles of anti-personnel mines or anti-detection mechanisms prohibited under Article 2 shall be reported to the Federal Ministry of the Interior within one month and shall be destroyed by the said Ministry not later than one year after the entry into force of this Federal Law upon reimbursement of costs.

1. Entered into force 1 January 1997. Published 10 January 1997 in *Bundesgesetzblatt* nr. 263/1996. Working translation provided by Federal Ministry of Justice.

Article 5 - Penalty
Whoever, and even if only by negligence, contravenes the prohibition of Article 2 of this Federal Law, shall be sentenced to imprisonment for up to two years, a fine up to 360 per diem rates, if the offence is not subject to a more severe penalty under any other Federal Law.

Article 6 - Confiscation and Forfeiture
1. Anti-personnel mines or anti-detection mechanisms as well as components thereof which are subject of an act punishable under Article 5 shall be confiscated by the Court order.
2. Machines and facilities used in the production of items under the prohibition set out in Article 2 can be declared forfeited by the Court. It shall be secured at the owner's expense that those items cannot be further used in contravention of the prohibition set out in Article 2.
3. Means used to transport items under the prohibition of Article 2 may be declared forfeited by the Court.
4. Items forfeiture according to paragraphs 2 and 3 shall become property of the Federation. Items confiscated under paragraph 1 shall become property of the Federation and must be reported to the Federal Ministry of the interior for destruction in accordance with Article 4.

Article 7 - Execution
Entrusted with the execution of this Federal Law are:
1. With respect to Article 3 paragraph 1 - the Federal Minister of the Interior and the Federal Minister of Defence,
2. With respect to Articles 5 and 6 - the Federal Minister of Justice and
3. With respect to the other provisions - the Federal Minister of the Interior.

Article 8 - Entry into Force
This Federal Law enters into force on 1st January 1997.

☛ **FINLAND: Finland's Position on Anti-personnel Landmines (APLS). Fact Sheet of the Finnish Ministry for Foreign Affairs, Political Department, 26 August 1997**[1]

The indiscriminate use of APLs in mostly internal conflicts around the world is causing widespread suffering to the civilian population. Finland supports effective international measures to put an end to this crisis through her support for the existing international norms, work for a total ban and participation in mine clearance in post-conflict areas.

Finland wants a global, verifiable and legally binding ban on APLs. Such a ban should ensure that civilians will not be terrorized with anti-personnel landmines.

To achieve an effective ban, involvement of the countries responsible for the crisis, including major producers and exporters, is necessary. Unilateral actions by countries such as Finland will not stop the landmine crisis.

Finland is actively working to launch negotiations on a total ban at the Geneva Conference on Disarmament which counts all the key countries as its members and also provides for the

1. For commentary, see Lauri Hannikainen at p. 436 et seq.

possibility of active participation by non-members who so wish. The recent appointment of a Special Coordinator to work on a mandate for APL negotiations at the Conference is a welcome step forward.

Norway is hosting an international conference in Oslo from 1 to 19 September to negotiate a ban on APLs. The conference is a part of the Ottawa process that has strengthened the momentum towards a total ban during the past year. Unfortunately it does not involve all the key countries.

Finland participates in the Oslo conference as an observer.

Finland is of the view that work at the Conference on Disarmament and within the Ottawa process can and should be mutually complementary. An effective end to the landmine crisis requires the involvement of both.

Finland has never exported any APLs, nor are any APLs being produced in Finland. Finland does not have any APLs or other landmines deployed anywhere in her territory. Finland maintains a stockpile of APLs for strictly defensive purposes. APLs are an integral part of the Finnish territorial defense doctrine. They would only be used in response to armed aggression against Finland. Given their importance to Finland's defence, any decision to destroy APLs and to bear the considerable cost of providing for the same defensive impact with other means would have to be made in the context of such a total ban that Finland regards as responding effectively to the global landmine crisis.

The viability of already existing international norms must be ensured. In particular, Finland stresses the need for early entry into force of and wide accession to the amended Protocol II of the Convention on Prohibitions or Restrictions on the use of Certain Conventional Weapons. Finland has been a party to the CCW Convention since its entry into force in 1983, and will ratify the amended Protocol in the nearest future.

Mine clearance and help for the victims of landmines remains a challenge that requires intensive international attention. The contribution of Finland to international mine clearance is growing. In 1997 Finland's national contribution will be approximately 3 million USD.

☛ ITALY: Rules for the Ban of Anti-personnel Land-mines, Law No. 374, October 29, 1997[1]

Article 1 (objectives)

1. It is forbidden to use, for whatever purpose, all types of anti-personnel mines, with the exception of the quantity provided for by Article 5, Paragraph 1, and for the exclusive use in demining operations training.

2. It is forbidden to pursue technological research, to manufacture, sell, transfer for whatever purpose, export, import, stockpile anti-personnel mines of all types or composition, or their components.

1. Published (in Italian) in *Supplemento ordinario alla Gazetta Ufficiale*, series generate, n. 276, 25 November 1995. For commentary, see Gargiulo, *supra* p. 323.

3. It is forbidden to use and transfer, for whatever purpose, patent rights for the manufacturing of anti-personnel mines or their components, in Italy and abroad, directly or indirectly, and to use and transfer, for whatever purpose, technologies suitable to manufacturing anti-personnel mines and their components.

Article 2 (definition)
1. 'Anti-personnel mine' means any munition or device which can be placed on, under, inside or near the ground or any surface area - and designed or adaptable - by means of specific mechanisms - so as to explode, cause an explosion or release incapacitating substances as a consequence of the presence, proximity or contact of a person.

Article 3 (obligations for anti-personnel mines holders)
Within 120 days from the entry into force of this Law, all Italian companies producing anti-personnel mines and their components, and whoever may hold anti-personnel mines and their components for whatever purpose, must report to the Carabinieri local headquarters and disclose the amount of mines or their components in their own possession. They must also, within the following 90 days, deliver all mines and their components to the Ministry of Defence, in accordance with the provisions of the existing law, to appropriate sites as indicated by the local Carabinieri headquarters.

Article 4 (obligations for owners of patent rights or technologies suitable to the manufacturing of anti-personnel mines)
1. Whoever may hold, for whatever purpose, patent rights or technologies suitable to the manufacturing of anti-personnel mines or their components must report to the Ministry of Industry and Trade within 60 days from the entry into force of the present Law.

Article 5 (destruction of stockpiles)
1. Within five years from the entry into force of this Law, the Ministry of Defence will see to the destruction of the stocks of anti-personnel mines assigned to or stockpiled by the Armed Forces, with the only exception of a limited amount, in no case exceeding the number of 10,000 mines, which can be renewed by means of importation, notwithstanding Article 1, Paragraph 2 of the present Law. These mines will exclusively be used for training in demining operations.
2. Within the same term as in Paragraph 1, the Ministry of Defence must also destroy all the anti-personnel mines handed over by private companies and any other holder, in accordance with Article 3 of this Law.
3. The expenses deriving from the implementation of Paragraph 1 and 2, estimated at 10 billion Italian lira per year in 1998 and 1999 respectively, will be covered by means of the 1998 and 1999 projections of the itemized budget registered (for the three year budget 1997-1999) under Chapter 6586 of the Ministry of Treasure state of provision concerning 1997, by partially resorting for this purpose to the budget accumulated for the Presidency of the Council of Ministers. The Minister of Treasure is authorized to introduce, by its own decrees, the necessary budget variations.

Article 6 (ministerial decree)
1. Within six months from the entry into force of the present Law, the Ministry of Defence, in concert with the Ministry of Foreign Affairs and the Ministry of Industry and Trade, will issue a decree outlining the rules for the destruction of the stockpiles of anti-personnel mines. These rules will also take into account the needs for environmental protection. The decree will also indicate the *ad hoc* official in charge and the responsible official at the Ministry of Defence. In addition to that, all quantities and types of anti-personnel mines held by the Armed Forces, and those delivered to the Ministry of Defence in accordance with Article 3, will be recorded in an appropriate Register. The date and means of destruction will be recorded in the same Register, as well as the disclosures made in accordance to Article 4 herein. The draft of the decree will be subject to the relevant Parliamentary Committees, which will express their evaluation within 20 days. The decree will then be published in the *Gazzetta Ufficiale.*

Article 7 (sanctions)
1. Whoever may use, with the exception of the provisions included in Article 5, Paragraph 1, manufacture, sell, transfer for whatever purpose, export, import, hold anti-personnel mines or their components, and whoever may use or transfer, directly or indirectly, patent rights or suitable technologies for the manufacturing, in Italy or abroad, of anti-personnel mines and their components, will be punished with 3 to 12 years of imprisonment and with a 500 million to 1,000 million Italian lira fine.
2. Whoever may infringe obligations provided in Articles 3 and 4 will be punished with 3 to 6 years of imprisonment and with a 200 to 500 million Italian lira fine. Guilty parties will also be banned from all public contracts for a period ranging from 5 to 10 years.
3. Sanctions provided in Paragraph 1 and 2 are reduced by half if the fact persecuted is of particularly small entity.

Article 8 (activities in favour of anti-personnel mines victims)
1. In Article 4, Paragraph 3 of the Law n. 49 'New Rules for Italian Cooperation with Developing Countries', dated 26th of February 1987, after item m), the following provision is added: m-bis) 'support to victims of anti-personnel mines through compensation, assistance and rehabilitation programmes'.

Article 9 (Ministers' competences and reporting to Parliament)
1. Ministers of Foreign Affairs, Defence and Industry and Trade will coordinatingly provide for the implementation of the present Law, therein including the destruction of anti-personnel mines, particularly the stockpile held by the Armed Forces, and all other anti-personnel mines taken into consideration by Articles 3 and 5.
2. The Ministers of Foreign Affairs, Defence and Industry and Trade will report to the Parliament every 6 months about the state of implementation of this Law. The Minister of Defence will also provide a yearly account of the ongoing destruction of stockpiles and related expenses and budget.

Article 10 (exemption from state secret and military secret)
1. State secret, as regulated in Law n. 801 of October 24, 1977 and in articles 202 and 256 of the Code of Criminal Procedure does not apply to what is provided for by the present Law, nor does the Military secret, as provided for by the Royal Decree n. 1161, July 11, 1941

☛ **USA: Protocols to the 1980 Conventional Weapons Convention**
Message From the President of the United States Transmitting Protocols to the 1980 Convention on Prohibitions or Restrictions on the Use of Certain Conventional Weapons Which May Be Deemed to Be Excessively Injurious or to Have Indiscriminate Effects: the Amended Protocol on Prohibitions or Restrictions on the Use of Mines, Booby-traps and Other Devices (Protocol II or the Amended Mines Protocol); the Protocol on Prohibitions or Restrictions on the Use of Incendiary Weapons (Protocol III or the Incendiary Weapons Protocol); and the Protocol on Blinding Laser Weapons (Protocol IV)

105TH CONGRESS, lst Session, Senate, Treaty Doc.105-1.
January 7, 1997. Protocols were read the first time and, together with the accompanying, papers, referred to the Committee on Foreign Relations and ordered to be printed for the use of the Senate.

Letter of transmittal
White House, January 7, 1997.
To the Senate of the United States:

I transmit herewith, for the advice and consent of the Senate to ratification, the following Protocols to the 1980 Convention on Prohibitions or Restrictions on the Use of Certain Conventional Weapons Which May Be Deemed to Be Excessively Injurious or to Have Indiscriminate Effects: the amended Protocol on Prohibitions or Restrictions on the Use of Mines, Booby-Traps and Other Devices (Protocol II or the amended Mines Protocol); the Protocol on Prohibitions or Restrictions on the Use of Incendiary Weapons (Protocol III or the Incendiary Weapons Protocol); and the Protocol on Blinding Laser Weapons (Protocol IV). Also transmitted for the information of the Senate is the report of the Department of State with respect to these Protocols, together with article-by-article analyses.

The most important of these Protocols is the amended Mines Protocol. It is an essential step forward in dealing with the problem of anti-personnel landmines (APL) and in minimizing the very severe casualties to civilians that have resulted from their use. It is an important precursor to the total prohibition of these weapons that the United States seeks.

Among other things, the amended Mines Protocol will do the following: (1) expand the scope of the original Protocol to include internal armed conflicts, where most civilian mine casualties have occurred; (2) require that all remotely delivered anti-personnel mines be equipped with self-destruct devices and backup self-deactivation features to ensure that they do not pose a longterm threat to civilians; (3) require that all nonremotely delivered anti-personnel mines that are not equipped with such devices be used only within controlled, marked, and monitored minefields to protect the civilian population in the area; (4) require that all anti-personnel mines be detectable using commonly available technology to make the task of mine clearance easier and safer; (5) require that the party laying mines assume responsibility for them to ensure against their irresponsible and indiscriminate use; and (6) provide more effective means for dealing with compliance problems to ensure that these restrictions are actually observed. These objectives were all endorsed by the Senate in its Resolution of Ratification of the Convention in March 1995.

The amended Mines Protocol was not as strong as we would have preferred. In particular, its provisions on verification and compliance are not as rigorous as we had proposed, and the transition periods allowed for the conversion or elimination of certain non-compliant mines are longer than we thought necessary. We shall pursue these issues in the regular meetings that the amended Protocol provides for review of its operation.

Nonetheless, I am convinced that this amended Protocol will, if generally adhered to, save many lives and prevent many tragic injuries. It will, as well, help to prepare the ground for the total prohibition of anti-personnel landmines to which the United States is committed. In this regard, I cannot overemphasize how seriously the United States takes the goal of eliminating APL entirely. The carnage and devastation caused by anti-personnel landmines-the hidden killers that murder and maim more than 25,000 people every year-must end.

On May 16, 1996, I launched an international effort to this end. This initiative sets out a concrete path to a global ban on anti-personnel landmines and is one of my top arms control priorities. At the same time, the policy recognizes that the United States has international commitments and responsibilities that must be taken into account in any negotiations on a total ban. As our work on this initiative progresses, we will continue to consult with the Congress.

The second of these Protocols - the Protocol on Incendiary Weapons is a part of the original Convention but was not sent to the Senate for advice and consent with the other 1980 Protocols in 1994 because of concerns about the acceptability of the Protocol from a military point of view. Incendiary weapons have significant potential military value, particularly with respect to flammable military targets that cannot so readily be destroyed with conventional explosives.

At the same time, these weapons can be misused in a manner that could cause heavy civilian casualties. In particular, the Protocol prohibits the use of air-delivered incendiary weapons against targets located in a city, town, village, or other concentration of civilians, a practice that caused very heavy civilian casualties in past conflicts.

The executive branch has given very careful study to the Incendiaries Protocol and has developed a reservation that would, in our view, make it acceptable from a broader national security perspective. This proposed reservation, the text of which appears in the report of the Department of State, would reserve the right to use incendiaries against military objectives located in concentrations of civilians where it is judged that such use would cause fewer casualties and less collateral damage than alternative weapons.

The third of these Protocols - the new Protocol on Blinding lasers - prohibits the use or transfer of laser weapons specifically designed to cause permanent blindness to unenhanced vision (that is, to the naked eye or to the eye with corrective devices). The Protocol also requires Parties to take all feasible precautions in the employment of other laser systems to avoid the incidence of such blindness.

These blinding lasers are not needed by our military forces. They are potential weapons of the future, and the United States is committed to preventing their emergence and use. The United States supports the adoption of this new Protocol.

I recommend that the Senate give its early and favorable consideration to these Protocols and give its advice and consent to ratification, subject to the conditions described in the accompanying report of the Department of State. The prompt ratification of the amended Mines Protocol is particularly important, so that the United States can continue its position of leadership in the effort to deal with the humanitarian catastrophe of irresponsible landmine use

William J. Clinton.
Department of State,
Washington, December 7, 1996.

The President,
The White House.

The President: I have the honor to submit to you, with a view to transmission to the Senate for advice and consent to ratification, three protocols to the Convention on Prohibitions or Restriction on the Use of Certain Conventional Weapons Which May be Deemed to be Excessively Injurious or to Have Indiscriminate Effects (the Convention):
(A) the Amended Protocol on Prohibitions or Restrictions on the Use of Mines, Booby Traps and Other Devices adopted at Geneva on May 3, 1996 (Protocol II or the Amended Mines Protocol);
(B) the Protocol on Prohibitions or Restrictions on the Use of Incendiary Weapons adopted at Geneva on October 10, 1980 (Protocol III or the Incendiary Weapons Protocol); and
(C) the Protocol on Blinding Laser Weapons adopted at Geneva on May 3, 1996 (Protocol IV).
Also submitted for transmittal for the information of the Senate is the report of the Department of State with respect to these Protocols, together with article-by-article analyses.

BACKGROUND

The Convention was concluded at Geneva on October 10, 1980, and signed by the United States on April 8, 1982. It entered into force on December 2, 1983, and, along with two of its Protocols, was ratified by the United States on March 24, 1995.

The Convention is part of a legal regime dealing with the conduct of armed conflict, including the four 1949 Geneva Conventions on the Protection of the Victims of War and the 1899 and 1907 Hague Conventions Respecting the Laws and Customs of War on Land. These important treaties attempt to reduce the suffering caused by armed conflicts and provide protection to the victims of war in a manner consistent with legitimate military requirements. The Convention, adopted October 10, 1980, contained three Protocols, each of which regulated the use of a particular type of conventional weapon thought to pose special risks of indiscriminate effects or unnecessary suffering. Protocol I, the Non-detectable Fragments Protocol, prohibits the use of – any weapon the primary effect of which – is to injure by fragments which in the human body escape detection by X-rays. Protocol II, the Mines Protocol, contains a detailed set of restrictions on the use of mines, booby-traps and similar devices, which are discussed at greater length below. Protocol III, the Incendiary Weapons Protocol, restricts the use of incendiary weapons in various ways.

In March 1995, the United States Senate gave its advice and consent to ratification of the Convention, including its Non-detectable Fragments Protocol and its Protocol. The Incendiary Weapons Protocol was not transmitted to the Senate at the time the Convention (and the two protocols) was transmitted and was instead given further study by the interagency community owing to certain military concerns. Those concerns have now been fully addressed. The First Review Conference for the Convention completed its review with the adoption of an amended Mines Protocol on May 3, 1996. Also at that session, the Conference adopted a new Protocol IV, the Blinding Laser Weapons Protocol.

(A) THE AMENDED MINES PROTOCOL

The amended Mines Protocol is, overall, a significant improvement over the 1980 Protocol and will, if widely observed, result in a substantial decrease in civilian casualties caused by the indiscriminate use of anti-personnel mines. The provisions of the amended Mines Protocol essentially reflect the practices already adopted by U.S. forces for the protection of the civilian population.

At the same time, the provisions of the amended Protocol, although improved, do not provide a complete solution to the serious problem of indiscriminate use of these devices. The amended Protocol will, however, continue to constitute a critical factor in our efforts to eliminate anti-personnel mines altogether and, in this regard is entirely consistent with your May 16, 1996, announcement of our policy to pursue an international agreement to ban use, stockpiling, production, and transfer of anti-personnel landmines.

For these reasons, the amended Protocol is desirable. It is consistent with U.S. military interests and humanitarian concerns. The earliest possible entry into force of the amended Protocol is therefore highly desirable. Accordingly, the United States should ratify it at the earliest possible date.

(B) THE INCENDIARY WEAPONS PROTOCOL

Protocol III - the Protocol on Incendiary Weapons-was a part of the original Convention package adopted at Geneva on October 10, 1980, but it was not sent to the Senate for advice and consent to ratification because of concerns about the acceptability of the Protocol from a military point of view. Incendiary weapons have significant - potential military value, particularly with respect to flammable military targets that cannot so readily be destroyed with conventional explosives. At the same time, these weapons can be misused in a manner that could cause heavy civilian casualties. In particular, the Protocol prohibits the use of air-delivered incendiary weapons against targets located in a city, town, village or other concentration of civilians, a practice which caused very heavy civilian casualties in past conflicts.

The Executive Branch has given very careful study to the Incendiaries Protocol and has developed a specific condition that would, in our view, make it acceptable from a broader national security perspective. This condition consists of a proposed reservation that would reserve the right to use incendiaries against military targets located in concentrations of civilians where it is judged that such use would cause fewer casualties and less collateral damage than alternative weapons. A good example of this would be the hypothetical use of incendiaries to destroy biological agents in an enemy storage facility where explosive devices might simply spread the agents with disastrous consequences for the civilian population.

(C) THE BLINDING LASER WEAPONS PROTOCOL

The provisions of the Blinding Laser Weapons Protocol, Protocol IV, if widely observed, will result in a substantially reduced risk of widespread development, proliferation and use of blinding laser weapons. The Protocol is intended to address this risk in a timely way, before such weapons become commonplace.

At the same time, lasers are absolutely vital to our modern military and the legitimate use of lasers for other military purposes is acknowledged by the Protocol. Indeed, lasers provide significant humanitarian benefits on and off the battlefield. They allow weapons systems to be increasingly discriminate, thereby reducing collateral damage to civilian lives and property.

The inevitable incidental or collateral effect of legitimate military use of lasers is also recognized and is explicitly not covered by this Protocol. The Department of Defense, will, nonetheless, continue to strive, through training and doctrine, to minimize these effects.

Blinding Laser Weapons Protocol is desirable therefore both because it reduces the potential risks of proliferation of blinding laser-weapons and because it clarifies the legitimacy of other types of battlefield lasers. It is fully consistent with U.S. military interests, Department of Defense policy and humanitarian concerns generally. Accordingly, the United States should ratify it at an early date.

CONDITIONS

The Senate is being asked to include a number of conditions, described in detail in the accompanying analyses, in its resolution of advice and consent to ratification. The texts of the three understandings to the amended Mines Protocol and the reservation to the Incendiary Weapons Protocol follow:

(A) THE AMENDED MINES PROTOCOL

1. The United States understands, with reference to Article 3, Paragraph 9 of the amended Mines Protocol, that an area of land can itself be a legitimate military objective for the purpose of the use of landmines, if its neutralization or denial, in the circumstances ruling at the time, offers a definite military advantage.
2. The United States understands that Article 5, Paragraph 2 of the amended Mines Protocol does not preclude agreement, in connection with peace treaties or similar arrangements, to allocate responsibilities under this subparagraph in a manner which nevertheless respects the essential spirit and purpose of the Article.
3. The United States understands that Article 7, Paragraph 2 of the amended Mines Protocol does not prohibit the adaptation in advance of other objects for use as booby-traps or other devices.

(C) THE INCENDIARY WEAPONS PROTOCOL

The United States declares, with reference to Article 2, Paragraphs 2 and 3 of the Incendiary Weapons Protocol, that it will reserve the right to use Incendiary weapons against military targets located in concentrations of civilians where it is judged that such use would cause fewer casualties and less collateral damage than alternative weapons.

CONCLUSION

The amended Mines Protocol, the Incendiary Weapons Protocol and the Blinding Laser Weapons Protocol contain restrictions which offer significant humanitarian benefit. Subject to the recommended conditions, all three are consistent with U.S. military requirements, and with existing U.S. military practices. Ratification by the United States will highlight our commitment on restricting or prohibiting unacceptable methods of warfare and, with respect to the amended Mines Protocol in particular, will materially advance our efforts to end the scourge posed by anti-personnel mines altogether. An article-by-article analysis of each of the three protocols is enclosed.

The Department of State, the Department of Defense and the Arms Control and Disarmament Agency join in recommending that the amended Mines Protocol, the Blinding Laser Weapons Protocol and the Incendiary Weapons Protocol be transmitted to the Senate for advice and consent to ratification, subject to the conditions previously described, at an early date.

Respectfully submitted, Warren Christopher.

Enclosures:
Tab (A) The Article-by-Article Analysis of the Amended Mines Protocol.
Tab (B) The Article-by-Article Analysis of the Incendiary Weapons Protocol.
Tab (C) The Article-by-Article Analysis of the Blinding Laser Weapons Protocol.

Article-by-Article Analysis of the Protocol on Prohibitions or Restrictions on the Use of Mines, Booby-traps and other Devices as Amended on 3 May 1996 Annexed to the Convention on Prohibitions or Restrictions on the Use of Certain Conventional Weapons which May be Deemed to be Excessively Injurious or to Have Indiscriminate Effects

(Protocol II as Amended on 3 May 1996)

The Protocol on Prohibitions or Restrictions on the Use of Mines, Booby-traps and Other Devices (Protocol II) is annexed to the Convention on Prohibitions or Restriction on the Use of Certain Conventional Weapons Which May be Deemed to be Excessively Injurious or to Have Indiscriminate Effects (the Convention).

The Convention, including Protocol II, as well as two additional protocols, was concluded at Geneva on October 10, 1980. The United States ratified the Convention and expressed its consent to be bound by its Protocol II, as well as its Protocol I on Non-Detectable Fragments on March 24, 1995.

In 1994, an international review of the Convention was begun to address, in particular, the strengthening of Protocol II. This international review process concluded in May of this year with the adoption of an amended Protocol II, including a revised Technical Annex (referred to herein variously as the amended Protocol or the amended Mines Protocol). It provides significant improvements over the current Protocol II, of 1980 (the 1980 Protocol). The provisions of the amended Protocol are analyzed, article-by-article, below.

Article 1 - Scope of Application

Article 1 consists of six paragraphs and addresses the scope of the Protocol.

Paragraph I establishes the material scope of application. Like the 1980 Protocol, the amended Protocol imposes a series of restrictions on the use of landmines, booby-traps and certain other delayed-action weapons. It applies to mines, both antipersonnel and anti-vehicle, laid to interdict beaches, waterway crossings or river crossings, but does not apply to the use of anti-shipmines at sea or in inland waterways.

Paragraph 2 expands the circumstances in which the provisions of the Protocol must be observed. The 1980 Protocol is limited to international armed conflicts and wars of national liberation, identified in Article 1(4) of Protocol 1 Additional to the 1949 Geneva Conventions. That is, by its terms, it applies only to situations of armed conflict between states or to cases in which peoples are fighting against colonial domination and alien occupation and against racist regimes in the exercise of their right of self-determination.

The amended Protocol encompasses all internal armed conflicts, incorporating by reference situations referred to in Article 3 common to the Geneva Conventions of 1949. (Common Article 3 concerns non-international armed conflict occurring within the territory of a state.)

The result is particularly significant in several respects. First, it is in internal conflicts (such as Cambodia and Angola) that the greatest civilian casualties from mines have occurred. Regulating and restricting the use of mines in such conflicts in the future will mean, if the Protocol is complied with, significant reductions in civilian deaths and injuries.

Second, since the requirements of the amended Protocol apply to all armed conflicts. whatever their political character, it gives no special status to liberation wars, as do Article 1(4) of Additional Protocol I and references thereto in Article 7 of the Convention itself. It was because of this special status and the subjectivity and political controversy that the reference to it injects into international humanitarian law that the United States declared at the time of its ratification of the Convention in March of 1995, that Article 7 of the Convention will have no effect in this respect.

Third, as provided for in paragraph 3, the amended Protocol will, if in force for a state involved in an internal armed conflict, govern that state's use of mines as well as the use of mines by the other party or parties to the conflict (that is, the insurgent group). There is no requirement that the adverse party or parties in the conflict meet specific criteria - e.g., be organized under responsible command and exercise some territorial control - as is the case in Protocol II Additional to the Geneva Conventions (the most recent attempt by the international community to improve the law applicable to internal conflicts).

Thus, although the amended Protocol expressly excludes from its scope of application situations of internal disturbances, such as riots, it does not permit the armed forces of a state - or of an insurgent group - to ignore its requirements in an armed conflict. It applies in all cases of non-international armed conflict and is therefore of broader application than Protocol II Additional to the Geneva Conventions.

As a result of this more comprehensive coverage, the cases where use of mines would technically be unregulated are quite few. Prospects that the amended Protocol will be observed by responsible militaries in all situations are therefore good, since few such militaries will wish to squander resources and material to maintain a double standard on the use of mines under such circumstances.

Finally, it was understood that certain provisions of the amended Protocol must be observed at all times. A statement to this effect was made part of the negotiating record by the delegation of Belgium, speaking on behalf of 24 other delegations, including the U.S. delegation, at the final plenary session of the Review Conference and was not contested by any other delegation.

This conclusion is supported, as well, by the scope of the Convention itself which makes clear that it and its annexed Protocols shall apply in situations referred to in Article 2 common to the Geneva Conventions of 22 August 1949. Common Article 2 refers specifically to provisions which shall be implemented in peace-time, a recognition that certain provisions must be observed at all times if they are to be implemented in good faith. Among the provisions of the amended Protocol that must be so observed are: the provisions regarding the recording, marking, monitoring and protection of areas containing mines; the provisions of Article 8 regarding transfers; and the provisions of Articles 13 and 14 regarding consultations and compliance. A statement to this effect was made part of the negotiating record by the U.S. Delegation, and was not contested by any other delegation.

Paragraphs 4 and 5 are a response to the concern that the expanded scope of the Protocol could be used as a pretext to violate the sovereignty of a state or intervene in its internal affairs. The provisions repeat verbatim Article 3 of Protocol II Additional to the Geneva Conventions.

An important point about paragraph 4 is that only 'legitimate' means may be used to 'defend the national unity and territorial integrity.' Therefore, even imperative needs of state security may not be invoked to justify breaches of the rules of the amended Protocol as such actions are, by definition, illegitimate.

Paragraph 5 concerns, specifically, the principle of non-intervention, and provides that nothing in the amended Protocol itself shall be invoked to justify intervention in the affairs of a High Contracting Party. This does not mean that any action to enforce the Protocol, such as a discussion of compliance issues in the periodic meetings of Parties under Article 13, could be considered unlawful intervention.

Finally, paragraph 6 is a response to the concern that the application of the amended Protocol to other than High Contracting Parties could affect the legal status of such parties or of territory in dispute. The paragraph meets that concern by clarifying that application of the amended Protocol to such parties will not change their legal status or the status of disputed territory. The language is drawn from a similar provision in paragraph 2 of Article 3 Common to the Geneva Conventions of 1949.

Article 2 - Definitions

Article 2 consists of 25 paragraphs, each providing a definition for a term used in the amended Protocol, including its technical annex. These definitions are not listed in any particular order of precedence, although it was generally recognized during the negotiations that the definition of 'mine', 'remotely-delivered mine', 'anti-personnel mine', and 'transfer' were particularly important.

Paragraph 1 of Article 2 defines 'mine' as a munition placed under, on or near the ground or other surface area and designed to be exploded by the presence, proximity or contact of a person or vehicle. It repeats the formula of the 1980 Protocol verbatim.

There are several noteworthy aspects of this definition. First, the term mine includes both anti-personnel and anti-vehicle mines, including anti-tank mines. Thus, where reference is made to mines, as in Article 3 concerning general restrictions on the use of mines, booby-traps and other devices, it is understood that both antipersonnel and anti-vehicle mines are being referenced.

The definition also contemplates that mines can be emplaced in a variety of ways - under, on or near the ground or other surface area. This makes clear that the critical defining characteristic of a mine is not its relationship to the ground or other surface area but rather its design function of being exploded by the presence, proximity or contact of a target, be that target a person or a vehicle. (This applies whether a munition is designed for this purpose in the factory, or adapted for this purpose in the field.)

It is also this characteristic, i.e., that the munition is 'designed' to be activated by the target, that distinguishes a mine from so-called unexploded ordinance or UXO. UXO is not covered by the Protocol, either the 1980 or the amended version. Unexploded ordinance is a result of a malfunction of a munition; UXO is not 'designed' in any sense, and, in particular, is not designed to be detonated by the presence, proximity or contact of person. Although UXO presents a serious problem that requires concerted attention, it is a problem outside the scope of Protocol II.

Paragraph 2 defines remotely-delivered mine, as a mine, not directly emplaced but delivvered by artillery, missile, rocket, mortar, or similar means, or dropped from an aircraft. Such mines pose particular hazards to civilians, in part because their location cannot be marked as accurately as mines placed by hand or by mechanical mine layers and in part because, emplaced from long distances, it is often difficult to ensure that civilians are excluded from areas containing such mines. This definition was developed, therefore, to clearly categorize such mines in order to subject them to specific, additional restrictions. These additional restrictions are set forth in Article 6.

Excluded from the definition of remotely-delivered mines (and therefore from the additional restrictions of Article 6) are mines delivered by a land-based system from less than 500 meters, provided that such mines are used in compliance with, *inter alia*, the provisions of Article 5, which concern restrictions on the use of anti-personnel mines which are not remotely-delivered. Such mines were exempted from the definition of remotely-delivered mines because, delivered in the prescribed manner, they can be accurately marked and civilian protections can be reliably maintained.

Paragraph 3 defines 'anti-personnel mine' as a mine primarily designed to be exploded by the presence, proximity or contact of a person and that will incapacitate, injure or kill one or more persons. This definition tracks closely with the definition of mine in paragraph 1. It adds, however, two elements.

The first is the word 'primarily' in the phrase 'Primarily designed'. This element was added to ensure that anti-tank mines equipped with anti-handling devices are not treated as anti-personnel mines. This was an important consideration for U.S. military operations. Anti-personnel mines are frequently used in conjunction with anti-tank mines to protect anti-tank mines against enemy removal during military operations. With increasing restrictions on the use of anti-personnel mines, it was clear, from a military perspective, that alternative means of protecting anti-tank mines against enemy removal during combat operations would be increasingly important.

One such common alternative is to equip anti-tank mines with anti-handling devices. But since such devices are, as a practical matter, intended to cause an anti-tank mine to detonate if handled by a person, there was concern that an anti-tank mine equipped with an anti-handling device would inadvertently fall within the definition of an anti-personnel mine, and be subject, therefore, to the additional constraints imposed on anti-personnel mines. Adding the word 'primarily' before 'designed' clarified that anti-tank mines that are equipped with anti-handling devices are not considered personnel mines as a result of being so equipped. This language was not intended to exclude from the restrictions on anti-personnel mines any munition designed to perform the function of an anti-personnel mine. This interpretation of the phrase was made part of the negotiating record through a statement by the German delegation at the final plenary session on behalf of 19 other delegations, including the U.S. delegation, and was not contested by any other delegation.

The second additional element in the anti-personnel mine definition is the reference to incapacitating, injuring or killing one or more persons. This description was understood to be broad enough to cover the range of hazards posed by anti-personnel mines. Additionally, the term 'incapacitating' does not restrict non-lethal weapon technology that may temporarily disable, stun or signal the presence of person but not cause permanent incapacity.

With respect to anti-personnel mines which have the potential to be either trip-wired or command-detonated, the definition applies when such mines are used with a trip-wire or are otherwise target-activated. When such mines are command-detonated, that is, exploded not by the target itself, but by an operator, they do not meet the definition of anti-personnel mine and are therefore not subject to the restrictions imposed on anti-personnel mines. They do, however, fall within the definition of 'other devices' in paragraph 7.

A well-known example of such a munition is the Claymore, a munition used for protection of installations and units in the field which can be configured for detonation either by command or by trip-wire. The Claymore and munitions like it are widely employed by many militaries, mostly in the command-detonated mode. But despite their widespread use, there is little evidence that such mines, even in trip-wired modes, contribute to the humanitarian problems associated with landmines.

Accordingly, the Protocol is deliberately structured so as not to prevent the traditional military use of the Claymore. In a command-detonated mode, the Claymore does not fall within the definition of antipersonnel mine. In a trip-wired mode, the Claymore is not excluded from the restrictions applicable to antipersonnel mines by reason of the definition in paragraph 3. Specifically, such mines, when used in a trip-wired mode, are covered by the definition but special, less restrictive rules in Article 5 apply to their use for a limited time – 72 hours – from their emplacement.

Finally, the term 'anti-tank mine' is not used or defined in the amended Protocol; such mines are referred to by the use of the phrase mines other than anti-personnel mines, which includes all mines designed to be exploded by the presence, proximity or contact of a vehicle. This formulation flows from the definitions for 'mine' and 'anti-personnel mine' when read in light of each other. Throughout this analysis mines other than anti-personnel mines are also referred to as anti-tank mines.

Paragraph 4 defines 'booby-trap' as any device or material which is designed, constructed, or adapted to kill or injure, and which functions unexpectedly when a person disturbs or approaches an apparently harmless object or performs an apparently safe act. This is the same definition used in the 1980 Protocol. It is understood to include, for example, a hand-grenade when attached to a door and rigged to explode when the door opens, as well as devices designed in advance to function as booby-traps.

Paragraph 5 defines 'other devices' as manually emplaced munitions and devices, including improvised explosive devices designed to kill, injure or damage and which are actuated manually, by remote control or automatically after a lapse of time. An example of such a device would be a Claymore-type munition in a command-detonated mode.

Specific prohibitions on the use of booby-traps and other devices are found in Article 7.

Paragraph 6 defines military objective, as, so far as objects are concerned, any object which by its nature, location, purpose or use makes an effective contribution to military action and whose total or partial destruction, capture or neutralization, in the circumstances ruling at the time, offers a definite military advantage. This is the same definition used in the 1980 Protocol and reflects a well-settled understanding of the term.

Paragraph 7 defines 'civilian objects' as objects which are not military objectives as defined in paragraph 6 of Article 2. Paragraph 6 and 7, therefore, read together, are exhaustive.

Paragraph 8 defines 'minefield' as a defined area in which mines have been emplaced and 'mined area' as an area which is dangerous due to the presence of mines. Although the terms are different, the provisions that apply to 'minefields' and 'mined areas' are the same in the Protocol.

Paragraph 8 also defines 'phoney minefield' as an area free of mines that simulates a minefield. Such phoney minefields are subject to all the provisions relevant to minefields and mined areas generally; there are no special rules for phoney minefields.

Paragraph 9 defines recording, as a physical, administrative and technical operation designed to obtain, for the purpose of registration in official records, all available information facilitating the location of minefields, mined areas, mines, booby-traps and other devices. This is a slight modification of the definition of recording, in the 1980 Protocol, adding references to 'mined areas' and 'other devices'. The reference to other devices is significant. The 1980 Protocol did not include such devices in its recording scheme. The amended Protocol has more rigorous recording requirements than the 1980 Protocol and expands the material scope of the recording requirements to include 'other devices'.

Paragraph 10 defines self-destruction mechanism, as an incorporated or externally attached automatically-functioning mechanism which secures the destruction of the munition into which it is incorporated or to which it is attached. Self-destruction (SD) mechanisms are required for all anti-personnel mines that are not marked and monitored in accordance with Article 5, as well as, under Article 6, all remotely-delivered anti-personnel mines. Detailed reliability and timing requirements for self-destruction mechanisms are specified in the Technical Annex.

Paragraph 11 defines 'self-neutralization mechanism' as an incorporated automatically-functioning mechanism which renders inoperable the munition into which it is incorporated. The term is used in Article 6 in relation to remotely-delivered mines other than anti-personnel mines. There are no technical specifications for self-neutralization mechanisms in the Technical Annex.

Paragraph 12 defines 'self-deactivating' (SDA) as automatically rendering a munition inoperable by means of the irreversible exhaustion of a component, for example, a battery, that is essential to the operation of the munition. Self-deactivation features are required as a backup for the self-destruction mechanisms required for all anti-personnel mines that are not marked and monitored in accordance with Article 5, as well as, under Article 6, all remotely-delivered anti-personnel mines. Detailed reliability and timing requirements for self-deactivation features are specified in the Technical Annex.

Paragraph 13 defines 'remote control' as control by commands from a distance.

Paragraph 14 defines anti-handling device, as a device intended to protect a mine and which is part of, linked to, attached to or placed under the mine and which activates when an attempt is made to tamper with the mine. A limited restriction concerning mines with such devices appears in Article 3(6).

Paragraph 15 defines transfer, as involving, in addition to the physical movement of mines into or from national territory, the transfer of title to and control over the mines, but does not involve the transfer of territory containing emplaced mines. This definition makes clear, therefore, that the transfer of areas of land (for example, in a peace agreement) is not constrained by the transfer restrictions of Article 8, even though mines may be present in the area.

Article 3 - General restrictions on the use of mines, booby-traps and other devices

Article 3 consists of 11 paragraphs and sets forth both general rules and a number of specific prohibitions regarding weapons to which the amended Protocol applies. It is a significant improvement over Article 3 of the 1980 Protocol, from which it is derived.

Paragraph 1 sets forth the material scope of the Article. In contrast to a number of other articles of the Protocol, Article 3 applies to all mines, both anti-personnel and anti-tank, booby-traps and other devices.

Paragraph 2 places the responsibility for these weapons on the party that employed them and obligates that Party to clear, remove, destroy or maintain them as specified in Article 10. This provision, in conjunction with paragraph 2 of Article 5 and the whole of Article 10 of the amended Protocol, establish a comprehensive set of procedures for fulfilling this responsibility both during and after armed conflict. These procedures are explored in detail in the discussion of Article 10.

Paragraph 3 prohibits the use of mines, booby-traps or other devices which are designed or of a nature to cause superfluous injury or unnecessary suffering. This rule is derived from Article 23 of the Annex to Hague Convention No. IV, 18 October 1907, embodying the Regulations Respecting the Laws and Customs of War on Land. It thus reiterates a proscription already in place as a matter of customary international law applicable to all weapons. It also implicitly makes clear that mines, booby-traps and other devices are not, *per se*, of a nature to cause unnecessary suffering, for if that were considered to be the case, no such rule would be necessary and they would be prohibited entirely.

Which types of such weapons might cause 'unnecessary suffering' can only be determined on a case-by-case basis, weighing the suffering caused against the military necessity for its use. One example of a prohibited device might be a mine or booby-trap that is filled with shards of glass. Such a weapon would likely be regarded as unnecessarily injurious because the shards would be undetectable by X-ray in the victim's body, and this would cause suffering that would be wholly unnecessary for its military purpose. (In any case, the device would be prohibited by Protocol I of the Convention on non-detectable fragments).

Paragraph 4 makes clear that mines, booby-traps and other devices must be used in compliance with the provisions of the Technical Annex and must themselves meet the technical specifications set forth therein. For example, anti-personnel mines used outside marked and monitored fields must be both self-destructing and self-deactivating in accordance with the precise timing and reliability standards set out in the Technical Annex.

Paragraph 5 prohibits the use of mines, booby-traps and other devices specifically designed to detonate by the presence of commonly available mine detectors as a result of their magnetic or other non-contact influence during normal use in detection operations. This provision is a result of concern with the possible development and proliferation of mines designed to impede demining activity. Although no state claimed to field such devices, in theory, mines could be adopted to detonate when a common mine detector is passed over them.

The provision clearly excludes situations where actual physical contact with mine detectors or abnormal use of mine detectors is required to detonate the mine. For example, a mine's trip-wire or tilt-rod (a type of vertical trip-wire) may be pulled or pushed in a sweep of a mine detector, setting off the mine. This would not constitute the use of a mine in contravention of this provision.

Paragraph 6 prohibits the use of a self-deactivating mine, either anti-personnel or anti-tank, that is equipped with an anti-handling device capable of functioning after the mine has deactivated. The intent is to avoid situations where a self-deactivating mine, the life of which is normally limited by the life of its battery is dangerous indefinitely as a result of a long-lived anti-handling device. This would defeat the purpose of the self-deactivation function by leaving a hazardous mine in place.

All remotely-delivered anti-personnel mines and all anti-personnel mines used outside of marked and monitored fields must include a self-deactivation feature and therefore would be subject to this rule. Anti-tank mines that are remotely delivered may be self-deactivating, although there is no absolute requirement that such mines have such a feature. (The United States had strongly supported a requirement in this regard but no consensus was possible.) In any case, where anti-tank mines are equipped with a self-deactivation feature, they may not have an anti-handling device capable of functioning after the mine has deactivated.

This provision was the result of lengthy discussion on anti-handling devices generally. During those discussions, the United States had proposed a ban on the use of all anti- handling devices on long-lived anti-personnel mines, that is, anti-personnel mines without SD/SDA. This was objectionable to many states. In the final analysis, the proscription on anti-handling devices that would outlive the self-deactivation feature for mines with a self-deactivation feature was the only proposal in this area that commanded consensus. It is a useful addition as it prevents, for example, the employment of anti-lift devices (a type of anti-handling device) that outlive the self-deactivation feature on self-deactivating mines.

Paragraph 7 codifies within Protocol II a well established customary principle of the law of war prohibiting the targeting of the civilian population as such, or individual civilians or civilian objects. It also prohibits the use of such weapons in reprisals against civilians.

Paragraph 8 prohibits indiscriminate use of mines, booby-traps and other devices and defines such use as placement which: (a) is not aimed at a military objective as defined in Article 2 or (b) employs a method or means of delivery which cannot be directed at a specific military objective, or (c) may be expected to cause incidental loss of civilian life or damage to civilian objects excessive in relation to the direct military advantage anticipated. This prohibition is already a feature of customary international law that is applicable to all weapons.

Paragraph 9 provides that several clearly separated and distinct military objectives located in a city, town, village or other area containing a similar concentration of civilians or civilian objects are not to be treated as a single military objective. This provision is derived from Article 51(5)(a) of Additional Protocol I to the 1949 Geneva Conventions. However, Article 51(5)(a) is limited in its application to attacks by bombardment, prohibiting the indiscriminate shelling of an entire city, town or village on the basis of the presence of several distinct military objectives. It states, when so limited, a principle we support and regard as customary international law.

However, when applied to mine warfare, this article could leave the misleading impression that it is illegal to use mines to deny enemy access to or use of an area containing civilians or civilian objects. Thus, throughout the negotiations and at the final plenary of the Review Conference, the United States made clear its understanding that, with respect to this provision, an area of land can itself be a legitimate military objective for the purpose of the use of landmines, if its neutralization or denial, in the circumstances ruling at the time, offers a definite military advantage. We recommend that the United States declare this understanding, as well, at the time of its acceptance of the amended Protocol.

Paragraph 10 builds a provision from the 1980 Protocol regarding precautions for the protection of Civilians. Like the 1980 version, it requires taking all feasible precautions to protect civilians from the effects of weapons to which the amended Protocol applies. The amended provision includes four examples of circumstances which should be taken into account when considering such precautions. They are: (a) the effect of mines upon the local civilian population for the duration of the minefield; (b) possible measures to protect civilians; (c) the availability and feasibility of alternatives; and (d) the military requirements for a minefield.

These general considerations are relevant to all mines, both antipersonnel and anti-tank, as well as the other weapons to which the amended Protocol applies.

Paragraph 11 provides that effective advance warning be given of any emplacement of mines, booby-traps and other devices which may affect the civilian population, unless circumstances do not permit. This provision is drawn from the 1980 Protocol, although there it applied only to the use of remotely-delivered mines. It now applies to the use of all weapons to which the amended Protocol applies.

Article 4 - Restrictions on the use of anti-personnel mines

One of the more important deficiencies of the 1980 Protocol is that it does not prohibit the use of non-detectable mines. A number of states have produced or deployed large numbers of non-detectable plastic mines which present a serious threat to civilians, peacekeepers, relief missions and mine-clearance personnel. Article 4 is designed to eliminate that deficiency with respect to anti-personnel mines.

This article consists of a single paragraph prohibiting the use of antipersonnel mines which are not detectable as specified in the Technical Annex. Specifically, paragraph 2 of the Technical Annex requires that anti-personnel mines have attached or incorporated-material that enables the mine to be detected by commonly available technical mine detection equipment and provides a response signal equivalent to a signal from 8 grams or more of iron in a single coherent presence of commonly available mine detectors as a result of their magnetic or other non-contact influence during normal use in detection operations. This provision is a result of concern with the possible development and proliferation of mines designed to impede demining activity. Although no state claimed to field such devices, in theory, mines could be adopted to detonate when a common mine detector is passed over them.

The provision clearly excludes situations where actual physical contact with mine detectors or abnormal use of mine detectors is required to detonate the mine. For example, a mine's trip-wire or tilt-rod (a type of vertical trip-wire) may be pulled or pushed in a sweep of a mine detector, setting off the mine. This would not constitute the use of a mine in contravention of this provision.

Paragraph 6 prohibits the use of a self-deactivating mine, either anti-personnel or anti-tank, that is equipped with an anti-handling device capable of functioning after the mine has deactivated. The intent is to avoid situations where a self-deactivating mine, the 'life' of which is normally limited by the life of its battery, is dangerous indefinitely as a result of a long-lived anti-handling device. This would defeat the purpose of the self-deactivated function by leaving a hazardous mine in place.

All remotely-delivered anti-personnel mines and all anti-personnel mines used outside of marked and monitored fields must include a self-deactivation feature and therefore would be subject to this rule. Anti-tank mines that are remotely delivered may be self-deactivating, although there is no absolute requirement that such mines have such a feature. (The United States had strongly supported a requirement in this regard but no consensus was possible.) In any case, where anti-tank mines are equipped with a self-deactivation feature, they may not have an anti-handling device capable of functioning after the mine has deactivated. (...)

Finally, it is, in the U.S. view, regrettable that the prohibition is limited to anti-personnel mines. Although the United States sought to apply this same requirement to anti-tank mines, it was not possible to achieve consensus on this proposal. As a unilateral matter, the United States will nonetheless observe a ban on transfer of anti-tank mines which fail to meet this detectability standard. We have invited other states to follow suit.

Article 5 - Restrictions on the use of anti-personnel mines other than remotely delivered mines

Another of the more important deficiencies of the 1980 Protocol is that it provides little effective protection for the civilian population against anti-personnel mines that remain active and dangerous for long periods. Such mines often cause civilian casualties for decades after they are laid. Articles 5 and 6 [are] designed to deal with that deficiency.

Article 5 consists of six paragraphs and contains key improvements over the 1980 Protocol regarding restrictions on anti-personnel mines that are not remotely-delivered.

The effect of the first four paragraphs is to require that all anti-personnel mines be kept within marked and protected minefields or be equipped with self-destruction (SD) mechanisms and self-deactivation (SDA) features in accordance with the Technical Annex to safeguard the civilian population.

With respect to the requirements to mark and protect minefields, paragraph 2 requires that all anti-personnel mines without SD/SDA be placed 'within a perimeter marked area which is monitored by military personnel and protected by fencing or other means, to ensure the effective exclusion of civilians from the area.' The marking must be of a distinct and durable character and must at least be visible to a person who is about to enter the perimeter-marked area. Paragraph 4 of the Technical Annex contains detailed specifications for the markings to be used, as well as an example of a readily understood warning sign.

In essence, the mine-laying party has the responsibility to take whatever measures are necessary under the specific circumstances to keep civilians out of the minefield. The U.S. military has maintained minefields for a number of years in Guantanamo and Korea that meet these standards, and is confident that these requirements are feasible and realistic.

Mines in such an area must be cleared before the area is abandoned unless the area is turned over to a state which accepts responsibility for the required protections and subsequent clearance.

With respect to this aspect of paragraph 2 on turning over territory containing mines, there was concern about potential unintended consequences in connection with peace treaties or similar arrangements. For example, it was feared that this requirement could impede negotiations where a party to the amended Protocol is negotiating the transfer of territory containing mines with a state not party.

It was widely understood, however, that this Paragraph does not preclude agreement among concerned states, in connection with such arrangements, to allocate responsibilities under this paragraph in another manner which respects the essential spirit and purpose of the Article. This interpretation of the provision was made part of the negotiating record through a statement by the Australian delegation at the final plenary session on behalf of 16 other delegations, including the U.S. delegation. No other delegation contested this statement on the record. We recommend that the United States declare this understanding, as well, at the time of its acceptance of the amended Protocol.

Paragraph 3 states the only exception to the marking, monitoring, protection and clearance requirement: when 'compliance is not feasible due to forcible loss of control of the areas as a result of enemy military action.' For the party that laid the mines, regaining control of the area means a renewed obligation to comply with the requirements to mark, monitor, protect and clear. If another party gains control of the area, paragraph 4 makes clear that it is obliged to meet such requirements to the maximum extent feasible.

Paragraph 5 imposes a requirement to take all feasible measures to prevent removal or degradation of the perimeter markings.

With respect to the self-destruct/self-deactivation (SD/SDA) requirement for anti-personnel mines used outside of marked, monitored and protected fields, paragraph 3 of the Technical Annex provides detailed specifications to ensure that such mines do not pose a long-term threat to the civilian population. At least 90 percent of antipersonnel mines equipped with SD/SDA features must destroy themselves within 30 days of emplacement and no more than 1 in 1000 may be capable of functioning as mine within 120 days after emplacement. Put another way, the overall reliability of the two systems working together meets the same reliability standard 99.9 percent – that the United Nations uses as its standard for deeming a field cleared in a humanitarian demining context. In practice, the safety of compliant mines will be even higher, since the design of a self-deactivating mine will inevitably render all mines inoperative within a brief period (typically, through the exhaustion of the battery powering the mine).

To secure these strict requirements and technical standards for SD/SDA it was again necessary to provide parties an option, tightly limited, to defer compliance with the self- destruct element for up to nine years from entry-into-force of the Protocol to permit states with large inventories of non-compliant mines to bring themselves into conformity with the new rules.

As with the option related to detectability, if a state determines it cannot immediately comply with the SD requirement for non-remotely-delivered anti-personnel mines used outside of marked and monitored fields, it may declare, with respect to mines produced prior to entry-into-force of the amended Protocol, that it will defer compliance. To the extent feasible, it must then minimize use of anti-personnel mines that do not comply. It must, however, with respect to such mines, comply with the requirements for self-deactivation.

In other words, for a limited time, a deferring party may use anti-personnel mines without SD outside of marked and monitored fields, provided such mines self-deactivate within 120 days in accordance with the requirements of the Technical Annex. By the end of the deferral period, and sooner if possible, any anti-personnel mine used outside of marked and monitored fields must be both self-destructing and self-deactivating. Moreover, because the deferral option only applies to mines produced prior to entry-into-force, there is a strong disincentive to produce such non-compliant anti-personnel mines after entry-into-force since such newly produced mines may not be lawfully used outside of marked and monitored fields under any circumstances. Finally, as noted above, the deferral period runs from the overall entry [in]to force of the amended protocol, rather than the date on which it enters into force for the particular state in question.

The last paragraph of Article 5 deals with Claymore-type mines when used in a trip-wired mode. It establishes a limited exemption from the marking and protection requirements of subparagraph 2(a) of the Article for such mines, defined as anti-personnel mines 'which propel fragments in a horizontal arc of less than 90 degrees and which are placed on or above the ground.' The exemption is restricted to a period of 72 hours from emplacement, at which point such mines are subject to the full set of protections required by subparagraph 2(a). (Typically, the personnel using the device will deactivate it and take it with them for protection at their next deployment point.) Furthermore, the exemption is contingent on (a) such mines being located in 'immediate proximity' to the military unit which emplaced them and (b) the area of their emplacement being monitored by military personnel 'to ensure the effective exclusion of civilians.' This is consistent with the practice of U.S. and other western military forces, which have safely used the Claymore for unit protection in the field for many years. (Claymores used in a command-detonated mode do not fall within the definition of 'anti-personnel mines' and are therefore not covered by Article 5.)

Article 6 - Restrictions on the use of remotely delivered mines

Article 6 consists of 4 paragraphs and deals with restrictions on the use of remotely-delivered mines (those delivered by aircraft or artillery). It is a significant improvement over the requirements of the 1980 Protocol, particularly with respect to remotely-delivered anti-personnel mines, the use of which is banned unless equipped with SD/SDA features as specified in paragraph 3 of the Technical Annex.

Paragraph 1 requires that all remotely-delivered mines, both anti-personnel mines and anti-tank mines, have their locations recorded in accordance with specifications set forth in the Technical Annex.

Paragraph 2 bans the use of long-lived remotely-delivered anti-personnel mines, that is, anti-personnel mines that are not self-destructing and self-deactivating in accordance with the specifications of the Technical Annex. This provision reinforces the Article 5 restrictions on anti-personnel-mines, in effect prohibiting all use of long-lived anti-personnel mines outside of marked, monitored and protected areas.

Again, to secure this strict requirement, it was necessary to provide parties an option to defer full compliance for up to nine years from entry-into-force of the amended Protocol; the intent being to enable states with large inventories of non-compliant mines to bring themselves into compliance with the new rules.

Thus, in the case of remotely-delivered anti-personnel mines, if a state determines that it cannot immediately comply with either the SD or SDA requirement, it may declare, with respect to such mines produced prior to entry-into-force of the amended Protocol, that it will defer compliance and, to the extent feasible, minimize use of such mines that do not comply. During the deferral period, it must, however, with respect to such remotely-delivered anti-personnel mines, comply with either the Technical Annex requirements for self-destruction or self-deactivation

Put another way, for a limited time, a deferring party may use remotely-delivered anti-personnel mines without both SD and SDA (it must have one or the other). By the end of the deferral period, and sooner if possible, all such mines must be both self-destructing and self-deactivating.

Significantly, transfers of remotely-delivered anti-personnel mines without both SD and SDA are immediately prohibited regardless of any deferral, in accordance with. Article 8 (2). Moreover, because the option to defer compliance only applies to remotely-delivered anti-personnel mines produced prior to entry-into-force, such mines produced after entry-into-force cannot lawfully be used or transferred unless they meet all requirements of the amended Protocol Like the parallel detectability provision, this has much the same effect as a production ban on long-lived remotely-delivered anti-personnel mines (i.e. those without both SD and SDA) since there is no economic utility in producing such a mine which can neither be used nor transferred.

Paragraph 3 applies to remotely-delivered mines that are not anti-personnel mines. It prohibits the use of such mines, unless, to the extent feasible, they are equipped with 'effective' self-destruction or self-neutralization mechanisms and back-up self-deactivation features. (The United States took the position that such mines should be equipped with self-deactivation and either self-destruction or self-neutralization, but many other delegations were unwilling to go so far with respect to anti-tank mines.) Unlike SD and SDA for anti-personnel mines, which are subject to strict technical specifications, there are no specific reliability standards and no timing requirement other than that these features be designed such that the anti-tank mine, if so equipped, will cease to function as a mine when it no longer serves the military purpose for which it was placed in position.

Paragraph 4 carries forward a provision from the 1980 Protocol, requiring advance warning of any deployment of remotely-delivered mines which may affect the civilian population unless circumstances do not permit.

Article 7 - Prohibitions on the use of booby-traps and other devices

Article 7 consists of three paragraphs and concerns the use of booby-traps and 'other devices'. It builds upon the booby-trap article of the 1980 Protocol, extending its prohibitions to 'other devices' and providing additional limitations aimed at safeguarding civilians.

Paragraph 1 prohibits booby-traps or other devices attached to or associated with any of a series of objects thought to pose particular dangers to civilians or other protected persons, including: internationally recognized protective emblems; sick, wounded or dead persons; medical facilities or equipment; children's toys or objects specially designed for children; and food or drink. The exception in paragraph l(g) of Article 7 does not, however, authorize kitchen utensils or appliances in military hospitals, military POW camps or military chapels to be booby-trapped.

Paragraph 2 prohibits the use of any booby-trap or other devices in the form of an apparently harmless portable object which is specifically designed and constructed to contain explosive material. This does not prohibit expedient adaptation of objects for use as booby-traps or other devices that are not designed or constructed for such use, and an understanding should be adopted at the time of ratification to make that clear. Such improvisation of booby-traps, for example to retard an enemy advance, does not pose the same sort of danger to the civilian population as the mass production of objects specifically designed as booby-traps toward which the provision was directed.

Paragraph 3 restricts the use of booby-traps and other devices. Use in cities, towns, villages or other areas containing a similar concentration of civilians is permitted only if combat between ground forces is taking place or appears imminent and (1) these weapons are placed in the close vicinity of a military objective or (2) measures are taken to protect civilians, such as the posting of warning sentries; the issuance of warnings or the erection of fences.

Article 8 - Transfers,

Article 8 consists of three paragraphs and deals with the transfer of mines. The proliferation and easy availability of these weapons significantly increases the threat to the civilian population. Although transfer restrictions in a law of war convention are uncommon, it was, in the U.S. view, essential to address this aspect of the problem as a means of further reducing indiscriminate and irresponsible use.

Paragraph 1(a) prohibits the transfer of all mines the use of which is prohibited by the amended Protocol, for example, anti-personnel mines which do not meet the detectability standards of the Technical Annex, remotely delivered anti-personnel mines which do not have SD/SDA features in accordance with the Technical Annex, and anti-personnel mines and anti-tank mines that are specifically designed to be detonated by the presence of common mine detectors.

Moreover, in paragraph 3 a political commitment is included to refrain from actions inconsistent with this subparagraph starting from the adoption of the Protocol (which occurred on May 3, 1996). Although such a political commitment does not legally bind the United States or prejudice the consideration of the amended Protocol by the United States Senate, it is in fact U.S. policy, pending entry into force, to observe all of the restrictions of the amended Protocol to the fullest extent possible from the time of adoption. This policy governs, as well, our observance of the provisions of Article B.

Paragraph 1(b) prohibits the transfer of mines to recipients other than states or state agencies authorized to receive such transfers. This rule is aimed at further limiting the availability of mines of all types to non-state entities, such as insurgent groups and terrorists.

Paragraph 1(c) requires that parties exercise restraint in the transfer of mines to all states and, with respect to any state not bound by the amended Protocol, prohibit all transfers of anti-personnel mines, unless such a state agrees to apply the amended Protocol. This provides assurance that such transfers will only be made to states that are committed to observing all the use restrictions of the amended protocol.

Paragraph 1(d) requires parties to ensure that any transfers made within the limitations of the Article otherwise comply with applicable norms of international law.

Paragraph 2 makes clear that a party's decision to defer compliance with certain provisions (as permitted in limited cases under the Technical Annex) does not release it from the transfer prohibition in subparagraph 1(a). Thus, as earlier discussed, a party may elect to continue to use, for example, non-detectable anti-personnel mines for up to nine years from entry into force of the Protocol, but that party remains bound not to transfer such mines during that period.

Article 9 - Recording and use of information on minefields, mined areas, mines, booby-traps and other devices

This article consists of 3 paragraphs and deals with the recording and use of information on all weapons subject to the Protocol, substantially improving the regime established by the 1980 Protocol.

Paragraph 1 requires parties to record all information on such weapons in accordance with the provisions of the Technical Annex. This is more expansive than the 1980 Protocol which imposed such a requirement only on minefields and booby-traps that were 'pre-planned'. Paragraph 1 of the Technical Annex provides specific guidelines for such recording. The party laying mines is required, among other things to record the location, perimeter and extent of minefields, and mined areas; the exact location of every mine, where feasible; and the type, number, emplacing method, type of fuse and life time, date and time of laying, anti-handling devices (if any) and other relevant information.

Paragraph 2 requires that records of all such information be retained. Immediately after the cessation of active hostilities, parties must take 'all necessary and appropriate measures, including the use of such information' to protect civilians from these weapons in areas under their control. At the same time, parties must also make such information available to other appropriate parties, including the Secretary General of the United Nations, unless in cases where forces of a party are in the territory of an adverse party, security interests require withholding the information.

Paragraph 3 clarifies that this Article is without prejudice to other Articles of the amended Protocol which deal with information about and removal of weapons subject to the Protocol.

Article 10 - Removal of minefields, mined areas, mines, booby-traps and other devices and international cooperation

Article 10 consists of 4 paragraphs and concerns the clearance or maintenance of minefields, as well as the disposition of other weapons subject to the Protocol. It also apportions responsibility for these obligations and constitutes a major improvement over the 1980 Protocol.

Paragraph 1 requires the clearance, removal, destruction or maintenance of protections for all such weapons without delay after the cessation of active hostilities.

Paragraph 2 of Article 10 imposes this responsibility on the party in the best position to fulfil the responsibility - that is, the party in control of the area containing the weapons.

Paragraph 3 requires that, if a party employed weapons in an area that, after the cessation of active hostilities, is under the control of another party, the party which employed the weapons has an obligation to provide certain limited assistance to the party in control of the area with respect to the safeguarding or removal of those weapons. For example, if a party laid mines in an area over which it lost control, it is required to provide to the party in control of the area, 'technical and material assistance necessary to fulfil' the removal or safeguarding responsibility set out in paragraph 1 of this Article. The provision of assistance is limited to that permitted by the party in control of the area and its scope and nature are unspecified.

Paragraph 4 requires that the parties endeavor to reach agreement 'at all times necessary' on the provisions of technical and material assistance to fulfil removal and safeguarding responsibilities for mines, booby-traps and other devices.

Article 11 - Technological cooperation and assistance

Article 11 consists of 7 paragraphs and deals with the exchange of equipment, material and information on the implementation of the amended Protocol and mine clearance. These provisions are designed to encourage these exchanges, which are necessary for prompt and effective mine-clearance operations and protocol implementation. No specific obligation exists to provide any particular type of assistance.

Paragraph 1 provides that each High Contracting Party undertakes to facilitate and has the right to participate in the fullest possible exchange of equipment and information concerning the implementation of the Protocol and mine clearance, and to refrain from 'undue' restrictions on the provision of mine-clearance equipment and information for humanitarian purposes. The United States and other Western delegations made clear that this would not affect the discretion of states to restrict or deny permission to export such items for national security or other valid reasons.

Paragraph 2 provides that each High Contracting Party undertakes to provide information for the mine clearance data base established within the UN system. Each party retains the right to determine the extent and type of information that it will provide.

Paragraph 3 provides that each High Contracting Party 'in a position to do so' shall provide assistance for mine clearance on a bilateral or multilateral basis. This language was specifically designed by Western delegations to reserve to contributing states the determination of whether, how, and how much to contribute. Paragraph 4 and 5 describe procedures by which High Contracting Parties may request assistance for these purposes.

Paragraph 6 provides that High Contracting Parties undertake, 'without prejudice to their constitutional and other legal provisions,' to transfer technology to facilitate implementation of the Protocol. Once again, this language was specifically designed by Western delegations to reserve to contributing states the ability to limit technology transfers in accordance with their laws.

The final paragraph notes the right of parties, where appropriate, to seek and receive, as necessary and feasible, technical assistance on relevant non-weapon technology as a means of reducing deferral periods.

Article 12 - Protection from the effects of minefields, mined areas, mines, booby-traps and other devices

Article 12 consists of 7 paragraphs and improves provisions in the 1980 protocol on the protection of international forces and missions from landmines and other covered weapons.

Paragraph 1 makes clear that these provisions do not obviate the need for host state consent to the entry of such missions into their territory (with the exception of UN peacekeeping forces and similar missions as provided in the UN charter), do not change the legal status of the territories or parties affected, and are without prejudice to any higher level of protection granted by international law, including decision of the UN Security Council.

Paragraph 2 applies to UN forces or missions, and to regional peacekeeping forces established pursuant to Chapter VIII of the Charter. Each High Contracting Party is required, so far as it is able, to take such measures as are necessary to protect such forces and missions from the effects of mines in any area under its control (including their removal if necessary), and to provide information on such mines to the head of the force or mission. Paragraphs 3, 4 and 5 provide similar protections for international humanitarian and fact-finding missions, and for the International Red Cross and national Red Cross or Red Crescent societies.

Paragraph 6 requires that such information provided in confidence not be released without the express authorization of the provider. Paragraph 7 requires respect for the laws of the host state, without prejudice to the requirements of the duties of such forces and missions.

Article 13 – Consultations of High Contracting Parties

Article 13 consists of 5 paragraphs and provides for regular meetings of parties to consider further improvements to the Protocol, exchange information and annual reports and review other issues related to the operation of the Protocol.

This adds a vital element to the 1980 regime, which contained no mechanism for consultations other than the complex review process which applies to the Convention as a whole. Meetings under this Article will concern only the Protocol itself, ensuring that the Parties take responsibility for keeping it effective and up-to-date with respect to the problems it is meant to address.

Specifically, paragraph 1 and 2 provide for annual conferences of parties Paragraph 3 describes the work of the conferences, including a review of the operation of the Protocol, preparation for review conferences, and consideration of the development of technologies to protect civilians. Paragraph 4 provides for annual reports by High Contracting Parties on these and other matters to advance of each annual conference. Paragraph 5 deals with the allocation of costs of these meetings.

The United States strongly supported these provisions, with the objective of creating a regular mechanism for encouraging the improvement of the Protocol and the consideration of alternatives to anti-personnel mines that could facilitate the achievement of the President's goal of total elimination.

Article 14 – Compliance

Article 14 consists of 4 paragraphs, and is modelled on provisions of the Geneva Conventions of 1949.

Paragraph 1 calls upon parties to take all appropriate steps, including legislative and other measures, to prevent and suppress violations of the amended Protocol. The imposition of such a responsibility is an important element in promoting compliance with the Protocol.

Paragraph 2 requires High Contracting Parties to impose penal sanctions against persons who violate provisions of the Protocol and in doing so, wilfully kill or cause serious Protocol and in doing so, wilfully kill or cause serious injury to civilians, and to bring such persons to justice. This obligation might be implemented with respect to such persons found on the territory of a party, either by prosecuting the offender or extraditing him to another appropriate state for prosecution. To ensure that the United States is able to carry out fully its obligations in this regard, the Executive Branch has expressed its support for further legislation providing jurisdiction to U.S. courts to enforce penal sanctions against such persons.

Paragraph 3 requires appropriate instruction and training for armed forces-personnel on their obligations under the Protocol. Paragraph 4 requires consultation and cooperation among parties to resolve any problems that may arise with regard to the interpretation and application of the Protocol.

Technical Annex

The Technical Annex consists of 4 paragraphs and an attachment. It provides substantial improvements over the current provisions on recording and marking of mines, including a requirement that mine records be kept at a level of command sufficient to ensure their safety, as well as a requirement that all mines produced after entry-into-force be marked to indicate, among other things, their country of origin and date of production.

It also provides detailed specifications for SD and SDA features and detectability, as well as their respective transition periods. It establishes specifications for internationally recognized signs for minefields and provides an example of an easy-to-understand international mine warning sign.

These provisions are described in detail above in connection with the relevant substantive provisions of the Protocol.

Summary

The provisions of the amended Protocol essentially reflect the practices already adopted by U.S. forces for the protection of the civilian population. Furthermore, in most cases, U.S. mines already meet or exceed the technical requirements established by the amended Protocol, including its Technical Annex. One exception is the 'M-14', a low- metallic anti-personnel mine which has a metallic signature below that required by the amended Protocol. Accordingly, the M-14 will either be modified to meet the requirement or disposed of, as circumstances require.

The amended Mines Protocol is consistent with U.S. military interests and humanitarian concerns and the United States should ratify it at the earliest possible date. Indeed, the earliest possible entry into force of the amended Protocol is highly desirable since the possible deferral periods for certain of the key technical requirements run from entry into force.

Article-by-Article Analysis of the Protocol on Prohibitions or Restrictions on the Use of Incendiary Weapons Annexed to the Convention on Prohibitions or Restrictions on the Use of Certain Conventional weapons Which May be Deemed to be Excessively-Injurious or to Have Indiscriminate Effects

(Protocol III)

The Protocol on Prohibitions or Restrictions on the Use of Incendiary Weapons (Protocol III or the Incendiary Weapons Protocol) is annexed to the Convention on Prohibitions or Restrictions on the Use of Certain Conventional Weapons Which May be Deemed to be Excessively Injurious or to Have Indiscriminate Effects (the Convention).

The Convention, including Protocol III, as well as two additional protocols, was concluded at Geneva on October 10, 1980. The United States ratified the Convention and expressed its consent to be bound by its Protocol II on Mines, Booby-traps and Other Devices, as well as its Protocol I on Non-Detectable Fragments, on March 24, 1995.

The President, in submitting the Convention to the Senate for consideration in 1994, recommended that the United States exercise its right to ratify the Convention accepting only the first two Protocols and not the Incendiary Weapons Protocol. As the President's transmittal message to the Senate indicated, there were concerns about the acceptability of certain of its restrictions from a military point of view that required further examination. After very careful study, a condition has been developed that makes the Protocol acceptable from a broader national security perspective. This condition is described in the analysis of the Protocol which follows. The Protocol consists of 2 articles.

Article 1

Article 1 defines various terms used in the Protocol's substantive provisions. Incendiary weapons are defined as any weapon or munition which is primarily designed to set fire to objects or to cause burn injury to persons through the action of flame, heat, or a combination thereof, produced by a chemical reaction of a substance delivered on the target. Accordingly, such weapons as high-explosive munitions and blast or fragmentation weapons are not covered by this protocol, even though they may have secondary burn effects on persons exposed or cause secondary fires. Similarly, laser weapons are not covered even if their primary effect is to set fire to objects or cause burn injuries, since they do not deliver burning substances on the target.

In addition, Article 1 specifically excludes from the definition of incendiary weapons: (1) munitions which may have incidental incendiary effects, such as illuminants, tracers, smoke or signalling systems; and (2) munitions combining penetration, blast or fragmentation effects with an additional incendiary effect, such as armor-piercing projectiles, fragmentation shells, explosive bombs and similar combined-effects munitions in which the incendiary effect is not specifically designed to cause burn injury to persons, but to be used against military objectives, such as armored vehicles, aircraft and installations or facilities. As a result, the Protocol only covers 'pure' incendiaries, such as napalm or the type of incendiary bombs used in World War II and Korea.

Article 2

Article 2 contains the Protocol's substantive restrictions. Paragraph 1 states that the civilian population as such and individual civilians or civilian objects may not be made the object of attack with incendiary weapons – a principle that applies to all weapons under customary international law.

The text of paragraph 2 prohibits the making of any military objective located within a concentration of civilians the object of attack by air-delivered incendiary weapons. Paragraph 3 prohibits other uses of incendiaries against military objectives located within concentrations of civilians, except when the target is clearly separated from the concentration of civilians and all feasible precautions are taken to limit the incendiary effects to the target and minimize civilian casualties. The proposed reservation of the United States as discussed below would revise the legal obligations of Article 2 on the United States so that the test of whether the use of an incendiary weapon is permitted in such circumstances would depend on whether it is judged that such use would cause fewer civilian casualties and less collateral damage than alternative weapons.

Paragraph 4 prohibits making forests or other kinds of plant cover the object of attack with incendiary weapons except when such natural elements are used to conceal combatants or other military objectives, or are themselves military objectives.

There have been a number of military reviews of the Incendiary Weapons Protocol since it was negotiated that raised concerns about the acceptability from a military point of view of paragraphs 2 and 3 of Article 2. Incendiary weapons have significant potential military value, particularly with respect to certain high-priority military targets. Incendiaries are the only weapons which can effectively destroy certain counter-proliferation targets such as biological weapons facilities which require high heat to eliminate bio-toxins. To use only high explosives would risk the widespread release of dangerous contaminants with potentially disastrous consequences for the civilian population. Certain flammable military targets are also more readily destroyed by incendiaries. For example, a fuel depot could require up to eight times the bombs and sorties to destroy using only high explosives rather than incendiaries. Such an increase means a significantly greater humanitarian risk of collateral damage. The United States must retain its ability to employ incendiaries to hold high-priority military targets such as these at risk in a manner consistent with the principle of proportionality which governs the use of all weapons under existing law.

Summary

Accordingly, we recommend that the United States, in accepting the Incendiary Weapons Protocol, reserve the right to use incendiary weapons against military targets located in concentrations of civilians where it is judged that such use would cause fewer casualties and less collateral damage than alternative weapons. With such a stipulation, the Incendiary Weapons Protocol is unobjectionable and should be ratified by the United States at an early date.

Article-by-Article Analysis of the Protocol on Blinding Laser weapons Annexed to the Convention on Prohibitions or Restrictions on the Use of Certain Conventional Weapons Which May be Deemed to be Excessively Injurious or to Have Indiscriminate Effects

(Protocol IV)

The Protocol on Blinding Laser Weapons (Protocol IV) is annexed to the Convention on Prohibitions or Restriction[s] on the Use of Certain Conventional Weapons Which May be Deemed to be Excessively Injurious or to Have Indiscriminate Effects (the Convention).

The Convention, including three annexed protocols, was concluded at Geneva on October 10, 1980. The United States ratified the Convention and expressed its consent to be bound by its Protocol II on Mines, Booby-traps and Other Devices, as well as its Protocol I on Non-Detectable Fragments, on March 24, 1995.

In 1994, an international review of the Convention was begun to address, in particular, the strengthening of the Mines Protocol. It also took under consideration the question of adopting a new protocol on blinding laser weapons. This international review process concluded in May of 1996 with the adoption of an amended Mines Protocol and a new Protocol IV on Blinding Laser Weapons. The provisions of the new Protocol are discussed, article by article, below.

The Blinding Laser Weapons Protocol consists of four articles.

Article 1

Article 1 prohibits the employment of 'laser weapons specifically designed, as their sole combat function or as one of their combat functions, to cause permanent blindness to unenhanced vision, that is to the naked eye or to the eye with corrective eyesight devices.' Article 1 also prohibits the transfer of any such weapon to any state or non-state entity.

This prohibition is fully consistent with the policy of the Department of Defense, which is to prohibit the use of weapons so designed. Although the prospect of mass blinding was an impetus for the adoption of the Protocol, it was not the intent of the Conference to prohibit only mass blinding. Accordingly, under both the Blinding Laser Protocol and Department of Defense policy, laser weapons designed specifically to cause such permanent blindness may not be used against an individual enemy combatant.

Article 2

Article 2 concerns lasers other than those described in Article 1 and obligates High Contracting Parties to take all feasible precautions to avoid the incidence of permanent blindness to unenhanced vision.

This requirement is also fully consistent with the policy of the Department of Defense which is to reduce, through training and doctrine, inadvertent injuries from the use of lasers designed for other purposes, such as range-finding, target discrimination, and communications.

Article 3

Article 3 provides that 'blinding as an incidental or collateral effect of the legitimate military employment of laser systems, including laser systems used against optical equipment, is not covered' by the Protocol.

Article 3 reflects a recognition of the inevitability of eye injury as the result of lawful battlefield laser use. It is an important measure in avoiding war crimes allegations where injury occurs from legitimate laser uses.

Article 4

Article 4 defines permanent blindness as 'irreversible and uncorrectable loss of vision which is seriously disabling with no prospect of recovery. Serious disability is equivalent to visual acuity of less than 20/200 Snellen measured in both eyes.'

This definition of the term 'permanent blindness' is of sufficient precision to prevent misuse or misunderstanding of the term which is a critical element of Article 1. It is also consistent with widely accepted ophthalmological standards.

Entry into force

The entry into force provision refers to the procedures contained in the main Convention. Those procedures provide that the new protocols, such as the Blinding Laser Weapons Protocol, will enter into force six months after twenty states have notified their consent to be bound.

Scope of application of the Protocol

The Protocol contains no provision regarding its scope of application. The Convention itself extends only to international armed conflicts (and to internal conflicts for 'national liberation'). At the time of drafting and adoption of the Protocol participants were aware that it was proposed to extend the scope of the Mines Protocol to internal conflicts. However, at the final session of the CCW Review conference, certain states were unwilling to extend the scope of the Blinding Laser Weapons Protocol, despite having done so for the Mines Protocol. As a result, the scope of the Blinding Laser Weapons Protocol is limited to the scope of the CCW

The United States favored an expanded scope of application for the Blinding Laser Weapons Protocol. As matter of policy, the United States will refrain from the use of laser weapons prohibited by the Protocol. Therefore, while the Blinding Laser Weapons Protocol does not legally apply all armed conflicts, it is U.S. policy to apply the Protocol to all such conflicts, however they may be characterized, and in peacetime.

Summary

The Protocol is fully consistent with U.S. military interests, Department of Defense policy and humanitarian concerns generally. Accordingly, the United States should ratify it at an early date.

☛ USA: US Policy on Landmines (Memorandum of the Secretary of Defense)

The Secretary of Defense Washington. CC 20301-1000 17 June [1997]
(. . .)
Subject: Implementation of the President's Decision on Anti-Personnel Landmines
I direct all elements of the Department of Defense to fully implement the President's new policy on Anti-Personnel landmines. The key elements of that policy follow:
The United States will aggressively pursue an international agreement to ban use, stockpiling, production, and transfer of anti-personnel landmines (APL) with a view to completing the negotiations as soon as possible.
The United States views the security situation on the Korean Peninsula as a unique case and in the negotiations of this agreement will protect our right to use APL there until alternatives become available or the risk of aggression has been removed.
Effective immediately, the United States will unilaterally undertake not to use, and to place in inactive stockpile status with intent to demilitarize by the end of 1999, all non- self-destructing APL not needed for

(a) training personnel engaged in demining and countermining operations, and

(b) to defend the United States and its allies from armed aggression across the Korean demilitarized zone.

Between now and the time an international agreement takes effect, the United States will reserve the option to use self-destructing/self-deactivating APL, subject to the restrictions the United States has accepted in the Convention on Conventional Weapons, in military hostilities to safeguard American lives and hasten the end of fighting.
Beginning in 1999, the Chairman of the Joint Chiefs of Staff will submit an annual report to the Secretary of Defense and the President outlining his assessment of whether there remains a military requirement for the exceptions noted above.
The Secretary of Defence is directed to undertake a programme of research, procurement, and other measures needed to eliminate the requirement for these exceptions and to permit both the United States and its allies to end reliance on APL as soon as possible.
The Department of Defense will undertake a substantial programme to develop improved mine detection and clearing technology and to share this improved technology with the broader international community. The Department of Defense will also significantly expand its humanitarian demining programme to train and assist other countries in developing effective demining programmes.
Please ensure your policies and programs are fully consistent with this new policy. In addition,

I am directing the following specific efforts:

Begin Research and Procurement of Alternatives
The Under Secretary of Defense for Acquisition and Technology will start a major development effort to:
Assess the full range of technology and identify promising alternatives for anti-personnel landmines;
Identify funding needs for development and procurement of alternatives at the fastest responsible rate for FY 98 and subsequent fiscal years; and
Provide a status report on these efforts to the maximum possible extent during the summer review, but no later than the start of the development of the FY1998 DoD Budget Estimate Submission this fall, outlining the research development and procurement phases and any critical gaps in capabilities.

Develop Operational Doctrine Tactics and Plans
The Chairman of the Joint Chiefs of Staff will:
Direct modification of war plans to account for no use of NSD APL (CINCUNC excepted);
Direct changes in war plans, joint doctrine and training to reduce and eliminate the reliance on APLs, consistent with the President's new policy; and
Direct the Services to begin development of tactics and Service doctrine eliminating the need to rely on self-destructing APLs in anticipation of prompt international agreement to ban all anti-personnel landmines. The Assistant Secretary of Defense for Strategy and Requirements will:
Review contingency plans and military operational plans to advise the USD(P) in meeting his statutory requirement to integrate plans;
Identify critical APL-related tasks needed to carry out military strategies and assess the capability of current and programmed forces to perform these critical tasks under provisions of the President's new policy; and
Monitor and provide policy input to the military requirements and processes for proposed alternatives for anti-personnel landmines.

Remove Non-Self-Destructing landmines
The Chairman of the Joint Chiefs of Staff will:
Initiate steps to remove all non-self-destructing APL (M-14 and M-16) from unit basic ammunition loads (CINCUNC excepted); and
Develop plans for removal of all NSD APL from pre-positioned stocks (CINCUNC excepted).
The Under Secretary of Defense for Acquisition and Technology will:
Provide the Services the appropriate guidance to complete removal, transport, and demilitarization of NSD APL not needed for (a) training or (b) defense of South Korea by 31 December 1999; and
Prepare a plan to assure demilitarization of all APL once an international agreement is reached or they are no longer certified as needed by the CJCS to the Secretary and the President.

Expand Humanitarian Demining R&D
The Assistant Secretary of Defense for Special Operations and Low Intensive Conflict, consistent with his demining responsibilities and in conjunction with the Under Secretary of Defense for Acquisition and Technology led Integrated Product Team (IPT) on landmine issues, will

accomplish and report the following through the USD(A&T):
Identify the most promising humanitarian demining R&D programs.
Provide a recommended program by August 31, 1996, outlining plans for (a) pursuing identified promising R&D programs: (b) developing a program for sharing appropriate demining technology with the broader international community; and (c) assessing how this technology effort can contribute to the broader humanitarian demining effort.

Expand Humanitarian demining Efforts
The Assistant Secretary of Defense for Special Operations and Low Intensive Conflict will outline proposals for 'significantly expanding' its humanitarian demining operations program by 1 August 1996. These proposals should include:
Quantitative expansion of current approaches;
Options for different approaches altogether, perhaps developed in consultation with other governments as well as non-governmental organizations involved in the demining effort;
Specific alternatives with substantive goals and associated timelines; and
Explanation of how these DoD efforts would contribute to the government-wide effort

Conclusion
The new policy on anti-personnel landmines strikes an important balance between military and humanitarian imperatives. Please ensure your component of the Department of Defense fully implements it.

4.11112 LASER WEAPONS AND OTHERS

☛ **Additional Protocol to the Convention on Prohibitions or Restrictions on the Use of Certain Conventional Weapons Which May Be Deemed to Be Excessively Injurious or to Have Indiscriminate Effects (Protocol IV on Blinding Laser Weapons), 13 October 1995**

ARTICLE 1
Article 1
It is prohibited to employ laser weapons specifically designed, as their sole combat function or as one of their combat functions, to cause permanent blindness to unenhanced vision, that is to the naked eye or to the eye with corrective eyesight devices. The High Contracting Parties shall not transfer such weapons to any State or non-State entity.

Article 2
In the employment of laser systems, the High Contracting Parties shall take all feasible precautions to avoid the incidence of permanent blindness to unenhanced vision. Such precautions shall include training of their armed forces and other practical measures.

Article 3
Blinding as an incidental or collateral effect of the legitimate military employment of laser systems, including laser systems used against optical equipment, is not covered by the prohibition of this Protocol.

Article 4
For the purpose of this Protocol, 'permanent blindness' means irreversible and uncorrectable loss of vision which is seriously disabling with no prospect of recovery. Serious disability is equivalent to visual acuity of less than 20/200 Snellen measured using both eyes'.

ARTICLE 2: ENTRY INTO FORCE
This Protocol shall enter into force as provided in paragraphs 3 and 4 of Article 5 of the Convention.

☛ **USA: Policy on Laser Weapons (Memorandum of the Secretary of Defense concerning blinding laser weapons, 17 Jan. 1997)**

(. . .)

SUBJECT: DOD Policy on Blinding Lasers
The statement below should replace the policy statement issued 29 August 1995.

The Department of Defense prohibits the use of lasers specifically designed to cause permanent blindness and supports negotiations to prohibit the use of such weapons. However, laser systems are absolutely vital to our modern military. Among other things, they are currently used for detection, targeting, range-finding, communications and target destruction. They provide a critical technological edge to US forces and allow our forces to fight, win and survive on an increasingly lethal battlefield. In addition, lasers provide significant humanitarian benefits. They allow weapon systems to be increasingly discriminate, thereby reducing collateral damage to civilian lives and property. The Department of Defense recognizes that accidental or incidental eye injuries may occur on the battlefield as the result of the use of lasers not specifically designed to cause permanent blindness. Therefore, we continue to strive, through training and doctrine, to minimize these injuries.

4.11122 CHEMICAL WEAPONS

☛ **USA: Message From the President to Congress Concerning the Advice and Consent of the Chemical Weapons Convention**

THE WHITE HOUSE. Office of the Press Secretary. April 25, 1997
TO THE CONGRESS OF THE UNITED STATES:

In accordance with the resolution of advice and consent to ratification of the Convention on the Prohibition of the Development, Production, Stockpiling and Use of Chemical Weapons and on

Their Destruction, adopted by the Senate of the United States on April 24, 1997, I hereby certify that:

In connection with Condition (1), Effect of Article XXII, the United States has informed all other States Parties to the Convention that the Senate reserves the right, pursuant to the Constitution of the United States, to give its advice and consent to ratification of the Convention subject to reservations, notwithstanding Article XXII of the Convention.

In connection with Condition (7), Continuing Vitality of the Australia Group and National Export Controls:

(i) nothing in the Convention obligates the United States to accept any modification, change in scope, or weakening of its national export controls;

(ii) the United States understands that the maintenance of national restrictions on trade in chemicals and chemical production technology is fully compatible with the provisions of the Convention, including Article XI(2), and solely within the sovereign jurisdiction of the United States;

(iii) the Convention preserves the right of State Parties, unilaterally or collectively, to maintain or impose export controls on chemicals and related chemical production technology for foreign policy or national security reasons, notwithstanding Article XI(2); and

(iv) each Australia Group member, at the highest diplomatic levels, has officially communicated to the United States Government its understanding and agreement that export control and nonproliferation measures which the Australia Group has undertaken are fully compatible with the provisions of the Convention, including Article XI(2), and its commitment to maintain in the future such export controls and nonproliferation measures against non-Australia Group members.

In connection with Condition (9), Protection of Advanced Biotechnology, the legitimate commercial activities and interests of chemical, biotechnology, and pharmaceutical firms in the United States are not being significantly harmed by the limitations of the Convention on access to, and production of, those chemicals and toxins listed in Schedule 1 of the Annex on chemicals.

In connection with Condition (15), Assistance Under Article X, the United States shall not provide assistance under paragraph 7(a) of Article X, and, for any State Party the government of which is not eligible for assistance under chapter 2 of part II (relating to military assistance) or chapter 4 of part II (relating to economic support assistance) of the Foreign Assistance Act of 1961:

(i) no assistance under paragraph 7(b) of Article X will be provided to the State Party; and

(ii) no assistance under paragraph 7(c) of Article X other than medical antidotes and treatment will be provided to the State Party.

In connection with Condition (18), Laboratory Sample Analysis, no sample collected in the United States pursuant to the Convention will be transferred for analysis to any laboratory outside the territory of the United States.

In connection with Condition (26), Riot Control Agents, the United States is not restricted by the Convention in its use of riot control agents, including the use against combatants who are parties to a conflict, in any of the following cases: (i) the conduct of peacetime military operations within an area of ongoing armed conflict when the United States is not a party to the conflict (such as recent use of the United States Armed Forces in Somalia, Bosnia, and Rwanda); (ii) consensual peacekeeping operations when the use of force is authorized by the receiving state, including operations pursuant to Chapter VI of the United Nations Charter; and (iii) peacekeeping operations when force is authorized by the Security Council under Chapter VII of the United Nations Charter.

In connection with Condition (27), Chemical Weapons Destruction, all the following conditions are satisfied:

(A) I have agreed to explore alternative technologies for the destruction of the United States stockpile of chemical weapons in order to ensure that the United States has the safest, most effective and environmentally sound plans and programs for meeting its obligations under the convention for the destruction of chemical weapons;

(B) the requirement in section 1412 of Public Law 99-145 (50 U.S.C. 1521) for completion of the destruction of the United States stockpile of chemical weapons by December 31, 2004, will be superseded upon the date the Convention enters into force with respect to the United States by the deadline required by the Convention of April 29, 2007;

(C) the requirement in Article III(1)(a)(v) of the Convention for a declaration by each State Party not later than 30 days after the date the Convention enters into force with respect to that Party, on general plans of the State Party for destruction of its chemical weapons does not preclude in any way the United States from deciding in the future to employ a technology for the destruction of chemical weapons different than that declared under that Article; and

(D) I will consult with the Congress on whether to submit a request to the Executive Council of the Organization for an extension of the deadline for the destruction of chemical weapons under the Convention, as provided under Part IV(A) of the Annex on Implementation and Verification to the Convention, if, as a result of the program of alternative technologies for the destruction of chemical munitions carried out under section 8065 of the Department of Defense Appropriations Act of 1997 (as contained in Public Law 104-208), I determine that alternatives to the incineration of chemical weapons are available that are safer and more environmentally sound but whose use would preclude the United States from meeting the deadlines of the Convention

In connection with Condition (28), Constitutional Protection Against Unreasonable Search and Seizure:

(i) for any challenge inspection conducted on the territory of the United States pursuant to Article IX, where consent has been withheld, the United States National Authority will first obtain a criminal search warrant based upon probable cause, supported by oath or affirmation, and describing with particularity the place to be searched and the persons or things to be seized; and

(ii) for any routine inspection of a declared facility under the Convention that is conducted on an involuntary basis on the territory of the United States, the United States National Authority first will obtain an administrative search warrant from a United States magistrate judge

In accordance with Condition (26) on Riot Control Agents, I have certified that the United States is not restricted by the Convention in its use of riot control agents in various peacetime and peacekeeping operations. These are situations in which the United States is not engaged in a use of force of a scope, duration and intensity that would trigger the laws of war with respect to U.S. forces.

In connection with Condition (4)(A), Cost Sharing Arrangements, which calls for a report identifying all cost-sharing arrangements with the Organization, I hereby report that because the Organization is not yet established and will not be until after entry into force of the Convention, as of this date there are no cost-sharing arrangements between the United States and the Organization to identify.
However, we will be working with the Organization upon its establishment to develop such arrangements with it and will provide additional information to the Congress in the annual reports contemplated by this Condition.

(...)

6.33 NATIONAL COURTS

☛ FRANCE: *Munyeshyaka*, Cour de Cassation of the French Republic, Chambre Criminelle, 6 January 1998. Nr. X 96-82.491 Pf. Nr. Y 96-82.492[1]

(. . .)

Considering that the disputed judgement has stated that the facts attributed to Wenceslas Munyeshyaka constituted, supposing they are established, the crimes of genocide, and complicity in genocide, and that the Juge d'Instruction [examining magistrate] of Privas was incompetent to examine the case;

With regard to the consideration that all the acts attributed to the suspect constitute the crime of genocide and complicity in genocide, as defined both in article 211-1 of the Penal Code and by the Convention for the Prevention and Punishment of the Crime of Genocide as approved by the General Assembly of the United Nations on 9 December 1948; that in internal penal law, the crime of genocide, as defined in article 211-1 of the Penal Code, is applied only when the criminal facts have been committed while executing a concerted plan, a condition that cannot be found for the acts of torture, which aims in a much more generic way at article 1 of the Convention of New York of 10 December 1984; that the competence of the Juge d'Instruction should only extend towards the highest penal meaning and the most specific, that of genocide, a violation distinct from torture and acts of barbarism as provided for by the Convention of New York of 10 December 1984 and punished by article 222 of the Penal code; that the Convention of 9 December 1948 does not

1. Unofficial translation by Ms. Louise Wesseling Plug. Printed in French in the *Revue générale de Droit international public*, tome 102, 1998/3, pp. 825-832, with a comment by Denis Alland and Frederique Ferrand.

provide for any rule on universal competence, that it extends competence to the tribunals of the state on whose territory the act has been committed or to an International Criminal Court; that a bill has been put forward in the Senate on 14 December 1995 to extend competence to the French judiciary in the case of the arrest in France of a Rwandan accused of genocide; that in the present state of our legislation this competence cannot be held; that in accordance with the dispositions of articles 689 and following of the Code of Penal Procedure, the presence of the suspect on the department of the Ardèche does not bring on the competence of the Juge d'Instruction of Privas to examine the crimes committed in a foreign country, by a foreigner against foreigners;

While the qualification of the facts have irrevocably been established by the Penal courts only, referred to in this case, the rule according to which the facts are punished in accordance with the highest penal expression cannot, in the examining phase, determine the competence of the French jurisdictions; it suffices that the facts can be included in a qualification that confers competence on the French jurisdictions so that these can examine the case, even if the facts could also be covered by a more serious or more specific qualification; that the French jurisdiction is competent to examine an offence committed in a foreign country by a foreigner, as soon as it covers the same facts as those which, under a different qualification, come under its competence; that while ruling that the Juge d'Instruction of Pivas was incompetent to examine the facts attributed to Wenceslas Munyeshyaka, namely both the crimes of genocide and of complicity in genocide and the acts that aim at article 1 of the Convention of New York of 10 December 1984, the Cour d'Appel has violated the texts referred to above.

As to the legal grounds:

Having seen articles 112-2, 1° of the Penal Code, 1 and 2 of the act nr. 96-432 of 22 May 1996, which bring about adaptation of French legislation to the dispositions of resolution 955 of the Security Council of the United Nations, instituting an international tribunal to judge the persons presumed responsible for acts of genocide or other grave offences of international humanitarian law, committed in 1994 on Rwandan territory;

Considering that, according to articles 1 and 2 of the above-mentioned act of 22 May 1996, the offenders or the accomplices of the acts that constitute, under articles 2 to 4 of the Statute of the International Tribunal, grave transgressions against the Conventions of Geneva of 12 August 1949, violations of the laws or customs of war, genocide or crimes against humanity, can, when they are found in France, be prosecuted and judged by the French jurisdictions, while applying the French law;

Considering that following from article 689-2 of the Penal Procedures Code that the French jurisdictions are competent, under the conditions provided by article 689-1 of the same Code, to judge persons who could be guilty, in a foreign country, of tortures, under article 1 of the Convention of New York of 10 December 1984, as soon as the criminal facts are susceptible to assume, according to French law, a qualification covered by the provisions of this article:

Considering that, in order to declare the Juge d'Instruction incompetent, the Chambre d'Accusation [Prosecution Department], after having decided that the prosecuted facts should be considered according to their highest penal meaning, states that they constitute the crimes of genocide and of the complicity in genocide, as provided for by article 211-1 of the Penal Code, and that the constitutive elements of these crimes are not included in the definition of the acts of torture that aims at article 1 of the Convention of New York of 10 December 1984;

But considering that in affirming that only the qualification of genocide was applicable in this case, the Chambre d'Accusation has misunderstood the above-mentioned article 689-2;

From which follows that cassation has been incurred as much for this reason as by virtue of the dispositions, mentioned in the act of 22 May 1996 applicable to the current legal procedures.

And considering that the cassation of the judgement of 20 March 1996 brings on the cassation of the judgement of the following 1 April pronouncing, as a consequence of the decision of incompetence, the inadmissibility of the filing of the action by Jean-Louis Nyilinkwaya and of the Galinier couple:

On these grounds,

I - Concerning the appeals of Jean-François Dupaquier, Eugénie Dupaquier, Calixte Kalinda, Jean-Paul Gouteux et Marie Gouteux against the judgement of 20 March 1996:
The appeals are declared inadmissible;
II - Concerning the appeals of Donation Rugema, Jeanne Mujawamaliya and Richard Nsanzabaganwa against the same judgement:
The appeals are dismissed;
III - Concerning the other appeals:
Nullifies And Annuls, in all its dispositions:

1) The judgement of the Chambre d'Accusation of the Cour d'Appel of Nimes, of 20 March 1996,
2) The judgement of the same Chambre d'Accusation of 1 April 1996,

And in order that it be judged again in accordance with the law,
Refers the case and the parties to the Chambre d'Accusation of the Cour d'Appel of Paris, appointed by special resolution of the Chambre du Conseil [council chamber];
States, that by applying article 609-1, second paragraph of the Penal Procedures Code, the Chambre d'Accusation referred to will be competent to prosecute the whole of the procedure;

(. . .)

☛ **THE NETHERLANDS: Supreme Court of the Netherlands (Hoge Raad Der Nederlanden). 11 November 1997. Criminal Division, No. 3717 Besch, ab**[1]

Decision on the appeal in cassation against a decision of the Court of Appeal in Arnhem military division, of 19 March 1997 in the criminal proceedings, against:

1. Unofficial translation by Mr. Peter Kell.

Darko Knesević, born in Banja Luka (former Yugoslavia) on 10 October 1964, resident in The Hague.

1. The disputed decision
After referral of the case by the Supreme Court (Hoge Raad) by decision of 22 October 1996, the Court of Appeal (Gerechtshof) - having improved and augmented the grounds - upheld a decision of 1 December 1995 of the Examining Magistrate (Rechter-Commissaris) responsible for dealing with criminal cases and also military cases, in which the application of the Public Prosecutor (Officier van Justitie) for the opening of a preliminary judicial inquiry was held to be non-admissible.

2. The appeals in cassation
2.1. Knesević lodged an appeal. On his behalf, M.J. van Basten Batenburg, attorney-at-law in The Hague, filed a notice of appeal in cassation in writing. The written document is appended to this decision and forms part of it.
2.2. The Procurator-General at the Court of Appeal also lodged an appeal. The Procurator-General filed a notice of appeal in cassation in writing. This written document too is appended to this decision and forms part of it.

3. The application of the Public Prosecutions Service
Van Dorst, the Advocate-General, entered an application that the appeals should be dismissed.

4. Course of the proceedings
4.1 On 1 November 1995 the Public Prosecutor applied for a preliminary judicial inquiry to be started in relation to Knesević, who was suspected of:

1. having intentionally and with premeditation taken the life of Smail Forić in Sivći in the municipality of Prijedor, situated in Bosnia and Herzegovina or in any event situated in the former Yugoslavia on or around 14 June 1992, or in any event in June 1992, in that the accused did intentionally and after calm deliberation and quiet consultation or in any event after a decision taken (shortly) before, fire a number of bullets from a firearm at the back of Forić from a distance of about 15 metres, as a result of which Forić was fatally wounded.

2. having intentionally and with premeditation taken the life of Jakupović (forename NN) in Sivći in the municipality of Prijedor, situated in Bosnia and Herzegovina or in any event situated in the former Yugoslavia on or around 14 June 1992, or in any event in June 1992, in that the accused did intentionally and after calm deliberation and quiet consultation or in any event after a decision taken (shortly) before fire a number of bullets from a firearm at the back of Jakupović from a distance of about 15 metres, as a result of which Jakupović was fatally wounded.

3. having, either together and in collusion with one or more other persons or alone, taken a group of imprisoned civilians from the sub-municipality of Sivći in the municipality of Prijedor, situated in Bosnia and Herzegovina or in any event situated in the former Yugoslavia, on or around 14 June 1992 or in any event in June 1992, to the Keraterm concentration camp, having threatened them with firearms, for the purpose of unlawfully transferring them to the control of the camp guards of the said concentration camp and/or moving them while they were in a helpless state;

4. having intentionally threatened the mother of Herima Besić with a firearm in or around the period of 15 June 1992 to 30 June 1992 in the municipality of Prijedor, situated in Bosnia and Herzegovina or in any event situated in the former Yugoslavia, in order to carry out a crime intended by the accused, namely of compelling Herima Besić and her sister, by force or other act and/or threat of force or other act, to submit to acts consisting entirely or in part of the sexual penetration of the body of the said Nerima Besić and her sister, the proposed crime having not been perpetrated solely as a result of a circumstance beyond the control of the accused, namely that Goran Valaula intervened, of in any event solely as a result of a circumstance independent of the will of the accused.

4.2 The application entails *inter alia*:
By acting in the manner described in points I, II, III and IV, the accused has been guilty of violating the laws and customs of war, as referred to in section 8 of the Wartime Criminal Law Act (Wet Oorlogstrafrecht), because:
1. the offences were committed by the accused when he, as a soldier or in any event as an armed person, was part of an armed group under the command of Colonel Arsić, or in any event under accountable command, which armed group was part of the (Bosnian) Serbian military units that were engaged in an armed conflict in the territory of the former Yugsoslavia with groups belonging, among others, to the Muslim community;
2. the armed conflict referred to above at 1 can be designated as an armed conflict as referred to in article 3 of the Geneva Convention relative to the Treatment of Civilian Persons in Time of War, of 12 August 1949, having regard to the findings of fact of, *inter alia*, the UN Committee of Experts, formulated pursuant to resolution 780/1992 of the Security Council;
3. the victims referred to at I/II/III/IV belonged to the Muslim community referred to at 1 above;
4. the offences described at I and II constitute violations of article 3, opening words, and 1A of the Convention referred to above at 2;
- the offence described at III constitutes a violation of article 3, opening words, and 1(b) and/or 1(c) of the Convention referred to above at 2;
- the offence described at IV constitutes a violation of article 3, opening words, and 1(c) of the Convention referred to above at 2.

4.3 The application is to the effect that the Examining Magistrate should immediately proceed to institute a preliminary judicial inquiry in respect of:
'assessment of jurisdiction and competence of the Military Division of Arnhem District Court (*Arrondissements - rechtbank*)'

4.4 By decision of 1 December 1995 the Examining Magistrate held that the above-mentioned application of the Public Prosecutor was not admissible, on the ground that - in brief - the Netherlands lacked jurisdiction regarding the offences mentioned in the application.

4.5 The Public Prosecutor appealed against the said decision of the Examining Magistrate. The District Court thereupon accepted that the Netherlands had jurisdiction with regard to the offences referred to in the application. After the Public Prosecutor has appealed in cassation against this decision - on a ground that is now no longer relevant - the decision of the District Court was quashed and the case was referred to the Court of Appeal (Military Division).

4.6 In the decision against which appeals have been lodged, the Court of Appeal upheld the decision of the Examining Magistrate, albeit after improving and augmenting the grounds. The Court of Appeal came to the conclusion in this decision that the Netherlands has jurisdiction and that the ordinary courts are empowered to take cognisance of the facts referred to in the application. The Court of Appeal gave the following reasons for this decision:
4.1. It has been submitted on behalf of D. Knesević that application of the Public Prosecutions Service must be declared inadmissible because the limitation of this application to the questions of jurisdiction and competence would constitute an abuse of due process and, furthermore, D. Knesević was not give timely notice of this application.
4.2. In the view of the Court of Appeal, the limited application submitted by the Public Prosecutions Service in this matter gives the opportunity for important questions of law relating to the further proceedings to be answered before an extensive investigation, which would also be damaging to the person concerned, is carried out. The Court of Appeal rejects the submission because the Public Prosecutions Service has not acted contrary to any principle of proper criminal procedure. The failure to notify D. Knesević at an earlier stage of the application against him has been rectified and he has now had sufficient time and opportunity to refute the application.
4.3 On the basis of the provisions of section 1 of the Wartime Criminal Law Act and taking account of the history of this legislation, it must be held that war crimes committed during a war or civil war or an armed conflict in which the Netherlands is not directly involved cannot be prosecuted here on the grounds of the provisions of this section and that the provisions of this Act are not applicable to them.
4.4 However, this outcome is implausible because the provision making the violation of the laws and customs of war a criminal offence was incorporated in sections 8 and 9 of the Wartime Criminal Law Act in order to fulfil the obligations to which the Netherlands is subject under the Red Cross Conventions. In this connection, it is provided in section 3 of the Wartime Criminal Law Act that Dutch criminal law is applicable, *inter alia,* to everyone who commits a crime described in sections 8 and 9 outside the European territory of the Kingdom of the Netherlands.
4.5 A reasonable interpretation of the law, partly based on the statement of defence and on the obligation contained in the Red Cross Conventions to try (or surrender) offenders, means that section 3 of the Wartime Criminal Law Act does not belong to the provisions referred to in section 1, which are applicable only to crimes committed during a war, civil war or armed conflict in which the Netherlands is directly involved, and that it instead applies at all times.
4.6 The Court of Appeal therefore considers that the Dutch courts are competent to take cognisance of the offences described in the application of the Public Prosecutor, but that the special provisions of the Wartime Criminal Law Act, including the provision designating the court that must take cognisance of these offences, are not applicable to them because section 1 of that Act is not applicable. This is why the court competent to hear the case is not the military court designated in the above-mentioned Act but the ordinary criminal courts, just as is the case in countries adjacent to the Netherlands.

5. Considerations preceding the assessment of the appeals

5.1 The bill that resulted in the Wartime Criminal Law Act was prepared by a commission instituted in 1948 under the chairmanship of J. Donner, the then President of the Supreme Court. This commission was given the task of ascertaining what provisions had to be made in terms of substantive and procedural law regarding 'treason', i.e., crimes against the security of the State committed in time of war and other offences deserving punishment and connected with war and occupation.

In discharging this assignment, the commission prepared a first draft of a bill for, *inter alia,* the Wartime Criminal Law Act, under which the provisions of that Act, including those that are now contained in section 3 (2) et seq., and in section 12 of the Wartime Criminal Law Act, would be applicable to crimes committed in the event of war or first being punishable in the event of war as described in the provisions referred to in section 1 of that draft. The latter provisions included the provisions now contained in sections 4-7 but not those now contained in sections 8 and 9 of the Wartime Criminal Law Act. In keeping within the terms of reference of the commission, the bill defined 'war' as: a war in which the Netherlands is involved.

At the suggestion of the international law expert Professor J.M.P. François, the commission added the present subsection 2 of section 1 of the Wartime Criminal Law Act to section 1 of its bill.

In the last stage of its work, the commission was asked to include provisions in its bill to implement the provisions of articles 49/50/129/146 in conjunction with articles 50/51/130/147 of the Red Cross Conventions of Geneva signed by the Netherlands on 8 December 1949, in which treaty provisions the States Parties undertook to introduce the statutory provisions necessary to make possible the effective punishment of every serious violation of these conventions, as referred to in the treaty provisions.

As a result of the latter, the commission incorporated in its preliminary draft the present sections 8 and 9, and the present part (1) of section 3, and also included a reference in section 1 to sections 8 and 9. It evidently went unnoticed in this connection - and also in the passage of the bill through parliament - that in this way the jurisdiction of the Dutch courts with regard to the violation of the laws and customs of war was confirmed, according to the letter of section 1 of the Wartime Criminal Law Act, only for those cases referred to in section 1, as a result of which the said treaty obligation was not completely fulfilled.

5.2. The intention of the government to comply in full in the Wartime Criminal Law Act with this treaty obligation is evident, *inter alia*, from the parliamentary history of the Act, in particular from the Explanatory Memorandum and the Memorandum of Reply relating to the relevant bill, which entail inter alia (Parliamentary Documents II, 1951-1952, 2258, no. 3, p. 6, and no. 5, p. 5):

'If no other power that is a party to the violated Convention requests the surrender of a prisoner of war who is in Dutch hands, it must be possible for this person to be tried by a Dutch court, even if the crime was committed abroad and even if the offence was not committed against a Dutch national and no Dutch interest has been harmed as a result';

(and)

'The provision included in section 3, at (1), makes the Dutch courts competent to take cognisance of war crimes irrespective of where and by whom they have been committed, i.e., even in those cases in which the crime was committed by a non-Dutch national outside the Netherlands in a war in which our country is not involved. It has been rightly noted in the Provisional Report that this provision must be regarded as an application of the so-called universality principle'.

5.3. In view of the considerations at 5.2, a reasonable interpretation of the law implies that, in accordance with the intention of the legislature that the treaty obligation entered into by the Netherlands should be complied with in full, section 1 of the Wartime Criminal Law Act must - despite its unclear wording in this respect - be taken to mean that the limitations contained in paragraphs 1, 2 and 3 of section 1 of the Wartime Criminal Law Act do not relate to sections 8 and 9 referred to therein, and also do not apply to section 3 and sections 10 et seq. of the Wartime Criminal Law Act.

6. Assessment of the disputed decision by reference to the ground of appeal advanced on behalf of Knesević
6.1 The Court of Appeal has evidently assumed in the disputed decision that the offences described and specified in detail in the application referred to above at 4.1 would, if proved, constitute actions contrary to the common article 3 of the Red Cross Conventions of Geneva of 1949 and consequently constitute the crime described in section 8 of the Wartime Criminal Law Act. Since this finding has not been disputed in the cassation proceedings, the same assumption may be used in assessing the ground of appeal.

6.2 The ground of appeal is evidently that the Court of Appeal wrongly took the view that the Dutch courts had jurisdiction in respect of the offences specified in the application for the institution of a preliminary judicial inquiry.

6.3 In view of what is held above at 5.3, section 1 of the Wartime Criminal Law Act must be interpreted in such a way that the provisions of that Act, including section 3, opening words and (1), and sections 10, 10(a) and 11, always apply to crimes as described in sections 8 and 9, without the limitations referred to in paragraph 1 or in paragraphs 2 or 3 of section 1.

6.4 The Court of Appeal therefore rightly held that the Dutch courts had jurisdiction with regard to the offences specified in the application for the institution of a preliminary judicial inquiry.

6.5 The ground of appeal is therefore unfounded.

7. Assessment of the grounds of appeal of the Procurator-General
7.1 The first ground of appeal is that the Court of Appeal wrongly considered that the court referred to in section 12, subsection 1, of the Wartime Criminal Law Act was not competent to take cognisance of the offences specified in the application for the institution of a preliminary judicial inquiry.

7.2 What is said in the Explanatory Memorandum and the Memorandum of Reply to the relevant bill concerning the military court is important in this connection (Parliamentary Documents 1950-1951, 2258, no. 3, pp. 12-13, and no. 5, pp. 8-9 respectively):

Explanatory Memorandum:
'It cannot be denied that a knowledge of the military situation is desirable for a proper assessment of wartime occupation crimes and war crimes. For example, there is the offence of taking service with the enemy, where it is necessary to decide whether a particular unit belongs to the armed forces of the enemy, and there are the complicated questions raised by the defence of obeying orders of a superior, which is raised by defendants who have committed war crimes in the military service of the enemy. The fact that these questions are often entirely or partly of a military nature was one of the reasons for proposing that after wartime occupation the trial of the crimes referred to in section 1 would be conducted by special courts. Under section 14, subsection 1, the courts (...) would be composed of legally qualified judges and military judges.'

Memorandum of Reply
'The similar nature of the offences to be tried after an occupation, irrespective of whether they have been committed by military personnel or civilians, was in any event considered to be an indication that both categories should be tried by the same court. In addition, there is the argument that foreign military personnel who have to be tried by a Dutch court for war crimes are not military personnel under current Dutch law, with the result that they should stand trial - at least under the present system - before the civil courts. This quickly leads to a conflict with the arrangement under the Geneva Convention, which provides that the same arrangement for trial should apply to both prisoners of war and a country's own military personnel. It could of course be provided that foreign war criminals should, in so far as they are military personnel, be tried before the military court. However, this would create a distinction between military and non-military war criminals, as a result of which the trial of cases involving this already tricky subject-matter would be divided between two different types of court. All these considerations have led to the decision (...) to confer jurisdiction for trying military personnel and civilians for crimes committed during an occupation, as referred to in section 1 of the bill, on one and the same court.

The Government was therefore faced with the same choice as Parliament, namely the choice between special courts and the ordinary civil courts. The Provisional Report mentions three reasons that have been advanced in the Explanatory Memorandum in favour of the chosen system. However, it does not mention the main argument, namely that it is stated in the Explanatory Memorandum that the crimes referred to in the draft are largely of a military nature. For example there is the question of the extent to which a defendant could and should have taken account in his individual situation of an official order or statutory regulation. Here, technical information is not sufficient for the court, since the answer to this question determines not only the question of guilt and innocence but also the sentence. The military element is therefore essential in the special criminal jurisdiction (...).'

7.3 In view of this and taking account of the considerations above at 5.3, the Court of Appeal wrongly held that the ordinary courts and not the military courts were competent to take cognisance of the offences referred to in the application.

7.4 In so far as the first ground of appeal of the Procurator General argues that the military court is competent to take cognisance of the offences referred to in the application, it is therefore advanced correctly. For the reasons set out below at 7.5., however, this does not result in cassation.

7.5 Although the Court of Appeal, as noted above at 7.3., wrongly held that the ordinary and not the military courts were competent to take cognisance of the offences referred to in the application, this need not result in cassation. The Court of Appeal has, after all, upheld the decision of the Examining Magistrate in which the Public Prosecutor was held not to be admissible in his application for the institution of a preliminary judicial inquiry. This decision of the Court of Appeal can be upheld because the objective of the Public Prosecutor in making the application has been achieved by the present decision of the Supreme Court. The objective was to obtain an answer to questions of law concerning the jurisdiction of the Netherlands and the competence of the military court. This answer has now been given. This is why the Public Prosecutor no longer has an interest in making his application and why it is right that the application of the Public Prosecutor should be declared inadmissible.

7.6. The grounds of appeal proposed by the Procurator General must therefore fail.

8. Conclusion

8.1 As none of the grounds of appeal can result in cassation, and the Supreme Court considers that there is no basis for quashing the disputed decision *ex officio*, the appeal is dismissed.

8.2 It should be noted that in principle there is no legal rule to prevent the granting of any new application for the institution of a preliminary judicial inquiry with a view to investigative activities.

9. Decision

The Supreme Court dismisses the appeals.

This decision has been given in chambers by the president of the Supreme Court, Hermans, as presiding judge, and by justices Bleichrodt, Corstens, Aaftink and Orie, in the presence of the clerk of the court, Bogaert, and was delivered at the public session of 11 November 1997.

☛ USA: in the Matter of Surrender of Elizaphan Ntakirutimana.
Misc. No.I-96-5. United States District Court for the Southern District of Texas, Laredo Division. 1997 U.S.dist.lexis 20714.
December 17, 1997, Entered

DISPOSITION: Government's request that ELIZAPHAN NTAKIRUTIMANA be surrendered to the International Tribunal for the Prosecution of Persons Responsible for Genocide and Other Serious Violations of International Humanitarian Law Committed in the Territory of Rwanda and Rwandan Citizens Responsible for Genocide or Other Such Violations Committed in the Territory of Neighbouring States DENIED.

(...)

JUDGES: MARCEL C. NOTZON, UNITED STATES MAGISTRATE JUDGE.

(...)

Pending before the Court is a request by the United States (the Government) for this Court to authorize the surrender of ELIZAPHAN NTAKIRUTIMANA (the Extraditee) to the International Tribunal for the Prosecution of Persons Responsible for Genocide and Other Serious Violations of International Humanitarian Law Committed in the Territory of Rwanda and Rwandan Citizens Responsible for Genocide or Other Such Violations Committed in the Territory of Neighbouring States (the Tribunal). For the reasons stated below, the Court DENIES this request and ORDERS the immediate release of the Extraditee.

FACTUAL BACKGROUND

The Extraditee is a 73 year old Rwandan citizen currently detained at the Webb County Law Enforcement Center. At the time of the events which form the basis of the charges against him, he was the President of the Seventh Day Adventist Church in Rwanda and was based in a church complex in Mugonero, Gishyita Commune, Kibuye Prefecture, Rwanda.[1] He is charged with luring several ethnic Tutsis to his church complex in the days immediately following the death of Rwandan President Habyarimana on April 6, 1994, and then organizing and leading an attack on his church complex on April 16, 1994, to kill all of these Tutsis. The Extraditee is an ethnic Hutu.[2] After the April 16, 1994 attack, the Extraditee is accused of leading armed bands of men into the countryside of the Bisesero region of Rwanda in an effort to hunt down and kill those Tutsis who survived the attack at Mugonero.[3] At some point after the attack on the Mugonero compound, the Extraditee was admitted to the United States and was legally residing with his son in Laredo, Texas, when he was arrested pursuant to these proceedings.[4]

On September 26, 1996, the Extraditee was provisionally arrested on the above charges. The Government timely submitted the packet containing the charges against the Extraditee, the official request for surrender from the tribunal and the documents intended to support that request on October 18, 1996. The instant request for surrender was made in the Government's 'Motion for Hearing on Request for the Surrender of Elizaphan Ntakirutimana,' filed on January 9, 1997 (Docket No. 19).

1. A Prefecture is roughtly equivalent to a State within the United States, and a Commune is roughly equivalent to a county within a state.

2. For many hundreds of years there has been ethnic fighting between Tutsis and Hutus in Rwanda. The Hutus are the ethnic majority in Rwanda and comprised 84% of the population in 1994. At that time Tutsis comprised 14% of the population of Rwanda. Historically, Tutsis have held disproportionate levels of wealth and political power in Rwanda dating back to British Imperialist days and beyond.

3. The Bisesero region is a mountainous region of Rwanda that spans two communes.

4. The record is unclear as to when the Extraditee arrived in the United States. The Government contends that he remained in Rwanda in the months following the Mugonero attack and led the attacks in the Bisesero region. The Extraditee contends that he fled the Mugonero compound on the morning of April 16, 1994, and did not return to the area. What is undisputed is that at some point the Extraditee was admitted to the United States and was residing here legally when he was arrested.

Since the filing of the request, the parties have submitted copious filings in this matter both on their own initiative and in response to directives from the Court. The Court has reviewed all of these filings, as well as all *amicus curiae*, prior to issuing this Memorandum and Order.

DISCUSSION

In matters of extradition, the Court must determine 1) whether the Court has jurisdiction to determine whether the fugitive is subject to surrender, and whether the Court has proper jurisdiction over the fugitive, 2) whether the fugitive is being sought for offenses which the applicable agreement permits surrender, and 3) whether there is sufficient evidence to establish the fugitive has committed the offenses for which he is being charged. See *Bingham* v. *Bradley*, 241 U.S. 511, 516-517, 60 L. Ed. 1136, 36 S. Ct. 634 (1916); *McNamara* v. *Henkel*, 226 U.S. 520, 523, 57 L. Ed. 330, 33 S. Ct. 146 (1913); *Ornelas* v. *Ruiz*, 161 U.S. 502, 508- 509, 40 L Ed. 787, 16 S. Ct. 689 (1896); *Austin* v. *Healey*, 5 F.3d 598, 600-01 (2nd Cir. 1993), cert. denied, *510 U.S. 1165, 114 S. Ct. 1192, 127 L Ed. 2d 542 (1994); Garcia-Guillem v. United States, 450 F.2d 1189, 1191* (5th Cir., 1971), cert. denied, *405 U.S. 989 (1972); Sayne v. Shipley, 418 F.2d 679, 683-84* (5th Cir., 1969), cert. denied, *398 U.S. 903, 26 L. Ed. 2d 61, 90 S. Ct. 1688 (1970); Zanazanian v. United States, 729 F.2d 624, 625-626* (9th Cir., 1984). As will be shown below, the instant request fails on the first and third prongs of the above inquiry.

Jurisdiction:
The Government seeks the surrender of the Extraditee pursuant to the 'Agreement on Surrender of Persons between the Government of the United States and the Tribunal' (Agreement) signed January 24, 1995, and the provisions of Section 1342 of Public Law 104-106. This section makes applicable to the instant case the procedures applicable to international extradition pursuant to *18 U.S.C 3184* et seq., and the interpretative case law pertaining to those procedures. Accordingly, Congress has instructed the Court to treat the Agreement as if it were a treaty of extradition negotiated between the United States and some other sovereign country. After much careful consideration, the Court is of the opinion that Congress cannot so instruct the Court and that Public Law 104-106, as it pertains to the Tribunal[5], is unconstitutional. Accordingly, the Court has no jurisdiction to hear the Government's requests and it will be dismissed.

On August 28, 1997, the Court invited the parties to comment on the authority of the Executive to negotiate treaties with parts of a multi-national body like the Tribunal and Congress' ability to effectuate such a treaty by enacting enabling legislation rather than adhering to a traditional ratification process by the Senate.

The Government cites the Court to four cases dealing with the United States-United Nations (U.N.) Headquarters Agreement for the proposition that the Executive has unlimited ability to make treaties and that courts have given effect to those agreements. See *Concerned Jewish Youth*

5. This same law authorized the surrender of persons to a similar U.N. tribunal investigating charges of genocide in the former Yugoslavia. The Court expresses no opinion on the Constitutional efficacy of those provisions.

v. McGuire, 621 F.2d 471 (2nd Cir., 1980), cert. denied, *450 U.S. 913, 67 L. Ed. 2d 337, 101 S. Ct. 1352 (1981); United States v. Palestine Liberation Organization,* et al., 695 F. Supp. 1456 (S.D.N.Y., 1988); *International Society for Krishna Consciousness, Inc. v. New York, 501 F. Supp. 684* (S.D.N.Y., 1980); *Greenberg v. Murphy, 329 F. Supp. 37* (S.D.N.Y., 1971). While these cases support, silently, the Executive power to make international agreements, none of these cases addressed whether the Headquarters Agreement itself is constitutional. Rather they were all concerned with regulating other activities tangentially related to the Headquarters Agreement.

McGuire and *International Society for Krishna Consciousness*, deal with restrictions on First Amendment activity around the U.N. Both found the minor restrictions on First Amendment rights immediately around the U.N. were justified by the need for the United States to uphold international agreements. They did not pass on whether the Headquarters agreement was properly enacted. Additionally, *United States* v. *Palestine Liberation Organization*, et al., which decided whether the Anti-Terrorism Act of 1988 authorized the closing of the PLO mission to the U.N., recognizes that there is a difference between treaties and other international agreements. However that difference was not important to the decision of the court and was not addressed. *United States v. Palestine Liberation Organization,* et al, *695 F. Supp. at 1458, n.3* ('We refer to the Headquarters Agreement as a treaty, since we are not concerned here with making a distinction among different forms of international agreement. The applicable law implicates all forms, including the Headquarters Agreement.').

Moreover, the Headquarters agreement was enacted pursuant to a treaty ratified with Senatorial advise and consent. The preamble to the agreement states, 'Whereas the Charter of the United Nations was signed on behalf of the United States on June 26, 1945, and was ratified on August 8, 1945, by the President of the United States, by and with the advice and consent of the Senate, and the instrument of ratification of the said Charter was deposited on August 8, 1945.' Joint Res. Aug. 4, 1947, c. 482, 61 Stat. 756 (emphasis added). Clearly, the Headquarters Agreement was made to effectuate a validly negotiated, signed and ratified treaty entered into by the United States. This places it in marked contrast to the Agreement with the Tribunal in the instant case.

While the cases cited by the Government tacitly support the assertion that the Executive may have unlimited ability to make international agreements, these cases have no bearing on how Executive agreements are constitutionally implemented. Thus they are of little value in the instant context.

Of more value is the justification given by the Government for Congressional enactment. The Government cites the Court to *Grin v. Shine, 187 U.S. 181, 191, 47 L. Ed. 130, 23 S. Ct. 98 (1902)* for the proposition that Congress may provide for the extradition of fugitives without treaty and without Executive action. The Court can find no support for this contention in the text of that case. Indeed *Grin* v. *Shine* involved an extradition of a fugitive to Russia, a country with which the United States had a valid extradition treaty. The wording seized upon by the Government ('Congress has a perfect right to provide for the extradition of criminals in its own way, with or without a treaty to that effect, and to declare that foreign criminals shall be surrendered upon such proofs of criminality as it may judge sufficient.' *Grin v. Shine, 187 U.S. at 191.*) pertains to the question of whether Congress could require more or less stringent proofs for surrendering a fugitive than those expressly contained in the treaty between Russia and the United States. It was not a statement by the Court that Congress can make extradition policy of its own accord. Indeed the entire res of the Shine case dealt with the application of provisions of a valid treaty between the United States and Russia. For the Government to claim that this case supports Congressional action in the field of extradition without a valid treaty is inapposite at best.

The Government also refers the Court to the provisions of *18 U.S.C.3181*(b)(1996) for the proposition that fugitives may be extradited without treaty. Section 3181(b) allows, 'the surrender of persons, other than citizens, nationals, or permanent residents of the United States, who have committed crimes of violence against nationals of the United States in foreign countries without regard to the existence of any treaty of extradition with such foreign government if the Attorney General certifies,' certain specific facts. *18 U.S.C. 3181*(b). However, despite this broad language, every case construing this section has required that a valid treaty exists between the United States and the country seeking extradition. See *Ivancevic v. Artukovic, 211 F.2d 565* (9th Cir, 1954), cert. denied *75 S. Ct. 28, 348 U.S. 818, 99 L Ed. 645,* reh'g. denied *75 S. Ct. 202, 348 U.S. 889, 99 L Ed. 698.* (Extradition from the United States to a foreign country may be accomplished only during existence of any treaty of extradition with such foreign government.); *U.S. ex rel. Saroop v. Garcia, 36 V.I. 353, 109 F.3d 165* (3rd Cir., 1997)(extradition treaty existed based on conduct between Trinidad and Tobago and the United States); *Kin-Hong v. United States, 926 F. Supp. 1180 (D.Mass 1996)*, supp. *927 F. Supp. 517*, reversed on other grounds, *83 F.3d 523* (3rd Cir., 1996)(Hong Kong's reversion to People's Republic of China (PRC) on July 1, 1997, will extinguish United States' authority to extradite individuals to Hong Kong). It is clear from these cases that, contrary to the Government's position, Congress has no independent authority to regulate extradition and that a treaty of extradition is required before extradition can occur.

For his part, the Extraditee claims, without citation, that there has never been an extradition from the United States that was not based on a treaty. While the Extraditee has not cited any authority for this assertion, the Court has found no instance where an extradition has occurred without a treaty. In none of the cases cited by either side in this dispute has there been an occasion where a fugitive was extradited absent a valid treaty. This fact convinces the Court that this is more than a mere matter of statistics.

The Constitution calls for the Executive to make treaties with the advice and consent of the Senate. Throughout the history of this Republic, every extradition from the United States has been accomplished under the terms of a valid treaty of extradition. In the instant case, it is undisputed that no treaty exists between the United States and the Tribunal. This is so even when, the Government insists, and the Court agrees, the Executive has the full ability and right to negotiate such a treaty. The absence of a treaty is a fatal defect in the Government's request that the Extraditee be surrendered. Without a treaty, this Court has no jurisdiction to act, and Congress' attempt to effectuate the Agreement in the absence of a treaty is an unconstitutional exercise of power. Accordingly, the Court finds that the provisions of Section 1342 of Public Law 104-106 are unconstitutional as they are applied to the Tribunal, and the Court dismisses the Government's request.

Probable Cause:
Assuming arguendo that Section 1342 of Public Law 104-106 is constitutional, the Court will proceed to an examination of whether there is probable cause to support the extradition of the Extraditee. The Court recognizes that the crimes of which the Extraditee is accused are crimes that are enumerated in the Agreement as supporting surrender. Thus the second prong of the Court's inquiry would be satisfied. The same cannot be said for the third prong.

The standard to be utilized in determining whether a fugitive is to be surrendered on the strength of the documents submitted by the requesting body is that of probable cause. *Escobedo v. United States, 623 F.2d 1098, 1102* (5th Cir.), cert. denied, 449 U.S. 1036, 66 L. Ed. 2d 497, 101 S. Ct. 612, reh'g. denied, 451 U.S. 934 (1980); *Garcia-Guillen* v. *United States*, 450 F.2d at 1192; *Jimenez* v. *Aristeguieta*, 311 F.2d 547, 562 (5th Cir., 1962). In making this determination, the Court is free to exercise its discretion in judging the credibility of the evidence presented as in any other domestic case where the Court would be required to make a determination of probable cause. *Parretti* v. *United States*, 112 F.3d 1363 (9th Cir., 1997). However, the Court is not allowed to hear live testimony from witnesses, allow discovery, or to consider evidence submitted by the fugitive that would contradict the evidence presented by the Government. See e.g., *Hooker* v. *Klein*, 573 F.2d 1360 (9th Cir.), cert. denied, 409 U.S. 869; *Collins* v. *Loisel*, 259 U.S. 309 at 316, 66 L Ed. 956, 42 S. Ct. 469; *Jimenez* v. *Aristeguieta*, 311 F.2d at 556. Following these principles, the Court finds that the Government has not carried its burden.

The support for the charges against the Extraditee comes from an affidavit filed by a Belgian police officer assigned to the Tribunal, Arjen Mostert. Officer Mostert has provided a 25 page affidavit which lays out the evidence against the Extraditee. The first eleven pages of his affidavit set out the history behind the creation of the Tribunal and recount, in a general way, the events that happened after the death of President Habyarimana in April of 1994.

When Officer Mostert finally begins his review of the attacks in which the Extraditee has been charged he offers a brief paragraph stating that the witnesses have not been offered any monetary reimbursement or other consideration for their testimony. None of the witnesses are identified, other than by a letter (i.e. A, B, C, etc.), and there is no other identifying information other than a general description that all witnesses are 'ordinary civilians.'

Officer Mostert states that twelve survivors of the attacks on Mugonero and Bisesero were interviewed, witnesses lettered A-L. There is no statement that these witnesses have given reliable information in the past, or that Officer Mostert in his experience finds them to be reliable. Officer Mostert admits that he did not interview all, or even a majority, of the witnesses, and that their testimony is, at times, taken from reports of other officers which he reviewed. There is no indication that either Officer Mostert, or the other officers who conducted the interviews, were fluent in Kinyarwanda, the language of Rwanda. There is also no indication that the witnesses were fluent in any language spoken by the interviewers.

Officer Mostert does not state when these interviews were conducted in relation to the attacks. It is clear that at least one witness (Witness 1) was interviewed on multiple occasions. It is not clear under what circumstances these interviews were conducted. Additionally, the affidavit fails to state when the charges against the Extraditee were first lodged (i.e. whether they were immediately lodged or whether they emerged over a period of time). Finally, there is not even any indication that these witnesses were placed under oath prior to making their statements.

Officer Mostert claims that four of the twelve witnesses (witnesses A, B, C and H) identified a picture of the Extraditee as a person who 'participated in the attack.' However, the affidavit fails to state when and under what conditions this photograph was shown to the witnesses, or whether the photograph was shown in conjunction with other photographs.

All of the above factors convince the Court that the possibility for inaccuracy or incredibility in the witnesses' statements is high. For that reason, the specific allegations against the Extraditee will be examined in light of the above factors.

Of the twelve witnesses only two claim that they observed the Extraditee during the attacks. All of the pertinent testimony will be discussed below. The Court will begin with the Mugonero attack.

Witness H states that he saw the Extraditee in the days immediately before the attack meeting with some of those who carried the attack out. He then states that once the attack began he saw the Extraditee, along with three others, armed with guns shoot at a group of Tutsis and that some of these Tutsis died. See Affidavit of Arjen Mostert at P. 18-19 P38. Taking this statement as true, the Court notes that Witness H does not state how he knew the group into which the Extraditee shot was composed of Tutsis. He does not state whether the group was armed nor does he state where in the complex this shooting took place. He does not say how long after the conflict began, which lasted all day, this shooting took place. This one sentence statement by Witness H is the only reference in the 25 pages of the affidavit wherein the Extraditee is accused of actually taking part in the attack at the Mugonero complex. None of the other witnesses can say that the Extraditee participated in the attack during that day. The most any other witness says is Witness I's statement that the Extraditee was 'among the attackers.' See Affidavit of Arjen Mostert at p. 20 P40.

There is no mention by any witness that the Extraditee committed a specific act, killed a friend or loved one, instructed others to kill or injure a friend or loved one, directed the assault or participated in any way other than the vague reference that he was 'among the attackers.' When examined in light of the factors mentioned above, such evidence is insufficient to convince the Court that probable cause exists to believe that the Extraditee participated in the attack on the Mugonero complex.

The same result is reached regarding the Government's allegations regarding the Bisesero attacks. Only Witness I claims to have seen the Extraditee kill or direct the killing of anyone in the Bisesero region. Witness I claims that he saw the Extraditee shooting at civilian Tutsis. See Affidavit of Arjen Mostert at p. 23-24, P48. Interestingly, Witness I does not make this claim until what is apparently his third interview on the matter. Id. In an earlier interview, Witness I merely claimed, once again, that the Extraditee was 'among the attackers' in the Bisesero region. Id.

Witnesses C and H claim they saw the Extraditee instruct other armed Hutus to take the roof off of a church so that it could not be used as a shelter. However, such an action would not constitute genocide as charged in the indictment.[6]

The only conceivably applicable section to the allegation that the Extraditee ordered that a roof be taken off of a church is (c). The Court cannot say in good conscience that, assuming as the Court must that the event occurred, taking the roof off of one church is inflicting conditions on the Tutsis calculated to bring about their physical destruction.

Once again, the affidavit cannot support the conclusion that the Extraditee participated in the Bisesero attacks. It is remarkable more for what it does not say than what it does say. The only allegation of attacks comes from one witness who did not remember until his third interview that the Extraditee had participated in attacks. When this witness did remember that fact, he provided no detail as to where these attacks occurred and who, if anybody, was killed. Additionally, he gave no specifics as to the time these shootings occurred. As with the rest of Officer Mostert's affidavit, Witness I spoke in generalities and gave no specific facts that would support the surrender of the Extraditee.

After careful consideration of the affidavit submitted by the Government, the Court finds that the information contained therein does not rise to the level of probable cause. Accordingly, the Government's request for surrender is denied.

CONCLUSION

In light of the findings made above, it is hereby ORDERED that the Government's request that ELIZAPHAN NTAKIRUTIMANA be surrendered to the International Tribunal for the Prosecution of Persons Responsible for Genocide and Other Serious Violations of International Humanitarian Law Committed in the Territory of Rwanda and Rwandan Citizens Responsible for Genocide or Other Such Violations Committed in the Territory of Neighbouring States is DENIED. Additionally, the U.S. Marshal's Service is DIRECTED to, forthwith, release ELIZAPHAN NTAKIRUTIMANA from custody in accordance with the findings contained in this Memorandum and Order.

IT IS SO ORDERED. (...)

6. Genocide is defined by the Tribunal in U.N. security counsel Resolution 955, Article 2, Paragraph 2 as:
'any of the following acts committed with the intent to destroy, in whole or in part, a national, ethnical, racial or religious group, as such:
(a) Killing members of the group;
(b) Causing serious bodily or mental harm to members of the group;
(c) Deliberately inflicting on the group conditions of life calculated to bring about its physical destruction in whole or in part;
(d) Imposing measures intended to prevent births within the group;
(e) Forcibly transferring children of the group to another group.'

7.1 NATIONAL POLICY STATEMENTS

☛ FRANCE: Advisory Opinion of the National Consultative Commission on Human Rights on the Adaption of the French Legal Order to the Convention of Humanitarian Law (As Adopted by the Plenary Assembly of 16 February 1998)[1]

THE FRENCH REPUBLIC Prime Minister
National Advisory Commission on Human Rights

– Is concerned to notice since a few years an aggravation of serious and massive violations of the most fundamental humanitarian norms;
– Considering that the first responsibility concerning the application and the respect of the rules on international human rights (I.H.R.) lies with the states and that these are under the obligation to repress the violations of I.H.R. and to adopt, to that effect, on an national level, legislation which permits the prosecution and the judgement of the persons responsible for these violations;
– Considering the state of the French legislation and jurisprudence regarding the international instruments that bind our country;
– Regretting in particular the restrictions that the French Jurisdictions encounter when exercising universal competence which is recognized by these instruments and which is used to prosecute more efficiently the actors of serious violations of international humanitarian law, whatever the nature of these violations, the location of the commission of the violation, and the nationality of the actors and victims;

The National Advisory Commission on Human Rights;

1 – Demands from the French government that legislative measures and/or regulatory measures are taken in order to assure:
– the appropriateness of the definitions of crimes under international Law on the one hand and under French Law on the other hand;
– a better definition of the conditions under which the French jurisdictions exercise universal competence;

I. – Concerning the conditions of the application in France of the Conventions of Geneva of 1949 and its additional Protocols

The National Advisory Commission on Human Rights;

2 – Recommends that an act be passed and promulgated for the purpose of the incorporation, in French criminal law and in criminal procedural law, of the relevant dispositions of the Conventions of Geneva, as well as of their two additional protocols and of the texts of IHL that binds our country, in such a way that the mechanism of repression and more specifically the universal competence as provided for by these texts can be applied in France.

1. Unofficial translation by Ms. Louise Wesseling Plug.

II - Concerning more generally the conditions of application in France of international texts of IHL

The National Advisory Commission on Human Rights;

– Aware of the difficulties encountered by the victims of violations of humanitarian law to provide evidence on the passage and the presence in France of the actors of violations of humanitarian law,

3 - Recommends that a circular letter be made by the Garde de Sceaux reminding the public prosecution departments that the victims of violations of the rules of IHL, notably those included in the laws that bring about the adaptation of the statutes of the two international criminal tribunals, as well as those concerning violations aimed at in the treaties that bind France and provide for a rule on universal competence, are admitted to file a civil action before a French Court of law under the conditions as provided for in the articles 2, 689 and following articles of the criminal procedures code.

4 - Recommends that in such a case the public prosecution departments receive instructions for the purpose of systematically investigating on the location on French territory the actors of violations so that the burden of this proof does not fall entirely upon the victims.

☛ FRANCE: Advisory Opinion on the Ratification by France of Protocol I Additional to the Conventions of Geneva (Adopted in plenary session on 8 January 1998)[1]

The National Advisory Commission on Human Rights;

1. Calling to mind its advisory opinion of 7 July 1994 on the implementation and the development of international humanitarian law;
2. Considering that France has ratified Protocol II of 8 June 1977 additional to the Conventions of Geneva of 12 August 1949;
3. Regretting that France has still not ratified Protocol I;
4. Regretting that this non-ratification prevents France from applying the regulations concerning armed conflicts as they have been adapted by Protocol I which binds almost 150 states; this reduces the possibilities of France for action on the part of its NGOs operating abroad;
5. Regretting as well that this non-ratification deprives France of the possibility to implement the dispositions relating to (and to participate in) the fact finding Commission as provided for by article 90 and of which the majority of the countries of the European Union are a member;
6. Considering the concordant interpretations relating to the importance of Protocol I regarding nuclear arms;
7. Sensitive to the many declarations of France in favour of action and international humanitarian law and considering, consequently, as an urgent necessity that France harmonizes these declarations with its conventional commitments among which should be those relating to Protocol I;

1. Unofficial translation by Ms. Louise Wesseling-Plug.

8. Taking into consideration the interpretative declarations, relating to the field of application of the text, adopted either at the moment of signing or at the moment of ratification, by several states willing to exclude nuclear arms from the dispositions of, notably, articles 1.4 and 96.3;

The National Advisory Commission on Human Rights;

Urges the government to reconsider the position of our country regarding this text and, under conditions of possible reservations or interpretative declarations which the government could believe should be put forward, to take the necessary initiatives so that Protocol I of 8 June 1977 can be ratified as soon as possible.

(I) Also included is the Convention of 10 December 1984 against torture, and other sufferings or cruel treatment, inhuman or degrading.

☛ USA: International and Operational Law Note: When Does the Law of War Apply: Analysis of Department of Defense Policy on Application of the Laws of War[1]

On 12 August 1996, the Chairman of the Joint Chiefs of Staff issued an instruction[2] that is intended to implement the Department of Defense Law of War Program.[3] With the following simple paragraph, this instruction established, as a matter of U.S. policy, the scope of applicability of law of war principles to U.S. operations:

The Armed Forces of the United States will comply with the law of war during the conduct of all military operations and related activities in armed conflict, however such conflicts are characterized, and unless directed by higher competent authorities, will apply law of war principles during all operations that are categorized as Military Operations Other Than War.[4]

This one paragraph elevated the imperative that judge advocates understand, and be prepared to articulate the 'principles of the law of war.' United States policy now extends the application of these principles to virtually every conceivable military operation.[5] While the imperative of

1. Reprinted from *The Army Lawyer*, Headquarters, Department of the Army, June 1998.

2. CHAIRMAN, JOINT CHIEFS OF STAFF INSTR. 5810.01. IMPLEMENTATION OF THE DOD LAW OF WAR PROGRAM, 12 Aug. 1996. Hereinafter JCS Instr. 5810.01.

3. U.S. DEP'T OF DEFENCE. Dir. § 100.77. DOD Law of War Program (10 July 1979) [hereinafter DOD Dir. § 100.77].

4. ICS Instr. 5810.01, *supra* n. 2, para. 4 1.

5. The United States Army defines Operations Other Than War as '[U]se of Army forces in peacetime . . . ' U.S. Dep't of Army Field Manual 100-5, Operations 2-8 (14 June 1993). Examples of peacetime use of the Army include 'disaster relief, nation assistance, security and advisory assistance, counterdrug operations, arms control, treaty verification, support to domestic civil authorities, and peacekeeping,' Id. At 2-0-1. The DOD Dictionary defines Operations Other Than War as follows:

Military operations other than war—(DOD) Operations that encompass the use of military capabilities across the range of military operations short of war. These military actions can be application of law of war principles to these operations is clear, the meaning of what constitutes 'principles of the law of war' is not. The instruction gives no indication as to which principles the Department of Defense is referring.[6]

Defining the 'principles' of the law of war is no simple task. While there may be little dispute that concepts such as military necessity, proportionality, and the prevention of unnecessary suffering fall within this definition, the instruction arguably encompasses a much more extensive list of concepts related to regulating the conduct of combatants during conflicts. The purpose of this note is to introduce judge advocates to a continuing series of practice notes, each of which will focus on a concept of the law of war which fall under the category of 'principle'.[7] These notes will improve the practictioner's understanding of law of war concepts that are potentially encompassed by the instruction.

To comprehend fully the significance of the instruction, a discussion of how the law of war is triggered as a matter of international law is essential. The law of war is an aspect of international law, which is a body of law that regulates the conduct of states.[8] As a general proposition, international law requires some 'justification' for intruding on the sovereign affairs of regulated states. In most cases, this 'justification' results from the consensual obligations assumed by a state in exchange for receiving the benefit of being a member of the regulated community.[9]

In the case of the law of war, it becomes binding on states (and therefore state actors) only if a state of conflict exists.[10] The extent of regulation is contingent on the nature of the conflict. If the

applied to complement any combination of the other instruments of national power and occur before, during, and after war. Also called MOOTW.
U.S. Dep't of Defense, Joint Publication 1-02, DOD Dictionary (23 Mar. 1994) (updated through April 1997).

6. See JCS Instr. 5810.01, *supra* n. 2.

7. See *supra* n. 2 and accompanying text.

8. International law . . . consisists of rules and principles of general application dealing with the conduct of states . . with these relations *inter se* . . .' Restatement Third of the Foreign Relations Law of the United States; 101 (1986).

9. See ANTHONY D'AMATO, INTERNATIONAL LAW ANTHOLOGY 41-48 (1994).

10. U.S. DEP'T OF ARMY. FIELD MANUAL 27-10, THE LAW OF LAND WARFARE 9 July 1956 (CI, 15 July 1976) [hereinafter FM27-10]. 'As the customary law of war applies to cases of international armed conflict and to forcible occupation of enemy territory generally as well as to declared war in its strict sense, a declaration of war is not an essential condition for the application of this body of law.' *Id* (emphasis added). See Geneva Convention for the Amelioration of the Condition of the Wounded and Sick in Armed Forces in the Field, Aug. 12 1949, Art. 2-3 T.I.A.S. No. 3362 [hereinafter GWS]; Geneva Convention for the Amelioration of the Condition of Wounded, Sick, and Shipwrecked Members at Sea, Aug. 12, 1949, art. 2-3, T.I.A.S No. 3363 [hereinafter GWS Sea]; Geneva Convention Relative to the Treatment of Prisoners of War, Aug. 12, 1949, art. 2-3 T.I.A.S. No. 3364 [hereinafter GPW]; Geneva Convention Relative to the Treatment of Civilian Persons in Time of War, Aug. 12, 1949, art. 2-3, T.I.A.S. No. 3365 [hereinafter GC]; 1977 Protocol I Additional to the Geneva Conventions. Dec. 12 1977, art. 1, 16 I.L.M. 1391; 1977 Protocol II

conflict results from a dispute between two states, the entire body of the law of war is 'triggered,' and the conduct and treatment of those involved or caught up in the conflict is regulated almost exclusively by international law.[11] If, however, the conflict is 'not of an international character,'[12] the extent of regulation imposed by the law of war is much more limited.[13] The extent of regulation is not significant to this discussion. Instead, the significance lies in the recognition that, as a matter of international law, the law of war becomes technically binding *only during periods of armed conflict or belligerent occupation*.

This fact explains the significance of the U.S. policy to extend application of law of war principles to 'all operations that are categorized as Military Operations Other Than War.[14] The impact of this policy is to extend application of these principles to operations that under international law would not necessarily trigger such application, because they do not involve 'conflict'.[15] Judge advocates who are unfamiliar with law of war concepts that arguably fall into the category of 'principles of the law of war' are therefore unprepared to provide the advice necessary to enable supported commands to comply with this instruction. The future installments in this series of practice notes will hopefully enable judge advocates to develop an understanding of some of these 'principles'.

7.21 NATIONAL LEGISLATION TO IMPLEMENT IHL TREATIES

☛ FINLAND: Chapter 11 Of the Revised Penal Code, Dealing With War Crimes And Crimes Against Humanity, 21 April 1995/578[16]

1 *War Crime*

(1) A person who in an act of war

1) uses a prohibited means of warfare or weapon;

2) abuses an international symbol designated for the protection of the wounded or sick; or

Additional to the Geneva Conventions, Dec. 12, 1977, art. 1, 16 I.L.M 1391 [hereinafter GPII]. One commentator notes:

> Humanitarian law also covers any dispute between two States involving the use of their armed forces. Neither the duration of the conflict, nor its intensity, play a role: the law must be applied to the fullest extent required by the situation of the persons and the objects protected by it.

Commentary on the Additional Protocols of 8 June 1977 to the Geneva Conventions of 12 August 1949, at 40 (Yves Sandoz et al. eds., 1987).

11. *See generally* FM 27-10, *supra* n. 10 at 9. See also RICHARD I. MILLER, THE LAW OF WAR 17-27 (1975).

12. See GWS, *supra* note 10, art. 3; GWS Sea, *supra* note 10, art. 3, GPW, *supra* note 10, art. 3; GC, *supra* note 10, art. 3.

13. See *supra* n. 12; see also GP II, *supra* n. 10.

14. JCS Instr. §810.01, supra n. 2, para 43.

15. See *supra* note 10 and accompanying text.

16. Source: Ministry of Justice, Finland.

3) otherwise violates the provisions of an international agreement on warfare binding on Finland or the generally acknowledged and established rules and customs of war under public international law shall be sentenced for a *war crime* to imprisonment for at least four months and at most six years.
(2) An attempt shall be punished.

2 *Aggravated War Crime*
(1) If in the war crime
1) several people are put in mortal danger;
2) very serious and extensive damage is caused to the economy; or
4) the offence is committed in an especially brutal or cruel manner and the offence is aggravated also when assessed as a whole, the offender shall be sentenced for an *aggravated war crime* to imprisonment for at least two and at most twelve years.
(2) An attempt shall be punished,

3 *Petty War Crime*
If the war crime, considering its consequences and the other relevant circumstances, is petty when assessed as a whole, the offender shall be sentenced for a *petty war crime* to a fine or to imprisonment for at most six months.

4 *Violation of Human Rights in a State of Emergency*
(1) A person who violates or fails to comply with the rules on the safeguarding of the wounded, the sick or the distressed, the treatment of prisoners of war and the protection of the civilian population, which according to the international agreements binding on Finland or the established rules of public international law are to be followed during war, armed conflict or occupation, shall be sentenced for the *violation of human rights in a state of emergency* to imprisonment for at least four months and at most six years.
(2) An attempt shall be punished.
(3) If the act referred to in this section, considering the nature of the violation, the minor significance of the consequences and the other relevant circumstances, is not serious when assessed as a whole, the offender shall not be sentenced for the violation of human rights in a state of emergency or an attempt thereof, but instead for the other offences manifest in the act.

5 *Aggravated Violation of Human Rights in a State of Emergency*
(1) If in the violation of human rights in a state of emergency
1) several people are put in mortal danger; or
2) the offence is committed in an especially brutal or cruel manner and the offence is aggravated also when assessed as a whole, the offender shall be sentenced for the *aggravated violation of human rights* to imprisonment for at least two and at most twelve years.
(2) An attempt shall be punished.

6 *Genocide*
(1) A person who for the purpose of entirely or partially destroying a race or national ethnic or religious group or another comparable group
1) kills members of the group;

2) inflicts grievous bodily or mental damage or illness to members of the group;
3) takes forcible measures to prevent procreation among the group;
4) forcibly moves children from one group to another; or
5) in another comparable manner impairs the survival of the group shall be sentenced for *genocide* to imprisonment for at least four years or for life.
(2) An attempt shall be punished.

7 *Preparation of Genocide*
A person who for the purpose referred to
1) conspires with another on genocide; or
2) makes a plan for genocide shall be sentenced for the *preparation of genocide* to imprisonment for at least four months and at most four years.

8 *Ethnic Agitation*
A person who spreads statements or other notices among the public where a certain race or national, ethnic or religious group or a comparable group is threatened, slandered or insulted shall be sentenced for *ethnic agitation* to a fine or to imprisonment for at most two years.

9 *Discrimination*
A person who in his trade or profession, service of the general public, exercise of official authority or other public function or in the arrangement of a public amusement or meeting, without a justified reason
1) refuses someone service in accordance with the generally followed Conditions;
2) refuses someone entry to the amusement or meeting or ejects him; or
3) places someone in an unequal or an essentially inferior position due to his race, national or ethnic origin, colour, language, sex, age, family ties, sexual preference, state of health, religion, political orientation, political or industrial activity or another comparable circumstance shall be sentenced, unless the act is punishable as industrial discrimination, for *discrimination* to a fine or to imprisonment for at most six months.

☛ PARAGUAY: Law No. 1160/97 Penal Code of the Republic of Paraguay
Adopted 26 November 1997[1]
[Excerpt]

TITLE 1
Chapter II
Application of the Law

Article 8. Acts against universally protected interests committed in a foreign country
1) Paraguayan penal law shall be also applied to the following acts committed in a foreign country:
1. the use of explosives, as regulated in article 203;

1. Unofficial translation provided by Professor Alfonso Velásquez.

2. attempts against the civil air and naval traffic, as regulated in article 213;
3. trade in human beings, as regulated in article 129;
4. narcotic and other dangerous drugs traffic, as regulated in articles 37 to 45 of Law 1340/88;
5. counterfeiting of currency, as regulated in articles 264 to 268;
6. genocide, as regulated in article 319;
7. other acts, that according to an international treaty, the Paraguayan state is obliged to persecute, even if they were committed in a foreign country.

2) Paraguayan laws shall be only applied in these cases upon the entry into the Paraguayan territory of the alleged criminal.

3) Application of Paraguayan laws will be excluded, if there is a final judgement from a foreign tribunal:
1. by which the author has been acquitted; or
2. if convicted to imprisonment, the sentence has been executed, or it has become inapplicable by virtue of statute of limitations, or a granted pardon.

TITLE VIII
Acts against the functions of the State

Chapter III
Acts against the exercise of public functions

Article 309. Torture

1) Anyone who with the intention of destroying or severely harming the personality of a victim or of a third party, and who is acting as a public functionary or in accordance with a functionary:
1. commits a punishable act against,
    a. physical integrity, in accordance with articles 110 to 112;
    b. freedom, in accordance with articles 120 to 122, and article 124;
    c. sexual autonomy, as prescribed in articles 128, 130 and 131;
    d. minors, in accordance with articles 135 and 136;
    e. the legality in the exercising of public functions, in accordance with articles 307, 308, 310 and 311; or
2. submits the victim to serious mental sufferings,

shall be punished with prison for no less than five years.

2) Paragraph 1) shall be applicable even in cases of the condition of functionary:
1. lacks of a valid juridical basis; or
2. it has been improperly arrogated by the author.

TITLE IX
Acts against the people

Article 319. Genocide

Anyone who, with the intention to destroy, in whole or in part, a national, ethnic, religious or social community or group:

1. kills or seriously harms members of the group;
2. inflicts on the community inhuman treatment or conditions of life that could cause its destruction in whole or in part;
3. forcibly or by means of intimidation, transfers children or adults to another group or places other than its habitual domiciles;
4. impedes the exercise of religion or the practice of custom;
5. imposes measures intended to prevent births within the group, and
6. forces the dispersion of the community,

shall be punished with prison for no less than five years.

Article 320. War crimes.
Anyone who, in violation of international laws of war, armed conflict or military occupation, commits against the civilian population, the wounded, the sick, or prisoners of war, the following acts:

1. homicide or serious harms;
2. inhuman treatments, including medical and scientific experiments;
3. deportation;
4. forced labour;
5. deprivation of freedom;
6. coercion to serve in the armed forces of the enemy, and
7. looting of private property and its deliberate destruction, especially those of a high economic and cultural value,

shall be punished with prison for no less than five years.

☛ PERU: Law No. 29626 Amending Certain Articles of the Penal Code and Incorporating Section XIV-A Concerning Crimes against Humanity 30 January 1991[1]

ARTICLE 1 - INCORPORATION OF SECTION XIV-A

Section XIV-A is hereby incorporated in the Penal Code, as follows:

'SECTION XIV - A CRIMES AGAINST HUMANITY

Chapter I

GENOCIDE

Article 319 - Any person who, with the intention of destroying, in whole or in part, a national, ethnic, social or religious group, commits any of the following acts, namely:

1. Translation provided by the International Committee of the Red Cross. Thanks to Professor Raúl Vinuesa and Mr. Jean-Marie Henckaerts.

1. Killing members of the group;
2. Causing serious bodily or mental harm to members of the group;
3. Deliberately inflicting on the group conditions of life calculated to bring about its physical destruction in whole or in part;
4. Imposing measures intended to prevent births within the group;
5. Forcibly transferring children of the group to another group, shall be liable to a term of imprisonment of not less than twenty years.

Chapter II

FORCIBLE DISAPPEARANCE

Article 320 - Any official or public servant who deprives a person of his liberty, ordering or committing acts that result in the duly proven disappearance of that person, shall be liable to a term of imprisonment of not less than fifteen years and shall be disqualified from holding office, in accordance with Article 36, Paras. 1 and 2.

Chapter III
TORTURE

Article 321 - Any official or public servant, or anyone acting with the consent or acquiescence of the former, who inflicts serious physical or mental pain or suffering on a person, or subjects him to conditions or treatment that destroy his personality or impair his physical or mental capacity, even if they do not cause physical pain or psychological distress, for the purpose of obtaining a confession or information from the victim or from a third party, or punishing him for any act that he has committed or is suspected of having committed, or intimidating or coercing him, shall be liable to a term of imprisonment of not less than five and not more than ten years. If the torture inflicted causes the death of the victim or injures him seriously and the perpetrator of the torture could have foreseen that result, the term of imprisonment shall be not less than eight and not more than twenty years in the case of death, and not less than six and not more than twelve years in the case of serious injury.

Article 322 - Any doctor or other health professional who participates in the crime referred to in Article 321 shall incur the same penalty as the perpetrators.

ARTICLE 2 - AMENDMENT OF ARTICLES 125 AND 128

Articles 125 and 128 of the Penal Code are hereby amended as follows:

'Article 125 - Anyone who endangers the life, or causes a serious and immediate threat to the health of a minor or a person incapable of looking after himself who is legally under his protection or *de facto* in his care, or abandons a minor or such a person in comparable circumstances, shall be liable to a term of imprisonment of not less than one and not more than four years.

Article 128 - Anyone who endangers the life or health of a person placed under his authority, guardianship, protection, care or supervision by depriving him of food or essential care, or subjecting him to excessive or inappropriate work, or applying excessive corrective or disciplinary measures, shall be liable to a term of imprisonment of not less than one and not more than four years.'

ARTICLE 3 - REPLACEMENT OF ARTICLE 129 OF THE PENAL CODE

Article 129 of the Penal Code is hereby replaced by the following wording:

'Article 129 - In the circumstances described in Articles 125 and 128, if serious injury or death results and could have been foreseen, the term of imprisonment shall be not less than three and not more than six years in the case of serious injury, and not less than four and not more than eight years in the case of death.'

ARTICLE 4 - MEDICAL EXAMINATION OF THE VICTIM
4.1 Any person may immediately request a medical examination of a torture victim or of any other person who is unable to appeal to the authorities himself
4.2 Forensic medical experts shall immediately assist in the examination of anyone who has been a victim of torture, without prejudice to the right of the accuser to call in any other doctor for verification of their findings.

ARTICLE 5 - PROCEDURE FOR ACTIONS REGARDING CRIMES AGAINST HUMANITY
Proceedings for crimes referred to in Section XIV-A shall be brought in the usual way before ordinary courts of law.

ARTICLE 6 - REPEALING CLAUSE
Article 1 of Law No. 25592, Chapter V of Section I of Volume 11 of the Penal Code and all other laws which are contrary to the present act are hereby repealed.

ARTICLE 7 - INCORPORATION OF THE FIFTH FINAL AND TEMPORARY PROVISION IN THE PENAL CODE
The Fifth Final and Temporary Provision is hereby incorporated in the Penal Code as follows:
'Five - Crimes of terrorism shall be governed by special laws.'

Hereby communicated to the President of the Republic for promulgation.
Done at Lima, 30 January 1998

☛ RWANDA: The Organic Law 8/96 of August 30, 1996 on the organisation of prosecutions for offences constituting the crime of genocide or crimes against humanity since 1 October 1990, entered into force on 1 September 1996

We, Pasteur BOSOMING,
President of the Republic;

THE TRANSITIONAL NATIONAL ASSEMBLY HAS ADOPTED AND WE SANCTION, PROMULGATE THE FOLLOWING ORGANIC LAW AND WE ORDER THAT IT BE PUBLISHED IN THE OFFICIAL JOURNAL OF THE REPUBLIC OF RWANDA.

The Transitional National Assembly meeting in its session of 9 August 1996;
Given the Fundamental Law of the Republic of Rwanda, in particular the Constitution of 10 June

1991, as amended and completed, in Articles 12, 33, 69 and 97 and the Earache Protocol of Agreement on Power-Sharing, in particular Articles 6 d), 26, 40, 72 and 73;
Given the Decree-Law n° 09/80 of 7 July 1980 establishing the Code of Judicial Organisation and Jurisdiction, in particular Article 8;
Given the Law of 23 February 1963 establishing the Code of Criminal Procedure, as amended;
Given the Decree-Law n° 21/77 of 18 August 1977 instituting the Penal Code as completed;
Given the genocide and crimes against humanity committed in Rwanda since 1 October 1990;
Given the need to adopt Provisions to prosecute and adjudicate the perpetrators of and accomplices in these crimes;
Given that the acts committed constitute offences provided for and punished under the Penal Code as well as the crime of genocide or crimes against humanity;
Given that the crime of genocide and crimes against humanity are provided for specifically in the Convention on the Prevention and Punishment of the Crime of Genocide of 9 December 1948, the Geneva Convention relative to the Protection of Civilian Persons in Time of War of 12 August 1949 and its additional Protocols, as well as the Convention on the Non-Applicability of Statutory Limitations to War Crimes and Crimes Against Humanity of 26 November 1968;
Given that Rwanda has ratified these three Conventions and has published them in the Official Gazette, but without having provided for penalties for these crimes;
Given that, as a consequence, the prosecutions must be based on the Penal Code;
Given that, in order to achieve reconciliation and justice in Rwanda, it is essential that the culture of impunity be eradicated forever;
Given that the exceptional situation in the country requires the adoption of specially adapted measures to satisfy the need for justice of the people of Rwanda;

ADOPTS:

CHAPTER I: GENERALITIES

Article 1

The purpose of this organic law is the Organisation of criminal proceedings against persons who are accused of having, since 1 October 1990, committed acts set out and sanctioned under the Penal Code and which constitute:

a) either the crime of genocide or crimes against humanity as defined in the Convention on the Prevention and Punishment of the Crime of Genocide of 9 December 1948, in the Geneva Convention relative to the Protection of Civilian Persons in Time of War of 12 August 1949 and its additional protocols, as well as in the Convention on the Non-Applicability of Statutory Limitations to War Crimes and Crimes Against Humanity of 26 November 1968, the three of which were ratified by Rwanda;

b) offences set out in the Penal Code which the Public Prosecution Department alleges or the defendant admits were committed in connection with the events surrounding the genocide and crimes against humanity.

CHAPTER II: CATEGORIZATION

Article 2

Persons accused of offences set out in Article 1 of this organic law and committed during the period between 1 October 1990 and 31 December 1994 shall, on the basis of their acts of participation, be classified into one of the following categories:

Category 1

a) persons whose criminal acts or whose acts of criminal participation place them among the planners, organisers, instigators, supervisors and leaders of the crime of genocide or of a crime against humanity;

b) persons who acted in positions of authority at the national, prefectoral, communal, sector or cell level, or in a political party, the army, religious organisations or in a militia and who perpetrated or fostered such crimes;

c) notorious murderers who by virtue of the zeal or excessive malice with which they committed atrocities, distinguished themselves in their areas of residence or where they passed;

d) persons who committed acts of sexual torture.

Category 2

Persons whose criminal acts or whose acts of criminal participation place them among perpetrators, conspirators or accomplices of intentional homicide or of serious assault against the person causing death.

Category 3

Persons whose criminal acts or whose acts of criminal participation make them guilty of other serious assaults against the person.

Category 4

Persons who committed offences against property.

Article 3

For the purposes of this organic law, an accomplice is a person who provided essential assistance in the commission of the offence or who, by any means, diverted criminal prosecution of persons referred to in Article 2 of this organic law or failed to give information about them.

The fact that any of the acts referred to in this organic law was committed by a subordinate does not relieve his superior of criminal responsibility if he knew or had reason to know that the subordinate was about to commit such acts or had done so and the superior failed to take the necessary and reasonable measures to punish or prevent such acts while these measures were available to him.

CHAPTER III: CONFESSION AND GUILTY PLEA PROCEDURE

SECTION 1 COMING INTO FORCE, ELIGIBILITY AND CONDITIONS

Article 4

The Confession and Guilty Plea Procedure shall come into force on the date this organic law is published to the Official Gazette and shall remain in force for eighteen (18) months; it may be renewed by presidential order for a period not longer than an additional eighteen months.

The Officer of the Public Prosecution Department responsible for the investigation shall inform the accused of the accused's right and interest to participate in the Confession and Guilty Plea Procedure. The Officer shall note on the record that the accused has been so informed.

Article 5

All persons who have committed offences set out in Article 1 have the right to participate in the Confession and Guilty Plea Procedure.

The right to participate, which cannot be denied, may be exercised at any time before the criminal file is brought to the attention of the President of the competent tribunal. This right can only be exercised once and the confession can be withdrawn at any time before it is pronounced again by the interested person before the court.

Notwithstanding the provisions of paragraph (1), persons who fall within Category 1, as defined in Article 2, shall not be eligible to the reductions in penalties set out in Articles 15 and 16.

Article 6

For the purposes of this Section, a confession is admissible if it includes:

a) a detailed description of all the offences set out under Article 1 that the applicant committed, including the date, time and the scene of each act, as well as the names of victims and witnesses, if known;

b) information with respect to accomplices, conspirators and all other information useful to the exercise of public prosecution;

c) an apology for the offences committed by the applicant;

d) an offer to plead guilty to the offences described by the applicant in accordance with the provisions of sub-paragraph (a).

The confession shall be recorded and transcribed by an Officer of the Public Prosecution Department and where the confession is submitted in writing, the Officer of the Public Prosecution Department shall request the applicant to confirm the confession. The applicant shall sign or mark with a fingerprint the record in the presence of the Officer of the Public Prosecution Department, who shall also sign the record.

The Public Prosecution Department shall inform the applicant of the Category within which the confessed acts place the applicant in order to allow the applicant to waive or confirm his choice to proceed with the Confession and Guilty Plea Procedure.

Where the applicant renounces his choice to proceed with the Confession and Guilty Plea Procedure, the applicant may withdraw the confession which shall then be inadmissible as evidence against the applicant in any subsequent proceedings.

Article 7
The Public Prosecution Department shall verify the accuracy and completeness of the confession and its compliance with the conditions stipulated in Article 6 within a maximum period of three months from the date of the signature of the record made in accordance with Article 6.
A record giving the reasons for the acceptance or rejection of the confession and offer to plead guilty shall be prepared following the verification; this record shall be signed by an Officer of the Public Prosecution Department.
Where a confession and offer to plead guilty is rejected, the Public Prosecution Department shall proceed with the investigation of the case in accordance with ordinary procedures and shall not accept a subsequent confession.

Article 8
Where the Public Prosecution Department accepts a confession and offer to plead guilty, an end of investigation memorandum containing the charges established by the confession shall be included in the case file and the file shall be forwarded to the competent court which shall then hear and determine the case.

Article 9
As investigations proceed, a list of persons suspected or accused of acts placing them within Category 1 shall be prepared and updated on a continuing basis by the Prosecutor General of the Supreme Court. This list shall be published three months after this organic law is published in the Official Gazette, and shall be periodically republished thereafter as it is updated.
Notwithstanding the provisions of Article 5, paragraph 3, a person who confesses and pleads guilty, and whose name was not published on the list of Category 1, shall not be placed in Category 1 if the confession is complete and accurate. If his confession should place him in Category 1, he shall be placed in Category 2.
Persons who shall have confessed their criminal acts before the list of names of Category 1 is published shall be placed in Category 1 if the acts they have committed place them there.
Where a person is later found to have committed offences that he has not confessed, he shall, at any time, be prosecuted for these offences and placed in the relevant Category.

SECTION 2
HEARING, ADJUDICATION AND EFFECTS OF THE CONFESSION AND GUILTY PLEA PROCEDURE

Article 10
Under the Confession and Guilty Plea Procedure, the hearing shall proceed as follows:
1. The clerk shall call the case;
2. The accused shall state his name;
3. The President of the bench shall ask the civil party to identify itself;
4. The clerk shall read the charges;
5. The Public Prosecution Department shall have the opportunity to be heard;
6. The clerk shall read the record of the confession and guilty plea and, if any, the document containing the confession;
7. The bench shall examine the accused to verify whether the confession and guilty plea have been

made in a voluntary manner with full knowledge of the case, including the nature of the charge, the sentence range and the absence of the right of appeal from the criminal provisions of the judgement to come;
8. The civil party shall state its claim;
9. The accused and, where applicable, any other person legally responsible shall present one after the other their defence to any civil claim or make any other statement in mitigation of their responsibility;
10. The bench shall receive the guilty plea and the hearing shall be declared closed.

Article 11
Where the confession has been rejected by the Public Prosecution Department following verification, as set out in Article 7, the accused may confirm to the bench at trial his request to participate in the Confession and Guilty Plea Procedure. The accused shall make the request after the clerk has read the charges, but no later than during his interrogation.
Where it is determined by the bench at the end of the hearing that the conditions included in Article 6 for a valid confession and guilty plea were met, the bench shall apply Articles 15 and 16.

Article 12
Where it is determined by the bench during the course of the hearing that the conditions for a valid confession and guilty plea are not met, the bench shall dismiss the confession and guilty plea. The bench shall similarly dismiss the confession and guilty plea where the accused waives his right to the confession procedure.
The competent court may requalify the charges that are before it.
Where the bench alters a charge based on facts which the applicant has admitted and confessed, the bench shall not dismiss the confession and guilty plea but shall order the reopening of the debates to allow the accused, after being advised of the new categorisation, to confirm or waive his choice to offer a confession and guilty plea.

Article 13
Where the bench dismisses the confession and guilty plea, it may schedule the case for trial at a later date or return it to the Office of the Public Prosecutor for completion of the investigation.

In any subsequent proceedings, the confession and accompanying guilty plea shall be inadmissible as evidence against the accused.

CHAPTER IV: PENALTIES

Article 14
The penalties imposed for the offences set out in Article 1 shall be those provided under the Penal Code, except:
a) that persons whose acts place them in Category 1 are liable to the death penalty;
b) that for persons whose acts place them in Category 2, the death penalty is replaced by life imprisonment;
c) where a confession and guilty plea have been accepted, in which case Articles 16 and 17 of this organic law apply;
d) that the acts committed by persons placed in Category 4 shall only give rise to civil damages

determined by amicable agreement between the parties with the assistance of the community, failing which the rules pertaining to criminal proceedings and civil actions shall apply. If the accused is sentenced to a term of imprisonment, the sentence is suspended.
For the application of this article, sub-paragraph (d), the conditions set out in article 97 of the Penal Code do not apply.

Article 15
Where a conviction is pronounced following a confession and guilty plea offered prior to prosecution, the penalty shall be reduced as follows:
a) persons whose acts place them within Category 2 shall be liable to a term of imprisonment of between 7 and 11 years;
b) persons whose acts place them within Category 3 shall be liable to a penalty equivalent to one-third of the penalty the tribunal would normally impose.

Article 16
Where a conviction is pronounced following a confession and guilty plea offered after prosecution, the penalty shall be reduced as follows:
a) persons whose acts place them within Category 2 shall be liable to a term of imprisonment of between 12 and 15 years;
b) persons whose acts place them within Category 3 shall be liable to a penalty equivalent to one-half of the penalty the tribunal would normally impose.

Article 17
Persons found guilty under this organic law shall be liable to the withdrawal of their civic rights in the following manner:
a) for persons whose acts place them within Category 1, the withdrawal for life of all civic rights;
b) for persons whose acts place them within Category 2, the withdrawal for life of civic rights as provided in Article 66 of the Penal Code, sub-paragraph 2, 3 and 5.
Persons whose acts place them within Category 3 shall incur the civic consequences provided by law.

Article 18
Notwithstanding the provisions of Article 94 of the Penal Code, a perpetrator who is sentenced for multiple crimes shall serve the most severe sentence.

CHAPTER V: SPECIALIZED CHAMBERS
SECTION 1
ESTABLISHMENT AND JURISDICTION OF SPECIALIZED CHAMBERS

Article 19
There are hereby established, within the Tribunals of First Instance and the military courts, Specialized Chambers with exclusive jurisdiction over the offences set out in Article 1.
Each Specialized Chamber may include several benches sitting simultaneously.
One or more of these benches shall be composed of magistrates for minors, which shall have exclusive jurisdiction over the offences set out in Article 1 committed by minors.

A Specialized Chamber may have several benches which may hear cases as itinerant Chambers in any location within its territorial jurisdiction for as long a period as its President deems necessary.
Chapter V and Chapter VI of this organic law are not applicable to cases where the accused is subject to special rules of jurisdiction by virtue of holding an official position.

SECTION 2
COMPOSITION OF SPECIALIZED CHAMBERS

Article 20
Each Specialized Chamber shall be comprised of such number of career or auxiliary magistrates as are deemed necessary and they shall be placed under the direction of a Vice-President of the Tribunal of First Instance or the military courts.
The Vice-President shall be responsible for the organisation and the assignment of duties within the Chamber.
Career magistrates and Presidents of the Specialized Chambers of the Tribunal of First Instance shall be named by order of the President of the Supreme Court, following a decision of the College of the President and the Vice-Presidents of the Supreme Court;
Career magistrates shall be named from among the magistrates of the Tribunal of First Instance of which the Specialized Chamber forms a part; Auxiliary magistrates and the President of the Specialized Chamber of the military courts shall be named in accordance with normal procedures.

Article 21
The bench of the Specialized Chambers shall be comprised of three magistrates with the President of the bench named by the President of the Chamber.

SECTION 3
THE PUBLIC PROSECUTION DEPARTMENT

Article 22
Officers of the Public Prosecution Department for the Specialized Chambers of the Tribunals of First Instance shall be named by the Prosecutor General of the Court of Appeal from among those assigned to the Office of the Public Prosecutor on proposal of the Public Prosecutor. They shall be supervised by the First Deputy designated for that purpose;
The Officers of the Public Prosecution Department of the Court of Appeal responsible for handling appeals from decisions of the Specialized Chambers are designated by the Prosecutor General of the Supreme Court upon proposal by the Prosecutor General of the Court of Appeal.
The Prosecutor General of the Supreme Court shall have supervision and general direction over the lower and higher level Offices of the Public Prosecutor with respect to matters relevant to the jurisdiction of the Specialized Chambers.

Article 23
The Officers of the Public Prosecution Department of the Specialized Chamber of the War Council shall be designated by the Military Auditor. The Military Auditor General of the Military Court shall designate the Officers of the Public Prosecution Department who shall have carriage of cases before this court.

CHAPTER VI: APPEALS AND REVIEW

Article 24

Decisions of the Specialized Chambers are subject to opposition and appeal; the limitation period for the filing of an appeal is fifteen days.

Appeals shall be based solely on questions of law or flagrant errors of fact.

Within a maximum period of three months following the filing of the file before the appellate court, the appellate court shall decide the admissibility of the appeal on the basis of the appeal documents. Where the appeal found to be admissible, the appellate court shall decide the appeal on its merits on the basis of the appeal documents. This decision is not subject to appeal or review.

Interlocutory rulings and decisions rendered subsequent to the acceptance of the confession and guilty plea are not subject to appeal or review, with the exception of civil interests flowing from these decisions.

Article 25

Notwithstanding the provisions of Article 24, where the appellate court condemns a person to death following an acquittal at first instance, the condemned person may, within fifteen days of conviction, apply for a review in cassation and the Court of Cassation may decide the case on its merits.

A review in cassation shall be based solely on questions of law or flagrant errors of fact.

Within a maximum period of three months following the filing of the file before the Court of Cassation, the Court of Cassation shall decide the admissibility of the application for review application based on the application documents. Where the review is found to be admissible, the Court of Cassation shall decide the application for review on its merits on the basis of the application documents. This decision is not subject to appeal or review.

Article 26

The Prosecutor General of the Supreme Court, on his own initiative and solely in the interests of the law may apply to the Court of Cassation for judicial review of any decision contrary to law rendered at the appellate level within three months of that decision.

CHAPTER VII: DAMAGES

Article 27

The Public Prosecution Department represents, as of right or upon request, the civil interests of minors and other legally incompetent persons who do not have legal representation.

Article 28

At any time, between the commencement of the investigation and the rendering of the final decision in a case, the President of the Specialized Chamber of the Court may, upon written application by an aggrieved party or the Public Prosecution Department, take all conservation measures necessary to safeguard the civil interests of the aggrieved party.

Article 29

The ordinary rules governing denunciations, complaints and civil actions are applicable to cases before the Specialized Chambers.

Victims acting either individually or through legally constituted associations for the defence of victims, represented by their legal representative or by a special representative designated according to their statutes, may request the commencement of a public prosecution by submitting a written petition setting out the grounds for the prosecution to the Public Prosecutor of the competent jurisdiction. The status of civil party shall be given to the petitioner. The civil party is exempt from the payment of legal fees.

Where the Public Prosecution Department has not instituted proceedings before the competent jurisdiction within six months of the submission of a petition, the civil party may commence a private prosecution, in which case the private party bears the burden of proof. The civil party is exempt from the payment of legal fees.

Civil and criminal convictions are open to appeal in accordance with Article 24. The person accused in the private prosecution shall be notified of the appeal and the appellate court shall decide the case in its entirety.

Article 30

Convicted persons whose acts place them within Category 1 under Article 2 shall be held jointly and severally liable for all damages caused in the country by their acts of criminal participation, regardless of where the offences were committed.

Persons whose acts place them within Categories 2, 3 or 4 shall be held liable for damages for the criminal acts they have committed.

Without prejudice to the rights of civil parties present or represented at trial, and at request of the Public Prosecution Department, the court shall award damages to victims not yet identified.

Article 31

The court having jurisdiction over the civil action shall rule on damages even where the accused has died during the course of the proceedings or has benefited from an amnesty.

Article 32

Damages awarded to victims who have not yet been identified shall be deposited in a Victims Compensation Fund, whose creation and operation shall be determined by a separate law. Prior to the adoption of the new law creating the Fund, damages awarded shall be deposited in an account at the National Bank of Rwanda opened for this purpose by the Minister responsible for Social Affairs and the Fund shall be used only after the adoption of the law.

CHAPTER VIII
MISCELLANEOUS AND FINAL PROVISIONS

Article 33

The Public Prosecution Department may institute proceedings against persons having no known domicile or residence in Rwanda or who are outside the country and against whom there are corroborating evidence of substantial evidence of guilt, whether or not such persons have been previously examined by the Public Prosecution Department.

Article 34

The time limit for the service of a subpoena shall be one month for persons having no known domicile or residence in Rwanda.

Where this is the case, a copy of the writ shall be posted on the main door of the court where the Chamber having jurisdiction over the case sits.

Article 35
Exceptions to joinder or indivisibility shall be raised before the court seized with the case and that court has exclusive jurisdiction to rule on the applicability of the exception; Applications requesting the withdrawal of magistrates shall be brought before the jurisdiction seized with the case;
Applications may be decided in conjunction with the merits of the case, or may be decided by interlocutory ruling from which there is no appeal or review.

Article 36
Persons prosecuted under the provisions of this organic law enjoy the same rights of defence given to other persons subject to criminal prosecution, including the right to the defence counsel of their choice, but not at government expense.

Article 37
Prosecutions and penalties for offences constituting the crime of genocide or crimes against humanity are not subject to a limitation period.

Article 38
Until the publication of the general law on the crime of genocide and the crimes against humanity, whoever commits any act constituting one or more of these crimes after 31 December 1994 shall be liable to the penalties provided by the Penal Code, and shall not be eligible to any penalty reduction as provided by this organic law.

Article 39
Unless otherwise provided in this organic law, all laws, including the Penal Code, the Code of Criminal Procedure and the Code of Judicial Organisation and Jurisdiction, shall apply to proceedings before the Specialized Chambers.

Article 40
This organic law is written in the three official languages of the Republic of Rwanda, the version in Kinyarwanda being considered as the original.

Article 41
This organic law comes into force on the date of its publication in the Official Gazette of the Republic of Rwanda.

Kigali 30/8/1996.

☛ SPAIN: Title XXIV of the Spanish Penal Code of 1995, passed by the Ley Orgánica [Organic Act] of Parliament 10/95 of 23rd November 1995[1]

TITLE XXIV
CRIMES AGAINST THE INTERNATIONAL COMMUNITY
CHAPTER ONE
CRIMES AGAINST THE IUS GENTIUM

Article 605
1. Anyone who kills a Head of a foreign State, or any other internationally protected person in Spain, will be sentenced to between twenty and twenty-five years in prison. Should there be other aggravating circumstances, the penalty imposed will be between twenty-five and thirty years in prison.
2. Anyone who causes the injuries established in article 149 to people mentioned in the paragraph above will be punished by a prison penalty of between fifteen and twenty years. Should the injuries caused be those established in article 150, prison penalty will be between eight and fifteen years, and between four and eight years for other injuries.
3. Any other crime committed against the people mentioned above, or against their official places, their private residences or their means of transport, will receive penalties that are in the upper half of the range stated in this code.

Article 606
1. Anyone who violates the personal immunity of a Head of another State or any other internationally protected person will be punished by a prison sentence of between six months and three years.
2. When the crimes included in this article and in the one above have no reciprocal penalty in the offended person's country, the penalty applied will be the one that is stipulated in this code for crimes against non-officials.

CHAPTER II
GENOCIDE CRIMES

Article 607
1. Anyone who should perpetrate any of the following acts, with the intent of partially or totally destroying a national, ethnic, racial or religious group, will be punishable by:
1st. A prison penalty between fifteen and twenty years if a member of one of these groups is killed. If two or more aggravating circumstances concur, the higher penalty will be imposed.
2nd. A prison penalty between fifteen and twenty years if a member of one of these groups is sexually attacked or receives any of the injuries established in article 149.
3rd. A prison penalty between eight and fifteen years if a person submits the group or some of its members to conditions that may put their lives in danger or perturb their health, or which may cause them any of the injuries established in article 150.

1. Translation provided by Professor Antoni Pigrau i Solé.

4th. A prison penalty between eight and fifteen years should the group or its members be obliged to displace or measures be taken that prevent them from leading their kind of life or from reproducing, or people be forced to change from one group to another.
5th. A prison penalty between four and eight years should injuries be caused that are different from those established in paragraphs two and three of this article.
2. The diffusion by any means of ideas or doctrines that condone or justify the crimes typified in the paragraph above in this article, or that attempt to rehabilitate regimes or institutions which defend practices that generate such crimes, will be punished by a prison penalty between one and two years.

CHAPTER III
CRIMES AGAINST PROTECTED PEOPLE AND PROPERTY IN THE EVENT OF ARMED CONFLICT

Article 608
For the purposes of this chapter, protected people will be defined as:
1st. The wounded, sick and shipwrecked, and medical and religious personnel, protected by the First and Second Geneva Convention of 12th August 1949 or by the Additional Protocol I of 8th June 1977.
2nd. Prisoners of war, protected by the Third Geneva Convention of 12th August 1949 or by the Additional Protocol I of 8th June 1977.
3rd. The civilian population and civilians, protected by the Fourth Geneva Convention of 12th August 1949 or by the Additional Protocol I of 8th June 1977.
4th. Non-combatants and Protecting Power personnel and their substitutes, protected by the Geneva Convention of 12th August 1949 or by the Additional Protocol I of 8th June 1977.
5th. Parliamentarians and their companions, protected by The Hague Convention of 29th June 1899.
6th. Anyone else who can be defined as such according to the Additional Protocol II of 8th June 1977 or any international Treaty to which Spain is a party

Article 609
Anyone who, during armed conflict, abuses the rights, or endangers the life, health or integrity of any protected person, inflicts torture or inhuman treatment, including biological experiments, causes great suffering or submits the said person to a medical act that is not required by the present state of health or by the generally accepted medical regulations that the Party responsible for the action would apply, in similar medical circumstances, to his or her fellow nationals who are not deprived of their liberty, will be punished by a prison sentence of between four and eight years and may also be obliged to pay any possible damages for the injuries caused.

Article 610
Anyone who, during armed conflict, uses methods or means of combat, or orders them to be used, which are prohibited or destined to cause unnecesary suffering or superfluous harm, as well as those that are conceived to cause, or with good reason are expected to cause, extensive, permanent and severe damage to the natural environment, endangering the health or the survival of the population, will be punished by a prison penalty of between ten and fifteen years, and may also be obliged to pay any damages for the injuries caused.

Article 611

In the event of armed conflict, in addition to any damages owing, a prison sentence of between ten and fifteen years will be given to anyone who should.

1st. Carry out or order indiscriminate or excessive attacks or use the civil population as an object of attack, reprisals or violent acts or threats in order to terrify them.

2nd. Violate the rules of International Law which are applicable to armed conflicts by destroying or damaging military ships or aircraft of an adversary or neutral party unnecesarily and without giving sufficient warning or taking the necessary measures to provide for the security of the personnel or to conserve the documentation on board.

3rd. Force a prisoner of war or a civilian to serve, in any way, in the armed forces of the opposing Party, or deprive them of their right to be judged in a regular and impartial way.

4th. Deport, move by force, take as hostage or illegally arrest any protected person.

5th. Move people of the occupying Party to the occupied territory and settle them there to reside on a permanent basis.

6th. Carry out, order or practise, with respect to any protected person, racial segregation and other inhuman and degrading practices based on unfavourable distinctions of character which involve insulting personal dignity.

7th. Unjustly prevent or delay the liberation or the repatriation of prisoners of war, prisoners or civilians.

Article 612

In the event of armed conflict, in addition to the sentence which corresponds to the results of such actions, a prison sentence of between three and seven years will be given to anyone who should:

1st. Knowingly violate the protection due to health units and health transport, prison camps, health and security areas, neutralized areas or sites for the internment of the civil population, and undefended areas and demilitarized zones, which are duly identified with signs or the appropriate distinctive signals.

2nd. Exercise violence on health or religious personnel, or members of medical missions or rescue teams.

3rd. Seriously injure, deprive or withhold the indispensable food or medical assistance required by protected people or subject them to humiliating or degrading treatment, induced or forced prostitution or any form of indecent assault, or omit to inform them in a comprehensible fashion, without justified delay, of their situation, or impose collective punishments for individual acts, or violate the prescriptions about accommodation for women and families or about special protection for women and children established in the international Treaties in which Spain is a party.

4th. Use unduly or in a perfidious fashion the distinctive protecting signs, emblems or signals established by and recognised in the international Treaties to which Spain is a party, particularly the distinctive signs of the Red Cross and the Red Crescent.

5th. Use unduly or in a perfidious fashion the distinctive flag, uniform, badge or emblem of neutral states, the United Nations, other states which are not part of the conflict or of the opposing Parties during attacks for the purpose of concealing, favouring, protecting or hindering military operations, except in those cases expressly established in the international Treaties to which Spain is a party.

6th. Use unduly or in a perfidious fashion the parliamentary or surrender flag, or threaten the inviolabilty of, or unduly retain, a parliamentarian or any accompanying person, Peace Keeping personnel or their substitutes, or a member of the International Inquiry Commission.
7th. Strip a cadaver, a wounded, sick, or shipwrecked person, a prisoner of war or an interned civilian of their personal effects.

Article 613
1. In the event of armed conflict, a prison sentence of between four and six years will be given to anyone who should:
a) Attack or subject to reprisals or hostile acts the cultural property or religious sites which are recognised as clearly being part of the cultural or spiritual heritage of the people or which have been specifically protected by special agreements, causing extensive destruction, whenever this property is not located in the immediate vicinity of military objectives and is not used to support the military effort of the adversary.
b) Attack or subject to reprisals or hostile acts the civil property of the adversary, thus causing its destruction, when, in the specific circumstances, it is of no defined military advantage or the said property makes no effective contribution to the military action of the adversary.
c) Attack, destroy, remove or make inoperative those assets that are essential for the survival of the civil population, except in the case that the adversary should use these assets to directly support a military action or exclusively as a means of subsistence for the members of their armed forces.
d) Attack or subject to reprisals those installations that contain dangerous forces, when such actions may produce the liberation of these forces but cause as a result considerable losses in the civil population, except in the case that such installations are regularly used in direct support of military operations and that such attacks are the only feasible means of ending such support.
e) Destroy, harm or take possession of things from another person, when there is no military necessity, force someone to surrender such things or carry out any other acts of pillage.
2. Should the cultural assets in question be under special protection or the action be of the utmost gravity, the higher penalty may be imposed.

Article 614
In the event of armed conflict, anyone who should carry out or order any other infringement or acts against the prescriptions of those international Treaties to which Spain is a party in relation to the management of hostilities, the protection of the wounded, sick and shipwrecked, the treatment of prisoners of war and civilians, and the protection of cultural assets, will be punished by a prison penalty of between six months and two years.

CHAPTER IV
COMMON PROVISIONS

Article 615
The provocation, conspiracy and proposition to commit the crimes established in this Title will be punishable by penalties one or two degrees below the penalty that would correspond to such crimes.

Article 616
Should any of the crimes established in this Title and in the previous one be committed by an authority or a public official, in addition to the penalty stipulated for the crime, said official will be disqualified from public service for a period between ten and twenty years. In the case of an individual, the judges or courts can impose the special disqualification from public employment or office for a period between one and ten years.

☛ **UK: Statutory Instruments 1998 No. 1754 Geneva Conventions. The Geneva Conventions Act (First Protocol) Order 1998**

Made 21st July 1998
Coming into force 28th July 1998

(...)

Her Majesty, in exercise of the power conferred on Her by section 7(3)(a) of the Geneva Conventions Act 1957(a), as amended by the Geneva Conventions (Amendment) Act 1995(b), is pleased, by and with the advice of Her Privy Council, to order, and it is hereby ordered, as follows:

Citation and commencement

1. This Order may be cited as the Geneva Conventions Act (First Protocol) Order 1998 and shall come into force on 28th July 1998.

Certification of declarations made on ratification of the First Protocol

2. It is hereby certified that when depositing the instrument of ratification of the First Protocol additional to the Geneva Conventions of 12th August 1949, that is to say the Protocol relating to the Protection of Victims of International Armed Conflicts (Protocol I) done on 10th June 1977, the reservations and declarations set out in the Schedule to this Order were made.

N H. Nicholls
Clerk of the Privy Council

(a) 1957 c. 52.
(b) c. 27.

SCHEDULE
(a) It continues to be the understanding of the United Kingdom that the rules introduced by the Protocol apply exclusively to conventional weapons without prejudice to any other rules of international law applicable to other types of weapons. In particular, the rules so introduced do not have any effect on and do not regulate or prohibit the use of nuclear weapons.
(b) The United Kingdom understands the term 'feasible' as used in the Protocol to mean that which is practicable or practically possible, taking into account all circumstances ruling at the time, including humanitarian and military considerations.

(c) Military commanders and others responsible for planning, deciding upon, or executing attacks necessarily have to reach decisions on the basis of their assessment of the information from all sources which is reasonably available to them at the relevant time.
(d) ARTICLE 1, paragraph 4 and ARTICLE 96, paragraph 3
It is the understanding of the United Kingdom that the term 'armed conflict' of itself and in its context denotes a situation of a kind which is not constituted by the commission of ordinary crimes including acts of terrorism whether concerted or in isolation.
The United Kingdom will not, in relation to any situation in which it is itself involved, consider itself bound in consequence of any declaration purporting to be made under paragraph 3 of Article 96 unless the United Kingdom shall have expressly recognised that it has been made by a body which is genuinely an authority representing a people engaged in an armed conflict of the type to which Article 1, paragraph 4, applies.
(e) ARTICLE 28, paragraph 2
Given the practical need to make use of non-dedicated aircraft for medical evacuation purposes, the United Kingdom does not interpret this paragraph as precluding the presence on board of communications equipment and encryption materials or the use thereof solely to facilitate navigation, identification or communication in support of medical transportation as defined in Article 8(f).
(f) ARTICLE 35, paragraph 3 and ARTICLE 55
The United Kingdom understands both of these provisions to cover the employment of methods and means of warfare and that the risk of environmental damage falling within the scope of these provisions arising from such methods and means of warfare is to be assessed objectively on the basis of the information available at the time.
(g) ARTICLE 44 paragraph 3
It is the understanding of the United Kingdom that:
- the situation in the second sentence of paragraph 3 can only exist in occupied territory or in armed conflicts covered by paragraph 4 of Article 1;
- 'deployment' in paragraph 3(b) means any movement towards a place from which an attack is to be launched.
(h) ARTICLE 50
In the view of the United Kingdom the rule in the second sentence of paragraph 1 applies only in cases of substantial doubt still remaining after the assessment referred to at paragraph (c) above has been made, and not as overriding a commander's duty to protect the safety of troops under his command or to preserve his military situation, in conformity with other provisions of the Protocol.
(i) ARTICLE 51 and ARTICLE 57
In the view of the United Kingdom, the military advantage anticipated from an attack is intended to refer to the advantage anticipated from the attack considered as a whole and not only from isolated or particular parts of the attack.
(j) ARTICLE 52
It is the understanding of the United Kingdom that:

– a specific area of land may be a military objective if, because of its location or other reasons specified in this Article, its total or partial destruction, capture or neutralisation in the circumstances ruling at the time offers definite military advantage;
– the first sentence of paragraph 2 prohibits only such attacks as may be directed against non-military objectives; it does not deal with the question of collateral damage resulting from attacks directed against military objectives.
(k) ARTICLE 53
The United Kingdom declares that if the objects protected by this Article are unlawfully used for military purposes they will thereby lose protection from attacks directed against such unlawful military uses.
(l) ARTICLE 54, paragraph 2
The United Kingdom understands that paragraph 2 has no application to attacks that are carried out for a specific purpose other than denying sustenance to the civilian population or the adverse party.
(m) ARTICLES 51-55
The obligations of Articles 51 and 55 are accepted on the basis that any adverse party against which the United Kingdom might be engaged will itself scrupulously observe those obligations. If an adverse party makes serious and deliberate attacks, in violation of Article 51 or Article 52 against the civilian population or civilians or against civilian objects, or, in violation of Articles 53, 54 and 55, on objects or items protected by those Articles, the United Kingdom will regard itself as entitled to take measures otherwise prohibited by the Articles in question to the extent that it considers such measures necessary for the sole purpose of compelling the adverse party to cease committing violations under those Articles, but only after formal warning to the adverse party requiring cessation of the violations has been disregarded and then only after a decision taken at the highest level of government. Any measures thus taken by the United Kingdom will not be disproportionate to the violations giving rise thereto and will not involve any action prohibited by the Geneva Conventions of 1949 nor will such measures be continued after the violations have ceased. The United Kingdom will notify the Protecting Powers of any such formal warning given to an adverse party, and if that warning has been disregarded, of any measures taken as a result.
(n) ARTICLES 56 and 85, paragraph 3c
The United Kingdom cannot undertake to grant absolute protection to installations which may contribute to the opposing Party's war effort, or to the defenders of such installations, but will take all due precautions in military operations at or near the installations referred to in paragraph 1 of Article 56 in the light of the known facts, including any special marking which the installation may carry, to avoid severe collateral losses among the civilian populations; direct attacks on such installations will be launched only on authorisation at a high level of command.
(o) ARTICLE 57, paragraph 2
The United Kingdom understands that the obligation to comply with paragraph 2(b) only extends to those who have the authority and practical possibility to cancel or suspend the attack.
(p) ARTICLE 70
It is the understanding of the United Kingdom that this Article does not affect the existing rules of naval warfare regarding naval blockade, submarine warfare or mine warfare.

EXPLANATORY NOTE
(This note is not part of the Order)
This Order, made under the Geneva Conventions Act 1957, as amended by the Geneva Conventions (Amendment) Act 1995, sets out the reservations and declarations made by the United Kingdom when ratifying Protocol I to the Geneva Conventions 1949. Section 7(3)(b) of the Act provides that for the purposes of the Act the Protocol shall be construed subject to and in accordance with such reservations and declarations. The text of the Protocol is in the Schedule to the 1995 Act. The Order will come into force on the date on which Protocol I enters into force in relation to the United Kingdom.

☛ USA: War Crimes Act of 1996
(Public Law 104-192, 110 Stat. 2104, 18 U.S.C. 2401)

A bill to amend title 18, United States Code, to carry out the international obligations of the United States under the Geneva Conventions to provide criminal penalties for certain war crimes.

Sec. 2. Criminal Penalties for Certain War Crimes
(a) In general, Title 18, United States Code, is amended by inserting after chapter 117 the following:

CHAPTER 118 - War Crimes

sec. 2401. War Crimes

(a) OFFENSE - Whoever, whether inside or outside the United States, commits a grave breach of the Geneva Conventions, in any of the circumstances described in subsection (b), shall be fined under this title or imprisoned for life or any term of years, or both, and if death results to the victims, shall also be subject to the penalty of death.
(b) CIRCUMSTANCES -The circumstances referred to in subsection (a) are that the person committing such breach or the victim of such breach is a member of the Armed Forces of the United States or a national of the United States (as defined in section 101 of the Immigration and Nationality Act).
(C) DEFINITIONS - As used in this section, the term 'grave breach of the Geneva Conventions' means conduct defined as a grave breach in any of the international conventions relating to the laws of warfare signed at Geneva 12 August 1949 or any protocol to any such convention, to which the United States is a party.

☛ USA: Expanded War Crimes of 1997
(House of Representatives - July 28, 1997)

SECTION 1. SHORT TITLE.

This Act may be cited as the 'Expanded War Crimes Act of 1997'.

SECTION 2. DEFINITION OF WAR CRIMES.

Section 2441 of title 18, United States Code, is amended

(1) in subsection (a), by striking 'grave breach of the Geneva Conventions' and inserting 'war crime';
(2) in subsection (b), by striking 'breach' each place it appears and inserting 'war crime'; and
(3) so that subsection (c) reads as follows:
(c) Definition. As used in this section the term 'war crime' means any conduct
(1) defined as a grave breach in any of the international conventions signed at Geneva 12 August 1949, or any protocol to such convention to which the United States is a party;
(2) prohibited by Articles 23, 25, 27, or 28 of the Annex to the Hague Convention IV, Respecting the Laws and Customs of War on Land, signed 18 October 1907;
(3) which constitutes a violation of common Article 3 of the international conventions signed at Geneva 12 August 1949, or any protocol to such convention to which the United States is a party and which deals with non-international armed conflict; or
(4) of a person who, in relation to an armed conflict and contrary to the provisions of the Protocol on Prohibitions or Restrictions on the Use of Mines, Booby-Traps and Other Devices as amended at Geneva on 3 May 1996 (Protocol II as amended on 3 May 1996), when the United States is a party to such Protocol, wilfully kills or causes serious injury to civilians.

TABLE OF CASES*

INTERNATIONAL

*The table of cases was compiled by Mrs. B.M. Hall, Elie, UK.

NATIONAL

Argentina

Federal Appeals Court

Supreme Court

Dolores Federal Court

Belgium

Military Court

Bosnia and Herzegovina

High Court of Sarajevo Canton Court

Canada

High Court of Justice

Federal Court

Court Martial Appeal Court

Court

INDEX

The index contains references to all matters of substance dealt with in the text of the articles. Detailed references to cases dealt with will be found in the accompanying Table of Cases. Multilateral agreements are indexed under *Agreements, multilateral, classified by subject*. The section on Correspondents' Reports is also indexed but for information on the practice of individual states regarding the principal instruments of international humanitarian law referred to (which are listed on page 398) the reader should consult the index under the states concerned. The index does contain, however, references to other material from this section, such as municipal legislation which is not purely concerned with the subject matter of the listed instruments: for example, references will be found to subjects such as amnesty, extradition, war crimes tribunals. Footnotes containing substantive material are also indexed, as are references to the work of scholars the first time such work is listed.

The index was compiled by Mrs. B.M. Hall, Elie, UK.

Abbreviations frequently used

g.r.	=	general references
ICTR	=	International Criminal Tribunal for Rwanda
ICTY	=	International Criminal Tribunal for the former Yugoslavia
IHL	=	International humanitarian law
p.a.r.	=	parties, accessions and ratifications
UN	=	United Nations Organisation
US	=	United States of America

MIX
Papier aus verantwortungsvollen Quellen
Paper from responsible sources
FSC® C105338

If you have any concerns about our products,
you can contact us on
ProductSafety@springernature.com

In case Publisher is established outside the EU,
the EU authorized representative is:
Springer Nature Customer Service Center GmbH
Europaplatz 3, 69115 Heidelberg, Germany

Printed by Libri Plureos GmbH
in Hamburg, Germany